Lívia Körtvélyessy, Alexandra Bagasheva, Pavol Štekauer (Eds.)
Derivational Networks Across Languages

Trends in Linguistics
Studies and Monographs

Editors
Chiara Gianollo
Daniël Van Olmen

Editorial Board
Walter Bisang
Tine Breban
Volker Gast
Hans Henrich Hock
Karen Lahousse
Natalia Levshina
Caterina Mauri
Heiko Narrog
Salvador Pons
Niina Ning Zhang
Amir Zeldes

Editor responsible for this volume
Chiara Gianollo

Volume 340

Derivational Networks Across Languages

Edited by
Lívia Körtvélyessy
Alexandra Bagasheva
Pavol Štekauer

DE GRUYTER
MOUTON

ISBN 978-3-11-077814-4
e-ISBN (PDF) 978-3-11-068663-0
e-ISBN (EPUB) 978-3-11-068680-7

Library of Congress Control Number: 2020931489

Bibliographic information published by the Deutsche Nationalbibliothek
The Deutsche Nationalbibliothek lists this publication in the Deutsche Nationalbibliografie;
detailed bibliographic data are available on the Internet at http://dnb.dnb.de.

© 2021 Walter de Gruyter GmbH, Berlin/Boston
This volume is text- and page-identical with the hardback published in 2020.
Typesetting: Integra Software Services Pvt. Ltd.
Printing and binding: CPI books GmbH, Leck

www.degruyter.com

Preface

This monograph examines derivational networks in 40 European languages. It combines a new theoretical perspective on the complexity of derivational processes in various languages with an examination of their typological characteristics. For that purpose, a new methodological approach has been introduced, including a number of parameters: the saturation value, the maximum derivational capacity, the maximum and average number of orders of derivation, and typical combinations of semantic categories and their blocking effects.

The point of departure for the theoretical considerations is the concept of the derivational paradigm that derives from the established concept of the inflectional paradigm. Recent decades witness to the fact that the original bias against derivational paradigms has been overcome and that this concept has already found its firm place in morphological investigations. Nevertheless, it appears that this monodimensional concept cannot provide us with a comprehensive picture of the complexity and diversity of derivational relations. This observation is reflected in the relevant literature in the use of a bidimensional concept of derivational nest or family. Still, this level of description is not sufficient either because it disregards the semantic aspect of derivational relations. Therefore, in this book, we introduce a tridimensional system of a derivational network that – in capturing the complexity of derivational relations – combines the 'vertical', paradigmatic dimension (all direct derivatives from a base word), the 'horizontal' dimension (all successive, linear derivatives from a base word), and the semantic dimension (semantic categories defining each derivational step).

Typologically, the research aims to identify the systematicity and regularity in developing derivational networks in the examined sample of languages and in individual language genera and/or families. This is supported by considerations about the role of word-classes, morphological types, and the differences and similarities between word-formation systems of the languages belonging to the same genus/family.

We wish to express our thanks to the dozens of morphologists who represent the sample languages in the individual language-specific chapters. This monograph would not have come into existence without their expertise and extensive cooperation. As a result, we can provide a picture of derivational networks in

---

Note: This research has been implemented with finanncial support from the VEGA 1/0002/17 research grant, and partly also from the Spanish State Research Agency (SRA, Ministry of Economy and Enterprise) and European Regional Development Fund (ERDF) (Ref. FFI2017-89665-P).

https://doi.org/10.1515/9783110686630-202

individual languages, language genera, and European languages as a whole (with the limitations stemming from the sample of languages).

The volume does not and cannot provide a complete picture of this topic in spite of its wide scope. However, it introduces a method that can be applied to other languages and other sample words selected by other criteria, for example, lexical fields.

Contents

Preface —— V

Abbreviations —— XI

Lívia Körtvélyessy, Alexandra Bagasheva, Pavol Štekauer, Salvador Valera
1   Introduction —— 1

Martina Ivanová, Božena Bednaříková
2   Introduction to Slavic languages —— 27

Alexandra Bagasheva
3   Derivational networks in Bulgarian —— 33

Zrinka Jelaska, Tomislava Bošnjak Botica
4   Derivational networks in Croatian —— 43

Božena Bednaříková
5   Derivational networks in Czech —— 53

Ewa Konieczna
6   Derivational networks in Polish —— 65

Viacheslav Shevchenko, Slávka Tomaščíková
7   Derivational networks in Russian —— 75

Gordana Štasni, Gordana Štrbac
8   Derivational networks in Serbian —— 85

Martina Ivanová
9   Derivational networks in Slovak —— 93

Katja Plemenitaš, Ines Voršič, Irena Stramljič Breznik
10   Derivational networks in Slovene —— 105

Nadia Yesypenko
11   Derivational networks in Ukrainian —— 115

Geri Popova, Maria Rosenberg
12 Introduction to Germanic languages —— 127

Hans Götzsche
13 Derivational networks in Danish —— 129

Jack Hoeksema
14 Derivational networks in Dutch —— 137

Gergana Popova
15 Derivational networks in English —— 147

Siebren Dyk
16 Derivational networks in Frisian —— 157

Martin Neef, Ayşe Yurdakul
17 Derivational networks in German —— 167

Thorsteinn G. Indridason
18 Derivational networks in Icelandic —— 179

John Ole Askedal
19 Derivational networks in Norwegian —— 189

Maria Rosenberg
20 Derivational networks in Swedish —— 203

Livio Gaeta
21 Introduction to Romance languages —— 213

Elisenda Bernal, Mercè Lorente
22 Derivational networks in Catalan —— 217

Vincent Renner
23 Derivational networks in French —— 229

María Belén Villar Díaz
24 Derivational networks in Galician —— 239

Livio Gaeta
25 Derivational networks in Italian —— 251

Alina Villalva
26 Derivational networks in Portuguese —— 261

Carmen Mîrzea Vasile
27 Derivational networks in Romanian —— 273

Ana Díaz-Negrillo
28 Derivational networks in Spanish —— 285

Maria Bloch-Trojnar, Silva Nurmio
29 Introduction to Celtic languages —— 295

Maria Bloch-Trojnar
30 Derivational networks in Irish —— 299

Silva Nurmio
31 Derivational networks in Welsh —— 309

Jurgis Pakerys
32 Introduction to Baltic languages —— 319

Agnė Navickaitė-Klišauskienė
33 Derivational networks in Latvian —— 323

Jurgis Pakerys
34 Derivational networks in Lithuanian —— 333

Dimitra Melissaropoulou, Angela Ralli
35 Derivational networks in Greek —— 347

László Palágyi, Erzsébet Tóth-Czifra, Réka Benczes
36 Introduction to Uralic languages —— 361

Reet Kasik
37 Derivational networks in Estonian —— 365

Kaarina Pitkänen-Heikkilä
38 Derivational networks in Finnish —— 373

László Palágyi, Erzsébet Tóth-Czifra, Réka Benczes
39 Derivational networks in Hungarian —— 385

Kaarina Vuolab-Lohi
40 Derivational networks in North Saami —— 399

Aslı Göksel
41 Introduction to Tatar and Turkish —— 409

László Károly
42 Derivational networks in Tatar —— 411

Aslı Göksel, Aysel Kapan
43 Derivational networks in Turkish —— 423

Seda Yusupova
44 Derivational networks in Chechen —— 435

Nina Sumbatova
45 Derivational networks in Dargwa —— 443

Xabier Artiagoitia
46 Derivational networks in Basque —— 455

Manana Topadze Gäumann
47 Derivational networks in Georgian —— 465

Benjamin Saade
48 Derivational networks in Maltese —— 475

Lívia Körtvélyessy, Alexandra Bagasheva, Pavol Štekauer, Salvador Valera, Ján Genči
49 Derivational networks in European languages: A cross-linguistic perspective —— 485

Index —— 609

Abbreviations

ABSTR	ABSTRACT
AN	ACTION NOUN
AOR	aorist
CAUS	CAUSATIVE
CVB	CONVERBIAL
DIM	DIMINUTIVE
DIR	DIRECTIONAL
DN	derivational network
EVAL	EVALUATIVE
GEN	genitive
INF	infinitive
INT	INTENSIFIER
INTR	intransitive
ITER	ITERATIVE
M	masculine
MANN	MANNER
NDR	noun deriving suffix
NEG	negation
NOM	nominative
PASS	passive
PL	plural
POSS	POSSESSIVE
RM	reflexive marker
SG	singular
SIM	SIMILATIVE
RM	reflexive marker
TR	transitive
VDER	verb deriving suffix

Lívia Körtvélyessy, Alexandra Bagasheva, Pavol Štekauer, Salvador Valera

1 Introduction

This monograph is aimed at the examination of derivational networks across European languages. The concept of a derivational network is not new. The first ideas of network regularities and the network organization of derivational morphology can be traced back to the 1960s in relation to the Dokulilean tradition in word-formation. Unfortunately, apart from an outline of general principles, very little has been done in the field since. In recent years, however, we have been witnessing a growing interest in derivational paradigms and larger derivational systems based on them. A brief overview of this direction of morphological research is presented in section 1.1.

In spite of, or better, precisely because of what is outlined in section 1.1, this volume is pioneering in terms of both the theory and its scope for a number of reasons:

(i) First and foremost, a new method of examination and comparison of derivational networks in various languages is introduced, including new criteria and parameters for their evaluation, including the maximum derivational network, the saturation value, the number of orders of derivation, the correlation between the paradigmatic capacity and the order of derivation, the typical combinability of semantic categories, and the blocking effects of semantic categories.

(ii) Research into word-formation paradigms is mostly exploratory even though the basic utility of paradigms is assumed to be explanatory, so in this sense the current research explores the applicability of word-formation paradigms in typological derivational research.

(iii) It introduces the idea of derivational networks relying on the concept of the derivational paradigm, extendable both vertically and horizontally. The *derivational network* is conceived as an intersection of *paradigmatic capacity* per *order of derivation*, and is evaluated in terms of the *structural richness* that is quantitatively represented by calculating the *saturation value*.

(iv) The vertical dimension operates with the narrow understanding of a paradigm as being applicable across the fluid boundary between inflection and derivation, while the horizontal incorporates specific features of word-formation families (understood narrowly as equal to series) as constituting one type of associative, paradigmatic relation.

https://doi.org/10.1515/9783110686630-001

(v) It introduces into the research of derivational networks a third dimension – a strong semantic perspective in the form of the classification of individual derivatives by means of *comparative semantic categories*. In other words, rather than representing the meaning of the derived word as a whole, a semantic category represents the derivational meaning of the affix attached to the word-formation base. Semantic categories constitute an open-ended set of theory-neutral, cross-linguistically applicable, comparative semantic concepts. For the purposes of this research, we utilize a list of 49 semantic categories that seem to exhaust the semantic specificity of the sample languages. As comparative concepts employed in typological research (Corbett 2010; Haspelmath 2010), these conceptualize prototypes abstracted from descriptive categories. An extensive investigation of the available non-decompositional models of semantic analysis of affixation phenomena and the calibration of posited onomasiological categories in comparative semantic concepts served as the basis for compiling the set applied here. (For a detailed presentation of the principles of the compilation of the list of comparative semantic categories employed in the research, see Bagasheva 2017.)

(vi) The research methodology rests upon a usage-based approach to language (see Barlow and Kemmer 2000; Bybee 2006), utilizing a bottom-up approach of analyzing actual data gathered in individual languages for drawing the respective derivational networks.

(vii) It is the first piece of *large-scale empirical research* into derivational networks. By implication, there has been no *cross-linguistic research* into derivational networks to date. This monograph presents and evaluates data from a sample of 40 languages from across Europe.

(viii) This makes it possible to draw generalizations and evaluate the role of the genetic factor, the morphological type,[1] the nature of a language's word-formation system, the word-class of the basic word, and the order of derivation in the construction, complexity and richness of derivational networks.

(ix) Last but not least, the data enables us to contribute to the discussion on the areal typology of European languages to determine a zonation according to the parameter of derivational network richness.

---

[1] When referring to morphological typology, we rely on the traditional classification proposed by Sapir (1921) and Skalička (2004–2006).

1.1 Previous research

As indicated above, the idea of complex and systematic relations among derivatives organized around a simple underived base word is not new. Relevant discussions can be found, for example, in the works of Czech and Slovak linguists from the 1960s and the following decades, inspired (as for many other word-formation issues) by Dokulil's seminal work (1962), with the fundamental theory systemized in Horecký et al. (1989) and Furdík (2004). This line of research is based on the principle of word-formation motivation as a universal principle encompassing and influencing almost the whole word-stock. Furdík (2004: 74) even speaks of derivational 'cases'. Then, the *derivational paradigm* is conceived as an ordered system of motivated units grouped around a single motivating unit and constituting motivation pairs with it (Horecký et al. 1989: 28–29; see example 1):

(1) *škola* 'school' *škol-ák* 'schoolboy'
    škol-ník 'school janitor'
    škôl-ka 'kindergarten'
    škol-stvo 'education system'
    škol-ička 'small school'   (Furdík 2004: 74)

A sequence of consecutive motivation pairs constitutes a derivational series (Dokulil 1962: 13) or chain (Zych 1999: 12). This is illusatrated in example (2), including seven orders of derivation:

(2) *hodný* 'worthy' >
    hodnota 'value' >
    hodnotiť 'evaluate' >
    zhodnotiť 'evaluate.RESULTATIVE' >
    zhodnocovať 'evaluate.DURATIVE' >
    zhodnocovateľ 'evaluator' >
    zhodnocovateľský 'evaluating' >
    zhodnocovateľsky 'in an evaluating manner'   (Furdík 2004: 74)

A system of derivational paradigms and series/chains organized around one basic underived (non-motivated) word constitutes a *derivational nest* (Horecký et al. 1989; Furdík 2004).

(3)
rezať 'to cut'	*rez-ač* 'cutter.AG'	*rezač-ka* 'cutter.AG.F'	
	rez-ačka 'cutter.INSTR'		
	rez-ák 'incisor'		
	rez 'cut.N'		
	reza-nie 'cutting'		
	rez-ba 'carving'	*rezb-ár* 'carver'	*rezbár-ka* 'carver. F'
			rezbárstvo 'woodcarving' *rezbár-sky* 'concerning woodcarving'
	rez-ivo 'lumber'		*rezb-ársky* 'in the woodcarving manner'
	rez-eň 'cutlet'	*rezn-ík* 'small cutlet'	
	rez-ina 'sawdust'		
	rez-ký 'brisk'		
	rez-ací 'cutting.ADJ'		
	reza-teľný 'cuttable'	*rezateľn-osť* 'cuttability'	
	rez-aný 'cut.PP'	*rezan-ka* 'noodle'	
		rezan-ec 'noodle'	
	od-rezať 'cut off.V'	*odrez-ok* 'shred'	
	v-rezať 'cut into'	*vrezať sa* 'cut into.REFLEXIVE'	
	nar-ezať 'slice'	*nárez* 'slice.N'	
		nareza-nie 'slicing'	
	etc.		(Horecký et al. 1989: 39–40)

This means that derivational nests are constituted by a set of derivational series in the syntagmatic direction and by a set of derivational paradigms in the paradigmatic dimension. A derivational nest covers motivated words with identical onomasiological marks but different onomasiological bases (Horecký et al. 1989: 31). As noted by Kardela (2015: 294), "[t]he theoretical import of the lexical nest should be obvious: the nests form a network of interrelated items which help state the complex derivational relations between the various lexical items and derivatives thereof."

Word-formation research in the recent period has brought renewed interest in complex derivational systems from various perspectives, including a revived interest in derivational paradigms. The discussion of paradigms in word-formation, as Blevins (2013) remarks, continues a venerable tradition in word-based models of the architecture of grammar dating back to ancient Greece. Despite vagaries of disparate development, all such models, including contemporary ones, according to Blevins, "project morphological analysis primarily upwards from the word, and treat the association of words with paradigms or other sets of forms as the most fundamental morphological task" (2013: 375).

Hathout and Namer (2016, 2019) propose a multi-level paradigm-based model, relying on the concepts of derivational family, arrangement relations, and the derivational paradigm. The derivational family is defined as a network of derivationally-related lexemes (e.g. *clarify, clarifier, clarifying, clarification*);

the arrangement relations (that correspond to the alignment relations discussed by Bonami and Strnadová 2019) connect the lexemes formed by the same derivational process. Hathout and Namer (2016) distinguish between the morpho-semantic (MS) and the morpho-formal (MF) levels of description. These levels of description of a derivational family are related by pairing individual morpho-formal units (e.g. *-ify* in *clarify*) with the corresponding morpho-semantic category (labeled 'concept'); in this case, it is *V_Event*, i.e. an Event represented by a verb. The individual morpho-formal units as well as morpho-semantic categories are interconnected to constitute modules that, as assumed by Hathout and Namer, represent systems of interpredictability between words (derivational family), concepts (MS) and formal patterns (MF).

(4) An example of a multi-level paradigm-based model (Hathout and Namer 2016)

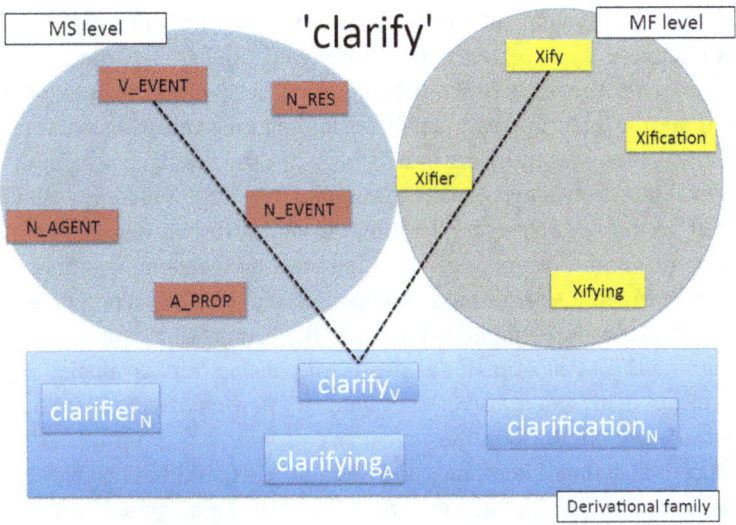

The concept of the derivational paradigm is also a point of departure for the discussion of more complex relations by Bonami and Strnadová (2016, 2019). They work with derivational (sub)families that exhibit key properties shared by inflection systems. Their understanding of the morphological subfamily is analogical to the definition of the derivational family by Hathout and Namer above, i.e. they define it as a set of morphologically related words. A paradigmatic system is then a collection of (partial) families that are aligned in terms of the content-based relations that their members entertain. The notion of alignment is purely content-based, and so it covers word pairs, such as *random, randomize*; *class, classify*; or *order*$_N$, *order*$_V$ – all these pairs are aligned through the CAUSATIVE relation. In general, they consider the content-based contrast between words to be the fundamental feature of paradigm structure.

Bonami and Strnadová emphasize the considerable similarity between inflectional paradigms and morphological families, which is projected onto their fairly liberal understanding of the morphological family: it permits inclusion in a single family of both inflectionally and derivationally-related words (e.g. *sing, sang, singer*). A specific feature of their approach is that the paradigmatic system does not allow for gaps (defectivity) or synonymy within a paradigm (overabundance) – they are purposefully ignored. Given this theoretical background and a number of analogies between inflectional and derivational paradigms, the authors give evidence that the method of computation of the predictability within inflectional paradigms is also applicable to that within derivational paradigms.

Rodrigues and Rodrigues (2017) speak of cross-paradigms conceived as "mental patterns dynamically organized around more than one axis." They distinguish between two main paradigmatic organizations, in particular, the lexeme-based and the affix-based paradigms. The former is illustrated with deverbal nouns, including various affixes adding the same Processual meaning to the ACTION represented by the basic verb, as in the Portuguese examples *avaliar* 'to evaluate' > *avaliação* 'evaluation', *matar* 'to kill' > *matança* 'slaughter', or *aterrar* 'to land' > *aterragem* 'landing'. In other words, this type of paradigmatic organization relies on various affixes adding the same meaning to word bases belonging to the same class of derivational base. The second type of paradigmatic organization employs one and the same affix, for instance, the Portuguese suffix *-ism(o)* in the series *medievalismo* 'medievalism', *espiritualismo* 'spiritualism', *luteranismo* 'Lutheranism', *newtonianismo* 'Newtonianism' and *figurativismo* 'figurativism'.

The central claim of Rodrigues and Rodrigues is that these two types of paradigmatic organization can interact to establish cross-paradigms. The ability of an affix to operate on derivational bases of different word-classes is semantically grounded and accounted for by what Libben (2014) labels as morphological superstates. An important condition for the formation of this kind of cross-paradigms is the size of the morphological family: the formation of cross-paradigms is, as suggested by Rodrigues and Rodrigues (2017), restricted to rich morphological families.

A different line of research into complex derivational relations is represented by tools and models employed by computer linguistics, for example, 'neural' models serving the completion of derivational paradigms, inspired by well-established models of inflectional paradigm completion (Cotterell et al.

2017) and computerized systems employed for the establishment of derivational nests (networks) in the Czech language (e.g. Pala and Hlaváčková 2007; Ševčíková and Žabokrtský 2014; Pala and Šmerk 2015).

1.2 Theoretical principles

The point of departure in our approach is the concept of *paradigm*. It has traditionally been discussed exclusively within the field of inflectional morphology. The idea of derivational paradigms has, for a long time, been called into question.[2] Nevertheless, there is significant parallelism between inflectional and derivational paradigms. The main points of *correspondence* are reviewed in what follows.

(i) Both of these types of paradigm operate within *word-classes*. Thus, there are, among others, substantival, verbal, adjectival and adverbial paradigms in inflection, which means that (inflectional) affixes are attached, respectively, to nominal, verbal, adjectival and adverbial bases. In derivation, in an analogical manner, paradigms are also based on nouns, verbs, adjectives and adverbs. The fact that the word-class can change in the process of derivation is not important (word-class changing affixation is a typical feature of derivational processes) in this respect because it does not affect the categorial foundation of either inflectional or derivational paradigms. The class-changing capacity of derivation bears on the two-dimensional system of derivational nests. The inflectional and derivational paradigms are, however, unidimensional systems that rely on the identity of the word-class of the basic word.

(ii) The inflectional paradigm is based on expressing certain (grammatical) *categories* by affixes (among other possible means), for example, CASE, NUMBER and GENDER in nouns. Analogically, derivational paradigms are also based on expressing certain (semantic) categories, for example, AGENT, PATIENT, INSTRUMENT, LOCATION, ABSTRACTION, ITERATIVITY, CAUSE, RESULT OF ACTION, DIMINUTIVENESS, AUGMENTATIVENESS, etc. *By implication, both types of paradigms are organized around the concept of category*.

(iii) Each of the grammatical categories can be realized, depending on the morphological type of a language, by *one or more form-meaning units*, including various affixes. Thus, for example, the nominative plural slot of the

---

2 For an overview of various approaches to derivational paradigms see Štekauer (2014) and Hathout and Namer (2019).

substantival paradigm in Slovak can be represented by *-i, -y, -ovia, -e, -á, -ia*, or *-tá* (their use depends on the formally determined gender of the particular noun and the nature of the word-final phoneme), and this establishes various substantival paradigms for the category of nouns (twelve in total). By the same token, one can analogically speak of *one or more form-meaning units* constituting derivational paradigms, for instance, within the semantic category of AGENT in English:

(5) (i)   verbal base + the suffix *-er* (*teacher*)
    (ii) nominal base + the suffix *-ist* (*pianist*)
    (iii) nominal base + the suffix *-ian* (*librarian*)
    (iv) nominal base + the semisuffix *-man* (*milkman*)
    (v)   verbal base + the suffix *-ist* (*typist*)
    (vi) verbal base + the suffix *-ee* (*escapee*)
    (vii) nominal base + the suffix *-eer* (*profiteer*)
    etc.

(iv) Both inflectional and derivational paradigms function as a *pattern* for new lexical items entering the system of a language. This means that both inflectional and derivational paradigms are controlled by the principles of *productivity*, *regularity* and *predictability*.

These analogies between inflectional and derivational paradigms can be completed with those proposed by Bonami and Strnadová (2016, 2019) using examples from Czech and French. These include points (v) through (vii) below.

(v) In a paradigmatic system, the formally unmarked cell (if any) need not be the same for all inflectional or derivational paradigms. In example (6a) from Czech, the same morphosyntactic feature is realized formally by different exponents: $X \sim X\mathring{u}$ vs. $Xa \sim X$ vs. $Xa \sim X\mathring{u}$ vs. $X \sim X$. The same kind of differential exponence can be illustrated for a derivational paradigm (6b), where we see the alternations $X \sim X\varepsilon$ vs. $Xi \sim X$ vs. $Xi \sim X\varepsilon$ vs. $X \sim X$:

(6) (a) Differential exponence in inflectional paradigms (example from Czech)

NOM. SG	GEN.PL	
hrad	hradů	'castle'
žena	žen	'woman'
táta	tátů	'dad'
stavení	stavení	'building'

(b) Differential exponence in derivational paradigms (example from French)

COUNTRY		INHABITANT	
France	'France'	Français	'French'
Russie	'Russia'	Russe	'Russian'
Albanie	'Albania'	Albanais	'Albanian'
Corse	'Corsica'	Corse	'Corsican'

(Bonami and Strnadová 2019: 180)

(vi) Both inflectional and derivational paradigms may use an exponence strategy that is a hybrid of two others (heteroclisis), as illustrated in (7). The contrast between nom.sg. and gen.pl. for *táta* is marked by a hybrid combination of the nom.sg. *žena* and the gen.pl. *hradů* (Xa ~ Xů). The same can be found in the derivational paradigm of (6b), where the contrast between *Albanie* and *Albanais* combines the exponents found in *Russie* (name of the country) and *Français* (inhabitant), i.e. Xi ~ Xɛ (Bonami and Strnadová 2019: 181):

(7)
NOM.SG	GEN.PL	COUNTRY	INHABITANT
hrad 'castle'	hradů	France 'France'	Français 'French'
táta 'dad'	tátů	Albanie 'Albania'	Albanais 'Albanian'

(vii) Some inflectional and derivational paradigms fail to mark the semantic difference with a corresponding form (syncretism) – this is a well-known violation of the principle of constructional iconicity proposed within the Natural Morphology theory (e.g. Dressler 2005):

(8)
nom.sg	gen.pl	country	Inhabitant
hrad 'castle'	hradů	**France** 'France'	Français 'French'
stavení 'building'	stavení	**Corse** 'Corsica'	**Corse** 'Corsican'

(Bonami and Strnadová 2016: 9)

This means for us that there seems to be only one substantial difference between the two types of paradigm: while the membership in inflectional paradigms is prototypically, due to the absence of competition, obligatory and automatic, the membership in derivational paradigms is prototypically, due to competition, facultative. As a result, while there are minimum gaps (but they do occur!) in the paradigms within the inflectional system, there are quite a lot of them in the derivational paradigmatic systems of natural languages. Related to this, while inflectional paradigms represent a closed system, derivational paradigms are an open system. This fact, however, does not project itself into a chaotic and vague nature of derivational paradigms. In fact, the opposite is true. In spite of numerous gaps, derivational paradigms are highly regular and predictable, which is guaranteed by the possibility to fill any empty slot with a potential word that fits the *paradigmatic system*. From this it follows that the only major difference between inflectional and derivational paradigms concerns the fact that, while the former is based on *actual units*, the latter relies on a combination of *actual and potential units* (see also Bauer 1997). In other words, as also pointed out by, among others, Boyé and Schalchli (2019) and Gaeta and Angster (2019), the difference between inflectional and derivational paradigms is basically of a *quantitative nature*.

In summary, while an inflectional paradigm is conceived as a system of forms of a single word, derivational paradigms can be treated as a system of complex words derived from a single word-formation base. This includes all *direct derivatives* from a single word-formation base (vertical dimension), as illustrated in the following example with the Slovak word *dom* 'house':

(9)   (i)   *dom*   'house'
       (ii)   *dom-ov*   'home'
       (iii)   *dom-ček*   'little house'
       (iv)   *dom-ík*   'little house'
       (v)   *dom-isko*   'large house'
       (vi)   *dom-ov* (adverb of direction)   'towards one's home'

In this case, we speak of the *paradigmatic capacity* of the word-formation base represented by the number of direct derivatives from the word-formation base (basic underived word).

In addition, there is another, syntagmatic dimension that should be taken into consideration, in particular, all linear derivations from a single word-formation base, as in (10):

(10) (a)   *dom*   *dom-ov*   *dom-ov-ina*   *dom-ov-in-ový*
             'house'   'home'   'homeland'   'related to a homeland'
     (b)   *dom*   *dom-ček*   *dom-ček-ový*
             'house'   'little house'   'related to a little house'
     (c)   *dom*   *dom-ík*   *dom-ík-ový*
             'house'   'little house'   'related to a little house'
     (d)   *dom*   *dom-isko*   *dom-isk-ový*
             'house'   'large house'   'related to a large house'

This dimension enables us to identify the number of affixation operations available for a given basic underived word. Each such affixation operation represents one order of derivation. By implication, this dimension identifies *orders of derivation*. In example (10), (a) shows three orders of derivation, while (b) through (d) permit two orders of derivation from the same simple underived word *dom* 'house'.

The concept of derivational orders makes it possible to extend the scope of paradigmatic capacity beyond the immediate, direct derivatives from basic words to all orders of derivation. In that case, we can speak of the *derivational capacity* of the word-formation base (basic, underived word). The derivational capacity can be examined for each order of derivation separately, or it can cover all orders of derivation.

Finally, each derivational step introduces (and therefore expresses and represents) a particular *semantic category*. In (10a) these are, respectively, LOCATION, LOCATION and QUALITY, in (10b) and (10c) DIMINUTIVE and QUALITY, and in (10d) AUGMENTATIVE and QUALITY. By implication, a combination of derivatives from the same base simultaneously identifies a combination of semantic categories realized in the process of consecutive derivations. Semantics thus functions as an indispensable third dimension of our model. Any order of derivation can include more than one semantic category, and one and the same category can be formally represented by more than one affix as, for example, in (10b) and (10c), where the 1st order of derivation from *dom* 'house' includes two different affixal representations of the semantic category of DIMINUTIVE. From this it follows that one and the same basic word can give rise to several paths of consecutive derivations, each of which has its specific number of derivatives representing specific semantic categories.

The paradigmatic capacity and the orders of derivation establish the *derivational network*, that is, a network of derivatives derived from the same word-formation base (simple underived word) with the aim of formally representing specific semantic categories.

Derivational networks may substantially differ from language to language in their complexity in terms of both the number of orders of derivation and the number of derivatives in each order. This is illustrated by a comparison of derivational networks for equivalent basic words: the Icelandic word *drekka* and the Bulgarian word *pie*, both meaning 'to drink'[3]:

---

[3] Due to the complexity of the derivational network for the Bulgarian word *pie* 'to drink', its derivational network is divided into three parts (Figures 1.1a, 1.2a and 1.3), each of which represents one order of derivation.

Figures 1.1–1.3 illustrate considerable differences between these two derivational networks in terms of both the number of derivatives and the number of orders.

The *maximum derivational network* results from the intersection ('horizontal' and 'vertical' derivations) of all implemented (actual) derivations found for all basic words of an examined sample within a particular word-class (see Figure 1.4).

In our example, the maximum derivational network for Bulgarian adjectives in the 1st order of derivation is 27 derivatives (the highlighted numbers). By adding up the maximum numbers for all orders of derivation, we get the maximum derivational network for the class of adjectives. In the case of Bulgarian adjectives, this is 88.

The concept of the *structural richness* of a derivational network of a single word-formation base is quantitatively represented by the *saturation value* calculated as a proportion between the number of actual derivatives in a particular derivational network and the maximum derivational network (cf. section 1.3.5).

1.3 Research project methodology and objectives

The research project from which this volume originates is aimed at the evaluation of a range of parameters defining derivational networks across languages: the paradigmatic capacity, the (maximum) derivational capacity, the order of derivation, the saturation value of derivational networks in individual languages and in language genera, typical combinations of semantic categories, and their potential blocking effects for a uniform sample of 30 words from 40 languages of Europe that yielded 1,200 derivational networks in total, an extremely rich source of data.

1.3.1 Sample of words

The point of departure is three word-classes, including nouns, verbs and adjectives. Each of these word-classes is represented by 10 simple underived words. Since each of the 30 basic words must be a simple underived word in each of the 40 sample languages, we chose Swadesh's core vocabulary counting 200 words because the chances of finding simple underived equivalents for core vocabulary words across the sample languages are relatively high. The first

	Agent	Location	Entitiy	Finitive	Directional	Saturative	Inceptive	Augmentative	Singulative	Diminutive	Desiderative
Quality											
1A pivăk											
1B piteen											
1C pijan											
1D pijač											
		1E pivnica									
			1F pivo								
			1G pitie								
			1H pijavica								
				1I dopie (si)							
				1J izpie							
					1K vpie (se)						
						1L napie (se)					
						1M opie (se)					
							1N zapie (se)				
							1O razpie (se)				
							1P propie (se)	1P nadpie			
								1Q prepie			
									1R otpie		
										1S popie	
										1T pijne	
											1U pie mu se

Figure 1.1: (a) Derivational network, 1st order, Bulgarian verb pie 'to drink'.

	1st order							
Quality	Resultative	Agent	Instrument	Process		State	Action	Manner
1A drekkanlegur								
				1B drekking				
				1C drekkandi				

Figure 1.1: (b) Derivational network, 1st order, Icelandic verb drekka 'to drink'.

selection identified 74 nouns, 54 verbs and 31 adjectives in total. Their equivalents in the sample languages were subsequently marked as simple or derived. This left us with 37 simple underived nouns, 12 simple underived verbs and 10 simple underived adjectives. Consequently, the sample of adjectives was 'naturally' identified. The samples of nouns and verbs were reduced to 10 each by eliminating those words that were excessively represented in Swadesh's semantic groups (Swadesh 1955). All in all, the resulting sample of 3x10 words includes only words that are simple, underived and, from a synchronic point of view, actively used in all 40 languages.

(11) | **Nouns** | **Verbs** | **Adjectives** |
|---|---|---|
| bone | cut | bad |
| eye | dig | new |
| tooth | pull | black |
| day | throw | straight |
| dog | give | warm |
| louse | hold | old |
| fire | sew | long |
| stone | burn | thin |
| water | drink | thick |
| name | know | narrow |

Importantly, each word was assessed and confirmed as an inherent part of the present-day wordstock of a particular language by an expert morphologist(s) of that language. By implication, the derivational networks based on these 30 simple underived words rely on synchronically productive affixation rules in each of the 40 languages covered in this research. One of the fundamental principles in developing individual derivational networks was the exclusion from the network of any archaic, obsolete, regional, or slang words.

2nd order

State	Female	Manner	Collective + (Entity)	Agent	Relational	Diminutive	Action	Saturative	Entity	Instrument	Inceptive	Abstraction	Quality
2A1 pivkost													
2C1 pijanstvo		2C2 pijano		2C3 pijanica	2C5 pijanski	2C6 pijaničak	2C7 pijanstva				2C8 vpijanči se		
	2D1 pijačka		2D2 pijačka	2C4 pijandur							2C9 opijanči se		
					2H1 pijavičen								
						2J1 poizpie		2J2 doizpie					
						2L1 ponapie (se)			2L3 napitka				
						2M1 poopie se							
						2N1 pozapie se						2N2 zapoj	
						2Q1 poprepie							
						2R1 pootpie							
						2T1 popijne				2S1 popivka			
										2S2 popivatelna	2U1 pripie mu se		2S3 popivatelen
											2U2 dopie mu se		

Figure 1.2: (a) Derivational network, 2nd order, Bulgarian verb pie 'to drink'.

2nd order	
Quality	**Action**
1A1 ódrekkanlegur	
1A2 ódrekkandi	
	1C1 sídrekkandi

Figure 1.2: (b) Derivational network, 2nd order, Icelandic verb drekka 'to drink'.

3rd order			
Agent	**Saturative**	**Diminutive**	**Pluriactionality**
3C4a pijandurnik	3C7a napijanstva (se)	3C6b popijanstva	
			3J1a izpoizpie
			3L1a izponapie

Figure 1.3: Derivational network, 3rd order, Bulgarian verb pie 'to drink'.

1.3.2 Sample of languages

The sample of 40 European languages was established in two steps. The primary source was the languages covered in Müller et al. (2015–2016). Their number was reduced on the basis of their data availability, i.e. according to the possibility of verifying the existence of derived words by means of representative dictionaries and/or corpora. An important reference guide in this respect was *Ethnologue*, in particular, its *Expanded Graded Intergenerational Disruption Scale* that includes 12 levels. Only levels 0–4 were taken into consideration because only languages falling within any of these five levels met the abovementioned criteria of representativeness (Table 1.1).

A list of the languages selected is given in Table 1.2.

1st order of derivation, Bulgarian, adjectives	Quality	Entity	State	Process	Inceptive	Resultative	Diminutive	Patient	Instrument	Manner	Temporal	Directional	Privative	Causative	Abstraction	Augmentative
	1	1	2			1	1		1					2		1
	1		1			1	3		1	1						2
			1			1			1		1	1	1			
			1			2								1	1	
	3	1		1		2	2		1					1		2
		1	3	1		1			1							
			2			1	2		1					3		2
	1		2	1	2	1	1		1							
	2		2			1			1					2		
			1	1			1	1								
Maximum derivational network	3	1	3	1	1	2	2	3	1	1	1	1	1	3	1	2

Figure 1.4: Maximum numbers of 1st order derivatives per semantic category – Bulgarian adjectives.

Table 1.1: Expanded Graded Intergenerational Disruption Scale (Ethnologue).

Level	Status	Description
0	International	The language is widely used between nations in trade, knowledge exchange, and international policy.
1	National	The language is used in education, work, mass media, and government at the national level.
2	Provincial	The language is used in education, work, mass media, and government within major administrative subdivisions of a nation.
3	Wider Communication	The language is used in work and mass media without official status to transcend language differences across a region.
4	Educational	The language is in vigorous use, with standardization and literature being sustained through a widespread system of institutionally supported education.

Table 1.2: Sample languages by language families and by genera (based on WALS).

Indo-European (29)	**Slavic** (9): Bulgarian, Croatian, Czech, Polish, Russian, Serbian, Slovak, Slovene, Ukrainian
	Germanic (8): Danish, Dutch, English, Frisian, German, Icelandic, Norwegian, Swedish
	Romance (7): Catalan, French, Galician, Italian, Portuguese, Romanian, Spanish
	Celtic (2): Irish, Welsh
	Baltic (2): Latvian, Lithuanian
	Greek
Uralic (4)	Estonian, Finnish, Hungarian, North Saami
Altaic (2)	Tatar, Turkish
Nakh-Daghestanian (2)	Chechen, Dargwa
Kartvelian (1)	Georgian
Afro-Asiatic (1)	Maltese
Isolate (1)	Basque

1.3.3 Semantic categories

For the sake of the semantic classification of each derived word, a provisional list of semantic categories was proposed and completed/modified in the course of the project's implementation, taking fine-grained nuances in different languages into consideration. The objective was to preserve a desired level of generalization without losing relevant distinctions (see Appendix 1). The overall semantic theory employed for devising a set of semantic categories is cast in constructionist (Booij 2010) and cognitive linguistic terms, at least in that it recognizes subsymbolic processes in networks as constitutive, since construction relations are obtained at all levels of linguistic patterning. The compiled set contains theory-neutral, cross-linguistically applicable, comparative semantic concepts (in Haspelmath's (2010) sense of the term 'comparative concept'). The semantic categories have been posited regardless of the formal means of their expression in different languages. In keeping with Croft's (2003) recommendations for enhancing cross-linguistic comparability, the semantic comparative categories allow for the examination of "the construction(s) or *strategies* used to *encode*" them in separate languages (Croft

2003: 14). The constructions can be read off the individual networks in each language, while the strategies can be detected in any alternative process employed in languages with poor derivational networks, where compensatory mechanisms, also known as "strategies", are identified.

Since comparative concepts are abstracted from descriptive categories as prototypes, the categories used in the individual chapters have been conceived on the basis of general typological considerations within the limits of typical meanings of affixation patterns in the European languages for which the categories have been posited. Bearing the underdetermination of lexical concepts (Evans 2009; Ludlow 2014) in mind and accepting that language is a complex adaptive system (Beckner et al. 2009) and that meaning in language is a synergetic, emergent phenomenon (Köhler 2011), the generation of meaning in derivational word-formation is a multifactorial process with particular meaning features not attributable to any single specific factor or constituent in a recoverable causal manner. With these preliminaries in mind, the set of semantic categories employed in building the networks are characterized by the following:

(i) they function as canonical points "from which the phenomena actually found can be calibrated" (Corbett 2010: 141) and, in that sense, they target common cross-linguistic specificities, not the peculiarities of individual languages;

(ii) they constitute "a special set of comparative concepts that are specifically created by typologists for the purposes of comparison" (Haspelmath 2010: 663) and are, in that sense, constructs, not part and parcel of the competence of speakers;

(iii) they are heterogeneous in terms of a number of criteria: a) the degree of granularity of the notional categories (in the sense that they combine different numbers of the ontological types discussed below); b) the number of cross-linguistic instantiations; and c) the typicality of individual semantic categories for a specific language;

(iv) their heterogeneity tries to avoid the association of comparative concepts with any specified word-class in any language, as well as distinctions between types of affixes (infixes, superfixes, prefixes, suffixes, etc.) and the associated problems of categorial headedness;

(v) the set of comparative concepts has been extracted from descriptive categories of individual languages. The language-specific categories were used as the lower limit of granularity, while the upper limit was determined by the *ontological types* defined by Cruse in dealing with lexical semantics, i.e. the "fundamental modes of conception that the human mind is presumably innately predisposed to adopt" (Cruse 2000: 49);

(vi) the degree of granularity can at best be illustrated, not explicated – e.g. RESULT OF ACTION is a subcategory of the basic ontological types, combining features of ACTION and STATE. Thus the employed semantic category RESULTATIVE is one level of generality removed from the ontological types. It is at that level that the comparative semantic concepts have been postulated;

(vii) each sense associated with a specific affix is accommodated under a separate semantic category from the set, and thus systematic polysemy in derivation can be captured;

(viii) when two inseparably linked meaning elements are associated with a single affix, two semantic categories are used to classify the derivative within a particular derivational step, e.g. Spanish *ojo* 'eye' > *oj-oso* 'a person having big eyes' labeled with PATIENT +AUGMENTATIVE; and

(ix) the semantic categories are associated with the last derivational step in a series, i.e. with the specific affix attached within this step, and derivatives are discretely arranged in orders of derivation so that the categories do not take into account the resultant lexical meaning of a specific derivative.

The set has been compiled on the basis of both semasiological (extensive reading of analyses of affixation phenomena on the basis of existing, actual words in various European languages) and onomasiological considerations (the onomasiological stance underlies the very cogitation of these concepts designed to incorporate possible words), even though the networks for the individual languages in the volume are based exclusively on existing, attested words.

1.3.4 Construction of derivational networks

Each contributor identified a derivational network for each of the 30 sample words for their language and calculated the saturation values of a derivational network:

a) for each sample word,
b) for the word-class of sample nouns, verbs and adjectives, and
c) for the whole sample of 30 words.

The development of derivational networks faces a number of theoretical problems primarily related to the fuzzy boundary between derivation and inflection (cf., for example, Scalise 1988; Dressler 1989; van Marle 1995; Booij 2006; ten Hacken 2014; Štekauer 2015). For illustration, the fuzzy boundary between past participles and their adjectival homonyms is one of many theoretical problems of this kind that have not found a unanimous solution either among theoretical morphologists or from a cross-linguistic perspective. Therefore, past participles and the words derived from them have not been included in the derivational networks within this project. Gradation, treated as an inflectional category in traditional grammars, has not been included in the derivational networks either, even if some authors consider it to be a derivational phenomenon. Similar problems bear on the status of combining forms, affixoids, polysemy, and semantic shift. Owing to unequal theoretical approaches to their derivational relevance, it was decided that combining forms be excluded from derivational networks. A list of them was compiled in order to keep to a unified approach across all languages. The same is true of affixoids unless a representative grammar or a reference book explicitly identifies a particular unit as an affix. If a language does not have any basic form, such as English infinitive, and if there are several inflected forms that can serve as the basis for the 1st order of derivation, all of these forms were taken as a single zero-degree base. Any transflexion, transposition, conversion, etc. were excluded from the scope of derivational networks. This fact, certainly, cannot but be reflected in the richness of the derivational networks. So, for example, in Basque, all verb formation is based on conversion. In addition, conversion is also highly productive for nouns and adjectives (cf. Chapter 46, this volume). The networks contain lexical items that are exclusively constructed by affixation processes. Only basic meanings, directly derived in the process of derivation, count. Last but not least, it was found that individual language genera face their own specific problems. These are discussed in brief introductions to the individual language groups.

1.3.5 Evaluation of derivational networks

Saturation value calculations are based on the concept of the *Maximum Derivational Network* (MDN) (see Figure 1.4 above and the relevant text). For its computation, it is necessary to identify the highest number of derivatives for a given semantic category from among all ten sample words (in our research) of a given word-class.

The MDN values enable us to calculate the saturation value for individual adjectives by means of the formula in (12):

(12)
$$SV = \frac{D}{MDN} \times 100(\%)$$

Legend:
SV Saturation value
D Number of derivatives
MDN Maximum derivational network

For illustration, the Bulgarian adjective *topâl* 'warm' has 27 derivatives. Its saturation value is obtained as 25: 88 × 100 = 28.41%.

In the 1st order, it produces 7 derivatives. These are related to the 1st order MDN, which is 27. Therefore, its 1st order saturation value is 7:27 × 100 = 25.93%.

This procedure makes it possible to calculate average saturation values for each word-class by orders of derivation (13):

(13) Bulgarian adjectives: Average values of saturation by orders of derivation:
1st order saturation 30.74%
2nd order saturation 18.79%
3rd order saturation 20.00%
4th order saturation 11.67%
5th order saturation 10.00%

As a result, each sample language is characterized in terms of the complexity of its derivational networks. Based on this data, the authors of language-specific chapters comment on the results according to a unified structure defined for all 40 language-specific chapters. That means that each language is evaluated and discussed within a separate chapter. Language genera that are represented by more than one language of this sample are introduced by chapters reflecting problems related to the construction of derivational networks in all the languages of the genus/family.

1.4 Structure of language-specific chapters

The structure of each language-specific chapter is as follows:
(i) A brief description of the word-formation system of a language in order to determine the role of affixation processes in the word-formation system of that language.
(ii) Computation of maximum derivational networks.
(iii) Computation of saturation values for each sample word in each of the three word-classes, i.e. nouns, verbs and adjectives, and for each of the word-classes as a whole.

(iv) Identification of the average number and the maximum number of orders of derivation for nouns, verbs and adjectives.
(v) Computation of the derivational capacity for each word-class in each order of derivation.
(vi) Examination of the correlation between semantic categories and orders of derivation.
(vii) Identification of those semantic categories that are typical of individual orders of derivation. In other words, an answer will be provided for the question 'Are any semantic categories characteristic of a particular order of derivation within a particular word-class of ten basic words?'
(viii) Identification of semantic categories that systematically block any further derivation at individual orders of derivation. While there has been extensive research into the combinability of derivational affixes, the data on the combinability of semantic categories without regard to the specific affixes that realize them may reveal additional explanations for the theory of affix combinations and the blocking effects of affixes.
(ix) Identification of typical combinations of semantic categories as an answer to the question 'Are any combinations of semantic categories typical of derivational networks of a given language?'
(x) Identification of multiple occurrences of semantic categories in a series of derivations from a single basic word.
(xi) Identification of the reversibility of semantic categories as an answer to the question 'Are there typical combinations of semantic categories of the sort AB/BA, meaning that two semantic categories can occur in a reversed order?'
(xii) For languages with small derivational networks, a brief explanation of what this means for the word-formation system of that language and how this paucity of derivatives is compensated for is given.
(xiii) Conclusions.

Any deviations from this structure are due to the absence of a particular phenomenon in a given language. Each of the proposed evaluation criteria that constitute the language-specific structure is designed to provide us with a picture of the derivational potential and its actualization and the nature of the derivational system of individual languages, with the emphasis on the role, function and combinability of semantic categories in the formation of new complex words. In addition, these criteria enable us to identify preferred word-formation strategies in various languages and genera.

The last chapter of this volume compares and evaluates the data for all 40 sample languages by individual parameters and draws conclusions from this analysis.

References

Bagasheva, Alexandra. 2017. Comparative semantic concepts in affixation. In J. Santana-Lario & S. Valera (eds.), *Competing patterns in English affixation*, 33–65. Bern: Peter Lang.
Barlow, Michale & Suzanne Kemmer (eds.). 2000. *Usage-based models of language*. Stanford: CSLI.
Bauer, Laurie. 1997. Derivational paradigms. In Geert Booij & Jaap van Marle (eds.), *Yearbook of Morphology*, 243–256. Dordrecht: Kluwer.
Beckner, Clay, Richard Blythe, Joan Bybee, Morten H. Christiansen, William Croft, Nick C. Ellis, John Holland, Jinyun Ke, Diane Larsen-Freeman & Tom Schoenemann. 2009. Language as a complex adaptive system. In Nick C. Ellis & Diane Larsen-Freeman (eds.), Language as a complex adaptive system. [Special issue]. *Language Learning* 59 (1). 1–26.
Blevins, James, P. 2013. Word-based Morphology from Aristotle to Modern WP (Word and Paradigm Models). In K. Alled (Ed.), *The Oxford Handbook of the History of Linguistics*, 375–395. Oxford: Oxford University Press.
Bonami, Olivier & Jana Strnadová. 2016. Derivational paradigms: pushing the analogy. Paper presented at the SLE conference, Naples, 31 August–3 September.
Bonami, Olivier & Jana Strnadová. 2019. Paradigm structure and predictability in derivational morphology. *Morphology* 29 (2). 167–197.
Booij, Gert. 2006. Inflection and derivation. In K. Brown (ed.), *Encyclopedia of Language and Linguistics*, 2nd edn., 654–661. Oxford: Elsevier.
Booij, Gert. 2010. *Construction Morphology*. Oxford: Oxford University Press.
Boyé, Gilles & Gauvin Schalchli. 2019. Realistic data and paradigms. *Morphology* 29 (2). 199–248.
Bybee, Joan. 2006. From usage to grammar: the mind's response to repetition. *Language* 82 (4): 711–733.
Corbett, Greville. 2010. Canonical Derivational Morphology. *Word Structure* 3 (2). 141–155.
Cotterell, R., E. Vylomova, H. Khayrallah, C. Kirov & D. Yarowsky. 2017. Paradigm completion for derivational morphology. arXiv:170809151.
Croft, William. 2003 [1990]. *Typology and Universals*, 2nd edn. Cambridge: Cambridge University Press.
Cruse, Alan. 2000. *Meaning in Language: An Introduction to Semantics and Pragmatics*. Oxford: Oxford University Press.
Dokulil, M. 1962. *Tvoření slov v češtině. Teorie odvozování slov*. [Word-formation in Czech. A theory of derivation]. Praha: Nakladatelství československé akademie věd.
Dressler, Wolfgang U. 1989. Prototypical differences between inflection and derivation. *Zeitschrift für Sprachwissenschaft und Kommunikationsforschung* 42. 3–10.
Dressler, Wolfgang U. 2005. Word formation in natural morphology. In Pavol Štekauer & Rochelle Lieber (eds.), *Handbook of word formation*, 267–284. Dordrecht: Springer.
Evans, Vyvyan. 2009. *How Words Mean*. Oxford: Oxford University Press.

Furdík, Juraj. 2004. *Slovenská slovotvorba*. Edited by Martin Ološtiak. Prešov: Náuka.
Gaeta, Livio & Marco Angster. 2019. Stripping paradigmatic relations out of the syntax. *Morphology* 29 (2). 249–270.
Haspelmath, Martin. 2010. Comparative concepts and descriptive categories in crosslinguistic studies. *Language* 86 (3). 663–687.
Hathout, Nabil & Fiameta Namer. 2016. Multi-level Paradigm-based Model of Competition in Word Formation. Paper presented at the 17th International Morphology Meeting, Vienna, 18–21 February.
Hathout, Nabil & Fiameta Namer. 2019. Paradigms in word-formation: what are we up to? *Morphology* 29 (2). 153–165.
Horecký, Ján, Klára Buzássyová & Ján Bosák. 1989. *Dynamika slovnej zásoby súčasnej slovenčiny*. Bratislava: SAV.
Kardela, Henryk. 2015. Lexical nests revisited: a cognitive grammar account. In R. Gregová, L. Körtvélyessy, S. Tomaščíková and S. Valera (eds.), A Festschrift for Pavol Štekauer. [Special issue]. *SKASE Journal of Theoretical Linguistics* 12 (3). 292–312.
Köhler, Reinhard. 2011. Laws of language. In Patrick Colm Hogan (ed.), *The Cambridge Encyclopedia of the Language Sciences*, 424–426). Cambridge: Cambridge University Press.
Libben, Gary. 2014. The nature of compounds: a psychocentric perspective. *Cognitive Neuropsychology* 31 (1–2). 8–25.
Ludlow, Peter. 2014. *Living Words: Meaning Underdetermination and the Dynamic Lexicon*. Oxford: Oxford University Press.
Müller, Peter O., Ingeborg Ohnheiser, Susan Olsen & Franz Rainer (eds.). 2015–2016. *Word-Formation. An International Handbook of the Languages of Europe*. Berlin: Mouton.
Pala, Karel & Dana Hlaváčková. 2007. Derivational Relations in Czech WordNet. In J. Piskorski and H. Tanev (eds.), *Proceedings of the Workshop on Balto-Slavonic Natural Language Processing: Information Extraction and Enabling Technologies*, 75–81. Madison: Omniopress.
Pala, Karel & Pavel Šmerk. 2015. Derivancze – Derivational Analyzer of Czech. In. P. Král and V. Matoušek (eds.), *Text, Speech and Dialogue. TSD 2015. Lecture Notes in Computer Science, vol. 9302*, 515–523. Springer: Cham.
Rodrigues, Alexandra S. & Pedro J. Rodrigues. 2017. Cross-paradigms or word formation patterns in interface: evidence from Portuguese. Paper presented at the ParadigMo Conference, Toulouse, 19–20 June.
Sapir, Edward. 1921. *Language: An Introduction to the Study of Speech*. New York: Harcourt, Brace and Company.
Scalise, Sergio. 1988. Inflection and derivation. *Linguistics* 26. 561–581.
Ševčíková, Magda & Zdeněk Žabokrtský. 2014. Word-Formation Network for Czech. In Nicoletta Calzolari, Khalid Choukri, Thierry Declerck, Hrafn Loftsson, Bente Maegaard, Joseph Mariani, Asuncion Moreno, Jan Odijk & Stelios Piperidis (eds.), *Proceedings of the 9th International Language Resources and Evaluation Conference (LREC 2014)*, 1087–1093. Paris: ELRA.
Skalička, Vladimír. 2004–2006. *Souborne dilo I–III*. Edited by F. Čermák, J. Čermák, P. Čermák & K. Poeta. Praha: Karolinum.
Swadesh, Morris. 1955. Towards Greater Accuracy in Lexicostatistic Dating. *International Journal of American Linguistics* 21 (2). 121–137.

Štekauer, Pavol. 2014. Derivational paradigms. In Rochelle Lieber & Pavol Štekauer (eds.), *The Oxford Handbook of Derivational Morphology*, 354–369. Oxford: Oxford University Press.

Štekauer, Pavol. 2015. The delimitation of derivation and inflection. In P.O. Müller, I. Ohnheiser, S. Olsen & F. Rainer (eds.), *Word-Formation. An International Handbook of the Languages of Europe*, 218–234. Berlin: Mouton.

Ten Hacken, Pius. 2014. Delineating derivation and inflection. In Rochelle Lieber & Pavol Štekauer (eds.), *The Oxford Handbook of Derivational Morphology*, 10–25. Oxford: Oxford University Press.

Van Marle, Jaap. 1995. The unity of morphology: on the interwovenness of the derivational and inflectional dimension of the word. In G. E. Booij & J. van Marle (eds.), *Yearbook of Morphology 1995*, 67–82. Dordrecht: Kluwer Academic Publishers.

Zych, Anna. 1999. *Struktura I semantyka polkich I roszjskich gniazd slowotwórczzch z przyimkami wyjściowymi nazywajacymi barwe*. Katowice: WUS.

Martina Ivanová, Božena Bednaříková
2 Introduction to Slavic languages

The first question to be discussed when investigating Slavic word-formation is the general status of word-formation in Slavic languages. According to linguistic tradition, word-formation is considered part of either morphology (as it is in Polish, cf. Nagórko 2016; partly in Czech, e.g. in Trávníček 1951; Dokulil et al. 1986; Bednaříková 2009; Štícha et al. 2013; etc.) or lexicology (as it is in Slovak, cf. Furdík 2004; partly in Czech, e.g. Hauser 1980).

Even if from the point of view of deductive typology (Skalička 1935), which assumes conversion as a typical word-formation process, word-formation is primarily based on affixation in Slavic languages. According to Furdík (2004: 64), 80% of words resulting from word-formation processes are affixally-derived words. Slavic languages have rich resources for word-formation. The affixation system is extremely productive and makes use of dozens, and sometimes hundreds, of affixes (Körtvélyessy 2016).

Within the domain of the word-formation status, the basic question is the boundary between inflection and derivation. The character of affixation as a morphological process differs according to its function. Basically, any morphological process is inherently additive. In derivation, in the sense of adding an affix (as a physical segment) to the base, the affix (be it prefix or suffix) bears the onomasiological function, while in inflection the affixation has the character of modification instead (see Mel'čuk 2000; Bednaříková 2009, 2011). In examples like *vod-a* (NOM.SG.) ~ *vod-u* (ACC. SG.) 'water', the affix replaces another affix, the inflection thus being a special subtype of modification. In affixation in the sense of derivation, there is an underlying word which is a member of the word-formational paradigm, whereas in affixation in the sense of modification/inflection there is no underlying word at all – none of the forms of the inflectional paradigm can be viewed as defining the others.

Generally, there are several potential problems regarding the status of lexical units as inflected or derived forms.

For example, the status of aspectual forms is open to debate. Some authors regard aspectual forms as grammatical (e.g. Kopečný 1962; Tichonov 1998) and others consider them as derivational (e.g. Maslov 1958, 1963; Sekaninová 1980; for detailed information, cf. Sokolová 2009). In some theoretical works, aspectual pairs differentiated by suffixes are considered part of inflection, whereas pairs differentiated by prefixes are considered part of word-formation. Other sources discussing inflection in general do not distinguish between perfectivization and imperfectivization but speak of aspect as non-prototypical inflection

(Dressler 1989) or inherent inflection (Booij 1996; Cetnarowska 2001). On the contrary, certain authors distinguish semantic changes brought about by prefixation that vary from neutral perfectivization to 'sublexical' modification in the so-called '*Aktionsarten*' and genuine lexical modification (Sussex and Cubberley 2006). Finally, some authors rest on the understanding that derivation and inflection constitute a continuum, situated between the poles of prototypical inflection and prototypical derivation, and allow for categories showing derivational and inflectional features at the same time (e.g. Dressler 1989; Manova 2005). Since there is no consistent and mutually compatible theory of verbal aspect in Slavic linguistics, a concept as a solution for the project has been adopted that allows for a so-called 'aspect pair' and, thus, two forms of the same lexeme. The respective forms of the aspectual pairs are neither examined in terms of direction of aspect polarity nor in terms of potential added onomasiological value (Furdík 2004).

Another problem is presented by nominal formations with the prefix *nie-/ne-*. Due to their productive nature, they are usually considered part of morphology, but this view is not generally accepted, e.g. Sokolová (1999) differentiates the status of forms: verbal forms with the prefix in question are considered examples of inflection (e.g. 'not work' has either a synthetic verbal form with a dependent prefix, e.g. *nepracovať* for Slovak or *nepracovat* for Czech, or an analytical verbal form with a free particle, e.g. *nie pracować* for Polish, *не рабóтя* for Bulgarian, *ne raditi* for Croatian, *ne raditi* for Serbian, *ne delati* for Slovenian, *не рабóтать* for Russian, *не працювáти* for Ukrainian, etc.), whereas adjectives and nouns with this prefix are examples of derivational forms (e.g. 'unhappy, unhappiness' – *nešťastný, nešťastie* for Slovak, *nešťastný, neštěstí* for Czech, *nieszczęśliwy, nieszczęście* for Polish, *nesretan, nesreća* for Croatian, *nesrečen, nesreča* for Slovenian, *nesrećan, nesreća* for Serbian, *нещáстен, нещáстие* for Bulgarian, *несчáстный, несчáстье* for Russian, *нещаслíвий, нещастя* for Ukrainian, etc.).

The most important problem, however, is the status of word coinage as such. As there is no clear boundary between inflection and word-formation, there is also no clear boundary between the functional status of the affixes. Even if the status is revealed, there are cases where, at first sight, clear inflectional affixes also play an important role in word-formation, at least as co-formants. The scope of word-formation affixation in Slavic languages generally includes prefixation, suffixation, reflexivization, and combined procedures. However, an important role is also obviously played by conversion, which, in Slavic linguistics, is preferably explained as a paradigmatic formation of new words, i.e. as a process that forms new words by a change of inflectional paradigm.

Another problem is that there is no unanimous interpretation of conversion in Slavic, so various phenomena have been subsumed under this term (Avramova and Baltova 2016: 3066). In their article on Bulgarian, the authors treat the formation of the deverbal noun *lov* 'hunt' from the verb *lov-í* 'to hunt', or the noun *uteh-a* 'comfort' from the verb *uteš-i* 'to comfort', as examples of paradigmatic derivation (conversion). Contrarily, Grčević (2016: 3008) regards deverbal nouns in Croatian, such as *zamjen-a* 'replacement' from the verb *zamijen-iti* 'to replace' or *napad-ø* 'attack' based on the present stem *napad-* of the verb *napasti* 'to attack', as the results of derivation, not conversion. According to Bulgarian works, the thematic formant actualizes the function of the word-formation affix *dim* 'smoke' – *dim-i* 'to smoke', so that *-i* is recognized as a word-formation affix (e.g. Radeva 2007). However, there are also other views. When identifying conversion in Bulgarian, Russian and Serbo-Croatian, Manova (2011: 30) makes reference to the generalized form of a word in Slavonic languages, which is given as shown below:

(1)　(PREF) – BASE – (DSUFF) – (TM) – (ISUFF)

In this template, DSUFF stands for a derivational suffix (which can have multiple realizations), TM for a thematic marker, and ISUFF for an inflectional suffix. Manova suggests that the output of conversion in the Slavonic languages under discussion has an empty derivational (DSUFF) slot (2011: 60), and it allows for the addition, deletion or replacement of inflectional affixes; for example, the addition of the thematic marker and the inflectional (infinitival) ending in the Russian noun-to-verb conversion *škól-a* 'school' → *škól-i-t'* 'to school, discipline', or the replacement of the verbal inflectional morphemes by the declensional morpheme, e.g. *dél-a-t* 'to do, make-impfv' → *dél-o* 'affair, business, deed-neut'. On the basis of this approach, *dim-i* can be described as an affixless conversion process, allowing the addition of the thematic morpheme. Nevertheless, the status of some morphemes is disputable. For example, Grčević (2016: 3011) treats Croatian denominal and deadjectival verbs, such as *kralj-evati* 'to reign' and *star-jeti* 'to grow old', as suffixal formations that contain the derivational suffixes *-evati* and *-jeti* added to the nominal base *kralj* 'king' or to the adjectival base *star* 'old'. Similarly, Nagórko (2016: 2844–5), among others, recognizes the dual (that is, inflectional and derivational) status of verbal theme markers, such as *-owa-* or *-i-*, and therefore she discusses the formation of denominal verbs in Polish such as *pan-owa-ć* 'to rule' (from *pan* 'lord') or *dziurk-owa-ć* 'to punch' (from *dziurk-a* 'hole') in the sections on derivation and on conversion in her article on Polish word-formation.

Related problems thus necessarily hold units as verbal adjectives and verbal nouns formed from verbs, namely from participles or transgressives, as verbal forms. All Slavic languages are typical of the participle-to-noun and the participle-to-adjective types of conversion. Verbal nouns (*čytanne* 'reading', *plâcenne* 'crying' in Belarusian; *pískaní* 'whistling', *škrábnutí* 'scratch' in Czech; *igranje* 'playing', *sedenje* 'sitting' in Slovene, etc.) are treated either as derivatives in selected works (cf. Lukašanec 2016; Bozděchová 2016; Breznik 2016; Karlík, Nekula and Rusínová 1995: 148; Karlík, Nekula and Pleskalová 2016), as paradigmatic forms of verb (e.g. Kopečný 1958: 132; Komárek et al. 1986), or simply as naming units formed from participles or transgressives by using inflectional morphological means (adopting the nominal or adjectival way of inflection).

In the light of the above-mentioned theories and theoretical concepts and with regard to the objectives of the whole project, all cases that are subject to the principle of conversion or affixless derivation have been excluded from the research. This applies in particular to deverbal adjectives and nouns with original thematic markers and original participative and transgressive affixes, although in linguistic development or in the development of linguistic theory, different interpretations could be made in individual Slavic languages. Also, inflectional affixes working as word-formational co-formants were not counted as relevant affixes (see *město* 'town' → *městský* 'urban', where the word-formational suffix *-sk* brings about the adjectival inflection represented by the nom.sg. desinence *-ý*), as they do not add any generalized word-formational meaning.

References

Avramova, Cvetanka & Julia Baltova. 2016. 167. Bulgarian. In Peter O. Müller, Ingeborg Ohnheiser, Susan Olsen & Franz Rainer (eds.), *Word-formation. An international handbook of the languages of Europe, Vol. 4*, 3049–3069. Berlin & New York: Mouton de Gruyter.
Bednaříková, Božena. 2009. *Word and Its Conversion*. Olomouc: Univerzita Palackého.
Bednaříková, Božena. 2011. Towards (Proto)typing of Morphological Processes. *Czech and Slovak Linguistic Review* I. 44–52.
Booij, Geert. 1996. Inherent versus contextual inflection and the split morphology hypothesis. In Geert Booij & Jaap van Marle (eds.), *Yearbook of morphology 1995*, 1–16. Dordrecht: Springer.
Bozděchová, Ivana. 2016. 158. Czech. In Peter O. Müller, Ingeborg Ohnheiser, Susan Olsen & Franz Rainer (eds.), *Word-formation. An international handbook of the languages of Europe. Vol. 4*, 2872–2891. Berlin & New York: Mouton de Gruyter.

Breznik, Irena Stramljič. 2016. 163. Slovene. In Peter O. Müller, Ingeborg Ohnheiser, Susan Olsen & Franz Rainer (eds.), *Word-formation. An international handbook of the languages of Europe. Vol. 4*, 2979–2998. Berlin & New York: Mouton de Gruyter.
Cetnarowska, Bozena. 2001. On inherent inflection feeding derivation in Polish. In Geert Booij & Jaap van Marle (eds.), *Yearbook of morphology 1999*, 153–183. Dordrecht: Springer.
Dokulil, Miloš, Karel Horálek, Jiřina Hůrková & Miloslava Knappová (eds.). 1986. *Grammar of Czech 1: Phonetics – Phonology – Morphonology – Word-formation*. Praha: Academia.
Dressler, Wolfgang U. 1989. Prototypical differences between inflection and derivation. *STUF-Language Typology and Universals* 42 (1). 3–10.
Furdík, Juraj. 2004. *Slovak Word-formation*. Edited by Martin Ološtiak. Prešov: Náuka.
Grčević, Mario. 2016. 164. Croatian. In Peter O. Müller, Ingeborg Ohnheiser, Susan Olsen & Franz Rainer (eds.), *Word-formation. An international handbook of the languages of Europe. Vol. 4*, 2998–3016. Berlin & New York: Mouton de Gruyter.
Hauser, Přemysl. 1980. *Study of Vocabulary*. Prague: SPN.
Karlík, Petr, Marek Nekula & Jana Pleskalová (eds.). 2016. *New Encyclopaedic Dictionary of Czech*. Prague: NLN.
Karlík, Petr, Marek Nekula & Zdenka Rusínová (eds.). 1995. *Reference Grammar of Czech*. Prague: Nakladatelství Lidové noviny.
Komárek, Miroslav, Jan Kořenský, Jan Petr & Jarmila Veselková (eds.). 1986. *Grammar of Czech. Morphology*. Prague: Academia.
Kopečný, František. 1958. *Foundations of Czech Syntax*. Prague: Státní pedagogické nakladatelství.
Kopečný, František. 1962. *Verbal Aspect in Czech*. Prague: Nakl. Československé akademie věd.
Körtvélyessy, Lívia. 2016. Word-formation in Slavic languages. *Poznan Studies in Contemporary Linguistics* 52 (3). 455–501.
Lukašanec, Alâksandr. 2016. 161. Belarussian. In Peter O. Müller, Ingeborg Ohnheiser, Susan Olsen & Franz Rainer (eds.), *Word-formation. An international handbook of the languages of Europe. Vol. 4*, 2932–2953. Berlin & New York: Mouton de Gruyter.
Manova, Stela. 2005. Derivation versus Inflection in Three Inflecting Languages. In Wolfgang U. Dressler, Dieter Kastovsky, Oskar E. Pfeiffer & Franz Rainer (eds.), *Morphology and its demarcations: Selected papers from the 11th Morphology Meeting, Vienna, February 2004*, 233–252. Amsterdam & Philadelphia: John Benjamins.
Manova, Stela. 2011. *Understanding morphological rules: with special emphasis on conversion and subtraction in Bulgarian, Russian and Serbo-Croatian*. Dordrecht: Springer.
Maslov, Jurij S. 1958. *Role of the So-called Perfectivization and Imperfectivization in the Process of the Slavic Verbal Aspect Formation*. Moscow.
Maslov, Jurij S. 1963. *Morphology of the Verbal aspect in contemporary Bulgarian Language*. Moscow & Leningrad.
Mel'čuk, Igor. 2000. Morphological processes. In Geert E. Booij, Christian Lehmann and Joachim Mugdan (eds.), *Morphologie / Morphology. Ein Internationales Handbuch zur Flexion und Wortbildung. An International Handbook on Inflection and Word-Formation. Volume 1*, 523–535. Berlin & New York: Walter de Gruyter.
Nagórko, Alicja. 2016. 156. Polish. In Peter O. Müller, Ingeborg Ohnheiser, Susan Olsen & Franz Rainer (eds.), *Word-formation. An international handbook of the languages of Europe. Vol. 4*, 2831–2852. Berlin & New York: Mouton de Gruyter Mouton.

Radeva, Vasilka. 2007. *In the world of words*. Sofia: Universitetsko izdavatelstvo "Sv. Kliment Ohridski".
Sekaninová, Ella. 1980. *Semantic Analysis of the Prefix Verb in Russian and Slovak*. Bratislava: Veda.
Skalička, Vladimír. 1935. *Zur ungarischen Grammatik*. Prague: Nakl. Filosofické fakulty University Karlovy.
Sokolová, Miloslava. 1999. Theoretical Foundations of Morphematic Processing of Slovak. In *Morfematický slovník slovenčiny*, 9–53. Prešov: Náuka.
Sokolová, Miloslava. 2009. Semantics of verbs and aspectual forms. In Martina Ivanová (ed.), *Aspektuálnosť a modálnosť v slovenčine*, 22–37. Prešov: Prešovská univerzita v Prešove.
Sussex, Roland & Paul Cubberley. 2006. *The Slavic Languages*. Cambridge: Cambridge University Press.
Štícha, František, Miloslav Vondráček, Ivana Kolářová, Ivana Hoffmannová, Jana Bílková & Ivana Svobodová. 2013. *Academic Grammar of Czech*. Prague: Academia.
Tichonov, Aleksandr. 1998. *Russian Verb: Problems of Theory and Lexicography*. Moscow: Academia.
Trávníček, František. 1951. *Grammar of Standard Czech. Volume 1*. Prague: Slovanské nakl.

Alexandra Bagasheva
3 Derivational networks in Bulgarian

3.1 General notes

Bulgarian is a typical inflectional Southern Slavonic language, with a high degree of synthetism preserved in the verbal system and a marked degree of analyticity achieved in the nominal system. However, "[t]he specific historical development of Bulgarian from a synthetic to an analytical nominal structure, which is unique within the Slavic language family, has not affected the stability of the Bulgarian word-formation system" (Avramova and Baltova 2015: 4). This stability concerns the almost invariable primacy of affixation as the most productive word-formation process in the language, followed by compounding. Unlike the ease of establishing morphological boundaries in agglutinating languages (e.g. Turkish), the separation of affixes from bases is not so straightforward in Bulgarian (for contrast, see Chapter 37 on Estonian, this volume). This does not, however, undermine the heavily affixating word-formation profile of the language, in which hundreds of derivational affixes are used for forming new lexical items from bases in almost all word-classes (nouns, adjectives, verbs, adverbs, numerals, etc.).

Two short notes that reveal further specificities of the adopted principles of data gathering are in order here. The first relates to the treatment of the formant *-nik*, which Warren (1990) classifies as a combining form, while all Slavists working on Bulgarian identify it as a very productive polysemous affix (Radeva 2007; Georgiev 1993; Stoyanov 1993; etc.). Bulgarian scholars include the following under the label affixoids: *eko-* 'eco-', *avto-* 'auto-', *geo-*, *vice-*, *-log*, *-fil* '-phile', *-fen* '-fan', *-gejt* '-gate', etc., claiming that "the products of 'affixoidization' should be treated as affixal formations and the respective formants as affixoids, i.e. as belonging to affixation" (Avramova and Baltova 2015: 5). In the calculations employed in the current chapter, *-nik* has been treated as a suffix, while the remainder of items in Warren's list (1990) have been excluded with the intent of bringing the data set into line with work done on other languages in the project.

The second note relates to the sources utilized in the process of gathering the data. The data (the attested derivatives) for the research were extracted from dictionaries (the *Multi-volume Dictionary of Modern Bulgarian*, the *Bulgarian Derivational Dictionary* and the *Bulgarian Dictionary*), the Bulgarian National Corpus and internet searches. Only actual words (without frequency counts) were included, without consideration of potential words. The data set does not contain words marked as obsolete, regional or technical in the sources.

3.2 Maximum derivational networks

The investigation of the nature of derivational networks for the three open classes of words in the language reveals that all three classes have a maximum of five orders of derivation with derivatives dropping significantly in number after the 3rd order, with only a single base from the studied sample in each word-class having a derivative in the 5th order. For nouns it is the base *oko* (eye) that saturates the 5th order, for verbs it is *dava/dade* (give), and for adjectives – *star* (old).

As can be seen from Table 3.1, verbs have the highest number of derivatives per semantic category in the first three orders of derivation and the greatest derivational potential, despite the fact that in the 4th order, deverbal derivation drops below that for adjectives and nouns as bases. Adjectives come second with comparatively rich maximum derivational networks, with nouns tailing behind.

Table 3.1: Maximum derivational networks per order of derivation for all three word-classes.

	1st order	2nd order	3rd order	4th order	5th order	Σ
Nouns	30	23	15	6	1	75
Verbs	51	61	22	2	1	126
Adjectives	27	33	21	6	1	88
TOTAL	108	117	58	14	3	300

3.3 Saturation values

Tables 3.2–3.4 below represent the saturation values of the networks of the 10 sample words in each class per order of derivation. Table 3.5 provides the average saturation values per order of derivation for each word-class.

As can be seen from the series of tables below, verbs are the most prolific derivational class, even though the saturation values per order of derivation are higher for adjectives in the 1st, 3rd and 4th orders of derivation. While only two bases in the class of verbs saturate the 4th order of derivation, *dava/dade* (give) and *gori* (burn), five adjective bases saturate it, as well as three within the noun class: *oko* (eye), *voda* (water) and *ime* (name).

For a full understanding of the information presented in Tables 3.2 to 3.5, a few explanatory comments are provided here. The resultant saturation values reflect some principles of exclusion applied to the data that might have slightly influenced the overall results. As the derivation of PRIVATIVE from adjectives

Table 3.2: Saturation values per order of derivation: Nouns.

Nouns		Saturation value	1st order	2nd order	3rd order	4th order	5th order
bone	kost	28	36.67	26.09	26.67	0	0
eye	oko	24	26.67	17.39	20	33.33	100
tooth	zâb	16	20	17.39	13.33	0	0
day	den	21.33	30	21.74	13.33	0	0
dog	kuče	17.33	23.33	26.09	0	0	0
louse	vâška	14.67	30	8.7	0	0	0
fire	ogân	18.67	30	21.74	0	0	0
stone	kamâk	22.67	30	34.78	0	0	0
water	voda	37.33	30	30.43	46.67	83.33	0
name	ime	20	13.33	21.74	33.33	16.67	0

Table 3.3: Saturation values per order of derivation, verbs.

Verbs		Saturation value	1st order	2nd order	3rd order	4th order	5th order
cut	reže	29.93	37.25	27.87	22.73	0	0
dig	kopae	25.55	35.29	24.59	9.09	0	0
pull	dârpa	17.52	19.61	19.67	9.09	0	0
throw	hvârlja	4.38	7.84	3.28	0	0	0
give	dava	40.15	25.49	47.54	50	50	100
hold	dârži	18.98	25.49	16.39	13.64	0	0
sew	šie	28.47	33.33	27.87	22.73	0	0
burn	gori	23.36	29.41	22.95	9.09	50	0
drink	pie	39.42	43.14	45.9	18.18	0	0
know	znae	11.68	7.84	14.75	13.64	0	0

Table 3.4: Saturation values per order of derivation: Adjectives.

Adjectives		Saturation value	1st order	2nd order	3rd order	4th order	5th order
narrow	tesen	18.18	37.04	6.06	19.05	0	0
old	star	30.68	37.04	18.18	42.86	16.67	100
straight	prav	11.36	22.22	12.12	0	0	0
New	nov	11.36	18.52	9.09	9.52	0	0
long	dâlâg	32.95	48.15	30.3	19.05	33.33	0
warm	warm	28.41	25.93	27.27	38.1	16.67	0
thick	debel	31.82	40.74	33.33	28.57	0	0
bad	loš	22.73	33.33	24.24	9.52	16.67	0
thin	tânâk	29.55	29.63	27.27	33.33	33.33	0
black	čeren	4.55	14.81	0	0	0	0

Table 3.5: Average saturation values per order of derivation for all three word-classes.

	1st order	2nd order	3rd order	4th order	5th order
Nouns	27	22.6	15.3	13.3	10
Adjectives	30.7	18.8	20	11.7	10
Verbs	26.5	25.1	16.8	10	10

with the prefix *ne-* (non) is extremely regular and the semantics of the output is uniform, such derivatives were not included in the calculations of the networks; only other affixal ways of expressing PRIVATIVE have been considered.

The adjective *prav* 'straight' is represented exclusively with its primary set of derivatives, relating to the spatial meaning of the adjective, contrary to the derivational family given in the *Derivational Dictionary*. The whole family of words associated with *pravo* 'law' are derived from a base which arises from conversion, and these derivatives are excluded from the calculations as their derivation without a meaning shift is synchronically not active, even though diachronically it has been claimed that the said base is a substantivized neuter form of the original adjective.

Counter Spencer's claims that reflexivization is a "type of word-formation that is not mediated through affixes as traditionally defined" (2015: 303), Körtvelyessy

(2016) recognizes reflexivization, realized synthetically or analytically, as postfixation. Postfixed reflexiveness is realized analytically via a clitic in Bulgarian, in contrast to Ukrainian and Russian (see Chapters 7 and 11, current volume), where reflexiveness is realized synthetically by an affix. Another notable contrast among the mentioned languages is the fact that, in Bulgarian, reflexiveness is not restricted to transitive verbs, and the products of the process vary significantly in terms of semantics. Reflexiveness has been interpreted as an affixal process here.

While there are semantic categories that are realized for all members of a word-class, there are cases where there is an overabundance of saturation instantiations for a particular semantic category with certain base words from a class, which subsequently influences the richness of the whole network. Admittedly, the proliferation of numerous non-synonymous derivations in a single semantic category is heavily dependent on the conceptual/ontological specificity of the base. Such is the case with the numerous DIRECTIONAL derivatives from the verbs *hvarli* 'throw' (whose meaning involves the components 'change in spatial positioning' and 'force') and the verb *dam* 'give' (which also ultimately involves spatial semantics, more specifically, 'change of positioning'). Almost all verbal prefixes can be attached to these bases, and the semantic changes in the resultant derivatives actualize changes in the trajectory. In the calculations, these derivatives have been lumped together under DIRECTIONAL.

3.4 Orders of derivation

All three classes have exactly one member that has a derivative in the 5th order of derivation. Standardly, all members of the three word-classes have derivatives up to the 3rd order of derivation, and the differences among them are slight in terms of the average number of active orders. Affixal derivation appears to be a rather productive and uniformly active word-formation process in Bulgarian as shown in Table 3.6.

Table 3.6: Maximum and average number of orders of derivation for all three word-classes.

	Maximum	Average
Nouns	5	3.0
Adjectives	5	3.1
Verbs	5	3.2

3.5 Derivational capacity

The telling fact that can be read off the table above is that verbs in Bulgarian have the highest derivational potential, twice as high as that of nouns, with adjectives coming closer to nouns than to verbs in their potential as bases for derivations. The same conslusions can be drawn from Tabes 3.7 and 3.8, respectively.

Table 3.7: Maximum and average derivational capacity for all three word-classes.

	Maximum	Average
Nouns	11	8.1
Adjectives	13	6.8
Verbs	22	13.5

Table 3.8: Average number of derivatives per order of derivation for all three word-classes.

	1st order	2nd order	3rd order	4th order	5th order
Nouns	8.1	5.2	2.3	0.8	0.1
Adjectives	6.8	6.2	4.2	0.7	0.1
Verbs	13.5	15.3	3.7	0.2	0.1

3.6 Correlation between semantic categories and orders of derivation

There are marked tendencies for strong correlations between certain semantic categories and orders of derivation per word-class, as follows: for nouns, QUALITY and DIMINUTIVE stand out, with all 10 nouns having derivatives in the QUALITY category and 9 in the DIMINUTIVE in the 1st order of derivation. RELATIONAL also stands out, with 9 nouns deriving lexemes in this category. In the 2nd order of derivation there is a tendency for nouns to saturate the category QUALITY to the highest degree – 7 nouns, without any other notable correlations in the remaining orders of derivation.

For adjectives, STATE, DIMINUTIVE and MANNER are unquestionable favourites in the 1st order of derivation, with STATE and DIMINUTIVE displaying a strong correlation as all 10 adjectives saturate these semantic categories. There is also a strong tendency for a correlation between the semantic category MANNER and the 1st order of derivation, with 8 out of 10 adjectives having derivatives for this category. In the 2nd order, a correlational tendency can be observed for the category DIMINUTIVE, with 8 adjectives out of 10 actualizing it. No marked tendencies can be detected in the remaining orders of derivation.

In the verb class, a marked correlation can be noted between the 1st order of derivation and the semantic category DIRECTIONAL, with 9 verbs with derivatives in that category. 8 of the verbs in the sample have derivatives in the categories DIMINUTIVE and ENTITY in the 1st order of derivation. There is a strong correlation between the 2nd order of derivation and the semantic category DIMINUTIVE, with all 10 verbs actualizing this category in the respective order. Though not very strong, there is a notable correlation between PLURIACTIONALITY and the 3rd order of derivation, with 7 verbs having derivatives in this semantic category in the 3rd order. No more notable correlations between a semantic category and an order of derivation within the class of verbs can be observed.

3.7 Semantic categories with blocking effects

The semantic categories MANNER and STATE show a tendency for blocking further derivation in the class of adjectives. In the substantive class, RELATIONAL shows a slight tendency for blocking further derivation, and in the verbal class, LOCATION and ABSTRACTION display mild blocking effects. In all three classes, FEMALE seems to have a blocking effect.

3.8 Typical combinations of semantic categories

For reasons of space, a single illustrative example has been chosen for each combination from the respective class.

In the nominal class, a tendency for the following combinations of semantic categories stand out: QUALITY > STATE (*zâbat* 'having big or many teeth' > *zâbatost* 'state of having big or many teeth') and QUALITY > PATIENT (*zâbat* 'having big or many teeth' > *zâbatko* 'a person with big or many teeth').

Notable combinations of semantic categories in subsequent orders of derivation in the adjective class are PATIENT > RELATIONAL (*starec* 'old man' > *starčeski* 'relating to an old man'), PATIENT > FEMALE (*starec* 'old man' > *starica* 'old woman') and PATIENT – DIMINUTIVE (*starec* 'old man' > *staričok* 'little old man').

In the verbal class, the most frequent combinations of semantic categories in consecutive orders of derivation are AGENT > RELATIONAL (*šivač* 'sewing man' > *šivaški* 'relating to a sewing man/sewing', AGENT > FEMALE (*šivač* 'sewing man' > *šivačka* 'sewing woman') and DIRECTIONAL > DIMINUTIVE (*izhvârli* 'throw away' > *poizhvârli* 'throw away a little; throw away slightly').

3.9 Multiple occurrence of semantic categories

In the substantive class, the semantic category DIMINUTIVE occurs subsequently in the 1st and 2nd orders of derivation, e.g. *oko* 'eye' > 1st order *oče* 'small eye' > 2nd order *očence*.

In the verb class, a single reoccurrence of a semantic category was detected in the 2nd and 3rd orders of derivation – PLURIACTIONALITY *dava/dade* 'give' > 1st order *prodade* 'sell' > 2nd order *izprodade* 'sell everything' > 3rd order *izponaprodade* 'sell everything'.

Adjectives do not seem to tolerate multiple occurrences of a semantic category in serial derivations. No further multiple occurrences of semantic categories could be established within the sample.

3.10 Reversibility of semantic categories

Within the sample of 10 words per word-class (nouns, adjectives and verbs), no reversal of semantic categories of the type AB/BA were registered. The same also applies to affixes.

3.11 Conclusions

In terms of the *saturation parameter* defined by Körtvelyessy (2016: 456) as "a numerical representation of the structural richness (diversity) of productive WF processes and types used to form new complex words", Bulgarian is a structurally rich language in which affixation surfaces as the most productive process, with various types used for constructing complex words.

Derivation from adjectives and verbs is productive and regular, with the exception of the colour adjective *čeren* 'black', which because of its semantics as a colour adjective is not as potent as the remaining adjectives in the sample. Nouns vary in terms of the number of derivatives in the 3rd order of derivation, while for the first two orders, most nouns have comparable numbers of derivatives.

Verbs are undeniably most productive as source words, followed by adjectives, with nouns tailing the productivity cline. Affixation is central to word-formation in Bulgarian and, despite the differences in derivational potential, words from all three classes (nouns, adjectives and verbs) participate actively in varied affixal derivations.

References

Avramova, Cvetanka & Julia Baltova. 2015. Bulgarian. In Peter O. Müller, Ingeborg Ohnheiser, Susan Olsen & Franz Rainer (eds.), *Word-Formation: An International Handbook of the Languages of Europe*. Berlin & New York: Mouton de Gruyter.
Georgiev, Stanyo. 1993. *Bulgarian Morphology*. Veliko Turnovo: "Abagar" Publishing House.
Körtvélyessy, Lívia. 2016. Word-formation in Slavic languages. *Poznan Studies in Contemporary Linguistics* 52 (3). 455–501.
Radeva, Vasilka. 2007. *In the world of words. Structure and meaning of derived words*. Sofia: Sofia University Publishing House "Saint Kliment Ohridski".
Spencer, Andrew. 2015. Derivation. In Peter O. Müller, Ingeborg Ohnheiser, Susan Olsen & Franz Rainer (eds.), *Word-Formation: An International Handbook of the Languages of Europe*, 301–322. Berlin & New York: Mouton de Gruyter.
Stoyanov, Stoyan. 1993. *Grammar of literary Bulgarian*. Sofia: Sofia University Publishing House "Saint Kliment Ohridski".
Warren, Beatrice. 1990. The importance of combining forms. In Wolfgang U. Dressler, Hans C. Luschützky, Oskar E. Pfeiffer & John R. Rennison (eds.), *Contemporary Morphology (Trends in Linguistics. Studies and Monographs 49)*, 111–133. Berlin & New York: Mouton de Gruyter.

Sources

Andrejchin, Ljubomir and Dimiter Popov (eds.). 1994. *Bulgarian Dictionary*, 4th edn. Sofia: Naouka i izkustvo.
Bulgarian Academy of Sciences (eds.). 2001–2015. *Dictionary of the Bulgarian Language*. Vols. 1–15. Sofia: Academic Publishing Company "Prof. Marin Drinov".
Institute for Bulgarian Language "Prof. L. Andreychin". Bulgarian National Corpus. http://search.dcl.bas.bg/ (last accessed 7 February 2018).
Penchev, Yordan (ed.), 1999, *Derivational Dictionary of Contemporary Literary Bulgarian*. Sofia: Academic Publishing Company "Prof. Marin Drinov".

Zrinka Jelaska, Tomislava Bošnjak Botica
4 Derivational networks in Croatian

4.1 General notes

Croatian is a fusional and a synthetic language, highly inflectional, just like most other Slavic languages. Affixation expands the Croatian vocabulary, with various types used for constructing complex words. Those are derived from all (lexical) word-classes via a large number of suffixes and prefixes, but just like in other Slavic languages, it is not always easy to separate affixes from their bases.

In Croatian, derivation determines both the word-class of a derivative and its semantic category. Derivation, especially suffixation, is by far the most productive process by which new words are formed. In contrast to prefixation, suffixation includes a change of grammatical category. There are at least 835 derivative affixes in Croatian (Babić 2002): 758 suffixes and 77 prefixes, or about a hundred more (Babić 1986) if they are differentiated according to parts of speech: 792 suffixes and 139 prefixes. However, less than half are synchronically productive, and different words yield derivatives to different degrees. Some derivational affixes are borrowed, mostly from Latin, Greek, German, and French.

The nature of prefixes in derivation in Croatian has been a matter of debate, as some recent grammatical descriptions have treated words formed with prefixes either as compounds (e.g. Težak and Babić 2009: 176) or a special (borderline) type of compound (e.g. Babić 2002), although they are often viewed as a derivational type (e.g. Barić et al. 1997: 295; Jelaska 2015: 62). Croatian linguists treat the negative element *ne-* mostly as a prefix.

As to the theoretical problem of distinguishing affixes proper and affixoids, some Croatian scholars (e.g. Silić and Pranjković 2005: 154–160) include *auto-, geo-, vice-, -log*, etc. under the label affixoids, while others include those within compounding or a special case of compounding (e.g. Barić et al. 1997: 289–290). In the calculations employed in the current chapter, none of the affixoids were included as, in the data set for this project, only affixes of Slavic origin are present in the Croatian set.

Derivations combined with clipping (e.g. *rezati* 'to cut' > *rez* 'cut' > *rezba* 'cut, incision' > *rezbariti* 'to carve' > *rezbarija* 'carving, fretwork'), or metaphorical extension (e.g. *rezati* > *rezak* 'biting'; *držati* 'hold' > *država* 'state'; *nov* 'new' > *novac* 'money') were excluded from the data analyzed in this chapter. Further data excluded from the analysis in this chapter (cf. the general introduction to Slavic languages) belong to aspectual verb pairs or chains that denote DURATION, e.g. the imperfective verbs *suzavati* and *suzivati* 'make narrow',

https://doi.org/10.1515/9783110686630-004

formed from the TERMINATIVE *suziti*; deverbal adjectives that denote QUALITY together with their PRIVATIVE pairs and RELATIONAL adjectives; and deverbal nouns with suffixes *-nje, -enje*, e.g. *znanje* 'knowledge', *suženje* 'constriction'.

Verbal adjectives (past participle) as inflectional forms are ruled out here, hence MANNER is mostly excluded from the data as many adverbs are formed by transformation from the neuter form of adjectives. Although it could be seen as coincidental, Croatian grammars (Barić et al. 1997: 274–275) speak of transformation rather than homophonic derivation as only such adverbs (verbal or not) have comparisons, the rest do not. If verbal adverbials were included in the data, MANNER would be highly productive. On the other hand, REFLEXIVE is included as postfixation (cf. the general introduction).

The attested derivatives for the research were extracted from three dictionaries: the *Dictionary of Croatian Language* (RHJ), the *Big Dictionary of Modern Croatian* (VRH), and the *Encyclopedic Dictionary of Croatian* (HER); three corpuses: the Croatian National Corpus (HNK), the Croatian Language Corpus (RIZNICA) and the Lexical Database of the Institute of Croatian Language and Linguistics; several other internet corpuses; and internet searches. Phonological variations, i.e. doublets in Standard Croatian, are excluded. Derivations marked as archaic or regional were excluded unless one of the dictionaries or internet searches could confirm their use. Thirty words in the sample yielded 1,720 derivatives: 397 nouns, 915 verbs and 408 adjectives.

4.2 Maximum derivational networks

All three word-classes have a maximum of five orders of derivation, with derivatives dropping significantly in number after the 3rd order of derivation, with only one or two bases from the studied sample in each word-class having a derivative in the 5th order. For nouns, it is the base *dan* 'day' which saturates the 5th order, for verbs it is *dati/davati* 'give' and *znati* 'know', and for adjectives it is *star* 'old' and *zao* 'bad'.

As can be seen from Table 4.1, nouns have the highest number of derivatives per semantic category in the 1st order of derivation, despite the fact that, from the 3rd order, noun derivation drops below that for verbs and adjectives as bases. From the 2nd order and in total, verbs have the highest number of derivatives per semantic category and the greatest derivational potential.

Table 4.1: Maximum derivational network per order of derivation for all three word-classes.

	1st order	2nd order	3rd order	4th order	5th order	Σ
Nouns	63	76	29	5	1	174
Verbs	62	122	94	29	7	314
Adjectives	37	46	45	15	4	147
TOTAL	168	244	168	49	12	635

4.3 Saturation values

The mean saturation values for the nouns (Table 4.2) range between 8% and 34%. *Voda* 'water' (34%) has the highest mean saturation value, but the only noun with a 5th order derivation (100%) is *dan* 'day'. In contrast, *vatra* 'fire', with the lowest mean saturation value (8%), is the only noun that lacks a 3rd order. Within the 1st order, *zub* 'tooth' has the highest saturation value (35%), while *uš* 'louse' has the lowest (8%).

Table 4.2: Saturation values per order of derivation, nouns.

Nouns		Saturation value (%)	1st order	2nd order	3rd order	4th order	5th order
bone	kost	19.54	22.22	23.68	6.9	0	0
eye	oko	30.46	31.75	27.63	37.93	20	0
tooth	zub	20.69	34.92	17.11	3.45	0	0
day	dan	32.76	23.81	25	62.07	80	100
dog	pas	18.97	19.05	26.32	3.45	0	0
louse	uš	9.2	7.94	6.58	17.24	20	0
fire	vatra	8.05	12.7	7.89	0	0	0
stone	kamen	26.44	31.75	28.95	10.34	20	0
water	voda	34.48	33.33	30.26	44.83	60	0
name	ime	27.59	23.81	30.26	31.03	20	0

The mean saturation values for the verbs (Table 4.3) range between 13% and 48%. *Dati* 'give' (48%) has the highest mean saturation value and a 5th order derivation, along with *znati* 'know'. In contrast, *šiti* 'sew', which has the lowest mean saturation value (13%), is the only verb that lacks a 4th order. Within the 1st order, *rezati* 'cut' has the highest saturation value (44%), while *držati* 'hold' has the lowest (23%).

Table 4.3: Saturation values per order of derivation, verbs.

Verbs		Saturation value (%)	1st order	2nd order	3rd order	4th order	5th order
cut	rezati	36.31	43.55	39.34	36.17	17.24	0
dig	kopati	27.39	30.65	32.79	24.47	13.79	0
pull	vući	34.39	32.26	44.26	31.91	13.79	0
throw	baciti	41.4	33.87	42.62	52.13	27.59	0
give	dati	48.41	29.03	48.36	62.77	51.72	14.29
hold	držati	20.06	22.58	20.49	20.21	17.24	0
sew	šiti	13.38	35.48	15.57	1.06	0	0
burn	gorjeti	17.2	24.19	21.31	11.7	6.9	0
drink	piti	17.83	24.19	17.21	18.09	10.34	0
know	znati	35.03	25.81	27.05	38.3	65.52	85.71

The mean saturation values for the adjectives (Table 4.4) range between 9% and 56%. *Nov* 'new' (56%) has the highest mean saturation value, while *star* 'old' and *zao* 'bad' have a 5th order derivation. In contrast, *uzak* 'narrow', which has the lowest mean saturation value (9%), is one of the five adjectives that lack a 4th order. Within the 1st order, *crn* 'black' has the highest saturation value (49%), while *zao* 'bad' has the lowest (14%).

The average saturation values per order of derivation for each word-class in the Croatian set (Table 4.5) are quite low in all orders, not reaching above 31 in the 1st order, 33 in the 2nd order, 30 in the 3rd order, 23 in the 4th order and 13 in the 5th order.

Table 4.4: Saturation values per order of derivation, adjectives.

Adjectives		Saturation value (%)	1st order	2nd order	3rd order	4th order	5th order
narrow	uzak	8.84	21.62	6.52	4.44	0	0
old	star	54.42	45.95	69.57	51.11	46.67	25
straight	ravan	17.01	24.32	21.74	11.11	6.67	0
new	nov	55.78	40.54	60.87	66.67	60	0
long	dug	34.01	35.14	47.83	33.33	0	0
warm	topao	11.56	24.32	15.22	2.22	0	0
thick	gust	12.93	24.32	15.22	4.44	6.67	0
bad	zao	27.21	13.51	13.04	24.44	93.33	100
thin	tanak	24.49	29.73	34.78	20	0	0
black	crn	31.29	48.65	36.96	24.44	0	0

Table 4.5: Average saturation values per order of derivation for all three word-classes.

	1st order	2nd order	3rd order	4th order	5th order
Nouns	24.13	22.36	21.724	22	10
Verbs	30.16	30.9	29.68	22.41	10
Adjectives	30.81	32.18	24.22	21.33	12.5

4.4 Orders of derivation

Table 4.6 shows that all word-classes have a maximum number of orders of derivation. All members of the three word-classes have derivatives up to the 3rd order, with the exception of the noun *vatra* 'fire', and the average number of derivations varies between 3–4 orders. Hence, affixal derivation appears as a productive and active word-formation process in Croatian.

Table 4.6: Maximum and average number of orders of derivation for all three word-classes.

	Maximum	Average
Nouns	5	3.6
Verbs	5	4.1
Adjectives	5	3.3

4.5 Derivational capacity

As can be seen in Table 4.7, verbs have the highest average derivational capacity (i.e. direct 1st order derivatives), nouns the middle, and adjectives have the lowest average value. The verb *rezati* 'cut' has the highest overall derivational capacity (27 derivatives in the 1st order).

Table 4.7: Maximum and average derivational capacity for all three word-classes.

	Maximum 1st order	Average 1st order
Nouns	22	13.9
Verbs	27	18.7
Adjectives	18	11.4

Table 4.8 shows that verbs are by far the most fruitful word-class in all orders. While adjectives yield the smallest number in the 1st and 2nd orders, nouns yield the smallest number in the 3rd, 4th and 5th orders. In the 4th order the difference is small, while in the 5th order all word-classes behave similarly, with little derivational output.

Table 4.8: Average number of derivatives per order of derivation for all three word-classes.

	1st order	2nd order	3rd order	4th order	5th order
Nouns	13.9	17	6.3	1.1	0.1
Verbs	18.7	37.4	27.9	6.5	0.7
Adjectives	11.4	14.8	10.9	3.2	0.5

4.6 Correlation between semantic categories and orders of derivation

There is a strong correlation between 1st order derivations of nouns and ENTITY (value 9), DIMINUTIVE, ACTION, and RELATIONAL (value 8); and between 2nd order derivations and RELATIONAL (value 10) and ABSTRACTION (value 8).

There is a strong correlation between 1st order derivations of verbs and the semantic category of TERMINATIVE (value 10); between 2nd order derivations and ABSTRACTION (value 10), RELATIONAL (value 9), and REFLEXIVE (value 8); between 3rd order derivations and POSSESSIVE (value 10), SIMILATIVE, RELATIONAL (value 9), and FEMALE (value 8); and between 4th order derivations and POSSESSIVE (value 8).

There is a strong correlation between 1st order derivations of adjectives and RELATIONAL (value 10) and ABSTRACTION (value 9); and between 2nd order derivations and RELATIONAL (value 9) and TERMINATIVE (value 8).

Hence, for all word-classes, there is a strong correlation between 2nd order derivations and RELATIONAL. In 1st order derivations, there is a strong correlation between RELATIONAL and nouns and adjectives, and in 2nd order derivations between ABSTRACTION and nouns and verbs.

4.7 Semantic categories with blocking effects

POSSESSIVE with the suffix *-ov*, *-ev* or *-in* blocks further derivation. ABSTRACTION with suffix *-ost* blocks anything but PRIVATIVE, and FEMININE blocks anything but POSSESSIVE. Other blockings in the derivational system depend, in addition to semantic categories, on the derivational suffix and word-classes.

4.8 Typical combinations of semantic categories

In the Croatian set, AGENT (or EXPERIENCER, PATIENT) – POSSESSIVE (e.g. *pas* 'dog' > *pset-ar* 'dog holder' > *pset-ar-ev* 'dog holder's'), AGENT – FEMININE – POSSESSIVE (*zub* 'tooth' > *zub-ar* 'dentist' > *zub-ar-ica* 'female dentist' > *zub-ar-ič-in* 'female dentist's') and AGENT – RELATIONAL (*zub* 'tooth' > *zub-ar* 'dentist' > *zub-ar-ski* 'dental') are typical for all word-forms, whilst TERMINATIVE or DIRECTIONAL often derive AGENT nouns (e.g. *is-kop-a-ti* 'to dig out' > *iz-kop-ač* 'digger'). For the verbal derivations, TERMINATIVE / DIRECTIONAL / CAUSATIVE – ABSTRACTION / REFLEXIVE are typical derivational sequences for verbs.

4.9 Multiple occurrence of semantic categories

The derivational system of Croatian does not reveal multiple occurrences of semantic categories on a systematic basis; however, it may occur sporadically in the derivational network of some words. The sample included RELATIONAL – ENTITY (+ AGENT) – RELATIONAL (*dn-ev-ni* – *dn-ev-n-ik* 'diary' – *dn-ev-n-ič-ki*; *dn-ev-n-ica* 'day wage' – *dn-ev-ni-čar* 'a man who earns day wage' – *dn-ev-n-ič-ar-ski*); QUALITY – QUALITY (*zl-o-ba-n* 'malicious' – *na-zl-o-ba-n* 'malicious'); ABSTRACTION – (ACTION – / QUALITY – / PRIVATIVE) – ABSTRACTION (e.g. *ime* 'name' – *imen-ic-a* 'noun' – *po-imen -ič-i-ti* 'make a noun' – *po-imen-ič-en-ost* 'nounness'; *zao* 'bad' – *zl-o* 'evil' – *zl-o-ba* 'malice', *zl-o-ba-n* 'malicious' – *zlo-b-n-ost* 'maliciousness'); and TERMINATIVE – TERMINATIVE (e.g. *po-dn-e* 'noon' – *po-po-dn-e* 'afternoon').

4.10 Reversibility of semantic categories

Two semantic categories may occur in a reversed order: one can derive in the order ATTENUATIVE (e.g. *star* 'old' > *po-star*) and then RELATIONAL (*po-star-i*) or, conversely, RELATIONAL (e.g. *star-i*) and then ATTENUATIVE (*o-star-iji*).

4.11 Conclusions

The Croatian set shows that words from all three word-classes participate actively in affixal derivations. The average number of derivational orders for all three word-classes ranges between 3.3 and 4.1, which means that there are a few 4th and 5th order derivations.

Thirty words in the sample yielded 1,720 derivatives, but single words yield derivatives to different degrees, ranging from 13 to 154. As the most productive words in the data, Croatian verbs yielded more derivatives (915) than adjectives (408) and nouns (397) combined. Verbs have the largest number of derivatives in all orders. The mean saturation values for verbs range between 13% and 48%, for nouns between 8% and 34%, and for adjectives between 9% and 56%. Nouns yielded the smallest number in the 3rd, 4th and 5th orders of derivation, while adjectives yielded the smallest number in the 1st and 2nd orders.

The highest number of derivatives in verbs could be related to much higher numbers of prefixes that attach to verbs compared to those that attach to nouns or adjectives. In the 1st order of derivation, 10 basic verbs yield 120 derived verbs (5 to 18 each) – 94% are derived by prefixes, while nouns and adjectives together yield 37 verbs (0 to 5 each) – only 35% are derived by prefixes.

Almost 86% of the given semantic categories (i.e. 42 of the 49 available) are covered by the Croatian derivatives. Hence, the derivational capacity of Croatian is very rich, given the semantics accounted for.

However, three of the given semantic categories are covered by more than 180 derivatives (RELATIONAL, ABSTRACTION, POSSESSIVE), seven by more than 50 derivatives (e.g. TERMINATIVE, FEMININE, REFLEXIVE, ENTITY, ABILITY, SIMILATIVE, and DIMINUTIVE), 12 by 20 to 50 derivatives (e.g. CAUSATIVE, RESULTATIVE, AGENT, INSTRUMENT, LOCATION, QUALITY, ACTION, DIRECTIONAL, AUGMENTATIVE, PRIVATIVE, PEJORATIVE, and CUMULATIVE), and the rest (20 derivatives) by less than 16 (e.g. PLURIACTIONALITY, SATURATIVE, MANNER, COLLECTIVE, PROCESS, PURPOSIVE, and PATIENT). Hence, this fact implies that Croatian makes use of other means, both morphological and syntactic, to account for some semantic categories.

References

Babić, Stjepan. 1986. *Tvorba riječi u hrvatskome književnom jeziku* [Word-formation in Literary Croatian Language]. Zagreb: Globus.
Babić, Stjepan. 2002. *Tvorba riječi u hrvatskome književnome jeziku* [Word-formation in Literary Croatian Language]. Zagreb: HAZU, Nakladni zavod Globus.
Barić, Eugenija, Mijo Lončarić, Dragica Malić, Slavko Pavešić, Mirko Peti, Vesna Zečević & Marija Znika. 1997. *Hrvatska gramatika* [Croatian Grammar]. Zagreb: Školska knjiga.
Jelaska, Zrinka 2015. *Basic Croatian Grammar*. Zagreb: HFD.
Silić, Josip & Pranjković, Ivo. 2005. *Gramatika hrvatskoga jezika*. [Grammar of the Croatian Language]. Zagreb: Školska knjiga.
Težak, Stjepko & Babić, Stjepan. 2009. *Gramatika hrvatskoga jezika*. [Grammar of the Croatian Language]. Zagreb: Školska knjiga.

Sources

HER. 2005. *Enciklopedijski rječnik hrvatskoga jezika* [Encyclopaedic Dictionary of the Croatian Language]. Zagreb: Novi liber.
HNK. *Croatian National Corpus*. http://filip.ffzg.hr/cgi-bin/run.cgi/first_form (last accessed 14 January 2018).
Hrvatski jezični korpus – Croatian language corpus. http://riznica.ihjj.hr/.
Hrvatski jezični portal. http://hrvatski.enacademic.com (last accessed 14 January 2018).

Hrvatski jezični portal – Znanje. hjp.znanje.hr/index.php?show=search_by_id&id=eF5nWxI%3D.

Jezikoslovac. http://jezikoslovac.com.

RHJ. 2000. *Rječnik hrvatskoga jezika* [Dictionary of the Croatian Language]. Zagreb: Školska knjiga.

VRH. 2015. *Veliki rječnik hrvatskoga standardnog jezika* [Big Dictionary of the Croatian Language]. Zagreb: Školska knjiga.

Božena Bednaříková
5 Derivational networks in Czech

5.1 General notes

Czech belongs to languages that are heavily inflecting (Štekauer and Lieber 2005: 6). Grammatical categories such as gender, number, case, person, aspect, etc. are expressed via affixes. Hence, affixation plays a crucial role in Czech morphology, and in grammars is usually described as a set of inflectional paradigms. The same is true in derivational morphology, which deals with deriving words from other words using affixes as well (Pala and Hlaváčková 2007: 75–76). In spite of the fact that Czech, as a typical inflectional language, is assumed to make use chiefly of conversion (Skalička 1935; Bednaříková 2009a), it has extensive derivational possibilities and a richly developed word-formation system closely intertwined with inflectional morphology (Bozděchová 2016: 2872). The most productive means of forming complex words is derivation, i.e. prefixation and suffixation. While in nominal word-formation, use is made of several hundreds of suffixes, prefixation is most frequent in deverbal derivation (Bozděchová 2016: 2875). According to recent research (Čermák 2010, 2012), nominal roots are most numerous, but most derivatives are linked to verbal roots. Roots then show a high degree of homonymy; in contrast, word-forming affixes (unlike inflectional affixes) have a rather weak functional homonymy (Čermák 2012: 47). Another typical feature of Czech derivation is the polysemy of affixes. Even so, there are several word-formation types that are characterized by high degrees of regularity, for example, the derivation of female nouns from their male counterparts and the derivation of DIMINUTIVES. Worth mentioning also are some suffixes with an almost constant function: *-tel* for AGENT nouns, *-ost* for abstract nouns, *-sk(ý)* for relational adjectives, *-c(í)* for deverbal adjectives denoting purposive meaning, etc. (Bozděchová 2016).

As mentioned above, derivation represents the chief word-formation process in Czech. Less frequent, but far more frequent and important than is reflected in studies of Czech word-formation, is conversion (Bednaříková 2009b; Čermák 2012). Undoubtedly, conversion increases the number of deverbal nouns and adjectives and denominal verbs and adjectives (for a discussion of conversion, see Chapter 1.1). Another word-formation process, composition, plays a less important role in Czech, even if a significant growth of compounds has been registered in the last decades (Lotko 2009), together with a very productive process of univerbization. But generally, morpho-suffixal word-formation prevails over morpho-syntactic word-formation in Czech (Bozděchová 2016: 2876).

As stressed in the general chapter on word-formation in Slavic, the character of affixation differs according to its function. In Czech, the situation is even more complex, as modification/inflection may have the role of a co-formant of word-formation (namely, suffixation as a type of affixation) – see examples like *voda* 'water' > *vod-ař-Ø* 'plumber', where *vod* is the word-formation base, *-ař* is the word-formation suffix, and *-Ø* is the zero desinence of NOM. SG., which represents the whole paradigm of masculine animate declension. Thus the word-formation formant has a complex character in Czech derivation, mainly in suffixation. It is a summary of all the features that help to increase the formal and semantic distance of the newly created word from the underlying base-word. While prefixation has nearly no power to affect the base of the word (the exceptions are rare – see *znát* 'know' > *poznat* 'get to know', where the function of the co-formant is manifested by the vocal alternation of the stem suffix), suffixation always has a central word-formation formant (suffix) and a related inflection brought by the respective word-formation suffix. It should be stressed that suffixes differ according to word-classes, i.e. there are differentiated suffixes for nouns, for adjectives and for verbs. Yet that is not all that matters. The Czech language belongs not only to languages with rich inflection, but also to languages with rather blurred boundaries between morphs. The connection of the word-formation suffix with the word-base is so tight that it is often accompanied by the overlapping of morphs and/or vocal or consonant alternations of the base.

The basic problem in developing derivational networks in Czech is to determine what derivation is and what derivation is not. It is not a usual problem to search for the boundary between inflection and derivation (because they are different types of affixation with different functions), but rather for the boundary between derivation and conversion. Generally, conversion is a morphological, formally non-additive process with an onomasiological/word-formation function whose central formant is a change in morphological characteristics (Bednaříková 2009b, 2011). Such a change primarily includes the change in word-class (there may be exceptions in Czech, such as *kámen* 'stone' > *kamení* 'stones, rocks') and thereby the change of inflection. Although conversion serves as an important word-formation process, the naming process itself is triggered by syntactic needs. The exclusion of conversion in developing derivational networks brings several consequences:

a) Verbal stem suffixes form part of an inflectional formant, and thus do not have the status of a word-formation suffix. Denominal and deadjectival verbs such as *kamenět* 'petrify', *vodnatět* 'get watery', *psovat* 'berate' and *jmenovat* 'name' do not participate in building the derivational network.

b) Deverbal nouns and adjectives whose word-base is either a participle (be it *-l* or *-n/t*) or a transgressive are formed by conversion, not by affixation

(suffixation). As such, they were also excluded (even if they are very frequent and productive); consider examples such as *řezání* 'cutting', *šití* 'sewing', *táhlý* 'prolonged', *hozený* 'thrown', *dopitý* 'drunk up', *kopající* 'digging' and *přiznavší* 'having confessed'.
c) The boundary between conversion and suffixation when forming adverbs seems to be very unclear. On the one hand, they may be handled as incongruent forms of adjectives (Komárek 2006); on the other, they establish a genuine word-class with a circumstantial function and as such are formed with specific suffixes: *-e*, *-y* or *-o*. Those suffixes bear the word-class characteristic but cannot be taken as real desinences with any inflectional function. For that reason, they were included in the derivational network.

Another problem which had to be dealt with was the role of prefixation in the verbal system. Most Czech verbs exist in so-called aspectual pairs (*kopat* 'dig' – *kopnout* 'have a dig'). The change of aspectual polarity is mostly realized by conversion (here by the change of conjugation), but there are some prefixes that may be believed to have a purely aspectual, and thus not word-formation, function. To avoid the unclear and arguable aspectual theory, all prefixes were considered as prefixes with a word-formation function and were thus included in the derivational network. Also included were ITERATIVES formed via suffixation (*držet* 'hold' > *držívat* 'be used to hold').

5.2 Maximum derivational networks

Table 5.1 shows that verbs exhibit the highest numbers of derivational networks in all orders and so in total. All three word-classes permit the 5th order, even if, for nouns and adjectives, the 5th order derivations are rather rare.

Table 5.1: Maximum derivational networks per order of derivation for all three word-classes.

	1st order	2nd order	3rd order	4th order	5th order	Σ
Nouns	31	57	33	6	2	129
Verbs	55	114	149	64	10	392
Adjectives	45	64	41	14	1	165
TOTAL	131	235	223	84	13	686

5.3 Saturation values

The average saturation values for the nouns vary greatly, as they range between 13% and 47% (see Table 5.2). The noun with the highest average saturation value is *oko* 'eye' (47%). In contrast, *veš* 'louse' has the lowest value (13%). Three of the nouns lack the 4th order of derivation, namely *pes* 'dog', *kámen* 'stone' and *jméno* 'name', while two of them permit the 5th order (*kost* 'bone' and *zub* 'tooth'). Within the 1st order, *zub* 'tooth' has the highest saturation value (58%), and *veš* 'louse' has the lowest one (only 6%).

Table 5.2: Saturation values per order of derivation, nouns.

Nouns		Saturation value (%)	1st order (%)	2nd order (%)	3rd order (%)	4th order (%)	5th order (%)
bone	kost	27.91	32.26	24.56	30.3	16.67	50
eye	oko	46.51	32.26	47.37	66.67	16.67	0
tooth	zub	37.21	58.06	42.11	12.12	16.67	50
day	den	16.28	19.35	12.28	18.18	33.33	0
dog	pes	20.16	35.48	17.54	15.15	0	0
louse	veš	13.18	6.45	17.54	12.12	16.67	0
fire	oheň	25.58	22.58	24.56	30.3	33.33	0
stone	kámen	36.43	51.61	47.37	12.12	0	0
water	voda	44.19	54.84	52.63	27.27	16.67	0
name	jméno	15.5	19.35	14.04	18.18	0	0

With regard to verbs (as shown in Table 5.3), the average saturation values again show a great deal of difference. The lowest and highest average saturation values are, respectively, 5% for *hodit* 'throw' and 47% for *řezat* 'cut' (the latter also has the highest saturation value within the 1st order, reaching 65%). The verb *hodit* 'throw' has no 3rd order of derivation. In contrast, three of the verbs (*dát* 'give', *šít* 'sew', and *znát* 'know') produce rather rich 5th orders of derivation.

The highest difference in average saturation values can be observed within adjectives (Table 5.4). While the highest average saturation value belongs to *starý* 'old' (60%), the lowest one belongs to *dlouhý* 'long' (12%). Moreover, *starý* 'old' stands out in the 1st order with a saturation value of 64%; *zlý* 'bad', on the

Table 5.3: Saturation values per order of derivation, verbs.

Verbs		Saturation value (%)	1st order (%)	2nd order (%)	3rd order (%)	4th order (%)	5th order (%)
cut	řezat	47.19	65.45	56.14	44.97	28.13	0
dig	kopat	22.96	41.82	25.44	22.82	6.25	0
pull	táhnout	19.64	49.09	34.21	7.38	0	0
throw	hodit	5.36	32.73	2.63	0	0	0
give	dát	45.66	27.27	30.7	51.68	75	40
hold	držet	13.01	30.91	17.54	7.38	4.69	0
sew	šít	29.59	36.36	20.18	30.87	32.81	60
burn	hořet	12.5	34.55	18.42	5.37	1.56	0
drink	pít	33.67	50.91	42.98	28.86	18.75	0
know	znát	18.88	29.09	21.05	16.11	14.06	10

Table 5.4: Saturation values per order of derivation, adjectives.

Adjectives		Saturation value (%)	1st order (%)	2nd order (%)	3rd order (%)	4th order (%)	5th order (%)
narrow	úzký	13.94	15.56	10.94	12.2	21.43	100
old	starý	60	64.44	68.75	56.1	21.43	0
straight	přímý	13.94	20	10.94	12.2	7.14	100
new	nový	47.88	26.67	46.88	70.73	57.14	0
long	dlouhý	12.12	24.44	9.38	4.88	7.14	0
warm	teplý	21.82	24.44	25.56	17.07	7.14	0
thick	tlustý	20.61	31.11	28.13	4.88	0	0
bad	zlý	18.79	6.67	20.31	34.15	7.14	0
thin	tenký	13.94	15.56	14.06	17.07	0	0
black	černý	24.85	37.78	25	14.63	14.29	0

other hand, has a saturation value reaching less than 7%. Two adjectives permit no 4th order of derivation (*tlustý* 'thick' and *tenký* 'thin'), while two of them produce 5th order derivations (*úzký* 'narrow' and *přímý* 'straight').

Table 5.5 gives the average saturation values per order of derivation for all the nouns, verbs and adjectives. The average values are similar for every order of the three word-classes except the 1st and the 5th ones (the adjectives are weaker in the 1st order but stronger in the 5th order than the other word-classes). The average saturation values are quite low, not reaching above 40% in the 1st order, 27% in the 2nd order, 25% in the 3rd order, 19% in the 4th order, and 20% in the 5th order.

Table 5.5: Average saturation values per order of derivation for all three word-classes.

	1st order	2nd order	3rd order	4th order	5th order
Nouns	33.22	30	24.24	15	10
Verbs	39.82	26.93	21.54	18.13	11
Adjectives	26.67	26.1	24.4	14.29	20

5.4 Orders of derivation

The maximum number of orders for the sample is five. Basically, Table 5.6 shows that the average number of orders for the nouns, verbs and adjectives does not vary.

Table 5.6: Maximum and average number of orders of derivation for all three word-classes.

	Maximum	Average
Nouns	5	3.9
Verbs	5	4
Adjectives	5	4

5.5 Derivational capacity

As can be seen from Table 5.7, the derivational capacity of verbs (i.e. direct 1st order derivatives) amounts to the highest average value. It even significantly exceeds the values of both nouns and adjectives. The rather high derivational capacity of verbs might be due to the fact that prefixation is often applied to verbs (see Chapter 1).

Table 5.7: Maximum and average derivational capacity for all three word-classes.

	Maximum	Average
Nouns	18	10.3
Verbs	36	21.9
Adjectives	29	12

As for the average derivational capacity in all orders and for all word-classes, Table 5.8 shows that, in the 1st order, the values may be easily correlated to those in Table 5.7. The numeric value of verbs is about twice that of nouns and adjectives in the 1st and 2nd orders, and the difference increases noticeably in the remaining orders of derivation. However, the table also shows little derivational output of the 5th order of derivation of all word-classes.

Table 5.8: Average number of derivatives per order of derivation for all three word-classes.

	1st order	2nd order	3rd order	4th order	5th order
Nouns	10.3	17.1	8	0.9	0.2
Verbs	21.9	30.7	32.1	11.6	1.1
Adjectives	12	16.7	10	2	0.2

5.6 Correlation between semantic categories and orders of derivation

The particular semantic category implemented for the majority of **nouns** in the first three orders is RELATIONAL. In the 1st and 2nd orders, 9 of the 10 sample nouns have the capacity to derive the RELATIONAL adjective (for the 3rd order the value is 8). The second most frequent semantic category is that of DIMINUTIVE, appearing in the 1st and 2nd orders with a value of 9. Besides RELATIONAL, the most frequently actualized category in the 3rd order is SIMILATIVE, reaching a value of 6. The 4th and 5th orders only have sporadic occurrences within several semantic categories. For Czech nouns, there is a strong correlation between the 1st and 2nd orders of derivation and their semantic categories of RELATIONAL and DIMINUTIVE. The 3rd order is then correlated with the category of RELATIONAL.

The strongest position among the semantic categories within **verbs** has the category of FINITIVE. Each of the 10 verbs in the 1st order has the capacity to derive a FINITIVE verb. The category of FINITIVE is then related to the categories of ITERATIVE and DIRECTIONAL, both of which have a value of 8. The 2nd order employs the categories of RELATIONAL and ABILITY (both 8) and the 3rd order the categories of PURPOSE (7) and RELATIONAL (7). Worth mentioning also is the 4th order that documents the strong derivational capacity of Czech verbs: the category of RELATIONAL appears again (7) followed by the category of FEMALE (6). One may conclude that, for Czech verbs, there is a firm correlation between the 1st order of derivation and the semantic category of FINITIVE and, to an extent, the related categories of ITERATIVE and DIRECTIONAL.

A similarly firm correlation between the 1st order and some semantic categories is true for Czech **adjectives.** All 10 adjectives derive ABSTRACTION and MANNER words. The 2nd and 3rd orders are then characterized by AUGMENTATIVE (9), followed in the 2nd order by RELATIONAL (8) and in the 3rd order by MANNER (8).

5.7 Semantic categories with blocking effects

As far as **nouns** are concerned, the only semantic category that reliably blocks any further derivation is RELATIONAL in the 3rd order. This applies to all 10 sample nouns. The blocking effect in the 1st order seems to be random, while the 2nd order tends to use MANNER as a derivational block. For **verbs** in the 1st order, a sort of blocking effect is played by ITERATIVE, in the 2nd order by MANNER, DIMINUTIVE, and also by ABILITY, and in the 3rd order by PURPOSE. Adjectival DIMINUTIVES seem to have a slight blocking role in the 1st derivational order of **adjectives**, while ABSTRACTION and MANNER are employed in both the 2nd and 3rd orders. The strongest blocking tendency may be found in the 3rd order in connection with the category of AUGMENTATIVE. Generally, there is no strict correlation between any semantic category and the individual word-classes, the only exception being the above-mentioned category of RELATIONAL in the 3rd derivational order of nouns.

5.8 Typical combinations of semantic categories

As for Czech **nouns**, the typical combination of semantic properties is based on the category of RELATIONAL that follows a noun (either a base-word or a coined noun) denoting AGENT (*zubař* 'dentist' > *zubařský* 'dentist's'), PATIENT (*kostlivec* 'skeleton' > *kostlivcový* 'skeletal'), INSTRUMENT (*kostice* 'bone in lingerie' > *kosticový* 'bony'), DIMINUTIVE (*kamének* 'small stone, pebble' > *kaménkový* 'stony') and LOCATION (*ohniště* 'campfire' > *ohnišťový* 'campfire's'). All 10 basic nouns are involved in this type of combination. Another semantic category that tends to appear in stable combinations (occurring in all 10 basic nouns) is MANNER: coined adjectives with the property of QUALITY, SIMILATIVE or RELATIONAL are then followed by an adverb which has/displays the respective meaning of MANNER (*kostnatý* 'bony' > *kostnatě* 'in a bony manner', *zubovitý* 'tooth-like' > *zubovitě* 'in a tooth-like manner', *nádenický* 'menial' > *nádenicky* 'in a menial manner'). For Czech, a chain of two DIMINUTIVES that come one after another (*očko* – *očičko* 'little eye') is typical (it appears in 8 of the 10 basic nouns).

A high degree of systematicity is to be found in Czech **verbs**. The category of DURATIVE regularly follows FINITIVE, CUMULATIVE, DIRECTIONAL or DISTRIBUTIVE and establishes the following regular series: DURATIVE – INSTRUMENT (*ořezávat* 'trim' > *ořezávátko* 'pencil sharpener'), DURATIVE – AGENT (*přidávat* 'add' > *přidavač* 'hodman'), DURATIVE – RESULT (*přidávat* 'add' > *přídavek* 'addition'), or DURATIVE – PURPOSE (*okopávat* 'hoe' > *okopávací* 'intended for hoeing'). The second verb in succession (except for the blocking PURPOSE – see above) is the basis for RELATIONAL, DIMINUTIVE, or, with AGENT, for FEMALE.

A similar systematicity is provided by Czech **adjectives**. In the derivational networks of all sample adjectives, the regular combinations AUGMENTATIVE – AUGMENTATIVE (*starší* 'older' > *nejstarší* 'the oldest') or MANNER – AUGMENTATIVE – AUGMENTATIVE (*teple* 'warmly' > *tepleji* 'warmer' > *nejtepleji* 'warmest') appear several times.

There are also tendencies that are valid for all three word-classes. What was said about RELATIONAL and MANNER in connection with nouns is evident in derivational networks of the whole sample. In addition, the semantic category of QUALITY strongly tends to establish a combination with ABSTRACTION or PATIENT.

5.9 Multiple occurrence of semantic categories

The reoccurrence of the same semantic category within one derivational chain of the base-word is rather rare in Czech. There are only two isolated examples within adjectives as base-words: ABSTRACTION – QUALITY – ABSTRACTION (*úzkost* 'anxiety' > *úzkostný* 'anxious' > *úzkostnost* 'being anxious' and *zlost* 'anger' > *zlostný* 'angry' > *zlostnost* 'being angry').

5.10 Reversibility of semantic categories

The research sample does not exhibit any reversed order of semantic categories. The only isolated example is RELATIONAL – PATIENT (*zubní* 'dental' > *zubnice* 'dental consonant'), as opposed to the regular PATIENT – RELATIONAL (*zubatec*$_N$ 'big-toothed' > *zubatcový*$_A$ 'big-toothed').

5.11 Conclusions

The derivational networks of the research sample and the data indicated in Tables 5.1–5.8 prove the highest structural richness belongs to networks developed by **verbs** as base-words. The maximum derivational network reaches a value of 392, the most numerous order in which is the 3rd order (149). Verbs also have the highest average saturation value, namely 39.82%. Nevertheless, when examining the respective sample words, the highest saturation value, i.e. the highest structural richness of the derivational network, is evinced in nouns by *oko* 'eye' and *voda* 'water', in verbs by *řezat* 'cut' and *dát* 'give', and in adjectives by the opposite pair of *starý* 'old' and *nový* 'new', all of which reach more than 45% (except *voda*, which 'only' reaches 44.19%), the adjective *starý* being the 'winner' with a value of 60%.

RELATIONAL, which has multiple roles in the derivational system, appears as the most specific semantic category. It is the most populous semantic category in the first three orders in nouns, even playing the role of a block for any further derivation in the 3rd one. Furthermore, it is highly correlated with all three derivational orders in nouns, with three orders (2nd–4th) in verbs, and with the 2nd order in adjectives. Another specificity should be mentioned in connection with verbs. One of the strongest positions among the semantic categories is occupied by FINITIVE, which is regularly followed by DURATIVE, thus establishing a firm combination of semantic categories. It is also due to the fact that both categories are phenomena of the so-called 'Aktionsart', a category on the edge of grammar and word-formation. In Czech it is realized by affixation, namely by word-formation suffixes.

References

Bednaříková, Božena. 2009a. Is Czech ideal representative of the inflectional language type? *Romanoslavica* XLV. 41–50.
Bednaříková, Božena. 2009b. *Word and Its Conversion*. Olomouc: Univerzita Palackého.
Bednaříková, Božena. 2011. Towards (Proto)typing of Morphological Processes. *Czech and Slovac Linguistic Review* I. 44–52.
Bozděchová, Ivana. 2016. 158. Czech. In Peter O. Müller, Ingeborg Ohnheiser, Susan Olsen & Franz Rainer (eds.), *Word-formation. An international handbook of the languages of Europe. Vol. 4*, 2872–2891. Berlin & New York: Mouton de Gruyter.
Čermák, František. 2010. *Lexicon and Semantics*. Prague: Nakladatelství Lidové noviny.
Čermák, František. 2012. *Morphematics and Word-formation of Czech*. Prague: Nakladatelství Lidové noviny.
Komárek, Miroslav. 2006. *Contributions to Czech Morphology*. Prague: Periplum.
Lotko, Edvard. 2009. *Comparative and Bohemian Studies*. Olomouc: Univerzita Palackého.
Pala, Karel & Dana Hlaváčková. 2007. Derivational relations in Czech Wordnet. In *Proceedings of the Workshop on Balto-Slavonic Natural Language Processing: Information Extraction and Enabling Technologies*, 75–81. Prague: Association for Computational Linguistics.
Skalička, Vladimír. 1935. *Zur ungarischen Grammatik*. Prague: Nakl. Filosofické fakulty University Karlovy.
Štekauer, Pavol & Rochelle Lieber (eds.). 2005. *Handbook of Word-Formation (Vol. 64)*. Springer.

Sources

Český národní korpus [Czech National Corpus]. https://www.korpus.cz/.
Internetová jazyková příručka [Internet Language Guide, Institute for Czech Language, Academy of Sciences of the Czech Republic]. http://prirucka.ujc.cas.cz/.
Příruční slovník jazyka českého (1935–1957) [Reference Dictionary of the Czech Language]. http://psjc.ujc.cas.cz/.
Slovník spisovného jazyka českého (1960–1971) [Dictionary of Standard Czech Language]. http://ssjc.ujc.cas.cz/.
Slovník spisovné češtiny pro školu a veřejnost [Dictionary of Standard Czech for School and Public]. http://prirucka.ujc.cas.cz/.

Ewa Konieczna
6 Derivational networks in Polish

6.1 General notes

Polish is a West Slavic language with a profusion of derivational and inflectional morphemes. Polish word-formation provides a wide range of morphological instruments aimed at forming new words, the commonest of which is affixation (Szymanek 2010). The principal derivational processes are prefixation and suffixation. Additionally, other techniques can be employed, such as prefixal-suffixal derivation and postfixation.

A remarkable feature of Polish affixation is affix stacking, i.e. "the occurrence of several distinct formatives in a particular derivative" (Szymanek 2010: 21), as well as the repetition of a single suffix, frequently employed in the formation of DIMINUTIVES. Double motivation is another characteristic of the Polish derivational system. For example, the formation of adjectives can be motivated by two nouns that are derivationally related: *górniczy* < *górnik* 'miner'/*górnictwo* 'mining' can be taken to refer either to miners or to mining (Szymanek 2010: 79). Last but not least, verbal prefixation in Polish constitutes a perfect example of the asymmetry of form and function (Beard 1995). A particular prefix may express several meanings and a given meaning may be conveyed by several prefixes. For example, the prefix *pod-* can be both DIRECTIONAL and DIMINUTIVE, as demonstrated by *budować* 'build' > *pod-budować* (*balkon*) 'to underpin (a balcony)' and *uczyć* 'teach' > *pod-uczyć* 'to teach sb the basics', respectively. The semantic category RESULTATIVE can be conceptualized by numerous prefixes, for instance by *z-* and *po-*, as in *z-drożeć, po-drożeć* 'to become expensive', created from the verbal base *drożeć* 'to become more expensive'.

Given this, the construction of derivational networks for nouns, verbs and adjectives involves the following problems. First of all, in the adjective derivational network, there are numerous cases of double motivation, predominantly of the following type: *wąziutki* [narrow.ADJ.DIM] (DIMINUTIVE)/*wąsko* [narrowly.ADV] (MANNER) > *wąziutko* [narrowly.DIM] (MANNER). In this case, the DIMINUTIVE form of the adjective is taken as the base on account of the fact that, in the Polish morphological tradition, the DIMINUTIVE form of the adverb is perceived as being created from the DIMINUTIVE adjective (Grzegorczykowa et al. 1999: 528).

Verbal prefixation has turned out to be another problematic area, not only due to prefix polysemy but also the overlap of the lexical and grammatical aspect. Consequently, if the prefixed deverbal derivative has several different meanings, it can be assigned to several distinct semantic categories. However, since prefixed verbs, with a few exceptions such as secondary imperfectives or ITERATIVES, are perfective by default, they have not been marked as RESULTATIVE if, in a particular derivative, a prefix possesses a lexical meaning that can be subsumed under one of the available semantic categories, such as DIRECTIONAL or DIMINUTIVE. If the lexical meaning of a prefix is bleached, the derivative can be included in the category RESULTATIVE. For example, *wy-pić* 'drink up', formed from *pić* 'drink', contains the prefix *wy-* 'out' which represents the liquid being moved out of the container in the process of drinking. Notwithstanding that, in this particular combination, the prefix *wy-* is not perceived by native speakers of Polish as a representative of the category DIRECTIONAL. Consequently, in cases like this one, prefixed verbs are assigned to the category RESULTATIVE.

Another complication is the interaction of the prefix semantics with the grammatical form of the object (Śmiech 1986). For instance, the meaning of the prefix *na-*, closely related to the spatial preposition *na* 'on', can be either CUMULATIVE, if the object cannot be perceived in terms of separate elements, as in the phrase *nakopać piasku* [on-dig.INF.CUM sand.UNCOUNT.GEN] 'to dig much sand', or it can be interpreted as DISTRIBUTIVE, if the activity can be seen as being aimed at members of the set, as in *nakopać ziemniaków* [on-dig.INF.DISTR potato.PL.GEN] 'to dig many potatoes'. Since the aim of the project did not involve contextualization patterns, the recognized dictionaries of the Polish language were consulted, and the verbs were assigned to the semantic category in accordance with the established prefix meaning provided by the dictionary.

As regards establishing the validity of derivatives for each item, they were included in the derivational networks if they were found either in the online or CD version of the dictionary of contemporary Polish (*Słownik Języka Polskiego PWN*) or the corpus of the contemporary Polish language (*Narodowy Korpus Języka Polskiego*), containing 1.5 billion words.

6.2 Maximum derivational networks

Table 6.1 presents the maximum derivational networks for nouns, verbs and adjectives.

As demonstrated above, verbs are characterized by the richest derivational networks in all orders, while nouns exhibit the poorest derivational capacity.

Table 6.1: Maximum derivational networks per order of derivation for all three word-classes.

	1st order	2nd order	3rd order	4th order	Σ
Nouns	26	25	5	3	59
Verbs	45	67	51	8	171
Adjectives	33	32	16	3	84
TOTAL	104	124	72	14	314

6.3 Saturation values

Tables 6.2–6.5 present saturation values for nouns, verbs and adjectives as well as the maximum derivational networks for all three word-classes.

Table 6.2: Saturation values per order of derivation, nouns.

Nouns		1st order	2nd order	3rd order	4th order	Total
bone	kość	33.33	35.71	12.5	0	30.3
eye	oko	18.52	7.14	25	33.33	15.15
tooth	ząb	48.15	7.14	0	0	22.73
day	dzień	18.52	3.57	25	66.67	15.15
dog	pies	29.63	3.57	0	0	13.64
louse	wesz	11.11	3.57	0	0	6.06
fire	ogień	18.52	7.14	0	0	10.61
stone	kamień	44.44	17.86	12.5	0	27.27
water	woda	33.33	53.57	37.5	0	40.91
name	imię	18.52	17.86	0	0	15.15

As is demonstrated by Table 6.2, the noun with the highest average saturation value (40.91) is *woda* 'water', which occurs despite the fact that this noun does not have any 4th order derivatives. The noun with the lowest average saturation value is *wesz* 'louse' (6.06). The reason for such a low saturation value for this noun, which produced only four derivatives that could be included in the sample, is its negative semantic potential, resulting in the derivation of predominantly pejorative lexemes that underwent a metaphorical shift, and hence had to be excluded. There are just two nouns with derivatives in all four orders – *oko* 'eye' and *dzień* 'day' – and as many as five nouns do not have any derivatives in the 3rd order. Consequently, the average saturation values for the 3rd and 4th orders of nouns are relatively low (11.25 and 10, respectively), far lower than those of verbs and adjectives. Likewise, the average saturation of the 2nd order is by far the lowest in all three word-classes studied, amounting to 15.71. However, the average saturation of the 1st order is only slightly lower than that of nouns and adjectives (see Table 6.5).

Consider the maximum derivational network and average saturation values for verbs in Table 6.3.

Table 6.3: Saturation values per order of derivation, verbs.

Verbs		1st order	2nd order	3rd order	4th order	Total
cut	ciąć	32.56	26.56	61.54	20	38.46
dig	kopać	46.51	48.44	13.46	0	34.32
pull	ciągnąć	41.86	43.75	34.62	40	40.24
throw	rzucać	27.91	37.5	1.92	0	21.89
give	dawać	18.6	14.06	9.62	30	14.79
hold	trzymać	16.28	10.94	5.77	20	11.24
sew	szyć	25.58	15.63	15.38	0	17.16
burn	palić	32.56	42.19	1.92	0	24.85
drink	pić	34.88	23.44	21.15	30	26.04
know	wiedzieć	4.65	3.13	5.77	0	4.14

As shown in Table 6.3, the verb with the highest average saturation value is *kopać* 'pull' (46.51), while the one with the lowest is *wiedzieć* 'know' (4.14). *Wiedzieć* is the only abstract verb in the sample and because it synchronically derives just one deverbal verb, *dowiedzieć się* 'find out', by means of prefixation, a major mechanism enabling the formation of morphologically complex verbs, the total saturation value for this verb is extremely low. The number of verbs generating the 4th order derivatives is the same as those that do not produce them, and amounts to five. While the average saturation of the 1st order is comparable with that of nouns (28.14 versus 27.41 for nouns), the average saturation values of the 2nd, 3rd and 4th orders are much higher than those for nouns (amounting to 26.56, 17.12 and 14, respectively) due to the extremely rich system of verbal prefixation in Polish and the phenomenon of affix stacking, which triggers numerous derivational chains, e.g. *ciągnąć* 'pull' > *wyciągnąć* (1st order, DIRECTIONAL) > *wyciągnąć się* (2nd order, REFLEXIVE); *wyciągać* (2nd order, ITERATIVE) > *wyciągać się* (3rd order, REFLEXIVE); or *powyciągać* (3rd order, DISTRIBUTIVE) > *powyciągać się* (4th order, REFLEXIVE).

Table 6.4 provides the relevant data for adjectives.

Table 6.4: Saturation values per order of derivation, adjectives.

Adjectives		1st order	2nd order	3rd order	4th order	Total
narrow	wąski	25	18.18	12.5	0	19.05
old	stary	43.75	12.12	6.25	0	22.62
straight	prosty	31.25	42.42	37.5	0	35.71
new	nowy	28.13	48.48	18.75	66.67	35.71
long	długi	25	18.18	12.5	66.67	21.43
warm	ciepły	43.75	36.36	0	0	30.95
thick	gruby	34.38	12.12	12.5	33.33	21.43
bad	zły	12.5	12.12	43.75	0	17.86
thin	cienki	28.13	18.18	0	0	17.86
black	czarny	31.25	30.3	6.25	0	25

The class of adjectives is the most homogenous with respect to total saturation values calculated for individual items: the ratio between the highest saturation value (35.71 for *prosty* and *nowy*) and the lowest one (17.86 for *zły* and *cienki*) is 2:1, while it is 6.75:1 for nouns and 9.7:1 for verbs. The average saturation values for all the orders of derivation are very much comparable to those of verbs. This seems to be caused by the fact that all adjectives derive at least one verb in the 1st order of derivation, e.g. *stary* 'old' > *starzeć się* 'get old' (REFLEXIVE), *gruby* 'fat' > *grubieć* 'start getting fat' (INCEPTIVE), or *długi* 'long' > *wydłużyć* 'make long' (RESULTATIVE). The derived verbs subsequently serve as inputs for further derivation, which has an effect on the saturation values due to the high productivity of verbal affixation.

Table 6.5 below presents the average saturation values for all the word-classes and for all the orders of derivation. While the values in the 1st order are quite uniform across the three word-classes, in the 2nd, 3rd and 4th orders, those for verbs and adjectives are significantly higher than those for nouns.

Table 6.5: Average saturation values per order of derivation for all three word-classes.

	1st order	2nd order	3rd order	4th order
Nouns	27.41	15.71	11.25	10
Verbs	28.14	28.71	18.27	15.45
Adjectives	30.31	24.85	15	16.67

6.4 Orders of derivation

As demonstrated by Table 6.6, none of the word-classes in the Polish sample are capable of producing more than four orders of derivation. The average number of orders of derivation is highest for verbs and lowest for nouns.

Table 6.6: Maximum and average number of orders of derivation for all three word-classes.

	Maximum	Average
Nouns	4	2.7
Verbs	4	3.5
Adjectives	4	3.1

6.5 Derivational capacity

Table 6.7 presents the maximum and average derivational capacities for the 1st order in all three word-classes. As can be seen, it is again verbs that score the highest, while nouns score the lowest both in terms of the maximum and the average derivational capacity.

As demonstrated in Table 6.8, derivational capacity in all orders is no different than that of the 1st order as regards their overall tendencies: verbs considerably

Table 6.7: Maximum and average derivational capacity for all three word-classes.

	Maximum	Average
Nouns	13	7.4
Verbs	20	12.1
Adjectives	14	9.7

Table 6.8: Average number of derivatives per order of derivation for all three word-classes.

	1st order	2nd order	3rd order	4th order
Nouns	7.4	4.4	0.9	0.3
Verbs	12.1	17	8.9	1.4
Adjectives	9.7	8.2	2.4	0.5

surpass both adjectives and nouns in terms of their average derivational capacity in the 2nd, 3rd and 4th orders of derivation. This is due to the fact that, as pointed out in section 6.3, each adjective derives at least one verb in the 1st order, which is not the case for nouns from the Swadesh list, as just four of them generate denominal verbs in the 1st order – *kamień* 'stone', *dzień* 'day', *woda* 'water', and *ząb* 'tooth' – which, in turn, produce few further derivatives.

6.6 Correlation between semantic categories and orders of derivation

For Polish nouns, there is a strong correlation between the 1st order of derivation and the semantic categories RELATIONAL (value 9) and DIMINUTIVE (value 8). AUGMENTATIVE (value 5) and QUALITY (value 5) are weakly correlated with the 1st order. There is also a weak correlation between the 2nd order and the semantic category QUALITY (value 5).

As regards verbs and correlations between semantic categories and the 1st order, the strongest one has been observed for the semantic category RESULTATIVE (value 8), and a weaker one for the semantic categories REFLEXIVE, DIMINUTIVE and DISTRIBUTIVE (value 7). There is a strong correlation between the

2nd order and ITERATIVE (value 9), while REFLEXIVE and QUALITY are only weakly correlated (value 6) with it. There is a weak correlation between the 3rd order and DISTRIBUTIVE (value 5).

For Polish adjectives, there is a strong correlation between the 1st order and the semantic categories of MANNER, DIMINUTIVE and RESULTATIVE (value 8). RESULTATIVE is also strongly correlated with the 2nd order (value 8), while DIMINUTIVE (value 7) and MANNER (value 6) are more weakly correlated with this order. There is a weak correlation between the 3rd order and QUALITY (value 6).

6.7 Semantic categories with blocking effects

For nouns, there is a strong blocking effect for AUGMENTATIVE (5/5)[1] and DIMINUTIVE (7/8) and a weak blocking effect for RELATIONAL (5/9) in the 1st order. In the 2nd order, there is a blocking effect for QUALITY (4/5). For verbs, there is a strong blocking effect for REFLEXIVE (6/7) in the 1st order and for DISTRIBUTIVE (5/5) in the 3rd order. For adjectives, there is a strong blocking effect for QUALITY (7/7), a relatively strong effect for PRIVATIVE (4/6) and a weak blocking effect for MANNER (5/8) as well as SIMILATIVE (4/8) in the 1st order. In the 2nd order, there is a blocking effect for DIMINUTIVE (4/5) and a weak blocking effect for RESULT (5/8) and MANNER (3/6).

6.8 Typical combinations of semantic categories

For nouns, there are no systematic combinations of semantic categories. For verbs, the following combinations are systematic: RESULTATIVE – ITERATIVE (*przeciąć* 'to cut in two' – *przecinać* 'to cut in two repeatedly'), RESULTATIVE – REFLEXIVE (*wypalić* 'to burn' – *wypalić się* 'to burn itself out'), ITERATIVE – DISTRIBUTIVE (*zaciągać* 'to drag repeatedly' – *pozaciągać* 'to drag many objects repeatedly'), ITERATIVE – INSTRUMENT (*zszywać* 'to sew up repeatedly' – *zszywacz* 'stapler'), DIMINUTIVE – ITERATIVE (*popić* 'to drink a little liquid' – *popijać* 'to

---

[1] The first numerical value represents the number of semantic categories that are blocked, while the second is the total number of bases from which a word derives in the respective semantic category. In the case of the semantic category DIMINUTIVE produced by nouns, the 7/8 notation means that eight nouns from the sample derive this semantic category and seven of them do not generate any further derivations.

drink a little liquid repeatedly') and DIRECTIONAL – ITERATIVE (*podrzucić* 'to toss' – *podrzucać* 'to toss repeatedly'). In the category of adjectives, it has been found that the following combinations are systematic: DIMINUTIVE – MANNER (*cieplutki* [warm.ADJ.DIM] – *cieplutko* [warm.ADV.DIM]), SIMILATIVE – MANNER (*czarniawy* 'blackish' [black.ADJ.SIM] – *czarniawo* [black.ADV.SIM] and PRIVATIVE – MANNER (*nieprosty* [straight.ADJ.PRIV] – *nieprosto* [straight.ADV.PRIV]).

6.9 Multiple occurrence of semantic categories

The phenomenon of the repeated occurrence of semantic categories in the series of derivations from a single initial word is the least robust in the semantic category of nouns: the category QUALITY reoccurs four times, DIMINUTIVE and PROCESS twice, and RELATIONAL, COLLECTIVE, RESULTATIVE and LOCATION reoccur just once. As regards the most frequent reoccurrence of semantic categories, which is that of QUALITY, it can be illustrated by a series of derivatives from the noun *kamień* 'stone' > *kamienisty* 'stony' (1st order QUALITY) > *kamienistość* 'being stony' (2nd order QUALITY).

With respect to verbs, REFLEXIVE reoccurs most frequently, viz. 10 times, while DISTRIBUTIVE and RESULTATIVE reoccur six times, DIMINUTIVE five times, INSTRUMENT and ITERATIVE three times, RELATIONAL, ACTION and LOCATION twice, and FEMALE, AGENT and AUGMENTATIVE just once. The multiple reoccurrence of REFLEXIVE can be exemplified by the following derivational chain, created from the base verb *palić* 'burn' > *wypalić* (1st order RESULTATIVE) > *wypallić się* (2nd order REFLEXIVE); *wypalać* (2nd order ITERATIVE) > *powypalać* (3rd order DISTRIBUTIVE) > *powypalać się* (4th order REFLEXIVE).

In the class of adjectives, the semantic category DIMINUTIVE reoccurs seven times, QUALITY and MANNER six times, REFLEXIVE three times, RESULTATIVE twice and LOCATION only once. The multiple reoccurrence of DIMINUTIVE can be exemplified by a series of derivations from the adjective *stary* 'old' > *stareńki* 'very old' (1st order DIMINUTIVE) > *starowinka* 'a very old lady' (2nd order DIMINUTIVE).

6.10 Reversibility of semantic categories

No instances of semantic categories occurring in a reversed order were attested in the Polish data.

6.11 Conclusions

As regards the results obtained for nouns, verbs and adjectives, all three word-classes have derivatives in the 4th order; however, the average number of orders is highest for verbs and lowest for nouns. The highest average saturation values were obtained for verbs for all orders and were lowest for nouns. The maximum and average derivational capacity for all the orders of derivation is highest for verbs and lowest for nouns. All in all, it is verbs that scored the highest, while nouns scored the lowest in all values, with adjectives occupying the middle position.

References

Beard, Robert. 1995. *Lexeme-Morpheme Base Morphology: A General Theory of Inflection and Word Formation*. Albany: SUNY Press.
Grzegorczykowa Renata, Roman Laskowski and Henryk Wróbel. (eds.). 1999. *Gramatyka Współczesnego Języka Polskiego. Morfologia – tom 1 i 2* (Grammar of contemporary Polish. Morphology – vols. 1 and 2). Warszawa: Wydawnictwo PWN.
Szymanek, Bogdan. 2010. *A Panorama of Polish Word Formation*. Lublin: Wydawnictwo KUL.
Śmiech, Witold. 1986. *Derywacja prefiksalna czasowników polskich* (Prefixal derivation of Polish verbs). Zakład Narodowy im. Ossolińskich.

Dictionaries and corpora

Narodowy Korpus Języka Polskiego. http://nkjp.pl.
Słownik Języka Polskiego PWN. https://sjp.pwn.pl.

Viacheslav Shevchenko, Slávka Tomaščíková
7 Derivational networks in Russian

7.1 General notes

In the modern Russian language, the most productive method of word-formation is affixation.

In Russian, nouns and adjectives are mostly formed by means of suffixes, and verbs – by means of prefixes. The combined suffixal-prefixal way of word-formation is mostly used for forming verbs and is less productive in the process of nouns formation. In modern Russian affixation has its grammatical peculiarities: prefixes are able to form the words of the same part of speech as the initial word; suffixes can be used to build words belonging to a different part of speech; and the suffixal-prefixal way can be used to form words of various parts of speech (Valgina et al. 2002).

A substantial part of affixes in the Russian language have been borrowed from other languages, including Greek (the prefixes *а-, ре-, про-, анти-* and others) and Latin (the suffixes *-ор, -ит, -ент, -ант* and others). The borrowed morphemes are usually elements of the borrowed words, but sometimes they are used to form words using the Russian roots (e.g. *ухажёр* 'boyfriend').

The problems that exist in the sphere of the Russian language morphology mainly concern the distinction between suffixes and verbal endings: some of the verbal endings are classified as word-formation suffixes, e.g. the verbal ending *ть* is considered to be an infinitive suffix by some scholars (Stepanova 2001).

The data for the present research has been taken from the word-formation dictionary of the modern Russian language (Ulyanova 2013) as well as from the Russian National Corpus (RNC).

7.2 Maximum derivational networks

According to the data presented in Table 7.1 below, the verbs display the richest maximum derivational networks in all orders and in total. The verbs also have the highest number in the 4th order derivations, whereas the number of nouns is 1. No data have been found for the 5th order.

Table 7.1: Maximum derivational networks per order of derivation for all three word-classes.

	1st order	2nd order	3rd order	4th order	5th order	Σ
Nouns	17	18	13	1	0	49
Verbs	32	34	22	5	0	93
Adjectives	18	23	5	0	0	46
TOTAL	67	75	40	6	0	188

7.3 Saturation values

The mean saturation values for nouns range between 8.16% and 30.61%, as shown in Table 7.2. Five words – *кость* 'bone', *глаз* 'eye', *камень* 'stone', *вода* 'water', and *имя* 'name' – have the same mean saturation value (30.61%). The word *вошь* 'louse' has the lowest mean saturation value (8.16%). Within the 1st order, the noun *глаз* 'eye' has the highest saturation value (64.71%) and *вошь* 'louse' has the lowest (11.76%). The word *имя* 'name' has the highest saturation value (44.44%) within the 2nd order. Four words – *глаз* 'eye', *зуб* 'tooth',

Table 7.2: Saturation values per order of derivation, nouns.

Nouns		Saturation value (%)	1st order (%)	2nd order (%)	3rd order (%)	4th order (%)	5th order (%)
bone	кость	30.61	29.41	38.89	23.08	0	0
eye	глаз	30.61	64.71	22.22	0	0	0
tooth	зуб	20.41	41.18	16.67	0	0	0
day	день	12.24	17.56	11.11	7.69	0	0
dog	собака	10.2	23.53	5.56	0	0	0
louse	вошь	8.16	11.76	5.56	7.69	0	0
fire	огонь	12.24	23.53	11.11	0	0	0
stone	камень	30.61	41.18	11.11	38.46	100	0
water	вода	30.61	17.65	27.78	53.85	0	0
name	имя	30.61	29.41	44.44	15.38	0	0

собака 'dog', and огонь 'fire' – have no 3rd order derivations. The word камень 'stone' is the only noun with a 4th order derivation.

In Table 7.3, the verb давать 'give' displays the highest mean saturation value (44.09%), and the verb рыть 'dig' has the lowest one (5.38%). The verb давать 'give' also has the highest value in the 1st and 2nd orders (50%). Within the 3rd order, жечь 'burn' displays the highest value (54.55%) and three verbs – резать 'cut', бросать 'throw' and шить 'sew' – have no 3rd order derivations. In the 4th order, the verb давать 'give' has the highest value (80%).

Table 7.3: Saturation values per order of derivation, verbs.

Verbs		Saturation value (%)	1st order (%)	2nd order (%)	3rd order (%)	4th order (%)	5th order (%)
cut	резать	11.83	3.13	29.41	0	0	0
dig	рыть	5.38	12.5	4.55			
pull	тянуть	13.98	17.65	31.82		0	0
throw	бросать	9.68	9.38	17.65	0	0	0
give	давать	44.09	50	50	18.18	80	0
hold	держать	13.98	29.41	9.09	20		0
sew	шить	9.68	18.75	8.82	0	0	0
burn	жечь	30.11	37.5	8.82	54.55	20	0
drink	пить	10.75	25	9.09		0	0
know	знать	10.75	15.63	8.82	4.55	20	0

The adjective тонкий 'thin' has the lowest mean saturation value (6.52%), whereas the words старый 'old' and тёплый 'warm' have the highest mean saturation value of 23.91%. Within the 1st order, the adjectives старый 'old', прямой 'straight', новый 'new' and толстый 'thick' have the same saturation value (22.22%); the adjective тёплый 'warm' has the highest saturation value (33.33%). In the 3rd order, the adjective старый 'old' displays the highest saturation value (40%); долгий 'long', тёплый 'warm' and плохой 'bad' have the same saturation value (20%). The rest of the adjectives are not represented in the 3rd order.

In Table 7.5, the average saturation values per order of derivation for all the nouns, verbs and adjectives in the Russian set are presented. Nouns have the

Table 7.4: Saturation values per order of derivation, adjectives.

Adjectives		Saturation value (%)	1st order (%)	2nd order (%)	3rd order (%)	4th order (%)	5th order (%)
narrow	узкий	10.87	16.67	8.7	0	0	0
old	старый	23.91	22.22	21.74	40	0	0
straight	прямой	21.74	22.22	26.09	0	0	0
new	новый	15.22	22.22	13.04	0	0	0
long	долгий	17.39	16.67	17.39	20	0	0
warm	тёплый	23.91	33.33	17.39	20	0	0
thick	толстый	13.04	22.22	8.7	0	0	0
bad	плохой	21.74	27.78	17.39	20	0	0
thin	тонкий	6.52	11.11	4.35	0	0	0
black	черный	10.87	16.67	8.7	0	0	0

Table 7.5: Average saturation values per order of derivation for all three word-classes.

	1st order	2nd order	3rd order	4th order	5th order
Nouns	30	19.45	14.62	10	0
Verbs	17.189	17.058	13.183	14	0
Adjectives	21.111	14.349	10	0	0

highest average saturation value in the 1st order (30%), whereas in other orders the values are fairly similar.

7.4 Orders of derivation

The maximum number of orders for the Russian set is four. In Table 7.6, we see that the average number for nouns, verbs and adjectives varies between two and three orders.

Table 7.6: Maximum and average number of orders of derivation for all three word-classes.

	Maximum	Average
Nouns	4	2.6
Verbs	4	2.8
Adjectives	3	2.5

7.5 Derivational capacity

According to the data presented in Table 7.7, verbs have the maximum derivational capacity (41), while adjectives have the lowest derivational capacity.

Table 7.7: Maximum and average derivational capacity for all three word-classes.

	Maximum	Average
Nouns	15	4.8
Verbs	41	7
Adjectives	11	6.5

As far as the average derivational capacity in all orders and for all word-classes is concerned, the data in Table 7.8 demonstrate that the verbs possess the highest derivational capacity in all orders. However, in the 1st order, nouns and verbs have almost equal values, and in the 2nd order, the values of nouns and adjectives are practically the same. In the 4th order, nouns and verbs demonstrate little derivational output.

Table 7.8: Average number of derivatives per order of derivation for all three word-classes.

	1st order	2nd order	3rd order	4th order	5th order
Nouns	5.1	3.5	1.9	0.1	0
Verbs	5.5	5.8	2.9	0.7	0
Adjectives	3.8	3.3	0.5	0	0

7.6 Correlation between semantic categories and orders of derivation

Among the nouns in the 1st order, the majority of derivatives are produced within the semantic categories DIMINUTIVE (18 derivatives), e.g. *глаз* 'eye' > *глазик* 'small eye' and *глазёнки* 'small pretty eyes', and QUALITY (17 derivatives), e.g. *кость* 'bone' > *костлявый* 'bony'. The DIMINUTIVE category is also represented in the 2nd order (7 derivatives), e.g. *день* 'day' > *денёчек* '(what a) day'. Another category present in the 2nd order is STATE (7 derivatives), e.g. *имя* 'name' > *именитость* 'eminence'. In the 3rd order, the most significant category is RESULTATIVE (4 derivatives), e.g. *кость* 'bone' > *окостенеть* 'ossify'. The other categories represented in the 3rd order are STATE (e.g. *вода* 'water' > *водянистость* 'wateriness') and QUALITY (e.g. *вода* 'water' > *паводковый* 'referring to a flood'). The only derivative in the 4th order refers to the category of STATE (*камень* 'stone' > *окаменелость* 'fossil'). The rest of the semantic categories in all orders are represented by 1–4 nouns.

As for the verbs, the derivatives in the 1st order mostly refer to the semantic categories ACTION (8 derivations), e.g. *бросать* 'to throw' > *бросок* 'a throw', and TERMINATIVE (6 derivatives), e.g. *давать* 'to give' > *выдать* 'to give out'. The categories REFLEXIVE (e.g. *резать* 'to cut' > *врезаться* 'to bump into'), ORNATIVE (e.g. *шить* 'to sew' > *вышить* 'to embroider') and DIRECTIONAL (e.g. *тянуть* 'to pull' > *оттянуть* 'to pull back') are each represented by 5 derivatives. In the 2nd order, the most widespread category is QUALITY (10 derivatives), e.g. *держать*$_V$ > *одержимый*$_A$ 'possessed'. The other categories that have the most derivatives are DIRECTIONAL (9 derivatives), e.g. *рыть* 'to dig' > *отрыть* 'dig up', and ACTION (9 derivatives), e.g. *знать*$_V$ 'to know' > *дознание*$_N$ 'investigation'. In the 3rd order, the majority of derivatives refer to the categories QUALITY (6 derivations), e.g. *знать*$_V$ 'to know' > *познавательный*$_A$ 'educational', and ACTION (5 derivatives), e.g. *жечь*$_V$ 'to burn' *выжигание*$_N$ 'burning off'. The 4th order is represented by the categories FEMALE (2 derivatives), e.g. *жечь*$_V$ 'to burn' > *поджигательница*$_N$ 'woman arsonist', and STATE (2 derivatives), e.g. *давать*$_V$ 'to give' *податливость*$_N$ 'amenability'. The categories ADDITIVE, QUALITY and PRIVATIVE have 1 derivative each in the 4th order. In general, the semantic categories in all orders are represented by 1–5 nouns.

As far as the adjectives are concerned, in the 1st order the most representative categories are DIMINUTIVE (10 derivatives), e.g. *плохой* 'bad' > *плохонький* 'poorish', and ABSTRACTION (6 derivatives), e.g. *новый*$_A$ 'new' *новшество*$_N$ 'novelty', which is quite understandable, because the characteristics of objects are easily compared and speakers often use these categories to express their evaluation of objects and phenomena. In the 2nd order, the majority of derivatives belong to the categories MANNER (6 derivatives), e.g. *прямой*$_A$ 'straight' *напрямик*$_{ADV}$ 'straight on', and CAUSATIVE (4 derivatives), e.g. *узкий*$_A$ 'narrow' > *сузить*$_V$ 'to narrow'. The other categories are represented by 1–3 derivatives. In the 3rd order, the PEJORATIVE, AUGMENTATIVE, STATE, ACTION and PRIVATIVE categories are represented by 1 derivative each.

7.7 Semantic categories with blocking effects

As far as the blocking effects for nouns are concerned, the semantic categories QUALITY, ACTION and INSTRUMENT block further derivation in the 1st order. Such semantic categories as ENTITY, STATE, ACTION and PRIVATIVE block further derivations in the 2nd order. In the 3rd order, further derivation is blocked by the CAUSATIVE, ACTION, DIMINUTIVE, STATE, QUALITY and PRIVATIVE categories.

Further derivations in the 1st order of the verbs are blocked by the ACTION, AUGMENTATIVE, TERMINATIVE, DIRECTIONAL and RESULTATIVE categories. In the 2nd order, further derivation is blocked by the QUALITY, ENTITY, PATIENT, INCEPTIVE, SATURATIVE and AUGMENTATIVE categories. ENTITY, STATE, ACTION, QUALITY block further derivation in the 3rd order.

In the 1st order of the adjectives, further derivation is blocked by such categories as ABSTRACTION, PRIVATIVE, MANNER, ACTION and REFLEXIVE. The DURATIVE, ACTION, CAUSATIVE, SPATIAL, RESULTATIVE, DIMINUTIVE and INSTRUMENT categories block further derivation in the 2nd order. In the 3rd order of adjectives, further derivation is blocked by the PRIVATIVE and ACTION categories.

Such semantic categories as ACTION, QUALITY, AUGMENTATIVE and STATE tend to block further derivation independently of the order in which they occur.

7.8 Typical combinations of semantic categories

The Russian set demonstrates that there are some typical and systematic combinations of semantic categories, e.g. PRIVATIVE-MANNER, AGENT-ABSTRACTION, AUGMENTATIVE-MANNER, and MANNER-SPATIAL (e.g. *недолгий* 'not long' > *недолго* 'not for a long time', *новатор* 'innovator' > *обновление* 'renewal', *преплохой* 'quite bad' > *плохонько* 'badly', *прямо* 'directly' > *выпрямить* 'straighten'), reflecting various derivations from adjectives to adverbs, from nouns to nouns and from adverbs to verbs.

As for the verbs, the analyzed derivations involve ACTION-PATIENT-PROCESS (e.g. *стареть* 'to keep on getting old' > *старичок* 'old man' > *постареть* 'to get old') and ACTION-DIRECTIONAL (e.g. *бросок* 'a throw' > *забросить* 'to throw far away'), involving derivations from verbs to nouns and from nouns to verbs. Other combinations include ACTION-INSTRUMENT-PRIVATIVE (e.g. *давать* 'to give' > *датчик* 'sensory device' > *недодать* 'give less'), ACTION-DIMINUTIVE (e.g. *глазеть* 'to stare' > *глазочек* 'small eye'), and QUALITY-AGENT-DIMINUTIVE (e.g. *водный* 'aquatic' > *подводник* 'submariner' > *водичка* 'water').

7.9 Multiple occurrence of semantic categories

The research has demonstrated that in Russian there are multiple reoccurrences in one derivational chain. The first case includes ACTION-ACTION (e.g. *давать* 'to give' > *отдача* 'the act of giving away', *резать* 'to cut' > *врезание* 'the act of cutting up'). Other cases include ADDITIVE-ADDITIVE (*додать* 'to give more' > *додавать* 'to keep on giving more'), DIRECTIONAL-DIRECTIONAL (*отдать* 'to give away' > *передавать* 'to hand over'), QUALITY-QUALITY (*одержимый* 'possessed' > *сдержанный* 'reserved'; *жженный* 'burned' > *выжженный* 'burned down'; *именной* 'nominal' > *именинный* 'related to some person'), SPATIAL-SPATIAL (*растянуть* 'to stretch something' > *вытянутый* 'stretched out'), ABSTRACTION-ABSTRACTION (*новшество* 'innovation' > *обновление* 'renewal'), MANNER-MANNER (*прямо* 'directly' > *прямехонько* 'completely straight'), and DIMINUTIVE-DIMINUTIVE (*толстенький* 'fatty' > *толстячок* 'fatty man'; *огонек* 'small fire' > *огонечек* 'tiny fire'; *зубок* 'small tooth' > *зубочек* 'tiny tooth').

7.10 Reversibility of semantic categories

We did not find instances of semantic categories occurring in a reversed order in the Russian data set.

7.11 Conclusions

According to the data in Table 7.1, verbs demonstrate the highest number of derivational networks in all orders and in total. Verbs also have the highest number in the 4th order derivatives, whereas the number of nouns is 1.

The mean saturation values for nouns range between 8.16% and 30.61%. Nouns have the highest average saturation value in the 1st order (30%), whereas in other orders the values are fairly similar. The maximum number of orders for the Russian set is four.

According to the data presented in Table 7.7, verbs have the maximum derivational capacity (41), whereas the adjectives have the lowest derivational capacity. As far as the average derivational capacity in all orders and for all word-classes is concerned, the data in Table 7.8 demonstrate that verbs possess the highest derivational capacity in all orders. However, in the 1st order, the values of nouns and verbs are almost equal, and in the 2nd order the values of nouns and adjectives are also practically the same. In the 4th order, nouns and verbs demonstrate little derivational output.

The results of the undertaken analysis demonstrate that the absolute majority of the semantic categories (28 of the 31 available labels) are covered by the Russian derivatives. This can be explained by the fact that the Russian language possesses a wide range of derivational means used for expressing the morphological and semantic relationships between words.

Reference

Stepanova, L. S. 2001. Suffiks ili okončanije? [Suffix or ending?]. *Russkij jazyk* 6. http://rus.1september.ru/article.php?ID=200100608.

Ulyanova, O. A. (ed.). 2013. *Slovoobrazovatěl'nyj slovar' sovremennogo russkogo jazyka* [Word-building dictionary of the modern Russian language]. Moskva: Adělant.

Valgina, N. S., D. E. Rozental' & M. I. Fomina. 2002. *Sovremennyj russkij jazyk* [The modern Russian language]. Moskva: Logos.

Sources

Russian National Corpus. http://www.ruscorpora.ru.

Gordana Štasni, Gordana Štrbac
8 Derivational networks in Serbian

8.1 General notes

Suffixation and prefixation are the main productive word-formation processes in Serbian. Compounding is not a typical feature of Serbian, and complex words are mostly loan translations from Greek and Latin. Conversion is the least productive word-formation process.

All autosemantic words can be derived by suffixation. The most numerous are nominal suffixes (there are more than 400 suffixes). Prefixation is the most productive in verb formation. Prefixes play a major role in changing the verbal aspect (Klajn 2002: 239–240). The main corpus of affixes in Serbian is composed of elements of domestic origin, but there are also affixes borrowed from Greek, Latin, and Turkish, as well as a small number of examples from other languages.

In Serbian, apart from prefixation and suffixation, there is also prefixal-suffixal derivation i.e. 'combined word formation' (Klajn 2002), which means adding a prefix and a suffix to the stem at the same time (prefix + stem + suffix).

Research has been conducted using a corpus taken from the *Dictionary of the Serbo-Croatian Literary Language* (1967–1976) and the *Dictionary of the Serbian Language* (2007). All the lexemes belonging to the contemporary Serbian language have been included in the corpus, while all the marked words (archaic, regional, etc.) have been left out. Some of the words had already been analyzed in *The Semantic-Derivational Dictionary. Part 1: Man – body parts* (2003).

Derivatives have been classified into semantic categories based on their primary meaning (as defined in a dictionary). There is a specific problem with the derivatives which denote the realia created as a result of an action. They can be found in two categories: RESULTATIVE and ENTITY. If the word has a predominantly objective meaning, the derivatives are classified within the category ENTITY. In the category PATIENT, there are both masculine and feminine nouns (e.g. *vašljiv* 'lousy' > *vašljiv-ac* 'the one who has lice' *m* and *vašljiv-ka* 'the one who has lice' *f*). The form *vašljivka* is not classified in the category FEMALE since it is motivated by the same adjective as the masculine noun. Derivatives formed from other word-classes are observed in the same way (e.g. *izdajnik* 'traitor' and *izdajnica* 'traitress'). The feminine nouns derived from the masculine belong to the category FEMALE (e.g. *zub-ar* 'dentist' and *zubar-ka* 'woman dentist').

In the Serbian language, reflexivity is a morpho-syntactic mark of verbs, rather than derivational. However, since reflexive forms have the role of motivating words in further derivations, they are included in the derivational network as follows: *baciti* 'to throw' > *pre-baciti se* 'overreach oneself'.

8.2 Maximum derivational networks

In Table 8.1 below, we can see that the verbs exhibit the highest numbers of derivational networks in all orders and, accordingly, in total. The derivatives of the 4th order are not numerous and those of the 5th order are rare.

Table 8.1: Maximum derivational networks per order of derivation for all three word-classes.

	1st order	2nd order	3rd order	4th order	5th order	Σ
Nouns	51	59	27	8	0	145
Verbs	93	124	114	55	6	392
Adjectives	74	100	70	23	2	269
TOTAL	218	283	211	86	8	806

8.3 Saturation values

As the results in Tables 8.2–8.5 show, the highest degrees of saturation are present in the adjective *prav* 'straight' (59.85%), the noun *oko* 'eye' (40.68%) and the verb *goreti* 'burn' (46.17%). Considered as a whole, for all three word-classes, there is a general tendency for the degree of saturation to decrease in value as the order of derivation increases. The higher orders of derivation (the 4th and the 5th) have almost half the saturation value of the lower orders (the 1st and the 2nd). Deviation from the general principle is noticed with verbs, where the 2nd and 3rd orders have higher degrees of saturation than the 1st.

8.4 Orders of derivation

The maximum number of orders for the Serbian sample is five. In Table 8.6, we can see that the average number for the nouns, verbs and adjectives varies from three to four orders.

Table 8.2: Saturation values per order of derivation, nouns.

Nouns		Saturation value (%)	1st order (%)	2nd order (%)	3rd order (%)	4th order (%)	5th order (%)
bone	kost	26.20	31.37	33.9	7.41	0	0
eye	oko	40.68	54.9	38.98	29.63	0	0
tooth	zub	31.03	39.22	33.9	18.52	0	0
day	dan	37.93	27.45	30.51	55.56	100	0
dog	pas	13.10	19.61	11.86	7.41	0	0
louse	vaš	8.27	7.84	13.56	0	0	0
fire	vatra	6.89	11.76	6.78	0	0	0
stone	kamen	31.72	39.22	30.51	25.93	12.5	0
water	voda	23.44	23.53	28.81	18.52	0	0
name	ime	19.31	21.57	20.34	14.81	12.5	0

Table 8.3: Saturation values per order of derivation, verbs.

Verbs		Saturation value (%)	1st order (%)	2nd order (%)	3rd order (%)	4th order (%)	5th order (%)
cut	seći	21.94	30.11	33.87	13.16	1.82	0
dig	kopati	18.88	24.73	27.42	11.4	7.27	0
pull	vući	23.21	35.48	25	22.81	1.82	0
throw	baciti	22.19	22.58	30.65	23.68	1.82	0
give	dati	36.99	23.66	45.16	37.72	41.82	16.67
hold	držati	26.02	23.66	33.06	28.07	12.73	0
sew	šiti	16.58	18.28	18.55	21.93	0	0
burn	goreti	46.17	27.96	50.81	50.88	56.36	50
drink	piti	20.92	27.96	23.39	19.3	9.09	0
know	znati	24.23	12.9	27.42	26.32	30.91	33.33

Table 8.4: Saturation values per order of derivation, adjectives.

Adjectives		Saturation value (%)	1st order (%)	2nd order (%)	3rd order (%)	4th order (%)	5th order (%)
narrow	uzak	4.83	9.46	4	2.86	0	0
old	star	23.79	33.78	27	14.29	8.7	0
straight	prav	59.85	27.03	55	88.57	95.65	100
new	nov	23.79	21.62	24	25.71	26.09	0
long	dug	17.47	25.68	14	15.71	13.04	0
warm	topao	11.15	17.57	11	4.29	13.04	0
thick	debeo	11.89	18.92	15	2.86	4.35	0
bad	loš	2.23	8.11	0	0	0	0
thin	tanak	22.30	18.92	24	20	34.78	0
black	crn	25.65	47.3	27	10	0	0

Table 8.5: Average saturation values per order of derivation for all three word-classes.

	1st order	2nd order	3rd order	4th order	5th order
Nouns	27.65	24.92	17.78	0	0
Verbs	24.732	31.533	25.527	16.364	10
Adjectives	22.84	20.1	18.43	19.57	10

Table 8.6: Maximum and average number of orders of derivation for all three word-classes.

	Maximum	Average
Nouns	4	3.1
Verbs	5	4.2
Adjectives	5	3.6

8.5 Derivational capacity

As follows from Table 8.7, the highest average value of derivational capacity is in the group of adjectives. The highest derivational capacity concerns the verb *vući* 'to pull'. Nouns have the lowest average derivational capacity, but the difference between nouns and adjectives is not statistically significant (2.8).

Table 8.7: Maximum and average derivational capacity for all three word-classes.

	Maximum	Average
Nouns	28	14.1
Verbs	33	23
Adjectives	35	16.9

As to the average derivational capacity in all orders and for all word-classes, Table 8.8 shows that the 2nd order of derivation has the highest average values.

Table 8.8: Average number of derivatives per order of derivation for all three word-classes.

	1st order	2nd order	3rd order	4th order	5th order
Nouns	14.1	14.7	4.8	1	0
Verbs	23	39.1	29.1	9	0.6
Adjectives	16.9	20.1	12.9	4.5	0.2

8.6 Correlation between semantic categories and orders of derivation

Considering the relation between semantic categories and orders of derivation, the following results have been obtained. As for the nouns, the category ENTITY is the most prominent among the derivatives of the 1st order (10), followed by

QUALITY and DIMINUTIVE (both 8). In the 2nd order, the other categories occur as follows: QUALITY (9), ENTITY and RELATIONAL (7). Among the 1st order derivatives motivated by the verbs, the most important category is CAUSATIVE (10), followed by DIMINUTIVE and RESULTATIVE (both 6). As for the other derivatives, the categories are classified as follows: in the 2nd order – ACTION and DURATIVE (both 10), AGENT and RESULTATIVE (both 7); in the 3rd order – ACTION (10), DURATIVE and QUALITY (both 6); and in the 4th order – ACTION (6). In the group of adjectives, among the 1st order derivatives with the highest number of occurrences, the most prominent semantic category is QUALITY (9 out of 10 adjectives have derivatives from this category). This category is followed by ENTITY and CAUSATIVE (both have 8 adjectives). As for the other derivatives, the categories are classified as follows: in the 2nd order – RELATIONAL (7) and CAUSATIVE (6); in the 3rd order – ACTION and DURATIVE (both 7); and in the 4th order – ACTION (7).

Based on these results, it can be concluded that there is a strong correlation in the group of adjectives between the 1st order derivatives and the category QUALITY; with nouns, this connection is seen in the category ENTITY; and as for verbs, it is in the category CAUSATIVE. It is interesting to draw attention to the expected relation between the derivatives of the 2nd and 3rd orders and the category ACTION in verbs.

8.7 Semantic categories with blocking effects

In the Serbian corpus, blocking is not a systematic occurrence, but rather a tendency within certain categories and orders of derivation. There is a general tendency for an increase in order of derivation to decrease the capacity for derivation in such a way that most semantic categories block further derivation in the 3rd, 4th, and 5th orders.

If we observe all three word-classes as a whole, blocking is most distinct in the RELATIONAL category, which is represented mostly by adjectives with limited semantic and derivational potential. In the categories AUGMENTATIVE and DIMINUTIVE, further derivation is blocked by their semantics, which comes down to referential value and the component of the augmented or decreased notion.

The QUALITY category is represented by adjectives and nouns that denote a certain characteristic. Further derivation is blocked only with nouns with the suffix *-ost*. These nouns have the function to nominate the characteristic denoted by the motivating adjective and serve as a means of nominalization, which is why they do not motivate further derivation. MANNER is a nonproductive category and blocks further derivation.

8.8 Typical combinations of semantic categories

As for the connections between semantic categories, we can talk about predictions rather than systematic and typical combinations, since they are often conditioned by the lexical semantics of concrete derivatives that are connected, as well as by their morphological marks. Thus, the units from the category RELATIONAL can be derived from nouns from different semantic categories, e.g. *bacač* 'thrower' (AGENT) > *bacački* 'related to thrower' (RELATIONAL), *država* 'state' (ENTITY) > *državni* 'related to a state' (RELATIONAL), etc. Nevertheless, the corpus has shown that some combinations of semantic categories occur more often than others. These will be analyzed on the level of the whole corpus, and not within specific word-classes. Among the most stable connections are:
a) QUALITY-QUALITY, which is established between an adjective with the meaning of quality and a noun of the same meaning (e.g. *zubat* 'toothy' and *zubatost* 'toothiness') or, less often, between two adjectives (e.g. *vodni* 'related to water' and *nizvodni* 'downstream');
b) ABILITY-PRIVATIVE (e.g. *popravljiv* 'reparable' and *nepopravljiv* 'irreparable');
c) ABILITY-QUALITY, which is established between an adjective and a noun (e.g. *zastariv* 'possible to become obsolete' and *zastarivost* 'possibility to become obsolete');
d) QUALITY-PATIENT (e.g. *vašljiv* 'lousy' and *vašljivac* 'one who has lice');
e) QUALITY-FEMALE (e.g. *bezočan* 'nefarious' and *bezočnica* 'a nefarious woman'); and
f) AGENT-FEMALE (e.g. *davatelj* 'giver' and *davateljka* 'giver' *f*).

8.9 Multiple occurrence of semantic categories

In the Serbian sample there are not many cases of multiple occurrences of semantic categories in one derivational chain. In all three word-classes, the most common reoccurrences are: QUALITY-QUALITY in the 1st and 2nd or the 2nd and 3rd orders of derivation (e.g. *kamen* 'stone' > *kamenit* 'stony' > *kamenitost* 'stoniness'; *piti* 'to drink' > *pitak* 'drinkable' > *pitkost* 'drinkables'; *prav* 'straight' > *pravda* 'justice' > *pravedan* 'rightful' > *pravednost* 'justness') and ENTITY-ENTITY in the 1st and 2nd orders of derivation (*kost* 'bone' > *koštunica* 'the fruit of a plant with a stem' > *koštuničarka* 'a kind of plant'; *goreti* 'to burn' > *ugar* 'a small piece of partly burned wood' > *ugarak* 'a small piece of partly burned wood'; *crn* 'black-burning' > *crnika* 'a kind of tree' > *crnikovina* 'the wood of this tree').

8.10 Reversibility of semantic categories

In the Serbian data, there are no instances of semantic categories occurring in the reversed order.

8.11 Conclusions

On the basis of the analyzed corpus, it can be concluded that affixation is a very productive derivational process in the Serbian language. The highest derivational capacity is seen with verbs (more than 1,000 derivatives), followed by adjectives (about 500 derivatives), and finally by nouns (more than 300 derivatives). It can be seen that prefixation is most common with verbs, while suffixation is most common with nouns and adjectives. Prefixal-suffixal derivation is less productive. It is also observed that as the order of derivation increases, the derivational capacity decreases.

The derivational capacity of verbs is reflected in the richness of semantic categories within their derivational networks. Systematic combinations of semantic categories have been noticed, but not connections between the categories in a reversed order.

References

Klajn, Ivan. 2002. *Word Formation in Contemporary Serbian Language. Part One: Compounding and Prefixation*. Belgrade & Novi Sad: Serbian Academy of Sciences and Arts, Matica Srpska.

Sources

Dictionary of Serbo-Croatian Literary Language. 1967–1976. Novi Sad & Zagreb: Matica Srpska, Matica Hrvatska.
Dictionary of the Serbian Language. 2007. Novi Sad: Matica Srpska.

Martina Ivanová
9 Derivational networks in Slovak

9.1 General notes

Derivation is considered the most productive word-formation process in the Slovak language: 80% of words resulting from word-formation processes are derivatives (Furdík 2004: 64). Derivation in Slovak distinguishes six derivative processes: prefixation, suffixation, postfixation, transflexion, reflexivization, and circumfixation. Basic derivational processes can either be affixal (suffixation, prefixation, postfixation, reflexivization, circumfixation) or non-affixal procedures (transflexion). The latest research, based on data from the *Slovak Dictionary of Root Morphemes* (cf. Sokolová, Ološtiak and Ivanová 2012), showed that the most productive affixation process is suffixation (76.7%), followed by prefixation (9.3%), circumfixion (7.8%), reflexivization (4%), and postfixation (0.034%) (cf. Ološtiak and Gianitsová-Ološtiaková 2015: 218).

The sources for the present research are two representative dictionaries by the Ľ. Štúr Institute of Linguistics, Slovak Academy of Sciences (KSSJ, SSSJ) and the *Slovak Dictionary of Root Morphemes* (2005, 2007, 2012). Derivation paradigms were completed by units whose usage was proved by data from the Slovak National Corpus or by internet searches (Google) to some extent.

9.2 Maximum derivational networks

Table 9.1 shows the calculations of the maximum derivational network for each order of derivation based on the number of derivatives in each semantic category for all word-classes.

It can be seen that the most prolific derivational networks in Slovak are typical of verbs, followed by adjectives and nouns. The reason for this possibly lies in the fact that verbs allow the forming of both prefixal derivatives with different spatial, temporal, and modal meanings as well as suffixal derivatives conceptualizing different aspects of event structure (such as AGENT, INSTRUMENT, LOCATION, RESULT, etc.) that can be expressed derivationally.

Table 9.1: Maximum derivational networks per order of derivation for all three word-classes.

	1st order	2nd order	3rd order	4th order	5th order	6th order	Σ
Nouns	47	45	27	5	1	0	125
Verbs	66	129	43	22	7	6	273
Adjectives	51	51	19	7	0	0	128
TOTAL	164	225	89	34	8	6	526

9.3 Saturation values

Table 9.2 shows the data regarding the saturation values of nouns for each order of derivation.

Table 9.2: Saturation values per order of derivation, nouns.

Nouns		Saturation value (%)	1st order (%)	2nd order (%)	3rd order (%)	4th order (%)	5th order (%)
bone	kosť	41.6	36.17	48.89	40.74	40	0
eye	oko	29.6	38.3	31.11	18.52	0	0
tooth	zub	32.8	34.04	42.22	22.22	0	0
day	deň	19.2	12.77	13.33	25.93	80	100
dog	pes	16	29.79	11.11	3.7	0	0
louse	voš	19.2	17.02	22.22	18.52	20	0
fire	oheň	12.8	17.02	15.56	3.7	0	0
stone	kameň	25.6	36.17	31.11	3.7	0	0
water	voda	42.4	42.55	53.33	33.33	0	0
name	meno	23.2	23.4	31.11	11.11	20	0

For the nouns in Table 9.2, the lowest and highest mean saturation values vary between 12.8% for *oheň* 'fire' and 42.4% for *voda* 'water'. *Voda* 'water' also has the highest value in the 1st order (42.55%). All nouns have 3rd order derivations, and four nouns produce 4th order derivations: *kosť* 'bone', *deň* 'day', *voš* 'lice' and *meno* 'name'. One noun, *deň* 'day', also has a 5th order of derivation.

Table 9.3 shows the data on the saturation values of verbs for each order of derivation.

Table 9.3: Saturation values per order of derivation, verbs.

Verbs		Saturation value (%)	1st order (%)	2nd order (%)	3rd order (%)	4th order (%)	5th order (%)
cut	rezať	24.34	42.42	24.81	9.3	4.55	0
dig	kopať	28.46	36.36	32.56	18.6	9.09	0
pull	ťahať	51.31	56.06	63.57	20.93	31.82	28.57
throw	hodiť/hádzať	30.34	28.79	34.11	34.88	9.09	14.29
give	dať/dávať	44.57	18.18	37.21	93.02	77.27	28.57
hold	držať	29.59	30.3	27.91	41.86	18.18	14.29
sew	šiť/ušiť	31.84	31.82	35.66	27.91	13.64	42.86
burn	horieť	9.74	21.21	6.98	6.98	0	0
drink	piť	20.6	36.36	17.83	13.95	4.55	14.29
know	vedieť	5.99	12.12	3.1	9.3	0	0

Among the verbs, the highest scores relate to the verbs *ťahať* 'pull' (51.31%) and *dať/dávať* 'give' (44.57%), while the lowest scores apply to the verbs *vedieť* 'know' (5.99%) and *horieť* 'burn' (9.74%). Six verbs produce 5th order derivations: *ťahať* 'pull', *hodiť/hádzať* 'throw', *dať/dávať* 'give', *držať* 'hold', *šiť/ušiť* 'sew' and *piť* 'drink'. One verb, *ťahať* 'pull', also produces the 6th order of derivation. The results suggest that the saturation value is determined by intentional types of verbs (cf. Buzássyová 1974). High scores are typical for agentive dynamic verbs of the first intentional type,[1] whereas non-agentive verbs from other intentional types score low.

In Table 9.4, the data on the saturation values of adjectives for each order of derivation are displayed.

---

[1] The first intentional type, a term introduced by E. Pauliny (1943), holds for verbs with subject and object complements.

Table 9.4: Saturation values per order of derivation, adjectives.

Adjectives		Saturation value (%)	1st order (%)	2nd order (%)	3rd order (%)	4th order (%)	5th order (%)
narrow	úzky	14.84	19.61	17.65	0	0	0
old	starý	42.97	50.98	43.14	31.58	14.29	0
straight	priamy	10.16	13.73	11.76	0	0	0
new	nový	41.41	29.41	39.22	73.68	57.14	0
long	dlhý	34.38	39.22	41.18	15.79	0	0
warm	teplý	33.59	43.14	27.45	26.32	28.57	0
thick	hustý	17.97	23.53	19.61	5.26	0	0
bad	zlý	15.63	13.73	13.73	21.05	28.57	0
thin	chudý	14.06	15.69	19.61	0	0	0
black	čierny	35.16	41.18	39.22	15.79	14.29	0

The adjective with the highest saturation value is *starý* 'old' (42.97%), while *priamy* 'straight' holds the lowest value (10.16%). The highest order of derivation, the 4th, holds for five adjectives: *nový* 'new', *zlý* 'bad', *teplý* 'warm', *starý* 'old' and *čierny* 'black'. In the case of adjectives, higher saturation values are typical of gradable adjectives denoting inherent qualities, whereas evaluative or non-gradable adjectives have lower saturation values.

Table 9.5 shows the calculations of the saturation values of word-classes as a whole by order of derivation.

Table 9.5: Average saturation values per order of derivation for all three word-classes.

	1st order	2nd order	3rd order	4th order	5th order
Nouns	28.72	30	18.15	16	10
Verbs	31.36	28.37	27.67	16.82	14.29
Adjectives	29.02	27.26	18.95	14.29	0

The highest saturation values in general are typical of Slovak verbs. The saturation value declines with successive orders of derivation. The only exception is in the case of nouns, as the 2nd order of derivation scores higher than the 1st order in nominal derivational networks.

9.4 Orders of derivation

Table 9.6 presents the average and the maximum number of derivational degrees within the examined sample of verbs, nouns and adjectives.

Table 9.6: Maximum and average number of orders of derivation for all three word-classes.

	Maximum	Average
Nouns	5	3.5
Verbs	6	4.3
Adjectives	4	3.1

In Table 9.6, we can see that the average number for the nouns, verbs and adjectives varies between 3.1–4.3 derivational degrees. As follows from Table 9.6, Slovak nouns show a higher number of derivation degrees with a lower number of derivatives, whereas Slovak adjectives have a lower number of derivation degrees with more numerous paradigms.

9.5 Derivational capacity

Table 9.7 shows the maximum and the average derivational capacity for individual word-classes in the 1st order of derivation.

Table 9.7: Maximum and average derivational capacity for all three word-classes.

	Maximum	Average
Nouns	20	13.2
Verbs	37	20.8
Adjectives	26	14.8

As the results show, the derivational capacity of the verbs (i.e. direct 1st order derivatives) amounts to the highest average value, whilst the nouns have the lowest average value. The results support the findings from works on Slovak word-formation (e.g. Ivanová, Kyseľová and Perovská 2015), suggesting that the typical function of verbs is that of motivating elements, whereas nouns typically fulfil the function of motivated elements.

Table 9.8 provides a summary of the average derivational capacity in all orders and all word-classes.

Table 9.8: Average number of derivatives per order of derivation for all three word-classes.

	1st order	2nd order	3rd order	4th order	5th order	6th order
Nouns	13.2	13.5	5.4	0.8	0.1	0
Verbs	20.8	36.6	12.1	3.7	0.6	0.6
Adjectives	14.8	13.9	3.6	1	0	0

As Table 9.8 shows, in the 1st and 2nd orders, the verbs reach the highest numbers followed by the adjectives and the nouns, which are quite similar. However, in the 3rd order, the nouns are more fruitful than the adjectives. From the 4th order, little derivational output can be traced in any of the word-classes.

9.6 Correlation between semantic categories and orders of derivation

The most characteristic semantic category of nouns in the 1st order is DIMINUTIVE, as 9 of 10 nouns derive a DIMINUTIVE unit (the exception is *meno* 'name'), e.g. *zúbok* 'tooth-DIM', *vodička* 'water-DIM'. 8 of the 10 nouns have 1st order derivations classified as RELATIONAL (the exceptions are *pes* 'dog' and *voš* 'lice' as they represent animal nouns, which usually form relational adjectives by means of transflexion in Slovak), e.g. *očný* 'of the eye' or *kostný* 'of the bone'. PRIVATIVE (e.g. *bezmenný* 'nameless', *bezzubý* 'toothless') and POSSESSIVE (e.g. *kamenistý* 'stony', *kostnatý* 'bony') are manifested by 7 of the 10 nouns. The most characteristic semantic category for nouns in the 2nd order is MANNER, as all 10 nouns derive a MANNER adverb, e.g. *kostnato* 'in a bony way' or *zubne* 'in a dental way' from 1st order adjective derivatives. RELATIONAL is the second most characteristic 2nd order category for all 10 nouns. Relational adjectives are formed from nominal derivatives of the 1st order that typically fall into the category of DIMINUTIVE (*ohník* 'fire-DIM' > *ohníkový* 'of fire-DIM'), ENTITY (*vodík* 'hydrogen' > *vodíkový* 'concerning hydrogen'), PATIENT (*podenka* 'dayfly' > *podenkový* 'of a dayfly'), or AGENT (*zubár* 'dentist' > *zubársky* 'dentist's'). In the 3rd order, 7 nouns derive a MANNER meaning. MANNER adverbs are derived from relational adjectives of the 2nd order, e.g. *vodácky* 'concerning paddling' or *kamenársky* 'concerning stone-cutting'. Otherwise, the rest of the semantic categories in all orders are represented by 1–3 nouns. Many nouns actually have more derivations under the label of the same semantic category, e.g. DIMINUTIVE nouns of the 1st order like *očko* 'eye-DIM', *očičko* 'eye-DIM', or *očinko* 'eye-DIM'.

The most characteristic semantic categories for verbs in the 1st order of derivation are ITERATIVE, DIRECTIONAL and RESULT. ITERATIVE is manifested by 9 of the 10 verbs (the exception is the static verb *vedieť* 'know'), e.g. *rezávať* 'be in the habit of carving' or *kopávať* 'be in the habit of digging'. 8 out of the 10 verbs derive verbs with a DIRECTIONAL meaning by means of prefixation (the exceptions are the static verbs *držať* 'hold' and *vedieť* 'know'). Slovak verbal prefixes can express a diversity of spatial meanings (crossing, approaching, entering, etc.), so it often occurs that many verbs actually have more derivations under the label of this semantic category in the same order, e.g. *vyrezať* 'cut out', *prerezať,* 'cut through', *vrezať* 'cut in'; *prehodiť/prehadzovať* 'throw over', *nadhodiť/nadhadzovať* 'throw up'; *vykopať* 'dig out', *podkopať* 'dig under'. RESULT is manifested by 8 of the 10 verbs (the exceptions are *hodiť/hádzať* 'throw' and *dať/dávať* 'give'), e.g. *rezba* 'carving', *rezanec* 'noodle', or *šev* 'seam'. In the 2nd order, REFLEXIVE (e.g. *kopnúť sa* 'kick oneself', *natiahnuť sa/naťahovať sa* 'stretch out oneself'), RELATIONAL (e.g. *rezbový* 'of carving', *kopáčsky* 'of digging') and ACTION (e.g. *obriezka* 'circumcision', *dodávka* 'delivery') are derived from 8 verbs. In verbs of the 3rd order, RELATIONAL is most common, represented by 9 verbs. Relational adjectives are derived from nouns of the 2nd order falling into the categories of INSTRUMENT or RESULT, e.g. *dodávkový* 'of a delivery truck', or *ohorkový* 'of (a) cigarette butt'. FEMALE (e.g. *dodávateľka* 'she-supplier'), MANNER (e.g. *pijansky* 'in a drunkard way') and STATIVE (e.g. *horľavosť* 'flammability') are manifested by 6 of the 10 verbs. MANNER (e.g. *dodatkovo* 'concerning addition') is produced by 6 verbs in the 4th order. The remaining semantic categories in all orders are derived from 1–3 verbs.

In the adjectives of the 1st order, STATIVE (e.g. *zlosť* 'anger, annoyance', *novosť* 'anger, annoyance') and MANNER (e.g. *dočierna* 'in black way', *spriama* 'erectly') are most common, and are represented by all 10 adjectives. 8 adjectives give rise to derivations with a CAUSATIVE meaning, e.g. *obnoviť/obnovovať* 'to renew' or *začierniť/začierňovať* 'to blacken' (the exceptions are *starý* 'old' and *chudý* 'thin'; the reason for this might lie in their semantics as they denote inherent qualities that cannot be caused externally). DIMINUTIVE is represented by 8 adjectives in the

1st order, e.g. *staručký* 'old-DIM' or *novučičký* 'new-DIM' (the exceptions are the negative evaluation adjective *zlý* 'bad' and the non-gradable adjective *priamy* 'straight', denoting an absolute inherent quality). The most characteristic semantic category for adjectives in the 2nd order is MANNER, represented by 8 adjectives. MANNER adverbs are usually derived from DIMINUTIVE adjectives, e.g. *staručko* 'oldly-DIM', *uzunko* 'narrowly-DIM', or *chudasto* 'thinly-DIM'. 7 adjectives give rise to derivations with a DIMINUTIVE meaning (e.g. *starček* 'old man-DIM', *obdĺžníček* 'rectangle-DIM'), or a PURPOSE meaning (e.g. *zatepľovací* 'for insulation', *predlžovací* 'for extension'). MANNER is yielded from 7 adjectives in the 3rd order, e.g. *zlostne* 'angrily', *dĺžkovo* 'of length', *novinovo* 'of newspapers', etc. The remaining semantic categories in the 4th order are derived from 1–2 adjectives.

9.7 Semantic categories with blocking effects

As to the blocking effects, for the nouns, the semantic categories AUGMENTATIVE (blocking in all 7 cases), MANNER (blocking in both cases) and FEMALE (blocking in both cases) usually block further derivations in the 1st order, and MANNER (blocking in all 19 cases), FEMALE (blocking in all 10 cases), STATIVE (blocking in all 10 cases) and ACTION (blocking in all 3 cases) block further derivations in the 2nd order. MANNER (blocking in all 16 cases), FEMALE (blocking in all 7 cases), PURPOSE (blocking in all 5 cases) and INSTRUMENT (blocking in all 4 cases) hamper further derivation in the 3rd order.

Further derivations in the 1st order of the verbs are blocked by the semantic categories of SATURATIVE (blocking in 10 out of 12 cases), ABSTRACTION (blocking in all 5 cases) and REFLEXIVE (blocking in all 4 cases). In the 2nd order, INSTRUMENT (blocking in 49 out of 50 cases), PURPOSE (blocking in all 34 cases),[2] RELATIONAL (blocking in 25 out of 29 cases),[3] FEMALE (blocking in all 7 cases) and STATIVE (blocking in all 6 cases) block further derivations. FEMALE (blocking in all 25 cases), MANNER (blocking in all 20 cases) and STATIVE (blocking in all 12 cases) hinder further derivations in the 3rd order.

In the 1st order of the adjectives, MANNER (blocking in all 18 cases) and TEMPORAL (blocking in both cases) hamper further derivations, and the same situation occurs with MANNER (blocking in all 38 cases), PURPOSE (blocking in all 12 cases), FEMALE (blocking in all 6 cases), REFLEXIVE (blocking in all 5 cases),

---

[2] The semantic category of PURPOSE blocks further derivations in case it applies to PURPOSE adjectives, e.g. *preťahovací* 'extending'.
[3] Only purely relational adjectives block further derivations, e.g. *rezancový* 'noodle-A'.

STATIVE (blocking in all 5 cases), TEMPORAL (blocking in all 4 cases) and ACTION (blocking in all 3 cases) in the 2nd order. The few occurrences of 3rd order derivations of adjectives are blocked by MANNER (blocking in all 14 cases), FEMALE (blocking in all 5 cases) and STATIVE (blocking in both cases).

9.8 Typical combinations of semantic categories

Slovak derivatives are typical for systematic combinations of semantic categories. Among these, the combination AGENT-FEMALE can be mentioned, e.g. *zubár* 'dentist' – *zubárka* 'she-dentist', or *vodák* 'paddler' – *vodáčka* 'she-paddler'. Feminization processes are highly productive in Slovak, feminine nouns can be formed from almost all personal masculine nouns.

Another typical combination of semantic categories is represented by RELATIONAL-MANNER: e.g. *kamenný* 'stony' – *kamenne* 'in a stony way', or *denníkový* 'of a diary' – *denníkovo* 'in a way concerning a diary'. The derivation of MANNER or ASPECT adverbs from relational adjectives is highly productive in Slovak.

The next combination is represented by RELATIONAL-STATIVE: e.g. *všivavý* 'lousy' – *všivavosť* 'lousiness', or *okatý* 'big-eyed' – *okatosť* 'the state of being big-eyed'. Here, the blocking effect is only connected with purely relational adjectives.

A typical combination of semantic categories is represented by the pairs CAUSATIVE-INSTRUMENT or CAUSATIVE-AGENT. Causative verbs usually derive INSTRUMENT or AGENT nouns, e.g. *zhusťovač* 'compressor' or *otepľovač* 'warmer'.

9.9 Multiple occurrence of semantic categories

The multiple occurrence of the same semantic categories is typical especially of Slovak nouns, and it concerns the semantic category RELATIONAL. Relational adjectives derive nominal units within the categories ENTITY or PATIENT from which other adjective derivatives within the RELATIONAL category are produced, e.g. *kôstkový* 'of (fruit) stone' (RELATIONAL) – *kôstkovica* 'stone fruit' (ENTITY) – *kôstkovicový* 'of stone fruit' (RELATIONAL), *zubový* 'dental' (RELATIONAL) – *zubovina* 'dentine' (ENTITY) – *zubovinový* 'of dentine' (RELATIONAL), *nádenný* 'daily' (RELATIONAL) – *nádenník* 'daily labourer' (PATIENT) – *nádennícky* 'of a daily labourer' (RELATIONAL), etc.

9.10 Reversibility of semantic categories

In the Slovak data set, no instances of semantic categories occurring in a reversed order were attested.

9.11 Conclusions

The present study has provided an analysis of derivation paradigms and semantic categories of 10 Slovak nouns, verbs and adjectives. The Slovak set shows that the average number of derivational orders for adjectives, nouns and verbs ranges between 3.1 and 4.3 (Table 9.6). Hence, there are few 4th or 5th order derivations, and a 6th order derivation is attested only in one verb paradigm.

Statistical research of the Slovak word-formation system allows for certain conclusions to be drawn regarding the investigated word-formation parameters.

The richest derivational networks are typical of Slovak verbs. The verbs exhibit the highest number of derivational networks in all six orders of derivation (Table 9.8). This can be explained on the basis of their semantic characteristics, as events and their participants that they conceptualize can be expressed by word-formation means in language. In spite of the fact that it is suffixation that is identified as the most productive derivational process in Slovak (cf. Chapter 9.1, this volume), within the system of verbs the central role is played by prefixation (cf. Ivanová, Kyseľová and Perovská 2015: 497). Prefixation is the main source of verbs derived from verbs. In Slovak, there is a rich set of prefixes with different spatial and aspectual meanings that can be added to a verb.

The poorest derivational networks are typical of Slovak nouns. This can be explained by the fact that nouns typically function as motivated units, not as motivating elements.

For the verbs and nouns, the average number of derivatives is higher in the 2nd order than in the 1st order. In contrast, the adjectives have a higher average number of derivatives in the 1st order (Table 9.8). For the nouns and adjectives, the average number of derivatives and the saturation value correlate: for the nouns, both are higher in the 2nd order than in the 1st order, while for the adjectives, both are lower in the 2nd order than in the 1st order. However, for the verbs, the average number of derivatives is higher in the 2nd order whereas the saturation value is higher in the 1st order. This can be explained by the fact that in the 1st order, verbs regularly form various prefixal derivatives opening the paradigmatic slots to be filled in the 2nd order, but they are not always actualized due to various semantic reasons.

Finally, four fifths of the semantic categories (39 of the 49 available labels) are covered by derivations in Slovak. This fact implies that Slovak relies hugely on derivation to account for the given semantic categories. Typical semantic categories can be stipulated for each word-class; however, the actualization of the potential paradigmatic gaps is determined by the semantics of the motivating units (the opposition concrete vs. abstract for nouns, the opposition agentive vs. non-agentive meaning, intentional type for verbs, the opposition iconic vs. evaluative semantics for adjectives, etc.).

References

Buzássyová, Klára. 1974. *Sémantika slovenských deverbatív*. Bratislava: Veda.
Furdík, Juraj. 2004. *Slovenská slovotvorba. Teória, opis, cvičenia*. Edited by Martin Ološtiak. Prešov: Náuka.
Ivanová, Martina, Miroslava Kyseľová & Veronika Perovská. 2015. Verbá. In Martin Ološtiak (ed.), *Kvalitatívne a kvantitatívne aspekty tvorenia slov v slovenčine*, 485–629. Prešov: Filozofická fakulta PU v Prešove.
Ološtiak, Martin & Lucia Ološtiaková-Gianitsová. 2015. Formálno-procesuálne aspekty slovotvornej motivácie. In Martin Ološtiak (ed.), *Kvalitatívne a kvantitatívne aspekty tvorenia slov v slovenčine*, 207–308. Prešov: Filozofická fakulta PU v Prešove.
Pauliny, Eugen. 1943. *Štruktúra slovenského slovesa*. Bratislava: Slovenská akadémia vied a umení.
Sokolová, Miloslava, Martin Ološtiak, Martina Ivanová, František Šimon, Katarína Vužňáková, Beáta Czéreová & Vladimír Benko. 2012 [2005, 2007]. *Slovník koreňových morfém slovenčiny*, 3rd edn. Prešov: FF PU.

Sources

KSSJ (Krátky slovník slovenského jazyka) [The Short Dictionary of the Slovak Language]. 2003. http://www.juls.savba.sk/kssj_4.html.
Slovenský národný korpus [The Slovak National Corpus]. http://korpus.juls.savba.sk/.
SSSJ, Slovník súčasného slovenského jazyka [The Dictionary of the Contemporary Slovak Language]. 2006, 2011, 2015. http://www.juls.savba.sk/pub_sssj.html.

Katja Plemenitaš, Ines Voršič, Irena Stramljič Breznik
10 Derivational networks in Slovene

10.1 General notes

Affixation and compounding are the core word-formation patterns in Slovene (Toporišič 2000, 2004; Vidovič Muha 2011). Affixation includes suffixation, prefixation and derivation through free morphemes (Toporišič 2000: 156–157). The most productive word-formation pattern is suffixation, with more than 300 suffixes used for the derivation of nouns, adjectives and verbs. The majority of suffixes derive nouns, which have masculine, feminine or neuter gender. 125 nominal suffixes are used for masculine nouns, 83 for feminine nouns and 28 for neuter nouns (Stramljič Breznik 2016: 2979–2998). The most productive nominal suffixes are *-ec*, *-ø*, *-ek* and *-ež* for masculine nouns; *-ica*, *-a* and *-ka* for feminine nouns, and *-(s)tvo*, *-(a/e/i)lo* and *-o* for neuter nouns (Toporišič 2000: 142–234). Adjectives can be formed with approximately 70 suffixes, the most productive of which are *-en*, *-ski* and *-ast*. Verbal word-formation, on the other hand, uses only 15 suffixes, the most frequent of which are *-ati*, *-iti* and *-(e/o)-vati*. Prefixation, including foreign prefixes, uses only 14 nominal, 4 adjectival, 20 nominal and adjectival, and around 40 verbal prefixes (Toporišič 2000: 142–234). At the boundary of the base and the affix, a range of predictable phonemic changes can occur, such as palatalization (*nog-* + *-ica* > *nož-ica* 'little foot/leg') (Toporišič 2000: 151–154).

The most productive word-formation process in Slovene is nominal suffixation. To this day, the majority of Slovene words are formed through nominal suffixation (Stramljič Breznik 2005: 505–520).

The Slovene language shares with other Slavic languages the theoretical problem of drawing a distinct line between inflection and derivation. Potential problems such as derivation through conversion, derivation of participial adjectives and gradation through prefixation (Toporišič 2000: 160, 203, 209) are excluded here, but the imperfectivization of perfective verbs (Toporišič 2000: 384–325) is included.

The sources draw on two dictionaries: the *SSKJ* (Dictionary of the Standard Slovene Language) by the Institute for the Slovene Language at the Slovene Academy of Sciences and Arts, and *The Slovene Etymological Dictionary* by Marko Snoj. Derivations marked as dialectal, archaic or very rare were mostly excluded from the networks unless searches on Google could show their use.

10.2 Maximum derivational networks

Table 10.1 shows that verbs exhibit the highest number of derivatives in individual semantic categories for all the orders. Nouns exhibit the lowest number in all the orders. Verbs and adjectives both permit a 5th order, while nouns permit only a 4th order.

Table 10.1: Maximum derivational networks per order of derivation for all 3 word-classes.

	1st order	2nd order	3rd order	4th order	5th order	Σ
Nouns	40	37	17	2	0	96
Verbs	68	91	63	33	9	264
Adjectives	43	59	62	18	5	187
TOTAL	151	187	142	53	14	547

10.3 Saturation values

For nouns, the mean saturation values range between 5.21% and 38.54%, as shown in Table 10.2. The noun with the highest saturation value is *zob* 'tooth' (38.54%), followed closely by *voda* 'water' (36.46%). In contrast, *oko* 'eye' has the lowest mean saturation value (5.21%) and is the only noun that lacks a 3rd order. *Kost* 'bone' is the only noun that has a 4th order. Within the 1st order, *voda* 'water' has the highest saturation value, and *dan* 'day' and *ogenj* 'fire' have the lowest (9.38%). Interestingly, the nouns with the highest and the lowest saturation value both denote body parts related to the head.

As Table 10.3 shows, the lowest and highest mean saturation values for verbs vary between *šivati* 'to sow' (13.64%), which is the only verb with no 4th order derivation, and *rezati* 'to cut' (46.59%). *Rezati* 'to cut' also has the highest value in the 1st and the 2nd orders. 2 verbs have a 5th order derivation, *piti* 'to drink' and *vedeti* 'to know'.

Table 10.4 shows that the mean saturation values for adjectives range between 6% and 40%, which is a range similar to that for nouns. The highest mean saturation value belongs to *raven* 'straight', while the lowest mean saturation belongs to *ozek* 'narrow'. In the 1st order derivation, the highest saturation value belongs to 2 adjectives, *nov* 'new' and *debel* 'thick'. 2 adjectives permit a 5th order derivation, the same as for verbs. But fewer adjectives than verbs permit a 4th order derivation: 5 adjectives, compared to 8 verbs.

Table 10.2: Saturation values per order of derivation, nouns.

Nouns		Saturation value (%)	1st order (%)	2nd order (%)	3rd order (%)	4th order (%)	5th order (%)
bone	kost	25	22.5	24.32	23.53	100	0
eye	oko	5.21	10	2.7	0	0	0
tooth	zob	38.54	35	29.73	70.59	0	0
day	dan	7.29	7.5	8.11	5.88	0	0
dog	pes	17.71	25	16.22	5.88	0	0
louse	uš	9.38	10	8.11	11.76	0	0
fire	ogenj	9.38	7.5	13.51	5.88	0	0
stone	kamen	28.13	32.5	29.73	17.65	0	0
water	voda	36.46	57.5	24.32	17.65	0	0
name	ime	28.13	22.5	35.14	29.41	0	0

Table 10.3: Saturation values per order of derivation, verbs.

Verbs		Saturation value (%)	1st order (%)	2nd order (%)	3rd order (%)	4th order (%)	5th order (%)
cut	rezati	46.59	57.35	61.54	39.68	9.09	0
dig	kopati	24.24	32.35	26.37	25.4	6.06	0
pull	vleči	20.08	27.94	31.87	6.35	3.03	0
throw	metati	19.7	27.94	26.37	14.29	0	0
give	dati	31.82	20.59	38.46	41.27	27.27	0
hold	držati	20.45	23.53	25.27	19.05	9.09	0
sew	šivati	13.64	27.94	15.38	4.76	0	0
burn	goreti	16.29	26.47	18.68	11.11	3.03	0
drink	piti	39.39	29.41	41.76	38.1	54.55	44.44
know	vedeti	20.08	16.18	13.19	19.05	39.39	55.56

Table 10.4: Saturation values per order of derivation, adjectives.

Adjectives		Saturation value (%)	1st order (%)	2nd order (%)	3rd order (%)	4th order (%)	5th order (%)
narrow	ozek	5.88	11.63	3.39	6.45	0	0
old	star	32.09	27.91	38.98	35.48	16.67	0
straight	raven	39.57	18.6	35.59	54.84	61.11	0
new	nov	23.53	34.88	33.9	14.52	0	0
long	dolg	15.51	25.58	15.25	6.45	16.67	40
warm	topel	12.3	18.6	16.95	8.06	0	0
thick	debel	30.48	34.88	45.76	24.19	0	0
bad	slab	21.93	30.23	25.42	19.35	5.56	0
thin	tanek	14.44	18.6	15.25	3.23	27.78	60
black	črn	20.86	32.56	25.42	16.13	0	0

Table 10.5 shows that the average saturation values for the Slovene dataset are relatively low, not reaching above 29% in the 1st order, 30% in the 2nd order, 22% in the 3rd order, 16% in the 4th order and 10% in the 5th order. The highest average saturation values pertain to verbs in all orders of derivation, followed by adjectives in 2nd place and nouns in 3rd place.

Table 10.5: Average saturation values per order of derivation for all 3 word-classes.

	1st order	2nd order	3rd order	4th order	5th order
Nouns	23	19.19	18.82	10	0
Verbs	28.97	29.89	21.91	15.15	10
Adjectives	25.35	25.59	18.87	12.78	10

10.4 Orders of derivation

As shown in Table 10.6, the maximum number of orders for the Slovene dataset is 5, with nouns permitting only a 4th order. Table 10.6 also shows that the average number for nouns, verbs and adjectives varies between 3 and 4 orders.

Table 10.6: Maximum and average number of orders of derivation for all 3 word-classes.

	Maximum	Average
Nouns	4	3.0
Verbs	5	4.0
Adjectives	5	3.7

10.5 Derivational capacity

Table 10.7 shows that the derivational capacity of verbs (i.e. direct 1st order derivatives) reaches the highest average value, while the derivational capacity of adjectives has the lowest average value. However, nouns have a higher maximum derivational capacity than adjectives, i.e. the noun *voda* 'water' yields 23 derivations in the 1st order.

Table 10.7: Maximum and average derivational capacity for all 3 word-classes.

	Maximum	Average
Nouns	23	9.2
Verbs	39	19.7
Adjectives	15	10.9

Table 10.8 shows that verbs have the highest average number of derivatives in all orders of derivation. Nouns have the lowest average derivational output, although the values become more similar in the 4th order. Nouns have no derivational output in the 5th order.

Table 10.8: Average number of derivatives per order of derivation for all 3 word-classes.

	1st order	2nd order	3rd order	4th order	5th order
Nouns	9.2	7.1	3.2	0.2	0
Verbs	19.7	27.2	13.8	5.0	0.9
Adjectives	10.9	15.1	11.7	2.3	0.5

10.6 Correlation between semantic categories and orders of derivation

In the 1st order, 9 out of 10 nouns yield derivations within the semantic category of DIMINUTIVE, followed by 8 nouns with derivations classified as RELATIONAL and 7 with derivations classified as LOCATION. The 2nd order shows a weaker correlation, with 7 nouns producing the category of RELATIONAL. The 3rd and 4th orders show a less characteristic pattern.

In the 1st order verbs, FINITIVE is the most common category, represented by 9 verbs, followed by the categories of AGENT and DIRECTION, both produced by 8 verbs. In the 2nd order, the characteristic numbers are similar, but apply to different semantic categories: 9 verbs produce the RELATIONAL category, followed by the categories DURATIVE and RESULTATIVE, both produced by 8 verbs. In the 3rd order, 8 verbs give rise to the category of ACTION, and 7 verbs to the category of RELATIONAL. In the 4th and 5th orders, there is a less characteristic pattern.

In the 1st order adjectives, QUALITY is most common, represented by 9 adjectives, followed by AUGMENTATIVE and CAUSATIVE, each realized by 8 adjectives, and MANNER, realized by 7 adjectives. In the 2nd order, RELATIONAL is predominant with 9 adjectives, followed by FINITIVE with 7 adjectives. In the 3rd order, ACTION is the most common with 8 adjectives. The 4th and 5th orders exhibit a less characteristic pattern.

All 3 word-classes have a strong correlation with RELATIONAL in the 2nd order and ACTION in the 3rd order. The strongest correlation with any semantic category in all 3 word-classes does not exceed 9 words.

10.7 Semantic categories with blocking effects

For nouns, there is a blocking effect for QUALITY in the 2nd order, exhibited by 6 nouns, DIMINUTIVE in the 1st order (3 nouns) and the 2nd order (2 nouns), COLLECTIVE in the 1st order (2 nouns), FEMALE in the 3rd order (2 nouns) and the 2nd order (1 noun), and SIMILATIVE in the 1st order (2 nouns) and the 2nd order (1 noun).

For verbs, there is a blocking tendency for FEMALE in the 2st order (5 verbs), the 3rd order (3 verbs) and the 4th order (2 verbs), ACTION in the 1st order (8 verbs), INSTRUMENT in the 2nd order (6 verbs), and DIMINUTIVE in the 2nd order (3 verbs) and the 3rd order (2 verbs).

For adjectives, there is a blocking effect for FEMALE in the 2nd order (5 adjectives) and the 3rd order (6 adjectives), and PROCESS in the 3rd order (4 adjectives).

All 3 word-classes have a general tendency for a blocking effect of DIMINUTIVE regardless of the order, and for FEMALE in the 2nd and higher orders.

10.8 Typical combinations of semantic categories

The most frequent combination of semantic categories for nouns is RELATIONAL/COMPOSITION/POSSESSIVE-QUALITY, exhibited by 6 nouns. This reflects a derivation by *-ost* from adjectives to nouns, e.g. *kamnit* 'made of stone' > *kamnitost* 'the quality of being made of stone'.

The most frequent combinations for verbs are AGENT-FEMALE, exhibited by 6 verbs, e.g. *kopati* 'dig', *kopač* 'digger' or *kopačica* 'female digger', and FINITIVE/DIRECTION-DURATIVE-ACTION, also exhibited by 6 verbs, e.g. *držati* 'to hold' > *zadržati* 'to hold back' > *zadrževati* 'to keep holding back' > *zadrževanje* 'the action of keeping holding back'.

The most frequent sequence of semantic categories for adjectives is CAUSATIVE-FINITIVE-ACTION/RESULTATIVE, exhibited by 8 adjectives, e.g. *slab* 'bad' > *slabiti* 'to weaken' > *oslabiti* 'to finish weakening' > *oslabitev* 'the action/result of finishing weakening'.

10.9 Multiple occurrence of semantic categories

For nouns, there are 4 cases: ACTION-ACTION (2 nouns), e.g. *kamen* 'stone' > *kamenjati* 'to stone' > *kamenjanje* 'stoning'; PROCESS-FINITIVE-PROCESS for the noun *kost* 'bone', e.g. *kost* 'bone' > *kosteneti* 'to turn into bone' > *okosteneti* 'to finish turning into bone' > *okostenenje* 'the process of finishing turning into bone'; DIMINUTIVE-DIMINUTIVE (2 nouns), e.g. *ogenj* 'fire' > *ognjič* 'little fire' > *ognjiček* 'little little fire'; and RELATIONAL-ENTITY-RELATIONAL for the noun *ogenj* 'fire', e.g. *ogenj* 'fire' > *ognjen* 'related to fire' > *ognjenik* 'volcano' > *ognjeniški* 'related to a volcano'.

For verbs, there are 2 cases: QUALITY-QUALITY, realized by 2 verbs, e.g. *vedeti* 'to know' > *zvedeti* 'to get to know' > *zvedav* 'knowledgeable' > *zvedavost* 'the quality of being knowledgeable', and FINITIVE-QUALITY-PRIVATIVE-QUALITY, realized by 1 verb: *držati* 'to hold' > *vzdržati* 'to hold up' > *vzdržen* 'restrained' > *nevzdržen* 'intolerable' > *nevzdržnost* 'the quality of being intolerable'.

For adjectives, there are also 2 cases: PROCESS-PROCESS (2 adjectives), e.g. *debel* 'thick' > *debeleti* 'to become thick' > *debeljenje* 'the process of becoming thick', and MANNER-MANNER (1 adjective): *tanek* 'thin' > *tanko* 'in a thin manner' > *natanko* 'in a thin manner'.

10.10 Reversibility of semantic categories

There is 1 instance, produced by the verb *vedeti* 'know', of 2 derivations from the 3rd order adjective *zaveden* 'of conscious nature', which are PRIVATIVE-MANNER and MANNER-PRIVATIVE: *nezaveden* 'unconscious' (PRIVATIVE) > *nezavedno* 'in an unconscious way' (MANNER), compared to *zavedoma* 'in a conscious way' (MANNER) > *nezavedoma* 'in an unconscious way' (PRIVATIVE).

10.11 Conclusions

The Slovene data show that nouns permit 4 orders of derivation, while verbs and adjectives both permit a 5th order (Table 10.6).

Verbs exhibit the richest derivational networks in the 1st, 2nd, 4th and 5th orders, while nouns have the lowest number in all 4 orders (Table 10.1).

Verbs also reach the highest average saturation values in all the orders, with adjectives in 2nd place and nouns in 3rd place (Tables 10.2–10.5). However, the overall highest saturation value (70.59% in the 3rd order) is manifested by a noun.

A similar pattern emerges for the average derivational capacity and the average number of derivatives per order of derivation (Tables 10.7–10.8). However, nouns reach a higher maximum derivational capacity than adjectives (Table 10.7).

The higher derivational outcome for verbs could be related to the higher number of prefixes that attach to verbs, combined with the higher semantic potential for derivation from verbs. The high semantic potential of individual nouns or adjectives also helps to account for the few deviations from the tendency for the highest values to occur in verbs, with adjectives in 2nd place and nouns in 3rd place.

Finally, the data show that 41 semantic categories out of 49 available labels are covered by Slovene derivations. Although there are some differences in the derivational potential and structural richness of the individual word-classes, overall, the derivational capacity of Slovene is rich.

References

Stramljič Breznik, Irena. 2005. Kvantitativne lastnosti slovenskega tvorjenega besedja v poskusnem besednodružinskem slovarju za črko B [Quantitative properties of Slovene complex words in the test dictionary of word families for entries starting in B]. *Slavistična revija* 53 (4). 505–520.
Stramljič Breznik, Irena. 2016. Slovene. In Peter O. Müller (ed.), *Word-formation; an international handbook of the languages of Europe*, Vol. 4, 2979–2998. Berlin & Boston: Mouton de Gruyter.
Toporišič, Jože. 2000. *Slovenska slovnica* [Slovene grammar], 4th edn. Maribor: Založba Obzorja.
Toporišič, Jože. 2004. *Slovenska slovnica* [Slovene grammar], 5th edn. Maribor: Založba Obzorja.
Vidovič Muha, Ada. 2011. *Slovensko skladenjsko besedotvorje ob primerih zloženk* [Slovene syntactic word-formation in the case of compounds], 2nd edn. Ljubljana: Znanstvena založba Filozofske fakultete.

Sources

SSKJ [Dictionary of the Standard Slovene Language]. 2014. Ljubljana: Založba ZRC.
Snoj, Marko. 2015. *Slovenski etimološki slovar* [Slovene Etymological Dictionary]. Ljubljana: Založba ZRC.

Nadia Yesypenko
11 Derivational networks in Ukrainian

11.1 General notes

In modern Ukrainian, the following types of word-formation processes are distinguished as the most productive: derivation (suffixal, prefixal, suffixal-prefixal, and postfixal methods), compounding and abbreviation (Plyushch 2005: 56; Vakaryuk and Pantso 2010: 35–37). Most of the derivational affixes are of native Ukrainian origin, and only a small part of them are borrowed. Thus, there are over 100 prefixes, about 20 of which are borrowed, and about 400 suffixes and their variants, over 20 of which are borrowed from other languages (Ponomariv, Rizun and Yu 2008: 132). In Ukrainian, both prefixation and suffixation are used for word-building and grammatical purposes. They alter the meaning of the base and change some grammatical properties of words (e.g. *вогонь*$_{N(masculine)}$ 'fire' > *вогневиця*$_{N(feminine)}$ 'lightning').

Prefixes occur mainly in nouns and adjectives, and occasionally in verbs. Prefixes in verbs usually indicate perfective and non-perfective aspects; in adjectives, they form the superlative degree of comparison. In the Ukrainian set, prefixes attach directly to the root morphemes (e.g. *різати* 'to cut' > *вирізати* 'to cut out') or another prefix (e.g. *повирізати* 'to resect'), so they do not change a part-of-speech paradigm, whereas suffixes derive words mainly by attaching to the base (e.g. *зуб*$_N$ 'tooth' > *зубець*$_N$ 'cog').

As to the theoretical problem of the prefix *не-* in Ukrainian, it involves negation, and can be found in adjectives (e.g. *новий*$_A$ 'new' > *неновий*$_A$ 'old') and nouns (e.g. *знати*$_V$ 'know' > *знання*$_N$ 'knowledge' > *незнання*$_N$ 'ignorance'). In contrast, Ukrainian verbs do not admit the prefix *не-* (the exception is *немати* 'not to have'), but favour the prefix *недо-* bearing the meaning of complete negation or partial fulfillment of the action (e.g. *пити*$_V$ 'drink' > *недопити*$_V$ 'unfinished drinking); '*не*', when used with verbs, is written separately, playing the role of a negative particle (e.g. *не пити* 'not to drink') (Plyushch 2005: 86).

Word-forming suffixes are divided into suffixes of mutation (from the Latin *mutatio*, meaning 'change'), transposition and modification. Mutational suffixes change the lexical meaning of a derived word, regardless of its part-of-speech affiliation (e.g. *різати*$_V$ 'cut' > *різьбяр*$_N$ 'engraver'). Transposition suffixes change a part-of-speech affiliation of a derived word while retaining its basic lexical meaning (e.g. *старий*$_A$ 'old' > *старість*$_N$ > 'old age/senility'). Modification suffixes change neither the part-of-speech affiliation nor the lexical meaning of a derivative, but they introduce emotional or evaluative connotations (e.g. старезний$_A$ 'old.AUGMENTATIVE', старесенький$_A$ 'old.DIMINUTIVE').

The suffix-prefixal word-formation process consists of the simultaneous attachment of the suffix and the prefix to the base: e.g. тонкий$_A$ 'thin' > витончення$_N$ 'thinning'.

The suffixal part of such words performs a part-of-speech affiliation role. The prefixal part of these words alters the lexical meaning, but in the verbs it also gives an indication of aspect (e.g. рити$_V$ 'dig' – дорити$_V$ 'to have dug'). The suffix-prefixal derivatives are found among Ukrainian nouns, adjectives, and verbs alike.

The sources draw from three dictionaries of Ukrainian word-formation processes. Present and past participles, being separate parts of speech in Ukrainian, were not classified as adjectives and were not included in the data.

11.2 Maximum derivational networks

In Table 11.1 below, we can see that adjectives exhibit the highest number of members of the derivational networks in total. Nouns and verbs demonstrate almost equal numbers of members of the derivational networks. 4th order derivations are rare, and only one of the three word-classes (nouns) permits a 5th order.

Table 11.1: Maximum derivational networks per order of derivation for all three word-classes.

	1st order	2nd order	3rd order	4th order	5th order	Σ
Nouns	25	21	18	6	1	71
Verbs	26	29	11	6	0	72
Adjectives	47	26	8	1	0	82
TOTAL	98	76	37	13	1	225

11.3 Saturation values

The mean saturation values for nouns range between 10% and 30%, as shown in Table 11.2. The noun with the highest mean saturation value is ім'я 'name' (30%), which also is the noun with the highest saturation value (50%) within the 4th order. In contrast, воша 'louse' has the lowest mean saturation value

(10%). This noun, along with *зуб* 'tooth', *собака* 'dog', and *вогонь* 'fire', lack the 3rd and 4th orders. Within the 1st order, *вогонь* 'fire' has the highest saturation value (56%), and *камінь* 'stone' has the lowest (4%).

Table 11.2: Saturation values per order of derivation, nouns.

Nouns		Saturation value (%)	1st order (%)	2nd order (%)	3rd order (%)	4th order (%)	5th order (%)
bone	кістка	25.35	16	23.81	38.89	33.33	0
eye	око	11.27	16	14.29	5.56	0	0
tooth	зуб	25.35	52	23.81	0	0	0
day	день	16.9	28	19.05	5.56	0	0
dog	собака	18.31	40	14.29	0	0	0
louse	воша	9.86	12	19.05	0	0	0
fire	вогонь	26.76	56	23.81	0	0	0
stone	камінь	22.54	4	38.1	27.78	33.33	0
water	вода	23.94	16	33.33	33.33	0	0
name	ім'я	29.58	8	33.33	44.44	50	100

For the verbs in Table 11.3, the lowest and highest mean saturation values vary between 15% for *знати* 'know' and 39% for *різати* 'cut', which also has the highest value in the 1st order (50%). One verb, *знати* 'know', has no 3rd or 4th orders. Three verbs have no 4th order derivations, namely *рити* 'dig', *пекти* 'burn' and *пити* 'drink', and none of the verbs permit the 5th order.

The adjectives in Table 11.4 are the most evenly distributed as to the saturation value per order. The mean saturation values range between 18% and 44%. The highest mean saturation value belongs to *старий* 'old' (44%). Moreover, *старий* 'old' stands out in the 1st order as well with a saturation value of 49%, and it is also the only adjective with a 4th order derivation (100%). In addition, there are five gaps (0%) in the 3rd order and none of the adjectives are recorded in the 5th order.

Table 11.5 gives the average saturation values per order of derivation for all nouns, verbs and adjectives in the Ukrainian set. We can see that the average values are quite similar for every order of verbs and adjectives. The average

Table 11.3: Saturation values per order of derivation, verbs.

Verbs		Saturation value (%)	1st order (%)	2nd order (%)	3rd order (%)	4th order (%)	5th order (%)
cut	різати	38.89	50	24.14	63.64	16.67	0
dig	рити	18.06	30.77	10.34	18.18	0	0
pull	тягнути[a]	23.61	3.85	37.93	36.36	16.67	0
throw	кинути	20.83	0	37.93	27.27	16.67	0
give	дати	19.44	34.62	10.34	9.09	16.67	0
hold	тримати	23.61	42.31	10.34	18.18	16.67	0
sew	шити	23.61	38.46	3.45	27.27	50	0
burn	пекти	25	38.46	24.14	9.09	0	0
drink	пити	20.83	34.62	13.79	18.18	0	0
know	знати	15.28	19.23	20.69	0	0	0

[a] The Ukrainian verbs *тягнути* 'to pull' and *кинути* 'to throw' possess not only the infinitive forming morpheme *-ти-*, but also the suffix *-ну-*, which, combined with the verbal base, adds a meaning of a sudden action or one-time action; from the grammatical perspective, it forms a perfective aspect of the verb.

saturation values are quite low, not reaching above 29% in the 1st order, 24% in the 2nd order, 23% in the 3rd order, and 13% in the 4th order, and 10% is the only saturation value for the nouns in the 5th order.

11.4 Orders of derivation

As mentioned previously (see Table 11.1), the maximum number of orders for the Ukrainian sample is five. In Table 11.6, we can see that the average number for nouns, verbs and adjectives varies between the 3rd and the 4th order.

Table 11.4: Saturation values per order of derivation, adjectives.

Adjectives		Saturation value (%)	1st order (%)	2nd order (%)	3rd order (%)	4th order (%)	5th order (%)
narrow	вузький	18.29	25.53	7.69	12.5	0	0
old	старий	43.9	48.94	38.46	25	100	0
straight	прямий	19.51	25.53	15.38	0	0	0
new	новий	28.05	21.28	38.46	37.5	0	0
long	довгий	19.51	19.15	19.23	25	0	0
warm	теплий	25.61	34.04	19.23	0	0	0
thick	товстий	28.05	36.17	23.08	0	0	0
bad	поганий	25.61	34.04	19.23	0	0	0
thin	тонкий	20.73	14.89	26.92	37.5	0	0
black	чорний	25.61	34.04	19.23	0	0	0

Table 11.5: Average saturation values per order of derivation for all three word-classes.

	1st order	2nd order	3rd order	4th order	5th order
Nouns	24.8	24.287	15.556	11.666	10
Verbs	29.232	19.309	22.726	13.335	0
Adjectives	29.361	22.691	13.75	10	0

Table 11.6: Maximum and average number of orders of derivation for all three word-classes.

	Maximum	Average
Nouns	5	2.98
Verbs	4	3.3
Adjectives	4	4.18

11.5 Derivational capacity

As follows from Table 11.7, the derivational capacity of adjectives (i.e. direct 1st order derivatives) amounts to the highest average value, whilst nouns have the lowest average value. The low derivational capacity of Ukrainian nouns might be assigned to the fact that there are other productive word-formation patterns, such as compounding, abbreviation and conversion.

Table 11.7: Maximum and average derivational capacity for all three word-classes.

	Maximum	Average
Nouns	14	6.2
Verbs	13	7.6
Adjectives	23	13.8

As to the average derivational capacity in all orders and for all word-classes, Table 11.8 indicates that, in the 1st order, the numbers are rather diverse for all three word-classes. In contrast, for the 2nd order, nouns, verbs and adjectives are quite similar. In the 3rd order, nouns and verbs show equal numbers, while adjectives are less productive. Little derivational output of three word-classes is registered in the 4th order, and in the 5th order, only nouns are attested.

Table 11.8: Average number of derivatives per order of derivation for all three word-classes.

	1st order	2nd order	3rd order	4th order	5th order
Nouns	6.2	5.1	2.8	0.7	0.1
Verbs	7.6	5.6	2.5	0.8	0
Adjectives	13.8	5.9	1.1	0.1	0

11.6 Correlation between semantic categories and orders of derivation

In the 1st order, 10 nouns from the list produce derivations within the semantic categories QUALITY and DIMINUTIVE, such as зуб$_N$ 'tooth' > зубчик$_N$ 'a little tooth'. 5 of the 10 nouns have 1st order derivations classified as AUGMENTATIVE (e.g. око$_N$ 'eye' > очище$_N$[1] 'a big eye'). ENTITY and QUALITY predominate in the 2nd order, since 7 of the 10 nouns are represented under this label, such as вогонь$_N$ 'fire' > вогневиця$_N$ 'lightning'. ACTION is the second most characteristic 2nd order category with 6 nouns. In the 3rd order, 4 nouns derive an ACTION meaning. The derivations in the 4th order include ACTION, ENTITY, QUALITY, COLLECTIVE meanings. Otherwise, the rest of the semantic categories in all orders are represented by 1–3 nouns.

The semantic categories in the 1st order of verbs are more evenly spread and more frequently represented overall. RESULTATIVE is manifested by 8 out of 10 verbs (e.g. різати$_V$ 'to cut' > обрізаний$_A$ 'cut-out'), SATURATIVE by 7 verbs, and DESIDERATIVE and PRIVATIVE by 6 verbs. 5 verbs give rise to DIMINUTIVE, DURATIVE and FINITIVE derivations. In the 2nd order, RESULTATIVE is derived from 9 out of the 10 verbs (the exception is пити$_V$ 'to drink') and PROCESS is produced by 5 verbs in the same order. PRIVATIVE is derived in 7 out of the 10 verbs in the 3rd order (the exceptions are тягнути$_V$ 'pull', кинути$_V$, 'throw', and знати$_V$ 'know'). ENTITY and PRIVATIVE dominate in the 4th order, being derived by 2 verbs each. The remaining semantic categories in all orders are derived from 1–4 verbs.

In adjectives recorded for the 1st order, AUGMENTATIVE and DIMINUTIVE are most common, represented by 9 out of the 10 adjectives (e.g. поганий$_A$ 'bad' > поганючий$_A$ 'very bad'). 8 adjectives give rise to derivations with a MANNER meaning (the exceptions are новий$_A$ 'new' and теплий$_A$ 'warm'), and 7 to an ACTION meaning (e.g. чорний$_A$[2] 'black' > чорніти$_V$ 'to blacken'). QUALITY and STATE are yielded from 6 adjectives, and PATIENT and ENTITY from 5 adjectives. In the 2nd order, PROCESS is derived from 6 adjectives, ACTION from 5 adjectives, and CAUSATIVE and QUALITY from 4 adjectives. PROCESS is represented by 3

---

[1] Variants of suffixational morphemes in Ukrainian words arise due to vowel and consonant gradation when the root ends with г, к, or х: [г]-[ж/з], [к]-[ч], [х]-[с] (e.g. окоN 'eye' > очнийA 'related to eyes', пектиV 'burn' > випічкаN 'pastry').

[2] Due to the restructure of a morphemic shape of a word, the whole morpheme or its part can transfer to another morpheme. As a result, one morpheme loses its meaning and a new wider morpheme appears. Ukrainian etymological roots and suffixes allow the formation of derived roots. For example, the suffix -н- in чорний 'black' belongs to etymological adjective-forming suffixes that joined the root, and now it is a constituent of the modern root чорн- (Hryshchenko 1978: 145–146).

adjectives in the 3rd order. The 4th order derivation is identified in ACTION. All other semantic categories in the different orders contain 1–3 derivations.

It is difficult to find equal patterns for all three word-classes, but common tendencies are revealed for nouns and adjectives, namely, the semantic categories DIMINUTIVE, AUGMENTATIVE and QUALITY, which predominate in the 1st order. ENTITY is represented to quite a high degree by nouns in the 2nd order of derivation, and PROCESS has a strong correlation with the adjectives in the 2nd order. For verbs, there is a rather strong correlation between the 1st order and RESULTATIVE, which also prevails in the 2nd order of verbs, and between the 3rd order and PRIVATIVE.

11.7 Semantic categories with blocking effects

Regarding blocking effects for the nouns in the Ukrainian data set, the semantic categories DIMINUTIVE and LOCATION block further derivations in the 1st order of derivation, and AGENT, QUALITY and AUGMENTATIVE block further derivations in the 2nd order. In the 3rd order, AUGMENTATIVE, DIMINUTIVE and PATIENT hinder further derivation.

Further derivations in the 1st order of the verbs are blocked by STATE, ENTITY, INCEPTIVE, LOCATION and PATIENT. In the 2nd order, AGENT, ENTITY, CUMULATIVE and DIRECTIONAL block further derivations. RESULTATIVE and CAUSATIVE block further derivations in the 3rd order.

In the 1st order of the adjectives, STATE, LOCATION, COLLECTIVE and RELATIVE hamper further derivations, and in the 2nd order, AGENT, QUALITY, ENTITY and CAUSATIVE hamper further derivations. The few occurrences of 3rd order derivations of adjectives are blocked by AGENT and ACTION.

In conclusion, some semantic categories, independently of the order in which they occur, tend to hamper further derivations, namely LOCATION, AGENT, ENTITY, STATE, QUALITY and CAUSATIVE.

11.8 Typical combinations of semantic categories

In the Ukrainian set, there are several typical and systematic combinations of semantic categories, such as QUALITY-AUGMENTATIVE (5 out of the 10 adjectives take part in this combination), QUALITY-DIMINUTIVE (all adjectives can form such a combination), QUALITY-ENTITY (half of the adjectives under study initiate this combination), QUALITY-STATE-PROCESS (7 out of the 10 adjectives serve as the initial source of this combination, e.g. *теплий*ₐ 'warm' > *тепличність*ₙ 'warmness' > *теплішання*ₙ 'getting warm'), and QUALITY-STATE-AGENT (4 out of the 10 adjectives are involved in this combination, e.g. *старий*ₐ 'old' > *старість*ₙ 'old age' > *стариган*ₙ 'an old man'), mainly reflecting derivations from adjectives to nouns. For verbal derivations, many combinations involve ACTION-PROCESS-RESULTATIVE (half of the verbs in the Ukrainian set perform in this derivational combination, e.g. *різати*ᵥ 'to cut' > *розрізання*ₙ 'cutting' > *розрізаний*ₐ 'cut apart'), ACTION-PROCESS-ENTITY (4 out of the 10 verbs can produce this combination, e.g. *дати*ᵥ³ 'to give' > *видання*ₙ 'publishing' > *видавництво*ₙ 'publishing house'), or ACTION-PROCESS-ENTITY-AGENT/FEMALE/ (4 out of the 10 verbs set up this combination, e.g. *шити*ᵥ 'to sew' > *шиття*ₙ 'sewing' > *вишиванка*ₙ 'a sewed shirt' > *вишивальниця*ₙ 'a sewer').

11.9 Multiple occurrence of semantic categories

There are three cases of multiple reoccurrence in one derivational chain. The first two cases consists of either just ACTION-ACTION (e.g. *тримати*ᵥ 'to hold' > *тримання*ₙ 'the action of holding') or ACTION-CAUSATIVE-ACTION (e.g. *рити*ᵥ 'dig' > *розритий*ₐ 'dug out' > *риття*ₙ 'the action of digging').

The other case is QUALITY-QUALITY, which occurs in some derivational chains of adjectives (e.g. *поганий*ₐ 'bad' > поганський*ₐ 'pagan').

11.10 Reversibility of semantic categories

In the Ukrainian data set, no instances of semantic categories occurring in a reversed order are revealed.

---

[3] The etymological root of the verb дати 'to give' has lost its original meaning in the words ви/да/ваний, ви/да/вати, ви/да/ватися, ви/да/вець, ви/да/вниця, ви/да/вницький, ви/да/вничий, ви/да/ний, ви/да/ння, ви/да/ти, переви/да/ти, and переви/да/ння, which all relate to 'publishing'. Polyuga (2001: 12) states that the appearance of new meanings in the derived words is an irreversible process. In some words this process is complete, in others it is still underway, and in others it is likely to happen, because the language is updating the meanings and, therefore, the morphemes.

11.11 Conclusions

The Ukrainian set shows that the average number of derivational orders for adjectives, nouns and verbs ranges between 2.98 and 4.18 (Table 11.6). 4th order derivations are rare, being more characteristic for verbs, and only nouns permit 5th order derivations.

Adjectives exhibit the highest numbers of derivational networks in total and the highest number of derivational networks in the 1st order (Table 11.1). The higher derivational outcome of the adjectives could be related to the higher number of DIMINUTIVE and AUGMENTATIVE suffixes that attach to adjectives compared to those that attach to nouns or verbs. The formation of adjectives involves suffixes of two groups: (1) those expressing diminution, augmentation, or subjective evaluations of the qualities of the subject, and (2) those expressing new shades, clarifying the meaning of the root. The derived adjectives are built on the adjectival base for the first group of suffixes, and on the substantival, verbal, and adverbial bases for the second group. Nouns and verbs attest almost equal numbers of derivational networks.

Adjectives and verbs have the overall highest saturation value: 29% in the 1st order (Table 11.5). For adjectives, the maximum derivational networks and the average number of derivatives are thus much higher in the 1st order, compared to the 2nd order (Tables 11.1 and 11.8). In contrast, the average saturation value for nouns is the almost the same in the 1st and 2nd orders (Table 11.5).

Finally, less than half of the semantic categories (i.e. 20 of the 49 available labels) are covered by the Ukrainian derivations. On the one hand, this fact implies that Ukrainian makes use of other means, whether morphological, morphological-syntactic, lexical-syntactic or lexical-semantic (Ponomariv, Rizun and Yu 2008), to account for the remaining semantic categories. However, on the other hand, the derivational capacity of Ukrainian is quite rich given the semantics accounted for. In addition, a number of paronymous words linked by the relation of sequential derivation make up word-forming chains that are frequently traced in Ukrainian word-formation processes.

References

Hryshchenko, A. P. 1978. *Adjectives in Ukrainian*. Kyiv: Naukova dumka.
Plyushch, M. Ya. 2005. *Grammar of Ukrainian: Volume I. Morpheme. Word-Building. Morphology*. Kyiv: Vyshcha Shkola.

Polyuga, L. M. 2001. *Dictionary of Ukrainian Morphemes*. Lviv: Svit.
Ponomariv, O. D., V. V. Rizun & L. Yu. Shevchenko. 2008. *Modern Ukrainian*. Kyiv: Lybid.
Vakaryuk, L. & S. Pantso. 2010. *Morphemics and Word-Building*. Ternopil: Bogdan.

Sources

Карпіловська, Є. А. 2002. *Кореневий гніздовий словник української мови: Гнізда слів з вершинами – омографічними коренями*. К.: Українська енциклопедія.
Полюга, Л. М. 2001. *Словник українських морфем*. Львів: Світ.
Сікорська, З. С. 1995. *Українсько-російський словотворчий словник*. К.: Освіта.

Geri Popova, Maria Rosenberg
12 Introduction to Germanic languages

The Germanic languages have compounding and derivation as their main word-formation patterns, whereas back-formation, blending, clipping and conversion are part of the minor word-formation processes (see individual chapters on several Germanic languages in Müller et al. 2016: 2387–2578).

Theoretical problems common to all the Germanic languages for the elaboration of derivational networks centre around four issues: (i) prefixes and suffixes as distinct from affixoids and combining forms; (ii) vowel changes; (iii) inflection vs. derivation, with present and past participles as a prominent case; and (iv) particle verbs.

The first issue is difficult to resolve on a pan-Germanic basis. Except for the neoclassical combining forms that are excluded from all derivational networks, independent of language, there are language-specific forms which have been dealt with independently for each individual chapter and language. As to the three last issues, there are some criteria that can serve as guidance. Regarding derivation via vowel change, one could argue for the exclusion of cases where the only 'symptom' of the derivational process is a vowel change (see Chapter 18 on Icelandic, for example), and for the inclusion of cases with a derivational affix plus a vowel change, as in the Swedish chapter (Chapter 20). The exclusion of present and past participles can be motivated if we separate form from function: participles are verb *forms* that can *function* as adjectives. There are of course various debates around the complexities of this issue; for English, the interested reader could refer to the work of, amongst others, Huddleston and Pullum (2002: 79–82), Spencer (2013, 2016), and Bauer et al. (2013: 306). Although the positions expressed by these authors differ, they can mostly be taken as an indication that participial adjectives are not the result of a straightforward derivational process. Some other phenomena that raise issues around the distinction between inflection and derivation are treated differently in the different chapters. For example, Chapter 17 on German takes the view that comparative and superlative forms of adjectives are part of derivation rather than inflection. This is in contrast to, for instance, English and Swedish, where comparative and superlative are considered to be inflectional. The exclusion of particle verbs is less complex and can be strongly motivated if we adopt the view that they are phrasal constructs (Los et al. 2012).

More generally, a number of the Germanic languages turn out to have relatively impoverished derivational networks (see remarks to that effect for English, Icelandic, and Frisian, for example). The authors of the respective chapters put forward different explanations for this, though some common themes emerge. All authors comment on the importance of Germanic compounding, and mention conversion as another contributing factor. Another important factor for many of the Germanic languages could be that a significant part of their morphology is of foreign origin, whereas the bases in the sample are mostly native. Frisian (alongside other Germanic languages) possibly compensates for the lack of derivation via syntactic means, as noted in Chapter 16. For Icelandic, the exclusion of vowel shift derivation may be significant, as is the role played by the rich inflectional system of the language (see chapter 18). In addition, for all Germanic languages, the exclusion of forms that are affix-like but cannot be considered uncontroversial derivational affixes, alongside the exclusion of the neoclassical formatives mentioned above, play a role.

In conclusion, it turns out that the different chapters on individual Germanic languages have occasionally taken different stances on these issues, which are made clear in the introductory part of each chapter.

References

Bauer, Laurie, Rochelle Lieber & Ingo Plag. 2013. *The Oxford Reference Guide to English Morphology*. Oxford: Oxford University Press.

Huddleston, Rodney & Geoffrey K. Pullum. 2002. *The Cambridge Grammar of the English Language*. Cambridge: Cambridge University Press.

Los, Bettelou, Corrien Blom, Geert Booij, Marion Elenbaas & Ans van Kemenade. 2012. *Morphosyntactic Change: A Comparative Study of Particles and Prefixes*. Cambridge: Cambridge University Press.

Müller, Peter O., Ingeborg Ohnheiser, Susan Olsen & Franz Rainer (eds.). 2016. *Word-Formation: An International Handbook of the Languages of Europe, Vol. 4*. Berlin & Boston: Mouton de Gruyter.

Spencer, Andrew. 2013. *Lexical Relatedness*. Oxford: Oxford University Press.

Spencer, Andrew. 2016. Two Morphologies or One? In Andrew Hippisley & Gregory Stump (eds.), *The Cambridge Handbook of Morphology (Cambridge Handbooks in Language and Linguistics)*, 27–49. Cambridge: Cambridge University Press.

Hans Götzsche
13 Derivational networks in Danish

13.1 General notes

Danish is a North Germanic language, belonging to, as it is called in Historical Linguistics, the East Scandinavian group of languages, thus including Danish and Swedish. Both Danish and Swedish have developed out of Old Norse, and the western dialects of Jutland have substantially changed their linguistic origins over the last thousand years to the extent that they are almost not distinguishable as successors of Old Norse. As for Danish in general, this has had a noticeable impact on the language's morphology and its potential for derivation.

In Modern Standard Danish there are only a minor number of affixes (see Götzsche 2016), and an even smaller number are productive. From the list of prefixes and suffixes provided by Skautrup (1968: 248–262), only a few are actually used in forming derivations in Danish. If one checks the NOD (1984: 593–597), ODS and DDO, it becomes apparent that, on the one hand, the borderline between compounds and derivations is not clear and, on the other hand, only a very small number of derivatives are used. This means that most of the derivatives mentioned by, for example, Skautrup are just employed in certain contexts, whereas semantic combinations otherwise expressed by derivations in typologically different languages are put together in Danish by compounding or, occasionally, by word orders. For example, in Finnish, the derivative *eläytyä* 'identify oneself with' has the base *elää* 'live', and the (most frequent) Danish equivalent is *leve sig ind i* 'identify oneself with' (in parallel with the Swedish *leva sig in i*). Accordingly many of the classical (Latin, Old Greek), historically conveyed affixes are now perceived as parts of roots, while the affixes of German origin (especially Low German) present one with a mixed picture.

13.2 Maximum derivational networks

It follows from the introductory remarks that Danish does not use derivation as a main tool in word-formation, and the numbers below display the potential of using a limited number of affixes for assigning new semantic categories to the 10 bases in each word-class. The most salient feature is that, with the words chosen, we have no derivations above the 2nd order. See table 13.1:

Table 13.1: Maximum derivational networks per order of derivation for all three word-classes.

	1st order	2nd order	Σ
Nouns	17	2	19
Verbs	30	1	31
Adjectives	15	2	17
TOTAL	62	5	67

13.3 Saturation values

As for the saturation values, the most interesting thing is that no values can be given for five out of the ten nouns since no derivations are found, due to the lack of derivation potentials. Most of the combinations with these gaps are either compounds (or borderline cases) or idiomatic expressions. See table 13.2:

Table 13.2: Saturation values per order of derivation, nouns.

Nouns		Saturation value (%)	1st order (%)	2nd order (%)
bone	ben	15.79	17.65	50
eye	oje	0	0	0
tooth	tand	0	0	0
day	dag	15.79	17.65	0
dog	hund	5.26	5.88	0
louse	lus	0	0	0
fire	ild	0	0	0
stone	sten	21.05	23.53	50
water	vand	31.58	35.29	0
name	navn	0	0	0

The verbs also present a case of derivational gaps, for the same reasons, viz. quasi-compounding or metaphorical meanings, and the other notable feature is that there is only one 2nd order instance. See table 13.3:

Table 13.3: Saturation values per order of derivation, verbs.

Verbs		Saturation value (%)	1st order (%)	2nd order (%)
cut	skære	16.13	16.66	0
dig	grave	25.80	26.66	1
pull	trække	0	0	0
throw	kaste	6.45	6.66	0
give	give	3.23	3.23	0
hold	holde	3.43	3.23	0
sew	sy	3.23	3.23	0
burn	brænde	16.13	16.66	0
drink	drikke	12.90	13.33	0
know	vide	9.68	10	0

This pattern is repeated in Table 13.4 on adjectives: four out of the ten words have no derivational potential and there is only one 2nd order option.

Table 13.4: Saturation values per order of derivation, adjectives.

Adjectives		Saturation value (%)	1st order (%)	2nd order (%)
narrow	dårlig	0	0	0
old	ny	29.41	33.33	0
straight	sort	0	0	0
new	lige	0	0	0
long	varm	5.88	6.66	1
warm	gammel	29.41	33.33	0
thick	lang	5.88	6.66	0
bad	tynd	0	0	0
thin	tyk	5.88	6.66	0
black	snæver	11.76	13.33	0

When summarizing the figures as average values, it is significant that it is hard to compute meaningful figures for 2nd order derivations, and the actual numbers in Table 13.5 may not be especially interesting given the background of the gaps presented above.

Table 13.5: Average saturation values per order of derivation for all three word-classes.

	1st order	2nd order
Nouns	20	0
Verbs	11.07	0
Adjectives	16.66	0

13.4 Orders of derivation

As can be inferred from the above, the figures for Danish on this score are very low.

Table 13.6: Maximum and average number of orders of derivation for all three word-classes.

	Maximum	Average
Nouns	2	1.12
Verbs	2	1.03
Adjectives	2	1.13

13.5 Derivational capacity

The figures for derivational capacities seem to underpin the conclusion mentioned above, viz. that Danish has very little capability for derivation. The information presented by the figures is, however, complicated by the linguistic details. Thus, it may be mentioned that the verb contributing to the maximum number in the verbs row in Table 13.7 is *grave* '(to) dig', but many of the word forms of this verb, e.g. *begrave* 'bury', were taken directly from Low German during the Middle Ages; this is the case with many of the verbs with the prefix *be-*: *beskære* 'trim', *begive*

Table 13.7: Maximum and average derivational capacity for all three word-classes.

	Maximum	Average
Nouns	7	1.4
Verbs	9	1.0
Adjectives	6	1.0

'set out', *beholde* 'keep', etc. So, it might be questioned whether the numbers give a correct picture of the productive derivational potentials of Danish.

The same question can be posed with regard to the figures in Table 13.8.

Table 13.8: Average number of derivatives per order of derivation for all three word-classes.

	1st order	2nd order
Nouns	3.4	0
Verbs	3.3	0
Adjectives	2.5	0

13.6 Correlation between semantic categories and orders of derivation

13.6.1 Nouns

As for Danish nouns, the most salient feature is that the basic derivational mechanism of moving meanings between word-classes is used. Thus, making verbs of ACTION or PROCESS out of nouns seems to be a traditional demand in language usage, like *sten* 'stone' > *forstene* 'petrify', and making an adjective out of a noun also seems to be adequate when making comparisons in the form of SIMILATIVES, like in the case of *hund* 'dog' > *hundeagtig* 'doglike, doggy'.

13.6.2 Verbs

Verbs might be expected to behave in the same way because talking about PROCESSES as ENTITIES may be a general necessity in communication,[1] but the Danish verb sample only confirms this to a certain extent, meaning that derivations making ENTITY meanings out of verbs are not overwhelmingly represented. Some examples may still be offered though: *sy* 'sew' > *syning* 'sewing, needlework'; *drikke* 'drink' > *drik* 'drink(s)', etc.

13.6.3 Adjectives

As might be expected, SIMILATIVE and QUALITY semantics are represented by numbers above 1 (one) in the set of affixes, but the numbers are not impressive: QUALITY = 2 and SIMILATIVE = 3. So the impression that Danish derivation is not a complicated business is, once again, upheld: e.g. *gammel* 'old' > *gammelagtig* 'elderly, oldish'.

13.7 Semantic categories with blocking effects

Because of the (extremely) low number of derivations above the 1st order, it is not appropriate to say anything general about potential blockings between levels of orders.

13.8 Typical combinations of semantic categories

The statement made in section 13.7 also goes for the potential for semantic combinations.

13.9 Multiple occurrence of semantic categories

This phenomenon is non-existent in Danish.

---

[1] Observe the general tendency to talk about the continuous flux of the world, in which we *go*, *run* and *sit*, as an entity: 'time' (cf. Filipović and Jaszczolt 2012).

13.10 Reversibility of semantic categories

This phenomenon is also non-existent in Danish.

13.11 Reasons for structurally poor derivational networks

To give reasons for (or assume the causes of) linguistic formation processes is not easy, and may be theoretically controversial. But in order to offer some kind of explanation for the poor derivational networks in Danish, one may point to the fact that Danish morphology has eroded over the years. Take, for instance, the orthographical rule that most, but not all, adjectives can be used as adverbs if a *-t* is affixed to the adjective: e.g. *svær* 'difficult' > *svært* 'difficultly'. In colloquial speech the -t is almost never pronounced, so series of derivatives are very difficult to produce in spoken Danish. Instead, the complex semantics of such series of derivatives in morphologically rich languages are expressed by compounds or syntactic constructions.

13.12 Conclusions

There is not much to add to the figures and the preliminary conclusions presented above. Danish is not a language that utilizes derivation as a prioritized tool in word-formation. Further research may need to give more attention to the context: which are the most important features in this austere affix environment, prefixes or suffixes? No doubt, suffixes are the ones utilized in productive word formation in Danish, to the extent that such suffixes are doubtlessly *not* free forms making compounds – this is the standard way of doing things in Danish. The paradigm of prefixes is quite another matter. Some Danish prefixes share semantics and some kind of syntactic behaviour with so-called particles in verb phrases, whereas other prefixes only share the word forms (orthographic or pronunciation features) with otherwise free forms, and not the semantics. This pattern is, as mentioned, complicated by the historical traces of the individual words, and this might need more historical analysis in order to illuminate the figures displayed above.

References

DDO = *Den Danske Ordbog*. 2003–2005. Kobenhavn: Det Danske Sprog- og Litteraturselskab.
Filipović, Luna & Katarzyna M. Jaszczolt. 2012. *Space and Time in Languages and Cultures*. Amsterdam & Philadelphia: John Benjamins Publishing Company.
Götzsche, Hans. 2016. 140. Danish. In Peter O. Müller, Ingeborg Ohnheiser, Susan Olsen & Franz Rainer (eds.), *Word-Formation: An International Handbook of the Languages of Europe, Vol. 4*, 2505–2524. Berlin & Boston: Mouton de Gruyter.
NOD = *Nye ord i dansk 1955–75*. 1984. København: Gyldendal.
ODS = *Ordbog over det danske Sprog*. 1918–1954. København: Det Danske Sprog- og Litteraturselskab.
Skautrup, Peter. 1968. *Det danske Sprogs Historie IV*. København: Det Dansk Sprog- og Litteraturselskab.

Jack Hoeksema
14 Derivational networks in Dutch

14.1 General notes

Dutch is the official language of the Netherlands and Flanders (Belgium). In the area of morphology, the differences between Netherlandish and Belgian Dutch are sufficiently minor to warrant a unified treatment in this chapter.

Dutch affixes can be divided into three groups: prefixes, suffixes and separable prefixes (Dutch has no infixes). The latter are also referred to as particles. Particle verbs are syntactically complex, and the prefix may have the status of an independent word, much like English particle verbs. However, when verbs are nominalized or adjectivized, the separable prefix becomes inseparable. The Dutch lexicon has a Romance stratum, with largely Romance affixes, and a Germanic stratum, with mostly Germanic affixes (De Haas and Trommelen 1993; Booij 2002). In addition, learned words may have affixes of Greek origin such as *pseudo-*, or *-itis*. Besides prefixes and suffixes, Dutch has a fair number of *affixoids*: independent words that have developed an affix-like meaning and use in compounds, and may be on their way to becoming real affixes (Booij and Hüning 2014). For the purposes of this chapter, only traditional prefixes and suffixes are considered, and separable prefixes and affixoids will be ignored. Derivations that do not occur as individual words but form part of longer words have not been included here, such as *weter* 'knower', which is part of the synthetic compound *allesweter* 'know-all', and *ogig* 'eyed,' which occurs in *blauwogig* 'blue-eyed' (Hoeksema 2014).

In preparing this chapter, numerous sources were used, such as WNT (*Woordenboek der Nederlandsche Taal*, online version), online newspapers (from Delpher.nl), and occasionally Google for relatively rare cases. Unproductive and semantically opaque derivations were excluded (e.g. *snede* 'cut$_N$' from *snijden* 'cut$_V$'), or *ontwerpen* 'design' from *werpen* 'to throw'. Old unproductive but common forms tend to block productive derivations, so for some words this decision has serious consequences (e.g. nominalizations of *geven* 'give' are mostly unproductive: *gave* 'act of giving, thing given', *gift* 'thing given', etc.). Semantic opacity is a matter of degree, and, in some cases, this chapter may have erred on the side of caution by also excluding cases like *verwerpen* 'reject', which may be seen as using a fairly transparent metaphor in which a physical action is turned into a judgement (throw away > reject). Such decisions also have important consequences for the results, given that they force us to remove higher order derivations as well, e.g. *verwerpelijk* 'despicable, worthy of rejection', *verwerpelijkheid* 'despicability'.

Productive and transparent affixes were included even in cases where the derived word is very infrequent. An example is the DIRECTIONAL suffix *-waarts*, which indicates the direction towards whatever is denoted by the stem noun. I included forms like *oogwaarts* 'towards the eye(s)' since it is attested and easy to understand, even though most speakers would not have much of a use for it.

14.2 Maximum derivational networks

Dutch derivational networks tend to be relatively poor compared to Slavic or Turkic. In Table 14.1, we present the maximum derivational networks per word-class and order of derivation. The differences between orders of derivation are clearly significant, but the differences among word-classes are marginal.

Table 14.1: Maximum derivational networks per order of derivation for all three word-classes.

	1st order	2nd order	3rd order	4th order	5th order	Σ
Nouns	9	6	2	0	0	17
Verbs	10	11	3	2	1	27
Adjectives	8	7	4	0	0	19
TOTAL	27	24	9	2	1	63

14.3 Saturation values

The saturation value for the individual nouns can be gleaned from Table 14.2. As the table shows, 3rd order derivations are absent for most nouns. All nouns in the sample have a DIMINUTIVE. For simple, concrete nouns, there is almost always a DIMINUTIVE in Dutch. Most nouns also give rise to privative adjectives in *-less* (except for *dag* 'day'). Since the suffix is productive and transparent, rare but attested cases such as *hondloos* 'dogless' were included. Some CAUSATIVES were removed from the data set, for reasons of semantic transparency, such as *vuren* 'to fire', which does not mean to cause or start a fire, but to fire a gun. The verb *stenigen* 'to stone, to kill by throwing stones' is likewise not fully transparent, and moreover has a semantically superfluous occurrence of the suffix *-ig*. Feminine endings were not considered, given that only one candidate, *hondin* 'female dog', was mentioned in the WNT, but this noun is obsolete. Had a

Table 14.2: Saturation values per order of derivation, nouns.

Noun		Sat. value (%)	1st order (%)	2nd order (%)	3rd order (%)
bone	been	65.2	81.8	60	0
eye	oog	21.7	45.5	0	0
tooth	tand	52.2	63.6	30	100
day	dag	4.4	9.1	0	0
dog	hond	30.4	45.5	20	0
louse	luis	39.1	54.6	30	0
fire	vuur	17.4	27.3	10	0
stone	steen	56.5	81.8	40	0
water	water	60.9	72.7	60	0
name	naam	30.4	36.4	30	0

different set of nouns been used, with more [+animate] cases, the category FEMININE would have been added.

The saturation values for the 10 Dutch verbs are given in Table 14.3. Some slots in the paradigm were maximally filled. All 10 verbs had AGENT/INSTRUMENT forms in -er. (I decided to make no difference between AGENT and INSTRUMENT readings.) Action nominalizations were somewhat less common due to frequent blocking by irregular forms (*werping 'throwing' is blocked by worp 'throw', for instance). Dutch has three productive action nominalization affixes: ge-, -ing, and -erij (Hoeksema 2014; Hüning 1999). The infinitive is likewise commonly used for action nominalizations (Booij 2015), but was not considered here due to its status as an inflectional category.

Table 14.3: Saturation values per order of derivation, verbs.

Verb		Sat. value (%)	1st order (%)	2nd order (%)	3rd order (%)	4th order (%)	5th order (%)
cut	snijden	55.6	53.3	73.3	33.3	0	0
dig	graven	47.2	66.7	40	33.3	0	0
pull	trekken	16.7	33.3	6.7	0	0	0

Table 14.3 (continued)

Verb		Sat. value (%)	1st order (%)	2nd order (%)	3rd order (%)	4th order (%)	5th order (%)
throw	werpen	19.4	26.7	20	0	0	0
give	geven	13.9	20	13.3	0	0	0
hold	houden	30.6	26.7	40	33.3	0	0
sew	naaien	30.6	46.7	26.7	0	0	0
burn	branden	41.7	33.3	60	33.3	0	0
drink	drinken	27.8	40	20	33.3	0	0
know	weten	30.6	13.3	20	100	100	100

The saturation values for the 10 Dutch adjectives are given in Table 14.4 below. Some categories were fully saturated, such as STATIVE in -*heid*. Negative adjectives were only found for the higher orders, since all 10 adjectives have lexical antonyms, which tend to block morphologically-derived antonyms (cf. Zimmer 1964 for English, but the Dutch situation is entirely comparable). Verbal derivations with *ver-* may undergo further derivation with -*baar* '-able'. Some *ver-* verbs

Table 14.4: Saturation values per order of derivation, adjectives.

Adjective		Sat. value (%)	1st order (%)	2nd order (%)	3rd order (%)	4th order (%)
narrow	nauw	32.1	18.2	38.5	50	0
old	oud	10.7	18.2	7.7	0	0
straight	recht	7.1	18.2	0	0	0
new	nieuw	64.3	63.6	53.9	100	0
long	lang	14.3	36.4	0	0	0
warm	warm	17.9	45.5	0	0	0
thick	dik	50	46.2	33.3	0	0
bad	slecht	17.9	18.2	23.1	0	0
thin	dun	46.4	54.6	38.5	50	0
black	zwart	46.4	72.7	38.5	0	0

had to be left out (*verouderen* 'to age, become old(er)', *verslechteren* 'to worsen', etc.), since they were based on comparatives, rather than the positive form of the adjective, and comparatives were kept out of the scope of this study. A few adjectives have DIMINUTIVES, denoting small persons or objects with the property associated with the adjective: e.g. *oudje* 'old-DIM = old person', *nieuwtje* 'new-DIM = (small) piece of news'. A different type of DIMINUTIVE is found with *warm* and *dun*, the adverbial forms of which are *warmpjes* and *dunnetjes*, which are formed by adding *-s* to a DIMINUTIVE ending. Semantically, these have been considered DIMINUTIVES, given that they have an attenuating character (*dunnetjes* = 'somewhat thinly').

In Table 14.5, the average saturation value for each word-class and order of derivation is displayed.

Table 14.5: Average saturation values per order of derivation for all three word-classes.

	1st order	2nd order	3rd order	4th order	5th order
Nouns	51.8	28	10	0	0
Verbs	36	32	26.7	10	10
Adjectives	40	24.6	25	0	0

14.4 Orders of derivation

As mentioned previously (Table 14.1), the maximum number of orders for the Dutch sample varies between three and five. In Table 14.6, we can see that the average number for the nouns, verbs and adjectives varies between 2–3 orders.

Table 14.6: Maximum and average number of orders of derivation for all three word-classes.

	Maximum	Average
Nouns	3	1.9
Verbs	5	2.8
Adjectives	3	2.1

14.5 Derivational capacity

Table 14.7 compares the maximum and average derivational capacities for 1st order derivations of the three word-classes in the sample.

Table 14.7: Maximum and average derivational capacity for all three word-classes.

	Maximum	Average
Nouns	9	5.7
Verbs	10	5.4
Adjectives	8	4.4

Finally, Table 14.8 compares the average number of derivatives in each order of derivation for the three word-classes.

Table 14.8: Average number of derivatives per order of derivation for all three word-classes.

	1st order	2nd order	3rd order	4th order	5th order
Nouns	5.7	2.8	0.2	0	0
Verbs	5.4	4.8	0.8	0.2	0.1
Adjectives	4.4	3.2	1	0	0

14.6 Correlation between semantic categories and orders of derivation

Among nouns, the semantic category DIMINUTIVE stands out in the 1st order of derivation, with 10 out of 10 nouns. In the 2nd order, the most prominent category is STATE (8 out of 10).

Among verbs, the semantic category AGENT is maximally represented in the 1st order of derivation (10 out of 10). In the 2nd order, DIMINUTIVE is most prominent (9 out of 10) and in the 3rd order, STATE (5 out of 10).

Among adjectives, finally, the semantic category STATE stands out in the 1st order of derivation (10 out of 10). In the 2nd order of derivation, the most prominent category is STATE (6 out of 10), and in the 3rd order it is once again STATE (3 out of 10).

14.7 Semantic categories with blocking effects

DIMINUTIVE by and large blocks any further derivation. The literature mentions a few exceptions such as *meisjesachtig* 'girlish' and *sprookjesachtig* 'fairytale-like', which have the DIMINUTIVE ending *-je* inside the attenuative derivational suffix *-achtig*, the *-s* being a linking phoneme (De Haas and Trommelen 1993: 311). However, these forms are special, since they concern words that are nowadays only used in the DIMINUTIVE form and are, moreover, not included in the present data set. Arguably, they belong to the morphological class of DIMINUTIVES, but not to the semantic category DIMINUTIVE.

The semantic category STATE usually blocks further derivation. A DIMINUTIVE ending may sometimes be attached, in which case the noun loses its more abstract meaning and denotes something more concrete. A case in point is *nieuwigheidje* 'little/minor novelty item', derived from *nieuwigheid* 'newishness, novelty', itself derived from *nieuwig* 'newish'. Given that the notional category STATE is no longer relevant here, such cases should not count as exceptions to the generalization that the category STATE blocks subsequent derivation.

14.8 Typical combinations of semantic categories

Common combinations of semantic categories are POTENTIAL-STATIVE (especially the suffix combination *-baarheid*), POTENTIAL-PRIVATIVE, PRIVATIVE-STATIVE, CAUSATIVE-AGENT, AGENT-FEMALE, AGENT-DIMINUTIVE, and CAUSATIVE-ACTION. Note that the order of the semantic categories is important and reflects the order of derivation: from a POTENTIAL one makes a STATIVE, not the other way around.

14.9 Multiple occurrence of semantic categories

The multiple occurrence of affixes and/or semantic categories is rare. As an example, Booij (2000: 365) suggests the form *werkeloosheidsloos* 'work-less-ness-less =

without unemployment', which is a possible, but not attested word, in which the private affix -*loos* '-less' appears twice.

The PRIVATIVE affixes *on-* 'un-' and -*loos* '-less' are incompatible, as are their counterparts in English (Siegel 1974). We may take this to be a consequence of a more general ban on double negation in the lexicon, similar to bans on a double *un-* (**ununimportant*). The above-mentioned Booij example is presumably immune to this ban because of the intervening affix -*heid*.

14.10 Reversibility of semantic categories

Dutch allows for some semantic categories to occur in both an A/B and a B/A order. However, such ordering issues were not found among the derivational paradigms of the 30 words in our sample.

14.11 Reasons for structurally poor derivational networks

In some cases, derivational networks were poor due to morphological irregularity. Such irregular forms were excluded. For example, many words derived from *dag* 'day' have a long vowel (e.g. *dagelijks* 'daily', *dagen* 'become day'), rather than the short vowel of *dag*. This is an exceptional feature, from a synchronic point of view, and is not shared by otherwise similar nouns such as *vlag* 'flag'. Semantically irregular derivations were also discarded, such as *langzaam* 'slow' from *lang* 'long', because they involve a change from length to speed (cf. also section 14.1).

14.12 Conclusions

Dutch is a typical Germanic language with some derivational morphology, albeit not over-abundant. Some categories (DIMINUTIVE for nouns, comparatives and superlatives for adjectives, AGENT for verbs) are very productive, others less so. Certain types of morphology are not well represented due to the choice of the 30 words (such as negative prefixation with *on-* 'un-') and the exclusion of particle verbs, irregular morphology and conversions.

For higher orders of derivation (2nd or higher), verbs tend to have more derived words than the other classes, but variation within the group of verbs is high, as it is in the other lexical classes. A slightly different sample in which some of the higher-yield verbs are replaced by lower-yield verbs would present a very different picture.

Some of the observations in the chapters for other Germanic languages hold for Dutch as well: for example, verbal prefixes play a big role in the 1st order derivations of Dutch. These prefixes tend to preserve the category and are hence input into the same suffixation processes as the stem verbs (e.g. agent-formation in *-er*).

The choice of basic nonderived adjectives meant that the PRIVATIVE prefix *on-* could not be used a lot: these tend to have lexical antonyms. As a result, this prefix, which operates on adjectives to produce adjectives, turns out to be more important for the nouns and verbs in our sample, since many of the deverbal and denominal adjectives have counterparts with this prefix.

References

Booij, Geert E. 2000. Inflection and derivation. In G. E. Booij, Christian Lehmann & Joachim Mugdan (eds.), *Morphologie: Ein Internationales Handbuch Zur Flexion und Wort-bildung, Vol. 1*. Berlin: Walter de Gruyter.
Booij, Geert E. 2002. *The Morphology of Dutch*. Oxford: Oxford University Press.
Booij, Geert E. 2015. The nominalization of Dutch particle verbs: Schema unification and second order schemas. *Nederlandse taalkunde* 20 (3). 285–314.
Booij, Geert E. & Matthias Hüning. 2014. Affixoids and constructional idioms. In Ronny Boogaart, Timothy Colleman & Gijsbert Rutten (eds.), *Extending the Scope of Construction Grammar*, 77–105. Berlin: Walter de Gruyter.
De Haas, Wim & Mieke Trommelen. 1993. *Morfologisch handboek van het Nederlands. Een overzicht van de woordvorming*. Den Haag: SDU.
Hoeksema, Jack. 2014. *Categorial Morphology*. London: Routledge.
Hüning, Matthias. 1999. *Woordensmederij. De geschiedenis van het suffix -erij*. Den Haag: Holland Academic Graphics.
Siegel, Dorothy C. 1974. *Topics in English morphology*. Cambridge, MA: MIT doctoral dissertation.
WNT = De Vries, Matthias, L. A. te Winkel et al. (eds.). 1882–1998. *Woordenboek der Nederlandsche Taal*, 29 volumes. The Hague: Martinus Nijhoff, Leyden: Sijthoff.
Zimmer, Karl E. 1964. *Affixal Negation in English and Other Languages: An Investigation of Restricted Productivity*. New York: Linguistics Circle of New York.

Gergana Popova
15 Derivational networks in English

15.1 General notes

This chapter covers the investigation of English derivational networks. Detailed descriptions of English derivation can be found in the work of, amongst others, Marchand (1969), Bauer (1983), Adams (2001), and Plag (2003). The preparation of the data sample was based on searches in the British National Corpus (BNC), the *Oxford English Dictionary* (OED), and the internet. Words marked as rare, obsolete or regional (e.g. *nameling, adname, foretooth, cutty*) in the OED were not included. On the advice of the project team, some unproductive patterns (*forgive, knowledge*) were left out too. Working with corpora and dictionaries meant that some derivatives, such as ones based on very productive patterns (e.g. prefixation with *un-* or suffixation with *-ness*), could go under the radar. Every attempt was made to test productive patterns against the words in the sample. This brought to the surface the issue of attested vs. possible words. For example, many of the verbs in the sample give rise to sequences like *pull > pullable > unpullable > unpullability*. But in some cases, it was difficult to find attestations, e.g. searches on Google returned no results, and so forms like *ungiveability* or *unsewability* were not included.

Another methodological issue centred around distinctions like affix, affixoid, and combining form. The guidance was to include only affixes and follow the categorization of an authoritative grammatical description. Accordingly, the chapter relies on the *Oxford Reference Guide to English Morphology* (Bauer et al. 2013), which in turn refers to theoretical principles laid down by Dalton-Puffer and Plag (2000). Words like *stoneware* or *waterscape* were excluded since *-ware* and *-scape* are classified as splinters, while others like *eyelike* and *firelike* were left out because *-like* is considered a compound form. Some forms (e.g. *multi-*, *super-*) were excluded despite being classified as prefixes by Bauer et al. (2013), either because they were on the list of combining forms recommended by the project, or in the interest of bringing the English data set into line with the work done on other languages.

15.2 Maximum derivational networks

English derivational networks are sparse and relatively shallow (see Tables 15.1 and 15.6 below). The highest depth, achieved for verbs and adjectives, is the 3rd order of derivation (for adjectives, only one derivative for one word was found in this order).

Table 15.1: Maximum derivational networks per order of derivation for all three word-classes.

	1st order	2nd order	3rd order	Σ
Nouns	22	11	0	33
Verbs	17	14	6	37
Adjectives	20	10	1	31
TOTAL	60	35	7	102

15.3 Saturation values

The derivational networks of the words in the sample can be discussed in terms of their saturation values (for all categories, see Table 15.5; for individual word-classes, see Tables 15.2–15.4 below). A network is fully saturated if all words have derivatives for the same semantic categories in all orders (and have precisely the same number of derivatives per semantic category in all cases). As the data below show, the saturation values for English are relatively low, so these conditions largely don't obtain. As discussed in section 15.6 below, some semantic categories are realized for all members of a word-class. However, some words can have more than one instantiation for a given category; for example, for *bone*, in addition to the PRIVATIVE *boneless*, we find also *debone* and *unbone*. Some words – for example the noun *dog*, which is linked to unique derivatives like *doggery*, *doggerel*, *doggess*, *dogship*, and *underdog* – have unusually rich derivational networks and so create unfilled cells for the other nouns in the sample. Thus *dog*, with 66.67%, has a higher saturation value than most of the other nouns. Saturation values for all nouns are shown in Table 15.2.

Similar points can be made for verbs. Some verbs give rise to less typical derivatives (e.g. *unhold*, *behold* and *withhold* from *hold*) for which others have no counterparts. Where such 'extra' forms give rise to further derivations (e.g. *upholder*,

Table 15.2: Saturation values per order of derivation, nouns.

Nouns	Saturation value (%)	1st order (%)	2nd order (%)
bone	35.48	30	45.45
eye	35.48	40	27.27
tooth	41.94	40	45.45
day	19.35	20	18.18
dog	67.74	68.18	63.64
louse	25.81	9.09	36.36
fire	12.9	13.64	18.18
stone	12.9	9.09	18.18
water	22.58	18.18	18.18
name	22.58	22.73	18.18

Table 15.3: Saturation values per order of derivation, verbs.

Verbs	Saturation value (%)	1st order (%)	2nd order (%)	3rd order (%)
cut	32.43	52.94	14.29	16.67
dig	32.43	35.29	35.71	16.67
pull	18.92	23.53	14.29	16.67
throw	18.92	23.53	14.29	16.67
give	10.81	17.65	7.14	0
hold	59.46	41.18	78.57	66.67
sew	27.03	29.41	35.71	0
burn	16.22	17.65	14.29	16.67
drink	35.14	35.29	28.57	50
know	24.32	23.53	28.57	16.67

upholding, upholdable, upholdability), gaps are created in more than one order of derivation. Sometimes, a fairly productive pattern like the ITERATIVES with *re-* is instantiated only for some verbs, e.g. *resew, redig*, but does not seem to be

Table 15.4: Saturation values per order of derivation, adjectives.

	Saturation value (%)	1st order (%)	2nd order (%)	3rd order (%)
narrow	16.13	20	10	0
old	32.26	40	20	0
straight	19.35	30	0	0
new	35.48	25	50	100
long	45.16	55	30	0
warm	25.81	35	10	0
thick	32.26	40	20	0
bad	16.13	20	10	0
thin	16.13	20	10	0
black	38.71	45	30	0

well-attested with others like *rethrow*, *repull*, though they do appear to be possible words.[1] The saturation values for verbs are given in Table 15.3.

For adjectives, too, some semantic categories are typical of all lexemes in the sample. Other categories are less saturated. For instance, only three adjectives have an attested morphological PRIVATIVE (*unstraight*, *unwarm*, *non-black*). Even though *un-* is generally characterized as a productive prefix in English, it is difficult to find attestations of forms like *unbad* or *unwarm*. This could be related to restrictions on *un-* prefixation like those discussed in Zimmer (1964: 41–45), e.g. restrictions on applying the prefix to evaluatively negative adjectives or monomorphemic adjectives which have monomorphemic antonyms. There is also another interesting source of gaps in the network. Like other adjectives in the sample, *black* forms a SIMILATIVE with *-ish*: *blackish*. However, unlike other adjectives, it has two other forms in this category: *off-black* and *blacky* (this latter is attested in the OED with the meaning 'somewhat black, blackish').[2] Adjectives also provide an interesting example of concealed regularity. Some have RESULTATIVES/CAUSATIVES, for example *blacken* or *straighten*. Others here have

---

[1] *Repull* is marked as obsolete and rare in the OED. Searches on Google suggest that the words may have some use, though mostly in technical registers. Given the emphasis in the project on productivity and general use, these words were therefore not included in the data set.

[2] It could be worth noting that in discussions of inflectional paradigms, analogous phenomena might be accommodated under the notion of overabundance (Thornton 2011).

genuine gaps: there is no morphological derivative like *newen or *warmen to render 'become/make new' or 'become/make warm' (though the latter meaning can be expressed by a conversion to the verb *warm*). Sometimes, however, there is only the appearance of a gap. For *long*, the relevant meaning is expressed by *lengthen* from *length*. Thus, the RESULTATIVE/CAUSATIVE for *long* appears in the 2nd order and so leaves a gap in the 1st order and, conversely, creates gaps for the other adjectives in the 2nd order. The saturation values for adjectives are shown in Table 15.4.

Table 15.5: Average saturation values per order of derivation for all three word-classes.

	1st order	2nd order	3rd order
Nouns	29	30.907	0
Verbs	30	27.143	21.669
Adjectives	33	16	10

The average saturation values per order of derivation for all word-classes are shown in Table 15.5.

15.4 Orders of derivation

As mentioned already, the networks are shallow. For nouns, the maximum number of orders of derivation is two and all nouns have derivatives in the 2nd order. Verbs and adjectives reach three orders of derivation, but whereas for verbs this is well represented (eight verbs have 3rd order derivatives), only one adjective (*new*) has one derivative in the 3rd order (*renewability*).

Table 15.6: Maximum and average number of orders of derivation for all three word-classes.

	Maximum	Average
Nouns	2	2
Verbs	3	2.6
Adjectives	3	2.1

15.5 Derivational capacity

One consequence of the outliers mentioned above are the differences between the maximum and the average derivational capacities for a certain word-class. The values for all three word-classes are shown in Table 15.7.

Table 15.7: Maximum and average derivational capacity for all three word-classes.

	Maximum	Average
Nouns	14	5.8
Verbs	9	5.1
Adjectives	11	6.6

The average number of derivatives therefore gives a fairer idea of derivational capacity. The values for all orders are given in Table 15.8 (there are no 3rd order derivatives for nouns, hence no value).

Table 15.8: Average number of derivatives per order of derivation for all three word-classes.

	1st order	2nd order	3rd order
Nouns	5.8	3.4	0
Verbs	5.1	3.7	1.3
Adjectives	6.6	1.9	0.1

15.6 Correlation between semantic categories and orders of derivation

Some of the general issues around assigning semantic categories to derivatives are discussed in the General Introduction to the volume and will not be reiterated here. As mentioned in the Introduction, where two labels were potentially applicable (e.g. both QUALITY and PRIVATIVE to a word like *nameless* or both ABILITY and PRIVATIVE to *unburnability*), an attempt was made, as far as was possible, to reflect the meaning that was most prominent at the last derivational step. There are some exceptions to this, however: since the project notes included both *readable* and *readability* as examples of ABILITY, the same logic was applied to the respective English derivatives and so both *pullable* and *pullability*, for instance, were coded as ABILITY. *Unpullability*, derived from the PRIVATIVE *unpullable*, was also coded as ABILITY.

All English nouns have realizations of the categories PRIVATIVE and QUALITY in the 1st order. The PRIVATIVE is most typically an adjective, expressing the quality of being characterized by the lack of the noun, e.g. *toothless, dayless, dogless*. All nouns have at least one other more general realization of the category QUALITY. For example, for *tooth*, there is *toothful, toothed, toothy,* and *toothsome*; for *fire*, however, there is only *fiery*. In the 2nd order of derivation, STATE is a typical category for all nouns, generally derived with *-ness*, e.g. *toothlessness, toothiness*.

For verbs, ABILITY (*diggable, drinkable*), ACTION (*digging, drinking*) and AGENT (*digger, drinker*) are represented for all words in the 1st order of derivation. In the 2nd order, the categories ABILITY (*diggability*) and PRIVATIVE (*undiggable*) are realized for 9 words. In the 3rd order of derivation for verbs, we find mostly derivatives of the ABILITY category, e.g. *uncuttability* (realized for 8 words).

For adjectives, three semantic categories are realized for all words in the 1st order: STATE, MANNER and SIMILATIVE, which are most often derived via suffixation with *-ness, -ly* and *-ish*, respectively. As this suggests, adverbs were included here as a derivational category, rather than as an inflectional one, though see for example Bauer et al. (2013: 322) on the relevant debate. No category is systematically represented in any other order.

15.7 Semantic categories with blocking effects

Given how shallow the networks are, it is difficult to comment on blocking effects.

15.8 Typical combinations of semantic categories

For all 10 nouns, STATE in the 2nd order combines with QUALITY in the 1st order (e.g. *bony > boniness*) and with PRIVATIVE in the 1st order (e.g. *boneless > bonelessness*). Typical for verbs are combinations of ABILITY in the 1st order with ABILITY and PRIVATIVE in the 2nd order (*cuttable > cuttability, cuttable > uncuttable*). These patterns hold for 9 and 10 words, respectively. PRIVATIVE in the 2nd order combines with ABILITY in the 3rd order (*uncuttable > uncuttability*). This is obtained for 8 words.

15.9 Multiple occurrence of semantic categories

For verbs, there are repetitions of ABILITY across the three orders, e.g. *cuttable, cuttability, uncuttability*.

15.10 Reversibility of semantic categories

For verbs, ABILITY and PRIVATIVE can occur in both orders, e.g. *cuttable > uncuttable* vs *uncuttable > uncuttability*.

15.11 Reasons for structurally poor derivational networks

Most striking for English is the relative paucity of networks, as defined by the specifications of the project. One explanation is the prominence in English of conversion and compounding (for more details on these, see Valera 2014 and Bauer 2017), both of which were specifically excluded under the brief. A further contributing factor stems from the fact that the selected sample words, all from the Swadesh list, are predominantly words of Anglo-Saxon origin. English, as pointed out for example by Marchand (1969), has morphological formatives of both native and foreign origin, with many foreign affixes not attaching themselves to native bases. The number of native affixes, especially prefixes, is relatively small (Marchand 1969: 129). Borrowing, points out Marchand (1969), displaced some native affixed words, and also in some cases led to the replacement of or restrictions on native affixes. Thus, this chapter relates primarily to English native bases and native affixes (with some exceptions, of course, such as the affixes *-able, re-* and, occasionally, *-al*). Inflection is not covered by the project and a decision was taken to exclude participles from the data sample, so there are no (present or past) participial adjectives.

15.12 Conclusions

English is a language with shallow and relatively sparsely populated derivational networks. As indicated above, this is partly due to the presence in English of both native and borrowed morphology and partly to the popularity of conversion and compounding. However, the derivational networks of English also show a stable kernel of paradigmaticity, with a good number of semantic categories being realized for all words in the sample. Such productive semantic categories can be found not only in the 1st, but also in the 2nd and (for verbs) even in the 3rd order of derivation. They are often co-extensive with the more familiar notion of productive word-formation patterns, but the adoption of a meaning-based approach allows us to gain a different perspective on the phenomena concerned and provides a suitable basis for comparisons with other languages.

Acknowledgements: I would like to thank the leaders of the MONIKA project, the participants in the workshop that took place in Košice in June 2018 under the auspices of the project, as well as my colleagues working on other Germanic languages (especially Jack Hoeksema, Martin Neef, and Maria Rosenberg) for their useful discussions and for spotting gaps and inaccuracies. Any remaining errors remain the sole responsibility of the author.

References

Adams, Valerie. 2001. *Complex Words in English*. Harlow: Longman.
Bauer, Laurie. 1983. *English Word-formation*. Cambridge: Cambridge University Press.
Bauer, Laurie. 2017. *Compounds and Compounding*. Cambridge: Cambridge University Press.
Bauer, Laurie, Rochelle Lieber & Ingo Plag. 2013. *The Oxford Reference Guide to English Morphology*. Oxford: Oxford University Press.
Dalton-Puffer, Christiane & Ingo Plag. 2000. Categorywise, some compound-type morphemes seem to be rather affix-like: On the status of *-ful*, *-type*, and *-wise* in Present Day English. *Folia Linguistica* 34 (3–4). 225–244.
Marchand, Hans. 1969. *The Categories and Types of Present-Day English Word-Formation: A Synchronic Diachronic Approach*, 2nd edn. München: C. H. Beck'sche Verlagsbuchhandlung.
Plag, Ingo. 2003. *Word-Formation in English*. Cambridge: Cambridge University Press.
Thornton, A. M. 2011. Overabundance (multiple forms realizing the same cell): A non-canonical phenomenon in Italian verb morphology. In Martin Maiden, John Charles Smith, Maria Goldbach & Marc-Olivier Hinzelin (eds.), *Morphological Autonomy: Perspectives From Romance Inflectional Morphology*, 358–381. Oxford: Oxford University Press.
Valera, Salvador. 2014. Conversion. In Rochelle Lieber & Pavol Štekauer (eds.), *Oxford Handbook of Derivational Morphology*, 154–168. Oxford: Oxford University Press.
Zimmer, Karl E. 1964. Affixal negation in English. *WORD* 20 (sup. 1). 21–45.

Siebren Dyk
16 Derivational networks in Frisian

16.1 General notes

Frisian is a West Germanic language, spoken by about 350,000 inhabitants of the province of Fryslân in the north of the Netherlands. The language is also known as West or Modern West Frisian, since other surviving branches of Frisian are still found in the north of Germany. These are East Frisian (about 2,000 speakers in the Saterland region) and North Frisian (about 6,000 speakers, along the west coast of Schleswig-Holstein). These varieties differ markedly from West Frisian and will not be dealt with here.

Frisian is a minority language and is under pressure from Dutch because all its speakers today are completely bilingual. This minority status may also have implications for the present investigation, as the data have been drawn from written sources. Written Frisian texts mainly consist of fictional prose.

The main source for the data was the *Wurdboek fan de Fryske Taal* (WFT), a scholarly dictionary covering Frisian between 1800 and 1975. In addition, the electronic corpus of the Fryske Akademy (TDB) was occasionally consulted. Extensive treatments of Frisian word-formation can be found in the work of Hoekstra (1998; for a shorter overview, see Hoekstra 2016) and the Frisian morphology section of the online *Taalportaal* (in English).

Derivation is one of the two main devices of Frisian word-formation, alongside compounding. Conversion is also fairly common, in particular in verb creation. Formations of this kind, such as $tosk_N$ 'tooth' > $toskje_V$ 'be teething', are excluded here. Also excluded is the very productive category of particle verbs. Most of them consist of an adposition (considered a prefix in some frameworks) and a verb; an example is *opjaan* 'give up'. In the spirit of the project, we therefore adhere to the traditional concept of derivational affixes. Suffixes that are traditionally considered as inflectional, for example the comparative and superlative of adjectives, are likewise excluded.

16.2 Maximum derivational networks

Verbs exhibit the highest numbers of derivational networks, in all orders, as shown in Table 16.1. They are also the only lexical category to reach the 4th order. Adjectives are the weakest category in the 1st order, but they clearly outnumber nouns in the 2nd order.

Table 16.1: Maximum derivational networks per order of derivation for all three word-classes.

	1st order	2nd order	3rd order	4th order	5th order	Σ
Nouns	33	4	0	0	0	22
Verbs	27	16	4	2	0	49
Adjectives	22	10	1	0	0	33
TOTAL	82	30	5	2	0	104

16.3 Saturation values

As Table 16.2 shows, the mean saturation values for nouns range from 14% (*tosk* 'tooth') to 45% (*stien* 'stone'). *Tosk*, along with *each* 'eye', does not appear in the 2nd order.

Table 16.2: Saturation values per order of derivation, nouns.

Nouns		Saturation value (%)	1st order (%)	2nd order (%)
bone	bonke	27.27	22.22	50
eye	each	18.18	22.22	0
tooth	tosk	13.64	11.11	25
day	dei	27.27	22.22	50
dog	hûn	27.27	22.22	50
louse	lûs	13.64	16.67	0
fire	fjoer	22.73	16.67	50
stone	stien	45.45	50	25
water	wetter	40.91	38.89	50
name	namme	18.18	16.67	25

For verbs, see Table 16.3, the lowest value is represented by *naaie* 'sew' (12%) and the highest by *baarne* 'burn' (41%). The verb *lûke* 'pull' is restricted to the 1st order, while *hâlde* 'keep' is the only verb that has a 3rd order derivation.

Table 16.4 shows that the set of adjectives has one member, namely *rjocht* 'straight', with an extremely low value: just 3%. Its low value is confirmed by

Table 16.3: Saturation values per order of derivation, verbs.

Verbs		Saturation value (%)	1st order (%)	2nd order (%)	3rd order (%)	4th order (%)
cut	snije	20.41	33.33	6.25	0	0
dig	grave	14.29	14.81	18.75	0	0
pull	lûke	18.37	33.33	0	0	0
throw	smite	12.24	11.11	18.75	0	0
give	jaan	18.37	25.93	12.5	0	0
hold	hâlde	28.57	25.93	37.5	25	0
sew	naaie	12.24	18.52	6.25	0	0
burn	baarne	40.82	48.15	43.75	0	0
drink	drinke	24.49	37.04	12.5	0	0
know	witte	38.78	25.93	43.75	75	100

Table 16.4: Saturation values per order of derivation, adjectives.

Adjectives		Saturation value (%)	1st order (%)	2nd order (%)	3rd order (%)
narrow	nau	21.21	27.27	10	0
old	âld	51.52	63.64	30	0
straight	rjocht	3.03	4.55	0	0
new	nij	45.45	40.91	50	100
long	lang	18.18	22.73	10	0
warm	waarm	21.21	22.73	20	0
thick	tsjok	12.12	13.64	10	0
bad	min	15.15	13.64	20	0
thin	tin	15.15	18.18	10	0
black	swart	24.24	27.27	20	0

the fact that it is restricted to the 1st order. On the other hand, *nij* 'new' is up at 45%, and is the only adjective that is represented in the 3rd order.

Table 16.5 shows the average saturation values per order. We can see that the percentages for the three lexical classes are more or less in the same range in the 1st order: 24% for nouns, 27% for verbs, and 25% for adjectives. In the 2nd order, nouns account for 33%, while verbs and adjectives are behind with 20% and 18% respectively.

Table 16.5: Average saturation values per order of derivation for all three word-classes.

	1st order	2nd order	3rd order	4th order
Nouns	23.89	32.5	0	0
Verbs	27.41	20	10	10
Adjectives	25.46	18	10	0

16.4 Orders of derivation

On average, as shown in Table 16.6, verbs are the most productive word-class in terms of possible orders of derivation, followed by adjectives and nouns. This is reflected in the maximum number of orders, which extends to four in the case of verbs, and is restricted to only two for nouns. Again, adjectives, with a maximum number of three orders, occupy the middle position.

Table 16.6: Maximum and average number of orders of derivation for all three word-classes.

	Maximum	Average
Nouns	2	1.7
Verbs	4	2.2
Adjectives	3	2

16.5 Derivational capacity

As shown in Table 16.7, verbs display the highest number of derivations in the 1st order (an average of 7.4), followed by adjectives (5.5) and nouns (4.3). However, for single items, it is the adjective *âld* 'old' that is most productive (14 derivatives), immediately followed by the verb *baarne* 'burn' (13). The adjective *âld* is special in that it has a number of lexicalized inflected forms (also comparatives and superlatives) that appear in the dictionaries, which we have included here. If it had been left out, *âld*'s counterpart *nij* 'new', with ten derivatives, would have led the class of adjectives. As for nouns, the most productive one is *stien* 'stone' (9).

Table 16.7: Maximum and average derivational capacity for all three word-classes.

	Maximum	Average
Nouns	9	4.3
Verbs	13	7.4
Adjectives	14	5.5

Table 16.8 shows the average number of derivatives per order. Once again, verbs are ahead in all orders. Nouns display the lowest numbers, although there is little difference between nouns and adjectives.

Table 16.8: Average number of derivatives per order of derivation for all three word-classes.

	1st order	2nd order	3rd order	4th order	5th order
Nouns	4.3	1.3	0	0	0
Verbs	7.4	3.2	0.4	0.2	0
Adjectives	5.5	1.8	0.1	0	0

16.6 Correlation between semantic categories and orders of derivation

As for nouns, the most common category in the 1st order is DIMINUTIVE (value 8). DIMINUTIVE formation is very productive in Frisian: from the present set, only *dei* 'day' and *namme* 'name' appear to be inappropriate candidates. Next best is ORNATIVE (value 6), whereby verbs, as well as adjectives, can be created by way of prefixation, mainly with the help of the suffix *-ich*, for example in *bonke*$_N$ 'bone' > *bonkich*$_A$ 'bony'. In the 2nd order, ABSTRACTION, with a value of 7, is by far the most common category. For verbal bases, the suffix -*ing* is used, as in *ûntwetterje*$_V$ 'drain' > *ûntwettering*$_N$ 'drainage'. For adjectival bases, the relevant suffix is -*ens*, as in *hûnich*$_A$ 'doggy' > *hûnigens*$_N$ 'dogginess', but we also find the suffix -*heid*. An example is *eachlik*$_A$ 'attractive, pleasing to the eye' > *eachlikheid*$_N$ 'attractiveness'. Other semantic categories for the 2nd order are negligible.

As for derivation in Frisian, verbal bases are the most active class. The most popular category in the 1st order is ACTION, with a value of 9. This can produce both nouns – mainly by the suffix -*erij*, for example in *snije*$_V$ 'cut' > *snijerij*$_N$ 'cutting' – as well as verbs. In that case, the derivative is headed by the prefix *be*- or *fer*-. Examples are *grave*$_V$ 'dig' > *begrave*$_V$ 'bury' and *naaie*$_V$ 'sew' > *fernaaie*$_V$ 'change by sewing'. The category AGENT has a value of 8. It is actualized by the very productive suffix -*er*, for example in *snije*$_V$ 'cut' > *snijer*$_N$ 'cutter'. Agentivity could be valued even higher if we also include the AGENT-FEMALE derivation *naaister*, from the verb *naaie* 'to sew' and the suffix -*ster*. The third semantic category is RESULTATIVE (value 7). Most of these derivations are produced through prefixation by *fer*- or *be*-, but in the present sample we also see a few words formed by the destructive prefix *te*-. An example is *snije*$_V$ 'cut' > *tesnije*$_V$ 'destroy by cutting'. The most prominent category in the 2nd order is ABSTRACTION (value 7). The derivations are mainly performed by the nominalizing suffix -*ing*, which is attached to verbal bases, as in *fergrave*$_V$ 'level' > *fergraving*$_N$ 'levelling'. In addition, some derived adjectival bases allow the nominalizing -*ens* or -*heid*.

The most characteristic semantic category for 1st order derivations from adjectives is ABSTRACTION. It has a value of 9, from 10 possible bases. This category is primarily used to transpose an adjective to a noun. Frisian has a few suffixes that can do this, the choice being partly dependent on the prosodic make-up of the base (Hoekstra 1990). As the 10 bases are all monosyllabic and hence end in a stressed syllable, the suffix -*ens* is the most relevant one, for example in *tsjok*$_A$ 'thick' > *tsjokkens*$_N$ 'thickness'. Occasionally, -*te* (*tsjokte*$_N$ 'thickness') and -*ichheid* also occur. An example of the latter suffix is *nij*$_A$ 'new' > *nijichheid*$_N$ 'newness'. Also relatively common (value 6) is SIMILATIVE, with the suffixes -*ich* and -*eftich*. *Nijich*$_A$ 'newish' and *nijeftich*$_A$ 'newish' can be derived in this way from *nij*$_A$ 'new'. For the 2nd order, ABSTRACTION is again the most popular category (value 7). This category applies to adjectival and verbal bases. As for the latter, the nominalizing suffix -*ing* is used, as in *ferâlderje*$_V$ 'grow old' > *ferâldering*$_N$ 'ageing'. Other semantic categories are marginal.

No common pattern can be observed for the 1st order in the three word-classes. It is conspicuous, however, that ABSTRACTION has such a high value in the 2nd orders of all lexical categories. This is due to the high productiveness of the suffixes -*ens*, -*heid* and -*ichheid* after adjectival bases and -*ing* after verbs.

16.7 Semantic categories with blocking effects

In Frisian, derivational potentiality rapidly decreases with each subsequent derivational cycle, with the result that we find only a few forms in the 3rd order. We might therefore expect the number of blocking categories to exceed the number of categories that permit further derivation.

Absolute blockers are DIMINUTIVE, SINGULATIVE, AGENT and UNDERGOER. For example, from *hûn* 'dog', one can derive the formations *hûnich* and *hûneftich* as SIMILATIVE and *hûnsk* as MANNER. However, it is impossible for the DIMINUTIVE *hûntsje* to act as a base for these semantic categories, cf. **hûntsjich*, **hûntsjeeftich* and **hûntsjesk*.

Blocking also applies to the fairly frequent category ABSTRACTION, as the only exceptional case is questionable in terms of word-formation.¹ SIMILATIVE also often blocks, while at the same time displaying some notable exceptions in this respect. On the other hand, we have some categories that permit derivation to move on to a higher order more often than not. These are ACTION, PROCESS, RESULTATIVE, ORNATIVE and QUALITY. For example, from the adjective *nij* 'new', we can derive the ACTION *fernije* 'renew' by adding the prefix *fer-*. From this, we can further derive *fernijer* (AGENT) and *fernijing*, which can represent ACTION and SINGULATIVE as well.

There are no indications that some specific blocking effects are restricted to certain derivational orders.

16.8 Typical combinations of semantic categories

ABSTRACTION is the most frequent derivational semantic category in the Frisian sample. Most often (six times), it is derived from ACTION, followed by QUALITY and SIMILATIVE, both of which form the basis for ABSTRACTION four times. Also worth mentioning is the combination PROCESS-ABSTRACTION, which occurs three times.

16.9 Multiple occurrence of semantic categories

There are only three derivational chains in which we can observe reoccurrences of the same semantic category. Most prominent is the verb *witte* 'know', with

---

[1] This concerns the word *bewitten* 'consciousness', marked in WFT as puristic and only occurring in the Frisian literary style. We assumed here that it derives from *witten* 'knowledge', since the alternative, the potential verbal base *bewitte*, does not exist and is not conceivable.

an ABSTRACTION in the 1st order (*witten* 'knowledge'), another ABSTRACTION in the 2nd order (*wittenskip* 'science'), followed by a third ABSTRACTION in the 4th order (*wittenskiplikens* 'scientific character'). The adjective *nij* 'new' has a 1st order ACTION in the verb *fernije* 'renew', and another ACTION in the 2nd order noun *fernijing* 'renewal'. The third case can be found with the noun *dei* 'day', which has a 1st order QUALITY derivation (*daachliks* 'daily'), followed by another (adverbial) QUALITY in *daachlikswei* 'daily'.[2]

All in all, we can conclude that multiple occurrence is rare in Frisian.

16.10 Reversibility of semantic categories

The reversed order of semantic categories did not occur in the Frisian material under study.

16.11 Reasons for structurally poor derivational networks

Frisian can be characterized as having a relatively poor derivational network. Quite a number of semantic categories are not represented derivationally, and many of those only occur sporadically. An alternative way to express the relevant meaning is syntactical, using a phrase that often includes one or more items that represent the meaning lexically. For example, INSTRUMENT may be expressed in a prepositional phrase with the preposition *mei* 'with'. The same preposition can act with respect to COMITATIVE. DURATIVE may be formulated by the preposition *oan* 'on' plus the article *it* 'it' plus the nominal infinitive, as in *it bern is oan it boartsjen* 'the child is playing'.

16.12 Conclusions

The derivational system of Frisian is relatively poor, as many semantic categories are not represented and the number of derivatives rapidly decreases with each consecutive derivational order.

---

[2] The source of the deviating stem might be found in either the irregular plural form *dagen* or in interference from the Dutch word *dagelijks*.

ABSTRACTION is the most popular semantic category overall, in particular after adjectival bases. Most often, it is derived from ACTION. Frequent semantic categories in the realm of nouns are DIMINUTIVE and ORNATIVE, and with verbs we see ACTION and AGENT in particular.

Verbs seem to be the most productive word-class: they may appear up to the 4th order, exhibit the highest numbers of derivational networks, and score highest in terms of saturation values. Nouns are the least productive, with adjectives occupying the middle position.

Some semantic categories appear to block consecutive derivation, namely DIMINUTIVE, SINGULATIVE, AGENT, UNDERGOER and ABSTRACTION. Multiple occurrences of a semantic category are very rare in Frisian, and reversed orders do not occur at all.

References

Hoekstra, Jarich. 1990. Adjectiefnominalisatie in het Fries [Adjective nominalization in Frisian]. *Interdisciplinair Tijdschrift voor Taal- en Tekstwetenschap 9*. 273–285.

Hoekstra, Jarich. 1998. *Fryske wurdfoarming* [Frisian word-formation]. Ljouwert/Leeuwarden: Fryske Akademy.

Hoekstra, Jarich. 2016. Frisian. In Peter O. Müller, Ingeborg Ohnheiser, Susan Olsen & Franz Rainer (eds.), *Word-formation. An International Handbook of the Languages of Europe, vol. 4*, 2451–2465. Berlin & Boston: Mouton de Gruyter.

Taalportaal. 2017. *Taalportaal: the linguistics of Dutch, Frisian and Afrikaans.* http://www.taalportaal.org.

TDB. 2017. *Taaldatabank Frysk* [Linguistic Database of Frisian]. https://fryske-akademy.nl/tdbport/.

WFT. 1984–2011. *Wurdboek fan de Fryske Taal / Woordenboek van de Friese Taal* [Dictionary of the Frisian Language], 25 volumes. Ljouwert/Leeuwarden: Fryske Akademy.

Martin Neef, Ayşe Yurdakul
17 Derivational networks in German

17.1 General notes

German as a typical Germanic language has a rich and productive morphology. The most productive type of lexeme formation is compounding, but derivation is also quite productive and exemplified by many different patterns (prefixes and suffixes, one circumfix). Another productive means of lexeme formation is conversion. Mostly, German has the properties that are presented in the general introduction to Germanic languages. Here, we focus on fuzzy cases.

Among the morpho-syntactic categories that pertain to the inflecting lexeme classes (verb, noun, adjective, determiner, pronoun), there is only one category that has received some discussion in the literature on German whether it actually is a case of inflection or rather of derivation. This is the category of comparison with the three subcategories positive (unmarked), comparative, and superlative. Based on the Latin tradition of grammar writing that predominates all work on Germanic languages, comparison is widely regarded as inflection, though of a rather untypical kind. Other evaluations, though, can also be found. For example, Hentschel & Weydt (2013: 198) see comparison at the border between inflection and lexeme formation. Only few researchers explicitly state that comparison belongs to lexeme formation (e.g. Olsen 1990: 139; cf. also Eisenberg 2013: 176–177, Duden 2016: 139; 372). For several reasons, we follow this latter analysis: Adjectives with a comparative marker add inflectional markers in the same way as adjectives without such a marker do. Comparison is not accessible to quite a large number of adjectives (cf. Duden 2016: 382–384). At the same time, few adverbs allow comparison forms (cf. Duden 2016: 582–583) but still no inflection proper (which is a defining criterion for adverbs). Comparative and superlative adjectives enter further lexeme formation processes like derivation (*vergrößern* 'to make sth. bigger') and compounding (*Kleinstwagen* 'microcar', lit. 'smallest car') in contrast to typical inflected word-forms. Finally, comparative and superlative adjectives are relational even if the base lexeme is non-relational (*weicher als Butter* 'softer than butter', *die teuerste Briefmarke der Welt* 'the most expensive stamp of the world'; Olsen 1990: 139) which indicates that the formal differences go beyond what is typically assumed from inflection. Consequently, the semantic category AUGMENTATIVE plays an important role in the derivational networks of German, which would not be the case if comparison were disregarded. Nevertheless, to keep the data comparable with the other languages in this volume, where the comparative and the superlative (including their derivatives) are disregarded for the derivational networks, these cases are not included here.

Next, conversion as a productive lexeme formation pattern in German needs to be addressed. In several cases, it is not apparent on first sight that two lexemes stand in a relation of conversion. An example is the basic noun *Fisch* 'fish' and the related verb *fischen* 'to fish' because of the obvious formal difference of the two words. However, verbal lexemes in German have as their citation form the infinitive which consists of a verbal stem plus an infinitive marker –(e)n. Hence, the stems of the verb and the noun are identical in this case, indicating that this is in fact a case of conversion. As conversion is different from derivation, conversion data are not included in the derivational networks. This leads to some gaps that need to be explained. We exclude, e.g., the derived noun *Tagung* 'meeting' as we analyze it as being derived from the converted verb *tagen* 'to meet' instead of from the simple noun *Tag* 'day' directly. On the other hand, we include the complex verb *befeuern* 'to make light' as directly derived from the simple noun *Feuer* 'fire' instead of from the converted verb *feuern* 'to shoot'. In such cases, semantic considerations are decisive.

Finally, we have a look at data that are controversial regarding the question whether they belong to derivation or to compounding. In verbal lexeme formation, in particular, compounding plays an important role (cf. Neef 2009: 389; the opposite opinion is expressed e.g. in Duden 2016: 675). Especially productive is the combination of prepositions and verbal stems. Such constructions fall in two formally distinct classes: On the one hand, there are particle verbs which appear as one word in some syntactic contexts and as two distinct words in others; hence their characterization as separable verbs (e.g. *untergehen* 'to sink, lit. 'under-go'). In accordance with the general introduction, we take this as a clear case of compounding (though some researchers regard it as a lexeme formation type in its own right; e.g. Duden 2016: 708; Weinrich 1993: 1032). However, among the complex verbs with a left element that is formally similar to a preposition, there are also many inseparable exemplars like *unterbrechen* 'to interrupt', lit. 'under-break'. While a number of grammars regard such elements as prefixes proper (e.g. Duden 2016: 709), we treat them as prepositions and the resulting complex verbs, consequently, as compounds. The reasons to regard the prepositions in question as prefixes may be semantic in nature: The semantic effects of prefixes proper and of prepositions as first elements in complex verbs are comparable. Moreover, the meaning of the preposition in a complex verb is often (though not necessarily) not clearly related to the free preposition. Both arguments, however, are not striking: The distinction of derivation and compounding is not a matter of semantics but of formal structure, and the fact that the meaning of an element in bound form differs to some extent from its free use is relevant in many other constructions as well, like semi-affixes that also do not fall under derivation but compounding. Thus, we have a rather strict view of the concept of derivation in German. In particular, we only regard the verbal prefixes *be–*, *ent–*, *er–*, *ge–*, *miss–*, *ver–*, and *zer–* as relevant for the discussion of derivational networks.

The main source of our research is the voluminous dictionary of word families (Splett 2009). An additional source is Fleischer and Barz (2012) who give an exhaustive list of German affixes. We used this list to create potential words with the thirty stems of the corpus. Then we checked whether these words actually exist by consulting a regular and a reverse dictionary (Dudenredaktion n.d., Muthmann 1991). Unattested potential words were controlled by internet searches (Google). In this way, we have, among other data, detected a word containing ten instances of the same prefix (*ur-ur- ... -alt*; cf. below), a singular case in German morphology.

17.2 Maximum derivational networks

As shown in Table 17.1, the verbs exhibit the highest and the nouns the lowest number of derivational networks in all (four) orders and in total. The highest number of orders is displayed by adjectives.

Table 17.1: Maximum derivational networks per order of derivation for all three word-classes.

	1st order	2nd order	3rd order	4th order	5th order	Σ
Nouns	21	9	3	1	0	34
Verbs	36	31	16	5	0	88
Adjectives	18	21	11	5	2	55
TOTAL	75	61	30	11	2	179

17.3 Saturation values

Table 17.2 shows that the noun *Wasser* 'water' has the highest saturation value (58.82%), whereas *Zahn* 'tooth', *Hund* 'dog', and *Name* 'name' are the nouns with the lowest saturation values (32.35% each).

According to Table 17.3, *ziehen* 'pull' demonstrates the highest saturation value (61.36%) and *wissen* 'know' the lowest one (14.77%) for the verbal derivations.

Table 17.2: Saturation values per order of derivation, nouns.

Nouns		Saturation value (%)	1st order (%)	2nd order (%)	3rd order (%)	4th order (%)	5th order (%)
Knochen	bone	47.06	42.86	66.67	33.33	0	0
Auge	eye	41.18	47.62	44.44	0	0	0
Zahn	tooth	32.35	38.1	33.33	0	0	0
Tag	day	41.18	38.1	33.33	66.67	100	0
Hund	dog	32.35	42.86	22.22		0	0
Laus	louse	35.29	33.33	44.44	33.33	0	0
Feuer	fire	44.12	33.33	66.67	66.67	0	0
Stein	stone	41.18	38.1	66.67	0	0	0
Wasser	water	58.82	42.86	88.89	66.67	100	0
Name	name	32.35	33.33	33.33	33.33	0	0

Table 17.3: Saturation values per order of derivation, verbs.

Verbs		Saturation value (%)	1st order (%)	2nd order (%)	3rd order (%)	4th order (%)	5th order (%)
schneiden	'cut'	26.14	27.78	29.03	25		0
graben	'dig'	25	27.78	32.26	12.5	0	0
ziehen	'pull'	61.36	52.78	64.52	68.75	80	0
werfen	'throw'	50	30.56	64.52	75	20	0
geben	'give'	34.09	30.56	35.48	37.5	40	0
halten	'hold'	50	41.67	58.06	56.25	40	0
nähen	'sew'	35.23	27.78	41.94	58.33	20	0
brennen	'burn'	25	25	29.03	25	0	0
trinken	'drink'	30.68	19.44	35.48	58.33	40	0
wissen	'know'	14.77	13.89	12.9	18.75	20	0

The adjective *alt* 'old' in Table 17.4 has the highest saturation value. In contrast, *gerade* 'straight' is the adjective with the lowest saturation value.

Table 17.4: Saturation values per order of derivation, adjectives.

Adjectives		Saturation value (%)	1st order (%)	2nd order (%)	3rd order (%)	4th order (%)	5th order (%)
schlecht	'bad'	20.97	16.67	14.29	27.27	60	50
neu	'new'	29.03	27.78	33.33	36.36	40	
schwarz	'black'	12.9	22.22	14.29	9.09	0	
gerade	'straight'	8.06	16.67	9.52	0	0	
warm	'warm'	25.81	38.89	28.57	18.18	20	
alt	'old'	35.48	33.33	19.05	36.36	40	50
lang	'long'	22.58	27.78	19.05	28.57	40	50
dünn	'thin'	27.42	44.44	28.57	50	0	
dick	'thick'	20.97	50	19.05	0	0	
eng	'narrow'	25.81	38.89	28.57	50	0	

As shown in Table 17.5, the average saturation value varies between the orders of derivation of all three word-classes. In the 1st and 2nd order, nouns reach the highest average saturation value (39.05% and 49.99%). Verbs have the highest average saturation value in the 2nd and 3rd order (40.32% and 43.54%). Adjectives behave in this respect like nouns in general, while the differences between the individual orders are rather small.

Table 17.5: Average saturation values per order of derivation for all three word-classes.

	1st order	2nd order	3rd order	4th order	5th order
Nouns	39.05	49.99	30	20	0
Verbs	29.72	40.32	43.54	26	0
Adjectives	31.67	21.43	19.99	20	15

17.4 Orders of derivation

In German, the maximum number of orders of nouns and verbs amounts to 4 and adjectives reaches 5, as given in Table 17.6. The average value of all three word-classes is approximately between 2.5 and 4.5.

Table 17.6: Maximum and average number of orders of derivation for all three word-classes.

	Maximum	Average
Nouns	4	2.8
Verbs	4	3.7
Adjectives	5	4.1

17.5 Derivational capacity

With the maximum number of 19 derivatives and an average value of 10.7 derivatives, the verbs in Table 17.7 have the highest capacity of derivation (in the 1st order), whereas the maximum number of noun and adjective derivatives (10 and 9 derivatives) and their average values (8.2 and 5.7 derivatives) are quite similar.

Table 17.7: Maximum and average derivational capacity for all three word-classes.

	Maximum	Average
Nouns	10	8.2
Verbs	19	10.7
Adjectives	9	5.7

As follows from Table 17.8, verbs show the highest average number of derivatives in all orders up to the 4th one. Adjectives represent the lowest average value of derivatives in the 1st order and nouns in the 3rd and 4th orders. Adjectives are the exclusive word-class with an average number beyond the 4th order of derivation.

Table 17.8: Average number of derivatives per order of derivation for all three word-classes.

	1st order	2nd order	3rd order	4th order	5th order
Nouns	8.2	4.5	0.9	0.2	0
Verbs	10.7	12.5	6.5	1.3	0
Adjectives	5.7	4.5	2.2	1	0.3

17.6 Correlation between semantic categories and orders of derivation

For German nouns, there is a strong correlation between the first order of derivation and the semantic categories DIMINUTIVE (e.g. *-lein* of *Äuglein* 'small eye') and QUALITY (e.g. *-ig* of *knochig* 'bony'). There are 9 of the 10 nouns which derive DIMINUTIVE as well as QUALITY words (value 9), followed by DIRECTIONAL (e.g. *-wärts* of *zahnwärts* 'toothways') and PRIVATIVE (e.g. *ent-* of ***ent**wässern* 'to dehydrate') (value 8 each). In the 2nd order, the most characteristic category for nouns is STATIVE (e.g. *-keit* of *Wässrig**keit*** 'wateriness') which appears in each of the 10 nouns. This class is followed by ACTION (e.g. *-ung* of *Benam**ung*** 'naming') (value 9). In the 3rd and 4th order of noun derivation, there is no correlation with semantic categories.

In the 1st order of verbal derivation, the most characteristic semantic classes are ACTION (e.g. *-erei* of *Graberei* 'digging'), AGENT (e.g. *-er* of *Gräber* 'digger'), and ABILITY (e.g. *-bar* of *brenn**bar*** 'burnable'), with a frequency of 9 derivatives each. The second most characteristic semantic class is PURPOSIVE (e.g. *be-* of ***be**graben* 'to inter') with 8 derivatives. With 9 derivatives each, the categories ACTION (e.g. *-ung* of *Verbrennung* 'combustion'), PRIVATIVE (e.g. *un-* of ***un**brennbar* 'unburnable'), ABILITY (e.g. *-bar* of *verbrenn**bar*** 'combustible') and FEMALE (e.g. *-in* of *Schneider**in*** 'tailoress') are the most frequent semantic classes in the 2nd order of verb derivation.

In the 3rd order derivations, 9 verbs derive FEMALE words (e.g. *-in* of *Beschneiderin* 'female circumciser'). Finally, ABILITY words (e.g. *-keit* of *Unbeschneidbar**keit*** 'uncircumcisability') (value 6) are the second most frequent derivatives.

The most characteristic semantic category in the 1st order of adjective derivation is STATIVE (e.g. *-heit* of *Schlechtheit* 'badness') (value 10), followed by QUALITY (e.g. *-lich* of *ältlich* 'oldish') and PATIENT (e.g. *-ling* of *Neuling* 'newcomer') (value 5 each), whereas the most frequent category in the 2nd order is ACTION (e.g. *-ung* of *Entwärmung* 'heat dissipation') with 9 derivatives, followed by STATIVE (e.g. *-heit* of *Ungeradheit* 'unstraightness') (value 7). A strong correlation occurs between the 3rd order of adjective derivation and the semantic class ABILITY (e.g. *-keit* of *Erwärmbarkeit* 'heatability') (value 6). ACTION (e.g. *-ung* in *Verlängerung* 'elongation/extension') (value 5) follows the category ABILITY in the 3rd order of adjective derivation. After the 3rd order of adjective derivation, no correlations to specific semantic categories were established.

17.7 Semantic categories with blocking effects

Irrespective of the order of derivation, FEMALE blocks any further derivation. There is, however, only one suffix (*-in* of e.g. *Schneiderin* 'tailoress') with this semantic category, so the effect can be attributed to this particular affix instead of the semantic category in general. STATIVE is a further semantic category with a blocking effect, represented by the suffix *-keit* of e.g. *Schneidbarkeit* 'cuttability'. An interesting semantic category is DIMINUTIVE (e.g. *-lein* of *Äuglein* 'small eye') that blocks derivation except with the same semantic category, so we find a double marking for DIMINUTIVE in some cases such as in *Knöchelchen* 'bonelet'. The suffixes *-el* and *-chen* are both DIMINUTIVE markers, so *Knöchelchen* results from the suffixation of *Knöchel* 'ankle' and this word from the suffixation of *Knochen* 'bone'. At a more detailed level, more correlations could be observed in the derivational behaviour of individual lexemes, but it is hard to observe any general tendencies in this respect. What seems clear, however, is that it is not the level of derivation that has any influence on blocking of the pertinent kind.

17.8 Typical combinations of semantic categories

All three word-classes (nouns, verbs, and adjectives) have the following combinations as typical semantic relations:
- AGENT-FEMALE (in 4 nouns, 10 verbs, 3 adjectives) (e.g. *Schneider* 'tailor' > *Schneiderin* 'tailoress')

- ABILITY-PRIVATIVE(-ABILITY) (in 2 nouns, 9 verbs, 3 adjectives) (e.g. *entzieh**bar*** 'withdrawable' > *un**entzieh**bar* 'unwithdrawable' > *Un**entzieh**barkeit* 'unwithdrawability')
- PRIVATIVE-ACTION (in 6 nouns, 5 verbs, 3 adjectives) (e.g. *entwärmen* 'to deheat' > *Entwärm**ung*** 'heat dissipation')

For 9 nouns and 4 adjectives, a characteristic semantic combination is QUALITY-STATIVE (e.g. *knoch**ig*** 'bony' > *Knoch**igkeit*** 'boniness'). Furthermore SIMILATIVE-STATIVE (e.g. *schwärz**lich*** 'blackish' > *Schwärz**lichkeit*** 'blackishness') constitutes a typical combination of categories for 6 nouns each and 1 adjective. Moreover, PURPOSIVE-ABILITY (e.g. *befeuern* 'to fire' > *befeuer**bar*** 'firable') is a frequent semantic combination for 8 basic verbs.

17.9 Multiple occurrence of semantic categories

In German, there is no recurrent semantic category in all 10 nouns, verbs and adjectives.

17.10 Reversibility of semantic categories

Within the examined sample of German derivatives, only ABILITY-PRIVATIVE/PRIVATIVE-ABILITY (e.g. *bewässer**bar*** 'waterable' (ABILITY) > *un**bewässer**bar* 'unwaterable' (PRIVATIVE) > *Un**bewässer**barkeit* (ABILITY) 'unwaterableness') is a pair of semantic categories that can occur in a reversed order.

17.11 Conclusions

The result for adjectives is somewhat blurred by the peculiar behaviour of the prefix *ur–* in combination with the lexeme *alt*. In this case, the prefix allows recursive affixation. In the pertinent databases, we have actually found rare occurrences (up to 14 instances) of *ur-*being attached to *alt*. It seems that there is no strict upper limit in this case, and we have refrained from noting data with more than 5 prefix occurrences. What is striking is that this prefix only attaches to a small number of adjectives and allows recursion only in the case of combination with the adjective *alt*. This phenomenon also shows up with some nominal bases of kinship terminology like *Ur-Ur-Großmutter* 'great-great-grandmother'. To give a more representative picture of the behaviour of adjectives in derivational networks, it may seem advisable to leave out the prefix *ur–* completely.

The saturation values of the three word-classes differ to a lesser degree from each other than the differences between the lexemes of one and the same word-class. Complexity stops at the 4th order for nouns and verbs and at the 5th order for adjectives (disregarding the prefix *ur-*). Regarding the average number of orders of derivations, adjectives have the highest value of all word-classes if *ur-* is included, but a lower value than verbs (3.5 compared to 3.7) if it is ignored. In any case, nouns show the lowest value in this category. With regard to the total number of data for the three word-classes, the picture is different: our data set contains 184 derived words based on simple nouns, 414 based on simple verbs, and 205 based on simple adjectives. Thus, verbs show by far the highest value of derivational capacity.

The number of semantic categories that we found attested in our data is not very high. The picture would be different if, particularly in the set of verbs, more data were taken into account. A number of otherwise unattested semantic categories have representatives among compound verbs with a preposition as the first element, a structural type that many grammars regard as instances of derivation. What is remarkable with regard to the combination of semantic categories is that DIMINUTIVE blocks any further derivation of semantic categories other than itself.

References

Duden. 2016. *Die Grammatik* [Grammar], 9th edn. Berlin: Dudenverlag.
Eisenberg, Peter. 2013. *Grundriss der deutschen Grammatik Band 1: Das Wort* [Outline of German Grammar. Volume 1: Word], 4th edn. Stuttgart & Weimar: Metzler.
Hentschel, Elke & Harald Weydt. 2013. *Handbuch der deutschen Grammatik* [Handbook of German Grammar], 4th edn. Berlin & Boston: de Gruyter.
Neef, Martin. 2009. IE, Germanic: German. In Rochelle Lieber & Pavol Štekauer (eds.), *The Oxford Handbook of Compounding*, 386–399. Oxford: Oxford University Press.
Olsen, Susan. 1990. Zum Begriff des morphologischen Heads [About the Term Morphological Head]. *Deutsche Sprache* 1990 (2). 126–148.
Weinrich, Harald. 1993. *Textgrammatik der deutschen Sprache* [Text Grammar of the German Language]. Mannheim: Dudenverlag.

Sources

Dudenredaktion. n.d. *Duden-Online*. www.duden.de/woerterbuch.
Fleischer, Wolfgang & Irmhild Barz. 2012. *Wortbildung der deutschen Gegenwartssprache* [Word-Formation in Present-Day German], 4th edn. Berlin: de Gruyter.
Muthmann, Gustav. 1991. *Rückläufiges deutsches Wörterbuch* [Reverse German Dictionary], 2nd edn. Tübingen: Niemeyer.
Splett, Jochen. 2009. *Deutsches Familienwörterbuch* [Dictionary of word families in German], 18 vols. Berlin & New York: de Gruyter.

Thorsteinn G. Indridason
18 Derivational networks in Icelandic

18.1 General notes

Derivation and compounding are the two main processes of productive word-formation in Icelandic. Derivation is divided into prefixation and suffixation, and is used for various purposes; for example, to express the opposite meaning of the base word, as in *þægur*_A 'obedient' > *ó-þægur*_A 'disobedient' (prefixation), or to derive a noun denoting action from a verb, like *skipa* 'to order' > *skip-un* 'an order' (suffixation). Derivation can also be expressed by means of a stem-internal vowel change, although this type is not productive, such as *bíða*_V 'to wait' > *bið*_N 'waiting' and *ljúka*_V 'to finish' > *lok*_N 'end', or it can be expressed through *i*-umlaut as in *langur*_A 'long' > *lengd*_N 'length' or *þungur*_A 'heavy' > *þyngd*_N 'weight'. Conversion is also possible, both from verb to noun like *koma*_V 'come' > *koma*_N 'arrival' and from noun to verb, like *leir*_N 'clay' > *leira*_V 'to play with clay'.

In prefixation, the prefixed element does not change the word-class of the base word, but prefixation does add meaning in most cases. Prefixes in Icelandic are divided into several categories depending on their semantic role (see Kvaran 2005: 125–130). Prefixes can be used to emphasize the meaning of the base, as in *aðal-* 'main'; they can express negative meaning, as in *van-* 'too little of something'; or they can denote position, as in *ná-* 'near', or that something is repeated, like *sí-* 'always'. Prefixes can vary in productivity (see e.g. Þorgeirsdóttir 1986 and Kvaran 2005).

Suffixation can form a word of a different word-class than the base word. It can, for example, derive a noun from a verb, but sometimes the word-class does not change. Suffixes, like prefixes, can also derive a different meaning from that of the base word, for example when a noun denoting an AGENT is derived from verbs, as in *kenna* 'teach' > *kenn-ari* 'teacher', or a noun denoting an INSTRUMENT is derived from a verb, as in *hreyfa* 'to move' > *hreyf-ill* 'motor'. Various linking elements can occur between the base word and the derivational suffixes, and they are usually interpreted as genitive endings, e.g. *dólg-s*(gen.sg. of nom.sg. *dólg-ur*)-*legur*(nom.sg.) 'rude' and *barn-a*(gen.pl. of nom.sg. *barn*)-*skapur*(nom.sg.) 'childishness'.[1] Derivational suffixes, like prefixes, vary in productivity. The suffix -*leg* is the most productive one, while suffixes like -*ari*, -*ing*, -*un*, and -*ug* are quite

---

[1] The suffixes in question originate historically from independent words through grammaticalization.

https://doi.org/10.1515/9783110686630-018

productive as well, but their productivity is considerably more limited than that of -*leg*. The suffixes -*ling* and -*ul* are semi-productive, while others like -*ald*, -*erni*, -*indi* and -*nað* have little or no productivity, i.e. few new forms are formed with them in the language today (see e.g. Indriðason 2008, 2016).

In developing derivational networks for Icelandic, some challenges were registered. In Icelandic there exist quite a number of word-forms that have a somewhat unclear status in word-formation, i.e. they are neither typical affixes nor independent words. Some of these can be categorized as prefixoids, like the bound intensifiers *hund-* 'dog', *ösku-* 'ash' and *band* 'thread' in *hund-skamma* lit. dog-scold, 'to scold forcefully', *ösku-illur* lit. ash-furious, 'absolutely furious' and *band-óður* lit. thread-mad, 'raving mad', respectively. Common to most of these intensifiers is that they can be translated as 'very' or 'extremely' (see Indriðason 2018). And there exist many suffix-like forms that are not easy to categorize either. They form nouns, such as -*fari* in *geim-fari* lit. space-traveller, 'astronaut', -*hýsi* as in *hjól-hýsi* lit. wheel-(small)house, 'caravan' and -*nætti* as in *lág-nætti* lit. low-night, 'midnight'. Others form adjectives, like -*lægur* in *land-lægur* lit. land-based, 'endemic', -*rækinn* in *skyldu-rækinn* lit. duty-fulfilling, 'conscientious' and -*gengur* in *hæg-gengur* lit. slow-walking, 'slow'. Many of these forms have been classified as affixoids and semi-words (see Indriðason 2016, 2018) and are thus excluded from the Icelandic networks since they do not fit in with the traditional definitions of prefix and suffix.

The two main sources of data were the electronic corpora *Íslenskur orðasjóður* (Corpus of Icelandic Websites) provided by Leipzig University, Germany, and *Mörkuð íslensk málheild* (Tagged Icelandic Corpus) provided by Stofnun Árna Magnússonar, University of Iceland.

18.2 Maximum derivational networks

In Table 18.1 below, verbs exhibit the highest number of derivational networks in the 1st and 2nd orders and the highest number in total (24), compared to adjectives (in second place with 17) and nouns (in third with 15). Note that no derivations are registered in the 4th or 5th order in any of the word-classes.

18.3 Saturation values

The mean saturation values in nouns range between 6.67% and 33.33%, as shown in Table 18.2. The noun with the highest saturation value is *tönn* 'tooth'

Table 18.1: Maximum derivational networks per order of derivation for all three word-classes.

	1st order	2nd order	3rd order	Σ
Nouns	12	2	1	15
Verbs	15	8	1	24
Adjectives	13	4	0	17
TOTAL	40	14	2	56

Table 18.2: Saturation values per order of derivation, nouns.

Nouns		Saturation value (%)	1st order (%)	2nd order (%)	3rd order (%)
bone	bein	6.67	8.33	0	0
eye	auga	6.67	8.33	0	0
tooth	tönn	33.33	25.00	50.00	100.00
day	dagur	20.00	25.00	0	0
dog	hundur	26.67	33.33	0	0
louse	lús	20.00	25.00	0	0
fire	eldur	13.33	16.67	0	0
stone	steinn	6.67	8.33	0	0
water	vatn	20.00	16.67	50.00	0
name	nafn	26.67	25.00	50.00	0

(33.33%), which also happens to be the only noun with a 3rd order value. On the other hand, the nouns *bein* 'bone', *auga* 'eye' and *steinn* 'stone' have the lowest mean saturation values (6.67%) and they also, along with several other nouns, lack a 2nd order. The noun *hundur* 'dog' has the highest value in the 1st order (33.33%), while *bein* 'bone', *auga* 'eye' and *steinn* 'stone' have the lowest values (8.33%).

The mean saturation values in verbs range between 4.17% and 45.83%, as shown in Table 18.3. The verb with the highest mean saturation value is *vita* 'know' (45.83%), while *halda* 'hold' has the lowest value (4.17%). The verb *henda* 'throw' is the only verb that has a 3rd order value. The verb *brenna* 'burn' has the

Table 18.3: Saturation values per order of derivation, verbs.

Verbs		Saturation value (%)	1st order (%)	2nd order (%)	3rd order (%)
cut	skera	25.00	40.00	0	0
dig	grafa	25.00	40.00	0	0
pull	toga	16.67	20.00	12.50	0
throw	henda	16.67	13.33	12.50	100.00
give	gefa	25.00	33.33	12.50	0
hold	halda	4.17	6.67	0	0
sew	sauma	12.50	20.00	0	0
burn	brenna	37.50	46.67	25.00	0
drink	drekka	25.00	20.00	37.50	0
know	vita	45.83	40.00	62.50	0

highest value in the 1st order (46.67%), followed by *skera* 'cut' and *grafa* 'dig' (both 40.00%), while the verb *halda* 'hold' has the lowest value (6.67%).

The mean saturation values in the adjectives range between 0% and 47.06%, as shown in Table 18.4. The adjective with the highest mean saturation value is *þykkur* 'thick' (47.06%), followed by *nýr* 'new' and *langur* 'long' (35.29%), while *heitur* 'warm' has the lowest value (0%). The adjectives *nýr* 'new', *langur* 'long' and *þykkur* 'thick' are the only adjectives that have 2nd order values. The adjective *þykkur* 'thick' also has the highest value in the 1st order (46.15%), followed by *nýr* 'new' (38.46%), but *heitur* 'warm' has the lowest value (0%).

Table 18.4: Saturation values per order of derivation, adjectives.

Adjectives		Saturation value (%)	1st order (%)	2nd order (%)
narrow	þröngur	11.76	15.38	0
old	gamall	23.53	30.77	0
straight	beinn	23.53	30.77	0
new	nýr	35.29	38.46	25
long	langur	35.29	30.77	50

Table 18.4 (continued)

Adjectives		Saturation value (%)	1st order (%)	2nd order (%)
warm	heitur	0	0	0
thick	þykkur	47.06	46.15	50
bad	slæmur	11.76	15.38	0
thin	mjór	23.53	30.77	0
black	svartur	17.65	23.08	0

Table 18.5 shows the average saturation value per order of derivation for all the nouns, verbs and adjectives in the Icelandic sample. The saturation value in the 1st order is highest in verbs (28.00%), followed by 26.20% for adjectives, and is lowest in nouns (19.20%). The same is true for the 2nd order, where verbs score highest, viz. 16.30%, but nouns (15.00%) score higher than adjectives (12.50%). In the 3rd order, verbs and nouns score alike at 10.00%. There are no examples of 3rd order derivations for adjectives; consequently, the saturation value for adjectives in the 3rd order is zero. Generally, there are few examples of 2nd and 3rd order derivations in the Icelandic sample.

Table 18.5: Average saturation values per order of derivation for all three word-classes.

	1st order	2nd order	3rd order
Nouns	19.20	15.00	10.00
Verbs	28.00	16.30	10.00
Adjectives	26.20	12.50	0

18.4 Orders of derivation

As shown above (Table 18.1), the maximum number of orders in the Icelandic sample is three. In Table 18.6, we can see that the average numbers of orders in nouns, verbs and adjectives lie between 1 and 1.5.

Table 18.6: Maximum and average number of orders of derivation for all three word-classes.

	Maximum	Average
Nouns	3	1
Verbs	3	1.5
Adjectives	2	1.2

18.5 Derivational capacity

In Table 18.7, there are figures for the average and maximum numbers of derivatives in the 1st order. Verbs have the highest value, and nouns, the lowest. The verb *brenna* 'burn' has the highest derivational capacity (7 derivations in the 1st order). The numbers in Table 18.7 show that a simple noun in Icelandic typically produces 2.3 derivations, a simple verb typically produces 4.2 derivations, and a simple adjective typically produces 3.4 derivations.

Table 18.7: Maximum and average derivational capacity for all three word-classes.

	Maximum	Average
Nouns	4	2.3
Verbs	7	4.2
Adjectives	6	3.4

In Table 18.8, the average derivational capacities for all orders and for all word-classes are presented. Verbs have the highest average capacity in the 1st and 2nd orders, while nouns have the lowest capacity in the same orders.

18.6 Correlation between semantic categories and orders of derivation

In the 1st order derivations in *nouns*, 4 out of the 10 nouns produce derivations within the semantic categories QUALITY and STATE, such as *bein* 'bone' > *beinlaus*$_A$

Table 18.8: Average number of derivatives per order of derivation for all three word-classes.

	1st order	2nd order	3rd order
Nouns	2.3	0.3	0.1
Verbs	4.2	1.3	0.1
Adjectives	3.4	0.5	0

'boneless' and *lús* 'louse' > *lúsugur*$_A$ 'lousy', and 3 out of the 10 produce derivations with the semantic category ACTION, such as *steinn* 'stone' > *steining*$_N$ 'stoning', followed by 2 out of 10 nouns with RESULTATIVE, AGENT and ITERATIVE derivations. In the 2nd order, only two categories produce derivations, viz. STATE with 2 out of the 10 nouns, such as *tönn* 'tooth' > *tannleysi*$_N$ 'toothlessness', and QUALITY with 1 out of 10 nouns: *nafn* 'name' > *nafnleysi*$_N$ 'anonymity'. Within the category AGENT, one finds the only derivation in the 3rd order in nouns, viz. *tönn* 'tooth' > *tannleysingi*$_N$ 'toothless individual'.

In the 1st order derivations of verbs, 6 out of the 10 produce derivations within the semantic category ACTION, such as *henda* 'throw' > *afhenda*$_V$ 'deliver', while 5 out of the 10 produce derivations within the semantic category INSTRUMENT, such as *toga* 'pull' > *togari*$_N$ 'trawler', and 4 out of the 10 produce derivations within the categories QUALITY, RESULTATIVE and AGENT. In the 2nd order, 3 out of the 10 verbs produce derivations within the semantic category QUALITY, such as *brenna* 'burn' > *torbrennanlegur*$_A$ 'difficult to burn', but 2 out of the 10 verbs produce derivations within the categories ACTION and AGENT. The only 3rd order derivation in the sample is in the category ACTION, viz. *henda* 'throw' > *endurafhending*$_N$ 'redeliverance'.

In the 1st order of derivations of adjectives, 7 out of the 10 produce derivations within the semantic category STATE, such as *mjór* 'thin' > *mjóni*$_N$ 'skinny', 6 out of the 10 within the category QUALITY, such as *beinn* 'straight' > *óbeinn*$_A$ 'indirect', and 5 out of the 10 within the category MANNER, such as *langur* 'long' > *aflangur*$_A$ 'oblong'. In the 2nd order, 2 out of the 10 adjectives produce derivations within the semantic category QUALITY, such as *langur* 'long' > *langsamlega*$_{Adv}$ 'by far'. No derivations were registered in the 3rd order.

It seems like QUALITY has a strong presence in all word-classes in the 1st order along with STATE, especially in nouns and adjectives, and the same tendency is also found in the 2nd order. Only two derivations were registered in the 3rd order, in the categories AGENT (nouns) and ACTION (verbs).

18.7 Semantic categories with blocking effects

In Icelandic, the derivational power of the system is severely reduced after the 1st order of derivations, and there are relatively few derivations in the 2nd order and only one derivation in the 3nd order in nouns and verbs, respectively, and none in adjectives.

Regarding the 1st order of nouns, the blocking categories are AGENT (2), ITERATIVE (1), RESULTATIVE (2), ACTION (3), PROCESS (1), MANNER (1) and SIMILATIVE (1). In the 2nd order, STATE (1) and QUALITY (1) block further derivations, and in the 3rd order, AGENT (1) blocks further derivations.[2]

Regarding the 1st order of verbs, the blocking categories are INSTRUMENT (1), RESULTATIVE (1), AGENT (1), STATE (1) and MANNER (1). In the 2nd order, PROCESS (1), AGENT (1), QUALITY (2), ACTION (1) and STATE (1) are the blocking categories. In the 3rd order of verbs, the blocking category is ACTION (1).

In the 1st order of adjectives, the blocking categories are STATE (7), MANNER (6), TEMPORAL (1), CAUSATIVE (1) and ACTION (1). In the 2nd order, the blocking categories are QUALITY (1), RESULTATIVE (1) and PROCESS (1).

To conclude, some semantic categories – independently of the order in which they occur – seem to restrain further derivation, namely categories like RESULTATIVE, ACTION, PROCESS and MANNER, but there appears to be no strong correlation between a semantic category and a particular order of derivation.

18.8 Typical combinations of semantic categories

In the Icelandic sample, there are several types of combination of semantic categories. Nearly all examples that were found are presented here. In nouns, there are combinations like STATE-AGENT (*tannleysi*$_N$ 'toothlessness' > *tannleysingi*$_N$ 'toothless individual'), STATE-STATE (*vatnslaus*$_A$ 'without water' > *vatnsleysi*$_N$ 'shortage of water') and QUALITY-QUALITY (*nafnlaus*$_A$ 'nameless' > *nafnleysi*$_N$ 'anonymity').

In verbs, there is PROCESS-PROCESS (*togun* 'towing' > *tognun*$_N$ 'sprain'), ACTION-ACTION (*afhenda*$_V$ 'deliver' > *afhending*$_N$ 'deliverance'), ACTION-AGENT (*útgefa*$_V$ 'publish' > *útgefandi*$_N$ 'publisher'), QUALITY-QUALITY (e.g. *brennanlegur*$_A$ 'burnable' > *torbrennanlegur*$_A$ 'difficult to burn'), AGENT-QUALITY (*vitni*$_N$ 'witness' > *forvitni*$_N$ 'curiosity') and AGENT-AGENT (*vitni*$_N$ 'witness' > *aðalvitni*$_N$ 'main witness').

---

[2] The number of basic words to which the blocking effect of individual semantic categories applies is shown in parentheses for each semantic category in question and for each word-class.

In adjectives, there is RESULTATIVE-QUALITY (*nýjung*$_N$ 'innovation' > *nýjungagirni*$_N$ 'innovativeness'), QUALITY-QUALITY (e.g. *langsamur*$_A$ 'prolonged' > *langsamlega*$_{Adv}$ 'by far'), ANTICAUSATIVE-ENTITY (e.g. *þykkna*$_V$ 'to thicken' > *þykkni*$_N$ 'extract') and ENTITY-PROCESS (e.g. *þykkni*$_N$ 'extract' > *þykknun*$_N$ 'thickening').

18.9 Multiple occurrence of semantic categories

There are several cases of multiple occurrence in one derivational chain. The first is STATE-STATE-AGENT, as in *tönn*$_N$ 'tooth' > *tannlaus*$_A$ 'toothless' > *tannleysi*$_N$ 'toothlessness' > *tannleysingi*$_N$ 'toothless individual'. Another one is ACTION-ACTION-ACTION, as in *henda*$_V$ 'throw' > *afhenda*$_V$ 'deliver' > *afhending*$_N$ 'deliverance' > *endurafhending*$_N$ 'redeliverance'. The third case is QUALITY-QUALITY, as in *brenna*$_V$ 'burn' > *brennanlegur*$_A$ 'burnable' > *torbrennanlegur*$_A$ 'difficult to burn'. The last case is AGENT-AGENT, as in *vitni*$_N$ 'witness' > *aðalvitni*$_N$ 'main witness'.

18.10 Reversibility of semantic categories

Reversed orders of semantic categories do not occur. This is clearly due to severe restrictions on the order of derivational suffixes in Icelandic, where the possibility of reversing the order depends, among other things, on selectional restrictions of each derivational suffix, e.g. the types of bases (number of syllables) it attaches to, types of word-classes, and semantic roles.

18.11 Conclusions

Icelandic is a language with a relatively small derivational network. By focussing on clear cases of prefixation and suffixation, excluding affixoids and other forms that are placed between a word and an affix and furthermore excluding derivation by vowel shift of Indo-European descent and derivation by conversion, the measurable derivational force of the Icelandic system is reduced considerably. The derivation is mainly placed in the 1st order category, as was found in the data, with a total of 99 derivations in nouns, verbs and adjectives compared to 21 in the 2nd order and two in the 3rd order. Some of these features explain why there is a considerable decline in the number of derivations in the 2nd order, only two 3rd order derivations and no 4th or 5th order derivations. Other possible explanations may be sought in the rich productivity of the compounding system, the rich inflectional morphology of Icelandic, where inflection expresses some of the categories often expressed by derivation in other languages, and in the multiple functions of syntactic expressions.

The most frequent semantic categories in the 1st order of derivations are QUALITY and STATE in nouns and adjectives, and ACTION in verbs.

References

Indriðason, Þorsteinn G. 2008. Um virkar og frjósamar orðmyndunarreglur í íslensku [On productive and profitable word-formation rules in Icelandic]. *Íslenskt mál* 30: 93–120.

Indriðason, Þorsteinn G. 2016. 143. Icelandic. In Peter O. Müller, Ingeborg Ohnheiser, Susan Olsen & Franz Rainer (eds.), *Word-Formation. An International Handbook of the Languages of Europe, vol. 4*, 2578–2600. Berlin & Boston: Mouton de Gruyter.

Indriðason, Þorsteinn G. 2018. On Bound Intensifiers in Icelandic. In Hans Götzsche (ed.), *The Meaning of Language*, 148–170. Newcastle: Cambridge Scholars Publishing.

Íslenskur orðasjóður [Corpus of text from Icelandic websites]. http://corpora.uni-leipzig.de/de?corpusId=isl_web_2005 (last accessed 20 December 2017).

Kvaran, Guðrún. 2005. Orð. *Handbók um beygingar- og orðmyndunarfræði (Íslensk tunga II)*. [Words. A handbook of inflectional and derivational morphology (Icelandic language II)]. Reykjavík: Almenna bókafélagið.

Mörkuð íslensk málheild [Tagged Icelandic corpus]. http://mim.hi.is (last accessed 20 December 2017).

Þorgeirsdóttir, Sigrún. 1986. *Um forskeyti í íslensku* [On prefixes in Icelandic]. Reykjavík: University of Iceland MA thesis.

John Ole Askedal
19 Derivational networks in Norwegian

19.1 General notes

Norwegian is a North Germanic language spoken by approximately five million people, mainly living in the Kingdom of Norway. Norwegian comes in two official varieties, Bokmål (BM; 'Book Language') and Nynorsk (NN; 'New Norwegian'), neither of which is internally uniform with regard to morphology or the phonological makeup of word forms to the same extent as most other European standard languages. In addition, there is a traditional, more uniform norm called Riksmål (RM; 'Language of the Realm'), which is, with marginal exceptions, included in the options of the official Bokmål norm as a 'moderate' variety.

In the following, I shall concentrate on the more common Bokmål variety used by about 90% of the population as the preferred written medium; differences between the two official varieties are in general not relevant to the descriptive tasks at hand. Where two semantically equivalent word forms exist in principle, I shall pick the one that appears to be more widespread in the modern language when a clear choice can be made; when that is not the case, two forms (one which coincides with Nynorsk) will be given.

19.1.1 Affixation in Norwegian

Norwegian possesses derivational suffixes as well as derivational prefixes. The various affixes are somewhat unevenly distributed among the various word-classes. According to Askedal (2016: 2536–2538), whose work is based on a number of authoritative sources, there are 47 more or less common noun-forming suffixes, 22 of which are native or naturalized suffixes of German origin, 7 specifically NN, and 18 of Romance or neoclassical foreign origin. There are 30 common adjective suffixes, comprising 12 native and naturalized German, 7 specifically NN, and 11 Romance and neoclassical suffixes (Askedal 2016: 2543–2543). Only three productive verb suffixes exist, which may also be considered variants (Askedal 2016: 2545).

Prefixes tell a different story. In Proto-Norse, most ancient Germanic prefixes were lost, including, in particular, the cognates of standard High German – *be-*, *er-*, *ge-*, and *ver-* – and their Middle Low German equivalents. In Modern Norwegian, verbs and adjectives as well as nouns show five or six autochthonous Nordic prefixes and an equal number of originally Middle Low or High

German prefixes (cf. Askedal 2016: 2541, 2544–2547). Prefixes are far more typical of verbs than of nouns and adjectives.

In particular, the number of verbs carrying the prefixes *an-*, *be-*, *er-*, and *for-* of German descent is large, due to an extended borrowing period that lasted for several hundred years. It should be noted, however, that although numerous verbs carry the prefixes in question, this does not necessarily mean that these prefixes are productive in the sense that they combine easily or freely with native Norwegian lexical material; in fact, rather the opposite appears to be the case (Enger and Conzett 2016: 288–289).

To these Nordic and originally German prefixes approximately 20 more or less common prefixes of neoclassical, Greek or Latin origin can be added in the domain of nouns and adjectives; with regard to verbs, their number may be somewhat lower (cf. Askedal et al. 2016: 179, 184–185, 190).

Prefixes affect the meaning of the word to which they are appended but not its word-class. Suffixes, on the other hand, most often effect a change of word-class.

Only a few autochthonous or originally German affixes are relevant in connection with the words in the Norwegian sample, and the neoclassical ones not at all. In addition to the affixes, Norwegian also possesses a number of 'linking' (or 'liaison') elements (above all *-e-* and *-s-*, as for instance in *holdning-s-løs* 'unprincipled, indecisive'). They are primarily found in compounds but occur in connection with a few suffixes, too. They are not counted as independent suffixes.

Confixes, which are mostly of foreign, neoclassical origin, are not empirically relevant in the present context. Native nouns that only occur as second elements in compounds, like *-drikker* (which appears to be obsolete in isolation) in *stordrikker* 'heavy drinker', are excluded, too.

Basically, word-formation by means of affixes is primarily a question of recurrent bound linguistic elements. The degree of productivity of such recurrent elements varies greatly, ranging from fossilization to coverage of the better part of a word-class.

Norwegian makes considerably less use of 'synthetic', affixal word-formation than a number of the other languages in the sample. Instead, compounding and various syntactic strategies are used, the latter betraying a bent towards overall typological 'analyticity'. One interesting construction type involving both the analytical and the synthetic typological options is provided by those verbs that may have a preposition or an adverb either as the 'free', non-bound part of a phrasal verb or as part of a composite verb stem. In such cases, there is often a difference in meaning between the two options, such as for *vende om* 'to turn around' vs. *omvende* 'to convert'; however, this is not always the case, e.g. *føye sammen* and *sammenføye*, both meaning 'to join, unite'. These observations are related to the more general fact that a great number of verbs, which, were they Slavic, would be analyzed as containing prefixes, are compounds from a Norwegian perspective.

19.1.2 Methodological issues

Prepositions, adverbs and similar forms functioning as lexical elements are not considered prefixes in verbs, but as parts of composite verbs, resulting in a clearly delimited group of true prefixes.

Ø-affixes or instances of word-formation by conversion or transposition, being non-affixal, are not accepted as data. Consequently, in certain instances, secondary derivations have to be described as 1st order derivations. For instance, the verb corresponding to *vann* 'water' is *vanne* 'to water, irrigate' with no manifest derivational affix; the *-e* at the end of the word is the infinitive ending, just as *-er* in *vanner* '(he/she/it) waters, irrigates' is the present tense ending. Hence, the action noun *vanning* 'watering, irrigation' either has to be omitted or described as a 1st order derivation from *vann* 'water'. Here, the latter option is chosen.

The relationship between the adjective *svart* 'black' and the corresponding CAUSATIVE verb *sverte* 'to blacken, polish; to tarnish' is treated similarly. The umlaut vowel in the verb is neither a suffix nor an infix, but the reflex of a Germanic derivational suffix that has left no other trace. Such cases are excluded from the data.

It seems intuitively natural to apply the notion of derivation to pairs of words where some sort of semantic relatedness is obtained. Thus, the CAUSATIVE verb *fortynne* 'to dilute' with the prefix *for-* is connected with the adjective *tynn* 'thin', and *besvare* 'to reply to, answer' is clearly derived from *svare* 'to answer, reply' with the transitivizing prefix *be-*. In a number of other prefix verbs, there is lexical root correspondence but no obvious general semantic relationship between a verb with a derivational affix and the corresponding verb without the affix; consider for instance the following: *dra* 'to pull' vs. *bedra* 'to betray' or *fordra* 'to tolerate, stand'; *kaste* 'to throw' vs. *forkaste* 'to reject'; *gi* 'to give' vs. *angi* 'to denounce, inform on' or *begi* 'to give up; (REFLEXIVE) to go'; and *skjære* 'to cut' vs. *forskjære* 'to mix one sort of wine or spirits with another'. Such instantiations of a derivational pattern are not part of the data. This decision is supported by the historical fact that the verbs in question were borrowed wholesale from Middle Low or High German; their meaning is the result of semantic developments in the variety of German from which they were borrowed, not of autochthonous Nordic semantic developments.

The semantic categories that serve to characterize derivational relationships basically form a closed conceptual universe. 2nd and higher order derivations form, in the normal state of affairs, sequences of different semantic categories (cf. section 19.9).

19.1.3 Sources

To establish the Norwegian data, *Norsk ordbok med 1000 illustrasjoner: Riksmål og moderat bokmål* (NO 2008) was used as the primary source. This modern one-volume BM/RM dictionary is a widely used and reliable guide to the non-Nynorsk variety of modern standard Norwegian, having more than 81,000 entries. It is supplemented by the recent digital BM/RM dictionary *Det Norske Akademis ordbok* (NAOB), which has approximately 225,000 entries and 300,000 authentic quotations. In most instances, the two dictionaries provide convergent information. To decide questions of occurrence and representativeness, recourse is taken to searches on Google. This is above all done in connection with theoretically possible, and intuitively natural, results of word-formation patterns that are productive elsewhere in the data but are not listed in the two dictionaries. In such cases, one attestation is considered in principle as sufficient proof of actual occurrence in the language. Theoretically possible derivations whose existence cannot thus be verified empirically are not accepted as data.

19.2 Maximum derivational networks

As shown in Table 19.1 below, nouns and adjectives are limited to 1st and 2nd order derivations. These orders predominate even in the case of verbs, but verbs allow for a small number of 3rd, 4th and 5th order derivations, too, the

Table 19.1: Maximum derivational networks per order of derivation for all three word-classes.

	1st order	2nd order	3rd order	4th order	5th order	Σ
Nouns	18	7	0	0	0	25
Verbs	14	12	3	1	1	31
Adjectives	17	10	0	0	0	27
TOTAL	49	29	3	1	1	83

latter being limited to the two verbs *vite* 'to know' and *drikke* 'to drink'. In view of this, the number of derivations is fairly similar in the three word-classes.

19.3 Saturation values

The mean saturation value for the nouns varies between 12% and 48% (cf. Table 19.2). The highest mean saturation value is found with *navn* 'name', sporting 48%, and the lowest with *tann* 'tooth' and *lus* 'louse', both showing 12%. Three nouns – *øye* 'eye', *tann* 'tooth', and *lus* 'louse' – have no 2nd order derivations. In the 1st order, *navn* 'name' has the highest saturation value with 39.39%, and *tann* 'tooth' and *lus* 'louse' have the lowest, showing 16.67%.

Table 19.2: Saturation values per order of derivation, nouns.

Nouns		Saturation value (%)	1st order (%)	2nd order (%)	3rd order (%)	4th order (%)	5th order (%)
bone	ben, bein	24	27.78	14.29	0	0	0
eye	øye	16	22.22	0	0	0	0
tooth	tann	12	16.67	0	0	0	0
day	dag	20	22.22	14.29	0	0	0
dog	hund	24	22.22	28.57	0	0	0
louse	lus	12	16.67	0	0	0	0
fire	ild	20	22.22	14.29	0	0	0
stone	sten, stein	28	22.22	42.86	0	0	0
water	vann	36	33.33	42.86	0	0	0
name	navn	48	38.39	71.43	0	0	0

In the case of the verbs shown in Table 19.3, the mean saturation values range from 3.23% with *kaste* 'to throw' to 29.03%, found for *holde* 'to hold' and *brenne* 'to burn'. The latter verb – *brenne* – is also, with 50%, the verb with the highest saturation value in the 1st order. The three verbs *dra* 'pull', *kaste* 'to throw', and *gi* 'to give' are limited to 1st order derivations; the remaining seven verbs also have 2nd order derivations and, as noted, *drikke* 'to drink' and *vite* 'to

Table 19.3: Saturation values per order of derivation, verbs.

Verbs		Saturation value (%)	1st order (%)	2nd order (%)	3rd order (%)	4th order (%)	5th order (%)
cut	skjære	25.81	35.71	25	0	0	0
dig	grave	16.13	21.43	16.67	0	0	0
pull	dra	9.68	21.43	0	0	0	0
throw	kaste	3.23	7.14	0	0	0	0
give	gi	6.45	14.29	0	0	0	0
hold	holde	29.03	42.86	25	0	0	0
sew	sy	9.68	14.29	8.33	0	0	0
burn	brenne	29.03	50	16.67	0	0	0
drink	drikke	32.26	35.71	33.33	33.33	0	0
know	vite	22.58	14.29	8.33	66.67	100	100

know' occur in the 3rd and 4th orders, too, and *vite* even occurs in a 4th and a 5th order derivation.

Concerning adjectives, the mean saturation values are on the whole more evenly distributed than in the two previous word-classes, ranging from 7.41% with *smal* 'narrow', *varm* 'warm' and *dårlig* 'bad' to 37.04% with *ny* 'new', *lang* 'long' and *tykk, tjukk* 'thick'. These two saturation values represent 6 of the total of 10 adjectives. Half the number of adjectives lack 2nd order derivations, viz. *gammel* 'old', *rett* 'straight', *varm* 'warm', *dårlig* 'bad' and *sort, svart* 'black'. The four adjectives *ny* 'new', *tykk, tjukk* 'thick', *tynn* 'thin' and *sort, svart* 'black' share the highest saturation value (35.29%) in the 1st order (cf. Table 19.4).

Table 19.5 presents the average saturation values per order of derivation for all nouns, verbs and adjectives in the Norwegian sample. The average saturation values are low and are almost identical in 1st order derivations in all three word-classes, where they range from 24.12% to 25.72%, while in the 2nd order they range from 13.33% to 22.86%. With nouns, 1st and 2nd order derivations have very similar saturation values. In the rather marginal 3rd, 4th and 5th order derivations, found only with verbs, the saturation values are uniformly 10%.

Table 19.4: Saturation values per order of derivation, adjectives.

Adjectives		Saturation value (%)	1st order (%)	2nd order (%)	3rd order (%)	4th order (%)	5th order (%)
narrow	smal	7.41	5.89	10	0	0	0
old	gammel	14.81	23.53	0	0	0	0
straight	rett	11.11	17.65	0	0	0	0
new	ny	37.04	35.29	40	0	0	0
long	lang	37.04	29.41	50	0	0	0
warm	varm	7.41	11.76	0	0	0	0
thick	tykk, tjukk	37.04	35.29	40	0	0	0
bad	dårlig	7.41	11.76	0	0	0	0
thin	tynn	33.33	35.29	30	0	0	0
black	sort, svart	22.22	35.29	0	0	0	0

Table 19.5: Average saturation values per order of derivation for all three word-classes.

	1st order	2nd order	3rd order	4th order	5th order
Nouns	24.44	22.86	0	0	0
Verbs	25.72	13.33	10	10	10
Adjectives	24.12	17	0	0	0

19.4 Orders of derivation

The maximum order attested in the Norwegian sample is five. This is only found once, in a derivation headed by the verb *vite* 'to know'. In the case of nouns and adjectives, the maximum order is two. With regard to maximum order, nouns and adjectives are roughly comparable. Verbs are slightly higher on the scale, due to the presence of 3rd, 4th and even 5th orders.

Table 19.6: Maximum and average number of orders of derivation for all three word-classes.

	Maximum	Average
Nouns	2	1.7
Verbs	5	2.1
Adjectives	2	1.5

19.5 Derivational capacity

In the Norwegian sample, nouns have the highest average derivational capacity, i.e. the ability to form 1st order derivations, and verbs the lowest. Adjectives appear (almost) in the mathematical middle. With the smallest possible margin, they have the lowest maximum derivational capacity but, on the other hand, there are four adjectives with six 1st order derivations ('new', 'thick', 'thin', 'black'). In comparison, one noun ('name') and one verb ('to burn') have seven 1st order derivations, and one noun ('water') and one verb ('to hold') have six 1st order derivations.

In the 2nd order, the average derivational capacity is virtually the same in all three word-classes Tables 19.7 and 19.8. Further orders are only attested in verbs, where their attestation decreases in perfectly harmonious mathematical order.

Morphologically, Norwegian is a fairly analytical language, albeit with ample productive possibilities of, in particular, NN compounding. This may go some way towards explaining the rather low derivational capacity exemplified by the Norwegian sample.

Table 19.7: Maximum and average derivational capacity for all three word-classes.

	Maximum	Average
Nouns	7	4.4
Verbs	7	3.6
Adjectives	6	4.1

Table 19.8: Average number of derivatives per order of derivation for all three word-classes.

	1st order	2nd order	3rd order	4th order	5th order
Nouns	4.4	1.6	0	0	0
Verbs	3.6	1.6	0.3	0.1	0.1
Adjectives	4.1	1.7	0	0	0

19.6 Correlation between semantic categories and orders of derivation

Of the altogether 49 semantic categories assumed in the project, 24, i.e. approximately half, are relevant in describing the Norwegian sample. Their empirical relevance varies from one occurrence in the case of ABSTRACTION, EXPERIENCER, ITERATIVE, MANNER and PEJORATIVE to 34 in the case of STATIVE. Eleven categories, i.e. almost half of the total number, occur in the 1st order only, these being AUGMENTATIVE, CAUSATIVE, EXPERIENCER, ITERATIVE, LOCATION, MANNER, PATIENT, PEJORATIVE, PURPOSIVE, RELATIONAL, and TEMPORAL. ABSTRACTION, FEMALE and RESULTATIVE only occur in the 2nd order. Only one category occurs in all derivational orders; this is STATIVE, which is also the only category occurring as the concluding step of the single instantiations of the 4th and 5th order derivations.

In the 1st order, 21 semantic categories occur in from 1 to 19 basic words in a total of 112 derivations. The four derivationally most productive semantic categories are ACTION (found in 19 basic words and 21 derivations), SIMILATIVE (in 13 words and 15 derivations), STATIVE (in 11 words and 12 derivations), and QUALITY (in 8 words and 9 derivations).

In the 2nd order, 11 semantic categories occur in from 1 to 10 words in 66 derivations. Here, the three most productive semantic categories are STATIVE (occurring in 10 words and 15 derivations), RESULTATIVE (in 8 words and an equal number of derivations), and ACTION (in 7 words and 8 derivations).

The three 3rd order derivations have STATIVE, QUALITY and PRIVATIVE as the concluding category, respectively; as noted, the 4th and 5th order derivations both end in STATIVE.

What the particularly productive semantic categories singled out here have in common is that they find formal expression in equally frequent and productive suffixes: STATIVE predominantly in *-het*, ACTION in *-ing*, SIMILATIVE in *-aktig*, QUALITY in *-et(e)* and *-ig*, and RESULTATIVE in *-ing* and *-else*.

The altogether 184 1st, 2nd, 3rd, 4th and 5th order derivations amount to an average of 6.13 derivations per basic word.

19.7 Semantic categories with blocking effects

LOCATION, as manifested in the *-eri* or *-e* suffix, e.g. *brenneri* 'distillery, still' or *rette* 'right or visible side', appears to preclude further derivation; this is also the case when PATIENT (e.g. *drikke* 'liquid for drinking'), INSTRUMENT (e.g. *sverte* '(black) polish'), ITERATIVE (e.g. *drikkeri* 'recurrent or constant drinking (of alcohol)'), or STATIVE (dimension, e.g. *lengde* 'length'), find expression in one of these suffixes, too.

The suffix *-er* designates AGENT or INSTRUMENT. In the former role, it permits the addition of the FEMALE suffix *-ske* (which is, however, becoming increasingly rare in the modern language), e.g. *syer* 'sewer, person whose occupation is sewing (regardless of natural gender)' and *syerske* 'female sewer'. The INSTRUMENT meaning precludes further derivation to FEMALE.

It may be noted that SIMILATIVE (e.g. *-aktig*) and RELATIONAL (e.g. *-messig*) combine more freely than the categories (suffixes) already mentioned, e.g. *sykepleierskeaktig* 'nurse-like' and, with a liaison *-s-*, *ernæringsmessig* 'nutrition-related'. (The Norwegian sample contains no such examples.)

The PRIVATIVE category (as expressed by the prefix *u-* 'un-', e.g. *udrikkelig* 'undrinkable') can neither be preceded nor followed by other derivational elements. This also goes for PURPOSIVE (e.g. *beholde* 'to keep') and CAUSATIVE (e.g. *fortynne* 'to dilute') when expressed by a prefix.

19.8 Typical combinations of semantic categories

The sample contains a total of 27 combinations of two semantic categories (including the combinations into which the few 3rd, 4th and 5th order derivations can be analyzed). Only two of the combinations form a sequence of the same category (cf. section 19.9).

The four most frequent combinations are ABILITY > STATIVE (6 attestations, e.g. *drikkelighet* 'drinkability', *fornybarhet* 'renewability'), QUALITY > STATIVE (5 attestations, e.g. *vandighet* 'wateriness'), SIMILATIVE > STATIVE (4 attestations, e.g. *hundeaktighet* 'canine appearance'), and CAUSATIVE > ACTION (4 attestations, e.g. *forlenging* 'lengthening'). The remaining combinations are attested three times or less; 13 are attested just once. Characteristically, the frequent combinations arise when a productive suffix expressing a specific meaning is attached to word ending in another productive suffix or prefix; consider the representative combinations in the examples already given (*-bar-het*, *-ig-het*, *-lig-het*, *-aktig-het*, *-for ... -ing*).

Another aspect of this is that certain semantic categories, or the affixes that serve to express them, attract specific other categories, and suffixes. The prime example is STATIVE, expressed by the suffix *-het*, which is attracted by ABILITY, QUALITY, and SIMILATIVE (cf. the above examples). A further example is RESULTATIVE, which is attracted by CAUSATIVE (e.g. *fornyelse* 'renewal'), ACTION (e.g. *benevnelse* 'designation'), and PROCESS (e.g. *forbening* 'ossification'), where RESULTATIVE is expressed by the typical *-else* suffix.

The combination AGENT-FEMALE (cf. section 19.7) was common in earlier stages of the language, producing scores of words like *sykepleierske* 'nurse'. Nowadays, female as well as male nurses are all called *sykepleier* without the FEMALE *-ske* suffix, i.e. with no marking of the gender difference.

19.9 Multiple occurrence of semantic categories

Given the identification procedure sketched in the general notes, which relies heavily on the availability of empirical attestation, 2nd order derivations show a moderate rate of occurrence in the Norwegian sample; higher orders are marginal. For this reason, it is to be expected that the reoccurrence of a semantic category within a derivational chain is rare indeed, and this expectation is borne out by the facts. We have noted only two examples: ACTION > ACTION in *begrave* 'to bury' > *begraving* 'burying' and PROCESS > PROCESS in *smalne* 'to become narrow' > *smalning* 'becoming narrow(er)'. There are cases on record, like *en-het-lig-het*, paraphrased as 'unit > uniform > uniformity', whose derivational patterning is, in semantic terms, *en* 'one' + STATIVE > QUALITY > STATIVE; however, such examples do not turn up in the sample.

19.10 Reversibility of semantic categories

The reversal of semantic categories does not exist as an option in Norwegian.

19.11 Reasons for structurally poor derivational networks

There appear to specific derivational as well as more general structural and typological reasons for the comparatively simple or 'shallow' character of the Norwegian derivational networks described here.

First, derivational suffixes appear in a fixed order and are, in the normal state of affairs, not reiterated, nor are they reversible; besides, the number of semantic categories they serve to express only amounts to half of the number deemed necessary and sufficient to adequately describe the total of 46 European languages dealt with.

Second, the overall development of the language since the Old Norse period has been one of steady transition from a highly synthetic language structure towards morphologically simplified analyticity, where compounding, in particular in nouns, and certain syntactic structures making use of prepositions perform tasks where derivational structures would be more naturally resorted to in other languages.

19.12 Conclusions

In the Norwegian sample, the average number of derivational orders for nouns, verbs and adjectives is 1.7, 2.1, and 1.5, respectively (Table 19.6). 1st and 2nd order derivations are more common by far; with nouns, their combined number amounts to 25, with verbs to 26, and with adjectives to 27. In contrast, 3rd, 4th and 5th order derivations are only found with verbs and here, their combined number amounts to a mere five. With regard to the more common 1st and 2nd order derivations, none of the three word-classes stands out. Obviously, simple, hierarchically 'shallow' derivations are highly favoured. The derivational network of the verb *vite* 'to know' stands out as particularly comprehensive.

The saturation value is in general higher in the 1st than in the 2nd and higher orders in the case of 20 out of the 30 words in the sample (Tables 19.2–19.4). Considering first the 1st and 2nd orders in nouns and adjectives, there are three nouns without 2nd order derivations. In the remaining seven nouns, the saturation value is higher in the 2nd order than in the 1st order in four cases. In the case of adjectives, five adjectives do not occur in 2nd order derivations; in the remaining five, the 2nd order derivations have the higher saturation value. Verbs behave somewhat differently from nouns and adjectives. 3rd and higher order derivations are restricted to *drikke* 'to drink' and *vite* 'to know'. The other eight verbs have 1st and 2nd order derivations, and in all these cases the 1st order derivations have the higher saturation value; this is also the case with *drikke* 'to drink', which adds 3rd order derivations with the same saturation value (33.33%) as the 2nd order derivations. *Vite* 'to know' follows the same pattern concerning the relationship between 1st and 2nd order derivations, but is distinguished by exhibiting the highest saturation value of all words in the sample with 100% in the 4th and 5th orders. The second highest saturation value in the sample is 71.43% in the 2nd order derivations of the noun *navn* 'name', which is followed by 66.67% for the 3rd order derivations of *vite* 'to know'.

As shown above (in section 19.6), the descriptive relevance of the 24 semantic categories is subject to a fair amount of variation. They are often associated with specific suffixes (cf. sections 19.7 and 19.8). Some suffixes are unambiguously associated with one semantic role (e.g. SIMILATIVE *-aktig*, RELATIONAL *-messig*); other suffixes are associated with different semantic categories (e.g. ACTION, RESULTATIVE, PROCESS or ENTITY *-ing*), and the same suffix may express different semantic categories (e.g. ABILITY *-bar*, *-lig*; LOCATION *-e*, *-eri*). Prefixes, although fewer in number, behave similarly. They may be unambiguous (e.g. AUGMENTATIVE *ur-*) or be associated with two or more semantic categories (e.g. ACTION or PURPOSIVE *be-*).

References

Askedal, John Ole. 2016. 141. Norwegian. In Peter O. Müller, Ingeborg Ohnheiser, Susan Olsen & Franz Rainer (eds.), *Word-Formation. An International Handbook of the Languages of Europe, vol. 4*, 2525–2554. Berlin & Boston: Mouton de Gruyter.
Askedal, John Ole, Tor Guttu, Per Egil Hegge, Inger-Lise Nyheim, Arthur O. Sandved, Ole Michael Selberg & Finn-Erik Vinje. 2017. *Norsk grammatikk*, 2nd edn. Oslo: Kunnskapsforlaget and Det Norske Akademi for Språk og Litteratur.
Enger, Hans-Olav & Philipp Conzett. 2016. Morfologi. In Helge Sandøy (ed.), *Norsk språkhistorie I: Mønster*, 213–315. Oslo: Novus.

Sources

NO = Guttu, Tor (ed.). 2008. *Norsk ordbok med 1000 illustrasjoner*, 2nd edn. Oslo: Kunnskapsforlaget.
NAOB = *Det Norske Akademis ordbok*. https://www.naob.no/s%C3B8k.

Maria Rosenberg
20 Derivational networks in Swedish

20.1 General notes

In conformity with other Germanic languages, compounding and derivation are the main productive word-formation processes in Swedish. Different liaison forms can occur, though arbitrarily applied (e.g. *barn-s-lig* 'child-s-ish'). There are about 200 derivational prefixes and suffixes, but not all of them are productive (Hultman 2003: 33). Many derivational affixes are borrowed, mostly from German, Greek, Latin or French (Thorell 1984: 69; Hultman 2003: 149–150; Kotcheva 2016: 2554). Given the data set for this project, i.e. Swadesh lists, only affixes of German origin are present in the Swedish set. In Swedish, both prefixation and suffixation alter the meaning of the base, but only suffixation implies a change of grammatical category (Kotcheva 2016: 2556). There are more prefixes that attach to verbs compared to prefixes that take nouns or adjectives as bases, but in contrast, there are a higher number of suffixes that derive nouns than those that attach to adjectives or derive adverbs; few suffixes derive verbs (two of Germanic origin and three of Romance origin) (cf. Hultman 2003: 54–56, 81–82, 147–150). In some derivational chains, vowel changes occur. Six such cases are included in the Swedish set.[1]

As to the theoretical problem of drawing a sharp line between affixes proper and affixoids and/or combining forms, one relevant example for Swedish involves the AUGMENTATIVE *jätte-* 'very' (literally 'giant') that can combine with most adjectives (e.g. *jättedålig* 'very bad'); another is the PRIVATIVE *-lös* '-less' (e.g. *tandlös* 'toothless'). Both cases are mostly classified as affixoids (cf. Söderbergh 1968: 30–31; Kotcheva 2016: 2556, 2562), and they are thus excluded from the Swedish networks.[2] In contrast, nearly all reference grammars and handbooks on Swedish word-formation distinguish between the prefix *för-* and the preposition or adverb *för* 'for' (Söderbergh 1968: 60; Teleman 1970: 54; Thorell 1984: 63–64; Josefsson 1998: 142–144; Hultman 2003: 149). I follow this position, so as to include derivations with *för-*.

Other potential problems, such as particle verbs as well as present and past participles that are verb forms but are used and mostly classified as adjectives

---

[1] (i) *namn*N 'name' > *nämna*V 'to mention'; (ii) *draga*V 'pull' > *bedraga*V 'to deceive' > *bedrägeri*N 'fraud'; (iii) *svart*A 'black' > *svärta*V 'to blacken'; (iv) *varm*A 'warm' > *värma*V 'to warm, heat'; (v) *lång*A 'long' > *länga*V 'to make longer'; and (vi) *trång*A 'narrow' > *tränga*V 'to corner, press, push'.
[2] Yet, Kotcheva (2016: 2568) lists a number of similar items (e.g. *döds-* 'dead-s' or *pytte-* 'tiny') as prefixes. In my opinion, such items would also be affixoids.

(Josefsson 1998: 147; Hultman 2003: 40), are ruled out here (cf. the general introduction to Germanic languages). Finally, the neuter form (with a final -*t*) of most Swedish adjectives (in particular those ending in -*ig*) can function as adverbials (Hultman 2003: 238).[3] Still, by adhering to the criterion of separating form from function, such adverbials are not included in the data (otherwise A-*t* with a MANNER label would be highly productive).

The sources draw from three dictionaries by the Swedish Academy (SAOB, SAOL, and SO). Derivations marked as rare, archaic or dialectal were mostly excluded unless internet searches (Google) could confirm their use to some extent.

20.2 Maximum derivational networks

In Table 20.1 below, we can see that the verbs exhibit the highest numbers of derivational networks in all orders and so in total. 4th order derivations are rare, and none of the three word-classes permits a 5th order.

Table 20.1: Maximum derivational networks per order of derivation for all three word-classes.

	1st order	2nd order	3rd order	4th order	5th order	Σ
Nouns	14	17	6	1	0	38
Verbs	21	23	8	1	0	53
Adjectives	17	9	7	1	0	34
TOTAL	52	49	21	3	0	125

20.3 Saturation values

The mean saturation values for the nouns range between 11% and 42%, as shown in Table 20.2. The noun with the highest mean saturation value is *vatten* 'water' (42%), which is also the only noun with a 4th order derivation (100%). In contrast, *öga* 'eye', which has the lowest mean saturation value (11%), is the only noun that lacks a 2nd order. Within the 1st order, *hund* 'dog' has the highest saturation value (64%), and *lus* 'louse' has the lowest (21%).

---

[3] Swedish nouns have two genders, arbitrarily assigned: common (uter) and neuter; common predominates.

Table 20.2: Saturation values per order of derivation, nouns.

Nouns		Saturation value (%)	1st order (%)	2nd order (%)	3rd order (%)	4th order (%)	5th order (%)
bone	ben	28.95	35.71	29.41	16.67	0	0
eye	öga	10.53	28.57	0	0	0	0
tooth	tand	26.32	42.86	11.76	33.33	0	0
day	dag	21.05	21.43	29.41	0	0	0
dog	hund	36.84	64.29	29.41	0	0	0
louse	lus	13.16	21.43	11.76	0	0	0
fire	eld	23.68	28.57	23.53	16.67	0	0
stone	sten	28.95	28.57	35.29	16.67	0	0
water	vatten	42.11	28.57	47.06	50	100	0
name	namn	36.84	42.86	29.41	50	0	0

For the verbs in Table 20.3, the lowest and highest mean saturation values vary between 8%, for *sy* 'sew', and 36%, for *hålla* 'hold'. *Skära* 'cut' has the highest value in the 1st order (52%). Two verbs, *gräva* 'dig' and *sy* 'sew', have no 2nd order derivations, and three verbs produce 4th order derivations: *hålla* 'hold', *bränna* 'burn' and *veta* 'know'.

Table 20.3: Saturation values per order of derivation, verbs.

Verbs		Saturation value (%)	1st order (%)	2nd order (%)	3rd order (%)	4th order (%)	5th order (%)
cut	skära	33.96	52.38	30.43	0	0	0
dig	gräva	11.32	28.57	0	0	0	0
pull	draga	33.96	42.86	30.43	25	0	0
throw	kasta	24.53	38.1	13.04	25	0	0
give	giva	28.3	23.81	34.78	25	0	0
hold	hålla	35.85	33.33	39.13	25	100	0
sew	sy	7.55	19.05	0	0	0	0
burn	bränna [a]	30.19	38.1	21.74	25	100	0

Table 20.3 (continued)

Verbs		Saturation value (%)	1st order (%)	2nd order (%)	3rd order (%)	4th order (%)	5th order (%)
drink	dricka	22.64	38.1	13.04	12.5	0	0
know	veta	26.42	19.05	26.09	37.5	100	0

[a]*Bränna* (transitive) instead of *brinna* (intransitive) was chosen as the Swedish counterpart to 'burn'.

The adjectives in Table 20.4 are more unevenly distributed as to the saturation value per order. The mean saturation values range between 9% and 53%. In addition, there are seven gaps (0%) in the 2nd and 3rd orders. The highest mean saturation value belongs to *lång* 'long', which also has a 4th order derivation, along with *tunn* 'thin'. Moreover, *lång* 'long' stands out in the 1st order with a saturation value of 71%.

Table 20.4: Saturation values per order of derivation, adjectives.

Adjectives		Saturation value (%)	1st order (%)	2nd order (%)	3rd order (%)	4th order (%)	5th order (%)
narrow	trång	26.47	17.65	33.33	42.86	0	0
old	gammal	8.82	17.65	0	0	0	0
straight	rak	17.65	35.29	0	0	0	0
new	ny	41.18	52.94	44.44	14.29	0	0
long	lång	52.94	70.59	22.22	42.86	100	0
warm	varm	35.29	41.18	33.33	28.57	0	0
thick	tjock	38.24	47.06	44.44	14.29	0	0
bad	dålig	8.82	17.65	0	0	0	0
thin	tunn	29.41	29.41	11.11	42.86	100	0
black	svart	38.24	52.94	44.44	0	0	0

Table 20.5 gives the average saturation value per order of derivation for all the nouns, verbs and adjectives in the Swedish set. We can see that the average values are quite similar for every order of the three word-classes. However, they are quite low, not reaching above 39% in the 1st order, 25% in the 2nd order, and 19% in the 3rd order.

Table 20.5: Average saturation values per order of derivation for all three word-classes.

	1st order	2nd order	3rd order	4th order	5th order
Nouns	34.286	24.704	18.334	10	0
Verbs	33.335	20.868	17.5	30	0
Adjectives	38.236	23.331	18.573	20	0

20.4 Orders of derivation

As mentioned previously (Table 20.1), the maximum number of orders for the Swedish sample is four. In Table 20.6, we can see that the average number for the nouns, verbs and adjectives varies between 2–3 orders.

Table 20.6: Maximum and average number of orders of derivation for all three word-classes.

	Maximum	Average
Nouns	4	2.6
Verbs	4	2.8
Adjectives	4	2.5

20.5 Derivational capacity

As follows from Table 20.7, the derivational capacity of the verbs (i.e. direct 1st order derivatives) amounts to the highest average value whilst the nouns have the

Table 20.7: Maximum and average derivational capacity for all three word-classes.

	Maximum	Average
Nouns	9	4.8
Verbs	11	7
Adjectives	12	6.5

lowest average value. However, the adjective *lång* 'long' has the highest overall derivational capacity (12 derivations in the 1st order). The rather low derivational capacity of the nouns might be due to the fact that Swedish has other available word-formation patterns, such as NN compounding, as well as syntactic means.

As to the average derivational capacity in all orders and for all word-classes, Table 20.8 shows that, in the 1st order, the verbs and adjectives have almost equal numbers. For the 2nd order, the nouns and verbs are quite similar, but the adjectives are less fruitful. In the 3rd and 4th orders, the nouns, verbs and adjectives behave quite similarly, with little derivational output.

Table 20.8: Average number of derivatives per order of derivation for all three word-classes.

	1st order	2nd order	3rd order	4th order	5th order
Nouns	4.8	4.2	1.1	0.1	0
Verbs	7	4.8	1.4	0.3	0
Adjectives	6.5	2.1	1.3	0.2	0

20.6 Correlation between semantic categories and orders of derivation

In the 1st order, 9 of the 10 nouns produce derivations within the semantic categories ACTION (the exception is *dag* 'day') and QUALITY (the exception is *öga* 'eye'), such as ben_N > $bena_V$ 'to bone' and $benig_A$ 'bony'. 8 of the 10 nouns have 1st order derivations classified as SIMILATIVE (7 nouns actually have two derivations under this label, mostly N-*artad* and N-*aktig*, e.g. $tand_N$ 'tooth' > $tandaktig_A$ or $tandartad_A$ 'similar to tooth'). ACTION likewise predominates in the 2nd order, since 9 of the 10 nouns are represented under this label (the exception is *öga* 'eye'), such as dag_N 'day' > $dagas_V$ 'to dawn' > $dagning_N$ 'dawn'. STATIVE is the second most characteristic 2nd order category with 5 nouns. In the 3rd order, 5 nouns derive a RESULTATIVE meaning. The only derivation in the 4th order has an ABILITY meaning. Otherwise, the rest of the semantic categories in all orders are represented by 1–3 nouns.

The semantic categories in the 1st order of the verbs are more widely spread and more frequently represented overall. ABILITY is manifested by 8 of the 10 verbs (e.g. $dricka_V$ 'to drink' > $drickbar_A$ 'drinkable'), AGENT by 7, and FEMALE (AGENT), ACTION and PURPOSIVE by 6 verbs. 5 verbs give rise to INSTRUMENT derivations (9 verbs, except *veta* 'know', thus produce AGENT and/or INSTRUMENT formations, e.g. *gräva*_V 'to dig' > *grävare*N 'who/with what one digs'). In the 2nd order, AGENT and STATIVE are derived from 5 verbs. STATIVE is produced by 6 verbs in the 3rd order and by the 3 verbs that derive the 4th order (e.g. *bränna*_V 'to burn' > *förbränna*_V 'to combust' > *förbränningsbar*_A 'combustible' > *förbränningsbarhet*_N 'combustibleness'). The remaining semantic categories in all orders are derived from 1–4 verbs.

In the 1st order of the adjectives, STATIVE is most common, represented by 9 adjectives (the exception is *gammal* 'old', where *ålderdom* 'old age, senescence' blocks *gammaldom/-het*). 8 adjectives give rise to derivations with an AUGMENTATIVE meaning (e.g. *varm*_A 'warm' > *urvarm*_A 'very warm'), and 6 to a PATIENT meaning (e.g. *ny*_A 'new' > *nying*_N 'newcomer'). SIMILATIVE, ACTION and CAUSATIVE are each yielded from 5 adjectives. In the 2nd order, CAUSATIVE and ACTION are derived from 4 adjectives each. ACTION is represented by 4 adjectives in the 3rd order. The two 4th order derivations are ABILITY. All other semantic categories in the different orders contain 1–3 derivations.

It is difficult to find patterns in common for the three word-classes. ACTION, however, is represented to a quite high degree by all word-classes in the 1st order. The nouns exhibit a strong correlation between the 1st order of derivation and ACTION, QUALITY and SIMILATIVE, and the 2nd order of derivation and ACTION. For the verbs, there is a rather strong correlation between the 1st order and ABILITY as well as AGENT, and between the 3rd and 4th order and STATIVE. For Swedish adjectives, the 1st order strongly correlates with STATIVE and AUGMENTATIVE.

20.7 Semantic categories with blocking effects

Regarding blocking effects, for the nouns, the semantic categories AGENT, ENTITY, MANNER and PATIENT block further derivation in the 1st order, and AGENT, AUGMENTATIVE, ENTITY, INSTRUMENT and MANNER block further derivations in the 2nd order. In the 3rd order, AGENT, ENTITY and INSTRUMENT hinder further derivation.

The 1st order of the verbs is blocked for further derivations by FEMALE (AGENT), ENTITY, INSTRUMENT, LOCATION and PATIENT. In the 2nd order, AGENT, ENTITY, FEMALE and INSTRUMENT block further derivations. FEMALE and MANNER block further derivations in the 3rd order.

In the 1st order of the adjectives, AUGMENTATIVE, ENTITY, MANNER and PATIENT hamper further derivations, and in the 2nd order, AGENT, FEMALE and INSTRUMENT hamper further derivations. The few occurrences of 3rd order derivations of adjectives are blocked by AGENT and INSTRUMENT.

In conclusion, some semantic categories, independently of the order in which they occur, tend to hamper further derivation, namely AUGMENTATIVE, ENTITY, FEMALE, INSTRUMENT, MANNER and PATIENT.

20.8 Typical combinations of semantic categories

In the Swedish set, there are several typical and systematic combinations of semantic categories, such as ABILITY-STATIVE, ABILITY-PRIVATIVE-STATIVE, QUALITY-AUGMENTATIVE, QUALITY-PRIVATIVE, QUALITY-STATIVE (e.g. *långsam*$_A$ 'slow' > *långsamhet*$_N$ 'slowness') and SIMILATIVE-STATIVE, mainly reflecting derivations from adjectives to nouns. For the verbal derivations, many combinations involve ACTION/CAUSATIVE-AGENT/FEMALE/INSTRUMENT, CAUSATIVE-ABILITY, CAUSATIVE-ACTION (-ABILITY), and ACTION-PURPOSIVE/PROCESS-RESULTATIVE (e.g. *giva*$_V$ 'to give' > *angiva*$_V$ 'to denounce, report' > *angiveri*$_N$ 'whistle-blowing').

20.9 Multiple occurrence of semantic categories

There are three cases of multiple reoccurrences in one derivational chain. The first two cases consist of just ACTION-ACTION (e.g. *stena*$_V$ 'to stone' > *stening*$_N$ 'the action of stoning') or ACTION-CAUSATIVE-ACTION (e.g. *tunna*$_V$ 'make/become thinner' > *förtunna*$_V$ 'dilute' > *förtunning*$_N$ 'the action of diluting').

The other case is STATIVE-STATIVE, which occurs in some derivational chains, such as the one with the relational suffix *-mässig* (e.g. *nyhet*$_N$ 'news' > *nyhetsmässig*$_A$ 'related to news' > *nyhetsmässighet*$_N$ 'the state of being related to news').

20.10 Reversibility of semantic categories

In the Swedish data set, no instances of semantic categories occurring in a reversed order are attested.

20.11 Conclusions

The Swedish set shows that the average number of derivational orders for adjectives, nouns and verbs ranges between 2.5 to 2.8 (Table 20.6). Hence, there are few 4th order derivations, and no 5th order.

The verbs exhibit the highest number of derivational networks in the 1st, 2nd and 3rd orders (Table 20.1). The higher derivational outcome of the verbs can be related to the higher number of prefixes that attach to verbs compared to those that attach to nouns or adjectives. As Barz (2016: 2388) notes for German, the word-formation of verbs has a different organization to that of nouns and adjectives: prefixation plays a more important role for verbs than suffixation. Hence, a similar remark can be made for Swedish.

However, the adjectives have the overall highest saturation value: 38% in the 1st order (Table 20.5). For the adjectives, the maximum derivational networks and the average number of derivatives are thus much higher in the 1st order compared to the 2nd order (Tables 20.1 and 20.8). In contrast, for the nouns and verbs, the maximum derivational networks are higher in the 2nd order than in the 1st order, and their average numbers of derivatives do not decline that much from the 1st to the 2nd order.

Finally, less than half of the semantic categories (22 of the 49 available labels) are covered by the Swedish derivations. On the one hand, this fact implies that Swedish makes use of other means, both morphological and syntactic, to account for the remaining semantic categories. But, on the other hand, the derivational capacity of Swedish is quite rich given the semantics accounted for. It might thus be possible that the German influence on the Swedish derivational system is heavier than in the other Scandinavian languages.

References

Barz, Irmhild. 2016. German. In Peter O. Müller, Ingeborg Ohnheiser, Susan Olsen & Franz Rainer (eds.), *Word-Formation: An International Handbook of the Languages of Europe*, Vol. 4, 2387–2410. Berlin & Boston: Mouton de Gruyter.
Hultman, Tor G. 2003. *Svenska Akademiens språklära* [The Grammar of the Swedish Academy]. Stockholm: Svenska Akademien.
Josefsson, Gunlög. 1998. *Minimal Words in a Minimal Syntax: Word Formation in Swedish*. Amsterdam & Philadelphia: John Benjamins.
Kotcheva, Kristina. 2016. Swedish. In Peter O. Müller, Ingeborg Ohnheiser, Susan Olsen & Franz Rainer (eds.), *Word-Formation: An International Handbook of the Languages of Europe*, Vol. 4, 2554–2578. Berlin & Boston: Mouton de Gruyter.

Söderbergh, Ragnhild. 1968. *Svensk ordbilding* [Swedish Word-Formation]. Stockholm: Norstedts.
Teleman, Ulf. 1970. *Om svenska ord* [About Swedish Words]. Lund: Gleerups.
Thorell, Olof. 1984. *Att bilda ord* [To Form Words]. Stockholm: Skriptor.

Sources

SAOB = *Svenska Akademiens ordbok* [The dictionary of the Swedish Academy]. http://www.svenska.se.
SAOL = *Svenska Akademiens ordlista* [The dictionary of the Swedish Academy]. http://www.svenska.se.

Livio Gaeta
21 Introduction to Romance languages

21.1 Introduction

Romance languages inherited a productive system of derivation from Latin, which however developed in partially independent and original ways. On the one hand, we observe cases of Latin affixes which underwent considerable expansion: for instance, the Latin suffix *-mentum* found in *impedīmentum* 'obstacle', *ornāmentum* 'ornament', etc. massively expanded in all Romance languages except Romanian, in which only relics survive in the form of Latinisms (e.g. *impediment, ornament*) while action nouns are productively formed with the help of the original inflectional ending of the Latin infinitive *-re*, as in *a schimba* 'to change' > *schimbare* 'change' (cf. Gaeta 2015).

On the other hand, new procedures were developed that resulted from different sources. One example in which all Romance languages apparently concur in a similar innovation is the adverb-forming suffix resulting from the well-known process of the grammaticalization of the Latin noun *mente(m)* 'mind' (cf. Detges 2015): e.g. Catalan *realment*, French *réellement*, and Galician, Italian, Portuguese, Romanian and Spanish *realmente* 'really'. The suffix is, however, productive to different degrees across the Romance languages: in Romanian, for instance, only a handful of adverbs formed with *-mente* are commonly used, and are, however, borrowings from Italian and French processes (see individual chapters on several Romance languages in Müller et al. 2016: 2600–2751).

21.2 Across inflection and derivation and the question of transflection

In the light of the development with respect to the Latin mother tongue, another general issue arises with regard to the distinction between inflection and derivation, concerning a number of cases which are traditionally held to lie at the edge of the continuum. Moreover, the general perspective adopted in the project of leaving out any instance of conversion, including so-called transflection, poses a number of challenges which require homogeneous and theoretically convincing choices.

In particular, the bar against conversion implies that one should leave out derivatives based on inflectional forms in the absence of any overt affix univocally referring to derivation. This means that, for instance, a derivative formed on the basis of the feminine past participle such as Fr. *gorger* 'to fill, saturate' > *gorgée* 'drink, swallow' has to be left out because the final vowel cannot be interpreted as a derivational affix, exactly as in its correspondents It. *bere* / Gal. / Port. / Sp. *beber* 'to drink' > It. *bevuta* / Gal. / Port. / Sp. *bebida* 'drink, swallow'. This goes hand in hand with the exclusion of any inflectional form used in a transposed function, as is typically the case for past participles used as adjectives as, for instance, Sp. *decidir* 'to decide' > *decidido* 'resolute'. In addition, one should consider that in some cases the suffix forming the past participle has given rise to a derivational suffix forming adjectives without a corresponding verb, such as Sp. *toga* 'robe' > *tog-ado* 'wearing a robe'. In this way, one might in principle interpret cases that look like conversions as being due to suffixation, as, for instance, Sp. *dentado* 'dentate' can in principle be formed either on the verb *dentar* 'to provide with teeth' or directly on the noun *dente* 'tooth'.

On the other hand, the original form of the Latin present participle has undergone different processes of reanalysis across the modern Romance languages, which might have different outcomes nowadays. Accordingly, different choices have to be taken for the single languages, as, for instance, the participial value is still alive in French, in contrast to its Italian correspondent: Fr. *la fille chantant l'hymne national* / It. **la ragazza cantante l'inno nazionale* 'the girl singing the national hymn'. Old present participles have developed different derivational values, ranging from AGENT nouns (e.g. Cat. *cantant*, Gal. / It. / Sp. *cantante* 'singer') to INSTRUMENTS (e.g. Cat. *tirant*, It. / Port. / Sp. *tirante* 'tie-rod', Cat. *tirants*, Gal. / Sp. *tirantes* 'braces'), property adjectives (e.g. Gal. / Port. / Sp. *cortante*, Cat. *tallant*, It. *tagliente* 'sharp'), etc.

In a similar way, the original suffix of the superlative has developed into a true elative in the modern Romance languages insofar as it has become irrelevant for syntax, as shown by the contrast between the Latin example in (1) and the Spanish one in (2):

(1) *ex his omnibus longe sunt humanissimi qui Cantium incolunt* (Caes. *Gall.* 5.14.1)
among his all.ABL.PL long.ADV are human.SUP.PL who Cantium inhabit.3PL
'of all people those who live in Cantium are by far the most human'

(2) *este actor es famosísimo* (*de todos)
this actor is famous.SUP of all
'this actor is very famous (*of all)'

In addition, the elative suffix has developed a number of restrictions, limiting its productivity to a different degree. For instance, in Spanish the so-called lexical elative is opposed to and blocks the morphological elative formed with the suffix *-ísimo*, while in French – except for a few established formations typical of the literary language such as *rarissime* 'very rare' and *richissime* 'very rich' – elatives formed with *-issime* are less entrenched than in other Romance languages like Italian, where it displays an extraordinary productivity, barely restricted by a small number of factors (cf. Rainer 2003). On the other hand, in several grammatical traditions, elatives formed with this suffix are nevertheless assigned to inflection.

21.3 Base allomorphy, suppletion and combining forms

Finally, the results of phonological change and of lexical stratification can lead to very different choices with regard to how to interpret allomorphy and suppletion (cf. Dressler 2015 for a general discussion). In general, cases of weak suppletion as, for instance, It. *caldo* 'warm' > *cal-ore* 'heat' and *occhio* 'eye' > *ocul-are* 'ocular' can be held to represent instances of base allomorphy, while strong suppletion cannot be counted on a par with the other derivatives, as shown on the one hand by It. *acqua* 'water' > *idr-ico* 'hydric' and on the other by Fr. *chaud* 'warm' > *chal-eur* 'heat', *oeil* 'eye' > *ocul-aire* 'ocular', etc. Clearly, the difference between weak and strong suppletion is difficult to draw and depends very much on the single examples in question. At any rate, the clear occurrence of an affix also has to be identified for weak suppletion, which forces the exclusion of cases like It. *nome* 'noun' > *nominare* 'to nominate' in which *-in-* cannot be interpreted as a verb-forming suffix.

Similar problems are provided by the difficult cline running from so-called neoclassical compounding down to affixation. It must be added that different criteria are adopted across the Romance languages for deciding between true affixation and the compounding of combining forms. For this reason, it is not possible to say a priori which choice has to be recommended, which instead relies very much on the single examples in question.

References

Detges, Ulrich. 2015. The Romance adverbs in *-mente*: a case study in grammaticalization. In Peter O. Müller, Ingeborg Ohnheiser, Susan Olsen & Franz Rainer (eds.), *Word-Formation: An International Handbook of the Languages of Europe, Volume 3*, 1824–1842. Berlin & Boston: Mouton de Gruyter.

Dressler, Wolfgang Ulrich. 2015. Allomorphy. In Peter O. Müller, Ingeborg Ohnheiser, Susan Olsen & Franz Rainer (eds.), *Word-Formation: An International Handbook of the Languages of Europe, Volume 1*, 500–516. Berlin & Boston: Mouton de Gruyter.

Gaeta, Livio. 2015. Action Nouns in Romance. In Peter O. Müller, Ingeborg Ohnheiser, Susan Olsen and Franz Rainer (eds.), *Word-Formation: An International Handbook of the Languages of Europe, Volume 2*, 1165–1185. Berlin & Boston: Mouton de Gruyter.

Müller, Peter O., Ingeborg Ohnheiser, Susan Olsen & Franz Rainer (eds.). 2016. *Word-Formation: An International Handbook of the Languages of Europe, Volume 4*. Berlin & Boston: Mouton de Gruyter.

Rainer, Franz. 2003. Studying restrictions on patterns of word-formation by means of the Internet. In Mark Aronoff and Livio Gaeta (eds.), Morphological Productivity. [Special issue]. *Italian Journal of Linguistics* 15 (1). 131–139.

Elisenda Bernal, Mercè Lorente
22 Derivational networks in Catalan

22.1 General notes

In Catalan, like in the rest of Romance languages, derivation and compounding are the most frequently used word-formation processes. Specifically, the most recent study on the formation of new words in Catalan has shown that two thirds of the identified neologisms were created by means of the language's own mechanisms and only one third of them were borrowings from other languages; within the former, derivation is the most productive mechanism, since prefixation and suffixation make up 23.7% of the total (Bernal, Cabré and Freixa 2015: 10).

According to the *Gramàtica de la llengua catalana* (2016), Catalan has 96 derivational suffixes (as well as 30 evaluative ones) and 56 prefixes. Nevertheless, not all of these are productive nowadays, nor to the same extent. Due to the different nature of prefixes and suffixes, phonological, morphological, syntactic and semantic differences can be found between them. These are briefly outlined below:

– Prefixation does not normally affect the grammatical category of the base it is added to (e.g. *història*$_N$ 'history' – *prehistòria*$_N$ 'prehistory'), while suffixation usually dictates the resulting word's category (e.g. *córrer*$_V$ 'to run' – *corredor*$_N$ 'runner'). However, in the Catalan lexicological tradition, prefixation is considered to have recategorizing properties, as in *fosc*$_A$ 'dark' – *enfosquir*$_V$ 'to dim, to darken' or *barca*$_N$ 'boat' – *embarcar*$_V$ 'to board' (see Cabré 1994, 2002; Institut d'Estudis Catalans 2016), in contrast to Spanish, where such cases are classified as instances of parasynthesis (Serrano-Dolader 1999).
– Both processes are recursive, yet despite their open character, not all combinations of bases and affixes are possible or infinite, even if the categorial or semantic restrictions that are imposed on the bases by the affixes are met. Thus, words often have no more than one prefix (e.g. *descarregar* 'to unload, to download'), and although recursion is possible (e.g. *antiantidroga* 'antiantidrug'), it is pragmatically unlikely (*?viceviceviceconseller* 'lit. deputy deputy deputy minister'). In the case of suffixes there is a general trend, halfway between morphology and pragmatics, which precludes the possibility of accumulating too high a number of suffixes, so that the application of more than four morphemes to a single base is almost nonexistent: e.g. *jardí* 'garden' – *jardiner* 'gardener' – *jardineria* 'gardening' – **jardineriós*. Furthermore, recursion is subject to the condition that the same suffix cannot be applied to a base that has been used to form a word in the immediately preceding derivational process: e.g. *vent* 'wind' – *ventós*

'windy' – *ventosós. Successive attachments of synonymous suffixes are likewise not tolerated, with the exception of evaluative suffixes: e.g. *ensenyar* 'to teach' – *ensenyament* 'teaching' – *ensenyamentació, but note *petit* 'small' – *petitó* 'very small' / *petitet* 'very small' – *petitonet* 'very small' (*petitetó).

The preparation of this chapter was based on the data on the derivational networks of selected words recorded in the academic dictionary *Diccionari de la llengua catalana* (DIEC2, 2007), which was supplemented with data recorded in the *Diccionari català-valencià-balear* (DCVB 1962).

22.2 Maximum derivational networks

In Table 22.1 below, it can be observed that nouns offer the highest number of derivational networks, followed closely by adjectives, although it should be noted that these are concerned primarily with 1st and 2nd order derivations; the 3rd order is quite limited and the 4th, anecdotal. None of the three word types reaches the 5th order.

Table 22.1: Maximum derivational networks per order of derivation for all three word-classes.

	1st order	2nd order	3rd order	4th order	5th order	Σ
Nouns	26	16	3	1	0	46
Verbs	18	17	2	0	0	37
Adjectives	18	17	6	1	0	42
Total	62	50	11	2	0	125

22.3 Saturation values

The mean saturation value for nouns (Table 22.2) is set between 2.27% for *poll* 'louse', which only generates 1st order derivatives – and very few indeed – and 47.73% for *pedra* 'stone', whose derived forms, nonetheless, only reach the 3rd order. In contrast to this, *dent* 'tooth' and *aigua* 'water', which reach the 4th order, have a lower mean value: 29.55%.

For verbs (Table 22.3), the lowest mean value is for the verb *cavar* 'dig', and the highest for the verb *tallar* 'cut', which is the only one to generate 3rd order

Table 22.2: Saturation values per order of derivation, nouns.

Nouns		1st order	2nd order	3rd order	4th order	5th order	Mean value
bone	os	26.83	8.11	25	0	0	18.18
eye	ull	17.07	21.62	0	0	0	17.05
tooth	dent	36.59	21.62	25	50	0	29.55
day	jorn	7.32	16.22	12.5	0	0	11.36
dog	gos	14.63	0	0	0	0	6.82
louse	poll	4.88	0	0	0	0	2.27
fire	foc	36.59	43.24	37.5	0	0	38.64
stone	pedra	63.41	40.54	12.5	0	0	47.73
water	aigua	26.83	32.43	25	50	0	29.55
name	nom	14.63	29.73	25	0	0	21.59

Table 22.3: Saturation values per order of derivation, verbs.

Verbs		1st order	2nd order	3rd order	4th order	5th order	Mean value
cut	tallar	48.57	53.13	50	0	0	50.7
dig	cavar	20	9.38	0	0	0	14.08
pull	estirar	28.57	21.88	0	0	0	23.94
throw	llançar	25.71	15.63	0	0	0	19.72
give	donar	31.43	0	0	0	0	15.49
hold	agafar	25.71	9.38	0	0	0	16.9
sew	cosir	28.57	21.88	25	0	0	25.35
burn	cremar	45.71	46.88	0	0	0	43.66
drink	beure	51.43	43.75	0	0	0	45.07
know	conèixer	22.86	46.88	50	0	0	35.21

derivatives alongside *conèixer* 'know' and *cosir* 'sew'. There is no verb that generates derived forms of the 4th or 5th order.

As for adjectives (Table 22.4), their mean values range between 8.6% for *dolent -a* 'bad' (which, alongside *estret -a* 'narrow', only generates 1st order derivatives)

Table 22.4: Saturation values per order of derivation, adjectives.

Adjectives		1st order	2nd order	3rd order	4th order	5th order	Mean value
narrow	estret -a	24	0	0	0	0	12.9
old	vell -a	36	15.63	0	0	0	24.73
straight	directe -a	18	12.5	10	0	0	15.05
new	nou nova	24	53.13	40	0	0	35.48
long	llarg -a	28	31.25	0	0	0	25.81
warm	calent -a	16	3.13	0	0	0	9.68
thick	gros grossa	28	6.25	0	0	0	17.2
bad	dolent -a	16	0	0	0	0	8.6
thin	fi fina	26	43.75	60	100	0	36.56
black	negre -a	36	18.75	0	0	0	25.81

and 36.56% for *fi fina* 'thin', which is the only adjective in the analyzed set to reach the 4th derivational order.

Table 22.5 shows the average saturation value per order of derivation for all the nouns, verbs and adjectives examined in the Catalan set. It can be seen that the resemblances between the orders in the three word types are pretty high, with differences between each word type barely exceeding eight points (in the 2nd order). It is also worth noting that the highest resemblance is found between nouns and adjectives, whose mean values are closest, at least in the first two orders. In any case, however, the mean saturation values are quite low, not reaching above 33% in the 1st order, 27% in the 2nd order, and 17% in the 3rd order.

Table 22.5: Average saturation values per order of derivation for all three word-classes.

	1st order	2nd order	3rd order	4th order	5th order
Nouns	24.88	21.35	16.25	10	0
Verbs	32.86	26.88	12.5	0	0
Adjectives	25.2	18.44	11	10	0

22.4 Orders of derivation

As mentioned above (Table 22.1), the maximum number of orders for the analyzed sample is four (and very limited). In the table below (Table 22.6), it can be observed that the average for verbs and adjectives is the same (2.2), even though verbs only reach the 3rd order whereas adjectives reach the 4th. In contrast, the average for nouns is noticeably higher, and it approximates three (2.7) for most cases.

Table 22.6: Maximum and average number of orders of derivation for all three word-classes.

	Maximum	Average
Nouns	4	2.7
Verbs	3	2.2
Adjectives	4	2.2

22.5 Derivational capacity

Table 22.7 relates the derivational capacity of the three word types: verbs and adjectives reach a maximum of 18 derivatives (i.e. direct 1st order derivatives). In the case of adjectives, this number is reached in two instances (*negre -a* 'black' and *vell -a* 'old'), which causes the mean value of adjectives to be higher than that of verbs and nouns. However, in the latter case, a much higher number of direct 1st order derivatives is reached (26), thanks to the derivatives of *pedra* 'stone'. Yet nouns have the lowest average overall (10.2), even though the three word types show a similar number of direct derivatives (between 10 and 12).

Table 22.7: Maximum and average derivational capacity for all three word-classes.

	Maximum	Average
Nouns	26	10.2
Verbs	18	11.5
Adjectives	18	12.6

If we consider all the orders (Table 22.8), we can see that the distance between word types grows at an exponential rate as we move from one level to the next: whereas in the 1st order the three types are pretty similar, the distance in the 2nd order is larger. Interestingly, adjectives, which generate more direct 1st order derivatives, reduce their value by half in the 2nd order, while the difference is not as marked for nouns and verbs. In the 3rd and 4th orders, the three types are quite similar: the derivational output is negligible for all the word-classes.

Table 22.8: Average number of derivatives per order of derivation for all three word-classes.

	1st order	2nd order	3rd order	4th order	5th order
Nouns	10.2	7.9	1.3	0.2	0
Verbs	11.5	8.6	0.5	0	0
Adjectives	12.6	5.9	1.1	0.1	0

22.6 Correlation between semantic categories and orders of derivation

In the 1st order, for nouns, the most frequent semantic categories include ACTION, COLLECTIVE, DIMINUTIVE and QUALITY (6 out of 10 cases), followed by the LOCATION and RELATIONAL categories (5 out of 10). In the 2nd order, the semantic category with the highest percentage of derivatives is AGENT (7 out of 10 cases), followed by QUALITY (6 out of 10 cases) and ACTION (5 out of 10). The denominal derivatives of the 1st and 2nd orders correlate with a total of 18 and 19 semantic categories respectively, quite a high dispersion rate, with an overlap among categories between the two orders of 60.87%. In the 3rd and 4th orders, the most frequent semantic category is ACTION (4 out of 10), which makes this semantic category the most productive in the denominal derivational networks.

As for verbs, the most common semantic category in the 1st order derivatives is also ACTION (in 100% of the cases), very closely followed by AGENT (9 out of 10 cases), with the vacant slot left by the verb *conèixer* 'know', which generates a derivative belonging to the category EXPERIENCER with the same suffix. In 7 of the 10 cases, the third semantic category is RESULTATIVE and, in 6 cases, the categories INSTRUMENT, QUALITY and ITERATIVE are also present. As we move to the second derivational order of verbs, the most frequent semantic categories are ACTION, QUALITY and DIMINUTIVE (7 out of 10 cases), followed by the RESULTATIVE (5 out of 10 cases), INSTRUMENT and AUGMENTATIVE categories (4 out of 10 cases). The 1st and 2nd order deverbal derivatives amount to a total of 19 and 15 semantic categories respectively, with a dispersion similar to that of nouns. The overlap among categories between the two derivational levels in the case of verbs is 65%. The few 3rd order deverbal derivatives are concentrated in the DIMINUTIVE and MANNER semantic categories.

In the 1st order of adjectives, the most frequent semantic category (10 out of 10 cases) is AUGMENTATIVE, which could be because the application of the AUGMENTATIVE category to predictive categories does not imply an increase in volume, but rather a degree of intensification, including the superlative derivatives in the case of adjectives. QUALITY is the second most frequent category (9 out of 10 cases), with the vacant slot left by *directe -a* 'straight', which also has a derivative in QUALITY, although of the 2nd order. Logically, the third most common category among the deadjectival derivatives is DIMINUTIVE (8 out of 10 cases), followed by PROCESS and ACTION (7 out of 10 cases). The dispersion rate of the semantic categories in the adjective derivatives is similar to that of nouns and verbs, with 19 different categories in both the 1st and 2nd orders, with an overlap of 65.22%. The few 3rd and 4th order derivatives also show high dispersion (ACTION is the category with most cases, and it only has 2 out of 10 in the 3rd order).

If we consider the quantitative results across the three word types, we can confirm that the most productive semantic categories in general are ACTION, with 45 derivatives (15 from nouns, 17 from verbs and 13 from adjectives), and QUALITY, with 40 derivatives (14 from nouns, 13 from verbs and 13 from adjectives). At a distance, the third most frequent semantic category for the three word types is AGENT, with 30 derivatives (13 from nouns, 12 from verbs and 5 from adjectives). AUGMENTATIVE and DIMINUTIVE, which can be considered semantic supercategories, since they include dimensional variation, intensity or degree variation, and the resources for affective expressivity, are also very common in the three categories: AUGMENTATIVE shows, in the cases examined, a total of 21 derivatives (6 from nouns, 4 from verbs and 11 from adjectives) and DIMINUTIVE, a total of 28 derivatives (10 from nouns, 10 from verbs and 8 from adjectives). From the list used for this project, out of the 49 semantic categories, we only used 27, or 55.10%, for the Catalan language.

22.7 Semantic categories with blocking effects

In Catalan it cannot be claimed that semantic categories possess blocking effects since, although certain trends may be noticed, there are always counterexamples that disprove this.

Thus, for nouns, we might even think that, in the 1st order, the semantic categories QUALITY and COLLECTIVE block subsequent derivations, because in 5 out of the 10 cases we find no derivation of the resulting forms in the 2nd order (as tentative as these results might be). Nevertheless, the fact that these categories do not appear in the 1st order for any of the three cases and, most notably, the confirmation that in two cases, *foc* 'fire' and *pedra* 'stone', these semantic categories (QUALITY and COLLECTIVE) allow the presence of derivatives in the 2nd order demonstrate the nonexistence of the blocking effects. A similar phenomenon can be found in the 2nd order in nouns: the derivatives that belong to the semantic categories of AGENT (6 out of 10 cases) and QUALITY (5 out of 10 cases) do not generate derivatives towards the 3rd order, but the instances examined in this paper do not exclude the possibility that other varied examples of 2nd order derivatives of the AGENT or QUALITY categories exist that may seamlessly generate derivatives for the 3rd order (e.g. *cavall* 'horse' > *cavaller*$_{AGENT}$ > *cavallerós*$_{QUALITY}$ > *cavallerositat*$_{QUALITY}$).

In the case of verbs, it is also difficult to claim that semantically motivated blocking exists since, although the 1st order derived forms of the semantic category AGENT do not generate new derivatives in the 2nd order in 7 out of 10 cases, it is evident that the Catalan language allows for many derivative words that refer to the AGENT category to generate new derivatives. The most abundant ones are found in the categories DIMINUTIVE and AUGMENTATIVE (e.g. *cuiner* 'cook' > *cuineret*; *modista* 'dressmaker' > *modisteta*; *corredor* 'runner' > *corredoràs*; *escriptora* 'writer' > *escriptorassa*), but the cases of AGENTS lexicalized as profession designations also generate derivatives in the category LOCATION (e.g. *modista* > *modisteria* 'dressmaker's trade'; *peixater peixatera* 'fishmonger' > *peixateria* 'fish market'; *comptador/comptadora* 'accountant' > *comptadoria* 'accounts department'). The dispersion of semantic categories and the concentration of derivational networks of verbs in two orders in most cases could explain the difficulty in finding clear cases of blocking, yet the point put forward here is that derivational blocking responds only to formal and pragmatic motives.

It should be borne in mind that, out of the 10 adjectives examined, two do not generate 2nd order derivatives, five only have 2nd order derivatives, two reach the 3rd order and only one reaches the 4th. The derivative forms of any order that do not produce new derivatives in the analyzed cases belong to the semantic categories AUGMENTATIVE and DIMINUTIVE. However, it should be remembered that the forms selected in this study are recorded in dictionaries and that this fact does not preclude the possibility that the Catalan language allows new derivatives to be generated from derived words that also refer to the AUGMENTATIVE and DIMINUTIVE categories (e.g. *dolent* 'bad' > *dolentot* > *dolenterot*; *estret* 'narrow' > *estretó* > *estretonet*). The semantic category QUALITY might seem to block new derivatives, if the cases that have no more than one (*dolent -a, estret -a*) or two derivational orders (*negre -a* 'black', *calent -a* 'hot', *vell -a* 'old', *llarg -a* 'long', *gros grossa* 'big'), or even the single case with four orders (*fi fina* 'thin'), are considered. Despite this, we insist on the fact that blocking effects in Catalan are linked fundamentally to morphology and not as much to semantic issues since, in the case of suffixation, when the QUALITY derivative is a noun the subsequent derivation is indeed blocked, yet when the QUALITY derivative is an adjective the subsequent derivation is allowed (e.g. *nou nova* 'new' > *novell -a* > *novellada* COLLECTIVE; *novellament* MANNER) and, furthermore, QUALITY derivatives can present prefixed derivatives (e.g. *negror* 'blackness' > *renegror*; *moralitat* 'morality' > *immoralitat* 'immorality').

22.8 Typical combinations of semantic categories

In the derivational networks of the analyzed units, the more frequent individual combinations (which appear in most cases) are QUALITY > QUALITY (21 cases), ACTION > ACTION (20), ENTITY > ACTION (15), ENTITY > LOCATIVE (13), ENTITY > COLLECTIVE (12) and ACTION > AGENT (10). For the rest of individual combinations, less than 10 cases were found. It must be noted that the individual combinations that are more frequent appear in the 1st order of derivation.

In Catalan, several combinations of semantic categories are frequent in derivational processes, such as LOCATION-base > ACTION > RESULTATIVE (e.g. *magatzem* 'warehouse' > *emmagatzemar* > *desemmagatzemar*); ENTITY-base > ACTION > RESULTATIVE (e.g. *tros* 'piece' > *trossejar* > *trossejament*); PROCESS-base > RESULTATIVE > RELATIONAL (e.g. *esdevenir* 'become' > *esdeveniment* > *esdevenimental*); ENTITY-base > AGENT > LOCATION (e.g. *flor* 'flower' > *florista* > *floristeria*); INSTRUMENT-base > ACTION (e.g. *martell* 'hammer' > *martellejar*); QUALITY-base > ACTION or PROCESS > PRIVATIVE (e.g. *lent* 'slow' > *alentir* > *desalentir*); ACTION or PROCESS > ITERATIVE (e.g. *pintar* 'paint' > *repintar*); and ENTITY-base > ACTION > INSTRUMENT – AGENT – LOCATION (e.g. *pasta* 'pastry' > *pastar* > *pastador*).

In the 10 cases of nouns we analyzed, the most frequent combinations across different derivational levels are: ENTITY-base > PROCESS > RESULTATIVE – ABILITY (e.g. *os* 'bone' > *ossi/òssia* > *ossificar* > *ossificació* – *ossificable*); ENTITY-base > ACTION – PROCESS > PRIVATIVE (e.g. *ull* 'eye' > *ullar* > *desullar*); ENTITY-base > PROCESS > COLLECTIVE – PRIVATIVE (e.g. *dent* 'tooth' > *dentar* > *dentadura* – *esdentar*); ENTITY-base > INSTRUMENT > AGENT (e.g. *ull* 'eye' > *ullera* > *ulleraire, ullerer/ullerera*); TEMPORAL-base > QUANTITY > AGENT – PROCESS – ACTION – ITERATIVE (e.g. *jorn* 'day' > *jornal* > *jornaler/jornalera* – *ajornalar* – *jornalejar*); ENTITY-base > LOCATIVE > QUALITY (e.g. *pedra* 'stone' > *pedregar* > *pedregós -osa*); and ENTITY-base > LOCATIVE >

CAUSATIVE > QUALITY > DIMINUTIVE (e.g. *aigua* 'water' > *aigual* > *aigualir* > *aigualit - ida* > *aigualidet -eta*).

In the derivational networks for the analyzed verbs, there are chained processes like the following: ACTION-base > ITERATIVE > ACTION – RESULTATIVE (e.g. *tallar* 'cut' > *retallar* > *retallada*); ACTION-base > QUALITY > DIMINUTIVE – AUGMENTATIVE (e.g. *estirar* 'pull' > *estirat -ada* > *estiradet -eta* – *estiradíssim -íssima*); ACTION-base > REVERSATIVE > RESULTATIVE > DIMINUTIVE (e.g. *cosir* 'sew' > *descosir* > *descosit* > *descosidet*); ACTION-base > RESULTATIVE > INSTRUMENT – PROCESS – QUALITY (e.g. *cremar* > *cremall* > *cremaller* – *cremallejar* – *cremallut, -uda*); and ACTION-base > ACTION > INSTRUMENT – LOCATION – RESULTATIVE (e.g. *beure* 'drink' > *abeurar* > *abeuradora* – *abeurador* – *abeurada*).

As for adjectives, some of the most recurring combinations are: QUALITY-base > ACTION > AGENT – QUALITY – RESULTATIVE (e.g. *nou nova* 'new' > *innovar* > *innovador -ora* – *innovació*); QUALITY-base > PROCESS – CAUSATIVE > QUALITY – CAUSATIVE (e.g. *negre -a* 'black' > *ennegrir* > *ennegridor -ora*); QUALITY-base > ACTION > INSTRUMENT (e.g. *calent -a* 'hot' > *encalentir* > *encalentidor*); QUALITY-STATE-base > PROCESS > PROCESS – CAUSATIVE (e.g. *vell -a* 'old' > *envellir* > *envelliment* – *envellidor -ora*); QUALITY-base > ACTION > PRIVATIVE (e.g. *fi fina* 'thin' > *afinar* > *desafinar*); and QUALITY-base > ACTION > AGENT – ACTION – ABILITY – RESULTATIVE/QUALITY/STATE > MANNER (e.g. *fi fina* 'thin' > *afinar* > *afinador -ora* – *afinació* – *afinable* – *afinat -ada* > *afinadament*).

At this point, we would like to highlight the fact that it is in the case of adjectives where the most homogenous patterns for derivation paths (with a maximum of three orders of derivation) can be found, since they all go through the combination QUALITY-base > ACTION – PROCESS. In the rest of the cases, the dispersion of semantic categories justifies why the combinations are very diverse.

22.9 Multiple occurrence of semantic categories

In Catalan, the change in word type by derivation facilitates the existence of combinations where semantic categories are repeated. In the analyzed data, we found cases of ACTION > ACTION (e.g. *ajornalar* > *ajornalament*; *foguejar* > *foguejament*; *cosir* > *cosit*; *agafar* > *agafada*; *conèixer* > *reconèixer* > *reconeixement*; *engrossir* > *engrossiment*); PROCESS > PROCESS (e.g. *ossificar* > *ossificació*; *ennegrir* > *ennegriment*); and QUALITY > QUALITY (e.g. *fogós -osa* > *fogositat*; *dolent -a* > *dolenteria*; *calent -a* > *calentor*; *llarg -a* > *llargada, llarguesa*; *vell -a* > *vellesa, vellura*; *gros grossa* > *grossària*; *estret -a* > *estretor, estretesa*).

22.10 Reversibility of semantic categories

In the Catalan data set, no instances of semantic categories occurring in a reversed order are attested.

22.11 Conclusions

The data analyzed for the Catalan language show that the average of the derivational orders for nouns, verbs and adjectives is set between 2.2 and 2.7 (Table 22.6). Only one noun (*aigua* 'water') and one adjective (*fi fina* 'thin') reach the 4th order, and no examples reach the 5th order.

Nouns constitute the morphosyntactic category with the highest number of derivational networks in the 1st order. In contrast to this, in the 2nd, 3rd and 4th levels, the results are very similar for the three word types (Table 22.1). The distance between the results of nouns and the other two categories can be explained by the fact that the volume of available suffixes that appear in the derivational networks for nouns is higher than the rest. Despite this fact, adjectives and verbs make up for this difference from the 2nd derivational order with a higher use of prefixes.

As for the mean saturation values, verbs are at the top of the list both in the 1st (32.86%) and 2nd orders (26.88%). In contrast, nouns have a higher value than adjectives in the 2nd and 3rd derivational levels (Table 22.5).

Lastly, the semantic categories present in the derivational networks analyzed do not exceed 50% of the available categories, which means that the Catalan language uses syntactic processes to cover the rest of the semantic categories. As stated above, the existence of semantic supercategories, which bring together items with different gradings or which correlate to the three word types, would explain the presence of semantic categories with a much higher frequency than others: ACTION, QUALITY, AGENT, AUGMENTATIVE and DIMINUTIVE. Even though some patterns are more recurring than others, we can state that the combination of semantic categories is quite diverse, and that it includes repetitions of categories in adjoining derivational orders. Blocking cannot be explained in Catalan based only on semantic constraints, but rather on morphology and pragmatics, as can be seen from the restriction on derivational orders.

References

Bernal, Elisenda, M. Teresa Cabré & Judit Freixa. 2015. Presentació. In Judit Freixa, Elisenda Bernal & M. Teresa Cabré (eds.), *La neologia lèxica catalana*, 9–11. Barcelona: Institut d'Estudis Catalans.
Cabré, M. Teresa. 1994. *A l'entorn de la paraula*, 2 vols. València: Publicacions de la Universitat de València.
Cabré, M. Teresa. 2002. La derivació. In Joan Solà, Maria Rosa Lloret, Joan Mascaró & Manuel Pérez Saldanya (eds.), *Gramàtica del català contemporani, vol. 1*, 731–774. Barcelona: Empúries.
Institut d'Estudis Catalans. 2016. *Gramàtica de la llengua catalana*. Barcelona: Institut d'Estudis Catalans.
Serrano-Dolader, David. 1999. La derivación verbal y la parasíntesis. In Ignacio Bosque and Violeta Demonte (eds.), *Gramática descriptiva de la lengua española, vol. 3*, 4683–4755. Madrid: Espasa.

Sources

DCVB = Alcover, Antoni M., Francesc de Borja Moll. 1962. *Diccionari català-valencià-balear*, 10 vols. Palma de Mallorca: Moll.
DIEC2 = Institut d'Estudis Catalans. 2007. *Diccionari de la llengua catalana*. Barcelona: Edicions 62 – Enciclopèdia Catalana.

Vincent Renner
23 Derivational networks in French

23.1 General notes

French commonly uses the morphological process of affixation in the formation of complex words, and derivational affixation is recognized to have three functions – a transpositional, a lexicon-expanding, and an evaluative function, to follow Laurie Bauer's (2004) terminology. Transpositional affixes aim at changing the lexical class of the base word, as in (1); lexicon-expanding affixes modify the denotational meaning of the base, as in (2); and evaluative affixes alter the connotational meaning of the base, as in (3):

(1a) *musée* 'museum' + *-al* '-al' > *muséal* 'museum-related'
(1b) *mondial* 'worldwide' + *-ité* '-ity' > *mondialité* 'worldwideness'

(2a) *abricot* 'apricot' + *-ier* 'tree' > *abricotier* 'apricot tree'
(2b) *a-* 'a-' + *mitose* 'mitosis' > *amitose* 'amitosis'

(3a) *chouette* 'nice' + *-os* '-y' > *chouettos* 'nicey'
(3b) *lapin* 'rabbit' + *-ou* '-y' > *lapinou* 'bunny'.

Establishing a derivational network markedly differs from grouping together the items of a word family. The outputs of affixation were included only if they appeared in one of the two largest standard general language dictionaries of Hexagonal French – the *Grand Robert de la Langue Française* (GRLF) and the *Trésor de la Langue Française* – or if they had been attested at least twice in reliable contexts returned by online search engine queries. A second limitation is that they were retained only if at least one 20th/21st-century output illustrating the same derivational pattern was listed in the GRLF. The present overview of the affixal capacity of French is thus slightly conservative given that the 30 simplex items of the core lexicon which constitute our study sample are centuries-old (most of them date back to the 11th and 12th centuries according to the GRLF) and that a number of their derivatives were institutionalized at a time when some affixes were still available, but which are not in the present-day state of the language. This is, for instance, the case for the deadjectival nominalizing suffixes *-eur* and *-esse*, which are both semantically equivalent to the English '-ness' and appear in derivatives like *chaleur* 'hotness', *longueur* 'length', *minceur* 'thinness', *épaisseur* 'thickness', *vieillesse* 'oldness', and *étroitesse* 'narrowness'.

Due to limitations of space, only one full derivational network is illustratively provided below (Figure 23.1). The network is structured around the simplex base form. All the 1st order derivatives stemming from the original base form are listed in the second column and each 2nd order derivative is listed on the same line as its 1st order base.

Base form	1st order derivatives (with semantic category)	2nd order derivatives (with semantic category)
coup(er)[a]	coupage; coupement (ACTION)	
	coupage; coupement (RESULTATIVE)	
	coupeur; coupeuse (AGENT)	
	coupeuse; coupoir (INSTRUMENT)	
	coupailler; coupasser (PEJORATIVE)	
	recouper (ITERATIVE)	recoupage; recoupement (ACTION)
	précouper (TEMPORAL)	précoupage (ACTION)
	surcouper (AUGMENTATIVE)	surcoupage (ACTION)
	coupable (ABILITY)	incoupable (PRIVATIVE); recoupable (ITERATIVE)

Figure 23.1: Derivational network for the verb couper 'to cut'.
[a]The -er infinitive suffix is inflectional and is thus disregarded in the derivational analysis.

23.2 Maximum derivational networks

To measure the structural richness of affixation, a virtual maximum derivational network can be computed for each order of derivation in each word-class, as shown in Table 23.1.

23.3 Saturation values

The degree of saturation, or relative saturation value, is presented in Tables 23.2–23.4 for each item of the three word-classes. In the class of nouns, there is a very wide gap between the highest and the lowest total saturation value (60), with a remarkable 0 value for two items: *feu* 'fire' and *eau* 'water'. This dramatically illustrates the frequent character of suppletion in French,

Table 23.1: Maximum derivational networks per order of derivation for all three word-classes.

Word-class	1st order	2nd order	3rd order	Σ
Nouns	21	33	6	60
Verbs	21	22	3	46
Adjectives	7	2	0	9
TOTAL	49	57	9	115

Table 23.2: Saturation values per order of derivation, nouns.

Noun		Saturation value (%)	1st order (%)	2nd order (%)	3rd order (%)
bone	os	60	38.1	66.67	100
eye	œil	1.67	4.76	0	0
tooth	dent	45	47.62	51.52	0
day	jour	3.33	4.76	3.03	0
dog	chien	5	14.29	0	0
louse	pou	13.33	19.05	12.12	0
fire	feu	0	0	0	0
stone	pierre	31.67	42.86	30.3	0
water	eau	0	0	0	0
name	nom	5	14.29	0	0

which has been repeatedly stressed in the linguistic literature (see e.g. Meillet 1913: 389). The adjective related to *feu* 'fire' is *igné* 'igneous' (from the Latin *igneus*); those related to *eau* 'water' are *aqueux* 'aqueous' (from the Latin *aquosus*) and *hydrique* 'hydric' (from the Greek *hudōr*). A majority of base nouns have a low 1st and 2nd order degree of saturation (under 20%), highlighting a somewhat limited general paradigmatic capacity.

In the verb category, there is a narrower gap between the extreme total saturation values (about 43%), but such a number still bears witness to a considerable heterogeneity of behaviours.

Table 23.3: Saturation values per order of derivation, verbs.

Verb		Saturation value (%)	1st order (%)	2nd order (%)	3rd order (%)
cut	couper	43.48	66.67	27.27	0
dig	creuser	43.48	42.86	50	0
pull	tirer	50	66.67	40.91	0
throw	lancer	28.26	33.33	27.27	0
give	donner	15.22	23.81	9.09	0
hold	tenir	15.22	19.05	9.09	33.33
sew	coudre	6.52	14.29	0	0
burn	brûler	28.26	57.14	4.55	0
drink	boire	17.39	23.81	9.09	33.33
know	savoir	13.04	4.76	18.18	33.33

Table 23.4: Saturation values per order of derivation, adjectives.

Adjective		Saturation value (%)	1st order (%)	2nd order (%)
bad	mauvais	44.44	57.14	0
new	nouveau	55.56	71.43	0
black	noir	88.89	85.71	100
straight	droit	22.22	28.57	0
warm	chaud	44.44	42.86	50
old	vieux	55.56	57.14	50
long	long	77.78	71.43	100
thin	mince	44.44	57.14	0
thick	épais	44.44	57.14	0
narrow	étroit	55.56	42.86	100

In the class of adjectives, the gap between the extreme total saturation values is again remarkably large at about 67%, but there is less overall heterogeneity than in the case of nouns and verbs, as 7 of the 10 adjectives have a value of 44.44% or 55.56%.

In Table 23.5, a bird's-eye view of the average saturation values per order of derivation is displayed, and it can again be underlined that the various percentages are fairly low, strikingly so in the case of nouns, mainly because of the commonplaceness of suppletion (e.g. œil 'eye' ~ oculaire 'ocular'; chien 'dog' ~ canin 'canine'; nom 'noun' ~ nominal 'nominal').

Table 23.5: Average saturation values per order of derivation for all three word-classes.

Word-class	1st order (%)	2nd order (%)	3rd order (%)
Nouns	18.57	16.36	10
Verbs	35.24	19.55	10
Adjectives	57.14	40	0

23.4 Orders of derivation

In Table 23.6, the variation in the number of attested orders of derivation is featured. Only verbs and nouns display three orders of derivation. Derivational richness is, however, somewhat limited in the case of verbs – nine items reach the 2nd order of derivation, but only three allow 3rd order derivation (e.g. *boire* 'to drink' > *buvable* 'drinkable' > *imbuvable* 'undrinkable' > *imbuvabilité* 'undrinkability') – and it is minimal for nouns, as it affects only one item, *os* 'bone', whose 3rd order derivatives are all technical terms from the domains of biology and medicine

Table 23.6: Maximum and average number of orders of derivation for all three word-classes.

Word-class	Maximum	Average
Nouns	3	1.4
Verbs	3	2.2
Adjectives	2	1.5

stemming from *ossification* (e.g. *os* 'bone' > *ossifier* 'ossify' > *ossification* 'ossification' > *surossiffication* 'overossification'). As for the class of adjectives, only two orders of derivation are attested and only half of the base words allow 2nd degree derivation (e.g. *long* 'long' > *longuet* 'longish' > *longuettement* 'longishly').

23.5 Derivational capacity

In Table 23.7, 1st order derivatives are examined cross-categorially. The class of adjectives exhibits the most homogeneity, with variation only between 2 and 6 outputs (respectively for the base adjectives *droit* 'straight' and *noir* 'black') and the maximum proportional deviation from the average is measured for nouns. In contrast to *feu* 'fire' and *eau* 'water', which have no derivatives, *dent* 'tooth', for instance, generates 5 nominal outputs (*dentée* 'bite', *dentier* 'dentures', *dentine* 'dentine', *dentiste* 'dentist', and *surdent* 'supernumerary tooth'), as well as 3 adjectival and 2 verbal outputs (respectively *denté* 'toothed', *dentaire* 'dental', *dental* 'dental', *édenter* 'to deprive of teeth', and *endenter* 'to tooth').

Table 23.7: Maximum and average derivational capacity for all three word-classes.

Word-class	Maximum	Average
Nouns	10	3.9
Verbs	14	7.4
Adjectives	6	4

In Table 23.8, a comparison of the numbers of derivatives in the different orders of derivation is drawn. If null and quasi-null average values are set aside, the most striking contrast opposes the class of nouns, which counts more 2nd order than 1st order derivatives, to that of verbs, which counts far fewer 2nd order than 1st order items. For denominal 2nd order derivatives, the distribution can be explained by the remarkable profitability of prefixation with the 2 adjectives *osseux* 'osseous' and *dentaire* 'dental' (e.g. LOCATIVE *interosseux* 'interosseous', *endodentaire* 'endodental', QUANTITIVE *uniosseux* 'uniosseous', *bidentaire* 'two-tooth', SIMILATIVE *pseudo-osseux* 'pseudo-osseous', *pseudo-dentaire* 'pseudo-dental', AUGMENTATIVE *hyperosseux* 'hyperosseous') in the specific context of scientific (biological/medical) terminology. For deverbal 2nd order derivation, profitability

Table 23.8: Average number of derivatives per order of derivation for all three word-classes.

Word-class	1st order	2nd order	3rd order
Nouns	3.9	5.4	0.6
Verbs	7.4	4.3	0.3
Adjectives	4	0.8	0

is mostly restricted to the addition of the ITERATIVE *re-* 're-', AUGMENTATIVE *sur-* 'over-' and PRIVATIVE *in-* 'un-' (e.g. *relancement* 'relaunch', *surcreusement* 'over-deepening', *indonnable* 'ungivable'), which may partly explain the comparatively low average value.

23.6 Correlation between semantic categories and orders of derivation

Turning to the distribution of individual affixes and semantic categories, it appears that their relative profitability varies substantially from one word-class to another. For nouns, it is striking to note that no single affix is used with half of the 10 base words. In contrast, a majority of verbs take the 1st order ITERATIVE *re-* 're-', AGENT *-eur/-euse* '-er' and ABILITY *-able* '-able'. In the 2nd order of derivation, the PRIVATIVE prefixation *in-* 'un-' is remarkably profitable as well as it applies to all the ABILITY deverbal adjectives (e.g. *lancer* 'to throw' > *lançable* 'throwable' > *inlançable* 'unthrowable'). As for the class of adjectives, it stands out in that it exemplifies the only cases of full 1st order profitability – the 10 adjectival bases realize AUGMENTATIVE *-issime* 'extremely' and MANNER *-ment* '-ly' – and also through the fact that all of its 8 2nd order derivatives realize MANNER *-ment* (e.g. *long* 'long' > *longuissime* 'extremely long' > *longuissimement* 'extremely longly').

Affixal rivalry may lead to the co-presence of full synonyms, as in (4):

(4a) *creusage ~ creusement* 'digging'; *empierrage ~ empierrement* 'stone surfacing' (ACTION and RESULTATIVE);
(4b) *édentement ~ édentation* 'lack of teeth' (RESULTATIVE);
(4c) *coupasser ~ coupailler* 'to cut in an irregular fashion' (PEJORATIVE);

(4d) *chiennerie ~ chiennaille* 'kennel of dogs' (COLLECTIVE);
(4e) *demi-long ~ semi-long* 'half-long' (SIMILATIVE).

It may also lead to some degree of specialization of the competing affixes, as illustrated by the INSTRUMENT suffixes and derivatives in (5):

(5a) *-ette*, in *tirette* 'bellpull', *tenette* 'lithotomy forceps';
(5b) *-oir*, in *coupoir* 'cutter', *creusoir* 'luthier's digger', *cousoir* 'sewing press', *brûloir* 'roasting machine';
(5c) *-eur*, in *lanceur* 'launch vehicle', *brûleur* 'burner';
(5d) *-euse*, in *coupeuse* 'cutting machine', *tireuse* 'photographic printing machine'.

INSTRUMENT *-ette* and *-oir* are used in nouns that typically denote implements, while *-eur* and *-euse* appear in nouns that typically denote machines.

23.7 Semantic categories with blocking effects

One remarkable limitation has been identified: MANNER (i.e. adverbialization in *-ment*) is the only semantic category with a blocking effect on deadjectival derivation.

23.8 Typical combinations of semantic categories

The co-presence of ABILITY, PRIVATIVE and STATIVE constitutes the only remarkably recurrent combination of semantic categories cross-categorially. Each of the 8 attested ABILITY deverbal adjectives generates a 2nd order PRIVATIVE output, and 5 of these items then allow 3rd order STATIVE derivation (see *imbuvabilité* 'undrinkability' in section 23.4 above).

23.9 Multiple occurrence of semantic categories

No remarkable multiple occurrences of the same semantic category have been noted in the derivational networks of French.

23.10 Reversibility of semantic categories

No remarkable reversibility of the ordering of semantic categories has been noted in the derivational networks of French.

23.11 Reasons for structurally poor derivational networks

As pointed out in section 23.3, a primary reason that explains why some derivational networks are relatively poor is suppletion. It can also be stressed that French commonly resorts to other lexicogenetic strategies: conversion is used for transpositional purposes to nominalize verbs (6) and adjectives (7); compounding is employed for lexicon-expanding purposes (8); and replication is utilized for evaluative purposes (9):

(6) *coup(er)* 'to cut' > *coupe* 'a cut';

(7) *mauvais* 'bad > (the) bad', *nouveau* 'new > (the) new';

(8a) *lance-satellites* (lit. 'launch$_V$-satellites') = *lanceur* 'launch vehicle';
(8b) *odontologie* 'odontology' = *dentisterie* 'dentistry';

(9) *chien* 'dog' > *chien-chien* 'doggy'; *os* 'bone' > *nonos* 'bone [+ evaluative].[1]

More broadly, French also frequently has recourse to non-morphological means to form new lexical units. This can, for example, be captured in the following synonymous pairs, which contrast an affixed form with an adjective-noun or noun-adjective construct (10), a noun-preposition-noun construct (11), and a simplex form (12):

(10a) *surnom* 'nickname' ~ *petit nom* (lit. 'little name');
(10b) *dentisterie* 'dentistry' ~ *médecine dentaire* (lit. 'dental medicine');

---

[1] For *os*, the partial left duplication takes place only after adding a prothetic syllable onset to the VC base.

(11a) *tenette* 'lithotomy forceps' ~ *pince à lithotomie* (lit. 'forceps to lithotomy');
(11b) *tirette* 'bellpull' ~ *cordon de sonnette* (lit. 'cord of bell');

(12) *dentine* 'dentine' ~ *ivoire* 'lit. ivory'.

23.12 Conclusions

French can be characterized by three main features: a limited derivational capacity overall (3rd order derivation is only marginally attested), fairly low saturation values in the different word-classes (under 60% for adjectives, under 40% for verbs, and under 20% for nouns), and wide gaps between individual saturation values in all word-classes and all orders of derivation.

References

Bauer, Laurie. 2004. The function of word-formation and the inflection-derivation distinction. In Henk Aertsen, Mike Hannay & Rod Lyall (eds.), *Words in their Places: A Festschrift for J. Lachlan Mackenzie*, 283–292. Amsterdam: Vrije Universiteit.

Grand Robert de la Langue Française, digital edition (v. 4.1). https://grandrobert.lerobert.com/ (accessed 9 March 2020).

Meillet, Antoine. 1913. La crise de la langue française. *Revue Politique et Littéraire – Revue Bleue* 51 (2). 385–390.

Trésor de la Langue Française, digital edition (v. 4). http://atilf.atilf.fr/dendien/scripts/tlfiv4/showps.exe?p=combi.htm (accessed 9 March 2020).

María Belén Villar Díaz
24 Derivational networks in Galician

24.1 General notes

As in the other Romance languages, word-formation in Galician makes ample use of two main processes: derivation and compounding. Only the first one is dealt with in this chapter, and our focus will mainly be on suffixation as it is the subprocess which generates the largest number of new units in Galician (Alonso Núñez 2000: 136), as is also the case in the neighbouring languages (Pena 1991: 81).

The (few) publications dealing with present-day derivation in Galician (González Fernández 1978; Pena 2005) emphasize the existence of a central and prototypical subsystem of derivation, that of deverbal nouns – and, more specifically, that of *nomina actionis* –, within the system of so-called heterogeneous derivation (Pena 2012: 327). In our derivational networks, however, a clear dominance of various patterns of deadjectival verbalization was found. This might seem to be a contradiction, but it is not if two considerations on the peculiarities of Galician are taken into account. First, it should be stressed that, alongside evaluative homogeneous derivation, the most productive derivational pattern in synchronic Galician is deadjectival verbal prefixal-suffixal derivation. To take an example, nine verbs with a CAUSATIVE and/or PROCESSUAL meaning have been derived from *vello* 'old' through the simultaneous concatenation of a prefix and a suffix: *avellar(se), avellentar(se), avelloar, avellouzar, envellecer, envellentar, revellar(se), revellirse,* and *revellecer* (these verbs are all quasi-synonyms meaning 'to age'; they can be distinguished through some degree of semantic specialization). Second, a number of units that are traditionally analyzed as deverbal derivatives were excluded from our data. Galician frequently resorts to morphological subtraction to form action nouns (e.g. *cortar* 'to cut' > *corta* 'a cut'; *cavar* 'to dig' > *cava* 'digging', *queimar* 'to burn' > *queima* 'burning') and this process, which used to be described as a type of back-formation (López Viñas 2012: 182), is now instead considered to be a case of conversion (Rainer 2012; Pena 2018).

The derivational networks of Galician were established using the resources compiled by the ILG (Institute of the Galician Language) and the lexicographical database of the dictionary of the RAG (Royal Galician Academy). Only those words with multiple occurrences in various 20th- and/or 21st-century textual sources were retained.[1] Words which were already attested under a derived form in Latin (e.g. *pronome* 'pronoun' < Lat. *pronomen*; *prolongar* 'to prolong' < Lat. *prolongare*) were excluded, and so were the cases of true suppletion, as in the units containing the learned elements *ocul-* (vs. *ollo* 'eye'), *acuat-* (vs. *auga* 'water') and *nomin-* (vs. *nome* 'name'). Cases of highly transparent base allomorphy – e.g. *petr-* (vs. *pedra* 'stone'), with an absence of the lenition of the voiceless dental plosive, and *os-* (vs. *óso* 'bone'), for which the absence of a diacritical mark indicates a difference of vocalic aperture, which is not perceived by all present-day speakers – were, however, retained. Finally, past participles with a resultative value were excluded, while those forms using *-ante* (*cortar* 'to cut' > *cortante* 'cutting, sharp') and *-ente* (*saber* 'to know' > *sabente* 'wise'), which are synchronically very distant from the original Latin present participles and are more and more frequent nowadays, especially in specialized terminologies, with an agentive value (e.g. *óso* 'bone' > *osificar* 'to ossify' > *osificante* 'ossifying agent'), were retained.

24.2 Maximum derivational networks

Table 24.1 highlights that the largest number of derivatives is generated in the word-class of adjectives and that only the 1st and 2nd orders of derivation are truly productive in Galician (the 3rd order only contains a few marginal items and no derivative is attested for the 4th or 5th orders).

Table 24.1: Maximum derivational networks per order of derivation for all three word-classes.

	1st order	2nd order	3rd order	4th order	5th order	Σ
Nouns	35	16	2	0	0	53
Verbs	30	23	4	0	0	57
Adjectives	43	17	2	0	0	62
TOTAL	108	56	8	0	0	172

---

[1] This led to discarding units that do exist (according to our linguistic competence) or could exist, but which were not attested in the consulted corpora (this especially concerns the diminutive suffixations *-iño*/*-iña* and the adverbialization *-mente*).

24.3 Saturation values

Table 24.2 shows that saturation varies greatly in the category of nouns, from 4.35% to 45.65%. The highest value (45.65%) is assigned to *pedra* 'stone', with *dente* 'tooth' closely behind (42.39%). These two nouns are the only ones that reach the 50% level of saturation for the 1st order of derivation. The lowest values have a saturation level under 10%. This is the case for *nome* 'name' (4.35%), *día* 'day' (7.67%), *ollo* 'eye' (9.78%) – whose low value can be partly explained by the phenomenon of learned suppletion mentioned above – and *can* 'dog' (5.43%), a noun which tends to resist derivation in Romance languages.[2] It is also to be noted that three of these four nouns have only 1st order derivatives (i.e. 0% saturation in the 2nd and 3rd orders).

Table 24.2: Saturation values per order of derivation, nouns.

Nouns		Saturation value (%)	1st order (%)	2nd order (%)	3rd order (%)	4th order (%)	5th order (%)
bone	óso	25	22.22	25.71	66.67	0	0
eye	ollo	9.78	16.67	0	0	0	0
tooth	dente	42.39	53.7	28.57	0	0	0
day	día	7.61	9.26	5.71	0	0	0
dog	can	5.43	9.26	0	0	0	0
louse	piollo	15.22	18.52	11.43	0	0	0
fire	fogo	31.52	29.63	37.14	0	0	0
stone	pedra	45.65	51.85	37.14	33.33	0	0
water	auga	21.74	29.63	11.43	0	0	0
name	nome	4.35	7.41	0	0	0	0

---

2 The percentages can be compared with those of the neighbouring languages, e.g. French *chien* and Portuguese *can*. Unlike the case of, for instance, Italian (*accanirsi*), in Galician, the vast majority of the derivatives that have a metaphorical meaning make use of another root, *perr-*, which is shared with Spanish (*emperrar / emperrenchar* 'to persist', *desemperrar / desemperrenchar* 'to stop persisting', *perrencha* 'caprice').

Table 24.3 shows a more balanced distribution for the category of verbs: two items, *tirar* 'to pull' and *beber* 'to drink', share the highest value (37.97%). Contrary to the general tendency, *tirar* has a higher value in its 2nd order of derivation (48.39%), which might be explained by the presence of several action nouns (e.g. *estirón* 'growth spurt', *estiramento* 'stretching', *retiramento* 'withdrawal'), which were obtained by suffixation rather than conversion. The lowest saturation values are found for the verbs *soster* 'to hold' (8.86%) and *dar* 'to give' (7.59%). For the latter, it should be noted that it coexists with the learned form *donar* (Lat. *donare*) and that *dar* is the only verb without any 2nd order derivative.

Table 24.3: Saturation values per order of derivation, verbs.

Verbs		Saturation value (%)	1st order (%)	2nd order (%)	3rd order (%)	4th order (%)	5th order (%)
cut	cortar	27.85	37.78	16.13	0	0	0
dig	cavar	29.11	28.89	29.03	33.33	0	0
pull	tirar	37.97	31.11	48.39	33.33	0	0
throw	lanzar	13.92	17.78	9.68	0	0	0
give	dar	7.59	13.33	0	0	0	0
hold	soster	8.86	11.11	6.45	0	0	0
sew	coser	24.05	26.67	16.13	66.67	0	0
burn	queimar	21.52	33.33	6.45	0	0	0
drink	beber	37.97	48.89	25.81	0	0	0
know	saber	18.99	28.89	6.45	0	0	0

In the category of adjectives, presented in Table 24.4, no base item has a saturation value below 10%. The highest value is for *negro* 'black' (44.87%), and immediately behind is *vello* 'old' (39.74%). These two high values can mainly be explained by their remarkable affinity with prefixal-suffixal derivation (see section 24.1 above). Unlike nouns and verbs, the adjectives are all productive down to the 2nd order of derivation, and two items have a noticeably higher 2nd order value – *novo* 'new' (28 > 58.33) and *longo* 'long' (26 > 66.67) – because of the use of several suffixes to form *nomina actionis*.

Table 24.5 gives all the average saturation values for each order of derivation and displays fairly low figures overall: under 30% for 1st order derivation, well

Table 24.4: Saturation values per order of derivation, adjectives.

Adjectives		Saturation value (%)	1st order (%)	2nd order (%)	3rd order (%)	4th order (%)	5th order (%)
narrow	estreito	15.38	18	12.5	0	0	0
old	vello	39.74	50	25	0	0	0
straight	dereito	24.36	24	29.17	0	0	0
new	novo	38.46	28	58.33	50	0	0
long	longo	37.18	26	66.67	0	0	0
warm	morno	23.08	34	4.17	0	0	0
thick	groso	14.1	16	12.5	0	0	0
bad	malo	10.26	12	8.33	0	0	0
thin	delgado	14.1	16	12.5	0	0	0
black	negro	44.87	60	12.5	50	0	0

Table 24.5: Average saturation values per order of derivation for all three word-classes.

	1st order	2nd order	3rd order	4th order	5th order
Nouns	24.815	15.713	10	0	0
Verbs	27.778	16.452	13.333	0	0
Adjectives	28.4	24.167	10	0	0

under 20% for 2nd order derivation (except for the category of adjectives, for the reasons given above) and around 10% for 3rd order derivation.

24.4 Orders of derivation

There exist three orders of derivation for each word-class in Galician, even though the average values in Table 24.6 conspicuously indicate that few base words – especially among the nouns – reach the 3rd order of derivation.

Table 24.6: Maximum and average number of orders of derivation for all three word-classes.

	Maximum	Average
Nouns	3	1.9
Verbs	3	2.2
Adjectives	3	2.2

24.5 Derivational capacity

The derivational capacity of present-day Galician is measured in Table 24.7. From an absolute standpoint, the maximum capacity for the 1st order of derivation is similar for the noun *dente* 'tooth' and the adjective *negro* 'black', which generated the highest number of derivatives (respectively, 29 and 30), while the most productive verb (*beber* 'drink') is far behind with only 22 derivatives. The average values are about the same for the three word-classes, with adjectives displaying a slightly higher capacity.

Table 24.7: Maximum and average derivational capacity for all three word-classes.

	Maximum	Average
Nouns	29	13.4
Verbs	22	12.5
Adjectives	30	14.2

Table 24.8 gives the average number of derivatives for all orders of derivation and shows a remarkable equality between the three word-classes in each order,

Table 24.8: Average number of derivatives per order of derivation for all three word-classes.

	1st order	2nd order	3rd order	4th order	5th order
Nouns	13.4	5.5	0.3	0	0
Verbs	12.5	5.1	0.4	0	0
Adjectives	14.2	5.8	0.4	0	0

as well as a virtual absence of derivational capacity in the 3rd order (an order in which the slight dominance of deadjectival units recedes).

24.6 Correlation between semantic categories and orders of derivation

In the 1st order of derivation, 9 out of 10 nouns generate DIMINUTIVE homogeneous derivatives (e.g. *óso* 'bone' > *osiño* 'little bone') while 8 out of 10 activate the category LOCATION (e.g. *óso* > *oseira* 'ossuary'). In 6 cases, the semantic values POSSESSIVE (e.g. *piollo* 'louse' > *piollento* 'lice-ridden') and PRIVATIVE (e.g. *piollo* > *despiollar* 'to pick lice off') are also activated. In the 2nd order, the categories ACTION and RESULTATIVE often coexist and are the most productive, with scores of 5 out of 10 (e.g. *pedra* 'stone' > *apedrar* 'lapidate' > *apredramento* 'lapidation'). The results for the 3rd order do not seem to be relevant as the three words concerned belong to different semantic categories.

For verbs, the most frequent semantic categories in the 1st order of derivation are ACTION and RESULTATIVE, with 9 and 8 verbs out of 10, respectively (e.g. *tirar* 'to pull' > *tirón* / *tiramento* 'a tug'). Then come AGENT, with 8 out of 10 (e.g. *tirar* > *tirador* 'shooter'), ABILITY, with 7 out of 10 (e.g. *soster* 'to hold' > *sostible* / *sostíbel* 'sustainable'), QUALITY (e.g. *tirar* > *tirante* 'tight') and INSTRUMENT (e.g. *tirar* > *tirador* 'a handle') with 6 out of 10. 5 verbs generate DIMINUTIVE 2nd order derivatives (e.g. *tirar* > *tirón* 'act of pulling' > *tironciño* 'act of pulling [+ evaluative]').[3] Out of the 3 verbs with 3rd order derivatives, 2 also generate DIMINUTIVE items (e.g. *tirar* > *estirar* 'to stretch' > *estirón* 'growth spurt' > *estironciño* 'growth spurt [+ evaluative]').

All adjectives generate DIMINUTIVE (e.g. *vello* 'old' > *velliño* 'old [+ evaluative]'), STATIVE (e.g. *vello* > *vellez* 'old age') and CAUSATIVE (e.g. *vello* > *envellecer* 'to age') derivatives (CAUSATIVES also often have a PROCESS reading); 9 adjectival bases lead to AUGMENTATIVE (e.g. *vello* > *vellísimo* / *revello* 'very old') derivations and 8 to MANNER derivations (e.g. *malo* 'bad' > *malamente* 'badly'). In the 2nd order of derivation, the categories ACTION and RESULTATIVE come first again (7 out of 10; e.g. *novo* 'new' > *renovar* 'to renew' > *renovación* 'renewing'); far behind come AGENT (e.g. *novo* > *renovar* > *renovador* 'renewing agent'), QUALITY (e.g. *novo* > *novidade* 'novelty' > *novidoso* 'novel') and MANNER (e.g. *malo* 'bad' >

---

[3] The evaluative character of diminutive suffixes, which is attested in many languages, is very salient in Galician.

malísimo 'very bad' > *malisimamente* 'very badly'). The results for 3rd order derivations are again irrelevant.

Several general conclusions can be drawn. It is in the word-class of adjectives that the highest degree of derivational productivity per semantic category is found: 10 out of 10 bases activate the categories DIMINUTIVE, CAUSATIVE/PROCESS and STATIVE. The first category, DIMINUTIVE, seems to be remarkably productive in Galician as it also includes 1st order denominal items as well as 2nd and 3rd order deverbal items. The second category, CAUSATIVE/PROCESS, is less present in denominal and deverbal derivations beyond the 1st order, but it stands out with the highest degree of saturation because of prefixal-suffixal derivation. The other salient feature of Galician is the presence of the semantic pair ACTION/RESULTATIVE, which is productive in all word-classes and orders of derivation.

24.7 Semantic categories with blocking effects

In the noun category, only a few semantic categories seem to trigger a blocking effect: virtually full blocking has been documented for DIMINUTIVE, and other blocking effects can be hypothesized for COLLECTIVE, LOCATIVE, POSSESSIVE and AGENT, even though they cannot be considered to be absolute.[4] These four categories also seem to block deverbal derivation, as does STATIVE. The category MANNER also has to be added for deadjectival derivation.

24.8 Typical combinations of semantic categories

Two distinct phenomena are relevant when scrutinizing typical combinations of semantic categories. First, in a number of derivatives, especially denominal ones, it is almost impossible to identify a unique value as two or more semantic

---

4 In our corpus-based research, no further derivation of any base word was attested for the four mentioned categories, but from a morphological standpoint we consider that adding an evaluative homogeneous suffix (of the DIMINUTIVE, AUGMENTATIVE or PEJORATIVE type) could be licit, as this type of suffixation is, as already stated, central to the derivational system of Galician: *dentadura* 'denture' > *dentaduriña* 'little denture' (COLLECTIVE > DIMINUTIVE), *oseira* 'ossuary' > *oseiriña* 'little ossuary' (LOCATIVE > DIMINUTIVE), *piollento* 'lice-ridden' > *piollentiño* 'lice-ridden [+ evaluative]' (POSSESSIVE > DIMINUTIVE), *fogueteiro* 'pyrotechnician' > *fogueteiriño* 'pyrotechnician [+ evaluative]' (AGENT > DIMINUTIVE).

categories seem to overlap[5]: POSSESSIVE-AUGMENTATIVE (e.g. *olludo* 'big-eyed'), POSSESSIVE-AUGMENTATIVE-PEJORATIVE (e.g. *osudo* 'who/which has prominent bones = scrawny'), and COLLECTIVE-DIMINUTIVE (e.g. *pedregullo* 'pile of small rocks'). Second, some so-called 'polyfunctional' affixes (Varela 2009: 44) generate derivatives (especially of the deverbal type) which are systematically given a double value: ACTION-RESULTATIVE (*-ción* / *-mento* / *-dura* / *-axe*; *lanzamento*, for example, not only means 'the act of throwing', but also the result of this act) or AGENT-INSTRUMENT (*-dor* / *-dora*; *lanzador*, for instance, not only means 'he who throws', but also 'an instrument to throw').

24.9 Multiple occurrence of semantic categories

Galician is not prone to semantic recursiveness. No salient example can be identified in our networks, even in the specific domain of evaluative derivation, in which other Romance languages like Spanish or Italian, for instance, can use the same suffix, or two similar suffixes, for intensification purposes (Varela 1999: 266).

24.10 Reversibility of semantic categories

No example of the reversibility of semantic categories is attested in our data.

24.11 Conclusions

The analysis of derivational networks in Galician shows that suffixation is by far the most productive subprocess. Prefixal-suffixal derivation comes second, and far behind is prefixation, a rare type of derivation that is limited to three semantic categories, LOCATION/TIME, ITERATIVE/AUGMENTATIVE and PRIVATIVE, in our data.

Derivation is very commonly used if one considers the total number of derivatives (see Table 24.1), but chain-derivation is moderately profitable as only two orders of derivation are truly attested in present-day Galician (see Table 24.6),

---

[5] In Galician, "it is especially frequent for two or more semantic types, which correspond to different paradigms, to coexist in one and the same derivative, which means that the meanings of the various paradigms do not always have clear boundaries; or, to put it differently, there are partial interparadigm intersections or overlappings" (Pena 2008: 565; our translation).

with an all-category average of 2.1 orders of derivation and an average of 0.36 derivatives for the 3rd order of derivation (see Table 24.8).

Our data lead to the conclusion that it is the word-class of adjectives that has the highest degree of derivational saturation thanks to the remarkable profitability of prefixal-suffixal derivation to form new deadjectival verbs.

As regards semantic types, the most frequently activated category is DIMINUTIVE/ATTENUATIVE. It is attested in combination with all types of bases, including verbal bases (e.g. *beber* 'to drink' > *bebiscar* 'to drink a small amount of liquid'), and in all orders of derivation. In the domain of heterogeneous derivation, the highest degree of productivity can be assigned to STATIVE and the pairs ACTION/ RESULTATIVE (with any base) and CAUSATIVE/PROCESS (with an adjectival base).

To conclude, we will point out that, in spite of its moderate profitability beyond the 2nd order of derivation, affixation, and suffixation in particular, is a remarkably productive process in the morphological system of present-day Galician.

References

Alonso Núñez, Aquilino. 2000. Os sufixos nominais diminutivos do galego actual [Diminutive nominal suffixes in present-day Galician]. *Verba* 27. 133–174.
González Fernández, Isabel. 1978. *Sufijos nominales en el gallego actual (Verba, anejo 11)*. Santiago de Compostela: Santiago University Press.
López Viñas, Xoán. 2012. *A formación de palabras no galego medieval: a afixación* [Word-formation in medieval Galician: Affixation]. A Coruña: Coruña University Press.
Pena, Jesús. 1991. La palabra: estructura y procesos morfológicos. *Verba* 18. 69–128.
Pena, Jesús. 2005. Os nomes denomináis de actividade, axentivos e instrumentais [Activity, action and instrument denominal nouns]. In Ana Isabel Boullón Agrelo, Xosé Luis Couceiro Pérez & Francisco Fernández Rei (eds.), *As tebras alumeadas* [The enlightened dark age], 423–431. Santiago de Compostela: Santiago University Press.
Pena, Jesús. 2008. La distinción entre centro y periferia aplicada al paradigma derivativo: el caso del sufijo -ería en español y en gallego. In Esther Corral Díaz, Lydia Fontoira Suris & Eduardo Moscoso Mato (eds.), *A mi dizen quantos amigos ey*, 565–571. Santiago de Compostela: Santiago University Press.
Pena, Jesús. 2012. Nombres denominales que expresan actividad y sus actantes o circunstantes. In Antonio Fábregas, Elena Feliu, Josefa Martín & José Pazo (eds.), *Los límites de la morfología. Estudios ofrecidos a Soledad Varela Ortega*, 327–339. Madrid: Autonomous University of Madrid Press.
Pena, Jesús. 2018. La Base de datos morfológica del español (BDME). In María Pilar Garcés (ed.), *Perspectivas teóricas y metodológicas en la elaboración de un diccionario histórico*, 17–61. Madrid & Frankfurt: Iberoamericana/Vervuet.
Rainer, Franz. 2012. Escarceos sobre la conversión sustantivo > adjetivo en español. In Antonio Fábregas, Elena Feliu, Josefa Martín & José Pazo (eds.), *Los límites de la*

morfología. Estudios ofrecidos a Soledad Varela Ortega, 369–382. Madrid: Autonomous University of Madrid Press.
Varela, Soledad. 1999. Sobre las relaciones de la morfología con la sintaxis. *Revista de filología española* 29. 257–281.
Varela, Soledad. 2009. *Morfología léxica: la formación de palabras*. Madrid: Gredos.

Sources

DdD = Santamaría, Antonio (ed.). 2006–2013. *Diccionario de diccionarios. Corpus lexicográfico da lingua galega* [Lexicographical Corpus of the Galician Language]. Instituto da Lingua Galega: Santiago de Compostela. http://sli.uvigo.es/ddd/ (last accessed December 2017).
DRAG = *Diccionario da Real Academia Galega* [Dictionary of the Royal Galician Academy]. González González, Manuel (ed.). 2012. *Real Academia Galega*. https://academia.gal/dicionario
RILG = Santamaría, Antonio (ed.). 2006–2017. *Recursos Integrados da Lingua Galega* [Integrated Resources of the Galician Language]. Instituto da Lingua Galega: Santiago de Compostela. http://sli.uvigo.es (last accessed December 2017).
TILG = Santamaría, Antonio (ed.). 2006–2013. *Tesouro Informatizado da Lingua Galega* [Computerized Thesaurus of the Galician Language]. Instituto da Lingua Galega: Santiago de Compostela. http://ilg.usc.es/TILG/ (last accessed December 2017).

Livio Gaeta
25 Derivational networks in Italian

25.1 General notes

With regard to the main questions discussed in the introductory chapter devoted to the Romance languages, a maximization approach has been adopted throughout this chapter on Italian (cf. Grossmann and Rainer 2004 for a detailed description of Italian word-formation). In particular, while – in accordance with the general design of the project – blatant cases of transflection have been left out from the sample (such as *bere* 'to drink' > *bevuta* 'drink', *discendere* 'to descend' > *discesa* 'descent', *nuotare* 'to swim' > *nuotata* 'swim', etc., which directly correspond to the feminine form of their respective past participles: *bevuto* 'drunk', *disceso* 'descended', *nuotato* 'swum', etc.), derivatives like *frustata* 'lash' and *martellata* 'hammer blow' have been included because a denominal interpretation is available. This is because of the suffix *-ata* that is found in denominal nouns like *pagliaccio* 'clown' > *pagliacciata* 'farce', which diachronically results from the reanalysis of the feminine past participle of 1st conjugation verbs (cf. Gaeta 2000). In these cases, a double motivation can be appealed to because we might take either the (denominal) verbs *frustare* 'to lash' and *martellare* 'to hammer' or the nouns *frusta* 'whip' and *martello* 'hammer' as a derivational base, relating the derivatives respectively either to the nominal base (via suffixation) or to the verbal base (via conversion). A similar approach has been adopted for cases in which an adjective can in principle be derived either from a verb via conversion (e.g. *occhiello* 'eyelet' > *occhiellare* 'to eyelet' > *occhiellato* 'eyeletted'), possibly accompanied by prefixation as in *osso* 'bone' > *disossare* 'to debone' > *disossato* 'deboned', or directly from a noun via suffixation (*occhiello* > *occhiell-ato*), possibly in combination with prefixation, as in *osso* > *dis-oss-ato*, on a par with clearly denominal nouns like *fortuna* 'luck' > *fortun-ato* 'lucky' and *grazia* 'grace' > *s-grazi-ato* 'ungraceful'. Notice that, in several cases, the intermediate verb does not occur or is rather infrequent with regard to the *-ato* derivative, as for instance in the case of *dente* 'tooth' > *dent-ato* 'dentate' and of the scarcely frequent conversion *dentare* 'to provide with teeth'. This makes a denominal derivation more plausible.

In accordance with the maximization approach, a number of patterns have also been included in the sample that are traditionally considered at the edge of the continuum between inflection and derivation. This concerns, for instance, the suffix of the so-called absolute superlative *-issimo*, which is traditionally assigned to inflection but is largely irrelevant for syntax, as shown by a comparison with the so-called relative superlative: *Gianni è bellissimo* 'Gianni is very beautiful' vs. *Gianni è il *bellissimo / più bello di tutti* 'Gianni is the most beautiful of all' (cf. Gaeta 2003), as well as the old form of the present participle, which has become in fact a suffix for AGENT nouns or adjectives (cf. Luraghi 1999). Finally, all instances of evaluative affixations have been included in the sample in spite of their problematic status with regard to prototypical derivation. A similar maximization approach has also been adopted for the difficult cline running from neoclassical compounding down to affixation. Following Iacobini (2004: 88), elements like *inter-*, *multi-*, *para-*, etc. have been included in the sample as they are commonly held to share the same properties of the prefixes with which they often form paradigmatic series. In contrast, other combining forms such as *tele-*, *video-*, *-fero*, *-logo*, etc. have been excluded because their behaviour is heterogeneous with regard to normal affixation.

The data mainly come from the two largest Italian dictionaries, the GDIU and the GDLI, and have been further enriched with the help of direct searches on the internet, while derivatives marked as rare, archaic or dialectal were mostly excluded.

25.2 Maximum derivational networks

Table 25.1 displays the maximum derivational networks per order of derivation that are relevant for the saturation value.

Table 25.1: Maximum derivational networks per order of derivation for all three word-classes.

	1st order	2nd order	3rd order	4th order	Σ
Nouns	35	43	11	4	93
Verbs	29	43	28	5	105
Adjectives	31	24	9	3	67
TOTAL	95	110	48	12	265

Note that the values for derivational networks are roughly similar in the 1st order, but they sharply decrease in the other orders for adjectives, while the opposite is true for verbs and nouns, where the values are even higher in the 2nd order than in the 1st. It is interesting to observe that the value for verbs in the

3rd order is quite high and in fact similar to that found in the 1st one. At any rate, the values for the 4th order are quite low for all word-classes.

25.3 Saturation values

In this section, the saturation values for the single word-classes are reported as they were elaborated in the general design of the project.

Table 25.2: Saturation values per order of derivation, nouns.

Nouns		Saturation value (%)	1st order (%)	2nd order (%)	3rd order (%)	4th order (%)
bone	osso	18.07	25.00	20.00	0.00	0.00
eye	occhio	30.72	35.94	37.14	8.70	0.00
tooth	dente	36.14	40.63	41.43	21.74	0.00
day	giorno	28.92	15.63	37.14	43.48	22.22
dog	cane	11.45	25.00	4.29	0.00	0.00
louse	pidocchio	13.86	26.56	8.57	0.00	0.00
fire	fuoco	48.80	39.06	51.43	52.17	88.89
stone	pietra	19.88	32.81	17.14	0.00	0.00
water	acqua	24.10	35.94	24.29	0.00	0.00
name	nome	18.67	18.75	18.57	21.74	11.11

It is interesting to observe that at least one top scorer is found in each of the three word-classes that displays a saturation value neatly surpassing or approximating the half of its derivational capacity: *tenere* 'to hold' for the verbs and *fuoco* 'fire' for the nouns, while among the adjectives, *lungo* 'long' and *nuovo* 'new' score equally and are closely followed by *caldo* 'warm'. Moreover, two members of this latter word-class clearly underexploit their capacity, namely *angusto* 'narrow' and *diritto* 'straight', with the effect of downsizing the general saturation value of this word-class with respect to the others. While this barely comes as a surprise given their lower frequency compared to their English correspondents, it is quite striking to observe that the verb *dare* 'to give' and the noun *cane* 'dog' score quite low, exploiting about – or even less than – one tenth of their derivational capacity in spite of their high frequency and familiarity. As for *dare*, this can arguably be

Table 25.3: Saturation values per order of derivation, verbs.

Verbs		Saturation value (%)	1st order (%)	2nd order (%)	3rd order (%)	4th order (%)
cut	tagliare	35.80	51.92	45.90	7.69	0.00
dig	scavare	16.05	23.08	16.39	10.26	0.00
pull	tirare	26.54	32.69	31.15	17.95	0.00
throw	gettare	9.88	13.46	13.11	2.56	0.00
give	dare	6.79	11.54	8.20	0.00	0.00
hold	tenere	64.81	36.54	77.05	82.05	70.00
sew	cucire	13.58	21.15	16.39	2.56	0.00
burn	bruciare	16.77	26.92	16.39	7.50	0.00
drink	bere	22.36	36.54	18.03	15.00	0.00
know	conoscere	35.40	25.00	40.98	35.00	62.50

Table 25.4: Saturation values per order of derivation, adjectives.

Adjectives		Saturation value (%)	1st order (%)	2nd order (%)	3rd order (%)	4th order (%)
narrow	angusto	4.65	8.33	3.13	0.00	0.00
old	vecchio	36.05	52.78	25.00	28.57	0.00
straight	diritto	4.65	11.11	0.00	0.00	0.00
new	nuovo	43.02	27.78	43.75	64.29	100.00
long	lungo	43.02	44.44	56.25	21.43	0.00
warm	caldo	39.53	33.33	43.75	50.00	25.00
thick	spesso	25.58	30.56	31.25	7.14	0.00
bad	cattivo	20.93	36.11	15.63	0.00	0.00
thin	sottile	20.93	27.78	25.00	0.00	0.00
black	nero	26.74	30.56	34.38	7.14	0.00

related to its reduced phonological size, which makes it a bad derivational basis. On the other hand, for *cane*, one might tentatively see the reason for its reduced saturation values in the 2nd and 3rd orders in its concrete reference, which is only partially exploited in the 1st order to convey more abstract and/or metaphorical meanings, similarly to the other noun *pidocchio* 'louse', which also scores quite low. Derivatives based on these extended meanings, however, are rarely open to further derivation. In addition, one should also consider the suppletive effect of the learned stems *cino-* and *pediculo-*, which are commonly used in terminologies and scientific or technical metalanguages. Concrete references that are rarely expandable metaphorically can also be held responsible for the reduced derivational capacity of the verb *cucire* 'to sew', while for *gettare* 'to throw', the competition with its near-synonym *lanciare* 'to launch, throw' can be invoked. At any rate, in the following table, the average saturation values per order of derivation are reported for all three word-classes.

On average, the values are quite homogeneous across the three word-classes.

Table 25.5: Average saturation values per order of derivation for all three word-classes.

	1st order	2nd order	3rd order	4th order
Nouns	29.53	26.00	14.78	12.22
Verbs	27.88	28.36	17.75	15.00
Adjectives	30.28	27.81	17.86	12.50

25.4 Orders of derivation

In the following table, the difference between the richness of nouns and verbs as derivational bases clearly stands out against the reduced derivational capacity of adjectives.

Table 25.6: Maximum and average number of orders of derivation for all three word-classes.

	Maximum	Average
Nouns	8	2.33
Verbs	9	2.63
Adjectives	6	1.69

25.5 Derivational capacity

This difference is also reflected in the following two tables, in which the maximum and the average derivational capacities for the three word-classes are reported with regard to the 1st order derivatives for all three word-classes.

Table 25.7: Maximum and average derivational capacity for all three word-classes.

	Maximum	Average
Nouns	26	18.9
Verbs	27	14.5
Adjectives	19	10.9

Table 25.8: Average number of derivatives per order of derivation for all three word-classes.

	1st order	2nd order	3rd order	4th order
Nouns	18.9	18.2	3.4	1.1
Verbs	14.5	17.3	7.1	1.2
Adjectives	10.9	8.9	2.5	0.5

25.6 Correlation between semantic categories and orders of derivation

There seems to be a certain correlation between saturation value and paradigmatic strength – the latter expressed by the total number of derivatives of the 1st order – in the 2nd order for all three word-classes (N_{2nd} = 0.46, V_{2nd} = 0.62, A_{2nd} = 0.63), while the correlation weakens and even becomes negative in the other orders (N_{3rd} = -0.03, V_{3rd} = 0.34, A_{3rd} = 0.34; N_{4th} = 0.19, V_{4th} = 0.17, A_{4th} = -0.05). This confirms the expectation that Italian apparently does not like long chains of affixes exceeding the 2nd order of derivation (cf. Gaeta 2005). Notice that the less robust correlation value obtained for nouns arguably depends on the low derivational capacity of *cane* and *pidocchio* discussed above.

Semantic categories typical of the 1st order of derivation are AUGMENTATIVE (present in 10 lexemes) MANNER (9), and DIMINUTIVE (7). It must be added that the other semantic category typical of adjectives in the 1st order is ABSTRACTION (10), but the suffixes mainly used to form abstracts, namely *-ità* and *-ezza*, are only marginally open to further derivation (cf. Gaeta 2005). This means that only verb-forming semantic categories, namely CAUSATIVE (6) and INCHOATIVE (3), provide bases which are further derived in the 2nd order for semantic categories like ACTION (8), ABILITY (7), AGENT (6), INSTRUMENT (5) and AGENT/FEMALE (4) with the addition of the semantic category MANNER (8), which is normally combined with bases displaying the elative suffix *-issimo* discussed above. Note the frequent occurrence of the conjoined categories AGENT/FEMALE, which is due to the highly productive suffix *-trice* (e.g. *nuovo* 'new' > *innovare* 'to innovate' > *innovatrice* 'innovator (fem.)'; cf. Gaeta 2010).

The picture for nouns and verbs is radically different. With regard to nouns, besides those relating to evaluative suffixes, namely DIMINUTIVE (10), AUGMENTATIVE (10) and PEJORATIVE (8), we observe a rich number of semantic categories typical of the 1st order which are distributed across different output word-classes: RELATIONAL (8), PRIVATIVE (7), QUALITY (7), AGENT (6), COLLECTIVE (6), LOCATION (6), ORNATIVE (6), SINGULATIVE (6), CAUSATIVE (5) and INSTRUMENT (5). This is reflected in 2nd order derivatives relating to semantic categories like ACTION (10), ABSTRACTION (7), AGENT (6), MANNER (6), ABILITY (5) and DIMINUTIVE (5). As for verbs, the semantic categories typical of the 1st order are ACTION (10), AGENT (10), ABILITY (9), AGENT/FEMALE (9), ITERATIVE (8), INSTRUMENT (7), DIMINUTIVE (6) and RESULTATIVE (6), which are reflected in 2nd order derivatives relating to semantic categories like ABILITY (10), ABSTRACTION (10), ACTION (9), AGENT (8), AGENT/FEMALE (8), and INSTRUMENT (6), which again give rise to 3rd order derivatives relating to ABSTRACTION (8) and, less typically, to ACTION (3) and AUGMENTATIVE (3).

25.7 Semantic categories with blocking effects

A certain number of factors of different natures can be held responsible for constraints on the derivational capacity of the lexemes. One factor of a phonological nature is the length of the base, as already pointed out for *dare*. Another factor is of a categorial nature, being connected either to the properties of a certain word-class or of a certain class of affixes. In this regard, the immensely productive suffix *-mente*, which is also the only suffix that forms adverbs, systematically excludes any further suffixation: *posteriore* 'posterior' > *posterior-mente* 'posterior-ADV' > **posteriorment-eggiare* (on productivity in Italian word-formation, cf. Gaeta and Ricca 2006). In terms of the derivational network adopted here, this restriction must be seen as a closing effect of the semantic category MANNER, which hampers any further derivation. More generally, adverbs are seldom possible bases of derivation: minor exceptions include *subito* 'immediately' > *subit-aneo* 'sudden', *indietro* 'backwards' > *indietr-eggiare* 'to move backwards', but *presto* 'soon' > **prest-aneo*, and *avanti* 'forwards' > **avant-eggiare*. The limited derivational capacity of *diritto* observed above also has to be seen from this viewpoint, since it is mainly used as an adverb.

On the other hand, the immense productivity of *-mente* must cede to bases displaying evaluative suffixes that generally hamper further derivations: *bello* 'beautiful' > *bell-ino* 'beautiful-DIM' > **bellina-mente*, *caldo* 'warm' > *cald-uccio* 'warm-DIM' > **calduccia-mente*, *cattivo* 'bad' > *cattiv-one* 'bad-AUG' > **cattivona-mente*, etc., unless a morphopragmatic trait [non-serious] is involved in the utterance, as in Manzoni's coinage *lungh-etta-mente* 'long-DIM-ADV'. Remarkably, the elative suffix *-issimo* does normally form adverbs: *cattiv-issima-mente* 'bad-AUG-ADV', *lungh-issima-mente* 'long-AUG-ADV', etc. The closing effect is not limited to *-mente*, but appears to be a general property of evaluative suffixes: *bellino* > **bellin-ezza*, *dolce* 'sweet' > *dolci-astro* 'sweet-PEJ' > **dolciastr-ificare*, etc. Again, in the terms adopted here, this restriction has to be seen as a closing effect of the semantic categories relating to evaluative meaning, namely DIMINUTIVE, AUGMENTATIVE (with the mentioned exception of *-issimo*) and PEJORATIVE.

25.8 Typical combinations of semantic categories

A number of chain-effects witnessing the derivational potential of the system can be observed, which are arguably related to the selective properties of the single affixes with regard to the input/output of the word-class.
- CAUSATIVE/ITERATIVE-ABILITY-ABSTRACTION: e.g. *caldo* 'warm' > *scaldare* 'to warm (up)' > *scaldabile* 'warmable' > *scaldabilità* 'warmability'; *cucire* 'to sew' > *ricucire* 'to re-sew' > *ricucibile* 're-sewable' > *ricucibilità* 're-sewability' (overall 7 cases)
- ABILITY-ABSTRACTION/PRIVATIVE-MANNER/ABSTRACTION: e.g. *conoscere* 'to know' > *conoscibile* 'knowable' > *conoscibilità* 'knowability' / *inconoscibile* 'unknowable' > *inconoscibilmente* 'unknowably' / *inconoscibilità* 'unknowability' (overall 7 cases)
- RELATIONAL-CAUSATIVE-ABSTRACTION(/ABILITY-ABSTRACTION): e.g. *fuoco* 'fire' > *focale* 'focal' > *focalizzare* 'to focalize' > *focalizzazione* 'focalization' / *focalizzabile* 'focalizable' > *focalizzabilità* 'focalizability' (overall 3 cases)

- QUALITY-PRIVATIVE-MANNER: e.g. *dente* 'tooth' > *dentato* 'toothed' > *sdentato* 'toothless' > *sdentatamente* 'toothlessly' (overall 3 cases)

These chains exploit the high productivity of verb-forming procedures as well as of certain affixes and affix combinations reflected in semantic sequences like ABILITY-ABSTRACTION and ABILITY-PRIVATIVE, which occur 43 and 13 times respectively in the sample.

25.9 Multiple occurence of semantic categories

Cases of multiple occurrences of the same semantic category are negligible, on the whole.

25.10 Reversibility of semantic categories

This phenomenon is non-existent in Italian.

25.11 Conclusions

To sum up, in Italian, the first two orders are considerably crowded with regard to the others, while no 5th order derivations occur. Verbs and nouns (in this order) clearly exhibit the highest number of derivational networks compared to adjectives, probably because of the closing effect of evaluative meanings (DIMINUTIVE, PEJORATIVE and, to an extent, AUGMENTATIVE) and of other semantic categories like MANNER and, to an extent, ABSTRACTION, which are particularly common with adjectives, especially in the 1st order. As a consequence, while the value for derivational networks of adjectives is quite high in the 1st order and sharply decreases in the others, the opposite is true for verbs and nouns, where the values are even higher in the 2nd order than in the 1st (Tables 25.1, 25.7 and 25.8). This is confirmed by the maximum and average number of orders of derivation, which are clearly lower for adjectives than the equivalent figures found for verbs and nouns (Table 25.6). In contrast, since the limits on the derivational capacity of adjectives result from the closing effects of certain meanings typically occurring in the 1st order, no repercussions are observed on the saturation value, which reflects the degree of actualization of the semantic categories that are activated at any order of derivation. In fact, similar values are obtained for all word-classes (Table 25.5), with the exception of nouns, where some misalignment has to be recorded (Table 25.2), probably because of the idiosyncratic properties of single lexemes that are due to the reduced size of the base or to the suppletive effect of learned stems.

References

Gaeta, Livio. 2000. On the Interaction between Morphology and Semantics: The Italian Suffix-ATA. *Acta Linguistica Hungarica* 47 (1–4). 205–229.
Gaeta, Livio. 2003. Produttività morfologica verificata su *corpora*: il suffisso *-issimo*. In Franz Rainer & Achim Stein (eds.), *I nuovi media come strumenti per la ricerca linguistica*, 43–60. Frankfurt/Main: Peter Lang.
Gaeta, Livio. 2005. Combinazioni di suffissi in italiano. In Maria Grossmann & Anna M. Thornton (eds.), *La formazione delle parole*, 229–247. Roma: Bulzoni.
Gaeta, Livio. 2010. On the viability of cognitive morphology for explaining language change. In Alexander Onysko & Sascha Michel (eds.), *Word Formation from Cognitive Perspectives*, 75–95. Berlin & New York: Mouton de Gruyter.
Gaeta, Livio & Davide Ricca. 2006. Productivity in Italian word-formation: A variable-corpus approach. *Linguistics* 44 (1). 57–89.
GDIU = De Mauro, Tullio (ed.). 1999. *Grande Dizionario Italiano dell'Uso*, 8 volumes. Turin: UTET.
GDLI = Battaglia, Salvatore et al. (1964–2009). *Grande Dizionario della Lingua Italiana*, 23 volumes. Turin: UTET.
Grossmann, Maria & Franz Rainer (eds.). 2004. *La formazione delle parole in italiano*. Tübingen: Niemeyer.
Iacobini, Claudio. 2004. Prefissazione. In Maria Grossmann & Franz Rainer (eds.), *La formazione delle parole in italiano*, 97–163. Tübingen: Niemeyer.
Luraghi, Silvia. 1999. Il suffisso *-ante/ente* in italiano: fra flessione e derivazione. In Paola Benincà, Alberto Mioni & Laura Vanelli (eds.), *Fonologia e Morfologia dell'italiano e dei dialetti d'Italia*, 539–550. Roma: Bulzoni.

Alina Villalva
26 Derivational networks in Portuguese

26.1 General notes

Word-formation in Portuguese relies largely on processes of affixation, namely suffixation and prefixation (Villalva and Gonçalves 2016). Although this distinction is traditionally acknowledged, the identification of the grammatical function of affixes in word structures leads to a different partition of affixes that aggregates all prefixes and all evaluative suffixes under the label of morphological modifiers, setting them apart from all derivational suffixes that are morphological predicates.

Derivation comprises processes forming adjectives (e.g. *bebí-vel* 'drinkable'), adverbs (e.g. *nova-mente* 'newly'), nouns (e.g. *escava-ção* 'excavation') and verbs (e.g. *nom-e-ar* 'to name'). It can also be accomplished by prefixal-suffixal derivation, which is particularly productive as a verb-forming resource (e.g. *en-velh-ecer* 'to grow old'). Most derivational suffixes have a Latin origin, either dating from the initial language state (e.g. *engenh-eir-o* 'engineer') or from a more recent neoclassical borrowing trend, usually mediated by another Romance language or even by English (e.g. *funcion-ári-o* 'employee'). Most deadjectival suffixes form STATE nouns (e.g. *nov-idad-e* 'newness'); denominal suffixes form relational adjectives (e.g. *dent-al* 'dental'); and they both form CAUSATIVE verbs (e.g. *a-long-ar* 'to elongate'; *em-pedr-ar* 'to cobble'). Deverbal suffixes typically form action nouns (e.g. *lança-ment-o* 'launching') and AGENT nouns (e.g. *corta-dor* 'cutter').

Morphological modifiers do not interfere with the grammatical properties of the base form (e.g. word-class, gender, conjugation). All modifier suffixes are evaluative, i.e. they convey a judgement on the base form, which is very often context-dependent – labels such as DIMINUTIVE, AUGMENTATIVE or PEJORATIVE merely reveal their typical interpretation. There are two series of evaluative suffixes: one is root-based (e.g. *car(a)* 'face' > *car-inha* 'face+inha') and the other is word-based (e.g. *unh(a)* 'nail' > *unha-zinha* 'nail+zinha'). The DIMINUTIVE suffixes -*inh(o/a)* and -*zinh(o/a)* are the most frequently used. The other evaluative suffixes are far less productive, except for the superlative adjective-forming suffixes -*íssimo* and -*zíssimo*. The distribution of these suffixes is multiply constrained. There are dialectal preferences (e.g. northern and central dialects prefer -*inh(o/a)* and -*zinh(o/a)* and southern dialects prefer -*it(o/a)* and -*zit(o/a)*); prosodic constraints (e.g. longer words reject root-based suffixes (?*apartamentinho* vs. *apartamentozinho* 'apartment+inho/zinho'; **jornalistinha* vs. *jornalistazinho* 'journalist+inho/zinho'); frequency effects (less frequent words reject the suffix -*inh(o/a)*, e.g. *olhinho* vs. ?*olhozinho* 'eye +inho/zinho' and ?*asminha* vs *asmazinha* 'asthma+inha/zinha'); and various types of lexical control (e.g. athematic words require the z-evaluative series – *mauinho* vs. *mauzinho*, *cãoinho* vs. *cãozinho*). The use of these suffixes is typically reserved for oral speech and informal registers, so the above-mentioned constraints are not felt as strong interdictions and this is why the margin for variation is wide.

The number of productive modifier prefixes is quite modest. Most of them originate in ancient Greek and Latin prepositions and adverbs – older prefixes are generally consensually accepted as such (e.g. *in-capaz* 'unable'), while neoclassical loans are often considered as roots (e.g. *super-velho* 'very old'). The distinction is spurious, however, since they all are modifiers irrespective of the lexical status.

The sources used for checking the existence of words in the Portuguese networks were the *Corpus de Referência do Português Contemporâneo* and Google Books (restricted to publications in European Portuguese).

26.2 Maximum derivational networks

Table 26.1 displays the maximal derivational networks from the Portuguese sample. Only three orders of derivation were documented. Overall, nouns and adjectives behave similarly in terms of maximum derivational networks, and they are both above the verbs' levels. The same observation applies to 1st and 2nd order results. In the 3rd order, adjectives clearly take the lead and verbs surpass nouns, albeit minimally.

Table 26.1: Maximum derivational networks per order of derivation for all three word-classes.

	1st order	2nd order	3rd order	Σ
Nouns	36	26	2	64
Verbs	26	18	3	47
Adjectives	31	23	10	64
TOTAL	94	68	15	175

26.3 Saturation values

An observation of the saturation values for the three word-classes reveals that the lowest mean saturation value is always approximately 6% and the highest mean saturation value is always close to 50%.

The Portuguese sample of nouns includes 8 masculine nouns (4 -*o* stem, 2 -*e* stem, 1 -*a* stem and 1 athematic) and 2 (-*a* stem) feminine nouns. Athematic nouns form a marginal stem class that tends either to block further derivation or to use an allomorph for that purpose – this is the case for *cão* 'dog' and its allomorph *can-* (e.g. *canil* 'kennel').[1]

Table 26.2 shows that the mean saturation values for nouns range between 6% and 50%. The noun with the highest mean saturation value is *dente* 'tooth', which is also one of the two cases with a 3rd order derivation. The noun with the lowest mean saturation value (*água* 'water') has only 1st order derivation,

Table 26.2: Saturation values per order of derivation, nouns.

Nouns		1st order (%)	2nd order (%)	3rd order (%)	Total (%)
bone	osso	36.11	26.92	0	31.25
eye	olho	25	3.85	0	15.63
tooth	dente	55.56	42.31	50	50
day	dia	11.11	15.38	0	12.5
dog	cão	22.22	0	0	12.5
louse	piolho	33.33	15.38	0	25
fire	fogo	38.89	34.62	0	35.94
stone	pedra	30.58	26.92	50	29.69
water	água	11.11	0	0	6.25
name	nome	16.67	19.23	100	20.31

---

1 The unmarked stem/gender classes for nouns in Portuguese are -*o* stem masculine (cf. *oss-o* 'bone') and -*a* stem feminine (cf. *pedr-a* 'stone'). However, the other two combinations are also possible: -*a* stem masculine (cf. *map-a* 'map') and the less common -*o* stem feminine (cf. *trib-o* 'tribe'). The remaining thematic classes include both masculine and feminine nouns (cf. masculine *dent-e* 'tooth', feminine *ment-e* 'mind'; masculine *ator* 'actor', feminine *atriz* 'actress'; masculine *avô* 'grandfather', feminine *avó* 'grandmother'). Stem and gender class membership is an idiosyncratic feature of each noun root.

which may be due to the fact that its root rivals with the equivalent neoclassical roots *aqu-* (e.g. *aquoso* 'watery') and *hidr-* (e.g. *hídrico* 'hydric').

The mean saturation values for verbs, as seen in Table 26.3, also range between 6% (for *dar* 'to give', which also lacks 2nd and 3rd order derivations) and 49% (for *cortar* 'to cut', although it does not have a 3rd order derivation). The low performance of the verb *dar* is probably explained by the fact that a single consonant forms the root – the phonetic fragility of the root often blocks further derivation. Finally, only two verbs (*cavar* 'to dig' and *lançar* 'to throw') have 3rd order derivations.

Table 26.3: Saturation values per order of derivation, verbs.

Verbs		1st order (%)	2nd order (%)	3rd order (%)	Saturation value (%)
cut	cortar	57.69	44.44	0	48.94
dig	cavar	23.08	27.78	66.67	27.66
pull	puxar	30.77	38.89	0	31.91
throw	lançar	34.62	38.89	33.33	36.17
give	dar	11.54	0	0	6.38
hold	segurar	19.23	5.56	0	12.77
sew	coser	19.23	5.56	0	12.77
burn	queimar	53.85	33.33	0	42.55
drink	beber	23.08	11.11	0	17.02
know	saber	15.38	27.78	0	19.15

The Portuguese sample of adjectives includes nine (*-o/-a* stem) variable adjectives and one athematic invariable adjective (*mau* 'bad').[2] Table 26.4 shows that the mean saturation values for adjectives range between 6% and 55%. The adjective with the highest mean saturation value is *velho* 'old', which is also one

---

[2] The stem and gender behaviour of adjectives is formally very similar to the behaviour of nouns. The major distinction sets apart gender-variable and gender-invariable adjectives, which means that the applicable classes are as follows: variable classes include *-o/-a* (e.g. *velho/velha* 'old'), zero/*-a* (e.g. *francês/francesa* 'French') and athematic/athematic (e.g. *mau/má* 'bad'); invariable classes include *-a* (e.g. *careca* 'bald'), *-e* (e.g. *leve* 'light'), zero (e.g. *capaz* 'able') and athematic (e.g. *ruim* 'bad'). Stem and gender class membership, as well as variability, are idiosyncratic features of each adjective root.

of the three with 3rd order derivations. The adjective with the lowest mean saturation value (*preto* 'black') is also the only one that has only 1st order derivations – this is probably due to the fact that it is a colour adjective.[3]

Table 26.4: Saturation values per order of derivation, adjectives.

Adjectives		1st order (%)	2nd order (%)	3rd order (%)	Saturation value (%)
narrow	estreito/a	25.81	4.35	0	14.06
old	velho/a	64.52	56.25	20	54.69
straight	direito/a	16.13	13.04	0	12.5
new	novo/a	45.16	69.57	60	56.25
long	longo/a	22.58	34.78	0	23.44
warm	morno/a	35.48	4.35	0	18.75
thick	grosso/a	35.48	39.13	0	31.25
bad	mau	25.81	26.09	40	28.13
thin	fino/a	29.03	26.09	0	23.44
black	preto/a	12.9	0	0	6.25

Table 26.5 displays the average saturation values for Portuguese nouns, verbs and adjectives, which are globally low (less than 31% for the 1st order, 28% for the 2nd and 20% for the 3rd). 1st order mean values are quite similar,

Table 26.5: Average saturation values per order of derivation for all three word-classes.

	1st order	2nd order	3rd order
Nouns	28.1	18.5	20
Verbs	28.85	23.33	10
Adjectives	31.29	27.39	12

---

[3] Colour adjectives form a peculiar set. Apart from often being formally similar to colour nouns, they cannot occur in a prenominal position (cf. **amarela casa* 'yellow house' vs. *nova casa* 'new house') and they resist superlative suffixation (cf. **amarelíssimo* 'yellow+*íssimo*').

but 2nd order values stretch from verbs in both directions, thus yielding a considerable distance between nouns and adjectives. In the 3rd order, verbs and adjectives have quite similar values, albeit half of the mean value of nouns.

26.4 Orders of derivation

As shown in Table 26.6, the maximum number of orders for the Portuguese sample is 3 and the average is lower than 2.5.

Table 26.6: Maximum and average number of orders of derivation for all three word-classes.

	Maximum	Average
Nouns	3	2.2
Verbs	3	2.3
Adjectives	3	2.4

26.5 Derivational capacity

The maximum derivational capacities of nouns and adjectives are identical, and they are both higher than the maximum capacity of verbs (cf. Table 26.7), which may be related to the fact that verbs are less prone to evaluative suffixation than nouns and adjectives.

Table 26.7: Maximum and average derivational capacity for all three word-classes.

	Maximum	Average
Nouns	20	10.1
Verbs	15	7.5
Adjectives	20	9.7

Table 26.8 shows that the maximum derivational capacity is always found in 1st order derivation. Noun and adjective values are always higher than verb values. 1st order nouns are slightly higher than 1st order adjectives, but 2nd and 3rd order adjectives have higher values than nouns.

Table 26.8: Average number of derivatives per order of derivation for all three word-classes.

	1st order	2nd order	3rd order
Nouns	10.2	4.8	0.4
Verbs	7.5	4.2	0.3
Adjectives	9.7	6.3	1.2

26.6 Correlation between semantic categories and orders of derivation

Table 26.9 shows that there is a strong correlation between saturation values and derivational strength in the 1st order of all word-classes. The 2nd order reveals a strong tendency for direct proportionality and, in the 3rd order, adjectives display a low level of correlation, whereas nouns and verbs display a low tendency to direct and indirect proportionality, respectively.

Table 26.9: Correlation between saturation values and derivational strength.

	1st order	2nd order	3rd order
Nouns	1	0.8	0.1
Verbs	1	0.7	-0.1
Adjectives	1	0.7	0.4

In the 1st order, all nouns and all adjectives generate words that fall under the category DIMINUTIVE (e.g. *oss-inho* 'bone+DIM', *estreit-inho/a* 'narrow+DIM'), and, eventually, they produce more than one DIMINUTIVE word: the 10 nouns produce 28 DIMINUTIVES (e.g. *foguinho, foguito, fogacho, fogozinho, fogaréu* 'fire+DIM') and the

10 adjectives produce 17 DIMINUTIVES (e.g. *velhinho, velhito, velhote* 'old+DIM'). The same holds for adjectives and the semantic category AUGMENTATIVE: the 10 adjectives produce 25 AUGMENTATIVES (e.g. *estreit-íssimo/a* 'narrow+AUG'). STATIVE is also a well-represented category for adjectives: 9 adjectives produce 17 STATIVE forms, though some are certainly more frequently used than others (e.g. *estreiteza* and *estreitura* 'narrowness'). The remaining categories (16 for nouns and 10 for adjectives) are less well documented: they affect 6 words or less. ITERATIVE is the most productive category for 1st order verbs (8 verbs, such as *relançar* 'to throw again', allow the formation of 9 ITERATIVE verbs), followed by AGENT (8 AGENT derivatives, such as *cavador* 'digger', for 7 verbs) and ACTION (15 ACTION derivatives, such as *queimadura* 'burn', for 6 verbs). The remaining 14 categories affect 5 verbs or less.

In the 2nd order, ACTION is a representative category for denominals (12 derivatives, such as *apedrejamento* 'stoning', for 7 words), and the same holds for deadjectivals (20 derivatives for 6 words). For 2nd order deverbals, the most prominent category is DIMINUTIVE (13 derivatives, such as *segurançazinha* 'safety +DIM', for 6 words). No significant figures stand up for any semantic category within the 3rd order derivatives.

In total, 27 semantic tags are required for the Portuguese sample. Most of them occur within the three word-classes, but some are much more frequent than others: AUGMENTATIVE, DIMINUTIVE and ACTION represent 40% of the total number of derivatives; 12 of the other categories represent 38.5% of the total (ABILITY, AGENT, CAUSATIVE, ENTITY, ITERATIVE, MANNER, PEJORATIVE, PRIVATIVE, RESULTATIVE, STATIVE, SUBITIVE and TEMPORAL).

The remaining 12 categories, representing 21.5% of the total number of derivatives, occur only with one or two word-classes. COLLECTIVE (e.g. *ossada* 'bones', *velhada* 'old people') and PROCESS (e.g. *envelhecer* 'to grow old', *engrossar* 'to thicken') occur with denominals and deadjectivals; QUALITY (e.g. *envelhecedor* 'aging', *cortante* 'cutting') and REVERSATIVE (e.g. *antienvelhecimento* 'anti-aging', *descoser* 'unsew') occur with deadjectivals and deverbals; and LOCATIVE (e.g. *pedreira* 'quarry', *bebedouro* 'drinker') occurs with denominals and deverbals. Finally, COMITATIVE (e.g. *consabedor* 'someone who shares knowledge') occurs only with 2nd order deverbals; COMPOSITION (e.g. *dentina* 'dentin') occurs with 1st order denominals; POSSESSIVE (e.g. *ossudo* 'bony') and RELATIONAL (e.g. *ósseo* 'osseous') occur with 1st and 2nd order denominals; INSTRUMENT (e.g. *puxador* 'doorknob') occurs with the three orders of deverbals; REFLEXIVE (e.g. *auto-renovação* 'self-renovation') occurs with 3rd order deadjectivals; and SIMILATIVE (e.g. *seminovo* 'semi-new') occurs with all three orders of deadjectivals.

26.7 Semantic categories with blocking effects

MANNER and some DIMINUTIVES and AUGMENTATIVES are systematic blocking categories. This is probably due to the fact that MANNER and z-evaluatives select fully inflected words: MANNER is realized by the suffix *-mente* that attaches to feminine singular adjectives (e.g. *novamente* 'newly'), and z-evaluatives such as *-zinho/a* (e.g. *pedrazinha* 'stone+DIM') or *-zão* (e.g. *mauzão* 'bad+AUG') typically attach to nouns and adjectives after inflection. The sample provides insufficient data for further assessment of blocking cases, however.

26.8 Typical combinations of semantic categories

A typical combination of semantic categories occurs between PROCESS/CAUSATIVE verbs[4] and ACTION/RESULTATIVE nouns[5] (sometimes also SUBITIVE nouns). The relationship is observable both in 1st order deverbal derivations (e.g. *puxão* 'tug', *lançamento* 'throw', *cosedura* 'stitching', *cortadela* 'superficial cut') and in 2nd order denominal and deadjectival derivations (e.g. *nomeação* 'nomination', *apedrejamento* 'stoning', *envelhecimento* 'aging', *afinação* 'tuning', *endireitadela* 'slight straightening').

Another typical combination holds between DIMINUTIVE and all the typical semantic categories of nouns: AGENT (e.g. *dentistazinho* 'dentist+DIM'); ACTION (e.g. *inovaçãozinha* 'innovation+DIM'); COLLECTIVE (e.g. *dentadurazinha* 'denture+DIM'); ENTITY (e.g. *fogueirinha* 'bonfire+DIM'); INSTRUMENT (e.g. *puxadorzinho* 'doorknob+DIM'); STATIVE (e.g. *maliciazinha* 'malice+DIM'); and SUBITIVE (e.g. *cortadelazinha* 'superficial cut+DIM').

---

[4] The distinction between CAUSATIVE and PROCESS verbs has no clear morphological correlates. The suffix *-ecer* (cf. *envelhecer* 'to grow old') is usually associated with a PROCESS reading, but the other verb-forming processes produce verbs that can have both readings (cf. *engrossar* 'to become thick', *engrossar* 'to turn X thick').
[5] The distinction between ACTION and RESULTATIVE nouns is equally opaque from a morphological point of view. Most deverbal action nouns gain a RESULTATIVE reading (cf. *adiamento* 'postponing', *adiamento* 'new deadline').

26.9 Multiple occurrence of semantic categories

Multiple occurrence is a typical feature of modifiers, however DIMINUTIVE is the only case found in this sample (e.g. *dentinhozinho* 'tooth+DIM+DIM', *pedrinhazinha* 'stone+DIM+DIM'). There is also one case of the reocurrence of evaluatives that belong to different semantic categories (*supermauzinho* 'AUG+bad+DIM').

26.10 Reversibility of semantic categories

In the Portuguese data set, no instances of semantic categories occurring in a reversed order are attested.

26.11 Reasons for structurally poor derivational networks

The size of the Portuguese derivational networks is constrained by some methodological choices. Regarding evaluative derivatives, only those that have a record in the reference sources have been considered, though many more are possible words. Loans that do not have a compositional structure in Portuguese have also been excluded (e.g. *costura* 'sewing', which is probably a French loan). This decision has a direct bearing on the size of the derivational paradigms, since many simple roots coexist with recent cognates that are used to form some derivatives (e.g. *direito* 'straight' vs. *direto* 'direct', which forms *indireto* 'indirect', *diretamente* 'directly, straightly') or neoclassical complex loans (e.g. *água* 'water' vs. *aquoso* 'watery', *aquatic* 'aquatic'; or *dentição* 'dentition', since the verb **dentir* is non-existent).

Furthermore, the exclusion of conversion helps to explain the scarcity of derivatives. Conversion is a productive non-morphological word-formation process in Portuguese (cf. Villalva 2013), and the output of conversion is very often also the supplement for further derivational interventions.[6]

---

[6] Note that four of the verbs in the sample are converted from adjectives (e.g. *cortar* 'to cut' from *curto* 'short', *segurar* 'to hold' from *seguro* 'safe') or nouns (e.g. *lançar* 'to throw' from *lança* 'spear', *cavar* 'to dig' from *cava* 'hole'). Since the base forms are not included in the sample, some of their derivatives are also excluded (e.g. *encurtar* 'to shorten', *seguramente* 'safely', *lanceiro* 'lancer', *cavidade* 'cavity').

Finally, the sample also excludes past participles (e.g. *aguada* 'watery preparation', *nomeada* 'fame', *empedrado* 'cobbled pavement', *refogado* 'stew') and, consequently, the derivatives that they potentiate (e.g. *aguadeiro* 'water carrier', *aguadilha* 'serosity', *nomeadamente* 'namely'). The status of these forms in Portuguese is quite complex (cf. Villalva 2009), but it has been argued that participial adjectives are not formed by inflection or by conversion. Note that all Portuguese verbs allow the inflection of a *-do* form, which is always invariable and is used to form periphrastic constructions with the auxiliary verb *ter* 'to have' (cf. *eu tenho viajado muito* 'I have travelled a lot'). The passive participle is not a verbal inflected form – it agrees, in gender and number, with the external argument (cf. *o livro foi pedido* 'the book was ordered', *as revistas foram pedidas* 'the journals were ordered'), but, of course, not all verbs are eligible (cf. **eu fui viajado* '*I was travelled'). Finally, some participles, though not eligible for passive constructions, may occur as deverbal adjectives (cf. *há pessoas muito viajadas* 'there are people who travel a lot'), which suggests that they are not obtained by conversion but by an independent deverbal *-d(o/a)* suffixation.

26.12 Conclusions

The Portuguese sample of derivational networks grasps a heterogeneous set of nouns, verbs and adjectives. They all allow the formation of immediate derivatives and often trigger 2nd order derivatives. The 3rd order is not always available though, and none of these words allow any further progression. Other Portuguese words may allow a 4th order of derivation (e.g. *in-des-monta-bil-idade* 'non-un-assemble-abl-ity'), even if this is not a type of structure that is commonly found. Furthermore, modification can be used systematically to increase the morphological complexity of any given noun or adjective (cf. *indesmontabilidade-zinha, super-indesmontabilidade, super-indesmontabilidade-zinha*). However, the usage of such words is highly constrained by specific pragmatic conditions; these affixes can be used, for instance, as irony markers. It is also worth noting that these derivational networks help to consolidate the opposition between derivation and modification. The frequency of modifier affixes, or at least some – namely DIMINUTIVE for nouns, AUGMENTATIVE for adjectives, and ITERATIVE for verbs –, is clearly higher than the frequency of derivational suffixes.

References

Villalva, Alina. 2009. A categoria 'particípio' e questões adjacentes. *Anais do Congresso Internacional da ABRALIN – João Pessoa 2009*. http://abralin.org/site/publicacao-em-anais/abralin-joao-pessoa-2009/.

Villalva, Alina. 2013. Bare Morphology. *Revista de Estudos Linguísticos da Univerdade do Porto* 8. 121–141.

Villalva, Alina & Carlos Alexandre Gonçalves. 2016. The phonology and morphology of word formation. In L. Wetzels, S. Menuzzi & J. Costa (eds.), *Handbook of Portuguese Linguistics*, 167–187. Oxford: Wiley-Blackwell.

Carmen Mîrzea Vasile
27 Derivational networks in Romanian

27.1 General notes

Derivation is the most important word-formation process in Romanian, suffixation being more productive than prefixation. Romanian has a rich inventory of affixes and allomorphs, whether inherited from Latin or borrowed from Slavic, Hungarian, Turkish, or, beginning from the end of the 18th century, from French, Italian and Latin. Back-formation (as well as blending, clipping or acronomy) is not a pre-eminent characteristic, whereas conversion distinguishes Romanian amongst other Romance languages. Besides adjective nominalization and past participle adjectivization, two highly productive patterns are adjective adverbialization and conversion of the supine into an action noun. In today's Romanian, compound words (concatenating free and combining forms) are less frequent than the affixed ones, the mechanism of compounding being more active as far as the nominal and the adjectival outputs are concerned. A descriptive overview of Romanian morphological derivation (the only word-formation process considered in our chapter) can be found in, amongst others, Fischer (1989), Vasiliu (2009), Croitor (2013), Rădulescu Sala (2015) and Grossmann (2016).

The derived forms discussed in this chapter belong to contemporary Romanian in general use. The sample data were mainly extracted from current dictionaries of Romanian (amongst which was DEX, the most important general dictionary of Romanian, and DA-DLR, the academic thesaurus dictionary). In order to provide evidence of the existence of a rare derivative, we also referred to the CoRoLa corpus (the first reference corpus for Romanian) and, whilst observing necessary care and discrimination, to internet archives accessed via searches on Google.

27.2 Maximum derivational networks

As can be seen from Table 27.1, all three word-classes have a maximum of four orders of derivation. For nouns and verbs, the sum of the highest numbers of derivatives per semantic category is comparable in the 1st and the 2nd orders of derivation (117 and 115, respectively), whilst in the 3rd order this sum falls to less than half (50). In the 4th order, the adjective *lung* 'long' has 1 derivative, and the verb *bea* 'drink' has 2 derivatives (under two different semantic categories).

Table 27.1: Maximum derivational networks per order of derivation for all three word-classes.

	1st order	2nd order	3rd order	4th order	Σ
Nouns	40	43	21	5	109
Verbs	39	52	17	2	110
Adjectives	38	20	12	1	71
TOTAL	117	115	50	8	290

As for nouns, there are 6 derivatives (under two different semantic categories): *ochi* 'eye' and *foc* 'fire', with 1 derivative, and *nume* 'name', with 4.

Verbs and nouns resemble one another with respect to their derivational potential (110 and 109, respectively); that of the adjectives (71) is much smaller. If, in the 1st order of derivation, all three word-classes have a similar derivational potential, in the other three orders adjectives are less productive. It is worth mentioning that both verbs and nouns have a higher derivational potential in the 2nd order than in the 1st order, whilst the derivational productivity of adjectives constantly decreases from the 1st order through to the 3rd order, with a considerable drop in the 4th order.

27.3 Saturation values

The saturation value of a sample word is deemed lesser or greater according to the number of available slots in a network it can fill and the extent to which it can produce derivatives in each semantic category. Many semantic categories are attested, some of which are not central, typical ones, and this lowers the saturation value of derivational networks. For example, on the one hand, there are unique instantiations of semantic categories such as SINGULATIVE (see *och-eadă* 'glance' across the 10 denominal networks), PEJORATIVE (see *negr-otei* 'nigger' within the deadjectival networks), or COMITATIVE (see *co-deține* 'co-hold' within the deverbal networks). On the other hand, one can see a remarkable affix rivalry and semantic micro-variation under a given semantic category (see the five 1st order DIRECTIONAL derivatives from *trage* 'pull' and the five 1st order DIMINUTIVES from *apă* 'water').

The three word-classes have a similar average structural richness (see Table 27.5 below). The saturation values per order of derivation for all three word-classes are not very high; they constantly decrease from the 1st order through to the 4th order. These relatively low average saturation values, as well as the extreme individual saturation values of sample words (see Tables 27.2–27.4), are necessitated by the numerous atypical semantic categories. This is due to the differences between sample words in terms of the suppletion of the base, the lexico-semantic domain they belong to, expressivity, the acceptability of a neologistic affix, etc. Some of these circumstances are mentioned in sections 27.5 and 27.6 (see also Moroianu 2013; Rădulescu Sala 2015).

Table 27.2: Saturation values per order of derivation, nouns.

Nouns		Saturation value (%)	1st order (%)	2nd order (%)	3rd order (%)	4th order (%)
bone	os	31.19	35	34.88	23.81	0
eye	ochi	33.94	42.5	37.21	14.29	20
tooth	dinte	34.86	57.5	34.88	0	0
day	zi	12.84	20	11.63	4.76	0
dog	câine	13.76	27.5	9.3	0	0
louse	păduche	12.84	30	4.65	0	0
fire	foc	35.78	42.5	20.93	57.14	20
stone	piatră	29.36	40	37.21	0	0
water	apă	13.76	32.5	4.65	0	0
name	nume	30.28	17.5	27.91	47.62	80

We should provide some additional explanations at this point. Firstly, the semantic categories PROCESS and RECIPROCAL are expressed regularly by reflexive constructions, which in Romanian, similarly to other Romance languages, are considered to belong to the syntax. This triggers the scarcity of the derivatives under these two important semantic categories. The second point relates to the category ABILITY. The typical strategy to express ABILITY in Romanian is to use a supine construction (a non-finite form of the verb preceded by the preposition *de*: e.g. *tăia* 'cut' → *de tăiat* 'cuttable'). Thus, the number of derivatives expressing ABILITY is not so high. The third point accounts for the rarity of *-ant/-ent* derivatives, which usually express the category ENTITY. The suffix *-ant/-ent* is more frequently associated with stems of foreign origin (1a) than with native ones (1b):

Table 27.3: Saturation values per order of derivation, verbs.

Verbs		Saturation value (%)	1st order (%)	2nd order (%)	3rd order (%)	4th order (%)
cut	tăia	10	25.64	1.92	0	0
dig	săpa	20.91	30.77	21.15	0	0
pull	trage	45.45	58.97	46.15	17.65	0
throw	arunca	11.82	23.08	7.69	0	0
give	da	11.82	12.82	13.46	5.88	0
hold	ține	38.18	30.77	44.23	41.18	0
sew	coase	11.82	28.21	3.85	0	0
burn	arde	20.91	38.46	13.46	5.88	0
drink	bea	46.36	30.77	44.23	82.35	100
know	cunoaște	24.55	35.9	19.23	17.65	0

Table 27.4: Saturation values per order of derivation, adjectives.

Adjectives		Saturation value (%)	1st order (%)	2nd order (%)	3rd order (%)	4th order (%)
narrow	îngust	14.08	21.05	10	0	0
old	vechi	18.31	28.95	10	0	0
straight	drept	25.35	21.05	40	16.67	0
new	nou	21.13	18.42	20	33.33	0
long	lung	42.25	47.37	25	50	100
warm	cald	30.99	23.68	45	33.33	0
thick	gros	26.76	31.58	25	16.67	0
bad	rău	15.49	18.42	15	8.33	0
thin	subțire	32.39	42.11	35	0	0
black	negru	49.3	55.26	50	33.33	0

Table 27.5: Average saturation values per order of derivation for all three word-classes.

	1st order (%)	2nd order (%)	3rd order (%)	4th order (%)
Nouns	34.5	22.33	14.76	12
Verbs	31.54	21.54	17.06	10
Adjectives	30.79	27.5	19.17	10

(1a) *ard-ent* ← *arde* 'burn' (< Fr. *ardent*), *pietrific-ant* (< Fr. *pétrifiant*)
(1b) *țin-ant ← *ține* 'hold', *arunc-ant ← *arunca* 'throw'

Another important point to make regards the semantic category MANNER: it is almost completely missing from our 30 derivational networks, because adverb formation with suffixes is a relatively unproductive process in Romanian. In contrast with other (standard) Romance languages, in Romanian, MANNER is expressed mainly by adverbs identical to the masculine / neuter singular form of the adjective, which is either primary and non-analyzable (2a) or derived by various affixes (2b), and conversion should be ignored here. Not a single core adjective derives a 1st order MANNER adverb.

(2a) *cald* 'warm(ly)', *rău* 'bad(ly)', *subțire* 'thin(ly)'
(2b) *căldur-os* 'warm(ly), cordial(ly)', *subțir-el* 'thinnish(ly)', *zil-nic* 'daily', *ne-în-foc-at* 'not enthusiastical(ly)'

Another compensatory strategy for expressing MANNER is the use of lexical expressions made up of *în mod/în chip* 'in the manner (of)', *din punct de vedere* 'from the point of view (of)' + adjective, *cu* 'with' + abstract noun, *ca* 'like' + concrete noun, etc.

In our 30 derivational networks, we found only three derived MANNER adverbs:

(3a) *beț-iv-ește* 'like a drunkard'
(3b) *beț-iv-ăn-ește* 'like a hard-drinker'
(3c) *câin-ește* 'like a dog, meanly'

27.4 Orders of derivation

As shown in Table 27.6, for all three word-classes, the maximum number of orders is four, the average being below 3. Each of the 30 base words generates

Table 27.6: Maximum and average number of orders of derivation for all three word-classes.

	Maximum	Average
Nouns	4	2.8
Verbs	4	2.7
Adjectives	4	2.8

derivatives in no less than two orders, and at least half of them (5 nouns, 6 verbs, 7 adjectives) have derivatives in the 3rd order. Three nouns (*ochi* 'eye', *foc* 'fire', *nume* 'name'), one adjective (*lung* 'long') and one verb (*bea* 'drink') attain four orders of derivation (see also supra, section 27.2).

27.5 Derivational capacity

As can be seen in Table 27.7 below, both the maximum and average derivational capacities are comparable for all three word-classes. The average derivational capacity of the nouns is a little higher (13.8) than that of the verbs (12.3) and of the adjectives (11.7). In Romanian, primary nouns, verbs, and adjectives typically derive between 11 and 14 complex words in the 1st order. The highest number of direct derivatives in the class of nouns is provided by *dinte* 'tooth' (23), whilst the lowest is provided by *nume* 'name' (7). In the case of the verbs, the extremities are *trage* 'pull' (23) and *da* 'give' (5). As for adjectives, *negru* 'black' has three times as many direct derivatives (21) as *rău* 'bad' or *nou* 'new' (both 7). However, the three groups of sample words exhibit homogeneity as far as their number of direct derivatives is concerned: about one third of the members of each category approach the average derivational capacity of their class.

Table 27.7: Maximum and average derivational capacity for all three word-classes.

	Maximum	Average
Nouns	23	13.8
Verbs	23	12.3
Adjectives	21	11.7

The average derivational capacity decreases in the 2nd order for all three categories of words (see Table 27.8). Verbs, however, maintain a value closer to that in the 1st order (11.2 vs. 12.3), and even achieve a higher maximum (24, for the same verb *trage* 'pull') than in the 1st order (23).

Table 27.8: Average number of derivatives per order of derivation for all three word-classes.

	1st order	2nd order	3rd order	4th order
Nouns	13.8	9.6	3.1	0.6
Verbs	12.3	11.2	2.9	0.2
Adjectives	11.7	5.5	2.3	0.1

We notice that the core nouns that have the highest total number of derivatives exhibit stem allomorphy (*foc* 'fire', *dinte* 'tooth', *ochi* 'eye', etc.) and can receive a wide range of neologistic affixes. The verbs *bea* 'drink' and *trage* 'pull' are the richest in derivatives. In the former case, expressivity plays an important role, whilst the latter's productivity is largely due to the fact that the native stem is included in a great number of loan-translations (Rom. *a-trage* vs. Fr. *attirer*, Rom. *dis-trage* vs. Fr. *distraire*). Due to complex reasons (amongst which are expressivity and inclusion in loan-blends), the adjectives *negru* 'black' and *lung* 'long' are the most productive.

27.6 Correlation between semantic categories and orders of derivation

The correlations between semantic categories that are expressed by more than 6 sample words in the 1st order of derivation are the following (the number of core words that derive a semantic category and the total number of derivatives under that semantic category can be found between parentheses): for nouns, DIMINUTIVE (9/28), CAUSATIVE (8/16), AUGMENTATIVE (7/8), AGENT (7/10), RELATIONAL (6/8), and COLLECTIVE (6/16); for adjectives, AUGMENTATIVE (10/22), CAUSATIVE (10/12), DIMINUTIVE (9/24), PRIVATIVE (8/8), and STATIVE (6/13); and for verbs, AGENT (10/10), AGENT+FEMALE (10/13), ITERATIVE (9/10), ENTITY (7/13), and ABILITY (7/7). The top two semantic categories correlated to the 2nd order are: for nouns, PRIVATIVE (7/10) and LOCATION (6/20); for adjectives, ABILITY (6/7) and ENTITY (5/8); and for verbs,

PRIVATIVE (9/26) and AGENT (5/14). Thus, for the 2nd order of derivation, except for the 9 core verbs deriving 26 PRIVATIVES, we did not notice any strong correlation with a given semantic category, although some tendencies exist.

Nouns and adjectives have an important number of 1st order DIMINUTIVES and AUGMENTATIVES. For example, *apă* 'water' derives 5 DIMINUTIVES (*ap-ică, ap-icică, ap-(i)șoară, ap-iță, ap-(u)șoară*) and *vechi* 'old', 4 AUGMENTATIVES (*arhi–vechi, super-vechi, stră-vechi, ultra-vechi*). The smaller number of denominal AUGMENTATIVES, compared with the number of deadjectival AUGMENTATIVES, is due to the fact that we have excluded[1] from our derivational networks the combinations of *super* with nouns (*super(-)foc* 'super fire', *super(-)câine* 'super dog', etc.). In Romanian reference works on word-formation, *super-* is considered to be a prefix. But, for this chapter, in line with the general principles of the volume, we decided to disregard occurrences of *super(-)* + noun, because the combination is quasi-regular, i.e. every noun has the possibility to be preceded by *super(-)*. In this case, the occurrence of *super(-)* implies that the speaker is impressed by a feature of the noun that is prominent in the given context. There are two possible interpretations of this usage of *super(-)* that justify its exclusion from Romanian derivative networks: (i) the extreme productivity of *super(-)* before nouns is a reason to consider it an inflexional-like affix; and (ii) *super(-)* could be interpreted as an invariable adjective placed before the noun.[2]

The total number of derivatives under some semantic categories is remarkable. Besides the data provided above, we must add that, in the 1st order, 5 nouns have 9 QUALITY derivatives and 5 different groups of verbs derive 13 AUGMENTATIVES, 8 INSTRUMENTS, and 8 LOCATION nouns. This fact bears witness to the affixal rivalry (see the examples from the DIMINUTIVE and AUGMENTATIVE series above) and to a number of specializations inside some semantic categories such as INSTRUMENT or ENTITY.

27.7 Semantic categories with blocking effects

The only certain observation to be made about the blocking effect of the semantic categories is that MANNER *-ește* adverbs do not allow further derivation. If

---

[1] The exception is *super-păduche* 'a medicine-resistant lice', which has a special meaning and is included in the network.
[2] In Romanian, the adjective follows the noun. The anteposition of the adjective is correlated with particular values (quite often, intensive values, as in our case). It should be added that the element *super(-)* before a noun can be spelled in three different ways: hyphenated, as a separate word, or directly attached to the noun. Thus, the spelling is irrelevant to its categorial status.

they clearly block diminution (otherwise accepted for primary adverbs and adverbialized adjectives), the subsequent negation is virtually possible in an oral repetitive pattern with a concessive value (4). The examples from (4a) were attested in our sources, while (4b) was not. A complex word like *super(-)câinește* 'very badly' is also theoretically possible, but was not attested.

(4a) *piatră, ne-piatră* 'stone or whatever', *rău, ne-rău* 'bad or otherwise'
(4b) *câin-ește, ne-câin-ește* 'like a dog or not'

27.8 Typical combinations of semantic categories

There are some recurrent combinations of semantic categories across all three word-classes. Within the 30 derivational networks, the following combinations are found quite frequently: RELATIONAL > LOCATION (20), ENTITY > DIMINUTIVE (16), CAUSATIVE > ENTITY (15), CAUSATIVE > ABILITY (14), CAUSATIVE > ITERATIVE (9), AUGMENTATIVE > AGENT (9), and CAUSATIVE > REVERSATIVE (7).[3] The semantic category PRIVATIVE can follow many categories, such as AGENT (16), ABILITY (13), ENTITY (8), RELATIONAL (7), and QUALITY (7). However, the important fact is that no recurrent combinations exist for all 10 sample words from the three word-classes for two given subsequent orders.

These combinations are not assigned exclusively to a word-class or to specific subsequent derivational orders. For example, a frequent combination of two semantic categories from the 1st and 2nd orders within the derivational networks of nouns (such as (5a-c)) is usually also found in other orders (5d), or across the derivational networks of sample verbs or adjectives in exactly the same orders of derivation (6a, b) or in other orders (6c).

(5a) *ochi* 'eye' > *ochi-os* (QUALITY) > *ne-ochi-os* (PRIVATIVE)
(5b) *os* 'bone' > *os-ifica* (CAUSATIVE) > *dez-os-ifica* (REVERSATIVE)
(5c) *nume* 'name' > *num-i* (CAUSATIVE) > *re-num-i* (ITERATIVE)
(5d) *nume* 'name' > *num-i* (CAUSATIVE) > *de-num-i* (CAUSATIVE) > *re-denum-i* (ITERATIVE) (cf. (5c))

---

[3] An apparently interesting combination occurs twice: *bețiv-an* 'hard-drinker' (AUGMENTATIVE) > *bețivăn-el* (DIMINUTIVE) and *pietr-oi* 'big stone' (AUGMENTATIVE) > *pietroi-aș* (DIMINUTIVE). The combination AUGMENTATIVE > DIMINUTIVE shows once again how productive the DIMINUTIVE affixes are in Romanian and illustrates the special semantics of evaluative affixes.

(6) a. *negru* 'black' > *negr-i* (CAUSATIVE) > *des-negr-i* (REVERSATIVE) (cf. (5b))
　　b. *nou* 'new' > *în-no-i* (CAUSATIVE) > *re-în-no-i* (ITERATIVE) (cf. (5c))
　　c. *rău* 'bad' > *rău-tate* (STATIVE) > *rău-tăc-ios* (QUALITY) > *ne-rău-tăc-ios* (PRIVATIVE) (cf. (5a))

27.9 Multiple occurrence of semantic categories

The semantic category DIMINUTIVE occurs twice in one single derivational network of one adjective (7). The semantic category CAUSATIVE has two occurrences within the networks of one noun (8a) and one adjective (8b). Note that the repeated semantic categories are next to each other.

(7)　*subțire* 'thin' > *subțir-el* (DIMINUTIVE) > *subțir-el-uț* (DIMINUTIVE)

(8)　a. *nume* 'name' > *num-i* 'name' (CAUSATIVE) > *de-num-i* (CAUSATIVE)
　　b. *lung* 'long' > *lung-i* (CAUSATIVE) > *pre-lung-i* (CAUSATIVE)

27.10 Reversibility of semantic categories

There are some couples of semantic categories that could occur in a reversed order. The usual orders exemplified in (9) can also be found reversed (10).

(9) a. ITERATIVE (*reînnoi* 'renew') > ABILITY (*reînnoibil* 'renewable')
　　b. STATIVE (*recunoștință* 'gratitude') > PRIVATIVE (*nerecunoștință* 'ingratitude')
　　c. STATIVE (*răutate* 'badness') > QUALITY (*răutăcios* 'malignant')
　　d. CAUSATIVE (*îngroșa* 'thicken') > ENTITY (*îngroșătură* 'calloused skin')

(10) a. ABILITY (*cunoscibil* 'knowable') > ITERATIVE (*recunoscibil* 'recognizable')
　　b. PRIVATIVE (*nedrept* 'unjust') > STATIVE (*nedreptate* 'injustice')
　　c. QUALITY (*ardent* 'ardent') > STATIVE (*ardență* 'ardour')
　　d. ENTITY (*ardei* 'pepper') > CAUSATIVE (*ardeia* 'pepper')

This flexibility in ordering the semantic categories could be correlated with the heterogeneous origins of Romanian affixes and also with the base allomorphy of many derivatives. Thus, no combination of two semantic categories is affected by a systematic reversibility across the 30 derivational networks.

27.11 Conclusions

The quantitative and qualitative analysis of the 30 derivational networks indicates that Romanian is a language with (at least) average structural diversity and irregularities in terms of word-formation. All three word-classes have a maximum of four orders of derivation and a similar average saturation value. Furthermore, the maximum and average derivational capacities are comparable: a primary noun, verb, or adjective typically has between 11 and 14 direct derivatives. Thus, verbs and nouns have a greater derivational potential than adjectives.

The relative randomness comes from the scarcity of the strong correlations between the semantic categories and the orders of derivation (there are only four semantic categories instantiated by all ten sample verbs and adjectives in the 1st order), from the possibility of the multiple occurrences of a semantic category (i.e. DIMINUTIVE and CAUSATIVE) in one single derivational chain, from the quite unstable combinations of semantic categories (for example, the combinations ITERATIVE > ABILITY or STATIVE > PRIVATIVE that can occur in a reversed order), as well as from atypical semantic categories (for example, SINGULATIVE and COMITATIVE).

This characteristic of Romanian word-formation should be associated with relatively inconsistent rules of combination between a variety of affixes of different origins and different allomorphic stems. In addition, the notable use of some specific types of conversion (such as adjective adverbialization and supine nominalization), as well as the strong suppletion of the bases and the semantic under-specializations, impoverish the derivational networks.

Acknowledgements: I would like to express my gratitude to the editors of the volume for their patience and support. Special thanks also to my colleagues Ion Giurgea, Irina Nicula and Alexandru Nicolae from the "Iorgu Iordan – Alexandru Rosetti" Institute of Linguistics of the Romanian Academy for their precious help during the various stages of the development of this chapter. Any remaining errors are the responsibility of the author.

References

Croitor, Blanca. 2013. Derivational morphology. In Gabriela Pană Dindelegan and Martin Maiden (eds.), *The Grammar of Romanian*, 599–606. Oxford: Oxford University Press.
Fischer, Iancu. 1989. Rumänisch: Wortbildungslehre. Formation des mots. In Günter Holtus, Michael Metzeltin & Christian Schmitt (eds.), *Die einzelnen romanischen Sprachen und Sprachgebiete von der Renaissance bis zur Gegenwart: Rumänisch, Dalmatisch /*

Istroromanisch, Friaulisch, Ladinisch, Bündnerromanisch (*Lexikon der Romanistischen Linguistik, vol. 3)*, 33–55. Tübingen: Max Niemeyer.

Grossmann, Maria. 2016. Romanian. In Peter O. Müller, Ingeborg Ohnheiser, Susan Olsen & Franz Rainer (eds.), *Word-Formation. An International Handbook of the Languages of Europe, vol. 4*, 2731–2751. Berlin & Boston: Mouton de Gruyter.

Moroianu, Cristian. 2013. *Lexicul moștenit – sursă de îmbogățire internă și mixtă a vocabularului românesc* [The inherited lexical elements – source of the internal and mixed means of the enrichment of the Romanian vocabulary]. București: Editura Muzeului Național al Literaturii Române, Colecția Aula Magna.

Rădulescu Sala, Marina 2015. From Latin to Romanian. In Peter O. Müller, Ingeborg Ohnheiser, Susan Olsen & Franz Rainer (eds.), *Word-Formation. An International Handbook of the Languages of Europe, vol. 3*, 1957–1975. Berlin & Boston: Mouton de Gruyter.

Vasiliu, Laura. 2009. Histoire interne du roumain: formation des mots / Interne Sprachgeschichte des Rumänischen: Wortbildung. In: Gerhard Ernst, Martin-Dietrich Gleßgen, Christian Schmitt & Wolfgang Schweickard (eds.), *Romanische Sprachgeschichte. Ein internationales Handbuch zur Geschichte der romanischen Sprachen / Histoire linguistique de la Romania. Manuel international d'histoire linguistique de la Romania, vol. 3*, 2710–2721. Berlin & New York: Walter de Gruyter.

Sources

CoRoLa = *Corpus computațional de referință pentru limba română contemporană* [The Reference Corpus of Contemporary Romanian Language]. http://corola.racai.ro/ (last accessed 15 July 2018).

DA = Academia Română. 1913–1949. *Dicționarul limbii române, A–B, C, D–De, F–I, J–Lojniță* [The dictionary of Romanian language, A–B, C, D–De, F–I, J–Lojniță]. București: Librăriile Socec & Comp. and C. Sfetea, Tipografia Ziarului "Universul", Monitorul Oficial și Imprimeriile Statului, Imprimeria Națională.

DEX = Academia Română. 2016. *Dicționarul explicativ al limbii române* [The explanatory dictionary of the Romanian language], 2nd edn. București: Univers Enciclopedic Gold.

DLR = Academia Română. 1965–2010. *Dicționarul limbii române. Serie nouă, D–E, J–Z* [The dictionary of Romanian language. New series, D–E, J–Z]. București: Editura Academiei Române.

Ana Díaz-Negrillo
28 Derivational networks in Spanish

28.1 General notes

Affixation is the main word-formation mechanism in Spanish. Bosque and Demonte (1999: 3) list over 300 affixes, of which 93 are prefixes and 208 are suffixes, and these are associated with a variety of semantic categories.

In Spanish, affixation comprises prefixation, suffixation and prefixal-suffixal derivation. Prefixation is predominantly word-class maintaining and is often associated with LOCATIVE, TEMPORAL, PRIVATIVE and AUGMENTATIVE meanings, as defined in this project. Suffixation may be class-maintaining, for example, in evaluative suffixation, which includes the meanings DIMINUTIVE, AUGMENTATIVE and PEJORATIVE, but it is predominantly word-class changing, in which case it covers the largest range of meanings, e.g. AGENT, ACTION, COLLECTIVE, RELATIONAL, POSSESSIVE, CAUSATIVE, PROCESS, etc. Prefixal-suffix derivation is class-changing and is limited to verb formation (e.g. *piedra* 'stone' > *a-pedr-ear* 'hit with stones') and largely confined to the semantic categories CAUSATIVE and ACTION.

The separation between suffixation and conversion in Spanish is subject to various interpretations, according to whether thematic vowels are viewed as lexical or inflectional material. Conversion is widely described in lexically related pairs of words that belong to two different word-classes and share the same base and a homonymic thematic vowel, e.g. *agua*$_N$ 'water' > *agua-r*$_V$, where *-a-* is a thematic vowel in both cases and *-r* is a verbal mark (cf., however, Real Academia Española 2011: 370). Still, if there is any subtraction, addition or suppletion of thematic vowels, the word-formation process described in the literature on Spanish word-formation varies. For Pena (1999: 4336–4338) and Varela Ortega (2009: 31–32), suffixation occurs if any of these three operations takes place. In contrast, for Escobar and Hualde (2010: 183), the thematic vowels are of an inflectional nature and consider pairs like *estrech-o*$_{Adj}$ 'narrow' > *estrech-ar*$_V$ 'make narrow(er)' as "verbalization without a derivational suffix", and hence it is conversion. This study follows the latter view and, therefore, leaves out this type of example in accordance with the structure of this volume.

Like other Romance languages, most of the Spanish vocabulary is Latin-based. A number of Spanish words in use nowadays were derived in Latin and not in Spanish. The approach of this study is synchronic, so the latter cases are within the scope of the Spanish derivational networks if the process is productive in Spanish (e.g. *nuevo* 'new' > *renovar* 'renew', Lat. *renovāre*). The main constraints in the derivational networks for Spanish are imposed by root suppletion. Derivations involving vocalic change and/or root extension have been included however (e.g. *piedra* 'stone' > *pedreg-oso*). Finally, any derivatives from Latin American Spanish have been excluded. For this study, the corpora used were set to retrieve data only from Castilian Spanish (*El Corpus del Español* and *Corpus de Referencia del Español Actual*, CREA) and, if there were any doubts, the derivative in question was checked against the online version of the *Diccionario de la Lengua Española* (Real Academia Española 2014), where Latin American Spanish derivatives and/or senses are marked.

28.2 Maximum derivational networks

The derivational networks for Spanish only reach up to the 3rd order of derivation (see Table 28.1). The 1st and 2nd orders of derivation show the highest values, while the 3rd order shows comparatively much lower values. Overall, nouns show the highest total values and verbs the lowest.

Table 28.1: Maximum derivational networks per order of derivation for all three word-classes.

	1st order	2nd order	3rd order	Σ
Nouns	46	33	5	84
Verbs	22	29	5	56
Adjectives	36	20	7	63
TOTAL	104	82	17	203

28.3 Saturation values

For most nouns, the saturation values tend to be lower in the 2nd and 3rd orders of derivation, as shown in Table 28.2. *Ojo* 'eye' shows the opposite tendency. This is explained by the high capacity of some specific *ojo* derivatives to yield further derivatives in subsequent orders of derivation. In particular, the 1st order derivative *ojeras* 'bags under the eye' shows a high capacity to derive 2nd order derivatives in the categories AUGMENTATIVE, DIMINUTIVE and POSSESSIVE. Similarly, the 2nd order derivative *ojeada* 'a quick look' has a high capacity to derive 3rd order derivatives in the category DIMINUTIVE.

Table 28.2: Saturation values per order of derivation, nouns.

Nouns		Saturation value (%)	1st order (%)	2nd order (%)	3rd order (%)
bone	hueso	13.1	19.57	6.06	0
eye	ojo	30.95	23.91	33.33	80
tooth	diente	41.67	50	36.36	0
day	día	9.52	8.7	12.12	0
dog	perro	25	43.48	3.03	0
louse	piojo	19.05	26.09	12.12	0
fire	fuego	14.29	21.74	6.06	0
stone	piedra	48.81	56.52	42.42	20
water	agua	15.48	21.74	9.09	0
name	nombre	10.71	19.57	0	0

The mean saturation values for verbs range between 46.43% (*tirar* 'pull') and 5.36% (*saber* 'know') (see Table 28.3 below). *Quemar* 'burn' shows the highest saturation value in the 1st order of derivation (63.64%). This is a result of the higher values in the semantic categories ACTION, RESULTATIVE and QUALITY. *Saber* 'know' shows the lowest saturation values in the 1st and 2nd orders of derivation.

Similarly to nouns, the saturation values for most of the verbs tend to become lower in the 2nd and 3rd orders of derivation. *Cavar* 'dig' and *tirar* 'pull' show the opposite tendency. This is explained by the fact that the 1st order derivatives *excavar* 'excavate' and *socavar* 'dig under' show a high capacity to derive 2nd and 3rd order derivatives, largely in the categories ACTION and RESULTATIVE. Likewise, the 1st order derivative *tirón* 'a sudden strong pull' has a high capacity to derive 2nd order derivatives, here in the categories AUGMENTATIVE and DIMINUTIVE.

The mean saturation values for adjectives range between a high of 63.49% for *viejo* 'old' and a low of 9.52% for *recto* 'straight' (see Table 28.4 below). The value for *viejo* 'old' is remarkably high in the 1st order of derivation, which is due to the fact that it gathers the maximum derivational saturation values in seven semantic categories. In two of them, AUGMENTATIVE and DIMINUTIVE, the values are comparatively high. In contrast, *recto* 'straight' derivatives do not reach the 2nd order. A number of 2nd and 3rd order derivatives involving semantic extension

Table 28.3: Saturation values per order of derivation, verbs.

Verbs		Saturation value (%)	1st order (%)	2nd order (%)	3rd order (%)
cut	cortar	17.86	31.82	10.34	0
dig	cavar	39.29	31.82	41.38	60
pull	tirar	46.43	45.45	51.72	20
throw	lanzar	19.64	27.27	13.79	20
give	dar	10.71	22.73	3.45	0
hold	sujetar	8.93	13.64	6.9	0
sew	coser	30.36	36.36	24.14	40
burn	quemar	35.71	63.64	20.69	0
drink	beber	12.5	27.27	3.45	0
know	saber	5.36	9.09	3.45	0

Table 28.4: Saturation values per order of derivation, adjectives.

Adjectives		Saturation value (%)	1st order (%)	2nd order (%)	3rd order (%)
narrow	estrecho	12.7	19.44	5	0
old	viejo	63.49	83.33	45	14.29
straight	recto	9.52	16.67	0	0
new	nuevo	49.21	30.56	70	85.71
long	largo	34.92	36.11	45	0
warm	tibio	12.7	13.89	15	0
thick	grueso	25.4	30.56	25	0
bad	malo	22.22	36.11	5	0
thin	delgado	34.92	38.89	35	14.29
black	negro	41.27	52.78	35	0

are recorded for this adjective, so they were excluded from the derivational network (e.g. *rectificar, rectificación, rectificable, irrectificable*, etc.).

Similarly to nouns and verbs, the saturation values for most of the adjectives tend to become lower in the 2nd and 3rd orders of derivation. A remarkable exception is *nuevo* 'new', which again is explained by the high capacity of some specific derivatives to yield further derivatives in subsequent orders of derivation. In particular, the 1st order derivatives *renovar* 'renew' and *novato* 'novice' derive a high number of derivatives in the 2nd order in a variety of semantic categories. Additionally, the 2nd order derivative *novedoso* 'innovative' derives a high number of 3rd order derivatives in a range of semantic categories.

Overall, as shown in Table 28.5, the average saturation values per order of derivation are low for nouns, verbs and adjectives, and show a decrease from the 1st order to the 3rd order of derivation.

Table 28.5: Average saturation values per order of derivation for all three word-classes.

	1st order	2nd order	3rd order
Nouns	29.13	16.06	10
Verbs	30.91	17.93	14
Adjectives	35.83	28	11.43

28.4 Orders of derivation

As discussed above (see Table 28.1), the derivatives in the Spanish sample stretch up to the 3rd order. As is also shown in Table 28.6, the 3rd order of derivation is hardly completed by nouns' and adjectives' derivatives.

Table 28.6: Maximum and average number of orders of derivation for all three word-classes.

	Maximum	Average
Nouns	3	2.1
Verbs	3	2.4
Adjectives	3	2.2

28.5 Derivational capacity

Table 28.7 shows that, on average, nouns and adjectives have a similar derivational capacity. In contrast, verbs show about half of the maximum and average derivational capacities of nouns and adjectives.

Table 28.7: Maximum and average derivational capacity for all three word-classes.

	Maximum	Average
Nouns	26	13.4
Verbs	14	6.7
Adjectives	30	12.9

Among the nouns, the maximum derivational capacity is demonstrated by *piedra* 'stone'. 7 other nouns show derivational capacity values equal to or above 10. 1st order derivatives in nouns are spread across 19 semantic categories, of which DIMINUTIVE and AUGMENTATIVE gather the highest number of derivatives (39 and 15 respectively, 40.3% of the derivatives in the 1st order). Among verbs, the maximum derivational capacity is shown by *quemar* 'burn'. Only one other verb shows a derivational capacity value equal to or above 10 (*tirar* 'pull', 10). 1st order derivatives in verbs are spread across 13 semantic categories, of which ACTION, QUALITY and RESULT gather the highest number of derivatives (10, 12 and 11 respectively, 49.3% of the derivatives in the 1st order). Among the adjectives, the maximum derivational capacity is provided by *viejo* 'old'. 6 other adjectives show derivational capacity values over 10. 1st order derivatives in adjectives are spread across 13 semantic categories, of which DIMINUTIVE and AUGMENTATIVE collect the highest number of derivatives (30 and 34 respectively, 49.6% of the derivatives in the 1st order).

In summary, 1st order derivatives of nouns and adjectives show capacity values that tend to be equal to or over 10, but this is rare in verbs. In addition, nouns and adjectives show their highest derivational capacities in the expression of evaluative meanings. In contrast, verbs do not yield 1st order derivatives in such semantic categories. This may explain the verbs' lower capacity value in Table 28.7. Still, on closer inspection, and by orders of derivation, Table 28.8 shows that the average number of verbs' derivatives in the 2nd and 3rd orders

Table 28.8: Average number of derivatives per order of derivation for all three word-classes.

	1st order	2nd order	3rd order
Nouns	13.4	5.2	0.5
Verbs	6.7	5.2	0.7
Adjectives	12.9	5.6	0.8

is similar to that of nouns and adjectives. This may partly be explained by the fact that, as mentioned earlier, three deverbal 1st order derivatives have a high derivational capacity (see section 28.3 above).

28.6 Correlation between semantic categories and orders of derivation

For nouns, the main semantic categories in question are DIMINUTIVE (derived from all 10 nouns, e.g. *huesito* 'small bone') and LOCATIVE (derived from 7 of the nouns, e.g. *pedrera* 'stone quarry'). In the 2nd and 3rd orders, the semantic categories are derived from no more than 6 of the nouns.

For verbs, the main semantic categories in question in the 1st order of derivation are ABILITY and QUALITY (derived from 8 of the nouns, e.g. *cosible* 'that can be sewn', *cortante* 'sharp, cutting'), and ACTION and RESULTATIVE (derived from 7 of the verbs, e.g. *lanzamiento* 'the action of throwing', *quemadura* 'a burn'). In the 2nd and 3rd orders, the semantic categories are derived from no more than 5 of the verbs.

For adjectives, the main semantic categories in question are DIMINUTIVE and STATIVE (derived from all 10 adjectives, e.g. *delgadito* 'slightly thin', *maldad* 'malice'), AUGMENTATIVE and MANNER (derived from 9 of the adjectives, e.g. *requetenuevo* 'extremely new', *estrechamente* 'narrowly'), and CAUSATIVE (derived from 7 of the verbs, e.g. *alargar* 'make longer'). In the 2nd order, ACTION and RESULTATIVE (derived from 7 of the adjectives, e.g. *ennegrecimiento* 'the action of blackening', *alargamiento* 'a result of lengthening') stand out. In the 3rd order, the semantic categories are derived from no more than 2 of the adjectives.

28.7 Semantic categories with blocking effects

A semantic category that systematically blocks further derivation in the Spanish sample is MANNER. This category was found in the nouns' 2nd order of derivation (e.g. *día* 'day' > *diariamente* 'daily') and in the adjectives' 1st, 2nd and 3rd orders of derivation (e.g. *estrecho* 'thin' > *estrechamente* 'narrowly', *delgado* 'thin' > *delgadísimamente* 'extremely thinly', *nuevo* 'new' > *novedosamente* 'innovatively').

28.8 Typical combinations of semantic categories

There are 92 different semantic category chains in the Spanish sample, typically consisting of 2 semantic categories (only 17 combinations consist of 3 semantic categories). This is consistent with the fact that most of the derivatives stand in the 1st and 2nd orders of derivation.

The attested chains show a low frequency overall. The chains showing the highest frequency (6 derivatives) are CAUSATIVE-ACTION/RESULTATIVE (e.g. *largo* 'long' > *alargar* 'make longer' > *alargamiento* 'the action/result of making longer') and LOCATIVE-ACTION/RESULTATIVE (e.g. *cavar* 'dig' > *excavar* 'excavate' > *excavación* 'excavation').

28.9 Multiple occurrence of semantic categories

The recursiveness of one category has been attested in the Spanish semantic category chains. However, the attested frequency is relatively low: ACTION-ACTION(-QUALITY/DIMINUTIVE) (e.g. *piedra*$_N$ 'stone' > *apedrear* 'hit with stones' > *apedreamiento* 'the action of hitting with stones') shows the highest frequency (5 derivatives).

28.10 Reversibility of semantic categories

Some semantic category chains may occur in a reversed order. However, their frequency is very low: QUALITY-STATIVE (*saber* 'know' > *sabedor* 'knowledgeable' > *sabiduría* 'wisdom') and STATIVE-QUALITY (e.g. *nuevo* 'new' > *novedad* 'innovation' > *novedoso* 'innovative') show the highest frequency (4 derivatives each).

28.11 Conclusions

Despite the relevance of affixation as a word-formation mechanism in Spanish, the Spanish derivatives of the sample rarely reach the 3rd order of derivation and represent only 27 of the 49 semantic categories in the project.

Nouns and adjectives show a higher number of maximum derivational networks and a higher derivational capacity than verbs. This may be partly explained by the relevance of evaluative derivation in these two word-classes, especially in the 1st order of derivation. Evaluative derivation is certainly highly productive in Spanish and largely denominal and deadjectival, but not deverbal. Evaluative morphology is also particularly favoured in colloquial discourse. The *Corpus del Español* contains data from online blogs, which may have had an effect on the number of evaluative derivatives in the networks.

Blocking does not seem to constrain the extension of the networks or the derivational capacity of the core vocabulary. MANNER is the only category that has been clearly shown to block further derivation, and is largely limited to the networks derived from the adjectives.

The Spanish sample is rich in terms of the types of combinations of semantic categories, but not in terms of the typicality of semantic category combinations. The range of category combinations that can occur in a reversed order is, limited and their frequency rather low.

References

Bosque, Ignacio & Violeta Demonte (eds.). 1999. *Gramática Descriptiva de la Lengua Española, Vol. 1* [Descriptive Grammar of the Spanish Language]. Madrid: Espasa Calpe.

Escobar, Anna María & José Ignacio Hualde. 2010. La estructura de las palabras: morfología. [The Structure of Words: Morphology]. In José Ignacio Hualde, Antxon Olarrea, Anna María Escobar & Catherine E. Travis (eds.), *Introducción a la Lingüística Hispánica* [Introduction to Hispanic Linguistics], 123–200. Cambridge: Cambridge University Press.

Pena, Jesús. 1999. Partes de la morfología. Las unidades del análisis morfológico. [Parts of Morphology: Units of Morphological Analysis]. In Ignacio Bosque and Violeta Demonte (eds.), *Gramática Descriptiva de la Lengua Española, Vol. 1* [Descriptive Grammar of the Spanish Language], 4305–4366. Madrid: Espasa.

Real Academia Española. 2011. *Nueva Gramática de la Lengua Española* [New Grammar of the Spanish Language]. Madrid: Espasa.

Varela Ortega, Soledad. 2009. *Morfología Léxica: la Formación de Palabras* [Lexical Morphology: Word-formation]. Madrid: Gredos.

Sources

Davis, Mark. 2016. *El Corpus del Español. Web/dialects* [The Corpus of Spanish. Web/Dialects]. https://www.corpusdelespanol.org/.

Real Academia Española. 2014. *Diccionario de la Lengua Española* [Spanish Language Dictionary]. Madrid: Espasa.

Real Academia Española. *Banco de Datos (CREA). Corpus de Referencia del Español Actual* [Dataset (CREA). Present-Day Spanish Reference Corpus]. http://corpus.rae.es/creanet.html.

Maria Bloch-Trojnar, Silva Nurmio
29 Introduction to Celtic languages

Major complicating factors in the process of compiling derivational networks in Irish and Welsh are the pervasive surface homonymy and functional ambiguity inherent in the terms 'verbal noun' (VN) and 'verbal adjective' (VA) employed in traditional grammars. The decision about where to draw the dividing line between inflection and word-formation is language-specific. The question of whether we are dealing with conversion or affix homonymy/polysemy can be resolved on system-internal grounds and has turned out not to be uniform in Irish and Welsh, which represent two distinct subgroups within the Celtic branch (Goidelic and Brittonic, respectively). The verbal noun (*ainm briathartha*) is one of the most complex categories of Irish grammar. It is used in all contexts where English uses a participle, an infinitive or a deverbal noun. The same phonological word may play the role of a non-finite form and a nominalization. Ó hAnluain (1999) distinguishes between VNs proper (*ainm briathartha ceart*), which function as non-finite verb forms, and VNs that behave like ordinary nouns (*gnáth-ainmfhocal*), i.e. they can be preceded by the definite article *an*, are modified by typical nominal modifiers such as adjectives, nouns in the genitive case, or numerals, and take plural and case inflection. However, he notes that category identification is not always obvious and many view this binary distinction as artificial on account of surface homonymy. According to Doyle (2001: 61), "in cases like this, it is difficult to speak of derivation from one category to another, since it is not clear what the base is. Rather, one can say that a given lexical item is a member of two categories, and only the syntactic context will tell us which one is involved in a particular example." The process of VN formation is most effectively accounted for by regarding the verbal root (rather than the verbal stem) as the base.[1] It is exception-ridden since it involves about 20 morphophonological exponents of varying productivity (e.g. *-(e)adh*, *-(i)ú*, *-t*, *-áil*, *-(e)amh*, *-(e)an*, *-úint*, *-int*). In addition, due to dialectal variation, there may be more than one VN form associated with a given verbal root (e.g. *seinn* 'play' > *seinm, seinniúint, seinnt*). This is as if English nominalizations in *-(at)ion*, *-ment*, *-al*, *-ure*, etc. were interchangeably featured in non-finite contexts. However, this formal overlap/indeterminacy is not complete, in that there are cases where the non-finite form and the nominalization differ (e.g. *folaigh* 'hide, cover, conceal' – *folú* 'hide.VN', *folachán* 'hiding, concealment', *ól* 'drink' – *ól*

---

[1] For a detailed account of the morphophonology of VNs, the reader is referred to Bloch-Trojnar (2006, 2008).

'drink.VN, drink.N', *ólachán* 'drinking, drink'). Nominalizations in Irish appear to tally with the traditional view, in that there is a categorial process yielding nouns with the semantics 'act(ion) of Verb-ing', and which show a systematic polysemy between an abstract action reading and more concrete meanings, such as result or object of activity. Therefore, for the purpose of this study, they are included in the derivational networks. However, an alternative analysis in which nominalizations are products of conversion cannot be definitively ruled out, a move that would diminish the derivational capacity of verbs.[2]

In Welsh, verbal nouns are formed by a range of suffixes added to the base, often, but not always, distributed according to the stem vowel, e.g. *car-u* 'love' and *torr-i* 'break, cut'.[3] Each verb regularly has a VN as part of its paradigm, and these have both verbal and nominal characteristics, as they do in Irish. In their nominal uses, they can, for instance, occur with the definite article and be modified by adjectives. On the other hand, verbal nouns are used in the construction [auxiliary verb] + [aspect marker] + [verbal noun] (Russell 2015: 1232–1236), e.g.

(1) mae   ef yn   cerdded
     be.3SG.PRES.INDIC he PRT walk.VN
     'he is walking'

Since VNs form a part of the paradigm of a verb, their nominal uses can be viewed as instances of conversion. Since conversion, or zero derivation, was excluded from the present study, VNs from verbal stems were not included in the

---

[2] There are several reasons why the author of the chapter on Irish has decided not to follow the conversion analysis. She is not aware of the existence of an analysis where such a relationship is explicitly and convincingly argued for. VN > N conversion poses serious formal, functional and semantic difficulties. The formation of infinitives in German or gerunds in English involves only one formal marker (*-en* and *-ing*, respectively), and the corresponding nouns show uniform actional semantics and belong to a single inflectional class. In Irish, there is a multitude of formal markers, it is not immediately evident which non-finite category should act as the base (the infinitive or present participle), the output is integrated into several declension classes (Carnie 2008), and the semantics of nouns shows the PROCESS/event-RESULT /object dichotomy. Furthermore, there are some complex issues relating to the relationship between abstract nouns with actional semantics and VNs, which seem to point to the opposite direction, i.e. N > VN conversion (Ó Cuív 1980, Wigger 1972: 209–212). There is no denying that VNs act as non-finite verb forms. However, to avoid the vexing question of directionality, it seems preferable not to regard nominalizations as derivationally related to them, as proposed by Doyle (2001), but to derive them from verbal bases, as suggested in Ó hAnluain (1999: 250), who lists VN formal markers in the section on word-formation.

[3] For further discussion, see Russell (1995: 260–277; 2015) and see Thomas (2006: 668–674) for a full list of suffixes.

derivational networks of Welsh verbs. However, there are also VNs built on nouns and adjectives, e.g. *du-o* 'turn black, darken (verbal noun)' from *du* 'black (adjective)' (see the chapter on Welsh for further discussion). These are clear instances of derivation and were included in the Welsh networks.

'Verbal adjectives' (VAs), corresponding in part to past participles in Germanic languages, among others, also warrant further discussion, e.g. Irish *póg-tha* 'kissed' and Welsh *rhodd-edig* 'given' (Ó Siadhail 1989: 198–200; Evans 1964: 165–166; see Russell 1995: 276, n. 2 for a comprehensive list of references). Whereas past participles in languages like English were excluded from this study since their adjectival uses can be argued to be the result of conversion from the verbal form, it can be argued that, synchronically, past participles in Welsh are adjectives derived from a verbal stem, and not the result of conversion. This is because the past participles no longer feature in fully 'verbal' contexts, but rather have been superseded by a construction using the verbal noun (see the chapter on Welsh for further discussion).

In Irish, on the other hand, the VA is still regularly used in verbal contexts. It discharges the role of the past/perfective participle and is used with the verb 'to be' to express the passive perfective aspect, and it also appears in resultative structures (Ó Sé 2004: 197; Doyle 2009: 144–146). In its adjectivized guise, the perfective participle, like any adjective, may appear predicatively after the copula or else fulfil an attributive function as a nominal postmodifier. In contrast to VNs, in morphological terms, the form of the VA is regular and productive and the addition of the two suffixes involved (*-ta/-te*, *-tha/-the*) is fully predictable from the phonological properties and the conjugation class of the verb. This prompts an analysis according to which such adjectives in Irish are products of conversion, and as such these are not included in the derivational networks.

In some derivational categories in Irish, we can observe a formal and semantic affinity with VNs and VAs. Such cases are treated as 1st order deverbal derivatives, and there are two equally plausible analyses. We can recognize the existence of the verbal stem in *-ta/-te*, *-tha/-the*, which is also deployed in derivation, or allow for more affix allomorphy (e.g. treating *-thóir* and *-tóir* as allomorphs of *-óir* in the formation of deverbal AGENT nouns). Consider some examples of the categories in question, where the derivative can be related to either the root or the extended stem:

(2) AGENT: *gearr, gearrtha* 'cut' > *gearrthóir* 'cutter', *ól, ólta* 'drink' > *óltóir* 'drinker'

(3) QUALITY: *dóigh, dóite* 'burn' > *dóiteach* 'burning, scorching; bitter, severe, annoying'

(4) ABILITY: *ól, ólta* 'drink' > *so-ólta* 'drinkable'

(5) ABSTRACTION: *cas, casta* 'twist' > *castacht* 'complexity, intricacy'

(6) RESULTATIVE: *gearr, gearrtha* 'cut' > *gearrthóg* 'cutting, snippet, cutlet'

In summary, the difficult categories for creating derivational networks in Irish and Welsh are the so-called verbal nouns and verbal adjectives, which straddle the boundary between inflection and derivation. While sharing many characteristics, they also differ significantly between the two languages, leading to different decisions being taken by the authors of the Irish and Welsh chapters in this volume: Welsh verbal nouns built on verbal stems were excluded while verbal adjectives were included, whereas the opposite is the case for Irish.

References

Bloch-Trojnar, Maria. 2006. *Polyfunctionality in Morphology. A Study of Verbal Nouns in Modern Irish*. Lublin: Wydawnictwo KUL.

Bloch-Trojnar, Maria. 2008. The morphology of verbal nouns in Modern Irish. *Éigse: A Journal of Irish Studies* 36. 63–81.

Carnie, Andrew. 2008. *Irish Nouns. A Reference Guide*. Oxford: Oxford University Press.

Doyle, Aidan. 2001. *Irish (Languages of the World/Materials 201)*. München: Lincom Europa.

Doyle, Aidan. 2009. Morphosyntactic change and the perfect passive of Irish. In Maria Bloch-Trojnar (ed.), *Perspectives on Celtic Languages*, 143–160. Lublin: Wydawnictwo KUL.

Evans, Simon D. 1964. *A Grammar of Middle Welsh*. Dublin: Dublin Institute for Advanced Studies.

Ó Cuív, Brian. 1980. The verbal noun ending in *-áil* and related forms. *Celtica* 13. 125–145.

Ó hAnluain, Liam. 1999. *Graiméar Gaeilge na mBráithre Críostaí* [Irish grammar by the Christian Brothers]. Baile Átha Cliath: An Gúm.

Ó Sé, Diarmuid. 2004. The 'after' perfect and related constructions in Gaelic dialects. *Ériu* 54. 179–248.

Ó Siadhail, Mícheál. 1989. *Modern Irish: Grammatical Structure and Dialectal Variation*. Cambridge: Cambridge University Press.

Russell, Paul, 1995. *An introduction to the Celtic languages*. London: Routledge.

Russell, Paul. 2015. Verbal nouns in Celtic. In Peter O. Müller, Ingeborg Ohnheiser, Susan Olsen & Franz Rainer (eds.), *Word-Formation: An International Handbook of the Languages of Europe*, 1230–1241. Berlin & Boston: Mouton de Gruyter.

Thomas, Peter Wynn. 2006. *Gramadeg y Gymraeg* [A grammar of Welsh], 3rd edn. Cardiff: University of Wales Press.

Wigger, Arndt. 1972. Preliminaries to a generative morphology of the Modern Irish verb. *Ériu* 23. 162–213.

Maria Bloch-Trojnar
30 Derivational networks in Irish

30.1 General notes

A description of word-formation in Irish cannot be conducted without due attention to the complex sociolinguistic context of a moribund language. It is only on the western fringes of the island, the so-called Gaeltacht areas, that Irish is still used as a medium of daily communication outside the educational system by about 20–40,000 speakers, who make up no more than 1% of the entire population (Hickey 2011: 10–12). Even these shrinking areas are affected by widespread diglossia, dialectal fragmentation, the haemorrhage of emigration of the young generation, and the immigration of speakers of English. The measures taken by government agencies to devise a formal standardized register and to rejuvenate the language have not always brought about the desired results (Ó Béarra 2007; Johnson 2009; Hickey 2011).[1] Paradoxically, word-formation strategies promoted by government bodies concerned with the preservation of the Irish language, such as the revival of old affixes and compounding patterns which have become obsolete in the spoken language, do not necessarily reflect the developments favoured by native speakers. According to Doyle, "it is no exaggeration to say that for the average speaker of the last few decades word formation has practically ceased to exist; words are simply taken over wholesale from English without changing their phonological or morphological shape" (2001: 58).[2]

Despite all these adversities, Irish is still a living spoken language and there is a fair number of resources that can be consulted to retrieve linguistically significant information. This paper deals with word-formation in Irish viewed as a whole, and so the main source of data is the standard *Irish-English Dictionary* (Ó Dónaill 1977), coupled with the *English-Irish Dictionary* (de Bhaldraithe 1959) and Dinneen's *Irish-English Dictionary* (1927). References are made to morphological descriptions of individual dialects (de Bhaldraithe 1953b; Ó Sé 2000; Ó Curnáin 2007), case studies of particular morphological categories (Doyle 1992; Bloch-Trojnar 2006) and traditional grammar and reference works concerning

---

[1] Traditional Late Modern Irish, as spoken in the Gaeltacht in the 1960s, is immune from English influence, whereas Non-Traditional Late Modern Irish or Neo-Irish, i.e. a variety influenced by English and L2 speakers of Irish, is affected at every linguistic level from sound to idiom (Ó Béarra 2007; Johnson 2009).
[2] For more information on the lexical encroachment of English, see e.g. de Bhaldraithe (1953a) and Doyle (1996a).

the learned word-formation of the standard language such as *Graiméar Gaeilge na mBráithre Críostaí* (Ó hAnluain 1999 [1960]), *Gramadach na Gaeilge agus Litriú na Gaeilge. An Caighdeán Oifigiúil* (1958) and 'The Irish language' (Ó Dochartaigh 1992). As the *Irish-English Dictionary* (Ó Dónaill 1977) is nowhere near as comprehensive as its English counterpart, the OED, it was necessary to conduct searches in the New Corpus for Ireland (Nua-Chorpas na hÉireann),[3] which has opened promising new vistas of research in the area of derivational morphology.

30.2 Maximum derivational networks

As is evident from Table 30.1 below, the maximum derivational network of nouns (with a maximum of 56 derivatives) is the highest of all lexical categories, the maximum for verbs being 38 and that of adjectives 39. There are marked differences between the numbers of maximum derivatives in particular orders and, compared to other classes, nouns have the highest values of maximum derivatives in the 1st and 2nd orders. The number of maximum derivatives in the 1st order of derivation in verbs is almost as high (or should one say just as low) as it is in the 2nd order. The maximum number of derivatives in the 3rd order is the same as for nouns. The total number of verbs is lowest of all three classes, the difference between verbs and adjectives being, however, negligible. Adjectives possess the highest number of maximum derivatives in the 3rd order. None of the three word-classes permit 4th and 5th order derivations.

Table 30.1: Maximum derivational networks per order of derivation for all three word-classes.

	1st order	2nd order	3rd order	4th order	5th order	Σ
Nouns	34	19	3	0	0	56
Verbs	18	17	3	0	0	38
Adjectives	20	14	5	0	0	39
TOTAL	72	50	11	0	0	133

---

[3] The New Corpus for Ireland (Nua-Chorpas na hÉireann) is a corpus of approximately 30 million words, created as part of the New English-Irish Dictionary project at Foras na Gaeilge. It contains a wide range of texts (fiction, factual texts, news reports, official documents, etc.) and also gives access to information concerning the frequency, dialect, genre, medium and native vs. non-native speaker usage of the searched items.

30.3 Saturation values

The mean saturation values for the nouns range between 7% (*fiacail* 'tooth', *madra* 'dog') and 54% (*cloch* 'stone'), as shown in Table 30.2. The noun with the highest mean saturation value also shows the highest saturation in the 1st and 2nd orders and, conversely, nouns with the lowest mean saturation exhibit the lowest saturation in the 1st and 2nd orders. Only two nouns (*cnámh* 'bone', *ainm* 'name') have 3rd order derivatives.

Table 30.2: Saturation values per order of derivation, nouns.

Nouns		Saturation value (%)	1st order (%)	2nd order (%)	3rd order (%)	4th order (%)	5th order (%)
bone	cnámh	21.43	17.65	26.32	33.33	0	0
eye	súil	14.29	14.71	15.79	0	0	0
tooth	fiacail	7.14	8.82	5.26	0	0	0
day	lá	17.86	20.59	15.79	0	0	0
dog	madra	7.14	8.82	5.26	0	0	0
louse	míol	16.07	20.59	10.53	0	0	0
fire	tine	16.07	20.59	10.53	0	0	0
stone	cloch	53.57	64.71	42.11	0	0	0
water	uisce	16.07	20.59	10.53	0	0	0
name	ainm	30.36	26.47	26.32	100	0	0

The mean saturation values for verbs are presented in Table 30.3 below. The verb with the lowest mean saturation value of 5% is *fuaigh* 'sew'. It is also the only verb that lacks a 2nd order. The verb with the highest mean saturation value, amounting to 39%, is *tarraing* 'pull', and it also has the highest saturation values in the 2nd and 3rd orders (41% and 67%, respectively). The verb *ól* 'drink' has the highest saturation in the 1st order (44%). Only three verbs (*tarraing* 'pull', *tabhair* 'give', *coinnigh* 'hold') give rise to 3rd order derivations.

The mean saturation values for adjectives, as shown in Table 30.4 below, range between 18% (*sean* 'old', *tiubh* 'thick') and 41% (*te* 'warm'). The adjective *cúng* 'narrow' has the highest value in the 1st order (55%), but lowest in the 2nd and 3rd. Five adjectives have 3rd order derivatives.

Table 30.5 presents the average saturation values per order of derivation for all three word-classes. Compared to the saturation of Irish nouns in particular

Table 30.3: Saturation values per order of derivation, verbs.

Verbs		Saturation value (%)	1st order (%)	2nd order (%)	3rd order (%)	4th order (%)	5th order (%)
cut	gearr	23.68	33.33	17.65	0	0	0
dig	tochail	10.53	11.11	11.76	0	0	0
pull	tarraing	39.47	33.33	41.18	66.67	0	0
throw	caith	18.42	16.67	23.53	0	0	0
give	tabhair	13.16	16.67	5.88	33.33	0	0
hold	coinnigh	10.53	11.11	5.88	33.33	0	0
sew	fuaigh	5.26	11.11	0	0	0	0
burn	dóigh	26.32	27.78	29.41	0	0	0
drink	ól	28.95	44.44	17.65	0	0	0
know	aithin	15.79	22.22	11.76	0	0	0

One of the distinctive traits of Irish is its impoverished inventory of stative verbs. At some point, Irish verbs lost their stative function and became essentially dynamic. Wagner (1959: 127) demonstrates that, in early Irish, there were stative verbs (e.g. *ad-ágathar* 'fears', *do-futhraccair* 'wishes', *ad-muinethar* 'remembers'), which in the modern language have been superseded by periphrastic constructions involving nouns, i.e. *ad-ágathar* > *tá eagla air* 'is fear on-him; he is afraid', *do-futhraccair* > *is áil leis; is mian leis* 'is wish with-him; he wishes', *ad-muinethar* > *tá cuimhne aige ar* 'is memory at-him about; he remembers'. By the same token, despite the fact that dictionaries list the verb *aithin* 'know, recognize', the most natural way of saying 'I know' is to use a periphrastic verb/predicate with a nominal, i.e. *tá aithne agam ar* 'is knowledge with-me on' or *tá a fhios agam* 'is its knowledge at-me'.

Table 30.4: Saturation values per order of derivation, adjectives.

Adjectives		Saturation value (%)	1st order (%)	2nd order (%)	3rd order (%)	4th order (%)	5th order (%)
narrow	cúng	30.77	55	7.14	0	0	0
old	sean	17.95	15	14.29	40	0	0
straight	díreach	28.21	40	21.43	0	0	0
new	nua	33.33	25	35.71	60	0	0
long	fada	30.77	45	14.29	20	0	0
warm	te	41.03	35	50	40	0	0

Table 30.4 (continued)

Adjectives		Saturation value (%)	1st order (%)	2nd order (%)	3rd order (%)	4th order (%)	5th order (%)
thick	tiubh	17.95	25	14.29	0	0	0
bad	dona	25.64	30	28.57	0	0	0
thin	tanaí	28.21	40	14.29	20	0	0
black	dubh	28.21	35	28.57	0	0	0

Table 30.5: Average saturation values per order of derivation for all three word-classes.

	1st order	2nd order	3rd order	4th order	5th order
Nouns	22.35	16.84	13.33	0	0
Verbs	22.78	16.47	13.33	0	0
Adjectives	34.5	22.86	18	0	0

orders of derivation, the differences in the average saturation for verbs in the respective orders are minute (not exceeding 23% in the 1st order, 17% in the 2nd and 14% in the 3rd). Adjectives possess the highest average of all word-classes across all orders.

30.4 Orders of derivation

All items save one (*fuaigh* 'sew') have derivatives in the 1st and 2nd orders of derivation. Table 30.6 demonstrates that there are no more than three orders for all lexical classes, with adjectives being most likely to give rise to 3rd order derivatives.

Table 30.6: Maximum and average number of orders of derivation for all three word-classes.

	Maximum	Average
Nouns	3	2.2
Verbs	3	2.2
Adjectives	3	2.5

30.5 Derivational capacity

As shown in Table 30.7 below, nouns have the highest derivational capacity in the 1st order of derivation, whereas verbs have the lowest.

Table 30.7: Maximum and average derivational capacity for all three word-classes.

	Maximum	Average
Nouns	22	7.6
Verbs	8	4.1
Adjectives	11	6.9

The average number of derivatives per order of derivation is presented in Table 30.8. In the 2nd order, the average derivational capacity of nouns is the same as that of adjectives, whereas in the 3rd order, adjectives give rise to the highest number of derivatives.

Table 30.8: Average number of derivatives per order of derivation for all three word-classes.

	1st order	2nd order	3rd order	4th order	5th order
Nouns	7.6	3.2	0.4	0	0
Verbs	4.1	2.8	0.4	0	0
Adjectives	6.9	3.2	0.9	0	0

30.6 Correlation between semantic categories and order of derivation

In the nominal domain there are no strongly correlated semantic categories for any order of derivation, i.e. weak correlations can be observed with the categories AUGMENTATIVE, QUALITY and CAUSATIVE (5/10) in the 1st order and with the category ACTION in the 2nd (6/10). For Irish verbs, there is a strong correlation between the 1st order of derivation and the semantic categories of ACTION and AGENT (9/10). There is no correlation with individual semantic categories for verbs in the 2nd and 3rd orders. As far as adjectives are concerned, there is a strong correlation between the 1st order and the semantic categories AUGMENTATIVE (10/10), ABSTRACTION

(9/10) and CAUSATIVE (8/10), and the 2nd order and the category ACTION (8/10). No correlation with individual semantic categories for adjectives in the 3rd order can be established.

30.7 Semantic categories with blocking effects

In denominal derivations, the semantic category ENTITY seems to exert a weak blocking effect in the 1st order, while ABSTRACTION and AUGMENTATIVE exert a weak blocking effect in the 2nd order. With regard to verbs, no categories seem to systematically block further derivations in the 1st, 2nd or 3rd order. A strong blocking tendency can be observed for the category AUGMENTATIVE in the 1st order of derivation in adjectives, whereas in the 2nd and 3rd orders, the category ABSTRACTION shows a weak blocking effect.

30.8 Typical combinations of semantic categories

In nominal derivations, a weak tendency can be observed for the CAUSATIVE-ACTION combination (e.g. *ainm* 'name' > *ainmnigh* 'nominate' > *ainmniú/ainmniúchán* 'nomination'). The combinations of semantic categories in the verbal domain are varied but do not show sufficient systematicity. Typical combinations of semantic categories based on adjectives include CAUSATIVE-ACTION (e.g. *tiubh* 'thick' > *tiubhaigh* 'thicken' > *tiúchan/ tiúchaint* 'thickening, concentration') and QUALITY-ABSTRACTION (e.g. *dubh* 'black' > *dubhach* 'gloomy' > *dubhachas* 'gloom').

30.9 Multiple occurrence of semantic categories

The multiple occurrence of categories is not impossible in Irish, as indicated by isolated cases of AUGMENTATIVE and ACTION in nouns (e.g. *cloch* 'stone' > *dea-chloch* 'good stone', AUGMENTATIVE > *fíor-dhea-chloch* 'really good stone', AUGMENTATIVE) and ENTITY, ABSTRACTION and ACTION in adjectives (e.g. *te* 'warm' > *teas* 'heat, hotness, warmth', ABSTRACTION > *teasaí* 'hot, warm', QUALITY > *teasaíocht* 'heat, warmth, ardour, passion, feverishness', ABSTRACTION). However, such phenomena can by no means be considered typical.

30.10 Reversibility of semantic categories

There are no instances of semantic categories occurring in reverse order in the Irish data set.

30.11 Reasons for structurally poor derivational networks

At the turn of the twentieth century, Irish was going through an intensive period of modernization marked by rapid vocabulary expansion, in which a terminological committee set up by the Gaelic League played an important role. Doyle (2015: 240–249) enumerates the following phenomena as sources of new lexical items:
1. borrowing with subsequent phonological and morphological adaptation,
2. calquing with the aid of native affixes,
3. semantic extensions,
4. substituting a descriptive phrase for a single word, and
5. reviving obsolete words and dormant morphological processes (such as compounding).

He points to a tension between native speakers, who favoured descriptive phrases in conversation, and the writers of the Gaelic League, who showed a preference for coining one-word equivalents of English terms. Native speakers were not actively involved in re-shaping the written language, and consequently, even though affixes seem to be available, in many cases their generality is not sufficient to be attested in the sample material. Descriptive phrases consisting of a noun followed by a qualifier (another noun in the genitive case) are the hallmark of Irish, e.g. *bean tí* 'woman of house, housewife', *smugairle róin* 'lit. spit of seal, jelly-fish'. Therefore, many semantic categories that are rendered by affixed formations in other languages have such compound equivalents in Irish (Doyle 1996b), e.g.
1. RELATIONAL: *taos fiacal* 'paste of teeth, dental paste',
2. ACTION: *gearradh na bhfiacal* 'cutting of the teeth, dentition',
3. FEMALE: *bean fuála* 'woman of sewing, sewing woman', and
4. INSTRUMENT: *inneall fuála* 'machine of sewing, sewing machine'.

Notably, there are other periphrastic structures to express categories such as
1. PRIVATIVE: *gan ainm* 'nameless',
2. MANNER: *go dona* 'badly', or
3. DIRECTIONAL: *caith amach, aníos, anuas, ar*, etc. 'throw out, up, down, on, etc.'

30.12 Conclusions

Due to system-internal and sociolinguistic factors, word-formation does not contribute substantially to lexical stock expansion in Modern Irish.

Irish derivationally expresses 26 of the 49 semantic categories identified for the purposes of this study. Adjectives are most likely to have 3rd order derivatives and show the highest average saturation values in the three orders available in Irish derivation. However, nouns have the highest average derivational capacity and exhibit the highest number of derivational networks and the highest values of maximum derivatives in the 1st and 2nd orders. Verbs lag behind due to the fact that Irish, like Germanic languages, shows a preference for root-particle rather than prefix-root combinations, as found in Slavic languages. In addition, the problems of differentiating between products of inflection and derivation arise mostly in the verbal domain.

References

Bloch-Trojnar, Maria. 2006. *Polyfunctionality in Morphology. A Study of Verbal Nouns in Modern Irish*. Lublin: Wydawnictwo KUL.
de Bhaldraithe, Thomás. 1953a. Nua-iasachtaí i nGaeilge Chois Fhairrge [New borrowings in the Irish of Cois Fhairrge]. *Éigse* 7. 1–34.
de Bhaldraithe, Thomás. 1953b. *Gaeilge Chois Fhairrge: An deilbhíocht* [The Irish of Cois Fhairrge. Morphology]. Baile Átha Cliath: Institiúid Ard-Léinn Bhaile Átha Cliath.
de Bhaldraithe, Thomás. 1959. *English-Irish Dictionary*. Baile Átha Cliath: An Gúm.
Dinneen, Patrick. 1927. *An Irish-English Dictionary (Being A Thesaurus Of The Words, Phrases And Idioms Of The Modern Irish Language)*. Dublin: Irish Texts Society by the Educational Company of Ireland.
Doyle, Aidan. 1992. *Noun Derivation in Modern Irish. Selected Categories, Rules and Suffixes*. Lublin: Wydawnictwo KUL.
Doyle, Aidan. 1996a. Nominal borrowings and word-formation in Irish. In Henryk Kardela and Bogdan Szymanek (eds.), *A Festschrift for Edmund Gussmann from his Friends and Colleagues*, 99–113. Lublin: Wydawnictwo KUL.
Doyle, Aidan. 1996b. Compounds and syntactic phrases in Modern Irish. *Studia Anglica Posnaniensia* 30. 83–96.
Doyle, Aidan. 2001. *Irish (Languages of the World/Materials 201)*. München: Lincom Europa.

Doyle, Aidan. 2015. *A History of the Irish Language. From the Norman Invasion to Independence*. Oxford: Oxford University Press.

Hickey, Raymond. 2011. *The Dialects of Irish: Study of a Changing Landscape*. Berlin & New York: Walter de Gruyter.

Johnson, Diarmuid. 2009. Some recent phonetic, syntactic and lexical change in Irish. In Maria Bloch-Trojnar (ed.), *Perspectives on Celtic languages*, 227–236. Lublin: Wydawnictwo KUL.

Ó Béarra, Feargal. 2007. Late Modern Irish and the dynamics of language change and language death. In Hildegard L. C. Tristram (ed.), *The Celtic Languages in Contact*, 260–269. Potsdam: Potsdam University Press.

Ó Curnáin, Brian. 2007. *The Irish of Iorras Aithneach. County Galway*. Dublin: Dublin Institute for Advanced Studies.

Ó Dochartaigh, Cathair. 1992. The Irish language. In Donald Macaulay (ed.), *The Celtic Languages*, 11–99. Cambridge: Cambridge University Press.

Ó Dónaill, Niall. 1977. *Foclóir Gaeilge–Béarla* [Irish-English Dictionary]. Baile Átha Cliath: An Gúm.

Ó hAnluain, Liam. 1999 [1960]. *Graiméar Gaeilge na mBráithre Críostaí* [Irish grammar by the Christian Brothers]. Baile Átha Cliath: An Gúm.

Ó Sé, Diarmuid. 2000. *Gaeilge Chorca Dhuibhne* [The Irish of West Kerry]. Baile Átha Cliath: Institiúid Teangeolaíochta Éireann.

Rannóg an Aistriúcháin. 1958. *Gramadach na Gaeilge agus Litriú na Gaeilge. An Caighdeán Oifigiúil* [Irish grammar and orthography. The standard version]. Baile Átha Cliath: Oifig an tSoláthair.

Wagner, Heinrich. 1958–1969. *Linguistic Atlas and Survey of Irish Dialects, Vols 1–4*. Dublin: Dublin Institute for Advanced Studies.

Wagner, Heinrich. 1959. *Das Verbum in den Sprachen der britischen Inseln*. Tübingen: Niemeyer.

Silva Nurmio
31 Derivational networks in Welsh

31.1 General notes

Affixation is a major way of deriving new words in Welsh.[1] Welsh affixes include many that were abstracted from Latin borrowings, such as the adjectival suffix *-us* (e.g. *deallus* 'intelligent', cf. *deall-* 'to understand') from the Latin suffix *-ōsus* (Russell 2015: 2774).

There are two kinds of Welsh words that pose a problem for a clear split into inflection and derivation: verbal nouns (from verbal bases) and SINGULATIVES. 'Verbal noun' or 'verb noun' (Welsh *berfenw*) is a traditional term for non-finite forms in the Celtic languages (which roughly correspond to participles, infinitives and deverbal nouns in languages like English); see the general introduction to the Celtic languages for more discussion. Unlike verbal nouns from verbal bases, verbal nouns formed from nouns and adjectives were included in this study, since these clearly involve adding a suffix to derive a new word, e.g. *llygad-u* 'to eye (verbal noun)' from *llygad* 'eye' (noun).[2]

Welsh has two SINGULATIVE-forming suffixes: *-yn* (masc.) and *-en* (fem.), e.g. *moch* 'pigs', *mochyn* 'a pig' (see Nurmio 2017 and references there). With bases that are count plurals (called 'morphological collectives' by Nurmio (2017)) like *moch*, the SINGULATIVE suffixes can be argued to form inflectional singular/plural pairs. These suffixes also attach to mass and non-nominal bases, however, e.g. *ceirch* 'oats', *ceirchen* 'a grain of oats', and in such cases the addition of the SINGULATIVE suffix is closer to derivation. The sample nouns included one morphological collective, *llau* 'lice', SINGULATIVE *lleuen* 'louse'. Here, the COLLECTIVE is the base for derivation, and the SINGULATIVE was not included as a derivative, since it was treated as an inflectional form. The suffixes *-yn/-en* also function as DIMINUTIVE suffixes when added to singular count noun bases. Such derivatives were included in this study, e.g. *caregyn* 'a small stone, pebble' (from *carreg* 'stone').

---

[1] For a detailed discussion of different affixes, see Russell (1990) and Zimmer (2000). Compounding is another main strategy, for which see Zimmer (2000) and Russell (2015).
[2] The reason that such verbal nouns were not analyzed as derived from verbal stems (e.g. *llygad* 'eye (noun)' > *llygad-* 'to eye' (verbal stem) > *llygad-u* (verbal noun)) is that the verbal noun is much more commonly used than inflected forms, which supports an analysis that the verbal noun is derived directly from the noun or adjective. This view also seems to be taken by Borsley et al. (2007: 68).

Another theoretical problem is the occasional use of the plural as a stem for adding affixes. In the sample for this study, this may be the case with e.g. *llygeidiog* 'having eyes, having large eyes'. It is not fully clear whether the base is the plural *llygaid* 'eyes' or the singular *llygad* 'eye', with vowel raising regularly caused by the suffix *-iog* (see Russell 1990: 39–60, 118, 2015: 2774). *Llygeidiog* occurs alongside its synonym *llygadog* based on the singular, and the two were counted as one entry for the purposes of this study, taking the former tentatively as a vowel alternation variant. However, the PRIVATIVE *dilygaid* 'eyeless' must have the plural as its base, and this form was excluded from the derivational network of 'eye'. The noun *dant* 'tooth' also has a different stem (*danhedd-*) for some derivatives, e.g. *danheddog* 'having teeth'. Russell (1990: 118–119) has shown that this stem is in origin the oblique stem of this noun, reflecting a preservation of an archaic Brittonic pattern where the oblique stem, not the nominative, was used in word-formation. Although diachronically *danhedd-* is not the plural, it is likely to be understood as such synchronically, and such derivatives were therefore excluded from the derivational network of *dant* 'tooth'.

The common AGENT and INSTRUMENT suffixes *-wr* (masc.) and *-wraig* (fem.), e.g. *torr-wr* 'cutter (person or implement)', from *gŵr* 'man' and *gwraig* 'woman' with an initial consonant mutation that deletes /g-/, are treated here as affixoids and were therefore excluded from the derivational networks.[3]

Welsh has the suffix *-edig*, which historically formed past participles from verbal bases, e.g. *toredig* 'broken, cut' from *torr-* 'to cut' (see Russell 1990: 78–79, 1995: 258–259). Synchronically, however, such derivatives are used as adjectives and do not feature in verbal constructions. The standard grammar by Thomas (2006: 675–676) lists *-edig* as an adjectival suffix, reflecting how it is viewed synchronically (see also Borsley et al. 2007: 69).[4] For the perfect aspect ('has done X'), Modern Welsh uses the construction *wedi* + verbal noun (the aspectual marker *wedi* is grammaticalized from the preposition *wedi* 'after'), e.g.

---

[3] See Russell 1989: 34–36, 1996: 121, 125 for further discussion. For other possible affixoids, see Russell (2015: 2772), and for other AGENT suffixes, see Zimmer (2000: 551–554).

[4] I have included *-edig* derivatives here, arguing that they should be regarded as adjectives synchronically, not as adjectives formed by conversion from a verbal form, even though this may be the case historically. The verbal connection is still apparent in the fact that intransitives often lack an *-edig* derivative, or it is otherwise only marginally attested (the present study only includes transitive verbs, however). The same argument applies to derivatives with the suffix *-adwy*, e.g. *llosgadwy* 'burnable' from *llosg-* 'to burn', which originally had a future participle or gerundive force (Evans 1964: 166) but is now an adjective-forming suffix.

(1) mae hi wedi mynd
be.3SG.PRES.INDIC she PRT go.VERBAL NOUN
'she has gone'

The sources used for creating the Welsh corpus are the *Dictionary of the Welsh Language* (Thomas et al. 1950–), the *Welsh Academy Dictionary* (Griffiths and Jones 1997), the searchable corpora of the Welsh National Corpora Portal (http://corpws.cymru), and the Welsh National Terminology Portal (http://termau.cymru). Native speaker judgements, and occasional Google searches, were used to verify derivatives whose present-day usage was not clear from the corpora and dictionaries.

31.2 Maximum derivational networks

Table 31.1 shows the maximum derivational network for each word-class per order of derivation. Verbs have the largest derivational networks in all orders. 3rd and 4th order derivatives are rare, and only verbs and adjectives have some 4th order derivatives.

Table 31.1: Maximum derivational networks per order of derivation for all three word-classes.

	1st order	2nd order	3rd order	4th order	∑
Nouns	35	15	1	0	51
Verbs	38	31	12	3	84
Adjectives	24	10	3	1	38
TOTAL	97	56	16	4	173

31.3 Saturation values

Tables 31.2–31.4 record the saturation values for nouns, verbs and adjectives, respectively, and Table 31.5 sums up the average saturation values for each word-class. There is much variation in the saturation values between different lexemes: the highest value for nouns is 50.98% (*enw* 'name') while the lowest is 5.88% (*llau* 'lice'). For verbs, the percentages are 66.67% (*gwybod-/gwybydd-* 'to know') and 1.19% (*rho(dd)-* 'to give'), and for adjectives, 39.47% (*newydd* 'new') and 13.16% (four adjectives have this percentage, see Table 31.4). The

Table 31.2: Saturation values per order of derivation, nouns.

Nouns		Saturation value (%)	1st order (%)	2nd order (%)	3rd order (%)
bone	asgwrn	13.73	17.14	6.67	0
eye	llygad	9.80	14.29	0	0
tooth	dant	15.69	17.14	13.33	0
day	dydd	21.57	28.57	6.67	0
dog	ci	17.65	14.29	20	100
lice	llau	5.88	8.57	0	0
fire	tân	13.73	17.14	6.67	0
stone	carreg	17.65	17.14	20	0
water	dŵr	19.61	28.57	0	0
name	enw	50.98	37.14	86.67	0

Table 31.3: Saturation values per order of derivation, verbs.

Verbs		Saturation value (%)	1st order (%)	2nd order (%)	3rd order (%)	4th order (%)
cut	torr-	11.9	23.68	3.23	0	0
dig	clodd-	8.33	15.79	3.23	0	0
pull	tynn-	17.86	23.68	6.45	25	33.33
throw	tafl-	8.33	18.42	0	0	0
give	rho(dd)-	1.19	2.63	0	0	0
hold	dal(i)-	9.52	13.16	9.68	0	0
sew	gwn-	3.57	7.89	0	0	0
burn	llosg-	22.62	23.68	32.26	0	0
drink	yf-	3.57	5.26	3.23	0	0
know	gwybod-/ gwybydd-	66.67	42.11	83.87	91.67	100

Table 31.4: Saturation values per order of derivation, adjectives.

Adjectives		Saturation value (%)	1st order (%)	2nd order (%)	3rd order (%)	4th order (%)
narrow	cul	13.16	20.83	0	0	0
old	hen	34.21	33.33	50	0	0
straight	syth	13.16	20.83	0	0	0
new	newydd	39.47	25	50	100	100
long	hir	13.16	20.83	0	0	0
warm	cynnes	18.42	25	10	0	0
thick	tew	28.95	29.17	40	0	0
bad	drwg	23.68	33.33	10	0	0
thin	tenau	26.32	41.67	0	0	0
black	du	13.16	20.83	0	0	0

Table 31.5: Average saturation values per order of derivation for all three word-classes.

	1st order	2nd order	3rd order	4th order
Nouns	19.999	16.001	10	0
Verbs	17.63	14.2	11.67	13.33
Adjectives	27.08	16	10	10

average saturation values in Table 31.5 are fairly low for all word-classes, generally staying below 20%, apart from the average of 27% for 1st order derivatives of adjectives.

31.4 Orders of derivation

Table 31.6 shows the maximum number of derivational orders for each of the three word-classes, followed by the average number of orders. Adjectives and verbs have 4th order derivatives (cf. Table 31.1), although the numbers are low (one adjectival derivative, four verbal ones), while nouns only have three orders.

Table 31.6: Maximum and average number of orders of derivation.

	Maximum	Average
Nouns	3	1.8
Verbs	4	2.1
Adjectives	4	1.6

Verbs have the highest average number of orders, although nouns and adjectives follow close behind. In all three word-classes, a word is likely to have more than one order of derivation.

31.5 Derivational capacity

Table 31.7 shows the maximum and the average derivational capacities for the three word-classes, calculated using the direct (i.e. 1st order) derivatives. A basic Welsh noun in our sample has on average seven direct derivatives, and the maximum number found is 13. Verbs have the highest difference between the average (6.7) and maximum (16 for *gwybod-/gwybydd-* 'know') number of derivatives, which means that there is considerable variation between lexemes.

Table 31.7: Maximum and average derivational capacity for all three word-classes.

	Maximum	Average
Nouns	13	7
Verbs	16	6.7
Adjectives	10	6.5

Table 31.8 shows the average number of derivatives per order of derivation for each word-class. The average Welsh noun in the sample has seven derivatives in the 1st order, 2.4 in the 2nd order, and 0.1 in the 3rd order. There is no major difference between word-classes in the 1st order of derivation, but in further orders verbs have more derivatives than nouns or adjectives.

Table 31.8: Average number of derivatives per order of derivation for all three word-classes.

Word-class	1st order	2nd order	3rd order	4th order
Nouns	7	2.4	0.1	0
Verbs	6.7	4.4	1.4	0.4
Adjectives	6.5	1.6	0.3	0.1

31.6 Correlation between semantic categories and orders of derivation

The most common semantic categories for nouns in the 1st order of derivation are QUALITY (value 9, i.e. 9 out of the 10 nouns have a derivative in this category), ACTION (value 7) and RELATIONAL (value 6). For 2nd order derivatives, ABSTRACTION (value 3) and PRIVATIVE (value 3) each occur with three words, and in the 3rd order we only find a single derivative, which comes under ACTION.

For verbs, the most common categories in the 1st order are QUALITY (value 7), ABILITY (value 6) and SINGULATIVE (value 4). In the 2nd order, these are QUALITY and ABSTRACTION (each with value 3). In the 3rd order, QUALITY occurs with two words (value 2), and in the 4th order, ABSTRACTION occurs with two (value 2).

For adjectives, the most common categories in the 1st order of derivation are STATIVE (value 9), ACTION (value 8) and PROCESS (value 7). In the 2nd order, these are QUALITY (value 4) and STATIVE (value 3). In the 3rd order, only two categories have any value at all (value 1 in each), namely ABSTRACTION and RELATIONAL.

Derivatives of 2nd to 4th orders are few in all three word-classes, and there appear to be no significant correlations between the order of derivation and semantic categories.

31.7 Semantic categories with blocking effects

With the Welsh words used in this study, 2nd order derivation is available for 19 out of the 30 sample words, most commonly for verbs. Only four words in total have a 3rd order derivative, while three of those also have a 4th order one. No word has 5th order derivatives. Not having a 2nd order derivative is, then, very common, and not having a 3rd or 4th order one is the norm. Because of the paucity of affixation beyond the 1st order, we cannot demonstrate that any particular semantic category systematically blocks further derivation.

31.8 Typical combinations of semantic categories

There are no combinations of semantic categories that can really be described as typical, due to the general poverty of derivation beyond the 1st order in Welsh, as discussed above. Some combinations occur in the networks of two different lexemes, e.g. PROCESS > PRIVATIVE for both *carreg* 'stone' and *llosg-* 'burn'. Only one combination, ACTION > QUALITY, occurs with three lexemes (*llosg-* 'burn', *clodd-* 'dig' and *ci* 'dog'); this is not enough to constitute typicality.

31.9 Multiple occurrence of semantic categories

There are six cases of multiple occurrences of a semantic category in one derivational chain. ABILITY > ABILITY occurs in the network of *torr-* 'to cut': *toradwy* 'broken; breakable' > *toradwyedd* 'breakability'. ACTION > ACTION is also found with *llosg-* 'to burn', and *ci* 'dog' has ACTION > QUALITY > ACTION. ABSTRACTION > ABSTRACTION is attested for *enw* 'name' and *gwybod-/gwybydd-* 'to know' and ABSTRACTION > QUALITY > ABSTRACTION for *gwybod-/gwybydd-* 'to know'. DIRECTIONAL > ABSTRACTION > QUALITY > ABSTRACTION occurs with *tynn-* 'to pull'. Finally, we find the chain REFLEXIVE > ABSTRACTION > REFLEXIVE for *gwybod-/gwybydd-* 'to know': *ymwybod* 'consciousness, awareness' > *ymwybyddiaeth* 'consciousness, awareness' > *hunanymwybyddiaeth* 'self-consciousness, self-awareness'.

31.10 Reversibility of semantic categories

The following pairs of semantic categories can occur in a reversed order of derivation (of the type AB/BA) in the network of one basic word: ABSTRACTION-PRIVATIVE (for the lexeme *gwybod-/gwybydd-* 'to know'), ABSTRACTION-QUALITY ('to know'), ABSTRACTION-REFLEXIVE ('to know'), CAUSATIVE-QUALITY (*enw* 'name'), and PRIVATIVE-QUALITY ('to know'). This means that, for instance, the network of *gwybod-/gwybydd-* 'to know' includes derivatives with a PRIVATIVE meaning based on a derivative denoting abstraction (e.g. *arwybod* 'awareness, cognition' > *diarwybod* 'unexpected, unaware'), and also a derivative with an abstract meaning based on one with a PRIVATIVE meaning (e.g. *anwybodus* 'ignorant, unknowing' > *anwybodusrwydd* 'ignorance').

31.11 Reasons for structurally poor derivational networks

Welsh has relatively poor derivational networks compared to many languages in this study. Many of the semantic categories are expressed by means other than derivational affixes. As already stated in the introduction, the categories AGENT and, sometimes, INSTRUMENT are often expressed with the affixoids *-wr* and *-wraig*, from *gŵr* 'man' and *gwraig* 'woman'.

The category DIMINUTIVE is most commonly expressed by periphrastic means by modifying a noun with the adjective *bach* 'small'. The derivational DIMINUTIVE suffixes *-yn*, *-en* and *-an* are not very commonly used, although three nouns in the sample have such DIMINUTIVES, which are accepted by native speakers as being possible in spoken usage: *asgwrn* 'bone' (dimin. *esgyrnyn*), *llygad* 'eye' (dimin. *llygedyn*) and *carreg* 'stone' (dimin. *cerigyn* and *caregan*). However, *llygedyn* is somewhat lexicalized, with most modern attestations having the meaning 'the smallest amount of; ray, glimmer', e.g. *llygedyn o obaith* 'a glimmer of hope'. Periphrasis is also the means of expressing semantic categories such as DESIDERATIVE, DIRECTIONAL, DURATIVE, FINITIVE, INCEPTIVE, etc.

HYPERONYMY and HYPONYMY are often expressed by compounding with the adjectival forms *uwch-* 'higher-ranking' (comparative of *uchel* 'high') or *is-* 'lower-ranking' (comparative of *isel* 'low'). The adjective *prif* 'principal, main' can also be used to denote hyperonomy (see Zimmer 2000: 25). New words formed with these adjectives are compounds rather than derivatives, since each adjective also exists as an independent word.

It should be noted that for many of the 30 basic words, there are many derivatives which are attested historically, but which are either no longer in use, or possibly never became productive once they were coined *ad hoc*. Searching through the main dictionary, *Geiriadur Prifysgol Cymru* (Thomas et al. 1950–), I often found derivatives with only one recorded attestation, and if no further examples could be found in corpora or on Google, such words were not included in the derivational networks.

31.12 Conclusions

The average number of derivational orders for the three word-classes in Welsh varies between 1.6 and 2.1; 3rd and 4th order derivations are very rare, and no lexeme in the sample has 5th order derivations. Of the three word-classes, verbs have the largest maximum derivational networks in all orders (see Table 31.1).

Adjectives have the highest overall saturation value in the 1st order (27%, Table 31.5). In the 2nd order, the saturation values vary between 16% (nouns and adjectives) and 14% (verbs), so there is a significant drop between the two orders for adjectives, while nouns and verbs do not change as much between the two orders.

Of the 49 semantic categories used in this study, 26 are available for Welsh lexemes. While some occur commonly for different lexemes (e.g. QUALITY and ACTION, see section 31.6 above), others are only attested once (e.g. HYPERONYMY, seen in *enw* 'name' > *cyfenw* 'surname'). All in all, almost half of the semantic categories are covered by means other than derivational morphology in Welsh, including compounding and periphrasis.

Acknowledgements: I would like to thank Laura Arman and Peredur Webb-Davies, as well as other members of the 2017 Welsh Linguistics Seminar, for providing native-speaker judgements on the derivational networks.

References

Borsley, Robert D., Maggie Tallerman & David Willis. 2007. *The Syntax of Welsh (Cambridge Syntax Guides)*. Cambridge: Cambridge University Press.
Evans, Simon D. 1964. *A Grammar of Middle Welsh*. Dublin: Dublin Institute for Advanced Studies.
Griffiths, Bruce & Dafydd Glyn Jones. 1997. *The Welsh Academy English-Welsh Dictionary/ Geiriadur yr Academi*. Cardiff: University of Wales Press. http://geiriaduracademi.org/ (accessed 20 March 2018)
Nurmio, Silva. 2017. Collective nouns in Welsh: a noun category or a plural allomorph? *Transactions of the Philological Society* 115(1), 58–78.
Russell, Paul. 1989. Agent suffixes in Welsh: native and non-native. *Bulletin of the Board of Celtic Studies* 36. 30–42.
Russell, Paul. 1990. *Celtic word-formation: the velar suffixes*. Dublin: Dublin Institute of Advanced Studies.
Russell, Paul. 1995. *An introduction to the Celtic languages*. London: Routledge.
Russell, Paul. 1996. "Verdunkelte Komposita" in Celtic. *Studia Celtica* 30. 113–125.
Russell, Paul. 2015. Welsh. In Peter O. Müller, Ingeborg Ohnheiser, Susan Olsen & Franz Rainer (eds.), *Word-Formation: An International Handbook of the Languages of Europe*, 2769–2781. Berlin & Boston: Mouton de Gruyter.
Thomas, Peter Wynn. 2006. *Gramadeg y Gymraeg* [A grammar of Welsh], 3rd edn. Cardiff: University of Wales Press.
Thomas, R. J., et al. (eds.), 1950–. *Geiriadur Prifysgol Cymru/A Dictionary of the Welsh Language*. Cardiff: University of Wales Press (2nd edition from 2003–, ed. Gareth, A. Bevan & P. J. Donovan et al., http://www.geiriadur.ac.uk (accessed 16 December 2017.))
Zimmer, Stefan. 2000. *Studies in Welsh word-formation*. Dublin: Dublin Institute for Advanced Studies.

Jurgis Pakerys
32 Introduction to Baltic languages

The Baltic branch of Indo-European survives in two languages, Latvian and Lithuanian. Both of them productively derive nouns, verbs, adjectives, and adverbs through prefixation and suffixation, but prefixation is notably more developed in the verbal domain. Interfixes are sometimes recognized in the Latvian linguistic tradition and refer to segments occurring before the suffixes that arguably play no independent derivational role (Kalnača 2014: 106–107; cf. Roché 2015 for the same interpretation of interfixes in Romance). The reflexive (middle) verbs are productively derived by the addition of affixal reflexive markers (RMs) and are discussed in more detail below. Both languages also allow the simultaneous addition of two affixes, such as prefix-suffix, prefix-RM, or suffix-RM.

The main questions to be answered while building the derivational networks of the Baltic languages in this project relate to the following: (1) the treatment of reflexive (middle) constructions, (2) the interpretation of some aspectual forms, (3) ambiguous orders of derivation, and (4) negative forms with respect to their inclusion in derivational networks and their order of derivation.

The interpretation of reflexive (middle) constructions[1] as inflectional or derivational is a well-known problem, and both the Latvian and Lithuanian linguistic traditions show certain variations (for an overview and for the arguments in favour of treating these constructions as inflectional rather than derivational, see Holvoet 2001: 183–189, 2015: 455–459). REFLEXIVE was included in the list of derivational categories of the present project, and without trying to claim anything new in the inflection versus derivation debate, these formations are also included in the Baltic derivational networks to enable cross-linguistic comparison, especially with genetically and areally related Slavic languages, which constitute a large part of the sample. Baltic reflexive formations typically function as anticausatives in Latvian, and as anticausatives and indirect reflexives (benefactives) in Lithuanian. To get an idea of how the inclusion of reflexive verbs influences the size of Baltic derivational networks, consider the following numbers: Latvian verbal derivational networks have 35 (7%) REFLEXIVES out of a total of 497 formations, while Lithuanian derivational networks have 80 (12.6%) out of a total of 635.

---

[1] These constructions have a broad range of functions and are termed 'reflexive' due to the original function of the reflexive pronominal clitic, which gradually became an affix. Alternatively, these constructions can also be called 'middle' to reflect their function, following the interpretation of Kemmer (1993). Adopting the terminological conventions of the present project, the term 'reflexive' is used henceforth.

https://doi.org/10.1515/9783110686630-032

Baltic reflexive verbs have affixal RMs, which appear as the last morpheme in all forms in Latvian, but only as the last morpheme in non-prefixed forms in Lithuanian, e.g. Latvian *vilkt* 'pull, drag' > *vilktie-**s** 'drag oneself', Lithuanian *traukti* 'pull' > *traukti-**s** 'shrink (intr.)'. In prefixed forms in Lithuanian, the RM is placed before the root, e.g. *ati-traukti* 'pull back (tr.)' > *at-**si**-traukti* 'pull back (intr.)'; an example of a Latvian form with a prefix where the RM is placed at the end is *at-vilkt* 'drag up' > *at-vilktie-**s*** 'drag oneself up'. In rare cases, the RM in Lithuanian appears before the first lexical prefix of the last derivational order if the verb contains two prefixes, e.g. *pri-pa-žinti* 'acknowledge' > *pri-**si**-pa-žinti* 'confess' (although such formations are not attested in the given sample of derivational networks). The appearance of the Lithuanian RM in two different positions reflects its former mobility as a clitic and can be interpreted as an instance of a Wackernagel affix (Nevis and Joseph 1993) or as an ambifix (Mugdan 2015: 268; see also Holvoet 2015: 457–460).

With regard to aspect, prefixed DIRECTIONAL formations in Latvian and Lithuanian express perfectivity and are at the same time FINITIVE, e.g. Latvian *griezt* 'cut (imperfective)' > ***iz**-griezt* 'cut out (perfective)', Lithuanian *pjauti* 'cut (imperfective)' > ***iš**-pjauti* 'cut out (perfective)'. As this is a regular relation, only DIRECTIONAL was marked in the Baltic derivational networks; FINITIVE was reserved for cases when a prefix added no spatial features to the derivative and only the endpoint was marked, e.g. Latvian *šūt* 'sew (imperfective)' > ***pa**-šūt* 'idem (perfective)', Lithuanian *siūti* 'sew (imperfective)' > ***pa**-siūti* 'idem (perfective)'. Lithuanian also has some imperfectivizing (DURATIVE) suffixations, which are absent in Latvian. In general, though, the Baltic languages do not possess a highly grammaticalized aspectual system of the Slavic, particularly Russian, type, despite a number of similarities. As a result, the Baltic formations related to aspectual distinctions are much more derivational than inflectional (for a discussion and further references, see Arkadiev et al. 2015: 31–35; Holvoet 2015: 463–464).

Baltic verbs with the structure prefix-root-suffix quite frequently allow two interpretations based on the order of their derivation: either the suffix is added first and then the prefix, or vice versa. For example, from the Lithuanian *deg-ti* 'burn (intr.)', one can derive a suffixal CAUSATIVE, *deg-**in**-ti* 'burn (tr.)', and then a FINITIVE can be formed by adding a prefix, ***su**-deg-in-ti* 'burn down (tr.)'; consider also the Latvian *deg-t* 'burn (intr.)' > *dedz-**inā**-t* 'burn (tr.)' (CAUSATIVE) > ***sa**-dedz-inā-t* 'burn down (tr.)' (FINITIVE). Alternatively, one can argue that a FINITIVE is derived first (*deg-ti* 'burn (intr.)' > ***su**-deg-ti* 'burn down (intr.)'), and a CAUSATIVE suffix is added later (> *su-deg-**in**-ti* 'burn down (tr.)'); consider also the Latvian *deg-t* 'burn (intr.)' > ***sa**-deg-t* 'burn down (intr.)' > *sa-dedz-**inā**-t* 'burn down (tr.)'. Some prefixed ITERATIVES also allow two interpretations, and the same problem is relevant for derived verbs with the structure prefix-root(-suffix)-RM (Latvian) or prefix-RM-root(-suffix) (Lithuanian), e.g. Latvian *vilkt* 'pull, drag' > *vilktie-s* 'drag oneself' (REFLEXIVE) > *at-vilktie-s* 'drag oneself up' (DIRECTIONAL), Lithuanian *siūti* 'sew (imperfective)' > *siūti-s* 'sew, have sewn for oneself (imperfective)' (REFLEXIVE) > *pa-si-siūti* 'sew, have sewn for oneself (perfective)' (FINITIVE) versus the alternative order of derivation – Latvian *vilkt* 'pull, drag (imperfective)' > *at-vilkt* 'drag up' (DIRECTIONAL) > *at-vilktie-s* 'drag oneself up' (REFLEXIVE), Lithuanian *siūti* 'sew (imperfective)' > *pa-siūti* 'sew (perfective)' (FINITIVE) > *pa-si-siūti* 'sew, have sewn for oneself (perfective)' (REFLEXIVE). The choice of the preferred order of derivation in such cases is left open to the authors of the individual chapters, and the interpretation chosen affects neither the number of orders nor the total number of derivatives. It should be mentioned, however, that the possibility of two alternative derivational histories shows that some verbal categories can occur in a reversed order (yet the order of morphemes in the final derivative remains the same), e.g. CAUSATIVE-FINITIVE vs. FINITIVE-CAUSATIVE or REFLEXIVE-DIRECTIONAL vs. DIRECTIONAL-REFLEXIVE, as illustrated above.

Prefixal negative (PRIVATIVE) derivatives in this survey are included for nouns, adjectives, and adverbs, but, following the traditional approach, verbs with negation are omitted (see e.g. Pavlovič 2015: 1367–1368 for an alternative view regarding Slavic). PRIVATIVE adverbs are interpreted as being derived from the corresponding positive ones, but a deadjectival interpretation would also be possible, e.g. Latvian *slikti* 'badly' > *ne-slikti* 'not badly', Lithuanian *blogai* 'badly' > *ne-blogai* 'not badly' versus Latvian *neslikt-s* 'not bad' > *neslikt-i* 'not badly', Lithuanian *neblog-as* 'not bad' > *neblog-ai* 'not badly'.

References

Arkadiev, Peter, Axel Holvoet & Björn Wiemer. 2015. Introduction: Baltic linguistics – State of the art. In Peter Arkadiev, Axel Holvoet & Björn Wiemer (eds.), *Contemporary Approaches to Baltic Linguistics*, 1–109. Berlin & New York: Mouton de Gruyter.
Holvoet, Axel. 2001. *Studies in the Latvian Verb*. Kraków: Wydawnictwo Uniwersytetu Jagiellońskiego.
Holvoet, Axel. 2015. Lithuanian inflection. In Matthew Baerman (ed.), *The Oxford Handbook of Inflection*, 447–464. Oxford: Oxford University Press.
Kalnača, Andra. 2014. *Typological Perspective on Latvian Grammar*. Berlin & Boston: De Gruyter Open Poland.
Kemmer, Susan. 1993. *The Middle Voice*. Amsterdam & Philadelphia: John Benjamins.

Mugdan, Joachim. 2015. Units of word-formation. In Peter O. Müller, Ingeborg Ohnheiser, Susan Olsen & Franz Rainer (eds.), *Word-Formation. An International Handbook of the Languages of Europe 1*, 235–301. Berlin & Boston: Mouton de Gruyter.

Nevis, Joel A. & Brian D. Joseph. 1993. Wackernagel affixes: Evidence from Balto-Slavic. *Yearbook of Morphology 1992*, 93–111. Dordrecht: Kluwer Academic.

Pavlovič, Jozef. 2015. Negation in the Slavic and Germanic languages. In Peter O. Müller, Ingeborg Ohnheiser, Susan Olsen & Franz Rainer (eds.), *Word-Formation. An International Handbook of the Languages of Europe 2*, 1360–1373. Berlin & Boston: Mouton de Gruyter.

Roché, Michel. 2015. Interfixes in Romance. In Peter O. Müller, Ingeborg Ohnheiser, Susan Olsen & Franz Rainer (eds.), *Word-Formation. An International Handbook of the Languages of Europe 1*, 551–568. Berlin & Boston: Mouton de Gruyter.

Agnė Navickaitė-Klišauskienė
33 Derivational networks in Latvian

33.1 General notes

In Latvian, affixation is the major process of forming new words (composition is another productive way). Different types of affixation can be distinguished in Latvian: prefixation, suffixation, and mixed word-formation types – viz. circumfixation (*ac-s* 'eye' > *pie-ac-is* 'eye flap') and prefixal-suffixal derivation (*akmen-s* 'stone' > *pār-akmeņ-oties* 'to turn into stone').[1] Latvian suffixes are used for deriving nouns, verbs and adjectives, whereas prefixation is the most productive process for deriving verbs. Circumfixation is characteristic of noun derivation, and prefixal-suffixal derivation is characteristic of verbs (Soida 2009; Auziņa et al. 2013: 190–299; Navickaitė-Klišauskienė 2016: 3107–3123).

As far as problematic cases are concerned, the question of productive derivational types should be taken into consideration. Some derivatives belonging to productive derivational types (e.g. *-tājs* for AGENT and *-šana* for ACTION) are potentially possible, but in reality they are not used. They are not even always included in dictionaries, nor are all of them usually available in the Latvian corpus, which is of a relatively small size. In such cases, internet searches were relied on. If no proper examples were found, the potential derivative was not included in the derivational network.

Prefixed *ne-* derivatives (PRIVATIVE) were included in the derivational networks if they were derived from nouns, adjectives or adverbs. Following the traditional point of view, derivatives formed from verbs were not included in the derivational networks (see Chapter 32).

In some cases, it is necessary to speak about different interpretations of the same derivational chain. This question usually arises when talking about derivations from verbs, in particular about derivatives belonging to the semantic categories of CAUSATIVE, FINITIVE and REFLEXIVE (see examples in Chapter 32).

---

[1] In Latvian, new words are derived by adding an inflection as a derivational formant. Such a way of forming new words is called paradigmatic derivation or flexation. In this case, inflections of derivatives fulfil a double function: they are affixes of both inflectional and derivational morphology. Words derived in this way have not been included in the derivational networks, however they comprise a large number of derivatives in the derivational networks of some analyzed words.

33.2 Maximum derivational networks

The most numerous derivational networks are typical of Latvian verbs (Table 33.1). Fewer derivatives are formed from the analyzed nouns and adjectives (taken together) than from verbs. Such differences are attributable to productive prefixed derivation and nouns (ACTION, AGENT, RESULTATIVE) being regularly derived from verbs. Looking at separate derivational orders, it can be very clearly seen that the maximum derivational capacity focuses on the 2nd order (only the largest number of nouns is derived in the 1st order). None of the words have 5th order derivatives, and the 4th order contains only a small number of derivatives (nouns do not have any 4th order derivatives).

Table 33.1: Maximum derivational networks per order of derivation for all three word-classes.

	1st order	2nd order	3rd order	4th order	5th order	Σ
Nouns	53	39	4	0	0	96
Verbs	153	276	66	2	0	497
Adjectives	59	83	33	4	0	179
TOTAL	265	398	103	6	0	766

33.3 Saturation values

The data in Table 33.2 indicate that the saturation values of nouns vary from 9% (*uguns* 'fire') to 50% (*ūdens* 'water'). All nouns have 1st and 2nd order derivatives. Only *uts* 'louse' and *ūdens* 'water' have 3rd order derivatives (with saturation values of 100% and 33% respectively). The already-mentioned word *ūdens* 'water' has the highest saturation values in the 1st (43%) and 2nd (62%) orders. The word *uguns* 'fire' has the lowest saturation value in the 1st order (9%), whereas in the 2nd order the noun *vārds* 'name' (6%) has the lowest saturation value.

Table 33.2: Saturation values per order of derivation, nouns.

Nouns		Saturation value (%)	1st order (%)	2nd order (%)	3rd order (%)	4th order (%)	5th order (%)
bone	*kauls*	30.95	30.43	37.5	0	0	0
eye	*acs*	26.19	30.43	25	0	0	0

Table 33.2 (continued)

Nouns		Saturation value (%)	1st order (%)	2nd order (%)	3rd order (%)	4th order (%)	5th order (%)
tooth	zobs	14.29	17.39	12.5	0	0	0
day	diena	11.9	13.04	12.5	0	0	0
dog	suns	21.43	26.09	18.75	0	0	0
louse	uts	23.81	13.04	25	100	0	0
fire	uguns	9.52	8.7	12.5	0	0	0
stone	akmens	26.19	26.09	31.25	0	0	0
water	ūdens	50	43.48	62.50	33.33	0	0
name	vārds	14.29	21.74	6.25	0	0	0

The data in Table 33.3 indicate that the saturation values of verbs vary from 8% (*zināt* 'know') to 53% (*rakt* 'dig'). The verb *zināt* 'know' has the lowest saturation value in the 1st and 2nd orders. In the 1st order, *dzert* 'drink' (45%) has the highest saturation value, whereas in the 2nd order *rakt* 'dig' (55%) moves up to first place again. The derivational networks of these two verbs (*dzert* 'drink' and

Table 33.3: Saturation values per order of derivation, verbs.

Verbs		Saturation value (%)	1st order (%)	2nd order (%)	3rd order (%)	4th order (%)	5th order (%)
cut	griezt	36.9	35.85	42.7	16	100	0
dig	rakt	52.38	39.62	55.06	72	0	0
pull	vilkt	23.21	28.3	25.84	4	0	0
throw	mest	34.52	30.19	34.83	40	100	0
give	dot	13.69	18.87	14.61	0	0	0
hold	turēt	16.67	20.75	16.85	8	0	0
sew	šūt	28.57	33.96	32.58	4	0	0
burn	degt	30.95	24.53	30.34	48	0	0
drink	dzert	51.19	45.28	50.56	68	0	0
know	zināt	7.74	11.32	6.74	0	0	0

rakt 'dig') are highly saturated in all derivational orders (however, they do not have 4th order derivatives). Only two verbs do not have 3rd order derivatives, namely *dot* 'give' and *zināt* 'know'. Only *griezt* 'cut' and *mest* 'throw' have 4th order derivatives.

Table 33.4 shows that the saturation values of adjectives vary from 8% (*biezs* 'thick') to 49% (*vecs* 'old'). The adjective *vecs* 'old' also has the highest saturation value in the 1st and 2nd orders – 59% and 45%, respectively. *Biezs* 'thick' has the lowest saturation values, namely 18% in the 1st order and 6% in the 2nd order. This adjective is the only one that does not have 3rd order derivatives. There are four adjectives that have 4th order derivatives, comparatively more than the earlier discussed nouns and verbs (compare Tables 33.3 and 33.4).

Table 33.4: Saturation values per order of derivation, adjectives.

Adjectives		Saturation value (%)	1st order (%)	2nd order (%)	3rd order (%)	4th order (%)	5th order (%)
narrow	šaurs	23.73	29.41	12.9	40	100	0
old	vecs	49.15	58.82	45.16	50	0	0
straight	taisns	28.81	23.53	22.58	50	100	0
new	jauns	42.37	52.94	45.16	20	0	0
long	garš	42.37	29.41	32.26	90	100	0
warm	silts	33.9	23.53	35.48	40	100	0
thick	biezs	8.47	17.65	6.45	0	0	0
bad	slikts	22.03	29.41	22.58	10	0	0
thin	plāns	15.25	29.41	9.68	10	0	0
black	melns	37.29	52.94	35.48	20	0	0

Table 33.5 provides the average saturation values of all analyzed word-classes. Higher saturation values in the 1st and 2nd orders is typical for nouns, whereas the saturation values of adjectives and verbs are more or less equal in all four derivational orders.

In the 1st order, the highest saturation value is typically provided by adjectives (as in the 3rd and 4th orders as well). Only in the 2nd order do verbs slightly exceed adjectives.

Table 33.5: Average saturation values per order of derivation for all three word-classes.

	1st order	2nd order	3rd order	4th order	5th order
Nouns	23.64	24.37	13.33	0	0
Verbs	28.87	31.02	26	20	0
Adjectives	34.71	27	33	40	0

33.4 Orders of derivation

As shown in Table 33.6, the 4th derivational order is characteristic of the derivational networks of verbs and adjectives. Nouns do not have any derivatives belonging to the 4th derivational order. The average number of derivational orders in Latvian nouns is slightly more than 2, whereas in verbs and adjectives this order increases to 3 and 3.3, respectively. The difference in the number of orders of nouns and adjectives is down to the tendency to derive verbs from adjectives, which, in turn, substantially expand a derivational network.

Table 33.6: Maximum and average number of orders of derivation for all three word-classes.

	Maximum	Average
Nouns	3	2.2
Verbs	4	3.0
Adjectives	4	3.3

33.5 Derivational capacity

Comparing the highest and average derivational capacities (considering only 1st order derivatives), which are reflected in Table 33.7, Latvian verbs stand out most in this respect. The derivational capacities of nouns and adjectives are very similar. The average number of 1st order derivatives varies between five and six.

As regards derivational capacity in all orders (Table 33.8), the verbs stand out again. The highest derivational capacity of verbs is reached in the 2nd order. However, it is substantially reduced in the 3rd order to 6.6, although it still remains the highest of all word-classes. As previously discussed with regard to Table 33.7, the average capacity of nouns and adjectives in the 1st order is similar, however, in the 2nd and 3rd orders adjectives exceed nouns in this respect.

Table 33.7: Maximum and average derivational capacity for all three word-classes.

	Maximum	Average
Nouns	10	5.3
Verbs	24	15.3
Adjectives	10	5.9

Table 33.8: Average number of derivatives per order of derivation for all three word-classes.

	1st order	2nd order	3rd order	4th order	5th order
Nouns	5.3	3.9	0.4	0	0
Verbs	15.3	27.6	6.6	0.2	0
Adjectives	5.9	8.3	3.3	0.4	0

33.6 Correlation between semantic categories and orders of derivation

When analyzing 1st order formations in the derivational networks of Latvian nouns, it is conspicuous that it is possible to form DIMINUTIVES from each noun under examination (10 words); fewer derivatives belonging to the semantic category of PRIVATIVE (6 words) can also be formed. In the 2nd order, the most common semantic categories are ABSTRACTION (7 words), MANNER (7 words) and DIMINUTIVE (5 words).

When analyzing 1st order derivatives in the derivational networks of Latvian verbs, three semantic categories could be distinguished, namely ACTION (all 10 words), FINITIVE (9 words) and AGENT (9 words). These categories dominate in other derivational orders, e.g. in the 2nd derivational order, derivatives belonging to the semantic category of ACTION are formed from all 10 verbs, AGENT from 9, FINITIVE from 8, and REFLEXIVE from 7. In the 3rd order, the semantic category of ACTION is distinguished: 8 derivational networks of verbs are supplemented with action verbs within this category.

In the 1st order of the derivational networks of Latvian adjectives, 3 semantic categories are distinguished, namely ABSTRACTION (10 words), SIMILATIVE (10 words) and MANNER (10 words). The semantic category of CAUSATIVE contains fewer words: verbs are derived from 8 base adjectives. It should be noted that a huge number of verbs are formed from the analyzed adjectives, and in the 2nd order the most numerous semantic categories are ACTION (9 words) and FINITIVE (8 words). Derivatives belonging to the semantic categories of MANNER (9 words) and DIMINUTIVE (8 words) are also formed from adjectives. In the 3rd order, the semantic category of ACTION (9 words) is distinguishable. A very limited number of derivatives belong to the 4th order, all of which are assigned to the semantic category of ACTION (4 words).

33.7 Semantic categories with blocking effects

As regards the derivation of the nouns under discussion, in the 1st order of derivational networks, the semantic category of DIMINUTIVE is the most distinctive. A DIMINUTIVE always blocks further derivation. A relatively clear-cut distinction appears within semantic categories themselves, which block further derivation. In the 2nd order of derivational networks this happens in all cases, namely within the categories of MANNER, ABSTRACTION and ACTION.

In all orders of verb derivation, the semantic category of ACTION blocks the further formation of words. Even in the derivational networks of verbs, the formation of derivatives belonging to the semantic category of RESULTATIVE is not as regular as ACTION, further formation from which is also blocked.

In the adjectives' derivations, the semantic category of MANNER blocks the further formation of words. Rare cases should be taken as exceptions, such as when a new derivative belonging to the semantic category of PRIVATIVE is produced from the derivative of MANNER with a *ne-* prefix, e.g. *slikt-s* 'bad' > *slikt-i* 'badly' > *ne-slikti* 'not badly'. If a verb is derived from a base adjective (in the analyzed derivational networks, it is derived in 9 cases out of 10), further derivation is always blocked by the semantic category of ACTION in the 2nd derivational order.

33.8 Typical combinations of semantic categories

Following a review of the derivational networks, it is possible to identify several combinations of semantic categories that could be regarded as typical:

- Typical combinations in the derivation of nouns are QUALITY/POSSESSIVE-MANNER (7 base nouns, e.g. *sunisk-s* 'doggy' > *sunisk-i* 'doggy') and QUALITY/POSSESSIVE-ABSTRACTION (7 base nouns, e.g. *ūdeņain-s* 'aqueous' > *ūdeņain-ums* 'aqueousness').
- In the formation of 9 verbs, the typical combination of FINITIVE-ACTION, e.g. *pašū-t* 'make clothes' > *pašū-šana* 'making (clothes)', is repeated. In some cases, this combination can be supplemented by the semantic category of REFLEXIVE, e.g. *pievilk-t* 'pull to' > *pievilk-ties* 'pull up' > *pievilk-šanās* 'pull up'. The combination of FINITIVE/DIRECTIONAL-RESULTATIVE (6 verbs) is also fairly common. The combination of CAUSATIVE-FINITIVE-ACTION, which is shown by 3 verbs, e.g. *šūdināt* 'get (clothes) made' > *pa-šūdinā-t* 'make clothes' > *pašūdinā-šana* 'making clothes', is less frequent.
- In the derivation of adjectives, the most typical combinations are SIMILATIVE-MANNER (8 words, e.g. *melngan-s* 'blackish' > *melngan-i* 'blackish (adv.)'), CAUSATIVE-FINITIVE-ACTION (8 words, e.g. *vecināt* 'make look old' > *no-vecinā-t* 'make older' > *novecinā-šana* 'making older') and ABSTRACTION-DIMINUTIVE (6 words, e.g. *siltums* 'warmth' > *siltumiņš*).

33.9 Multiple occurrence of semantic categories

The multiple occurrence of semantic categories, with only a few exceptions, is a rather rare phenomenon in the Latvian language. Even though the derivational chain DIMINUTIVE-DIMINUTIVE is fundamentally intrinsic to Latvian, it is not reflected in the analyzed nouns in the derivational networks.

Several notable examples can be found in the derivational networks of adjectives; in two derivational networks, the semantic category chain SIMILATIVE-SIMILATIVE is repeated: *meln-s* 'black' > *meln-īgs* 'blackish' > *melnīg-snējs* 'swarthy' and *gar-š* 'long' > *gar-ens* 'longish' > *garen-isks* 'longish'. Such derivational types are not productive in Latvian, however.

33.10 Reversibility of semantic categories

A brief description and several examples are given in the introductory chapter to the Baltic languages (see Chapter 32).

33.11 Reasons for structurally poor derivational networks

Out of all 30 analyzed derivational networks in Latvian, it can clearly be seen that larger derivational networks are more typical of verbs and adjectives. Fewer derivatives are formed from nouns, e.g. the derivational network of *uguns* 'fire' is represented by only four derivatives, *diena* 'day' by five derivatives, and *vārds* 'name' and *zobs* 'tooth' have six derivatives each. The reason for this is not always easy to find. One possibility is that the derivational networks of nouns are narrowed by composition, another process of word-formation competing with affixation. The other reasons could be semantic, for instance, in Latvian the noun *vārds* refers not only to 'name', but also to 'word' (it creates a rather large derivational network), and the noun *zobs* means not only 'tooth', but also 'tine' or 'prong'.

33.12 Conclusions

A close analysis of the Latvian material shows irregularly abundant derivational networks (Table 33.1). The maximum number of derivatives is typical of verbs. This can be explained by regular verbal-noun derivations and the active use of prefixes as a derivational formant. Fewer derivatives constitute the derivational networks of adjectives, however adjectives exceed nouns. This is due to the greater capabilities of adjectives to form verbs and subsequently expand the derivational network. Such distribution is shown not only by the general number of derivatives, but also by the number of derivatives in separate derivational orders.

In all derivational networks, the largest recorded number of derivational orders is four (verbs and adjectives). A slightly higher average number of orders is typical of adjectives (Table 33.6). The derivational networks of nouns have fewer orders. 3rd order derivatives were only recorded in two derivational networks (the average number of orders is 2.2).

The average saturation value of the derivational networks of adjectives is slightly higher than that of verbs and nouns (for the 1st, 3rd and 4th orders). Verbs exceed adjectives only in the 2nd order in this respect (Table 33.5).

38 semantic categories were found in the 30 analyzed derivational networks. Naturally, not all categories are characterized by a huge number of derivatives, e.g. PURPOSIVE, ORNATIVE, or RECIPROCAL (each recorded as few as one derivative). The most numerous and typical semantic groups for all analyzed word-classes are ACTION, FINITIVE, RESULTATIVE, REFLEXIVE and AGENT.

References

Auziņa, Ilze, Ieva Breņķe, Juris Grigorjevs, Inese Indričāne, Baiba Ivulāne, Andra Kalnača, Linda Lauze, Ilze Lokmane, Dace Markus, Daina Nītiņa, Gunta Smiltniece, Baiba Valkovska & Anna Vulāne. 2013. *Latviešu valodas gramatika* [Grammar of Latvian], Rīga: LU Latviešu valodas institūts.

Navickaitė-Klišauskienė, Agnė. 2016. Latvian. In Peter O. Müller, Ingeborg Ohnheiser, Susan Olsen & Franz Rainer (eds.), *Word-Formation. An International Handbook of the Languages of Europe 5*, 3107–3123. Berlin: Mouton de Gruyter.

Soida, Emīlija. 2009. *Vārddarināšana*. Rīga: Latvijas Universitāte.

Sources

Corpus of Latvian language. www.korpuss.lv (accessed 2016–2018).
Dictionary of Modern Latvian (*Mūsdienu latviešu valodas vārdnīca*). http://www.tezaurs.lv/mlvv.
Dictionary of the Latvian language (*Latviešu literārās valodas vardnīca*). http://www.tezaurs.lv/llvv

Jurgis Pakerys
34 Derivational networks in Lithuanian

34.1 General notes

Lithuanian productively uses suffixation to derive nouns, verbs and adjectives, while prefixation is much more frequent in verbal than in nominal and adjectival derivations. Reflexive (middle) verbs are derived by the addition of the reflexive marker (RM), which takes its position depending on the morphemic structure of the base (see more on this category and its marker in Chapter 32). Lithuanian also employs composition and paradigmatic derivations, but these are out of the scope of the present study.[1]

The use of lexemes included in the derivational networks (DNs) was checked in 2017–2018 using the following sources: (1) the *Dictionary of Modern Lithuanian* (DŽ), (2) the Corpus of Contemporary Lithuanian (CCL), and (3) online texts indexed by Google. In the case of the dialectal and possibly archaic lexemes listed in DŽ, preference was given to CCL and online data. However, one should bear in mind that the search functions provided by the CCL and Google are limited and some omissions and misjudgements are still possible.

In nominal and adjectival derivational networks, some cases were found where the lexemes could be interpreted either as prefixal derivations or as compounds consisting of a preposition and a noun. For example, either *be-dant-is* 'toothless' is based on the prepositional phrase *be dant-ų* (without tooth-GEN.PL) 'without tooth', or *be-* is recognized as a PRIVATIVE prefix. In this study, the traditional prefixal interpretation was adopted (Ulvydas 1965: 590; Stundžia 2016: 3097; see an alternative view in Paulauskienė 1994: 95). The Lithuanian prescriptive tradition does not recognize INSTRUMENTS derived with the suffixes used to form AGENTS, but derivatives of this type are quite productive and were included based on their attestations in the CCL and online texts.

For verbs, the suffix *-y-ti* occurring in the infinitive stem is traditionally interpreted as a derivational suffix (Ulvydas 1971: 244; Ambrazas 2005: 396, 399; Stundžia 2016: 3100), but it is absent from other stems and arguably functions as an inflection-class marker (Pakerys 2011). Following this interpretation, formations containing *-y-ti* only in the infinitive stem were not included.

---

[1] For more details and further references, see the latest overview of Lithuanian word-formation by Stundžia (2016).

https://doi.org/10.1515/9783110686630-034

Finally, it should be mentioned that the adjective *šilt-as* (warm-NOM.SG.M) 'warm' used in the basic word list (cf. Chapter 1.3.2) may be interpreted as derived in the suffix *-t-* from *šil-ti* (get.warm-INF) 'get warm' (Ulvydas 1965: 552; Ambrazas 2005: 223); however, this type is non-productive and very limited, hence the lexeme was considered acceptable for the basic word list. (Other notes relevant for both Latvian and Lithuanian derivations can be found in Chapter 32.)

34.2 Maximum derivational networks

As can be seen in Table 34.1 below, verbs produced the largest derivational networks, while nouns and adjectives had similarly sized maximum derivational networks in the 1st order; however, in total, adjectives produced larger derivational networks than nouns due to significant expansion in the 2nd and 3rd orders. With regard to the total numbers of derivatives, the verbs of the sample produced 635 formations, followed by adjectives (379), then nouns (152). None of the words had 5th order derivations, and nouns had only a few formations in the 3rd order and derived none in the 4th order.

Table 34.1: Maximum derivational networks per order of derivation for all three word-classes.

	1st order	2nd order	3rd order	4th order	5th order	Σ
Nouns	29	23	4	0	0	56
Verbs	56	98	45	5	0	204
Adjectives	26	37	19	3	0	85
TOTAL	111	158	68	8	0	345

The size of verbal derivational networks can be explained by the ability of verbs to derive regular nominal formations and numerous prefixal derivatives, which in turn develop their sub-networks. The derivational networks of adjectives were larger than those of nouns because adjectives exhibit some paradigmaticity (see comments above Table 34.4) and also productively derive verbs, which help expand the adjectival networks in the 2nd and 3rd orders. (This pattern is typical for qualitative adjectives, and in our sample all adjectives belonged to this class.)

34.3 Saturation values

The saturation values of nominal derivational networks ranged from 9% to 46% (see Table 34.2 below). The smallest derivational networks were for *utėlė* 'louse' and *ugnis* 'fire', while the most saturated ones belonged to *vardas* 'name', *kaulas* 'bone' and *šuo* 'dog'. In some cases, a high saturation value in the 1st order seemed to warrant a high total saturation, but this was not always the case. For example, *šuo* 'dog' had a saturation of 48% in the 1st order but dropped to 26% in the 2nd order, while *vardas* 'name' and *kaulas* 'bone' had lower values in the 1st order (41%) compared to that of *šuo* 'dog', but succeeded in maintaining the pace of the expansion of their derivational networks in the 2nd order (43% and 39%, respectively).

Table 34.2: Saturation values per order of derivation, nouns.

Nouns		Saturation value (%)	1st order (%)	2nd order (%)	3rd order (%)	4th order (%)	5th order (%)
bone	kaulas	39.29	41.38	39.13	25	0	0
eye	akis	33.93	27.59	47.83	0	0	0
tooth	dantis	17.86	31.03	4.35	0	0	0
day	diena	14.29	17.24	8.7	25	0	0
dog	šuo	37.5	48.28	26.09	25	0	0
louse	utėlė	8.93	10.34	8.7	0	0	0
fire	ugnis	8.93	10.34	8.7	0	0	0
stone	akmuo	33.93	37.93	30.43	25	0	0
water	vanduo	30.36	31.03	26.09	50	0	0
name	vardas	46.43	41.38	43.48	100	0	0

For verbs, the smallest derivational network belonged to *žinoti* 'know' (saturation value of 3%), and the most developed derivational networks were for *traukti* 'pull' (62%) and *pjauti* 'cut' (52%), as shown in Table 34.3 below. Similarly to nominal derivational networks, a highly saturated 1st order does not necessarily warrant a high total saturation. For a lexeme to develop a well-saturated derivational network, the 1st order is important, but the derivational network needs to be constantly developed in the following orders. For example, *mesti* 'throw'

Table 34.3: Saturation values per order of derivation, verbs.

Verbs		Saturation value (%)	1st order (%)	2nd order (%)	3rd order (%)	4th order (%)	5th order (%)
cut	pjauti	52.45	48.21	51.02	62.22	40	0
dig	kasti	35.78	39.29	36.73	33.33	0	0
pull	traukti	62.25	51.79	66.33	62.22	100	0
throw	mesti	41.18	35.71	47.96	35.56	20	0
give	duoti	13.73	21.43	10.2	13.33	0	0
hold	laikyti	16.18	25	13.27	13.33	0	0
sew	siūti	33.82	32.14	35.71	28.89	60	0
burn	degti	24.02	26.79	18.37	28.89	60	0
drink	gerti	28.43	42.86	28.57	13.33	0	0
know	žinoti	3.43	7.14	2.04	2.22	0	0

had a lower saturation value in the 1st order (36%) than *gerti* 'drink' (43%), but it kept expanding its derivational network in the 2nd order (48%), while *gerti* 'drink' started to lose to its competitors (29%). The top two lexemes, *traukti* 'pull' and *pjauti* 'cut', already scored highly in the 1st order and, most importantly, maintained their saturation in the 2nd and 3rd orders.

As can be seen in Table 34.4 below, the saturation values of adjectival derivational networks ranged from 34% for *šiltas* 'warm' to 64% for *juodas* 'black'. As noted above, a relatively high 1st order score needs to be maintained in the subsequent orders to develop a well-saturated derivational network.

Table 34.5 presents the average saturation values across word-classes and orders. Adjectival derivational networks in particular stand out. In the 1st order (average saturation of 56%), adjectival derivational networks were still far away from the saturation seen in typical inflectional paradigms, but these derivational networks seemed to be the most regular of all word-classes. Deverbal ACTIONS, denominal DIMINUTIVES and some other categories are productive, but as a whole, they are unable to offset a certain paradigmatic effect of the productive deadjectival categories. As noted earlier, qualitative adjectives also differ from nouns in their ability to derive regular verbal formations in the 1st order, which in turn seems to help maintain relatively high average saturation values in the 2nd and 3rd orders, which are filled by many deverbal formations.

Table 34.4: Saturation values per order of derivation, adjectives.

	Adjectives	Saturation value (%)	1st order (%)	2nd order (%)	3rd order (%)	4th order (%)	5th order (%)
narrow	siauras	41.18	46.15	35.14	52.63	0	0
old	senas	48.24	69.23	40.54	42.11	0	0
straight	tiesus	36.47	38.46	37.84	36.84	0	0
new	naujas	44.71	57.69	32.43	47.37	66.67	0
long	ilgas	44.71	50	40.54	42.11	66.67	0
warm	šiltas	34.12	46.15	27.03	36.84	0	0
thick	storas	44.71	61.54	37.84	36.84	33.33	0
bad	blogas	40	57.69	29.73	36.84	33.33	0
thin	plonas	48.24	53.85	40.54	52.63	66.67	0
black	juodas	63.53	76.92	64.86	52.63	0	0

Table 34.5: Average saturation values per order of derivation for all three word-classes.

	1st order (%)	2nd order (%)	3rd order (%)	4th order (%)	5th order (%)
Nouns	29.65	24.35	25.00	0	0
Verbs	33.036	31.02	29.33	28.00	0
Adjectives	55.77	38.65	43.68	26.67	0

33.4 Orders of derivation

The maximum number of orders of derivation was three for nouns (2.6 on average) and four (3.5 on average) for verbs and adjectives (see Table 34.6). Again, the difference between nouns and adjectives can be explained by the productive formation of deadjectival verbs, which produce corresponding verbal derivational networks; conversely, the lower numbers of nominal orders of derivation seem to be primarily limited by less productive denominal verbs.

Table 34.6: Maximum and average number of orders of derivation for all three word-classes.

	Maximum	Average
Nouns	3	2.6
Verbs	4	3.5
Adjectives	4	3.5

34.5 Derivational capacity

The derivational capacity, which is measured as the number of direct 1st order derivatives, was highest for verbs, reaching a maximum of 29 and an average of 18.5 (see Table 34.7). In this respect, verbs surpassed nouns by a factor of a little more than two, while adjectives fell in between. As noted earlier, the high derivational capacity of verbs results from their ability to derive numerous prefixal formations and regular deverbal nominals. Adjectives have a higher derivational capacity than nouns because they have more paradigmatic derivational networks and derive more verbs than nouns do.

Table 34.7: Maximum and average derivational capacity for all three word-classes.

	Maximum	Average
Nouns	14	8.6
Verbs	29	18.5
Adjectives	20	14.5

When the average number of derivatives across orders is considered (Table 34.8), one notices a decreasing trend for nouns, while adjectival derivational networks maintain their capacity in the 2nd order and then start decreasing in the 3rd order. Verbal derivational networks, however, behave differently: they skyrocket to a peak in the 2nd order and then dip into a sudden decline in the 3rd order. Verbal and adjectival patterns seem to be explained by derived verbs in the 1st order; as mentioned above, verbs are usually able to derive large numbers of prefixal formations, while deadjectival verbs are regular but much lower in number, hence the difference in the number of further derivations in the 2nd order.

Table 34.8: Average number of derivatives per order of derivation for all three word-classes.

	1st order	2nd order	3rd order	4th order	5th order
Nouns	8.6	5.6	1	0	0
Verbs	18.5	30.4	13.2	1.4	0
Adjectives	14.5	14.3	8.3	0.8	0

34.6 Correlation between semantic categories and orders of derivation

In the 1st order, all 10 nouns from the basic word list derived DIMINUTIVES, 8 nouns had RELATIONAL adjectives, and 7 nouns had POSSESSIVE and PRIVATIVE formations. In the 2nd order, the top categories were ABSTRACTIONS (typically derived from POSSESSIVE adjectives, attested in 8 derivational networks) and deverbal ACTIONS (attested in 7 derivational networks), followed by FINITIVES (in 6 derivational networks). The 3rd order contained ACTION nominals only (in 6 derivational networks). In sum, the 1st order reflects the productivity of Lithuanian denominal DIMINUTIVES and some denominal adjectival categories (RELATIONAL, POSSESSIVE, PRIVATIVE). Further orders show expected patterns for the respective word-classes, as noted for verbs (deriving ACTIONS) and adjectives (deriving ABSTRACTIONS) below; it should be noted, however, that in the verbal derivational networks discussed below, DIRECTIONAL formations surpass FINITIVE ones.

All 10 verbs derived ACTIONS in the 1st order and the majority of them also had AGENT and DIRECTIONAL formations (9 and 8, respectively). In the 2nd order, all verbs derived in the 1st order had ACTIONS, 9 derivational networks contained REFLEXIVES, and 8 derivational networks had AGENTS. The 3rd and 4th orders were again dominated by deverbal ACTIONS (attested in 10 and 5 derivational networks, respectively). In sum, verbal derivational networks are good representations of the general productivity of ACTION, REFLEXIVE, DIRECTIONAL, and AGENT formations in Lithuanian.

The 1st order of derivation of the adjectives shows the certain paradigmatic effect noted earlier. For all 10 lexemes, this order includes at least one formation for each of the seven categories: ABSTRACTION, PRIVATIVE (as negative), MANNER, AUGMENTATIVE (as intensive), SIMILATIVE (as attenuative), PATIENT (as a bearer of QUALITY) and PROCESS. The CAUSATIVE derivation is absent only for 'old', because this slot is taken by a deverbal formation (*sen-ti* (grow.old-INF) 'grow old' > *sen-din-ti* (grow.old-CAUS-INF) 'make old', while the verbal STATIVE is only realized for 'black' and 'bad'. In the 2nd order, all 10 derivational networks contain derivations for ACTION and DIMINUTIVE (mostly deverbal), 9 derivational networks include REFLEXIVES, and 8 derivational networks have FINITIVES; out of the deadjectival categories, MANNER is the most frequent (realized in 8 derivational networks) and is always derived from SIMILATIVES of the 1st order. The 3rd order is characterized by ACTIONS (attested in 10 derivational networks) and REFLEXIVES (in 9 derivational networks), while in the 4th order, only ACTION is available (in 5 derivational networks). To conclude, the 1st order is characterized by a large number of categories realized for all, or almost all, bases. Further orders producing verbs are similar to nominal derivational networks, whereby FINITIVE formations are frequent and DIRECTIVES are uncommon, which is understandable given the largely non-spatial semantics of these verbs.

In general, the occurrence of particular categories seems to be more related to the word-classes of available bases than to orders, and typically productive categories for a given word-class are realized.

34.7 Semantic categories with blocking effects

For nominal derivational networks, a typical blocking category in the 1st order was DIMINUTIVE, with the exception of when a further DIMINUTIVE was derived, e.g. *vard-as* (name-NOM.SG) 'name' > *vard-el-is* (name-DIM-NOM.SG) 'dear, cute name' > *vard-el-yt-is* (name-DIM-DIM-NOM.SG) 'a very cute name'. In the 2nd order, derivation stopped in the categories of ABSTRACTION and ACTION, and in the 3rd order, the terminal category was ACTION (but note some examples of possible further derivation from these categories below).

ACTION is typically a blocking category in all orders of verbal derivational networks and it may only occasionally derive further DIMINUTIVES, such as *met-im-as* (throw-AN-NOM.SG) 'throw (as in a basketball game)' > *met-im-uk-as* (throw-AN-DIM-NOM.SG), especially when the base undergoes some concretization. Denominal DIMINUTIVES frequently behave as terminal categories, as mentioned above, but deverbal DIMINUTIVES differ by usually allowing further derivation.

For adjectives, the typical blocking categories in the 1st order are MANNER and ABSTRACTION. In the 2nd order, MANNER, ACTION, AGENT, and INSTRUMENT hamper further derivation, while in the 3rd and 4th orders, ACTION is the most frequent terminal category. It should be noted, however, that ABSTRACTIONS may derive some DIMINUTIVES in Lithuanian, such as *skan-us* (tasty-NOM.SG.M) 'tasty' > *skan-um-as* (tasty-ABSTR-NOM.SG) 'flavour, tastefulness' > *skan-um-ėl-is* (tasty-ABSTR-DIM-NOM.SG) 'diminutive of flavour (with some emphasis)', but they were not attested in the sample of derivational networks examined in the present study. The same applies to AGENTS and INSTRUMENTS, which may allow further derivatives (denominal verbs, DIMINUTIVES, etc.), but none occurred in the adjectival derivational networks of the sample. The blocking effect of MANNER, however, seems to be related to the semantic category of the base: in general, adverbs in Lithuanian allow the formation of PRIVATIVES (with negation), but in blocking cases, the adverbs were derived from SIMILATIVES (attenuatives), which most probably hampered the further formation of PRIVATIVE (negative) derivatives.

34.8 Typical combinations of semantic categories

There were no typical noun > noun category combinations noted in derivational networks beginning with nouns. Of the (noun >) adjective > noun cases, POSSESSIVE-ABSTRACTION, such as *ak-is* (eye-NOM.SG) 'eye' > *ak-yl-as* (eye-POSS-NOM.SG.M) 'having good eyes, sharp-sighted' > *ak-yl-um-as* (eye-POSS-ABSTR-NOM.SG) 'watchfulness', was quite common, being attested in 8 derivational networks (9 formations in total) that began with a noun from the basic word list and in 2 derivational networks (2 formations in total) that began with a verb from that list. PROCESS-ACTION (5 formations in 5 derivational networks) and PROCESS-FINITIVE-ACTION (6 formations in 5 derivational networks) were less frequent.

The typical category combinations beginning with a verb were DIRECTIONAL-ACTION, such as *kas-ti* (dig-INF) 'dig' > *iš-kas-ti* (DIR-dig-INF) 'dig out' > *iš-kas-im-as* (DIR-dig-AN-NOM.SG) 'digging out' (51 formations in 8 derivational networks of simplex verbs and 2 formations in 1 derivational network derived from complex verbs), and its extended version with the RM, DIRECTIONAL-REFLEXIVE-ACTION (33 cases in 5 derivational networks). Less common was FINITIVE-ACTION (5 formations in 5 derivational networks of simplex verbs), which was also found in the derivational networks of deadjectival and denominal verbs (see above and below). REFLEXIVE-ACTION was found in 6 formations belonging to 6 derivational networks of simplex verbs. (When complex prefixless verbs are included, 2 more formations can be added.) Another combination was DIRECTIONAL-ITERATIVE/DURATIVE, as in *kas-ti* (dig-INF) 'dig' > *at-kas-ti* (DIR-dig-INF) 'dig up' > *at-kas-inė-ti* (DIR-dig-ITER-INF) 'dig up (as ITERATIVE or imperfective)' (19 formations in 3 derivational networks of simplex verbs, 15 of which also derive ACTIONS). Of the denominal formations in verbal derivational networks, the combination INSTRUMENT-DIMINUTIVE stood out (10 formations in 4 derivational networks).

For adjectives (adjective > adjective), SIMILATIVE-MANNER (13 formations in 8 derivational networks of simplex adjectives and 5 formations in 3 derivational networks from derived adjectives) and MANNER-PRIVATIVE (9 formations in 8 derivational networks of simplex adjectives) can be identified as quite common combinations. An example is the following: *sen-as* (old-NOM.SG.M) 'old' > *sen-ok-as* (old-SIM-NOM.SG.M) 'somewhat old' > *sen-ok-ai* (old-SIM-MANN) 'quite a while ago', *sen-as* (old-NOM.SG.M) 'old' > *seni-ai* (old-MANN) 'long time ago' > *ne-seni-ai* (NEG-old-MANN) 'not long ago'. Other typical combinations belong to the type (adjective >) verb > noun, including PROCESS-ACTION (12 formations in 10 adjectival derivational networks), PROCESS-FINITIVE-ACTION (8 formations in 5 adjectival derivational networks), CAUSATIVE-REFLEXIVE-ACTION (8 formations in 8 derivational networks), CAUSATIVE-FINITIVE-REFLEXIVE (8 formations in 6 derivational networks), and CAUSATIVE-INSTRUMENT (9 formations in 7 derivational networks).

Some of these combinations are quite trivial because their second members are simply productive and thus are independent of the first members. For example, if a new verb is derived (irrespective of the above-mentioned category of the base), it will probably have a productive ACTION nominal, and when new adverbs enter the lexicon, many of them can be negated (MANNER-PRIVATIVE). The formation of the POSSESSIVE, however, can be held at least partly responsible for the further derivation of ABSTRACTION because POSSESSIVE adjectives are qualitative, and qualitative adjectives (not relational ones) can derive ABSTRACTIONS. In a similar fashion, CAUSATIVES create a precondition for the formation of REFLEXIVES and INSTRUMENTS because they are usually derived from transitives. Consider also the case of DIRECTIONAL-DURATIVE: DIRECTIONAL prefixes make the verbs perfective, which is a necessary precondition for the DURATIVE (imperfective) to be formed.

34.9 Multiple occurrence of semantic categories

The multiple occurrence of semantic categories is, in general, rare in Lithuanian derivation, with the exception of the suffix stacking of adjectival AUGMENTATIVES (intensifiers): ten cases were found with two suffixes and one case with three suffixes: *nauj-ut-ėl-ait-is* (new-INT-INT-INT-NOM.SG.M) 'very very new'. Suffix stacking in nominal DIMINUTIVES is also possible and was attested in one case with two affixes: *vard-el-yt-is* (name-DIM-DIM-NOM.SG) 'a very cute name'.

Of the cases when a multiple occurrence was interrupted by another category, the combination ABSTRACTION-SIMILATIVE-ABSTRACTION was noted in two derivational networks, as in *nauj-as* (new-NOM.SG.M) 'new' > *nauj-ov-ė* (new-ABSTR-NOM.SG) 'novelty' (ABSTRACTION) > *nauj-ov–išk-as* (new-ABSTR-SIM-NOM.SG.M) 'new-fashioned' (SIMILATIVE) > *nauj-ov–išk-um-as* (new-ABSTR-SIM-ABSTR-NOM.SG) 'novelty' (ABSTRACTION).

34.10 Reversibility of semantic categories

Verbs with the structure prefix(-RM)-root(-suffix) may allow alternative interpretations of their derivational history, which means that some categories can occur in the reverse order (see a short discussion and some examples in Chapter 32). The most frequent categories expressed by the prefixes in these cases are DIRECTIVE and FINITIVE. The RM has a number of meanings subsumed in this study under the label of REFLEXIVE, while the suffixes typically denote CAUSATIVE or ITERATIVE actions. However, it should be noted that the end result (the ordering of morphemes) is always the same, irrespective of the assumed order of derivation.

34.11 Conclusions

The largest derivational networks were produced by verbs, followed by adjectives, then nouns. The maximum number of orders was four, attested in verbal and adjectival derivational networks (both having 3.5 orders on average), while nouns had smaller derivational networks (2.6 orders on average, with a maximum of three). The same ranking of the word-classes is also achieved when the derivational capacity is measured. The size of verbal derivational networks can be explained by productive prefixal derivation and the regular formation of deverbal nominals, while adjectives surpass nouns in their ability to derive verbs more regularly and show a more developed derivational paradigmaticity.

In regard to saturation values, high numbers in the 1st order do not necessarily warrant well-saturated derivational networks overall. For a lexeme to develop an extensive derivational network, a relatively high level of saturation needs to be maintained in the orders following the initial one. The average saturation values of adjectival derivational networks stand out and can be recognized as the most paradigmatic, followed by those of verbs and nouns.

The occurrence of semantic categories in different orders reflects their general productivity and seems to be mostly related to the word-classes of available bases in a given order. Some category combinations can be regarded as trivial because their second members are largely independent of the first ones and reflect general productivity. However, a number of categories can be argued to provide certain preconditions for further derivation, such as POSSESSIVE-ABSTRACTION, CAUSATIVE-REFLEXIVE, CAUSATIVE-INSTRUMENT, and DIRECTIONAL-DURATIVE. The categories usually blocking further derivation are denominal DIMINUTIVES, deverbal and deadjectival ABSTRACTIONS, deverbal ACTIONS (all with some attested or possible exceptions) and deadjectival MANNER formations derived from SIMILATIVES (attenuatives).

The multiple occurrence of categories was attested in the cases of stacked AUGMENTATIVE (intensive) and denominal DIMINUTIVE suffixes and in the chain ABSTRACTION-SIMILATIVE-ABSTRACTION. The reversibility of categories can be recognized in the cases when the addition of the RM, verbal prefixes (mostly expressing FINITIVE and DIRECTIVE) and suffixes (marking ITERATIVE and CAUSATIVE) allows alternative interpretations of the order of derivation. However, the order of morphemes in the derivative is always the same, irrespective of the history of derivation.

Acknowledgements: I would like to thank Alexandra Bagasheva, Lívia Körtvélyessy, Pavol Štekauer, and Salvador Valera for their many helpful comments and suggestions on this chapter and on the introduction to the Baltic languages. Many thanks also to Agnė Navickaitė-Klišauskienė for the great discussions we had while working on the Baltic derivational networks and writing our respective chapters, and to Cristina Aggazzotti for her insightful remarks and meticulous editing of my texts.

References

Ambrazas, Vytautas (ed.). 2005. *Dabartinės lietuvių kalbos gramatika* [Grammar of Modern Lithuanian], 4th edn. Vilnius: Mokslo ir enciklopedijų leidybos institutas.
CCL = *Corpus of Contemporary Lithuanian*. http://corpus.vdu.lt/en/ (accessed 2017–2018).
DŽ = *Dabartinės lietuvių kalbos žodynas* [Dictionary of Modern Lithuanian]. Edited by Stasys Keinys, 6th edn. Vilnius: Lietuvių kalbos institutas.
Pakerys, Jurgis. 2011. *On derivational suffixes and inflectional classes of verbs in Modern Lithuanian. Lietuvių kalba 5*. http://www.lietuviukalba.lt/index.php/lietuviu-kalba/article/view/30/24 (accessed 29 March 2018).
Paulauskienė, Aldona. 1994. *Lietuvių kalbos morfologija: Paskaitos lituanistams* [Lithuanian Morphology: Lectures for the Students of Lithuanian Philology]. Vilnius: Mokslo ir enciklopedijų leidykla.

Stundžia, Bonifacas. 2016. Lithuanian. In Peter O. Müller, Ingeborg Ohnheiser, Susan Olsen & Franz Rainer (eds.), *Word-Formation. An International Handbook of the Languages of Europe 5*, 3089–3106. Berlin: Mouton de Gruyter.

Ulvydas, Kazys (ed.). 1965. *Lietuvių kalbos gramatika 1* [Grammar of Lithuanian 1]. Vilnius: Mintis.

Ulvydas, Kazys (ed.). 1971. *Lietuvių kalbos gramatika 2* [Grammar of Lithuanian 2]. Vilnius: Mintis.

Dimitra Melissaropoulou, Angela Ralli
35 Derivational networks in Greek

35.1 General notes

Greek is an independent branch of the Indo-European family. Nowadays, it consists of several varieties which are spoken in the modern world – both inside and outside Greece – by a total of approximately 14–15 million people. For the purposes of this contribution, we will use the term Greek to refer to Standard Modern Greek in general, while special terms will be used to denote varieties other than Standard Modern Greek, if necessary.

From a typological point of view, Greek is generally considered to be a synthetic system of the fusional type, showing a rich morphological structure in inflection and the word-formation domains, that is, derivation and compounding (Ralli 2005, 2013, 2015). Word formation is highly saturated by affixal means, producing new lexemes of all major categories, nouns, verbs, adjectives and adverbs, while non-affixal derivation, as for instance conversion, is not unknown, although less frequent. Structurally, Greek is a stem-based language (cf. Ralli 2005), and derivational affixes, i.e. prefixes or suffixes, attach to the left or the right side of the stem accordingly ([pref-stem]) ([stem-suf]). Both prefixation and suffixation are very productive processes, but suffixes are more numerous than prefixes. Prefixes do not generally change the grammatical category of the base to which they attach, while suffixes may act as category-changing ones.

Serious difficulties with respect to the compilation of an affixal corpus are caused by various lexicalization levels of derived words, both structural and semantic, due to the substantial enrichment of the Greek lexicon with words, roots/ stems and affixes originating from Ancient Greek, a process which has occurred in the last two centuries. For instance, a respectable number of derivational prefixes deriving from Ancient Greek prepositions render the semantic transparency of their prefixed formations difficult. For example, the prefix <δια-> ðia- in verbal forms such as <διαβλέπω> ðia'vlepo 'to foresee' ('vlepo 'to see') and <διαγράφω> ðia'γrafo 'to delete' ('γrafo 'to write') does not always have the same semantic contribution to its formations. Given the fact that an unpredictable meaning may develop in derivational affixation, we have chosen to include this type of form in our corpus so as not to impoverish the wealth of prefixed derived elements in Greek. On the contrary, we have decided to exclude [+ learned] affixoids (mainly suffixoids) such as <-λογος> -loγos (Ralli 2008) which, despite their bound character, produce items sharing more similarities with compounds than with derived words (e.g. <γλωσσο-λόγος> γloso-'loγos 'linguist'). Finally, possible words that are at the base of actual ones have been taken into consideration, such as <σκυλάρι> sci'lari 'little dog', which is presupposed for the formation of the actual word <σκυλαράκι> scila'raki 'very little dog'. Note that, sometimes, possible words appear in dialectal dictionaries. For instance, sci'lar(i) is frequently used in the Aivaliot and Lesbian dialects (Ralli 2017).

The sources of our contribution are based on two major Modern Greek dictionaries (INS and Babiniotis 2012) and a special dictionary of derived and compound words (Babiniotis 2016). The relevant data were filtered – adding or excluding derivatives accordingly – through internet search engines (Google) in order to confirm their actual use and take into consideration the above-mentioned peculiarities of the Greek language regarding the absence of semantic transparency and [+/– learned] forms.

35.2 Maximum derivational networks

As shown in Table 35.1, adjectives exhibit the highest numbers of derivational networks in the first two orders of derivation (Σ = 66). They are followed by nouns, which score a lower total (Σ = 62), while verbs occupy third position (Σ = 50). 4th order derivations are rare, while none of the three word-classes permit a 5th order derivation.

Table 35.1: Maximum derivational networks per order of derivation for all three word-classes.

	1st order	2nd order	3rd order	4th order	5th order	Σ
Nouns	22	23	17	0	0	62
Verbs	28	18	4	0	0	50
Adjectives	31	25	9	1	0	66
TOTAL	81	66	30	1	0	178

35.3 Saturation values

Beginning with nouns, the mean saturation values range between 6.45% and 56.45%, as depicted in Table 35.2. The noun with the highest saturation value is 'kokalo 'bone' (56.45%), while the noun with the lowest saturation value is fo'tça 'fire' (6.45%), which is also the only one lacking a 2nd order derivation.

Table 35.2: Saturation values per order of derivation, nouns.

Nouns		Saturation value (%)	1st order (%)	2nd order (%)	3rd order (%)	4th order (%)	5th order (%)
bone	<κόκκαλο> 'kokalo	56.45	50	69.57	47.06	0	0
eye	<μάτι> 'mati	38.71	36.36	39.13	41.18	0	0
tooth	<δόντι> 'ðondi	29.03	45.45	21.74	17.65	0	0
day	<(η)μέρα> (i)'mera	22.58	31.82	8.7	29.41	0	0
dog	<σκύλος> 'scilos	25.81	40.91	30.43	0	0	0
louse	<ψείρα> 'psira	32.26	45.45	21.74	29.41	0	0
fire	<φωτιά> fo'tça	6.45	18.18	0	0	0	0
stone	<πέτρα> 'petra	45.16	63.64	43.48	23.53	0	0
water	<νερό> ne'ro	35.48	22.73	39.13	47.06	0	0
name	<όνομα> onoma'	38.71	40.91	47.83	23.53	0	0

Focusing on the 1st order derivations, 'petra 'stone' exhibits the highest saturation value (63.64%), while fo'tça 'fire' (18.18%) has the lowest.

For verbs demonstrated in Table 35.3, the mean saturation values range between 78% for 'kovo 'to cut' and 8% for 'ksero 'to know'. The verb with the lowest saturation value, in both the average and the 1st order derivations, is 'ksero 'to know', which remarkably lacks 2nd and 3rd order derivations.

Interestingly, adjectives, demonstrated in Table 35.4, seem to be subject to more even saturation values per order. Their mean saturation values range between 31.82% and 50%. For this category, several 4th order derivations occur, contrary to the categories of nouns and verbs. The adjective that exhibits the highest mean and 1st order saturation values is 'mavros (50%), which is also among the adjectives with a 4th order derivation.

In Table 35.5, the average saturation values per order of derivation for all three categories are provided. It is shown that the average saturation values are not exactly similar for all three word-classes. In particular, the values are quite high in the 1st (48.22%) and 2nd (45.56%) orders of verbs.

Table 35.3: Saturation values per order of derivation, verbs.

Verbs		Saturation value (%)	1st order (%)	2nd order (%)	3rd order (%)	4th order (%)	5th order (%)
to cut	<κόβω> 'kovo	78	85.71	72.22	50	0	0
to dig	<σκάβω> 'skavo	56	64.29	50	25	0	0
to pull	<τραβώ> tra'vo	38	39.29	38.89	25	0	0
to throw	<πετώ> pe'to	40	39.29	44.44	25	0	0
to give	<δίνω> 'ðino	54	53.57	61.11	25	0	0
to hold	<κρατώ> kra'to	46	42.86	50	50	0	0
to sew	<ράβω> 'ravo	58	53.57	61.11	75	0	0
to burn	<καίω> 'ceo	44	46.43	38.89	50	0	0
to drink	<πίνω> 'pino	38	42.86	38.89	0	0	0
to know	<ξέρω> 'ksero	8	14.29	0	0	0	0

Table 35.4: Saturation values per order of derivation, adjectives.

Adjectives		Saturation value (%)	1st order (%)	2nd order (%)	3rd order (%)	4th order (%)	5th order (%)
narrow	<κακός> ka'kos	46.97	41.94	52	55.56	0	0
old	<νέος> 'neos	31.82	38.71	20	33.33	100	0
straight	<μαύρος> 'mavros	50	48.39	40	77.78	100	0
new	<ίσιος> 'isjos	36.36	25.81	36	66.67	100	0
long	<ζεστός> ze'stos	39.39	29.03	40	66.67	100	0
warm	<γέρος> 'jeros	45.45	38.71	48	66.67	0	0
thick	<μακρύς> ma'kris	37.88	32.26	52	22.22	0	0
bad	<λεπτός> le'ptos	34.85	22.58	48	33.33	100	0
thin	<χοντρός> xo'dros	36.36	38.71	40	22.22	0	0
black	<στενός> ste'nos	34.85	35.48	28	44.44	100	0

Table 35.5: Average saturation values per order of derivation for all three word-classes.

	1st order	2nd order	3rd order	4th order	5th order
Nouns	39.55	32.18	25.88	0	0
Verbs	48.22	45.56	32.5	0	0
Adjectives	35.16	40.4	48.89	60	0

35.4 Orders of derivation

As already mentioned in section 35.2 (cf. Table 35.1), the maximum number of orders for the Greek sample is four. However, as can be seen in Table 35.6, the average number for nouns and verbs is 2.6–2.8, while the corresponding number for adjectives reaches a value of 3.6, since several 4th order derivations are attested.

Table 35.6: Maximum and average number of orders of derivation for all three word-classes.

	Maximum	Average
Nouns	3	2.8
Verbs	3	2.6
Adjectives	4	3.6

35.5 Derivational capacity

Regarding the derivational capacity, demonstrated in Table 35.7, verbs seem to exhibit the highest average value, while nouns have the lowest one. Amongst all 30 words in the three word-classes, the verb 'kovo 'to cut' has the highest overall derivational capacity (counting 24 1st order derivatives).

Turning now to the average derivational capacity of all three classes per word order, as summarized in Table 35.8, in the 1st order, verbs and adjectives exhibit higher numbers (11–13.5 approximately) compared to nouns, which score around 9. In the 2nd order, the difference has somehow been eliminated, since all three

Table 35.7: Maximum and average derivational capacity for all three word-classes.

	Maximum	Average
Nouns	14	8.7
Verbs	24	13.5
Adjectives	15	10.9

categories range between approximately 7.5 and 10. Lastly, in the 3rd order, while nouns and adjectives behave similarly, verbs use minimal affixal derivational means.

Table 35.8: Average number of derivatives per order of derivation for all three word-classes.

	1st order	2nd order	3rd order	4th order	5th order
Nouns	8.7	7.4	4.4	0	0
Verbs	13.5	8.2	1.3	0	0
Adjectives	10.9	10.1	4.4	0.6	0

35.6 Correlation between semantic categories and orders of derivation

Beginning with the adjectives, in the 1st order of derivation, DIMINUTIVE (value 10) and AUGMENTATIVE (value 10) are the most common semantic categories, since all 10 adjectives produce a DIMINUTIVE and an AUGMENTATIVE word, followed by those of MANNER (value 9) and ACTION (value 9). In the 2nd order of derivation, the semantic category ITERATIVE (value 10) is most characteristic, followed by DIMINUTIVE, ACTION, MANNER and RESULT (each value 9), while the category ATTENUATIVE gives a relatively high score (value 8). In the 3rd order of derivation, the semantic category ACTION (value 9) is typical, followed by PATIENT (value 8), MANNER (value 7) and ITERATIVE (value 7). Thus, for Greek adjectives, there is a strong correlation between evaluative categories (DIMINUTIVE and AUGMENTATIVE) and the 1st order of derivation; a correlation exists between DIMINUTIVE, ACTION, MANNER and RESULT and the 2nd order; and ACTION and PATIENT correlate with the 3rd order.

Turning to nouns, in the 1st order of derivation, the most characteristic semantic category is DIMINUTIVE (value 10), since all 10 nouns create a DIMINUTIVE word, followed by AUGMENTATIVE (value 9) and ACTION (value 8). In the 2nd order of derivation, the most typical semantic categories are DIMINUTIVE, PATIENT, and RESULT (each value 7), followed by ACTION, ATTENUATIVE and ITERATIVE (each value 6). In the 3rd order of derivation, PATIENT (value 8) takes precedence over the other semantic categories, followed by RESULT, SATURATIVE and PRIVATIVE (each value 6). Therefore, as for adjectives, in Greek nouns, correlations exist between DIMINUTIVE and AUGMENTATIVE and the 1st order of derivation, between DIMINUTIVE, PATIENT and RESULT and the 2nd order, and between PATIENT and the 3rd order.

Finally, with respect to verbs, the most common semantic categories in the 1st order of derivation are DIMINUTIVE, AUGMENTATIVE and SATURATIVE (each value 10), followed by ITERATIVE (value 9). In the 2nd order of derivation, DIMINUTIVE (value 9) and PATIENT (value 9) are the most frequent, while PRIVATIVE (value 8) comes next. DIMINUTIVE (value 8) is again the most typical semantic category in the 3rd order of derivation. As for the other categories, the strongest correlation exists between the 1st order of derivation and DIMINUTIVE and AUGMENTATIVE. The other correlations are between DIMINUTIVE, PATIENT and the 2nd order and between DIMINUTIVE and the 3rd order.

35.7 Semantic categories with blocking effects

By comparing the blocking semantic categories for all 10 adjectives per order of derivation, a number of conclusions can be reached. The comparison is schematically given as follows:

A. Blocking semantic categories for adjectives
   1st order: DIMINUTIVE, 2nd order: DIMINUTIVE, **3rd order: MANNER** (7/10 basic words)
   1st order: ACTION, 2nd order: ITERATIVE, **3rd order: PATIENT** (8/10 basic words)
   1st order: ACTION, 2nd order: SATURATIVE, **3rd order: PATIENT** (8/10 basic words)
   1st order: ACTION, 2nd order: RESULT, **3rd order: DIMINUTIVE** (7/10 basic words)
   1st order: ABSTRACTION (5/10 basic words)
   1st order: COLLECTIVE (2/10 adjectives)

B. Blocking semantic categories for nouns
   1st order: ACTION, 2nd order: REVERSATIVE, **3rd order: PATIENT** (6/10 basic words)
   1st order: ACTION, 2nd order: ITERATIVE, **3rd order: PATIENT** (6/10 basic words)

1st order: ACTION, 2nd order: ATTENUATIVE, **3rd order: PATIENT** (6/10 basic words)
1st order: ACTION, 2nd order: SIMILATIVE, **3rd order: PRIVATIVE** (6/10 basic words)
1st order: AUGMENTATIVE (9/10 basic words)
1st order: PEJORATIVE (4/10 basic words)

C. Blocking semantic categories for verbs
1st order: RESULT, 2nd order: DIMINUTIVE, **3rd order: DIMINUTIVE** (10/10 basic words)
1st order: SIMILATIVE, **2nd order: PRIVATIVE** (6/10 basic words)
1st order: DIMINUTIVE, **2nd order: PATIENT** (10/10 basic words)
1st order: AGENT, **2nd order: FEMALE** (3/10 basic words)
1st order: CONCOMITANT **2nd order: PATIENT** (4/10 basic words)
1st order: ENTITY (3/10 basic words)
1st order: LOCATION (3/10 basic words)

A contrastive look at all three orders of derivation in the three word-classes reveals that certain semantic categories (such as PRIVATIVE, FEMININE, COLLECTIVE, PEJORATIVE, and DIMINUTIVE) tend to block further derivations. These findings constitute corroborative evidence for the claims put forward by Melissaropoulou (2011) and Melissaropoulou and Ralli (2010), although in a different vein, according to which, in Modern Greek, certain suffixes (e.g. the Greek DIMINUTIVES -*itsa* and -*aci*) are marked as [+ closing].

35.8 Typical combinations of semantic categories

In the Greek data set, the following typical and systematic combinations of semantic categories (occurring with at least seven basic words) have been traced per word-class:

A. Adjectives
(i) ACTION-ITERATIVE-PATIENT
(1)   ζεστός > ζεσταίνω > ξαναζεσταίνω > ξαναζεσταμένος
       ze'stos > ze'steno > ksanaze'steno > ksanazesta'menos
       'warm' 'to warm'   'to re-warm'   're-warmed'

(ii) ACTION-SATURATIVE-PATIENT
(2) ζεστός > ζεσταίνω > παραζεσταίνω > παραζεσταμένος
    ze'stos > ze'steno > paraze'steno > parazesta'menos
    'warm' 'to warm' 'to over-warm' 'over-warmed'

(iii) ACTION-SATURATIVE-ITERATIVE-PATIENT
(3) μαύρος > μαυρίζω > παραμαυρίζω > ξαναπαραμαυρίζω > ξαναπαραμαυρισμένος
    'mavros > ma'vrizo > parama'vrizo > ksanaparama'vrizo > ksanaparamavri'zmenos
    'black'   'to blacken' 'to over-blacken' 'to over-blacken again' 'over-blackened again'

(iv) ACTION-ATTENUATIVE-PATIENT
(4) ζεστός > ζεσταίνω > ψιλοζεσταίνω > ψιλοζεσταμένος
    ze'stos > ze'steno > psiloze'steno > psilozesta'menos
    'warm' 'to warm' 'to warm a bit' 'slightly warmed'

(v) ACTION-RESULT-DIMINUTIVE
(5) μαύρος > μαυρίζω > μαύρισμα > μαυρισματάκι
    'mavros > ma'vrizo > 'mavrizma > mavrizma'taci
    'black' 'to blacken' 'blackening' 'blackening.DIM'

B. Nouns
(i) ACTION-PATIENT
(6) πέτρα > πετρώνω > πετρωμένος
    'petra > pe'trono > petro'menos
    'stone' 'to petrify' 'petrified'

(ii) ACTION-SATURATIVE-PATIENT
(7) μάτι > ματιάζω > παραματιάζω > παραματιασμένος
    'mati > ma'tçazo > parama'tçazo > paramatça'zmenos
    'eye' 'to put the evil eye' 'to put the evil eye to excess' 'excessively affected the evil eye'

(iii) ACTION-ITERATIVE-PATIENT
(8) μάτι > ματιάζω > ξαναματιάζω > ξαναματιασμένος
    'mati > ma'tçazo > ksanama'tçazo > ksanamatça'zmenos
    'eye' 'to put the evil eye' 'to put the evil eye again' 're-affected by the evil eye'

(iv) ACTION-REVERSATIVE-PATIENT
(9) ψείρα > ψειρίζω > ξεψειρίζω > ξεψειρισμένος
'psira > psi'rizo > ksepsi'rizo > ksepsiri'zmenos
'louse' 'to scrutinize' 'to clean of lice' 'cleaned of lice'

(v) ACTION-ATTENUATIVE-PATIENT
(10) μάτι > ματιάζω > ψιλοματιάζω > ψιλοματιασμένος
'mati > ma'tçazo > psiloma'tçazo > psilomatça'zmenos
'eye' 'to put the evil eye' 'to put the evil eye again' 'slightly affected by the evil eye'

C. Verbs
(i) ITERATIVE-PATIENT
(11) κόβω > ξανακόβω > ξανακομμένος
'kovo > ksana'kovo > ksanako'menos
'to cut' 'to cut again' 'cut again'

(ii) DIMINUTIVE-PATIENT
(12) κόβω > ψιλοκόβω > ψιλοκομμένος
'kovo > psilo'kovo > psiloko'menos
'to cut' 'to cut into small pieces' 'cut into small pieces'

(iii) AUGMENTATIVE-PATIENT
(13) καίω > πολυκαίω > πολυκαμένος
'ceo > poli'ceo > polika'menos
'to burn' 'to burn a lot' 'burned a lot'

(iv) SATURATIVE-PATIENT
(14) καίω > παρακαίω > παρακαμένος
'ceo > para'ceo > paraka'menos
'to burn' 'to burn to excess' 'burned to excess'

(v) RESULT-DIMINUTIVE-DIMINUTIVE[1]
(15) κόβω > κόψιμο > κοψιματάκι > ψιλοκοψιματάκι
'kovo > 'kopsimo > kopsima'taci > psilokopsima'taci
'to cut' 'cut[ting]' 'little cut[ting]' 'little cut[ting].DIM'

---

[1] It could also be interpreted as ATTENUATIVE, depending on the context.

35.9 Multiple occurrence of semantic categories

From all semantic categories in the three word-classes of Greek, only one, DIMINUTIVE, occurs repeatedly in the derivation series. The number of occurrences and the members of each word-class that are susceptible to multiple occurrence are shown in the following lists.

A. Nouns

Number of occurrences	Nouns
2	‹μάτι› 'mati 'eye', ‹δόντι› 'ðondi 'tooth', ‹σκύλος› 'scilos 'dog', ‹πέτρα› 'petra 'stone', ‹νερό› ne'ro 'water', ‹όνομα› 'onoma 'name'

B. Verbs

Number of occurrences	Verbs
2	‹κόβω› 'kovo 'to cut', ‹σκάβω› 'skavo 'to dig', ‹τραβώ› tra'vo 'to pull', ‹πετώ› pe'to 'to throw', ‹δίνω› 'ðino 'to give', ‹κρατώ› kra'to 'to hold', ‹ράβω› 'ravo 'to sew', ‹καίω› 'ceo 'to burn'

C. Adjectives

Number of occurrences	Adjectives
2	‹νέος› 'neos 'new', ‹γέρος› 'jeros 'old', ‹μακρύς› ma'kris 'long', ‹λεπτός› le'ptos 'thin',
3	‹κακός› ka'kos 'bad', ‹μαύρος› 'mavros 'black', ‹ζεστός› ze'stos 'warm', ‹χοντρός› xo'dros 'thick'

As demonstrated above, although recursiveness involving repetition of the same item is not generally acceptable in Greek derivational affixation, it is quite common in diminution. However, this is what occurs in Standard Modern Greek, as opposed to a number of dialectal varieties, where there is a different situation (Melissaropoulou 2006, 2007; Melissaropoulou and Ralli 2008).

35.10 Reversibility of semantic categories

The possibility of an alternative order in the combination of semantic categories exists in Greek due to structural reasons, since certain Greek prefixes can combine with both verbs and deverbal adjectives (coming from past participles).

(16) a. Adjective-ACTION-PATIENT-SATURATIVE
ζεστός > ζεσταίνω > ζεσταμένος > παραζεσταμένος
ze'stos > ze'steno > zesta'menos > parazesta'menos
'warm' 'to warm' 'warmed' 'over-warmed'
b. Adjective-ACTION-SATURATIVE-PATIENT
ζεστός > ζεσταίνω > παραζεσταίνω > παραζεσταμένος
ze'stos > ze'steno > paraze'steno > parazesta'menos
'warm' 'to warm' 'to over-warm' 'over-warmed'

35.11 Conclusions

In this article, we presented the results of a quantitative analysis of a sample of 30 Greek basic words (10 items per word-class), according to a new approach in derivational morphology, the so-called derivational network. Although the sample is small, the results are revealing of the tendencies and the properties of Greek derivational affixation, as encoded in the derivational network schemata.

As can be seen from the above-mentioned quantitative results, Greek is not a system with poor derivational networks. It actually displays a very rich derivational network, concentrated in the first three degrees (orders of derivation). In contrast, the 4th order is minimally operative (attested only in adjectives with a very low frequency), while the 5th one seems to be absent, at least for the words under examination.

References

Melissaropoulou, Dimitra. 2006. *I morfologiki diadikasia tou ypokorismou sti dialektiki poikilia tis Ellinikis – Sygkrisi me tin Koini Nea Elliniki* [The process of diminution in Greek dialectal variation and its comparison with Standard Modern Greek]. Patras: University of Patras MA thesis.
Melissaropoulou, Dimitra. 2007. *Morfologiki perigrafi kai analysi tou Mikrasiatikou idiomatos Kydonion kai Mosxonision: i paragogi lekseon* [Morphological description and analysis of

the Asia Minor dialect of Kydonies and Moschonisia: the derivation of words]. Patras: University of Patras PhD dissertation.

Melissaropoulou, Dimitra. 2011. Remarks on the combinability of derivational suffixes in Greek and its dialectal variation. In M. Janse, B. Joseph, P. Pavlou, A. Ralli & S. Armosti (eds.), *Studies in Modern Greek Dialects and Linguistic Theory*, 157–168. Nicosia: Research Centre of Kykkos Monastery.

Melissaropoulou, Dimitra & Angela Ralli. 2008. Headedness in Diminutive Formation: Evidence from Modern Greek and its Dialectal Variation. *Acta Linguistica Hungarica* 55. 183–204.

Melissaropoulou, Dimitra & Angela Ralli. 2010. Greek derivational structures: restrictions and constraints. *Morphology* 20. 343–357.

Ralli, Angela. 2005. *Morfologia* [Morphology]. Athens: Patakis.

Ralli, Angela. 2008. Greek deverbal compounds with bound Stems: A case of neoclassical formations in Modern Greek. *Southern Journal of Linguistics (SJL)* 29 (1/2). 150–173.

Ralli, Angela. 2013. Greek. *Revue Belge de Philologie et d'Histoire* 90. 939–966.

Ralli, Angela. 2015. Greek. In Peter O. Müller, Ingeborg Ohnheiser, Susan Olsen & Franz Rainer (eds.), *Word-Formation. An International Handbook of the Languages of Europe*, 3138–3156. Berlin: Mouton de Gruyter.

Ralli, Angela. 2017. *Leksiko dialektikis pikilias Kydonion Moschonision ke vorioanatolikis Lesvou* [Dictionary of the dialectal varieties of Kydonies, Moschonisia and North-Eastern Lesbos]. Athens: Foundation of Historical Studies.

Sources

Babiniotis, Georgios. 2012. *Dictionary of Modern Greek*. Athens: Center of Lexicology.

Babiniotis, Georgios. 2016. *Dictionary of Derived and Compound Modern Greek Words*. Athens: Center of Lexicology.

INS. 2017. *Dictionary of Standard Modern Greek*. Institute of Modern Greek Studies (Manolis Triantafyllidis Foundation). http://www.greek-language.gr/greekLang/modern_greek/tools/lexica/triantafyllides/search.html?lq=.

László Palágyi, Erzsébet Tóth-Czifra, Réka Benczes
36 Introduction to Uralic languages

36.1 General issues in Uralic derivation

Providing a succinct summary of derivation in the Uralic language family is a challenging, if not a "practically impossible" task (Kiefer and Laakso 2014: 1), due primarily to the internal diversity of the language family (Abondolo 1998; Collinder 1960, 1969; Marcantonio 2003), which is comparable to the diversity inherent in the Indo-European language family and to the immensely rich derivational system that each of the languages in the family possesses.[1] (Note also that the respective languages have been very unevenly researched and/or documented – see Kiefer and Laasko 2014.) The Uralic language family consists of six main branches (on taxonomical issues, see Salminen 2002): Finnic, Mari, Mordvin, Permic, Ugric and Samoyedic. As far as the languages of the present volume are concerned, Estonian, Finnish and (central-south) Saami belong to the Finnic branch (Itkonen 1997; Laakso 2000; Sammallahti 1998), while Hungarian is an Ugric language (Honti 1979; Kálmán 1988).

Uralic languages are agglutinative; each bound morpheme typically represents one morphological category. Nevertheless, full agglutination is an exception rather than the rule; plenty of counterexamples abound (see, for example, Hungarian *ház-am* 'my house' in *látom a ház-am-Ø* 'I see my house', where the accusative is not represented with a distinct morpheme). Derivational morphology is chiefly suffix-based in all Uralic languages (similarly to inflectional morphology). However, prefixes can occur (see, for example, negative prefixation in North Saami, *eahpe-čielgass* 'unclear'). Derivation-like prefixes that modify the meaning of the verb and which might even change its argument structure are generally common in Ugric languages (Kiefer and Honti 2003). Such prefixes (also referred to as 'preverbs' in the literature) differ from Romance, Slavic or German verbal prefixes, since they are not inseparable from the verbal base. Although it is disputed whether the phenomenon is a borrowing or an Ugric heritage that originated in Proto-Ugric, verbal 'prefixation' plays an important role in a number of the languages of the family, especially Hungarian.

---

[1] The two standard works on the history of derivation in Uralic are Györke (1934) and Lehtisalo (1936); for a more recent overview, see Kangasmaa-Minn (1987), Kiefer and Laakso (2014), and Laakso (2015).

Distinguishing between inflexional and derivational suffixes on the basis of their productivity is often difficult (see, for example, the wholly productive Finnish *-va/-vä*, which forms the present active participle of verbs). Still, prototypical derivational suffixes are closer to roots/stems and can be followed by inflexional suffixes. In addition, complex derivational morphemes also occur (see, for example, Hungarian *-hat-ó/-ható* '-able'). Derivation can be supported by phrases (e.g. Hungarian *hatalom* 'power' → **hatalm-ú* 'possessing power', *nagy hatalom* 'big power' → *nagy hatalm-ú* 'powerful'), and derivational suffixes can be attached to inflexional forms (e.g. Hungarian *nagyobb* 'bigger' → *nagyobb-ít* 'make somebody/something bigger').

A substantial number of Uralic derivational suffixes are polyfunctional and polysemic; thus, there are no sharp boundaries between the assortment of noun-derivational and verb-derivational affixes (Laakso 1997), which might have acted both as nominalizers and verbalizers (e.g. the Proto-Uralic **-j* in Finnish *muista-* 'to remember' → *muist-i* 'memory'; *muna* 'egg' → *mun-i-* 'to lay'), contributing to different kinds of meanings within the very same lexical category (e.g. the Proto-Uralic **-j* in Finnish *leipä* 'bread' → *leip-o* 'to bake bread', *pien-* 'small' → *pien-i* 'to make sth. small', *harava* 'rake' → *harav-oi* 'to rake', etc.).

Generally speaking, the meaning of the derivative is often non-compositional or not predictable (e.g. Finnish *paljas* 'naked' → *paljas-taa* 'reveal'), as it is motivated by the compositional elements, though plenty of counterexamples also exist that point exactly to the predictability of certain forms (e.g. Finnish *syö-* 'to eat' → *syö-ttä-* 'to feed'). The morphophonology of derivation is mostly governed by vowel harmony (Abondolo 1996); note, however, that Estonian is an exception. Furthermore, Uralic languages are typically characterized by a lack of grammatical gender. Consequently, unlike most Slavic, Romance and German languages, the feminine gender (as in occupations) is expressed via composition and not by affixation (if it is expressed at all). See the following section for a brief overview of the lexical and semantic categories.

36.2 Lexical and semantic categories

Nouns and adjectives can be treated as neighbouring lexical categories with no clear boundary between them. The inflexional pattern of adjectives differs from nouns only partially, and both lexical categories can be characterized by multifunctional derivational suffixes (Finnish *-lAinen*, e.g. *eri-lainen* 'different$_A$', *vuokra-lainen* 'tenant$_N$'). Although the literature does not traditionally describe noun-adjective pairs as conversions in, for example, Finnish and Hungarian, there are plenty of cases that are ambiguous at best (e.g. Hungarian *ismerős* 'familiar$_A$' – *ismerős* 'acquaintance$_N$'; *hódító* 'conquering$_A$' – *hódító* 'conqueror$_N$').

In spite of certain (unproductive) multifunctional suffixes (e.g. Hungarian *halász(ik)* 'to fish', *hal-ász* 'fisherman'; Finnish *pain-i* 'wrestling', *pain-i-* 'to wrestle'), typically there is a clear-cut boundary between verbs and nouns, which is also confirmed by a lack of productive noun-verb conversion in Uralic languages. Adverbs and adjectives are even more distinct than verbs and nouns, because the former pair does not usually share any attachable suffixes. Productive deverbal suffixes are usually larger in number than denominal suffixes; the latter are, nevertheless, more common than deadjectival suffixes (which are poorly represented in Uralic languages).

References

Abondolo, D. 1996. Vowel rotation in Uralic: Obug[r]ocentric evidence. *SSEES Occasional Papers 31*. London: School of Slavonic and East European Studies.
Abondolo, D. (ed.). 1998. *The Uralic languages*. London & New York: Routledge.
Collinder, B. 1960. *Comparative Grammar of the Uralic Languages*. Stockholm: Almqvist & Wiksells.
Collinder, B. 1969. *Survey of the Uralic Languages*. Stockholm: Almqvist & Wiksells.
Györke, J. 1934. *Die Verbildungslehre des Uralischen*. Tartu.
Honti, L. 1979. Characteristic features of Ugric languages (observations on the question of Ugric unity). *Acta Linguistica Academiae Scientiarum Hungaricae 29*. 1–26.
Itkonen, T. 1997. Reflections on Pre-Uralic and the "Saami-Finnic protolanguage". *Finnisch-Ugrische Forschungen 54*. 229–266.
Kálmán, B. 1988. The history of Ob-Ugric languages. In D. Sinor (ed.), *The Uralic Languages: Description, History and Foreign Influences*. Handbuch der Orientalistik 8/1, Leiden: Brill.
Kangasmaa-Minn, E. 1987. Functional derivation in Finno-Ugric. *Papers on derivation in Uralic. Szegeder und Turkuer Beitrage zur Uralischen Derivation*, 5–27. Szeged: Univ. Szeged de Attila József Nominata.
Kiefer, F. & J. Laasko. 2014. Uralic. In Rochelle Lieber & Pavol Štekauer (eds.), *The Oxford Handbook of Derivational Morphology*, 3308–3325. Oxford: Oxford University Press.
Kiefer, F. & L. Honti. 2003. Verbal 'Prefixation' in the Uralic Languages. *Acta Linguistica. Hungarica* 50 (1–2). 137–153.
Laakso, J. 1997. On verbalizing nouns in Uralic. *FUF* 54 (3). 267–304.
Laakso, J. 2015. The history of word-formation in Uralic. In P. O. Müller, I. Ohnheiser, S. Olsen & F. Rainer (eds.), *Word-Formation: An International Handbook of the Languages of Europe*, 2061–2078. Berlin: Mouton de Gruyter.
Laakso, J. (ed.). 2000. *Facing Finnic. Castrenianumin toimitteita 59*. Helsinki: Finno-Ugrian Society.
Lehtisalo, T. 1936. *Die Primären ururalischen Ableitungssuffixe* [The Primary Proto-Uralic derivational suffixes]. Suomalais-Ugrilaisen Seuran Toimituksia LXXII.

Marcantonio, A. 2003. The Uralic Language Family: Facts, Myths and Statistics. *Publications of the Philological Society 35*. Oxford: Blackwell.

Salminen, T. 2002. Problems in the taxonomy of the Uralic languages in the light of modern comparative studies. *Лингвистический беспредел: сборник статей к 70-летию А. И. Кузнецовой*, 44–55. Москва: Издательство Московского университета.

Sammallahti, P. 1998. *The Saami languages: an introduction*. Kárášjohka: Davvi Girji.

Reet Kasik
37 Derivational networks in Estonian

37.1 General notes

Estonian is a typical agglutinating Finno-Ugric language that uses a large number of suffixes in inflection and word-formation. It is usually rather easy to separate suffixes from stems. The existence of prefixes in Estonian has been a matter of debate, however. Some grammatical descriptions (e.g. Erelt et al 1995: 595) have treated the negative prefixoids *eba* 'un-' and *mitte* 'non-' as prefixes; however, more recent treatments have regarded them as bound bases, and when they form complex words, these are treated as compounds (e.g. Kasik 2015: 105–107).

There are about a hundred derivative suffixes in Estonian, but some are synchronically unproductive. Derivative suffixes include about 10 verb-forming suffixes, about 40 noun-forming suffixes, about 10 adjective-forming suffixes, and about 10 adverb-forming suffixes (Kasik 2015). Complex words are derived from all the word-classes, including deictic and function words. Derivatives of some semantic categories (such as INSTRUMENTAL, RESULTATIVE, ENTITY, and LOCATION) have been systematically created by terminologists to address specific needs in Estonian-language terminology (Erelt 2007: 177–185). Derivation from adjectives and verbs is productive and regular; by contrast, nouns yield derivatives to varying degrees. A small number of noun bases have large numbers of derivatives, while almost half of the simple bases do not have any or only a single derivative (Rätsep 2002: 84–96).

The sources used in this paper draw from the Estonian dictionary compiled by the Institute of the Estonian Language (EKSS) and the Estonian corpus of web-based texts etTenTen.

37.2 Maximum derivational networks

Table 37.1 below shows that verbs exhibit the highest number of derivational networks in the 1st and 2nd orders, and hence also overall. Adjectives exhibit the highest number of derivational networks in the 3rd order.

Table 37.1: Maximum derivational networks per order of derivation for all three word-classes.

	1st order	2nd order	3rd order	4th order	5th order	Total
Nouns	31	25	10	1	0	67
Verbs	38	40	26	10	2	116
Adjectives	25	30	27	10	0	92
TOTAL	94	95	63	21	2	275

37.3 Saturation values

The mean saturation values for the nouns range between 7% and 72%, as shown in Table 37.2. The noun with the highest mean saturation value is *vesi* 'water' (72%), which is also the only noun with a 4th order derivation (100%); *koer* 'dog' and *täi* 'louse' have the lowest mean saturation values (7%). Within the 1st order, *vesi* 'water' has the highest saturation value (58%), and *täi* 'louse' has the lowest (10%).

Table 37.2: Saturation values per order of derivation, nouns.

Nouns		Saturation value (%)	1st order (%)	2nd order (%)	3rd order (%)	4th order (%)
bone	luu	19.4	22.58	24	0	0
eye	silm	17.91	25.81	16	0	0
tooth	hammas	31.34	25.81	48	10	0
day	päev	23.88	25.81	24	20	0
dog	koer	7.46	12.9	4	0	0
louse	täi	7.46	9.68	8	0	0
fire	tuli	19.4	19.35	28	0	0
stone	kivi	29.85	32.26	36	10	0
water	vesi	71.64	58.06	80	90	100
name	nimi	25.37	29.03	32	0	0

For the verbs in Table 37.3, the lowest and highest mean saturation values vary between 7% for *õmblema* 'sew' and 57% for *teadma* 'know'. *Hoidma* 'hold' and *teadma* 'know' have the highest values in the 1st order (39%).

Table 37.3: Saturation values per order of derivation, verbs.

Verbs		Saturation value (%)	1st order (%)	2nd order (%)	3rd order (%)	4th order (%)	5th order (%)
cut	lõikama	15.52	26.32	17.5	3.85	0	0
dig	kaevama	17.24	31.58	20	0	0	0
pull	tõmbama	23.28	34.21	27.5	11.54	0	0
throw	viskama	13.79	28.95	12.5	0	0	0
give	andma	35.34	36.84	50	26.92	0	0
hold	hoidma	37.93	39.47	45	42.31	0	0
sew	õmblema	6.9	15.79	5	0	0	0
burn	põlema	19.83	18.42	27.5	11.54	20	0
drink	jooma	28.45	34.21	30	30.77	0	0
know	teadma	56.9	39.47	62.5	53.85	100	100

For the adjectives in Table 37.4, the mean saturation values range between 24% (*kitsas* 'narrow') and 45% (*uus* 'new'). Within the 1st order, *pikk* 'long' has the highest saturation value (56%), and *lahja* 'thin' has the lowest (16%).

Table 37.4: Saturation values per order of derivation, adjectives.

Adjectives		Saturation value (%)	1st order (%)	2nd order (%)	3rd order (%)	4th order (%)
narrow	kitsas	23.91	28	26.67	18.52	20
old	vana	27.17	40	30	22.22	0
straight	sirge	39.13	28	53.33	40.74	20
new	uus	45.65	28	40	59.26	70
long	pikk	44.57	56	56.67	25.93	30
warm	soe	34.78	20	33.33	48.15	40
thick	paks	20.65	20	23.33	18.52	20
bad	halb	30.43	20	43.33	29.63	20
thin	lahja	25	16	33.33	25.93	20
black	must	34.78	52	46.67	11.11	20

Table 37.5 gives the average saturation values per order of derivation for all the nouns, verbs and adjectives in the Estonian set. We can see that the average values are quite similar for every order of the three word-classes. The average saturation values are also quite low, not reaching above 31% in the 1st order, 39% in the 2nd order, and 30% in the 3rd order.

Table 37.5: Average saturation values per order of derivation for all three word-classes.

	1st order	2nd order	3rd order	4th order	5th order
Nouns	26.129	30	13	10	0
Verbs	30.526	29.75	18.078	12	10
Adjectives	30.8	38.67	30	26	0

37.4 Orders of derivation

Out of the 10 adjectives in the sample, nine yield derivatives of the 4th order; one (*vana* 'old') only has derivatives of the 3rd order. Among the nouns, only one (*vesi* 'water') yields derivatives of the 4th order; three nouns have derivatives of the 3rd order, and six have derivatives of the 2nd order. Among the verbs, one (*teadma* 'know') yields derivatives of the 5th order and one (*põlema* 'burn') has derivatives of the 4th order; five verbs yield derivatives of the 3rd order and three have derivatives of the 2nd order.

Table 37.6: Maximum and average number of orders of derivation for all three word-classes.

	Maximum	Average
Nouns	4	2.5
Verbs	5	3
Adjectives	4	3.9

37.5 Derivational capacity

Among the three word-classes, verbs have the greatest derivational capacity (Table 37.7), while the noun *vesi* 'water' has the largest number of 1st order derivatives.

Table 37.7: Maximum and average derivational capacity for all three word-classes.

	Maximum	Average
Nouns	18	8.1
Verbs	15	10.3
Adjectives	15	8.6

Adjectives and verbs yield the largest number of 2nd order derivatives, and nouns yield the largest number of 1st order derivatives. 3rd order derivatives are most numerous from adjectives, less numerous from verbs, and the least numerous from nouns (Table 37.8).

Table 37.8: Average number of derivatives per order of derivation for all three word-classes.

	1st order	2nd order	3rd order	4th order	5th order
Nouns	8.1	7.5	1.3	0.1	0
Verbs	11.6	11.9	4.7	1.2	0.2
Adjectives	8.6	11.6	8.1	2.6	0

37.6 Correlation between semantic categories and orders of derivation

Derivation from adjectives is the most regular. The adjective *paks* 'thick' has the smallest number of derivatives (19) and *uus* 'new' has the largest (42). Estonian adjectives reveal strong correlations between 1st order derivation and the semantic categories MANNER (value 10) and PROCESS (value 10), between 2nd order derivation and the semantic categories MANNER (value 9), PROCESS (value 9), and CAUSATIVE (value 8), and between 3rd order derivation and the semantic categories ACTION (value 9), PATIENT (value 9), and AGENT (value 8).

Derivation from nouns is irregular. The nouns *koer* 'dog' and *täi* 'louse' have the smallest number of derivatives (5) while *vesi* 'water' has the largest number (48). A strong correlation exists only between 1st order derivation and the semantic categories DIMINUTIVE (value 10) and PRIVATIVE (value 9) and between 2nd order derivations and the semantic category MANNER (value 9).

Derivation from verbs is regular in two orders of derivation. Among the verbs, *õmblema* 'sew' has the smallest number of derivatives (8) and *teadma* 'know' has the largest number (66); the other verbs have 16–44 derivatives. A strong correlation was found between 1st order derivation and the semantic categories ABILITY (value 10), ACTION (value 9), AGENT (value 9), RESULTATIVE (value 8), and PATIENT (value 8), and between 2nd order derivation and the semantic categories ABILITY (value 10), ACTION (value 9), and AGENT (value 9).

37.7 Semantic categories with blocking effects

Regarding blocking effects, for the nouns, the semantic categories DIMINUTIVE and COLLECTIVE block further derivation in the 1st order, MANNER in the 2nd order, and PROCESS in the 3rd order.

Further derivations in the 1st order of the verbs are blocked by INSTRUMENTAL. In the 2nd order, ABILITY blocks further derivations. MANNER, ACTION and ABILITY block further derivations in the 3rd order.

In the 1st order of the adjectives, DIMINUTIVE, STATIVE and MANNER hamper further derivations, and in the 2nd order, MANNER, PROCESS and STATIVE prevent further derivations. In the 3rd order, MANNER and STATIVE block further derivations, and MANNER also in the 4th order.

MANNER and DIMINUTIVE are semantic categories that block further derivations throughout the derivational system, independently of the order in which they occur.

37.8 Typical combinations of semantic categories

In Estonian, derivation primarily determines the word-class of a derivative and, secondarily, its semantic category. 1st and 2nd order derivatives or 2nd and 3rd order derivatives of the same base word may belong to the same semantic category but a different word-class. 10 adjectives produce derivations within the semantic category PROCESS (verb)-PROCESS (noun), and 10 verbs produce derivations within the category ABILITY (adjective)-ABILITY (noun). A typical combination among the adjectives is PROCESS-CAUSATIVE-ACTION/AGENT/PATIENT (9) (e.g. *uus* 'new' > *uue-ne* 'renew (intr.)' > *uue-n-da* 'renew sth' > *uue-n-da-mine* 'renewal'/*uue-n-da-ja* 'innovator'/*uue-n-da-tu* 'what was renewed'). Typical combinations among the nouns are PRIVATIVE-STATIVE/MANNER (9) (e.g. *nimi* 'name' > *nime-tu* 'nameless' > *nime-tu-s* 'namelessness'/*nime-tu-lt* 'namelessly'), POSSESSIVE-STATIVE/MANNER (4) (e.g. *hammas* 'tooth' > *hambu-line* 'toothed, dentate, serrated' > *hambu-lis-us* 'serratedness'/ *hambu-lise-lt* 'serratedly') and SIMILATIVE-STATIVE/MANNER (3) (e.g. *koer* 'dog' > *koera-lik* 'dog-like, doggish' > *koera-likk-us* 'doggishness'/*koera-liku-lt* 'doggishly'). A typical combination among the intransitive verbs is CAUSATIVE-AGENT/ACTION (5) (e.g. *põlema* 'burn' > *põle-ta* 'burn sth.' > *põle-ta-ja* 'one who burns sth.'/*põle-ta-mine* 'burning').

37.9 Multiple occurrence of semantic categories

The derivational system of Estonian does not reveal multiple reoccurrences of semantic categories on a systematic basis; it may, however, occur sporadically in the derivational network of some adjectives. In this vein, the sample included *uus* 'new' – *uue-ne* 'renew (intr.)' (PROCESS verb) – *uue-n-da* 'renew sth' (CAUSATIVE) – *uue-n-d-u* 'renew' (PROCESS verb) and *soe* 'warm' – *sooj-us* 'warmth' (STATIVE) – *sooj-us-lik* 'thermal, heat-related' (RELATIONAL) – *sooj-us-likk-us* 'thermality, condition of being thermal' (STATIVE).

37.10 Reversibility of semantic categories

When deriving verbs from adjectives, the semantic categories PROCESS and CAUSATIVE may occur in a reversed order (AB/BA); one can derive a PROCESS verb from an adjective and then a CAUSATIVE verb from the latter (e.g. *uus* 'new' – *uue-ne* 'renew' (PROCESS) – *uue-n-da* 'renew sth.' (CAUSATIVE)) or a CAUSATIVE from an adjective and a PROCESS verb from the latter (e.g. *rikas* 'rich' – *rikas-ta* 'enrich' (CAUSATIVE) – *rikas-t-u* 'become rich' (PROCESS)); however, such examples did not occur in the sample. The sequence of derivation depends on the phonological structure of the base verb.

37.11 Conclusions

The Estonian set shows that the average number of derivational orders for adjectives, nouns and verbs ranges between 2.5 (nouns) and 3.9 (adjectives) (Table 37.6). Verbs exhibit the highest number of derivational networks in the 1st and 2nd orders, and adjectives are highest in the 3rd order (Table 37.1). The average saturation values per order of derivation for all the nouns, verbs and adjectives are quite similar for every order of the three word-classes. However, adjectives have the highest saturation values: 31% in the 1st order, 39% in the 2nd order, 30% in the 3rd order, and 26% in the 4th order (Table 37.5).

For the nouns, the maximum derivational networks and the average number of derivatives are higher in the 1st order than in the 2nd order (Tables 37.1 and 37.8). In contrast, for the verbs and adjectives, the maximum derivational networks and the average number of derivatives are higher in the 2nd order than in the 1st order.

The Estonian derivational affixes are suffixes. Less than half of the semantic categories (24 of the 49 available labels) are covered by the Estonian derivations. This implies that Estonian makes use of other means, both morphological and syntactic (especially compounding), to account for the remaining semantic categories. On the other hand, the derivational capacity of Estonian is quite rich, at least within the semantic range covered.

References

Erelt, Mati, Reet Kasik, Helle Metslang, Henno Rajandi, Kristiina Ross, Henn Saari, Kaja Tael & Silvi Vare. 1995. *Eesti keele grammatika I. Morfologia. Sõnamoodustus* [Estonian Grammar I. Morphology. Word-formation]. Tallinn: Estonian Academy Publishers.
Erelt, Tiiu. 2007. *Terminiõpetus* [Terminology]. Tartu: Tartu University Press.
Kasik, Reet. 2015. *Sõnamoodustus* [Word-formation]. Tartu: Tartu University Press.
Rätsep, Huno. 2002. *Sõnaloo raamat* [Book of Words]. Tartu: Ilmamaa.

Sources

EKSS = *Eesti keele seletav sõnaraamat* [Explanatory Dictionary of the Estonian Language]. 2009. Tallinn: Institute of Estonian Language. http://www.keeleveeb.ee.
etTenTen. http://www.keeleveeb.ee/etTenTen.

Kaarina Pitkänen-Heikkilä
38 Derivational networks in Finnish

38.1 General notes

Derivation in Finnish is accomplished mainly through suffixation, and prefixation is not characteristic of Finnish word-formation. Finnish has systematically avoided verbal prefixes even though it has been influenced by many languages that have them. It does, however, have certain prefix-like particles that form compounds with verbs (Bikupska 2018: 15). Nouns and adjectives in present-day Finnish, it will be noted, may have short compounding forms (often borrowed, e.g. *anti-*, *eko-*, *semi-*) that could also be seen as prefixes (Tyysteri 2015: 125). Possible word-formation with prefixes is excluded from the Finnish data in this research. The only clear cases would be *epätietoinen* 'unaware' (negative *epä-* + *tietoinen* 'conscious, aware' < *tietää* 'know') and its further derivatives, which are considered compounds in Finnish and are therefore also excluded from this data.

Finnish has almost 200 derivational types, including over 100 nominal and adjectival suffixes and about 50 verbal suffixes. Pitkänen-Heikkilä (2016) describes the most common of these in English. The *Iso suomen kielioppi* ([*Comprehensive Finnish Grammar*], 2004) introduces 48 types of noun derivatives, 27 types of verb derivatives, 7 types of adverb derivatives and 15 types of adjective derivatives, excluding participles, ordinal numbers and comparison forms (Hakulinen et al. 2004: 195–196, 297–298, 365). Lauri Hakulinen (1967) lists a total of 88 denominal nominal suffixes, 46 deverbal nominal suffixes, 31 deverbal verbal suffixes and 17 denominal verbal suffixes (Hakulinen 1967: 246). Many Finnish derivational types do not appear in this research because certain types can only be added to certain root types, and the 30 chosen base words do not include all of them.

It is worth pointing out that complete derivational maps are very difficult to produce in Finnish. Intuition does not necessarily yield all derivatives in productive use, and many are typically excluded from Finnish dictionaries (e.g. Hakulinen et al. 2004: 186). Established derivatives that appear in dictionaries tend to have some lexical meaning. Researchers seeking information on the actual usage of intuition-based derivatives may, however, find it from corpora or the internet, e.g. by using Google.

It should also be taken into consideration that derivational series are not always clear in suffixal derivation (e.g. Räisänen 1978; Hakulinen et al. 2004: 182). It is possible to construe the verbal derivatives *kaveta* (PROCESS 'become narrower'), *kaventaa* (CAUSATIVE 'make narrower') and *kaventua* (PROCESS 'become narrower') for the 1st order of derivation from the adjective *kapea* 'narrow', for example, but, as will be shown in this study, the following derivational series is also feasible: *kapea* > PROCESS *kaveta* > CAUSATIVE *kaventaa* > ANTICAUSATIVE *kaventua*.

Derivation produces new words, whereas inflection does not. The distinctions between the two are not always clear, however. In particular, denominal verbs and deverbal nouns in Finnish include many borderline cases. Finnish words with the suffix *-minen*, for example, may be categorized as infinitive forms of verbs, or they may be totally excluded from nominal forms. Most commonly, however, they can be decoded as infinitives only with regard to some special syntactic tasks, or otherwise as action name derivatives (Häkkinen 1990: 102).

Given the exclusion of participles in this study, certain common semantic categories show little or no attestation in this research. For example, UNDERGOER (AGENT participle, e.g. *leikkaama* 'to be cut by somebody') does not exist, ABILITY (e.g. active and passive participles *leikkaava*$_A$ 'cutting' and *leikattava*$_A$ 'cuttable', and their further derivatives STATE *leikkaavuus*$_N$ 'piercingness', STATE *leikattavuus*$_N$ 'possibility to be cut') are rare, and QUALITY (e.g. the participles *leikattu*$_A$ 'operated on; cut; sterilized', *leikannut*$_A$ 'operating; cutting; sterilizing') is even more rare. I have included only the *mAtOn*-suffix that produces PRIVATIVE (*leikkaamaton*$_A$ 'uncut') derivatives and is the negative equivalent of the AGENT participle.

It was challenging to find 30 real, underived words in Finnish for this study because many words that are perceived as simple words nowadays are historically derivatives. For example, *ommella* 'sew' is not an old underived simplex – the suffix *-ele-* is also transparent (*ompele-*). Because this project examines derivatives synchronically, I took in this word, too. As a consequence, however, the derivational map of this word does not allow for some typical 1st order suffixes because the base word already has this ITERATIVE suffix. In addition, the adjectival base *kapea* 'narrow' is historically a derivative. The suffix *-eA* is transparent, but the root and the meaning are not, and because of this, *eA* derivatives are often categorized as simplexes (e.g. Hakanen 1973). The oldest Finnish simplex roots have two syllables and end in *a* or *ä*. The sample of 30 words also includes different words (e.g. 'warm' *lämmin*: *läm-pi-mä-*), but from the point of view of modern Finnish they can be examined as simplex.

The equivalent of 'hold' in Finnish is *pitää*, which is a highly polysemous word. In addition to meaning 'hold', it also means 'like', 'must' and 'keep'. The equivalent of 'burn' is either *palaa* (intransitive) or *polttaa* (transitive). *Palaa* does not produce derivatives in most semantic categories, so the verb *polttaa* was selected.

It is impossible to find all the actual derivatives without conducting more elaborate research. Derivatives of the 1st order are often to be found in dictionaries (e.g. the frequently used *Kielitoimiston sanakirja* [*The Dictionary of Standard*

Finnish]), whereas further orders should be searched for in Kielipankki (The Language Bank of Finland) corpora using Korp searches, or via the internet using Google searches. The verbal derivatives of the adjective *paha* 'bad' in the 1st order of derivation, for instance, include PROCESS *paheta* 'get worse', CAUSATIVE *pahoittaa* 'make worse (somebody's feelings)' and INCHOATIVE *pahastua* 'become offended', all of which appear in *Kielitoimiston sanakirja*. Korp searches in Kielipankki yield further derivations in the ITERATIVE category, e.g. (*pahastua* >) *pahastella* in the 2st order and (*paheta* > *pahentaa* >) *pahennella* in the 3rd order. Only one of these verbs, however, (*pahoittaa* 'make worse (somebody's feelings)') has a PRIVATIVE derivative (*pahoittelematon* in the 3rd order) according to an internet search, although it is intuitively clear that the two other ITERATIVE derivatives can also be combined with the PRIVATIVE suffix -*mAtOn* (*pahentelematon, pahastelematon*).

Established, lexicalized derivatives are excluded from the data, which is why some common Finnish derivative types seem to be rare. Derivatives that occur as lexicalized forms may, at the same time, block their productive use as derivatives. Many Finnish two-syllable verb roots that end in *a* or *ä* (e.g. *vetää: vedä-* 'pull', *antaa: anna-* 'give', *kaivaa: kaiva-* 'dig'), for example, produce RESULTATIVE *Os*-derivatives (*vedos, annos, kaivos*). Many of these derivatives are lexicalized, however, and have special, established meanings (*vedos* 'proof', *annos* 'portion', *kaivos* 'mine'), and are excluded from this study. Even if they are structurally transparent, they are not necessarily easy to recognize as derivatives of those roots.

38.2 Maximum derivational networks

As Table 38.1 shows, the typical number of derivational orders in Finnish is three. The derivation of almost half (14) of the 30 words is in the 4th order. There are rare cases of words with derivatives in the 5th order.

Table 38.1: Maximum derivational networks per order of derivation for all three word-classes.

	1st order	2nd order	3rd order	4th order	5th order	Σ
Nouns	33	34	21	7	2	97
Verbs	34	37	19	9	1	100
Adjectives	27	54	27	12	2	122
TOTAL	94	125	67	28	5	319

38.3 Saturation values

As Tables 38.2–38.4 show, the highest mean saturation values per word-class are 57% for verbs (*leikata* 'cut'), 52% for adjectives (*uusi* 'new'), and 46% for nouns (*päivä* 'day'). The lowest mean values are 8% for nouns (*täi* 'louse'), 11% for verbs (*polttaa* 'burn') and 13% for adjectives (*musta* 'black').

Table 38.2: Saturation values per order of derivation, nouns.

Nouns		Saturation value (%)	1st order (%)	2nd order (%)	3rd order (%)	4th order (%)	5th order (%)
bone	luu	24.74	24.24	35.29	19.05	0	0
eye	silmä	35.05	42.42	41.18	28.57	0	0
tooth	hammas	29.9	42.42	32.35	19.05	0	0
day	päivä	46.39	30.3	44.12	52.38	100	100
dog	koira	15.46	30.3	14.71	0	0	0
louse	täi	8.25	18.18	5.88	0	0	0
fire	tuli	25.77	24.24	32.35	23.81	14.29	0
stone	kivi	42.27	27.27	58.82	52.38	14.29	0
water	vesi	29.9	36.36	32.35	28.57	0	0
name	nimi	40.21	36.36	58.82	33.33	0	0

Table 38.2 shows that the highest saturation value of nouns within the 1st order is 42% (*silmä* 'eye' and *hammas* 'tooth'), 59% in the 2nd order (*kivi* 'stone' and *nimi* 'name') and 52% in the 3rd order (*päivä* 'day' and *kivi* 'stone'). The old Finnish noun *täi* 'louse' has the lowest saturation value in the 1st, 2nd and 3rd orders of derivation. The nouns *koira* 'dog' and *täi* 'louse' do not have derivations in the 3rd order, three nouns have derivations of the 4th order, and only one (*päivä* 'day') has a derivation of the 5th order.

Table 38.3 shows that one verb has a 5th order derivation (*tietää* 'know') and four have 4th order derivations. The verb *leikata* 'cut' has the highest saturation values (76% and 68%) in the 1st and 2nd orders, but in the 3rd order the highest value (47%) is for *pitää* 'hold' and *tietää* 'know', whereas that of the verb *leikata* is only 32%.

As Table 38.4 shows, the adjectives with the highest saturation values (48%) in the 1st order are *uusi* 'new' and *paha* 'bad'; in the 2nd order, the highest value

Table 38.3: Saturation values per order of derivation, verbs.

Verbs		Saturation value (%)	1st order (%)	2nd order (%)	3rd order (%)	4th order (%)	5th order (%)
cut	leikata	57	76.47	67.57	31.58	0	0
dig	kaivaa	29	41.18	29.73	21.05	0	0
pull	vetää	24	38.24	29.73	0	0	0
throw	heittää	23	32.35	27.03	10.53	0	0
give	antaa	21	23.53	27.03	5.26	22.22	0
hold	pitää	34	23.53	40.54	47.37	22.22	0
sew	ommella	19	23.53	16.22	21.05	11.11	0
burn	polttaa	11	20.59	10.81	0	0	0
drink	juoda	19	29.41	18.92	10.53	0	0
know	tietää	31	23.53	16.22	47.37	77.78	100

Table 38.4: Saturation values per order of derivation, adjectives.

Adjectives		Saturation value (%)	1st order (%)	2nd order (%)	3rd order (%)	4th order (%)	5th order (%)
narrow	kapea	26.23	22.22	9.26	48.15	58.33	50
old	vanha	27.05	29.63	18.52	29.63	41.67	100
straight	suora	19.67	18.52	20.37	29.63	0	0
new	uusi	52.46	48.15	75.93	29.63	16.67	0
long	pitkä	38.52	40.74	20.37	70.37	50	0
warm	lämmin	27.87	33.33	31.48	29.63	0	0
thick	paksu	20.49	29.63	22.22	14.81	8.33	0
bad	paha	38.52	48.15	27.78	48.15	41.67	50
thin	ohut	25.41	22.22	7.41	40.74	75	50
black	musta	13.11	22.22	12.96	11.11	0	0

(76%) is attested for *uusi*, but in the 3rd order it is 70% for *pitkä* 'long'. The words *suora* 'straight', *lämmin* 'warm' and *musta* 'black' have no 4th order derivations, yet *kapea* 'narrow', *vanha* 'old', *paha* 'bad' and *ohut* 'thin' all attest 5th order derivations.

As Table 38.5 shows, the average saturation values for all three word-classes do not differ critically in this data set in the 1st order of derivation: verbs have a slightly higher average value (33%) than adjectives (31%) and nouns (31%). The average saturation value in the 2nd order is 36% for nouns, 28% for verbs, and 25% for adjectives. The differences are clearer in the later orders of derivation: adjectives have higher saturation values (35%) than nouns (28%) and verbs (19%) in the 3rd order, and adjectives have clearly higher values than nouns and verbs in the 4th and 5th orders. The reason for the big differences in average values is the lack of 3rd order derivation in some base words.

Table 38.5: Average saturation values per order of derivation for all three word-classes.

	1st order	2nd order	3rd order	4th order	5th order
Nouns	31.21	35.59	28.42	12.86	10
Verbs	33.24	28.38	19.47	13.33	10
Adjectives	31.48	24.63	35.19	30	25

38.4 Orders of derivation

The maximum number of orders in the Finnish data is five for nouns, adjectives, and verbs. As Table 38.6 shows, the average number for nouns and verbs is 3.2, and 4.1 for adjectives. The low average for nouns and verbs reflects the fact that there are also two adjectives and two verbs that attest only two orders (*koira* 'dog', *täi* 'louse', *vetää* 'pull', *polttaa* 'burn').

Table 38.6: Maximum and average number of orders of derivation for all three word-classes.

	Maximum	Average
Nouns	5	3.2
Verbs	5	3.2
Adjectives	5	4.1

38.5 Derivational capacity

The derivational capacity, as shown in Table 38.7, covers only 1st order derivatives. The average derivational capacity in the Finnish data set is between 8.5 and 11.3, even if the differences between the maximum capacities are bigger. The verb *leikata* 'cut' has the highest derivational capacity, with 26 1st order derivatives. The maximum derivational capacity for nouns is 14, versus 13 for adjectives; they occur with the words *silmä* 'eye', *hammas* 'tooth' and *uusi* 'new'. Of the verbs, *leikata* has an exceptional capacity (26), and the others have only 7–14 1st order derivatives.

Table 38.7: Maximum and average derivational capacity for all three word-classes.

	Maximum	Average
Nouns	14	10.3
Verbs	26	11.3
Adjectives	13	8.5

There is no significant difference in average derivational capacity between nouns, verbs and adjectives. As illustrated in Table 38.8, however, adjectives have a higher derivational capacity than nouns and verbs in the 2nd–5th orders. The differences are clearest in the 3rd order of derivation: nouns and verbs have an average of 5.4 and 3.8 derivatives, respectively, whereas adjectives have 8.5 derivatives on average. The most prolific adjective in the 3rd order is *pitkä* 'long', with 19 derivatives. One verb (*tietää* 'know'), one noun (*päivä* 'day') and four adjectives (*kapea* 'narrow', *vanha* 'old', *paha* 'bad', *ohut* 'thin') have 5th order derivatives (e.g. *paha* 'bad' > CAUSATIVE *pahoittaa*$_V$ 'make worse (somebody's feelings)' > ITERATIVE *pahoitella*$_V$ > PRIVATIVE *pahoittelematon*$_A$ > STATIVE *pahoittelemattomuus*$_N$).

Table 38.8: Average number of derivatives per order of derivation for all three word-classes.

	1st order	2nd order	3rd order	4th order	5th order
Nouns	10.3	12.1	5.4	0.9	0.2
Verbs	11.3	10.1	3.8	1.2	0.1
Adjectives	8.5	13.3	8.5	3.2	0.5

38.6 Correlation between semantic categories and orders of derivation

All the nouns in the 1st order produce derivatives within the semantic categories SIMILATIVE and PRIVATIVE (e.g. *kivi* > *kivimäinen* 'stonelike' and *kivetön* 'without stone'), and 9 produce derivatives within the POSSESSIVE category (e.g. *kivi* > *kivellinen* 'with stone', the exception is *päivä* 'day', which has the POSSESSIVE suffix *-llinen* in its lexicalized use in *päivällinen* 'dinner'; I have categorized the productive use of this suffix as QUALITY: *päivällinen* 'of the day'). The category QUALITY has 8 nouns that produce adjectives mainly with the suffix *-inen* (e.g. *kivinen* 'stony'). In the 2nd order, the semantic category STATIVE has 1–5 derivatives in each of the 10 noun bases, as all SIMILATIVE, PRIVATIVE and QUALITY adjectives can be derived with the suffix *-UUs* (e.g. *kivimäisyys* 'stonelikeness', *kivettömyys* 'lacking stones', *kivisyys* 'stoniness'). ACTION is also quite a common category in the 2nd order of derivation, 8 nouns being represented under this label even with 4 different derivatives (e.g. *kivi* 'sten' > *kivittää* 'to stone' > *kivitys* 'stoning'; the exceptions are *koira* 'dog' and *täi* 'louse', which have no verb derivations in the 1st order).

All the verbs in the 1st order produce derivatives within the semantic categories ACTION, AGENT and PRIVATIVE (e.g. *leikkaus* 'cutting, surgical operation', *leikkaaja* 'cutter', *leikkaamaton* 'uncut'). In the 2nd order, the semantic category STATIVE has 10 verbs that produce property names (e.g. *leikkaamattomuus* 'having not been cut' [lit. 'uncutness']), and ACTION and AGENT have 8 verbs that produce ACTION and AGENT names (e.g. *leikkely* 'cutting, dissecting', *leikkauttaja* 'one who has something cut'; the exceptions are *ommella* 'sew' and *tietää* 'know').

There is a strong correlation in Finnish adjectives between the 1st order of derivation and the semantic categories STATE, PROCESS, ATTENUATIVE and MANNER. All these categories have 1–3 derivatives in any of the 10 adjectival bases of the sample (e.g. *paha* 'bad' > STATE *pahuus* 'badness', PROCESS *paheta* 'get worse', ATTENUATIVE *pahahko* 'fairly bad' and MANNER *pahasti* 'badly'). An equally strong correlation is also present in the 2nd order of derivation and the semantic categories PRIVATIVE and ACTION, as well as between the 3rd order of derivation and the semantic category ACTION. These categories in the 2nd order have 1–12 derivatives (e.g. *pahuudeton*$_A$ 'without badness', *paheksunta*$_N$ 'thinking ill of somebody, disapproval'), and ACTION in the 3rd order has 1–4 derivatives (e.g. *pahastuttaminen*$_N$ 'offending, displeasing', *pahoittelu*$_N$ 'expression of regret') in each of the 10 adjectival bases of the sample.

38.7 Semantic categories with blocking effects

Blocking effects in Finnish are typically morphological, and hence are also extensive, i.e. *-UUs*, which produces property names, and *-sti*, which produces adverbs, block further derivation in this data set. Thus, the semantic categories STATIVE (10 nouns in the 2nd order, e.g. *päivittäisyys*$_N$ 'dailiness', *koiramaisuus*$_N$ 'dog likeness') and MANNER (6 nouns in the 2nd order, e.g. *hampaattomasti*$_{ADV}$ 'without teeth, toothlessly', *kivisesti*$_{ADV}$ 'stonily') block further derivation. With verbs, too, the semantic category STATIVE (10 verbs in the 2nd order and 7 verbs in the 3rd order, e.g. *leikkaamattomuus*$_N$ 'having not cut; having not been cut') blocks further derivation. In addition, further derivations of adjectives are not possible in the categories STATIVE (e.g. 10 adjectives in the 1st order, such as *vanhuus*$_N$ 'old age', and 9 in the 3rd order, such as *uudistamattomuus*$_N$ 'being unreconstructed') and MANNER (10 adjectives in the 1st order, such as *pahasti*$_{ADV}$ 'badly', and 5 in the 2nd order, such as *lämpimähkösti*$_{ADV}$ 'rather warmly').

Although adverbs ending *-sti* can usually be formed from adjectives, on the semantic level, not all adjectives are suitable for expressing MANNER or quantity. Examples of these include adjectives that express colour, age, shape or size and indicate a permanent and inherent property (e.g. ?*sinisesti* 'blue-ly', ?*vanhasti* 'old-ly', *kolmivuotiaasti 'three-year-old-ly') (Hakulinen et al. 2004: 367–368). However, some such derivatives are recorded with metaphorical uses in this data set: e.g. *mustasti* 'black-ly', *paksusti* 'thick-ly', *vanhasti* 'old-ly, oldish'.

38.8 Typical combinations of semantic categories

Koivisto (2013) introduced Finnish derivation series using examples in which as many as five suffixes are attested, which according to Koivisto is the maximum number of consecutive suffixes in a root. Such complex derivatives are often difficult to understand, however, and are rarely used (Koivisto 2013: 180, 186).

Every verb derivative can be further derived with the suffix *-mAtOn*, which produces privative adjectives, and further with the suffix *-UUs*, which produces property names (e.g. *leikata* 'cut' > PRIVATIVE *leikkaamaton*$_A$ 'uncut' > STATIVE *leikkaamattomuus*$_N$ 'having not cut; having not been cut'). All 10 adjectives and 8 nouns (blocks with *täi* 'louse' and *koira* 'dog') in the sample of Finnish data have verb derivatives of the 1st order (semantic categories CAUSATIVE and/or PROCESS). Thus, typical combinations are CAUSATIVE-PRIVATIVE-STATIVE (e.g. *päivä* 'day' > CAUSATIVE *päivätä*$_V$ 'date' > PRIVATIVE *päiväämätön*$_A$ 'undated' > STATIVE *päiväämättömyys*$_N$ 'undatedness') and PROCESS-PRIVATIVE-STATIVE (e.g. *musta* 'black' > PROCESS *mustua*$_V$ 'become black' > PRIVATIVE *mustumaton*$_A$ 'impossible to be blackened' > STATIVE *mustumattomuus*$_N$ 'being impossible to be blackened'). In addition, a typical combination for adjective bases is the verbal series PROCESS-CAUSATIVE-ANTICAUSATIVE (10 PROCESS in the 1st order of derivation, a further 9 CAUSATIVE in the 2nd order, and 5 ANTICAUSATIVE in the 3rd order, e.g. *paha* 'bad' > PROCESS *paheta*$_V$ 'get worse' > CAUSATIVE *pahentaa*$_V$ 'make worse' > ANTICAUSATIVE *pahentua*$_V$ 'get worse').

In addition, it is possible to derive ACTION and AGENT names from all verbs. Typical combinations are CAUSATIVE-ACTION and CAUSATIVE-AGENT, as well as PROCESS-ACTION and PROCESS-PATIENT. For example, 8 nouns, 10 adjectives and 8 verbs have action names in the 2nd order, whereas 6 nouns, 7 adjectives and 8 verbs have AGENT names in the 2nd order as they have verbal derivatives in the 1st order (e.g. *nimi* 'name' > CAUSATIVE *nimittää*$_V$ 'nominate' > ACTION *nimitys*$_N$ 'nomination'; *nimi* 'name' > CAUSATIVE *nimetä*$_V$ 'to name' > AGENT *nimeäjä*$_N$ 'who gives the name'; *leikata* 'cut' > CAUSATIVE *leikkauttaa*$_V$ 'to have something cut by somebody' > ACTION *leikkauttaminen*$_N$ 'having something cut by somebody'; *tuli* 'fire' > CAUSATIVE *tulittaa*$_V$ 'to fire, shoot' > AGENT *tulittaja*$_N$ 'who fires').

38.9 Multiple occurrence of semantic categories

CAUSATIVE verbs are productive in Finnish, and many can be derived further for the meaning of commission: such derivatives can be called CURATIVES. For example, all 10 adjectives in the sample have CAUSATIVE verbs in the 1st or 2nd order of derivation, and they all have new CAUSATIVE (CURATIVE) verbs in the 2nd or 3rd order. It is a CAUSATIVE-CAUSATIVE combination that is typical of Finnish, for example, *lämmin* 'warm' > *lämmittää*$_V$ 'to warm, heat' > *lämmityttää*$_V$ 'to have something (e.g. house) heated', *pitkä* 'long' > *pitkittää*$_V$ 'prolong, lengthen' > *pitkityttää*$_V$ 'to have something (e.g. time) lengthened', *ohut* 'thin' > *ohentaa*$_V$ 'to thin, dilute' > *ohennuttaa*$_V$ 'to have something (e.g. hair) thinned'.

38.10 Reversibility of semantic categories

Certain semantic categories may occur multiple times in series of derivations in which consecutive adjective and adverb suffixes are possible, and also in the opposite order. For example, MANNER-QUALITY and QUALITY-MANNER are possible even in the same series, e.g. *pitkä* 'long' > MANNER *pitkittäin*$_{ADV}$ 'lengthwise' >

QUALITY *pitkittäinen*_A 'longitudinal' > MANNER *pitkittäisesti*_ADV 'longitudinally'. The adverbs *pitkittäin* and *pitkittäisesti* are almost synonymous, however, and this is accordingly a unique case. There is also a noun that attests the MANNER-QUALITY series (*silmä* 'eye' > MANNER *silmäkkäin*_ADV 'eyeball to eyeball' > QUALITY *silmäkkäinen*_A), but it cannot be derived further to MANNER (*silmäkkäisesti*_ADV is a potential and possible Finnish word, but I did not find any occurrences of it).

38.11 Conclusions

The average number of derivational orders ranges between 3.2 and 4.1 in the Finnish data set. As Koivisto (2013: 186) claims, it is possible to form longer combinations with suffixes, but very long formations may well be difficult to use and understand. There are three nouns, four verbs and seven adjectives that have 4th order derivations, and one noun, one verb and four adjectives that have 5th order derivations. Adjectives yield the richest derivational maps, with 10 base words producing 354 derivatives: the most productive base is *uusi* 'new' with 64 derivatives. The count of derivatives among the 10 nouns is 288, the most productive being *päivä* 'day' with 44. With regard to verbs, the derivational map produces 268 derivatives, and *leikata* 'cut' is the most productive with 57.

In sum, the derivatives of the 30 Finnish base words are assigned to 31 different semantic categories based on the data used for this study. The most frequent categories are ACTION, AGENT, PATIENT, QUALITY, POSSESSIVE, SIMILATIVE, ATTENUATIVE, DURATIVE, PRIVATIVE, PROCESS, CAUSATIVE, ITERATIVE, STATE and MANNER. Some categories are used rather seldom: these include ENTITY, DIMINUTIVE, REFLEXIVE, SUBITIVE, INSTRUMENTATIVE, ANTICAUSATIVE, EXPERIENCER, LOCATION, AUGMENTATIVE, RESULTATIVE and COLLECTIVE. Derivatives in the ABILITY, INCHOATIVE, OCCUPATION, FEMININE, RELATIONAL and TEMPORAL categories are the rarest in this data set. In some cases, the reason for the low frequency (ABILITY, INCHOATIVE, RESULTATIVE) or total absence (UNDERGOER) is that the chosen base words do not represent all possible semantic and morphological types, and because of the exclusion of participles. Although the abundance of deverbal verbal suffixes (e.g. in the categories DURATIVE, ITERATIVE, REFLEXIVE and SUBITIVE) is considered one of the distinguishing features of Finnish compared to Indo-European languages (e.g. Karlsson 2015: 278), they are not strongly emphasized in this data set. This is, however, possibly reflected in Table 38.5, which shows the highest saturation values for verbs in the 1st order of derivation, for nouns in the 2nd order, and for adjectives in the 3rd order.

References

Bikupska, Anna-Maija. 2018. *Verbi verbistä: Puolan ja suomen johdetun verbileksikon merkitysrakenteen vertailua* [A verb for a verb: A comparative study of the semantic structure of derived verb lexicon in Polish and Finnish University of Helsinki]. http://hdl.handle.net/10138/232239.

Hakanen, Aimo. 1973. *Adjektiivien vastakohtasuhteet suomen kielessä* [Opposite relations of adjectives in Finnish]. SKST 311. Helsinki: SKS.

Hakulinen, Lauri. 1967. *Suomen kielen rakenne ja kehitys*. [The structure and development of the Finnish language.] Third, revised edition. Helsinki: Otava.

Hakulinen, Auli, Maria Vilkuna, Riitta Korhonen, Vesa Koivisto, Tarja Riitta Heinonen & Irja Alho. 2004. *Iso suomen kielioppi* [The Comprehensive Finnish Grammar]. SKST 950. Helsinki: SKS.

Häkkinen, Kaisa. 1990. *Mistä sanat tulevat? Suomalaista etymologiaa* [Where words come from? Finnish etymology]. Tietolipas 117. Helsinki: SKS.

Karlsson, Fred. 2015. *Finnish. An Essential Grammar*, 3rd edn. London & New York: Routledge.

Koivisto, Vesa. 2013. *Suomen sanojen rakenne* [Structure of Finnish words]. Helsinki: SKS.

Pitkänen-Heikkilä, Kaarina. 2016. 176. Finnish. In Peter O. Müller, Ingeborg Ohnheiser, Susan Olsen & Franz Rainer (eds.), *Word-Formation. An International Handbook of the Languages of Europe, Vol 5*, 3209–3228. Boston & Berlin: Mouton de Gruyter.

Räisänen, Alpo. 1978. Kantasanan ja johdoksen suhteesta [From the relationship between base and derivative]. *Virittäjä* 100. 321–344.

Tyysteri, Laura. 2015. *Aamiaiskahvilasta ötökkätarjontaan. Suomen kirjoitetun yleiskielen morfosyntaktisten yhdyssanarakenteiden produktiivisuus* [Productivity of morphosyntactic compound structures in written Finnish standard language]. Annalis Universitatis Turkuensis C: 408. Scripta Lingua Fennica Edita. Turku.

Sources

Borin, Lars, Markus Forsberg & Johan Roxendal. 2012. *Korp – the corpus infrastructure of Språkbanken*. https://korp.csc.fi/.

Kielipankki. *The Language Bank of Finland*. https://www.kielipankki.fi/language-bank/.

Kielitoimiston sanakirja [Dictionary of standard Finnish]. https://www.kielitoimistonsanakirja.fi/

László Palágyi, Erzsébet Tóth-Czifra, Réka Benczes
39 Derivational networks in Hungarian

39.1 General notes

Due to its agglutinating nature, Hungarian is a morphologically complex language with a high frequency of affixational word-formation patterns (as opposed to other means of word-formation, such as conversion; Comrie 1987; Palágyi 2016). Thus, its rich system of derivational affixes makes Hungarian especially suitable – and highly relevant – for the study of derivational networks.[1] Two significant consequences follow from this property of Hungarian that deserve particular attention in the present study.

First, there is a high degree of differentiation between the various morphological classes, which also implies that there is an abundance of affixes in Hungarian morphology that fall somewhere in between the derivational-inflectional continuum.[2] One such transient form is the modal *-hAt* derivational affix referring to ability or possibility (e.g. *tanul* 'learn' > *tanulhat* 'can learn').

Second, there is also a wealth of synonymous (Keszler 2000: 310), multifunctional (Kenesei 2014) and polysemous (Kugler and Simon 2017; Tóth-Czifra 2015; Fekete 2013) meaning networks within the stock of derivational affixes. Thus, the same function can be expressed by multiple and synonymous derivational affixes (e.g. *kutya* 'dog' > *kutyuli, kutyi, kutyus, kutyuska* 'doggie'). At the same time, exactly the opposite situation also occurs – i.e. one derivational affix is able to express multiple functions (e.g. the deverbal *-Ó* affix can refer to an EVENT, an AGENT, an INSTRUMENT, a property or a LOCATION). It is a relatively common phenomenon that the multifunctional property of the derivational affix is based on either a correlation in experience (durability entailing a loss in intensity – see, e.g., Szili 2014: 4) or on an antecedent-consequence relationship (e.g. *-Ás* forms expressing both the ACTION and the result of the action, as in *kér* 'ask' > *kérés* 'asking', *kérés* 'request').

In line with a usage-based approach to language (see Barlow and Kemmer 2000), our analyses are based on linguistic patterns observable in natural language use, extracted from the *Hungarian Gigaword Corpus* (Oravecz, Váradi and

---
[1] See especially Kiefer and Laasko 2014: 486–489, Kenesei, Vago and Fenyvesi 1998: 351, and Dressler and Ladányi 2000: 103 for an elaboration.
[2] This particular property is not limited to Hungarian; it is characteristic of agglutinative languages in general: "Data from agglutinative languages do not support such a strict separation of inflectional and derivational markers" (Plungian 2001: 188).

Sass 2014; henceforth HGC) by searching for [core vocabulary units].* and .*[core vocabulary units].* The resulting data thus represent a bottom-up, not top-down, approach.

As a second step in the analysis, we cross-checked the data obtained from the HGC with the *Hungarian Etymological Dictionary* (Benkő 1984) to ensure that the derivatives were in fact related to those particular bases that we had identified. This step was crucial for the elimination of false friends (e.g. *tartózkodik* 'stay somewhere' and its derivatives are not related to *tart* 'hold' (an item that is listed in the core vocabulary) but rather to *tartózik* 'hold back', which is no longer a part of synchronic language use). The bottom-up approach entailed that, when identifying the semantic categories, we relied on the meaning addition of the derivative as compared to the immediate base – not on the canonical meaning of the suffix that is typically provided in various grammars.

With respect to the selection of the derivatives that we included in the study, we restricted our analysis to a somewhat narrow definition of what counts as a derivational suffix (in alignment with the general principles of the volume). Consequently, we left out affixoids as well as affixes considered as either transient (Keszler et al. 2000) or inflectional (e.g. Kiefer 2000; É. Kiss, Kiefer and Siptár 2003), the latter exemplified primarily by highly productive participial affixes (*-Ó* present participle, *-(V)tt* past participle and *-vA* adverbial participle), and the *-hAt* (ABILITY), *-hAtÓ* (MANNER), and *-hAtAtlan* (un ... able) suffixes.

With regard to semantic categorization, verbal derivatives posed the greatest challenge. On the one hand, the derivational network of verbs is considerably more elaborate and productive than that of the nouns or adjectives; on the other hand, these verbal derivatives activate the most abstract, temporal meanings. As for the individual semantic categories, we interpreted the DURATIVE category more generally (following Comrie 1976) – thus, any verbal derivative that does not evoke any salient aspectual or aktionsart meaning and which encompasses a wider time frame is considered as DURATIVE. The derivation *víz* 'water' > *vizez* 'to water' is a case in point. In our data, the majority of affixations in *-(V)z* denominals are interpreted as DURATIVE. Due to the highly schematized character of the affix, it does not carry any specifications in terms of aspect or aktionsart; instead, it only indicates the ENTITY > ACTION conversion/meaning shift. Such schematicity correlates with high productivity (see Ladányi 2007). When it comes to derivatives formed with verbal prefixes, such derivatives are always polysemous. Here we focused on the aspectual, aktionsart or figurative meaning, as opposed to the secondary, DIRECTIONAL function of the prefix (for example, we considered the primary meaning of *felad* as 'to give up, abandon' or that of *feldob* as 'to cheer up'); accordingly, such derivatives were categorized as RESULTATIVE, FINITIVE, SINGULATIVE, SATURATIVE, etc.

39.2 Maximum derivational networks

As it is indicated in Table 39.1, typically nouns have the most extended derivation network in Hungarian, including even 5th order derivations. Adjectives, by contrast, show a lesser degree of derivational richness, not only in terms of forming the basis of multiple derivational sequences (we see no instances for 5th order derivations and only seven instances for 4th order derivations), but also in the terms of derivational diversity. That is, adjective-based derivations show fewer instances of 1st, 2nd and 3rd order derivations than nouns and verbs; however, this is only relative to the other two word classes. In sum, the table shows clear evidence for the richness of Hungarian affixational morphology.

Table 39.1: Maximum derivational networks per order of derivation for all three word-classes.

	1st order	2nd order	3rd order	4th order	5th order	Σ
Nouns	27	43	40	15	4	145
Verbs	40	45	29	8	2	128
Adjectives	20	41	20	7	0	88
TOTAL	87	129	89	30	6	341

39.3 Saturation values

The mean saturation values for the nouns range between 12% and 53% (see Table 39.2). The noun with the highest mean saturation value is *szem* 'eye' (53.25%), which is also one of the two nouns with a 5th order derivation (75%). Remarkably, *nap* 'day', which has the lowest mean saturation value (11.71%), also has a 5th order derivation. In contrast, within the 1st order, *kutya* 'dog' has the highest saturation value, but lacks 4th and 5th order derivations.

For the verbs in Table 39.3, the lowest and highest mean saturation values vary between 13% for *ás* 'dig' and 50% for *tart* 'hold'. The latter has the highest value in the 1st order (42.5%). Two verbs, *húz* 'pull' and *iszik* 'drink', have no 3rd order derivations, and two verbs, *tart* 'hold' and *ad* 'give', produce 4th order derivations; the latter is the only verb with a 5th order derivation.

The adjectives in Table 39.4 are slightly more unevenly distributed with regard to the saturation value per order. The mean saturation values range between 10% and 55%. The highest mean saturation value belongs to *új* 'new', which also

Table 39.2: Saturation values per order of derivation, nouns.

Nouns		Saturation (%)	1st order (%)	2nd order (%)	3rd order (%)	4th order (%)	5th order (%)
bone	csont	19.53	25.92	23.25	12.5	20	0
eye	szem	53.25	44.44	53.48	57.5	66.66	75
tooth	fog	18.75	33.33	30.23	5	0	0
day	nap	11.71	18.51	4.65	12.5	20	25
dog	kutya	14.06	44.44	11.62	2.5	0	0
louse	tetű	11.71	18.51	11.62	10	6.66	0
fire	tűz	22.65	29.62	27.9	20	6.66	0
stone	kő	35.93	25.92	44.18	37.5	12.5	0
water	víz	35.15	33.33	34.88	47.5	13.33	0
name	név	25.78	22.22	32.55	30	6.66	0

Table 39.3: Saturation values per order of derivation, verbs.

Verbs		Saturation (%)	1st order (%)	2nd order (%)	3rd order (%)	4th order (%)	5th order (%)
cut	vág	28.22	32.5	44.44	6.89	0	0
dig	ás	12.9	17.5	17.77	3.44	0	0
pull	húz	22.58	40	26.66	0	0	0
throw	dob	18.54	20	24.44	13.79	0	0
give	ad	46.77	40	44.44	44.82	87.5	100
hold	tart	50	42.5	71.11	41.37	12.5	0
sew	varr	19.35	22.5	28.88	6.89	0	0
burn	ég	38.7	32.5	51.11	41.37	0	0
drink	iszik	16.12	27.5	20	0	0	0
know	tud	29.83	22.5	35.55	41.37	0	0

Table 39.4: Saturation values per order of derivation, adjectives.

Adjectives		Saturation (%)	1st order (%)	2nd order (%)	3rd order (%)	4th order (%)
narrow	szűk	37.5	20	36.58	70	0
old	öreg	34.09	45	39.02	25	0
straight	egyenes	19.31	30	17.07	20	0
new	új	54.54	45	43.9	70	100
long	hosszú	30.68	50	29.26	20	14.28
warm	meleg	51.13	40	60.97	45	0
thick	vastag	15.9	30	14.63	10	0
bad	rossz	10.22	30	15	0	0
thin	vékony	26.13	30	26.82	30	0
black	fekete	36.36	45	34.14	40	14.28

has a 4th order derivation, along with *hosszú* 'long' and *fekete* 'black'. Moreover, *hosszú* 'long' has the highest saturation value in the 1st order (50%).

Table 39.5 gives the average saturation values per order of derivation for all the nouns, verbs and adjectives in the Hungarian set. Adjectives have the highest values for the 1st and 3rd orders, while verbs have the highest values for the 2nd order. The average saturation values are evenly balanced in the first three orders; nevertheless, they are at the same time also quite low, not going above 37% in the 1st and 2nd orders and not surpassing 33% in the 3rd order.

Table 39.5: Average saturation values per order of derivation for all three word-classes.

	1st order	2nd order	3rd order	4th order	5th order
Nouns	25.62	27.43	23.5	15.24	10
Verbs	29.75	36.44	19.99	10	10
Adjectives	36.5	31.73	33	12.85	0

39.4 Orders of derivation

The maximum number of orders for the Hungarian sample is five; adjectives, however, lack a 5th order. The average number of derivations for nouns, verbs and adjectives is nevertheless relatively stable, varying between three and four orders.

Table 39.6: Maximum and average number of orders of derivation for all three word-classes.

	Maximum	Average
Nouns	5	3.6
Verbs	5	3.1
Adjectives	4	3.3

39.5 Derivational capacity

Very generally speaking, the affixational patterns of the verbal paradigm are significantly more detailed and productive than the nominal or the adjectival outputs. This particular phenomenon might be explained by the relative paucity of tenses in Hungarian, which is compensated for by the rather large stock of verbal prefixes (such as RESULTATIVE, TELIC and SINGULATIVE). This explains the relatively high maximum number of verbs in the first two orders (see Tables 39.6, 39.7 and 39.8). Nevertheless, there is a correlation between the relatively low number of verbal derivatives and blocking from the 3rd order onwards. We believe that this is due to the relatively early appearance of the PROCESS and ACTION categories, which mostly block any further derivation. These semantic categories are related to deverbal nominals and typically emerge earlier among the verbs (typically in the 2nd order) (e.g. verbal *dob* 'to throw' > 1st order *bedob* 'to throw in' > ACTION 2nd order *bedobás* 'throw-in'; adjectival *szűk* 'narrow' > 1st *szűkít* 'to narrow' > 2nd *leszűkít* 'to narrow down' > ACTION 3rd *leszűkítés* 'narrowing down'; nominal *csont* 'bone' > 1st *csontoz* 'to bone' > 2nd *kicsontoz* 'to unbone' > ACTION 3rd *kicsontozás* 'boning').

Table 39.7: Maximum and average derivational capacity for all three word-classes.

	Maximum	Average
Nouns	12	8
Verbs	17	11.9
Adjectives	10	7.3

Table 39.8: Average number of derivatives per order of derivation for all three word-classes.

	1st order	2nd order	3rd order	4th order	5th order
Nouns	8	11.8	9.4	2.6	0.4
Verbs	11.9	16.4	5.8	0.8	0.2
Adjectives	8.6	11.6	8.1	2.6	0

39.6 Correlation between semantic categories and orders of derivation

39.6.1 Verbs

1st order
ACTION (9 out of 10 verbs derive an ACTION word, value: 9), followed by RESULTATIVE (value: 8) and CAUSATIVE (value: 7)
2nd order
ACTION (value: 10), CAUSATIVE (value: 9), QUALITY (value: 9)
3rd order
ACTION (value: 7)

Two observations can be made with regard to the category of verbs. First, for Hungarian verbs, the category of ACTION seems to be the most dominant in all the derivational orders. Due to the general and unlimited productivity of the deverbal *-ás* affix, resulting in nouns with the very schematic meaning of ACTION (e.g. *iszik* 'to drink' → *ivás* 'drinking'), it is not possible to ascertain a specific correlation with either one of the derivational orders. In fact, the unlimited productivity of the *-ás* affix has a considerable impact on the occurrence of individual semantic categories and the order of derivation of the other two word-classes as well (see below). Second, the correlation between CAUSATIVE and REFLEXIVE is a consequence of the parallel productivity of passive and active verbs (e.g. *melegít* 'to warm/heat' – *melegedik* 'to become warm').

39.6.2 Nouns

1st order
DURATIVE (value: 9), DIMINUTIVE (value: 8), QUALITY (value: 8), PRIVATIVE (value: 7)
2nd order
ACTION (value: 8), MANNER (value: 8), REFLEXIVE (value: 6), STATIVE (value: 6)
3rd order
ACTION (value: 8), RELATIONAL (value: 6)

As expected, the category of ACTION overweighs the other word-class-specific correlations among nouns, too. The reason behind the strong correlation between 1st order derivatives of Hungarian nouns and the semantic category of DURATIVE is due to our broad interpretation of the category (for further details, see section 39.2 above), as a result of which the majority of N > V derivations (verb outputs with no sharp aspectual or aktionsart markers) fall into this particular semantic category. The category of DIMINUTIVE, however, seems to be a word-class-specific semantic category, showing a strong correlation with 1st order nominal derivatives. Further, the CAUSATIVE-REFLEXIVE correlation that is observable among the verbal derivatives (see section 39.6.1) result in ACTION-PROCESS pairs in the case of nouns.

39.6.3 Adjectives

1st order
REFLEXIVE (value: 10), CAUSATIVE (value: 9), MANNER (value: 8)
2nd order
RESULTATIVE (value: 9), PROCESS (value: 9), ACTION (value: 8)
3rd order
PROCESS (value: 9), ACTION (value: 9), RELATIONAL (value: 7)

Yet again, the highly productive *-ás* affix is a dominant category overall among the adjectives as well. The category of MANNER is also noteworthy here, due to the productivity of Adj > Adv derivations.

39.7 Semantic categories with blocking effects[3]

Verbs: 1st order: AGENT (2 out of 10 base verbs block further derivation in the 1st order, value: 2) *(vágó)*
2nd order: ACTION (value: 8) *(ivás)*, INSTRUMENT (value: 4) *(fölvarró)*, **MANNER** (value: 5) *(varrottan)*, RELATIONAL (value: 6) *(varrodai)*
3rd order: ACTION (value: 7) *(tudósítás)*, AGENT (value: 2) *(tudósító)*, **MANNER** (value: 5) *(tudatosan)*
4th order: ACTION (value: 3) *(tudatosítás)*

Nouns: 1st order: DIMINUTIVE (value: 8) *(csontocska)*, POSSESSIVE (value: 6) *(csontú)*
2nd order: AGENT (value: 1) *(csontozó)*, ACTION (value: 7) *(csontozás)*, **DIMINUTIVE** (value: 1) *(csontika)*, MANNER (value: 8) *(csontosan)*, PROCESS (value: 2) *(nevezés)*
3rd order: ACTION (value: 8) *(megnevezés)*, PROCESS (value: 4) *(kövesülés)*, RELATIONAL (value: 6) *(szemészeti)*
4th order: ACTION (value: 3) *(megneveztetés)*, PROCESS (value: 6) *(megcsontosodás)*

Adjectives: 1st order: STATIVE (value: 5) *(feketeség)*
2nd order: MANNER (value: 4) *(szűkösen)*, PROCESS (value: 7) *(szűkülés)*
3rd order: ACTION (value: 7) *(leszűkítés)*, RELATIONAL (value: 7) *(szűkítési)*, MANNER (value: 3) *(szükségtelenül)*, PROCESS (value: 9) *(leszűkülés)*

Typical end points in the paradigms are ACTION, PROCESS, MANNER and RELATIONAL – i.e. there is a plethora of prefixed verbal derivatives that are formed by attaching the *-ás* suffix to the verbal base. Examples include the following: DURATIVE *(tart* 'hold') – TELIC *(megtart* 'hold/retain') – ACTION *(megtartás* 'retention').

39.8 Typical combinations of semantic categories

Two of the characteristic and reoccurring features of all three paradigms (especially in the case of adjectival derivatives) are the QUALITY (base, *szűk* 'narrow' >

---

[3] Bold type signifies categories that systematically block any further derivation; normal type is used for categories that *typically* block any further derivation (but with exceptions) – see main text for a brief discussion.

REFLEXIVE (*szűkül* 'to narrow') > PROCESS (*szűkülés* 'narrowing') (observable in 17 out of 30 base words, value: 17) and the QUALITY (base, *szűk* 'narrow') > CAUSATIVE (*szűkít* 'to narrow') > ACTION (*szűkítés* 'narrowing') sequences (value: 14). These sequences are in some cases complemented by an intermediate RESULTATIVE step, forming a QUALITY (*meleg* 'warm') > REFLEXIVE (*melegedik* 'to warm') > RESULTATIVE (*felmelegedik* 'to warm up') > PROCESS (*felmelegedés* 'warming up') chain (value: 11). They can also be followed by a RELATIONAL end point (e.g. *szűkítési* 'of a narrowing property'), forming a QUALITY > CAUSATIVE > ACTION > RELATIONAL (value: 4) or a QUALITY > REFLEXIVE > PROCESS > RELATIONAL (value: 3) chain. In three cases, the QUALITY > CAUSATIVE > RESULTATIVE > ACTION > RELATIONAL combination is also observable. Needless to say, such sequences also highlight the detailedness of the verbal paradigm (as compared to the other two sets), since it is the REFLEXIVE, CAUSATIVE and RESULTATIVE verbal derivations that make these chains predominantly productive.

39.9 Multiple occurrence of semantic categories

Recursiveness was generally rare in the Hungarian data; however, it does seem that certain semantic chains (QUALITY > STATIVE/ABSTRACTION > QUALITY > STATIVE/ABSTRACTION and QUALITY > MANNER > QUALITY > MANNER) and typical combinations make recursiveness possible in Hungarian to a limited extent. For example, the semantic category of QUALITY (by the suffix *-(O)s*) and STATIVE/ABSTRACTION (by the suffix *-sÁg*) occurs repeatedly in *szükségesség*: QUALITY (*szűk* 'narrow') > STATIVE/ABSTRACTION (*szükség* 'need') > QUALITY (*szükséges* 'necessary') > STATIVE/ABSTRACTION (*szükségesség* 'necessity').[4] In addition, the semantic category of QUALITY (by the suffix *-(O)s*) and MANNER (by the suffixes *-ÓlAg* and *-An*) occurs repeatedly in *újólagosan*: QUALITY (*új* 'new') > MANNER (*újólag* 'newly') > QUALITY (*újólagos* 'recent/new') > MANNER (*újólagosan* 'newly').

39.10 Reversibility of semantic categories

In close correlation with recursiveness (see above), the QUALITY-STATIVE/ABSTRACTION combination was not very typical in the data, but this was the

---

[4] This recursiveness is generally made possible by the metaphorical extension of the 1st order (cf. *egész* 'whole' → *egészség* 'health' → *egészséges* 'healthy' → *egészségesség* 'healthiness').

only one that was reversible, appearing as both QUALITY > STATIVE/ABSTRACTION (*vizes* 'wet' > *vizesség* 'of a wet quality') and STATIVE/ABSTRACTION > QUALITY (*szükség* 'need' > *szükséges* 'necessary').

39.11 Conclusions

The rich derivational system of Hungarian contains a very diverse scope of affixes, ranging from semantically rich forms that span parts of speech (e.g. N > V) all the way to more schematic, highly productive and inflection-like elements. This derivational continuum manifests itself in the networks themselves: affixes situated towards the derivational end of this continuum are typically located in the 1st order of the networks. It can be generally stated that a larger proportion of such affixes in the 1st order results in larger (and lengthier) networks. At the same time, highly productive, semantically schematic and inflection-like affixes usually emerge towards the end of the derivational networks, from the 3rd order onwards. The deverbal *-ás* nominal suffix proved to be very productive. This feature explains the often-held view in Hungarian morphological literature that such derivatives should be regarded as equivalent to the infinitival category (Antal 1977). From a diachronic point of view, they do bear such traces (Adamikné Jászó 1991); thus, they can have an active-passive sense, and they are the only nouns in Hungarian that can be modified by adverbs.

The verbal derivational paradigm proved to be more detailed and definitely more productive than that of the nouns or the adjectives. Verbal prefixes play an especially substantial role in this regard by actively contributing to the novel aktionsart (and often metaphorical and metonymical) senses of the derivatives (e.g. *beég* lit. 'to burn in', fig. 'getting embarrassed'; *feltüzel* 'to set sth. afire'; *leiszik vkit* lit. 'to spill drink on sth.', fig. 'to drink more than sb.'). Accordingly, the final element in the derivational sequence is typically a prefixed verbal derivative, completed by the above-mentioned *-ás* derivative.

Verbs formed from nouns and adjectives are usually non-compositional in the sense that the meaning of the base determines the meaning of the derivative by elaborating the base-suffix relation (cf. *köv-ez* 'to stone', *csont-oz* 'to unbone', *viz-ez* 'to add water'). This is also the reason why derivatives formed with identical suffixes can end up in different semantic categories.

Last but not least, the derivational network is also affected by the cultural context (e.g. the DIMINUTIVES of *kutya* 'dog'). At the same time, the semantic structure of the derivative reflects our knowledge structure of the world (see, for example, the vast number of NON-AGENTIVE, REFLEXIVE, and PROCESS nouns for substances: *kő* 'stone', *csont* 'bone', *tűz* 'fire', *víz* 'water').

References

Adamikné Jászó, Anna. 1991. *Az igenevek* [Participles]. In Loránd Benkő (ed.), *A Magyar nyelv történeti nyelvtana I* [A historical grammar of the Hungarian language I], 319–352. Budapest: Akadémiai Kiadó.
Antal, László. 1977. *Egy új magyar nyelvtan felé* [Towards a new Hungarian grammar]. Budapest: Magvető.
Barlow, Michale & Suzanne Kemmer (eds.). 2000. *Usage-based models of language.* Stanford: CSLI.
Benkő, Loránd (ed.). 1984. *A magyar nyelv történeti-etimológiai szótára* [A historical etymological dictionary of the Hungarian language]. Budapest: Akadémiai Kiadó.
Comrie, Bernard. 1976. *Aspect: An Introduction to the Study of Verbal Aspect and Related Problems (Cambridge Textbooks in Linguistics).* Cambridge: Cambridge University Press.
Comrie, Bernard. 1987. *The world's major languages.* New York: Oxford University Press.
Dressler, Wolfgang U. & Mária Ladányi. 2000. Productivity in word formation (WF): a morphological approach. *Acta Linguistica Hungarica* 47. 103–144.
É. Kiss, Katalin, Ferenc Kiefer and Péter Siptár. 2003. *Új magyar nyelvtan* [New Hungarian grammar]. Budapest: Osiris.
Fekete, István. 2013. Hungarian *gyerekestül* versus *gyerekkel* ('with [the] kid'). *AHEA: E-Journal of the American Hungarian Educators Associatison* 6. 1–25.
Kenesei, István. 2014. On a multifunctional derivational affix: Its use in relational adjectives or nominal modification and phrasal affixation in Hungarian. *Word Structure* 7. 214–239.
Kenesei, István, Robert M. Vago & Anna Fenyvesi. 1998. *Hungarian.* London: Routledge.
Keszler, Borbála, Judit Balogh, Lea Haader, Nóra Kugler, Kirsztina Laczkó & Klára Lengyel. 2000. *Magyar Grammatika* [Hungarian Grammar]. Budapest: Nemzeti Tankönyvkiadó.
Keszler, Borbála. 2000. *A szóképzés* [Word-formation]. In Borbála Keszler, Judit Balogh, Lea Haader, Nóra Kugler, Kirsztina Laczkó & Klára Lengyel (eds.), *Magyar Grammatika* [Hungarian Grammar], 307–320. Budapest: Nemzeti Tankönyvkiadó.
Kiefer, Ferenc & Johanna Laakso. 2014. Derivation in Uralic. In Rochelle Lieber & Pavol Štekauer (eds.), *Oxford Handbook of Derivational Morphology*, 716–737. Oxford: Oxford University Press.
Kiefer, Ferenc (ed.). 2000. *Strukturális magyar nyelvtan: Morfológia* [The structure of Hungarian: Morphology]. Budapest: Akadémiai Kiadó.
Kugler, Nóra, Gábor Simon. 2017. A felismerőképesség határán. Az összetett szó mint emergens szemantikai konstrukció [On the borders of recognizability: Compounds as emergent semantic constructions]. In Edit Kádár and N. Sándor Szilágyi (eds.), *Összetételek és nyelvleírási modellek* [Compounds and models of language description], 95–131. Kolozsvár: Erdélyi Múzeum-Egyesület.
Ladányi, Mária. 2007. *Produktivitás és analógia a szóképzésben* [Productivity and Analogy in Derivation]. Budapest: Tinta Kiadó.

Oravecz, Csaba, Tamás Váradi & Bálint Sass. 2014. The Hungarian Gigaword Corpus. *Proceedings of LREC*, 1719-1723.
Palágyi, László. 2016. A magyar főnév és melléknév kognitív szerveződésének alapjai és konverziós viszonyai [The foundations of the cognitive organisation of Hungarian nouns and adjectives and their conversion relations]. *Nyelvtudományi Közlemények* 112. 207-241.
Plungian, Vladimir A. 2001. Agglutination vs. flection. In Martin Haspelmath, Ekkehard König, Wulf Oesterreicher, and Wolfgang Raible (eds.), *Language typology and language universals: An international handbook (HSK)*, 669-678. Berlin: de Gruyter.
Szili, Katalin. 2014. A hanghatások és az emberi testrészek mozgásainak képe a magyar nyelvben [Sound effects and body part movements as reflected in Hungarian]. *Magyar nyelvőr* 138. 1-16.
Tóth-Czifra, Erzsébet. 2015. Suffixation and what else? A cognitive linguistic analysis of the Hungarian deverbal suffix -Ó. *Studia Linguistica Hungarica* 30. 5-31.

Kaarina Vuolab-Lohi
40 Derivational networks in North Saami

40.1 General notes

Compounding and derivation are the main productive word-formation processes in the North Saami language. There are mostly derivational suffixes; in North Saami, there are only two prefixes: *eahpe-* and *sahte-*. The prefix *eahpe-* and the suffix *-meahttun* have been borrowed from the Finnic languages, and there is no formal way of deriving words for females from those for males or vice versa (Sammallahti 1998: 91, 108, 240). Derivation is possible within word-classes as well as across categories. There are very productive suffixes operating within categories, such as the DIMINUTIVE suffix *-š* in nouns, e.g. *geađggáš*, as well as the CAUSATIVE, ITERATIVE (FREQUENTATIVE-CONTINUATIVE), DIMINUTIVE and momentary suffixes in verbs, e.g. *čuohppat* 'to cut' > CAUSATIVE e.g. *čuohpahit*, ITERATIVE *čuohpadit*, DIMINUTIVE *čuohpastit*. Derivation across categories is also very productive for some deverbal nouns, e.g. action nouns ending in *-n/-pmi* and *-muš/-moš*, such as *čuohppan* 'cutting' and *čuohppamuš* 'having to cut' from *čuohppat* 'to cut' (Sammallahti 1998: 88–89).[1]

The preparation of the data sample was based on searches in the Nielsen (1979), Sammallahti (1989), and Sammallahti and Nickel (2006) dictionaries, as well as in the *Álgu etymological database of the Saami languages* and the *Frequency list of North Sámi lemmas*. Working only with dictionaries was problematic, because not all derivative words from a base are included. For instance, dictionaries rarely include derived words with deverbal suffixes, such as the DIMINUTIVE *-st-* (e.g. *borastit*), the SUBITIVE *-l-* (e.g. *borralit*), and particularly the passive *-(oj)uvvot* (e.g. *borrojuvvot*) and the inchoative *-goahtit* (e.g. *borragoahtit*). The passive suffix *-(oj)uvvot* and the inchoative *-goahtit* are very productive as well. As a native speaker, I had to rely on my capacity as much as I could, in addition to performing web searches (Google) to confirm their use. In North Saami, it is also possible to use the same derivational suffix twice in spoken language, e.g. *viehkat* 'to run' > *viehka-l-astte-stit* (INCHOATIVE, DIMINUTIVE, DIMINUTIVE), or *njuoskat* 'get wet' > *njuoska-d-adda-di-šgoahtit* (CAUSATIVE, ITERATIVE, CAUSATIVE, INCHOATIVE), but it would have been too challenging to

---

[1] Descriptions of North Saami derivations can be found in Sammallahti (1998) and also in grammars, amongst others, by Nielsen (1979), Nickel and Sammallahti (2011), and Svonni (2015).

https://doi.org/10.1515/9783110686630-040

try and gather all such instances. The best approach would have been to ask informants as to the actual use of such sequences.

40.2 Maximum derivational networks

The derivational networks of North Saami are rich. In Table 40.1 below, we can see that verbs exhibit the highest numbers of derivational networks in all orders and so in total, e.g. verbs have 26 semantic categories in the 1st order, whereas adjectives have only 14. The greatest depth is the 5th order of derivation. The number of derivatives within the 3rd order of derivation is almost equal across word-classes. The biggest difference between the 1st and 2nd orders of derivation occurs for nouns.

Table 40.1: Maximum derivational networks per order of derivation for all three word-classes.

	1st order	2nd order	3rd order	4th order	5th order	Σ
Nouns	23	38	25	8	3	97
Verbs	56	62	22	4	2	146
Adjectives	33	36	23	11	1	104
TOTAL	112	136	70	23	6	347

40.3 Saturation values

In Table 40.2, the highest mean saturation value is that of *čalbmi* 'eye' (51.5%), and *beana* 'dog' has the lowest mean saturation value (4%). Within the 1st order, *čáhci* 'water' and *čalbmi* 'eye' have the highest saturation value (48%), and *beana* 'dog' has the lowest (9%), not having rich derivational networks in North Saami. Within the 2nd order, *namma* 'name' has the highest saturation value (68.5%).

For the verbs in Table 40.3, the lowest and highest mean saturation values vary between 19% for *goarrut* 'sew' and 57% for *geassit* 'pull'. *Goarrut* has no 3th order derivations, but five verbs produce 4th order derivations: *čuohppat* 'cut', *geassit* 'pull', *suohpput* 'throw', *buollit* 'burn' and *juhkat* 'drink'.

The lowest mean saturation values for the adjectives are those of *bahá* 'bad' and *boaris* 'old' (16.5%), as shown in Table 40.4. The highest mean saturation

Table 40.2: Saturation values per order of derivation, nouns.

Nouns		Saturation value (%)	1st order (%)	2nd order (%)	3rd order (%)	4th order (%)	5th order (%)
bone	dákti	29.9	34.78	23.68	40	25	0
eye	čalbmi	50.52	47.83	36.84	52	100	100
tooth	bátni	25.77	39.13	21.05	24	25	0
day	beaivi	29.9	47.83	34.21	16	12.5	0
dog	beana	4.12	8.7	2.63	4	0	0
louse	dihkki	30.93	13.04	23.68	60	37.5	0
fire	dolla	20.62	17.39	15.79	32	25	0
stone	geađgi	35.05	30.43	47.37	32	12.5	0
water	čáhci	38.14	47.83	34.21	44	25	0
name	namma	47.42	43.48	68.42	40	0	0

Table 40.3: Saturation values per order of derivation, verbs.

Verbs		Saturation value (%)	1st order (%)	2nd order (%)	3rd order (%)	4th order (%)	5th order (%)
cut	čuohppat	50	44.64	48.39	59.09	75	100
dig	roggat	21.23	32.14	17.74	9.09	0	0
pull	geassit	56.85	39.29	64.52	86.36	50	0
throw	suohpput	31.51	32.14	29.03	40.91	25	0
give	addit	52.05	44.64	67.74	40.91	0	0
hold	doallat	28.77	28.57	23.87	22.73	0	0
sew	goarrut	19.18	25	22.58	0	0	0
burn	buollit	24.66	26.79	25.81	18.18	25	0
drink	juhkat	46.58	41.07	51.61	50	50	0
know	diehtit	37.67	35.71	38.71	50	0	0

Buollit (intransitive) instead of *boaldit* (transitive) was chosen as the North Saami counterpart for 'burn'.

Table 40.4: Saturation values per order of derivation, adjectives.

Adjectives		Saturation value (%)	1st order (%)	2nd order (%)	3rd order (%)	4th order (%)	5th order (%)
narrow	gárži	27.88	18.18	33.33	39.13	18.18	0
old	boaris	16.35	12.12	19.44	21.74	9.09	0
straight	njuolgat	75.96	60.61	77.78	82.61	100	100
new	ođas	34.62	21.21	47.22	43.48	18.18	0
long	guhkki	33.65	48.48	30.56	30.43	9.09	0
warm	liekkas	37.5	27.27	47.22	47.83	18.18	0
thick	gassat[a]	20.19	24.24	16.67	26.09	9.09	0
bad	bahá	16.35	27.27	13.89	13.04	0	0
thin	Seaggi[b]	28.85	33.33	33.33	26.09	9.09	0
black	čáhppat	35.78	42.42	41.67	30.43	9.09	0

[a]*Gassat* 'thick, fat (of round objects)' instead of *assái* 'thick (of flat things)' was chosen as the North Saami counterpart for 'thick'.
[b]*Seaggi* 'thin (the opposite of *gassat*)' instead of *asehaš* 'thin (of flat things)' was chosen as the North Saami counterpart for 'thin'.

value belongs to *njuolgat* 'straight' (76%), which also has 5th order derivations. Moreover, *njuolgat* 'straight' stands out in the 1st order with a saturation value of 60.5%, in the 2nd order with 78%, and also in the 3rd order with a saturation value of 82.5%.

Table 40.5 gives the average saturation values per order of derivation for all the nouns, verbs and adjectives in the North Saami set. We can see that the average values are higher in the 1st, 2nd and 3rd orders of derivation for verbs than for nouns and adjectives, but in the 4th order, nouns have the highest average values (25%).

Table 40.5: Average saturation values per order of derivation for all three word-classes.

	1st order	2nd order	3rd order	4th order	5th order
Nouns	33.044	30.788	34.4	26.25	10
Verbs	34.999	40	37.727	22.5	10
Adjectives	31.513	36.111	36.087	19.999	10

40.4 Orders of derivation

The maximum number of orders for nouns, verbs and adjectives in the North Saami sample is five. The average number varies between 3.5 and 4, as shown in Table 40.6.

Table 40.6: Maximum and average number of orders of derivation for all three word-classes.

	Maximum	Average
Nouns	5	3.9
Verbs	5	3.5
Adjectives	5	4.0

40.5 Derivational capacity

As follows from Table 40.7, the derivational capacity of the verbs (i.e. direct 1st order derivatives) amounts to the highest average value, whilst the nouns have the lowest average value. However, the verbs *čuohppat* 'cut' and *addit* 'give' have the highest overall derivational capacity (25 derivations in the 1st order).

Table 40.7: Maximum and average derivational capacity for all three word-classes.

	Maximum	Average
Nouns	11	7.6
Verbs	25	19.6
Adjectives	20	10.4

As for the average derivational capacity in all orders and for all word-classes, Table 40.8 shows that, in the 1st and 2nd orders, verbs clearly have higher numbers than adjectives and nouns. The derivational capacity is highest in the 2nd order for all word-classes. In the 3rd order, the derivational capacity for all word-classes is quite similar.

Table 40.8: Average number of derivatives per order of derivation for all three word-classes.

	1st order	2nd order	3rd order	4th order	5th order
Nouns	7.6	11.7	8.6	2.1	0.3
Verbs	19.6	24.8	8.3	0.9	0.2
Adjectives	10.4	13.0	8.3	2.2	0.1

40.6 Correlation between semantic categories and orders of derivation

In the 1st order, 9 of the 10 North Saami nouns produce derivations within the semantic category QUALITY, e.g. *dáktái* 'bony', *čalbmeš* 'who sees well', *čázas* 'very wet'. 8 of the 10 nouns produce derivations within the semantic category RESULTATIVE, such as *dákti*$_N$ 'bone' > *dáktat*$_V$ 'petrify, dry, harden (of plants)' and *čáhci*$_N$ 'water' > *čáhcut*$_V$ 'become soaked, wet through'. 7 of the nouns produce derivations within the semantic category PRIVATIVE, such as *bátni*$_N$ 'tooth' > *báneheapme*$_A$ 'toothless, having bad teeth'. 6 of the 10 nouns produce derivations within the semantic category DIMINUTIVE, e.g. *geadgi*$_N$ 'stone' > *geadggáš*$_N$, *beana*$_N$ 'dog' > *beatnagaš*$_N$; the DIMINUTIVE suffix -š can also produce an ENTITY meaning, e.g. *beaivi* 'day' > *beaivváš* 'sun'. In the 2nd order, RESULTATIVE predominates; all 10 nouns are represented under this label, such as *báneheapme*$_A$ > *bánehuvvat*$_V$ 'become toothless'. PROCESS is the second most characteristic 2nd order category with 8 derived nouns. In the 3rd order of derivation, 10 nouns derive a PROCESS meaning. In the 4th order, 6 nouns derive an ACTION meaning. The only derivation in the 5th order also has an ACTION meaning.

Categories of verbs that are systematically represented in the 1st order of derivation are ACTION (e.g. *geassit*$_V$ 'pull' > *geassin*$_N$), INCHOATIVE (e.g. *geassigoahtit*$_V$) and QUALITY (e.g. *geassil*$_A$). 9 of the 10 nouns produce derivations within the semantic categories CAUSATIVE (e.g. *čuohppat*$_V$ 'cut' > *čuohpahit*$_V$), RESULTATIVE (e.g. *čuhppojuvvot*$_V$ 'to be cut (off by somebody)'), SUBITIVE (e.g. *čuohppalit*$_V$ 'cut in haste or quickly'), and PATIENT (e.g. *addit*$_V$ 'give' > *addes*$_A$, *addeš*$_A$ 'too fond of giving'). 8 verbs produce derivations within the semantic category AGENT, e.g. > *čuohppi*$_N$. In the 2nd order of derivation, the categories ACTION (e.g. *čuohpadit*$_V$ 'be cutting' > *čuohpadeapmi*$_N$) and AGENT (e.g. *čuohpadit*$_V$ > *čuohpadeaddji*$_N$) are systematically realized, as is, with some exceptions, the INCHOATIVE (e.g. *čuohpadit*$_V$ > *čuohpadišgoahtit*$_V$). In the 3rd order of derivation for verbs, there are mostly derivates with an ACTION meaning, e.g. the ITERATIVE verb *čuohpadaddat*$_V$ > *čuohpadaddan*$_N$. In the 4th order, 4 verbs derive an ACTION meaning, and in the 5th order, 1 verb derives an ACTION meaning.

In the 1st order of adjectives, RESULTATIVE is most common category, represented by all 10 adjectives, e.g. *boaris* 'old' > *boarásmit*$_V$ 'become old'. 9 adjectives give rise to derivations with a STATE meaning (e.g. > *boarisvuohta*$_N$) and 8 apiece to ACTION (e.g. *guhkki*$_A$ 'long' > *guhkidit*$_V$ 'lengthen') and PERCEPTIVE meanings (e.g. *boaris*$_A$ 'old' > *boarášit*$_V$ 'consider too old'). 8 adjectives also have an ENTITY meaning (e.g. *ođas* 'new' > *ođut*$_N$ 'animal or thing which one has recently obtained'). In the 2nd order of derivation of adjectives, the categories ACTION (e.g. *njulget*$_V$ 'straighten' > *njulgen*$_N$), PROCESS (e.g *boarásmuvvat*$_V$ 'become old' > *boarásmuvvan*$_N$), AGENT (e.g. *njulget*$_V$ 'straighten' > *njulgejeaddji*$_N$) and INCHOATIVE (e.g. *boarášit*$_V$ 'consider too old' > *boarášišgoahtit*$_V$) are systematically realized. In the 2nd order, CAUSATIVE is derived from 6 adjectives. In the 3rd order, the semantic categories ACTION and PROCESS are systematically realized. The three 4th order derivations are ACTION (5 adjectives) PROCESS (3 adjectives) and INCHOATIVE (1 adjective). In the 5th order of derivation, 1 verb derives an ACTION meaning.

40.7 Semantic categories with blocking effects

For North Saami nouns, the semantic categories with blocking effects seem to be DIMINUTIVE and MANNER. The semantic category DIMINUTIVE blocks further derivations in the 1st order for 6 out of 10 nouns, e.g. *beana* 'dog' > *beatnagaš*, and MANNER for 5 nouns. In the 2nd order, PROCESS hinders further derivations for 8 nouns, the semantic categories ACTION and AGENT for 7 nouns, and STATE for 6 nouns. In the 3rd order of derivation, PROCESS blocks further derivations for 10 nouns, ACTION for 8 nouns, and AGENT for 6 nouns. In the 4th order, ACTION blocks further derivations for 6 nouns and PROCESS for 5 nouns out of 10.

The semantic categories in the 1st order of the verbs are more spread out and more frequently represented overall. In the 1st order, the semantic category ACTION blocks 10 out of 10 verbs, e.g. *addit* 'to give' > *addin*$_N$, AGENT blocks 9 verbs, e.g. *goarrut* 'to sew' > *goarrun*$_N$, and ENTITY blocks 4 verbs. In the 2nd order of derivation, ACTION and AGENT hinder further derivations for 10 verbs and PROCESS for 6 verbs. In the 3rd order of derivation, ACTION blocks 9 out of 10 verbs, PROCESS blocks 6 verbs, and AGENT blocks 3 verbs. In the 4th order, ACTION hinders further derivation for 2 verbs.

In the 1st order of adjectives, ENTITY, MANNER, QUALITY, RECIPROCAL, TEMPORAL and LOCATION block further derivation. The semantic category ENTITY blocks 7 out of 10 adjectives, e.g. *čáhppat* 'black' > *čáhput*$_N$ 'black quadruped', and MANNER and QUALITY hinder further derivations for 4 adjectives. In the 2nd order, ACTION, PROCESS and AGENT each hinder further derivation for all 10 adjectives, and PATIENT for 4 adjectives. In the 3rd order, ACTION and PROCESS each block further derivation for all 10 adjectives, and AGENT for 8 adjectives. In the 4th order, ACTION and PROCESS each block further derivations for 4 adjectives.

40.8 Typical combinations of semantic categories

North Saami nouns have several typical and systematic combinations of semantic categories. 8 of the 10 nouns have the combination RESULTATIVE > PROCESS, e.g. *dákti* 'bone' > *dáktat*$_V$ > *dáktán*$_N$, 5 nouns have the combination RESULTATIVE > INCHOATIVE > PROCESS, e.g. *dihkki* 'louse' > *dihkkat*$_V$ > *dihkkagoahtit*$_V$ > *dihkkagoahtin*$_N$, and 4 have PRIVATIVE > RESULTATIVE > INCHOATIVE > PROCESS, e.g. *čalbmi* 'eye' > *čalmmeheapme*$_A$ > *čalmmehuvvat*$_V$ > *čalmmehuvvagoahtit*$_V$ > *čalmmehuvvagoahtin*$_N$.

Verbs also have several typical and systematic combinations of semantic categories. All 10 verbs have the combination CAUSATIVE > ACTION, e.g. *geassit* 'pull' > *geasehit*$_N$ > *geaseheapmi*$_N$, and 9 have SUBITIVE > ACTION, e.g. *addit* 'pull' > *addilit*$_V$, CAUSATIVE > ACTION, e.g. *goarrut* 'sew' > *goaruhit*$_V$, and CAUSATIVE > AGENT. 8 verbs also have the combination CAUSATIVE > INHCOATIVE > ACTION, e.g. *juhkat* 'drink' > *jugahit*$_V$ > *jugahišgoahtit*$_V$ > *jugahišgoahtin*$_N$.

For all 10 adjectives, a typical combination of semantic categories is RESULTATIVE > PROCESS, e.g. *guhkki* 'long' > *guhkkut*$_V$ > *guhkkun*$_N$, while 7 adjectives have PERCEPTIVE > ACTION/AGENT, e.g. *ođđa* 'new' > *ođašit*$_V$ > *ođašeapmi*$_N$ / *ođašeaddji*$_N$. 9 adjectives have the combination RESULTATIVE > INCHOATIVE > PROCESS, e.g. *čáhppat* 'black' > *čáhpodit*$_V$ > *čáhpodišdoahtit*$_V$ > *čáhpodišgoahtin*$_N$, and 7 have RESULTATIVE > CAUSATIVE > INCHOATIVE > PROCESS, e.g. *gassat* 'thick' > *gassut* > *gassudit*$_V$ > *gassudišgoahtit*$_V$ > *gassudišgoahtin*$_N$.

40.9 Multiple occurrence of semantic categories

There are only a few cases of multiple occurrences in some derivational chains. 4 of the 10 nouns have multiple occurrences of ACTION > ACTION, e.g. *dihkki* 'louse' > *dihkket*$_V$ 'delouse' > *dihkke*$_N$ 'delousing'. Only 2 of the 10 verbs have multiple occurrences of the semantic categories ABILITY > ABILITY, e.g. *juhkat* 'drink' > *jugahit*$_V$> *jugahit*$_V$ 'be drinkable' > *jugahahtti*$_A$ 'drinkable'. Adjectives also have some cases of multiple occurrences; 2 of the 10 have ACTION > ACTION, e.g. *liekkas* 'warm' > *liekkadit*$_V$ 'warm up, heat' > *liekkadeapmi*$_N$ and RESULTATIVE > RESULTATIVE, e.g. *dákti* 'bone' > *dáktadit*$_V$ 'to get stringy, woody'. There are also 3 that have CAUSATIVE > CAUSATIVE (> ACTION), e.g. *njuolgat* 'straight' > *njuget*$_V$ 'straighten' > *njulgehit*$_V$ 'get to straighten' (> *njulgeheapmi*$_N$).

40.10 Reversibility of semantic categories

In the North Saami data set, no instances of semantic categories occurring in a reversed order are attested.

40.11 Conclusions

The derivational networks of North Saami are rich. A good number of semantic categories are realized for all words (especially verbs) in the sample. Productive semantic categories can be found even in the 4th order of derivation. Some semantic categories with blocking effects, independently of the order in which they occur, tend to hamper further derivation, namely deverbal nouns derivated as a PROCESS, ACTION or AGENT.

Verbs exhibit the highest number of maximum derivational networks in the 1st and 2nd orders (Table 40.1). The verbs have the highest average number of derivatives in the 2nd order. In the 3rd order of derivation, the average number of derivatives is almost equal for all word-classes (Table 40.8). Verbs also have the highest average saturation values: 35% in the 1st order, 38% in the 2nd order, and 37% in the 3rd order (Table 40.5).

The average number of derivational orders for adjectives, nouns and verbs ranges between 3.5 and 4 (Table 40.6). Hence, there are few 5th order derivations, but as indicated in the general notes, in spoken language, it is possible to use the same derivational suffix twice.

References

Nickel, Klaus & Pekka Sammallahti. 2011. *Nordsamisk grammatikk*. Karasjok: Davvi Girji.
Sammallahti, Pekka. 1998. *Saami Languages*. An Introduction. Kárášjohka: Davvi Girji.
Svonni, Mikael. 2015. *Davvisámegiella – sánit ja cealkagat. Láidehus sámi lingvistihkkii.*
    Kiruna: Ravda Lágádus.

Sources

Álgu etymological database of the Saami languages. http://kaino.kotus.fi/algu/.
Giellatekno: Frequency list of North Sámi lemmas. http://giellatekno.uit.no/words/lists/sme/
    l-freq.N.html.
Nielsen, Konrad 1979 [1932–1962]. *Lappisk (samisk) ordbok. Grunnet på dialektene i Polmak,
    Karasjok og Kautokkeino*, 2nd edn. Oslo: H. Aschehoug & Co.
Sammallahti, Pekka. 1989. *Sámi-suoma sátnegirji*. Ohcejohka: Jorgaleaddji Oy.
Sammallahti, Pekka & Klaus Nickel. 2006. *Sámi-duiskka sátnegirji*. Karasjok: Davvi Girji.

Aslı Göksel
41 Introduction to Tatar and Turkish

Tatar and Turkish belong to the Turkic language family (Johanson 1998: 82–83; Boeschoten 1998: 13–14; see also Berta 1998 and Csató and Johanson 1998).

The typical word-formation strategy in Tatar and Turkish is affixation, which can produce words with multiple suffixes. Tatar and Turkish have fronting harmony in their suffixes and, on a smaller scale, rounding harmony. Suffixes that start with plosives and affricates assimilate in voicing to the last segment of their host. Many of the suffixes have unstable initial segments, and hiatus resolution is done by the elision of the first vowel or consonant of the suffix. Final stress in Tatar and Turkish occurs on the last suffix in complex words (with various exceptions). Both languages have clear morpheme boundaries and although these languages are considered to have a one-to-one relationship between form and meaning, many irregularities exist. To a much lesser extent than affixation, conversion exists as a category-changing derivational mechanism.

Having an overwhelmingly agglutinative nature, both languages would be expected to have more derivatives in every category. Although the maximum order for derivations was four in Tatar and five in Turkish, many derivational grids remained empty. One of the reasons for this is because compounding, a productive word-formation process, especially in Tatar, was not represented as word-formation category. Worth mentioning with respect to compounding, affixoids (such as the modal marker -(y)AbIl in Turkish) were also not taken into consideration as derivational markers. Another reason for the underrepresentation of the full derivational capacity of the languages in question was the elimination of certain suffixes for which a pure derivational description was not possible. An example is the action nominalizer -U in Tatar which, in this study, only appears in complex morphemes. Forms containing participles is another case in point. The passive suffix -Il in Turkish has been left out as a derivational marker since it is also an inflectional suffix, although it occurs in bases for further derivation.

References

Berta, Árpád. 1998. Tatar and Bashkir. In Lars Johanson & Éva Ágnes Csató (eds.), *The Turkic Languages*, 283–300. London: Routledge.

Boeschoten, Hendrik. 1998. The speakers of Turkic languages. In Lars Johanson & Éva Ágnes Csató (eds.), *The Turkic Languages*, 1–15. London: Routledge.
Csató, Éva Á. & Lars Johanson. 1998. Turkish. In Lars Johanson & Éva Ágnes Csató (eds.), *The Turkic Languages*, 203–235. London: Routledge.
Johanson, Lars. 1998. The history of Turkic. In Lars Johanson & Éva Ágnes Csató (eds.), *The Turkic Languages*, 81–125. London: Routledge.

László Károly
42 Derivational networks in Tatar

42.1 General notes

Tatar is an agglutinative language with rich synthetic morphology both in category-defining and category-changing domains. Bound morphemes are typically suffixes in Tatar. Most Tatar derivational suffixes are of Turkic origin. Those found in the derivational networks are Turkic without exception.

Due to vowel harmony and contact assimilation, bound morphemes in Tatar can have different, predictable morphophonemic variants. Capital letters will be used to indicate the morphophonemes appearing in harmonic suffixes.

The academic dictionaries by Golovkina (1966), Ganiev (2004) and Asylgaraev et al. (2007) have been used to identify derivational networks of Tatar. In cases where these dictionaries did not provide enough information about semantics, the *Text Corpus of the Modern Tatar Language* by Saykhunov, Ibragimov and Khusainov (2017) was also consulted.

In the analysis, 66 suffixes expressing 27 semantic categories were identified. Only the categories ABSTRACTION, AGENT, CAUSATIVE, DIMINUTIVE, ITERATIVE, PERCEPTIVE, PRIVATIVE, QUALITY, RECIPROCAL, SIMILATIVE, STATE and UNDERGOER appear in all three word-classes.

The action nominalizer in *-U* was not considered in the analysis, but some complex suffixes based on it were added to the derivational networks, such as *-UčE*, forming AGENTS from verbal bases, and *-UčAn*, expressing QUALITY for most of the cases; see e.g. *tek-* 'to sew' > *tegüče* 'tailor' and *tartïn-* 'to feel shy' > *tartïnučan* 'shy', respectively. Other complex suffixes based on verbal adjectives or verbal nouns were also added to the derivational networks, such as *-KAnlEk* (< *-KAn* and *+lEk*), expressing STATE or ABSTRACTION; see e.g. *birel-* 'to be given' > *birelgänlek* 'devotion'.

The double use of ITERATIVE (*-(E)štEr-kAlA-* or *-kAlA-(E)štEr-*) is relatively frequent in Tatar; see e.g. *kis-* 'to cut' > *kiskälä-* 'to cut repetitively' > *kiskäläšter-* 'to cut repetitively'. Usually there is no semantic difference, but only a stylistic difference between the single and double forms. The double use of CAUSATIVE, such as *-DEr-t-*, *-t-DEr-* or *-(E)r-t-*, is also a frequent phenomenon in Tatar. The semantic difference here, however, can vary greatly; see e.g. *bel-* 'to know' > *belder-* 'to inform' > *beldert-* 'to inform; to cause to inform' and *eč-* 'to drink' > *ečer-* 'to give drink' > *ečert-* 'to give drink'.

The suffixes *+lAn-* (< *+lA-* and *-(E)n-*) and *+lAš-* (< *+lA-* and *-(E)š-*) are compound affixes, but are regarded as one unit if the intermediate form in *+lA-* is not attested; see e.g. *söyäk* 'bone' > **söyäklä-* > *söyäklän-* 'to ossify, to become bony'. Several derivational suffixes in Tatar are polyfunctional; see e.g. +*lEk*, which is capable of expressing seven different semantic categories: STATE, ABSTRACTION, LOCATION, ABILITY, INSTRUMENT, OCCUPATION and RELATIONAL. On the other hand, certain semantic categories can be expressed by several suffixes. For example, UNDERGOER can be yielded by +*A*-, +*lA*-, +*lAn*-, +*lAš*-, +(*E*)*k*-, +*sEn*-, +(*A*)*r*-, +(*A*)*l*-, +(*A*)*y*-, -(*E*)*l*- and -(*E*)*n*-.

42.2 Maximum derivational networks

In Tatar, verbs produce the biggest derivational networks in every order. Derivations of the 4th order are extremely rare and no example of a 5th order derivation is attested, see Table 42.1.

Table 42.1: Maximum derivational networks per order of derivation for all three word-classes.

	1st order	2nd order	3rd order	4th order	5th order	∑
Nouns	18	19	5	1	0	43
Verbs	34	27	10	0	0	71
Adjectives	14	14	6	1	0	35
TOTAL	66	60	21	2	0	149

42.3 Saturation values

As Table 42.2 shows, nouns have relatively low mean saturation values, ranging from 6.98% to 48.84%. It is the word *su* 'water' that most thoroughly saturates the possible paradigmatic slots. The words *et* 'dog', *bet* 'louse' and *ut* 'fire' have the lowest mean saturation value (6.98%). *Et* 'dog', *ut* 'louse' and *söyäk* 'bone' even lack 2nd order derivatives. Within the 1st order, *kön* 'day' has the lowest saturation value (5.56%), whereas *küz* 'eye' and *su* 'water' have the highest (50%). Slots in the 3rd order are only filled by three nouns, and only the word *at* 'name' is capable of producing 4th order derivatives.

The verbs in Table 42.3 represent a more even distribution of mean saturation values. There is only one verb, *tek-* 'to sew', that has an extremely low value (8.45%). The verb *kis-* 'to cut' has the highest saturation value (55.88%) in the 1st

Table 42.2: Saturation values per order of derivation, nouns.

Nouns		Saturation value (%)	1st order (%)	2nd order (%)	3rd order (%)	4th order (%)	5th order (%)
bone	söyäk	16.28	38.89	0	0	0	0
eye	küz	41.86	50	42.11	20	0	0
tooth	teš	23.26	27.78	15.79	40	0	0
day	kön	13.95	5.56	26.32	0	0	0
dog	et	6.98	16.67	0	0	0	0
louse	bet	6.98	11.11	5.26	0	0	0
fire	ut	6.98	16.67	0	0	0	0
stone	taš	13.95	27.78	5.26	0	0	0
water	su	48.84	50	63.16	0	0	0
name	at	18.6	16.67	10.53	40	100	0

Table 42.3: Saturation values per order of derivation, verbs.

Verbs		Saturation value (%)	1st order (%)	2nd order (%)	3rd order (%)	4th order (%)	5th order (%)
cut	kis-	50.7	55.88	48.15	40	0	0
dig	kaz-	14.08	17.65	11.11	10	0	0
pull	tart-	40.85	35.29	51.85	30	0	0
throw	at-	12.68	20.59	7.41	0	0	0
give	bir-	14.08	17.65	11.11	10	0	0
hold	tot-	29.58	41.18	22.22	10	0	0
sew	tek-	8.45	14.71	3.7	0	0	0
burn	yan-	15.49	11.76	25.93	0	0	0
drink	eč-	14.08	17.65	14.81	0	0	0
know	bel-	40.85	29.41	51.85	50	0	0

order. Four verbs have no 3rd order derivatives and no verb is capable of producing 4th order derivatives.

As Table 42.4 shows, the adjectives have the most even distribution of mean saturation values, ranging from 14.29% to 37.14%. The colour word *kara* 'black' has the highest value in the 1st order (57.14%). The 3rd order also displays an even distribution; only the word *iske* 'old' has no derivatives in this order. There is, however, only a single derivative in the 4th order.

Table 42.4: Saturation values per order of derivation, adjectives.

Adjectives		Saturation value (%)	1st order (%)	2nd order (%)	3rd order (%)	4th order (%)	5th order (%)
narrow	tar	28.57	21.43	28.57	50	0	0
old	iske	22.86	35.71	21.43	0	0	0
straight	turï	25.71	14.29	28.57	50	0	0
new	yaŋa	17.14	14.29	14.29	33.33	0	0
long	ozïn	20	21.43	14.29	33.33	0	0
warm	jïlï	17.14	21.43	7.14	33.33	0	0
thick	kalïn	14.29	21.43	7.14	16.67	0	0
bad	yaman	37.14	28.57	42.86	33.33	100	0
thin	nečkä	22.86	21.43	28.57	16.67	0	0
black	kara	37.14	57.14	28.57	16.67	0	0

The average saturation values in Table 42.5 are considered to be quite low, remaining below 29% for all word-classes. The average values are very similar in the 1st order, but nouns drop significantly in the 2nd order. This shows that nouns generally have a lower capability of saturating the possible paradigmatic slots in this order.

Table 42.5: Average saturation values per order of derivation for all three word-classes.

	1st order	2nd order	3rd order	4th order	5th order
Nouns	26.113	16.843	10	10	0
Verbs	26.177	24.814	15	0	0
Adjectives	25.715	22.143	28.333	10	0

42.4 Orders of derivation

As Table 42.6 shows, the average number of orders is significantly smaller for the noun word-class. There are three derivational networks, *bet* 'louse', *et* 'dog' and *ut* 'fire', with only 1st order derivatives. There is no higher order than the 4th one, and only the words *yaman* 'bad' and *at* 'name' have 4th order derivatives (one for each). Since the 3rd order already has a low number of derivatives, it is often impossible to draw firm conclusions regarding this order.

Table 42.6: Maximum and average number of orders of derivation for all three word-classes.

	Maximum	Average
Nouns	4	2.1
Verbs	3	2.6
Adjectives	4	3

42.5 Derivational capacity

The network size varies greatly, particularly in the noun word-class. The biggest network, *kis-* 'to cut', includes 36 derivatives, whereas the words *et* 'dog', *bet* 'louse' and *ut* 'fire' produce only three derivatives. Regarding adjectives and nouns, the average size is 8.5 words per network. The average size of the derivational networks for the verb word-class is 17.1.

In the 1st order, as Table 42.7 shows, the verb word-class has the highest derivational capacity, with a maximum of 19 derivatives. The average derivational capacity of verbs (8.9) also stands out significantly. The other two word-classes do not differ greatly from one another.

Table 42.7: Maximum and average derivational capacity for all three word-classes.

	Maximum	Average
Nouns	9	4.7
Verbs	19	8.9
Adjectives	8	3.6

As Table 42.8 shows, the average number of derivatives gradually decreases by order of derivation. Verbs have the highest average number in the 1st and 2nd orders, but the value drops significantly in the 3rd order. Nouns and adjectives show fairly similar figures. 4th order derivatives are extremely rare in Tatar, and there are only two examples identified in the derivational networks:
1) *yaman* 'bad' > *yamansu* 'sad, sorrowful' > *yamansula-* 'to grieve, to be sad' > *yamansulan-* 'to sorrow, to feel grief over' > *yamansulandïr-* 'to make sad', and
2) *at* 'name' > *ata-* 'to name, to nominate' > *atak* 'fame' > *ataklï* 'famous, well-known' > *ataklïlïk* 'fame, reputation'.

Table 42.8: Average number of derivatives per order of derivation for all three word-classes.

	1st order	2nd order	3rd order	4th order	5th order
Nouns	4.7	3.2	0.5	0.1	0
Verbs	8.9	6.7	1.5	0	0
Adjectives	3.6	3.1	1.7	0.1	0

42.6 Correlation between semantic categories and orders of derivation

42.6.1 Nouns

In the 1st order, the most typical semantic category is POSSESSIVE (9); see e.g. *söyäk* 'bone' > *söyäkle* 'having bone, bony'. PRIVATIVE (7), DIMINUTIVE (5) and UNDERGOER (5) are also frequent in this order; see e.g. *küz* 'eye' > *küzsez* 'eyeless, blind', *teš* 'tooth' > *tešček* 'little tooth', and *taš* 'stone' > *tašlan-* 'to become petrified', respectively. There is no typical category in the 2nd order, wherein the category AGENT has the highest value (4). Typicality cannot be discussed for the 3rd order.

The semantic categories LOCATION, MANNER, ORNATIVE and RELATIONAL are only attested in this word-class.

42.6.2 Verbs

In the 1st order, the most typical categories are UNDERGOER (9), CAUSATIVE (9) and AGENT (8); see e.g. *kis-* 'to cut' > *kisel-* 'to become cut', *kaz-* 'to dig' > *kazït-* 'to cause to dig', and *at-* 'to throw' > *atučï* 'gunner, rifleman', respectively. CAUSATIVE (7) and ABSTRACTION (7) are the most typical categories in the 2nd order. UNDERGOER and QUALITY each have a value of 5. Due to the low number of derivatives, typicality cannot be discussed in the 3rd order.

The semantic categories COMITATIVE, CUMULATIVE, ENTITY, INTENSIVE, PLURIACTIONALITY and SINGULATIVE are only attested in this word-class.

42.6.3 Adjectives

In the 1st order, the most typical semantic categories are UNDERGOER (7) and STATE (7); see e.g. *yaŋa* 'new' > *yaŋar-* 'to become renewed, to revive' and *yaman* 'bad' > *yamanlïk* 'badness', respectively. These are followed by CAUSATIVE (5); see e.g. *kara* 'black' > *karala-* 'to make black, to blacken'. Only CAUSATIVE is typical for the 2nd order; each of the 10 adjectives derives in this category. A dozen other semantic categories are represented by 3 or fewer examples. In the 3rd order, the most frequent categories are CAUSATIVE (7) and UNDERGOER (7).

Regarding the overall typicality of semantic categories, UNDERGOER has a strong correlation with the 1st order in all three word-classes.

42.7 Semantic categories with blocking effects

42.7.1 Nouns

DIMINUTIVE (5/5 examples) and SIMILATIVE (3/4 examples) block further derivations in the 1st order; see e.g. *söyäk* 'bone' > *söyäkček* 'ossicle' and *söyäkčel* 'like bone', respectively. Due to the insufficient number of examples, no further tendencies can be defined, but the category MANNER has a possible blocking effect in any order where it appears.

42.7.2 Verbs

ACTION (4/5 examples) and AGENT (8/9 examples) block further derivations in the 1st order; see e.g. *bir-* 'to give' > *bireš* 'giving, handing over' and *bel-* 'to know' > *belüče* 'expert', respectively. AGENT (5/5 examples), ACTION (3/3 examples) and DIMINUTIVE (2/2 examples) tend to block further derivations in the 2nd order.

42.7.3 Adjectives

SIMILATIVE (6/7 cases), STATE (6/7 cases) and ABSTRACTION (3/3 cases) block further derivations in the 1st order; see e.g. *kara* 'black' > *karača* 'somewhat black', *nečkä* 'thin' > *nečkälek* 'thinness' and *iske* 'old' > *iskelek* 'the old way of life; conservatism', respectively. In the 2nd order, only the category STATE has a blocking effect; see e.g. *yaman* 'bad' > *yamansu* 'sad, sorrowful' > *yamansulïk* 'sadness'. ACTION and AGENT seem to have a blocking effect, but there are not enough examples to speak about tendencies.

DIMINUTIVE and SIMILATIVE tend to block further derivations in any order where they appear. AGENT and ACTION also tend to block further derivation. Although there is a low number of MANNER derivatives in the analyzed data, this category also blocks further derivation in any order.

42.8 Typical combinations of semantic categories

42.8.1 Nouns

The derivational networks of nouns represent 38 different combinations of 17 semantic categories, therefore no typicality can be identified. The most frequent combination is PERCEPTIVE-PERCEPTIVE (3), but all are derived from the word *su* 'water'; see e.g. *su* 'water' > *susa-* 'to be, or feel thirsty' > *susaučï* 'thirsty'.

42.8.2 Verbs

Altogether, 23 semantic categories are represented in 57 combinations. Most of them are represented by a small number of examples. Although no typicality can be identified, the most frequently appearing combinations are CAUSATIVE-CAUSATIVE

(5) and CAUSATIVE-UNDERGOER (4); for the latter, see e.g. *yan-* 'to burn' > *yandïr-* 'to burn, to set on fire' > *yandïrïl-* 'to become burnt'.

42.8.3 Adjectives

Typical combinations for the adjectives are UNDERGOER-CAUSATIVE (7) and UNDERGOER-CAUSATIVE-UNDERGOER (5); for the former, see e.g. *iske* 'old' > *isker-* 'to become worn' > *iskert-* 'to wear out'.

42.9 Multiple occurrence of semantic categories

42.9.1 Nouns

Recursiveness is not typical in this word-class. There are three examples of the combination PERCEPTIVE-PERCEPTIVE, but all are derived from the word *su* 'water'; see e.g. *su* 'water' > *susa-* 'to feel thirsty' > *susankïra-* 'to feel thirsty'. A single case of ABSTRACTION is also attested; see ORNATIVE-ABSTRACTION-QUALITY-ABSTRACTION in *at* 'name' > *ata-* 'to name, to nominate' > *atak* 'fame' > *ataklï* 'famous, well-known' > *ataklïlïk* 'fame, reputation'.

42.9.2 Verbs

The only two recursive semantic categories that appear frequently in Tatar are CAUSATIVE (6) and ITERATIVE (3); see e.g. *kaz-* 'to dig' > *kazït-* 'to cause to dig' > *kazïttïr-* 'to cause to cause to dig' and *at-* 'to throw' > *atkala-* 'to throw repetitively' > *atkalaštïr-* 'to throw repetitively', respectively.

42.9.3 Adjectives

The recursiveness of CAUSATIVE is common in this word-class (10); see e.g. CAUSATIVE-REFLEXIVE-CAUSATIVE in *kara* 'black' > *karala-* 'to blacken' > *karalan-* 'to blacken oneself' > *karalandïr-* 'to blacken'. UNDERGOER is less frequent (5); see e.g. UNDERGOER-CAUSATIVE-UNDERGOER in *ozïn* 'long' > *ozïnay-* 'to become long' > *ozïnayt-* 'to lengthen, to make long' > *ozïnaytïl-* 'to get lengthened'. There is one example for STATE, namely STATE-QUALITY-STATE in *turï* 'straight' > *turïlïk* 'straightness' > *turïlïklï* 'true' > *turïlïklïlïk* 'truth, the state of being true'.

42.10 Reversibility of semantic categories

The reverse order of semantic categories is not typical in Tatar, and the noun word-class has no examples of it at all.

42.10.1 Verbs

The following combinations could be found among the verbs: ABSTRACTION-QUALITY (2) vs. QUALITY-ABSTRACTION (2); CAUSATIVE-PLURIACTIONALITY (1) vs. PLURIACTIONALITY-CAUSATIVE (1); CAUSATIVE-RECIPROCAL (1) vs. RECIPROCAL-CAUSATIVE (1); CAUSATIVE-UNDERGOER (4) vs. UNDERGOER-CAUSATIVE (1); QUALITY-UNDERGOER (1) vs. UNDERGOER-QUALITY (1); and ITERATIVE-RECIPROCAL (2) in *kis-* 'to cut' > *kiskälä-* 'to cut repetitively' > *kiskäläš-* 'to cut one another repetitively' vs. RECIPROCAL-ITERATIVE (1) in *kis-* 'to cut' > *kiseš-* 'to cut one another' > *kiseškälä-* 'to cut one another repetitively'.

42.10.2 Adjectives

The adjective word-class also has some sporadic examples of reversibility: CAUSATIVE-REFLEXIVE (1) vs. REFLEXIVE-CAUSATIVE (1); CAUSATIVE-UNDERGOER (3) vs. UNDERGOER-CAUSATIVE (7); and QUALITY-STATE (2) in *yaman* 'bad' > *yamansu* 'sorrowful, sad' > *yamansulïk* 'sadness' vs. STATE-QUALITY (1) in *turï* 'straight' > *turïlïk* 'straightness' > *turïlïklï* 'true'.

42.11 Reasons for structurally poor derivational networks

The derivational networks of *bet* 'louse', *et* 'dog' and *ut* 'fire' are extremely small, each having only three derivatives. It is worth noting that *etle* 'having dog' and *etsez* 'having no dog, without dog', derived from *et* 'dog', are only attested in the *Text Corpus of the Modern Tatar Language*. None of them are mentioned in the standard academic dictionaries.

It is not clear why these three words are unable to build regular-sized networks, but it is very likely that the semantics of the base words constrain the possible number of derivatives.

A commonly used compensatory strategy is to form new words by means of compounding, which is especially productive in the domain of noun formation (see Károly 2016).

42.12 Conclusions

Although Tatar is an agglutinative language and derivation is a major strategy in forming new words, the identified derivational networks can be considered to be relatively small. The average number of orders is not high (2.566) and 4th order derivation is extremely rare. There is obviously a large difference between the derivational networks of the three word-classes.

The paradigmatic capacity of derivation is generally low in Tatar; possible derivational slots often remain empty. The low paradigmatic capacity is due to various factors, but the working hypothesis adopted here is that it often originates from semantic constraints. For instance, several derivational suffixes are capable of expressing different semantic categories, and the actual realization is greatly dependent on the semantics of the base. The suffix -*KEč* can express ABILITY, QUALITY, INSTRUMENT, and OCCUPATION; see e.g. *kis-* 'to cut' > *kiskeč* 'capable of cutting' and *tot-* 'to hold' > *totkič* 'handle'. Similar to this, the verbalizer +*lA-* is able to denote the semantic categories CAUSATIVE, STATE, INSTRUMENTAL, ORNATIVE, and RESULTATIVE; see e.g. *küz* 'eye' > *küzlä-* 'to spy' and *su* 'water' > *sula-* 'to moisten'.

References

Asylgaraev, Šaripzjan N. et al. (eds.). 2007. *Tatarsko-russkij slovar'* 1–2 [Tatar-Russian dictionary]. Kazan': Magarif.
Ganiev, Fuat A. (ed.). 2004. *Tatarsko-russkij slovar'* [Tatar-Russian dictionary]. Kazan': Tatarskoe knižnoe izdatel'stvo.
Golovkina, O. V. (ed.). 1966. *Tatarsko-russkij slovar'* [Tatar-Russian dictionary]. Moskva: Sovetskaja Énciklopedija.
Károly, László. 2016. Tatar. In Peter O. Müller, Ingeborg Ohnheiser, Susan Olsen & Franz Rainer (eds.), *Word-Formation. An International Handbook of the Languages of Europe 5*, 3398–3413. Berlin & Boston: Mouton de Gruyter.
Saykhunov, Mansur R., Tavzikh I. Ibragimov & Rustem R. Khusainov (eds.). 2017. *Text Corpus of the modern Tatar language*. http://www.corpus.tatar/.

Aslı Göksel, Aysel Kapan
43 Derivational networks in Turkish

43.1 General notes

Next to compounding, the predominant word-formation process in Turkish is affixation, which is almost exclusively done through suffixation. A few loan prefixes occur in calcitrated forms, and some stems have acquired prefixal status after the Language Reform of the 1930s (Lewis 2000). Conversion targets only about 50 roots (Uygun 2009), and base modification occurs in a handful of examples (Bacanlı 2016, Göksel 2019).

According to Uzun et al. (1992), there are 191 derivational suffixes that attach to major lexical categories in Turkish, most of which are polysemous. 144 of these suffixes derive nominals[1] and 80 of them take nominal bases (see Göksel and Kerslake 2005; Korkmaz 2009), pointing to a larger presence of nominal (nouns and adjectives) than verbal categories. However, the few verb-deriving suffixes are more productive than noun-deriving suffixes (Korkmaz 2009). Nakipoğlu and Üntak (2008) point out that of the 4,669 verbs in Turkish, all but 221 are derived.

As a general note on suffixation, there are a number of phonological processes that play a role in the form of the allomorphs. The vowels in a suffix are harmonized with respect to fronting, as a result of which a suffix has allomorphs with front and back vowels, and in addition, if a suffix has a high vowel, it is harmonized with respect to rounding. Further, the initial consonants of suffixes assimilate to the previous segment in terms of voicing. Finally, as Turkish does not allow vowel sequences, hiatus resolution either creates a buffer consonant at morpheme boundaries or the initial vowel of a suffix is deleted in such an environment.

For the Turkish data, the *Comprehensive Turkish Dictionary* of the Turkish Language Association (TDK) has been used as the primary source. Where the TDK dictionary lacked possible and potential derivations which we, as native speakers, assumed might exist, we searched for that derivation on search engines to verify whether it was in usage. Those that appeared more than once in conversational or other contexts, i.e. those that were not cases of hapax legomenon, were included. In contrast, we considered entries from dictionaries other than the TDK that appeared on search engines as unreliable sources.

---

[1] Some of these suffixes were borrowed from dialects or other Turkic languages, or were revived from Old Turkic (see Lewis 2000: 86–101).

43.2 Maximum derivational networks

The maximum derivational networks of the three word-classes are shown in Table 43.1. The verbal category has the highest maximum derivational networks in all orders except in the 5th order. Nouns and adjectives are similar in their number of maximum derivational networks compared to the verbal category. However, nouns and verbs are dissimilar in one respect. Considering each order of derivation, only adjectives have a continuous decrease in their number of maximum derivational networks. Nouns and verbs have their peak in the 2nd order and then they gradually decrease in their number of maximum derivational networks.

Table 43.1: Maximum derivational networks per order of derivation for all three word-classes.

	1st order	2nd order	3rd order	4th order	5th order	Σ
Nouns	20	25	16	8	4	73
Verbs	24	35	22	10	2	93
Adjectives	19	16	14	9	2	60
TOTAL	63	76	52	27	8	226

43.3 Saturation values

Although nominals appear to be a more robust class than verbs vis-à-vis affixes and the bases they apply to, nouns, adjectives and verbs are identical in terms of the order of derivation they allow (all go up to the 5th order). The class that differs most in terms of the span between the lowest and highest saturation values is adjectives (lowest 10, highest 60), compared to nouns (lowest 9.59, highest 54.79) and verbs (lowest 15.05, highest 58.06). The lexical item with the highest saturation values is the adjective *dar* 'narrow' with 88.89 in the 4th order, followed by the verb *bil* 'know' with 86.36 in the 3rd order and then by the noun *göz* 'eye' with 81.25 in the 3rd order.

Table 43.2 shows that the highest and lowest saturation values for nouns are 54.79% and 9.59% respectively. All of the base words can have derivations up to the 3rd order, but only three base words derive to the 4th order and only one to the 5th order. What is interesting here is that the base word with the highest saturation value is not the one that has derivations up to the 5th order. Both of the lexical items with the highest and the lowest saturation values, *göz* 'eye' and *bit* 'louse' respectively, derive up to the 3rd order.

Table 43.2: Saturation values per order of derivation, nouns.

Nouns		Saturation value (%)	1st order (%)	2nd order (%)	3rd order (%)	4th order (%)	5th order (%)
bone	kemik	16.44	25	20	12.5	0	0
eye	göz	54.79	35	80	81.25	0	0
tooth	diş	32.88	40	40	37.5	0	0
day	gün	16.44	25	24	6.25	0	0
dog	köpek	23.29	35	20	18.75	25	0
louse	bit	9.59	10	12	12.5	0	0
fire	ateş	16.44	25	24	6.25	0	0
stone	taş	28.77	35	24	43.75	12.5	0
water	su	34.25	35	48	37.5	0	0
name	ad	39.73	20	28	37.5	100	100

Table 43.3: Saturation values per order of derivation, verbs.

Verbs		Saturation value (%)	1st order (%)	2nd order (%)	3rd order (%)	4th order (%)	5th order (%)
cut	kes	46.24	54.17	40	63.64	20	0
dig	kaz	40.86	41.67	48.57	40.91	20	0
pull	çek	55.91	50	68.57	63.64	20	0
throw	at	30.11	41.67	40	18.18	0	0
give	ver	17.2	33.33	22.86	0	0	0
hold	tut	33.33	54.17	42.86	13.64	0	0
sew	dik	29.03	37.5	31.43	31.82	0	0
burn	yan	15.05	29.17	17.14	4.55	0	0
drink	iç	38.71	41.67	57.14	27.27	0	0
know	bil	58.06	29.17	45.71	86.36	100	100

Table 43.3 shows that for the verbal category, *bil* 'know' has the highest saturation value, which is 58.06%, and *yan* 'burn' has the lowest, which is 15.05%. The verb with the highest saturation value, *bil* 'know', is the only verb that derives up to the 5th order. In contrast, the verb with the lowest saturation value, *yan* 'burn', is not the verb that has the fewest number of derivational orders, which instead is the verb *ver* 'give', which derives only up to the 2nd order.

As shown in Table 43.4 a have the highest discrepancy between the highest and the lowest saturation values. The highest saturation value is 60% for *dar* 'narrow' and the lowest saturation value is 10% for *uzun* 'long'. In addition, adjectives are the only category with base words that do not derive further than the 2nd order.

Table 43.4: Saturation values per order of derivation, adjectives.

Adjectives		Saturation value (%)	1st order (%)	2nd order (%)	3rd order (%)	4th order (%)	5th order (%)
narrow	dar	60	36.84	56.25	85.71	88.89	0
old	eski	15	36.84	12.5	0	0	0
straight	düz	36.67	21.05	50	57.14	22.22	0
new	yeni	48.33	31.58	50	78.57	33.33	50
long	uzun	10	26.32	6.25	0	0	0
warm	sıcak	25	36.84	18.75	21.43	22.22	0
thick	kalın	30	36.84	37.5	21.43	22.22	0
bad	kötü	48.33	21.05	50	71.43	55.56	100
thin	ince	26.67	26.32	31.25	42.86	0	0
black	siyah	33.33	31.58	31.25	50	22.22	0

Table 43.5 shows that in terms of the orders of derivation, the saturation value of the nominal category is the lowest among the three lexical categories. Verbs have the highest saturation values in the 1st and the 2nd orders, and adjectives have the highest saturation values in the rest of the orders. On average, adjectives have the highest saturation value as well.

Table 43.5: Average saturation values per order of derivation for all three word-classes.

	1st order	2nd order	3rd order	4th order	5th order
Nouns	28.5	32	29.375	13.75	10
Verbs	41.252	41.428	35.001	16	10
Adjectives	30.526	34.375	42.857	26.666	15

43.4 Orders of derivation

Although all lexical categories can derive into a 5th order, which is the maximum, the average number of derivational orders is higher for adjectives than the other two lexical categories, as shown in table 43.6.

Table 43.6: Maximum and average number of orders of derivation for all three word-classes.

	Maximum	Average
Nouns	5	3.4
Verbs	5	3.4
Adjectives	5	3.7

It should be noted that, in Turkish, lexical items may undergo derivations beyond the 5th order. Some of these cases are not presented in the data. For example, *göz-le-n-e-bil-ir-lik* (eye-VDER-PASS-CVB-POSS-AOR-NDER) 'observability' is not listed in our data because affixoids (here, *bil* (POSS)) and conversion, here exemplified by the participle (i.e. the word form before the final NDER suffix), are not included in the study.

43.5 Derivational capacity

The highest derivational capacities, both the maximum and the average, belong to the verbal category in Turkish. The derivational capacities of nouns and adjectives are more or less the same. However, while the maximum derivational capacity of nouns is higher than that of adjectives, on average the nouns have a lower derivational capacity than the adjectives.

Table 43.7: Maximum and average derivational capacity for all three word-classes.

	Maximum	Average
Nouns	8	5.7
Verbs	13	9.9
Adjectives	7	5.8

Even though verbs have the highest derivational capacity, the average number of derivatives for each order of verbs is not the highest among all the lexical categories. The average number of derivatives in the 1st, 2nd and 3rd orders is highest in verbs. This average is highest in the 4th order in adjectives and in the 5th order in nouns. The overall highest number of derivatives per order of derivation can be seen in the 2nd derivational order of verbs.

Table 43.8: Average number of derivatives per order of derivation for all three word-classes.

	1st order	2nd order	3rd order	4th order	5th order
Nouns	5.7	8	4.7	1.1	0.4
Verbs	9.9	14.5	7.7	1.6	0.2
Adjectives	5.8	5.5	6	2.4	0.3

43.6 Correlation between semantic categories and orders of derivation

There is a high occurrence of the semantic category STATE in all orders of derivation, regardless of the lexical category of the base. It is worth mentioning that there is only one exception to this: the 1st order of nouns. In the 1st order, STATE interacts with 10 base adjectives and 10 base verbs but only 2 base nouns (*köpek* 'dog' and *su* 'water'). Instead, for the 1st order of nouns, there is a strong tendency for the semantic categories QUALITY, ACTION and PRIVATIVE to occur. In the 1st order, all base nouns are derived in the semantic category QUALITY and 7 of the 10 base nouns are derived in the categories ACTION and PRIVATIVE. In the 2nd order, 10 verbs, 9 nouns (except for *gün* 'day'), and 9 adjectives (except for *uzun* 'long') interact with the semantic category STATE. In the 3rd order, all 10 nouns, 9 verbs (except for *ver* 'give'), and 8 adjectives (except for *eski* 'old' and *uzun* 'long') are derived in the category STATE. Only the derivation of adjectives is worth mentioning for the 4th order: 7 of them are derived in the category STATE.

ACTION is similar to STATE, in this respect. There is a high tendency for all orders of derivation to include the category ACTION except for one: the 1st order of adjectives. For the 1st order, all 10 base verbs and 7 base nouns (except for *kemik* 'bone', *gün* 'day', and *köpek* 'dog') are derived in the category ACTION, but only 1 adjective is derived in this semantic category. Instead, the 1st order of adjectives is strongly correlated with the semantic categories AUGMENTATIVE, DIMINUTIVE, and SIMILATIVE. 9 of the 10 base adjectives are derived in AUGMENTATIVE (except for *kötü* 'bad') and 7 of the 10 base adjectives are derived in the DIMINUTIVE and SIMILATIVE categories in the 1st order. In the 2nd order, ACTION interacts with 9 nouns (except for *gün* 'day'), 9 verbs (except for *yan* 'burn.INTR'), and 9 adjectives (except for *uzun* 'long'). In the 3rd order, 8 of the 10 nouns, adjectives, and verbs are derived in this category.

In addition to STATE and ACTION, higher orders of derivation of adjectives and verbs tend to correlate with other semantic categories as well. In the 2nd order of derivation, 7 out of 10 adjectives correlate with PROCESS and CAUSATIVE, while in the 3rd order, 7 adjectives correlate with CAUSATIVE. As for the verbal category, the 1st derivational order correlates with CAUSATIVE (9 out of 10 verbs), PROCESS (9 out of 10 verbs), and RESULTATIVE (8 out of 10 verbs), whereas in the 2nd order, 8 out of 10 verbs are correlated with CAUSATIVE and QUALITY.

43.7 Semantic categories with blocking effects

Blocking occurs across the board. In adjectives, the semantic categories that systematically block further derivation happen to be different for the 1st and higher orders. In the 1st order, the lexical items that are derived in AUGMENTATIVE, SIMILATIVE, and DIMINUTIVE do not tend to undergo further derivation. For example, the derivational outcome of *ince* 'thin' > *ip-ince* 'very thin' does not typically derive into the 3rd order. There is only one exception to this. The DIMINUTIVE derived from *uzun* 'long' may derive one more time: *uzun-ca* 'longish' > *uzun-ca-cık* 'longish.EVAL'. For the 2nd and higher orders of derivation, systematic blocking, without exceptions, can be observed in the category ACTION. However, STATE and PROCESS are also worth mentioning since there is a pattern in their blocking: they block further derivation only if the derived form is a nominal. Other semantic categories might also show blocking effects, however these are neither as widespread nor as systematic as the ones mentioned above.

In nouns, DIMINUTIVES and SIMILATIVES block further derivations in the 1st order. For example, there is no 3rd order derivation after the following derivation: *köpek* 'dog' > *köpeğ-imsi* 'doglike'. In the 2nd and higher orders, the semantic category ACTION has a blocking effect depending on the lexical category.

In nouns and adjectives, the semantic categories that have a blocking effect vary among the derivational steps. This contrasts with verbs. In verbs, if a semantic category blocks derivation in the 1st order, it also blocks it in the other derivational steps. From the 1st order, STATE, ACTION, and PROCESS block further derivation if the output category of the derivation is not verbal. DIMINUTIVE blocks derivation in a few instances and RESULTATIVE blocks it with a few exceptions. The derivational sequence of *bil* 'know' > *bil-gi* 'knowledge' > *bil-gi-li* 'knowledgeable' could be given as an example for such an exception.

We can summarize the generalizations as follows: the systematic blocking of derivation is restricted to the categories MANNER, AUGMENTATIVE, DIMINUTIVE, and SIMILATIVE. These categories block further derivation among all lexical categories, with very few exceptions. The semantic categories STATE, ACTION, and PROCESS block further derivation if the lexical items that are derived in these categories also happen to be in the nominal category. Otherwise, blocking occurs sporadically.

43.8 Typical combinations of semantic categories

After deriving a lexical item into the verbal category, further derivation in the semantic categories STATE, ACTION, and PROCESS is typical in Turkish. For example, following the derivation *dar* 'narrow' > *dar-al* 'to become narrow', a form like *dar-al-ma* 'the state of becoming narrow' is expected. Other typical and systematic combinations occur in the categories CAUSATIVE-INSTRUMENTAL, e.g. ince 'thin' > *ince-l* 'to become thin' > *ince-l-t* 'to cause to become thin' > *ince-l-t-ici* 'thinner'. CAUSATIVE-PROCESS and REFLEXIVE-STATE are also commonly observed.

43.9 Multiple occurrence of semantic categories

Recursiveness occurs with the category CAUSATIVE. For example, *yeni* 'new' > *yeni-le* 'to make something new' can undergo one more derivation, as in *yeni-le-t* 'to cause to make (st.) new'. The 2nd order derivative has the categorial function of creating a verb, and the recursivity has the effect of adding a new AGENT.

43.10 Reversibility of semantic categories

In our data, only two pairs of semantic categories can occur in a reversed order: CAUSATIVE-PROCESS and AGENT-STATE. Some pairs have identical affixes save for the order they occur in, e.g. *yeni-lik-çi* (new-STATE-AGENT) 'a person who adheres to/supports the state of novelty' vs. *yeni-ci-lik* (new-AGENT-STATE) 'the state of being a person supporting novelty'.

43.11 Reasons for structurally poor derivational networks

Affixation is a productive morphological operation in Turkish, as a result of which the output is a substantial derivational network.

43.12 Conclusions

Derivational affixes have been investigated in terms of their categorial properties, their semantic contribution to the word form, and their concatenation properties (Sebüktekin 1971; Uzun 1993; Aksan 1998; Korkmaz 2009; Uygun 2009, among others), but the present study is the first of its kind to investigate the concatenative power of semantic categories in derivational paradigms in Turkish.

The study has singled out the role of affixation as a derivational mechanism; however, two cases of affixation have been excluded from the study. One of these is participles that are derived by affixation but which have nevertheless been left out of the investigation as they are conversions of inflected verbs. The other category is affixoids. These are affixal modal verbs that are productive in deriving various semantic categories (e.g. POSSIBILITY). The inclusion of these two categories would have changed the results considerably.

There are a few potential problems in developing derivational networks based solely on affixation. One has to do with the presence of alternative mechanisms for the expression of certain semantic categories, e.g. compounding for AUGMENTATIVE (*kötü* 'bad' > *kötü kötü* 'consistently bad') and a phrasal construction for SIMILATIVE (*ince* 'thin' > *ince gibi* 'like thin'). Another, less pervasive problem is the loss of the association between the derivatives of bound stems, e.g. *uzun* 'long' and *uza* 'to become long' cannot be reflected, as *uz-* is a bound stem. These have been omitted as they do not manifest well-behaved affixation. This too has affected the results.

Many stems in Turkish have synonyms as a result of the centuries-long influence of Arabic and Persian on Turkish. For example, the words for 'black' are *kara* (Turkic) or *siyah* (Persian). We found that the one with the Turkic origin generated more idiomatic meanings in the derivatives, and therefore we chose the borrowed *siyah* as the base word, since metaphorical meanings were also excluded from the study.

The study reinforces the presence of a well-known categorization in Turkish: that between nominals (nouns and adjectives) and verbs (see Uygun 2009 and references therein). Here, we see the distinction drawn between these two syntactic categories as it is manifested in derivation. For example, the saturation levels in the 1st and 2nd order derivations in nouns and adjectives are comparable, whereas verbs have a much higher saturation value (Table 43.5). The same applies to the average number of derivatives per order of derivation, where nouns and adjectives show similarities (Table 43.8), and the average and maximum derivational capacities (Table 43.7). Future studies will no doubt shed new light on the various topics discussed in this paper.

Acknowledgements: We would like to thank Prof. Dr. Alexandra Bagasheva, Prof. Dr. Lívia Körtvélyessy, Prof. Dr. Pavol Štekauer, and Dr. Salvador Valera not only for their comments on the manuscript but also for initiating the research programme that has led to the present study and for inviting us to the Derivational Networks Workshop in Danišovce, Slovakia, which took place from April 27–29, 2017. Aslı Göksel's contribution was supported by a grant from Boğaziçi University Research Fund 11500, and Aysel Kapan's contribution was supported by Dil Uygulama ve Araştırma Merkezi (Language Application and Research Centre) at Boğaziçi University.

References

Aksan, Mustafa. 1998. Durum değişikliği eylemleri türetimi ve anlambilimsel kısıtlamalar [The derivation of change of state verbs and semantic blocking]. In Yeşim Aksan & Mustafa Aksan (eds.), *XII. Dilbilim Kurultayı Bildirileri*, 197–208. Mersin Üniversitesi Yayınları.

Bacanlı, Eyüp. 2016. *Türk Dillerinde Düzensizlikler* [Irregularities in Turkic Languages]. Ankara: Etkileşim Yayınevi.

Göksel, Aslı. 2019. *Morphology in Altaic Languages. Oxford Research Encyclopedia of Linguistics*. Retrieved 8 Mar. 2020, from https://oxfordre.com/linguistics/view/10.1093/acrefore/9780199384655.001.0001/acrefore-9780199384655-e-526.

Göksel, Aslı & Celia Kerslake. 2005. *Turkish, A Comprehensive Grammar*. London: Routledge.

Korkmaz, Zeynep. 2009. *Türkiye Türkçesi Grameri: Şekil Bilgisi* [Grammar of the Turkish of Turkey: Morphology]. Ankara: Türk Dil Kurumu.
Lewis, Geoffrey. 2000. *The Turkish Language Reform, A Catastrophic Success*. Oxford University Press.
Nakipoğlu, Mine & Aslı Üntak. 2008. A complete verb lexicon of Turkish based on morphemic analysis. *Turkic Languages* 12 (2). 221–280.
Sebüktekin, Hikmet. 1971. *Turkish English Contrastive Analysis*. The Hague: De Gruyter.
Uygun, Dilek. 2009. *A split model for category specification: Lexical categories in Turkish*. Boğaziçi: Boğaziçi University PhD dissertation.
Uzun, Nadir Engin. 1993. *Türkiye Türkçesinde Sözlüksel Yapı [Lexical structure of the Turkish of Turkey]*. Ankara: Ankara Üniversitesi Yayınları PhD dissertation.
Uzun, Nadir Engin, Leyla Uzun, Yeşim Aksan & Mustafa Aksan. 1992. *Türkiye Türkçesinin Türetim Ekleri: Bir Döküm Denemesi* [The Derivational Affixes of Turkish: An Essay on Documentation]. Ankara: Şirin Kırtasiye.

Source

Türk Dil Kurumu Büyük Türkçe Sözlük [Turkish Language Assosiation Comprehensive Turkish Dictionary]. http://www.tdk.gov.tr.

Seda Yusupova
44 Derivational networks in Chechen

44.1 General notes

The Chechen language is one of the Nakh languages of the Iberian-Caucasian group of languages. Word-formation, as well as many other areas of linguistics, is insufficiently studied in the Chechen language. A big contribution to this area was made by the Chechen philologist Chokayev, who believes that in the Nakh languages, composition is more developed than just as an affixation. The other point of view is that affixation is used much more widely than it is considered to be (Halidov 2013: 366–670; Vagapov 2009). In the Chechen language, the following processes of word-formation are recognized: composition, affixation (prefixation and suffixation), a phonetic way, and conversion (Chokayev 2010: 74; Aliroyev 2005: 42). The suffixation of nouns cannot be called very productive, as only some suffixes function to form new words (Chokayev 2010: 235).

According to the Chechen lists of words, derivation from verbs is formed by suffixation for the formation of adjectives and verbal nouns (masdar, by the addition of the suffixes *r* and *m*). The CAUSATIVE meaning is expressed with the help of *iyta*, and potential possibility by *dala*. Some derivations from verbs reveal vowel sound changes in the root, e.g. *tega* 'sew' – *to'gurg* 'the thing that is being sewn' or *haa* 'know' – *huurg* 'informed'. There are many derivational nets with prefixes in the list of the selected verbs.

Adjectives add the suffix *dan* to form verbs. There are more suffixes that attach to verbs and adjectives than to nouns. The derivatives from nouns are mostly adjectives. More suffixes derive adjectives, nouns and verbs than derive adverbs in the networks.

The derivational networks have been made on the basis of the Chechen-Russian dictionaries (Matsiyev 1961, 2010; Ismailov 2009).

44.2 Maximum derivational networks

In Table 44.1, according to the data from the dictionaries, the quantity of derivational networks is greatest in verbs. Only verbs had a 3rd order derivation, and none of the three word-classes showed a 4th order derivation.

Table 44.1: Maximum derivational networks per order of derivation for all three word-classes.

	1st order	2nd order	3rd order	4th order	5th order	∑
Nouns	3	0	0	0	0	3
Verbs	11	19	1	0	0	31
Adjectives	8	3	0	0	0	11
TOTAL	22	22	1	0	0	45

44.3 Saturation values

The nouns with the highest saturation value in a network are *b'arg* 'eye' (50%) and *ce* 'name' (57%). The lowest saturation value (16%) is illustrated in the words *hi* 'water', *da'ahk* 'bone' and *tulg* 'stone'. None of the 10 nouns have 2nd order derivations. The mean saturation values vary from 16% to 57%.

Table 44.2: Saturation values per order of derivation, nouns.

Nouns		Saturation value (%)	1st order (%)	2nd order (%)	3rd order (%)	4th order (%)	5th order (%)
bone	da'ahk	16.67	16.67	0	0	0	0
eye	b'arg	50	50	0	0	0	0
tooth	c'erg	16.67	16.67	0	0	0	0
day	de	33.33	33.33	0	0	0	0
dog	zhala	33.33	33.33	0	0	0	0
louse	meza	33.33	33.33	0	0	0	0
fire	c'e	16.67	16.67	0	0	0	0
stone	t'ulg	16.67	16.67	0	0	0	0
water	hi	16.67	16.67	0	0	0	0
name	c'e	57.14	57.14	0	0	0	0

Among the verbs, the most saturated is *khiysa* 'throw' (46%). The lowest number of derivatives is shown by *latto* 'hold' (3%). Three verbs, *ahka* 'dig' (11%), *latto* 'hold' (3%) and *miyla* 'drink' (8%), exhibit only 1st order derivation. *Daga* 'burn' (16%) is the only verb that has a 3rd order.

Table 44.3: Saturation values per order of derivation, verbs.

Verbs		Saturation value (%)	1st order (%)	2nd order (%)	3rd order (%)	4th order (%)	5th order (%)
cut	hado	11.29	10.71	12.12	0	0	0
dig	ahka	17.74	39.29	0	0	0	0
pull	iyza	35.48	32.14	39.39	0	0	0
throw	khiysa	46.77	35.71	57.58	0	0	0
give	dala	11.29	14.29	9.09	0	0	0
hold	latto	3.23	7.14	0	0	0	0
sew	tega	24.19	32.14	18.18	0	0	0
burn	daga	16.13	21.43	9.09	100	0	0
drink	miyla	8.06	17.86	0	0	0	0
know	haa	24.19	17.86	30.3	0	0	0

Among the adjectives, the following have the highest number of derivatives: *niysa* 'right' (55%), *ia'rzha* 'black' (35%), *dutka* 'thin' (25%), *vokkha* 'old' (20%) and *von* 'bad' (11%). The lowest saturation value is 5%, demonstrated by *deha* 'long' and *mela* 'warm'. Three adjectives, *kerla* 'new', *gotta* 'narrow' and *stoma* 'thick', have a saturation value of 15%. Four adjectives have 2nd order derivations: *niysa* 'straight', *kerla* 'new', *dutka* 'thin' and *ia'rzha* 'black'.

Table 44.4: Saturation values per order of derivation, adjectives.

Adjectives		Saturation value (%)	1st order (%)	2nd order (%)	3rd order (%)	4th order (%)	5th order (%)
narrow	gotta	15	18.75	0	0	0	0
old	vokkha	20	25	0	0	0	0
straight	niysa	55	50	75	0	0	0

Table 44.4 (continued)

Adjectives		Saturation value (%)	1st order (%)	2nd order (%)	3rd order (%)	4th order (%)	5th order (%)
new	kerla	15	12.5	25	0	0	0
long	deha	5	6.25	0	0	0	0
warm	mela	5	6.25	0	0	0	0
thick	stomma	15	18.75	0	0	0	0
bad	von	10	12.5	0	0	0	0
thin	dutka	25	18.75	50	0	0	0
black	ia'rzha	35	31.25	50	0	0	0

Table 44.5: Average saturation values per order of derivation for all three word-classes.

	1st order	2nd order	3rd order	4th order	5th order
Nouns	25.7	0	0	0	0
Verbs	22.8	17.5	10	0	0
Adjectives	20	20	0	0	0

The most productive class of words turned out to be verbs; it has also more derivatives in the 1st order. In second place are adjectives, followed by nouns, which have few derivatives, more often zero nets.

44.4 Orders of derivation

Table 44.6: Maximum and average number of orders of derivation for all three word-classes.

	Maximum	Average
Nouns	1	0.2
Verbs	3	0.6
Adjectives	2	0.4

The verbs illustrate the most orders of derivation with three; the adjectives have two and nouns one. The latter have approximately identical indicators, but these concern only certain words, not the entire list of basic words.

44.5 Derivational capacity

Table 44.7: Maximum and average derivational capacity for all three word-classes.

	Maximum	Average
Nouns	4	1.8
Verbs	29	6.4
Adjectives	11	3.2

In a derivational network of verbs, there are more words (maximum 29) than for nouns and adjectives (maximum 4–11).

Table 44.8: Average number of derivatives per order of derivation for all three word-classes.

	1st order	2nd order	3rd order	4th order	5th order
Nouns	1.8	0	0	0	0
Verbs	6.4	5.8	0.1	0	0
Adjectives	3.2	0.8	0	0	0

In the 1st order, all classes of words have more derivatives than in the subsequent orders; the nouns on average have empty gaps starting from the 2nd order, and the adjectives from the 3rd order.

44.6 Correlation between semantic categories and orders of derivation

According to the results of the analysis of the nouns, the derivatives of the 1st order have the semantic category of QUALITY.

Among the verbs, the derivatives more often reflect PROCESS and ACTION. 4 verbs produce derivations of the semantic category REFLEXIVE. In the 1st order, 5 of the 10 verbs present the semantic category CAUSATIVE. 5 verbs out of the 10 derive the meaning PROCESS in the 1st order, and 4 of the 10 in the 2nd order. 8 of the 10 verbs have derivations within the category ACTION in the 1st order, and 7 of the 10 produce derivations with the category of CAUSATIVE. In the 2nd order, 5 verbs come under the category of PROCESS.

5 adjectives have the categories of QUALITY and STATE. In the 2nd order, 3 adjectives reveal a CAUSATIVE category. 3 adjectives out of the 10 derive ACTION and CAUSATIVE meanings. 5 adjectives out of the 10 have the categories of QUALITY and STATE in the 1st order.

In Chechen, there is no strict correlation between semantic categories and orders of derivation.

44.7 Semantic categories with blocking effects

Nouns of the 1st order are blocked by such semantic categories as MANNER, STATE and TEMPORAL. In the 1st order of the verbs, PROCESS hampers further derivations and, in the 2nd order, CAUSATIVE blocks further derivations. In the 1st order of the adjectives, STATE blocks further derivations, and in the 2nd order, they are blocked by CAUSATIVE and QUALITY.

44.8 Typical combinations of semantic categories

In Chechen, ACTION-CAUSATIVE (e.g. *chuahka* 'to dig' – *chuahkiyta* 'make sb. dig in') is a typical combination of semantic categories for verbs. For adjectives, there are 4 cases of QUALITY-STATE (e.g. *gottanig* 'narrow' – *gottalla* 'narrowness') and QUALITY-STATE (e.g. *stommanig* 'thick' – *stomalla* 'thickness').

44.9 Multiple occurrence of semantic categories

A review of the derivational chains shows multiple reoccurrences of the following semantic categories: ACTION-ACTION, especially concerning verbal nouns (e.g. *iyzo* 'pull' – *iyzor* 'stretching'), ACTION-CAUSATIVE ACTION (e.g. *chudala* 'give, bring, show (the document)' – *chudaliyta* 'make sb. give smth.'), QUALITY-QUALITY (e.g. *kerlanig* 'new' – *kerlahoyn* 'innovative'), and PATIENT-PATIENT (e.g. *vokhaha* – 'senior', *vokkhanig* 'elder').

44.10 Reasons for structurally poor derivational networks

The reason for poor derivational networks in a language may be an insufficiently developed lexicography, which is partly true of Chechen, or a difficult system of word-formation in a language, which is rather inclined to a composition that complicates the enrichment and replenishment of the language by new words. An important and key factor may also be the functioning and development of the language within bilingualism, which exerts a considerable impact on the use of a language and its potential, as well as on its incentives for preservation and survival. The Chechen language did not develop fully in this respect and was rather in a stiffened condition, and, at the same time, Russian was actively getting into the Chechen language and words were being borrowed in their initial form, without being modified and processed. In the severe conditions of there being a lack of any other language for the transfer of and obtaining information, people are forced to use the means of the language they possess and so raise the possibilities for the development and replenishment of a language by new words, and its requirement for communication, education and work moves the language forward. But in the case of the Chechen language, the situation is a bit different due to bilingualism.

44.11 Conclusions

According to the results of the analysis of the derivational networks of the nuclear words selected at the initial stage of the project in different languages, it is possible to draw some conclusions on derivational peculiarities in the Chechen language. Firstly, the theory about the tendency of the Chechen language to composition is confirmed, as it is one of the most productive and active ways of word-formation; affixal means are also involved in this process. Secondly, the derivational orders vary from one to three. Thirdly, the verbs have the highest number of steps and derivational chains, as well as a prevalence of prefixes, while the adjectives have fewer steps and fewer derivatives (a maximum of two), as do nouns, where only one order of derivation is traced.

References

Aliroev I.Yu. 2005. Samouchitel' chechenskogo yazika /RAN. In-t yazikoznaniya. Izd.2-e. – M.: Academia, 184.
Chokaev K.Z. 2010. Morfologiya chechenskogo yazika. – Grozniy: Izd-vo ANCHR, 384.
Halidov, A.I. 2013. *Grammatika chechenskogo yazika. Tom 1. Vvedenie v grammatiku. Fonetika. Morfemika. Slovoobrazovanie.* Grozniy: Groznenskiy rabochiy.
Ismailov A.T. 2009. Dosh-Slovo. *Razmishleniya o rodnom yazike.* Elista: ZAOp 'NPP Dzhangar'.
Matsiyev A.G. 1961. *Chechen-Russian Dictionary.* Moskva: Gosudarstvennoe izdatelstvo inostrannih i nacionalnih slovarey.
Matsiyev A.G. 2010. *Chechen-Russian Dictionary.* Grozniy: FGUP IPK Groznenskiy rabochiy.
Vagapov A. 2009. Million slov chechenskok yazika.

Nina Sumbatova
45 Derivational networks in Dargwa

45.1 General notes

Dargwa is a language of the Nakh-Daghestanian (East Caucasian) language family spoken in the Republic of Daghestan (Russian Federation). The total number of speakers is more than half a million, but the language consists of several very different dialects, most of which are not mutually understandable. Dargwa has a standard variant that was created in the 1920s, but this variant is mainly used in education and several mass media platforms, not for oral communication. This paper is based on data for the dialect of Tanti, which is close to the Tsudakhar dialect (Sumbatova and Lander 2014). The data were collected in the course of fieldwork in the village of Tanti in 2016–2017.[1]

Like other languages of the East Caucasian family, Dargwa is a morphologically ergative, left-branching language with very rich, mainly agglutinative inflectional morphology. It has complex nominal systems with especially numerous forms with locative semantics as well as branched verbal systems with many TAM-paradigms and different non-finite forms, including participles, converbs, infinitives and deverbal nouns.

Dargwa makes extensive use of affixation, but in most cases this affixation is traditionally treated as inflection. In fact, there is no clear borderline between inflection and derivation: in most cases, the authors just follow tradition, which is, in turn, based to a remarkable degree on the traditions of Russian grammar (for word-formation in Dargwa, see Sumbatova 2016). I shall also adhere to the descriptive tradition as presented, for example, in the basic grammar of Dargwa (Abdullaev 1954) and some other descriptive works (Xajdakov 1985; Musaev 1999, 2002; van den Berg 2001, etc.). These works deal mainly with Standard Dargwa, but as the system of Tanti is similar to the standard language, the decisions relevant for Standard Dargwa are perfectly applicable to the data for the dialect. Some of the decisions are listed below.

Dargwa (including Tanti) has a number of derivational markers whose only function is to change the lexical class (part of speech) of a certain unit. Some of

---

[1] I express my sincerest gratitude to my consultant Magomed Mamaev and his family.

Note: This research was supported by RSF grant no. 17-18-01184.

these affixes are universal in the sense that they can modify words of different lexical classes. In Tanti, the most widely used transcategorial affixes are -*dix:* (derives abstract nouns from words of different lexical classes, example (1)) and -*se* (derives adjectives, example (2)).

(1) ʁ˳*abza* 'hero' > ʁ˳*abza-dix*[2] 'heroism', *razi* 'glad' > *razi-dix* 'gladness', *w.ams:ur* '(he is) tired' (finite verbal form) > *w.ams:ur-dix*[3] 'being tired', *čet:i.b* 'above' > *čet:i.b-dix* 'being above, victory' (Sumbatova 2013: 150)

(2) *q:uʁa* > *q:uʁa-se* 'beautiful', *hišt:u.b* 'here' > *hišt:u.b-se* '(the one) located here' (Sumbatova 2013: 151)

The suffix -*le* derives adverbs from adjectival stems:

(3) *ʔaˤχ-le* 'well', *q:alaba-le* 'fast', *q:ijan-ne* 'difficult (ADV)' (*n* + -*le* > *nne*), *ʔaˤʔni-le* 'necessarily'

In the derivational networks, the transcategorial affixes are taken into account, with the exception of the most occasional and marginal derivations (example (5)).

The main problem with the nominal paradigms is that some forms that are traditionally treated as usual case forms (the genitive, comitative and locative forms) show properties of derivations. In particular, these forms can be the bases of certain derivations, and attach the derivational affix -*se* to form adjectives:

(4) ʕúˤli 'eye'
genitive -*la*: ʕúˤl-la > ʕúˤl-la-se 'belonging to the eye' (adjective)
inessive -*c:e.b*: ʕúˤl-li-c:e.b[4] 'in the eye' > ʕúˤl-li-c:e.b-se 'situated in the eye'
superessive -*ja.b*: ʕúˤl-li-ja.b 'on the eye' > ʕúˤl-li-ja.b-se 'situated on the eye'
subessive -*gu.b*: ʕúˤl-li-gu.b 'under the eye' > ʕúˤl-li-gu.b-se 'situated under the eye'

In principle, the operations of attaching a case marker and the attributive marker -*se* are, to a certain degree, recursive:

---

[2] The suffix -*dix:* is realized as -*dix* at the end of a word.
[3] Here and below: a point separates a gender marker from the rest of the word form.
[4] -*li* is the oblique stem marker.

(5) ʕúʕli 'eye':
ʕúʕl-li-gu.b 'under the eye' (subessive) >
ʕúʕl-li-gu.b-se 'situated under the eye' (adjective derived from the subessive form) >
ʕúʕl-li-gu.b-se-ja.b 'on the one situated under the eye' (superessive of the adjective derived from the subessive)) >
ʕúʕl-li-gu.b-se-ja.b-se 'situated on the one that is situated on the eye' (adjective derived from the superessive form of the adjective derived from the subessive), etc.

In this chapter, we do not regard case forms as derivational markers and do not include operations like those illustrated in (5) in the derivational framework – first, because we decided to follow the tradition and, second, because most such forms, though being easily derived, remain occasional.

In the verbal domain, the problem of demarcation between inflection and derivation is even more complicated. In this paper, we treated all participles, converbs and infinitives as parts of verbal paradigms. Note that we treated masdars (with the suffix -ni) as a verbal form, since they are productively and uniformly derived from all verbal stems and do not show any essential variation in meaning:

(6) b.ut'-/b.urt'-[5] PF/IPF 'cut' (infinitives but'-iž/burt'-iž) > b.ut'-ni/b.urt'-ni 'cutting'
b.aχ-/b.alχ PF/IPF (infinitives baxiž/balxiž) > b.aχ-ni/b.alχ-ni 'learning'/ 'knowing'

Two types of deverbal nouns were included in the derivational networks. These are the deverbal nouns with the suffix -ala (they are not absolutely productive and their meaning is not absolutely standard) and the deverbal nouns with the transcategorial suffix -dix:, because this suffix cannot be viewed as a marker of a verbal category.

One more problem relates to the analogous derivations from different verbal stems. Almost all verbs in Dargwa have two roots: perfective and imperfective (cf. b.aχ- 'learn', b.alχ- 'know'), each of which forms several stems that are further used as bases for inflectional forms. In many cases, the two roots (or two or more verbal stems) are also used to form different derivations, which retain the semantic opposition of the two stems:

---

5 The slash separates the perfective and imperfective root.

(7) b.urqːiž 'dig out' (PF) / uqːiž 'dig' (IPF)
b.urqːiž > b.urqː-ub-dix: 'the fact that something has been dug out'
uqː-iž > uqː-u-dix: 'the process of digging'

(8) b.uciž 'catch' (PF) / b.urciž 'hold' (IPF)
b.uciž > gu-b.uciž 'put someting under something (once)' (PF)
b.urciž > gu-b.urciž 'put something under something (several times or constantly)' (IPF)

In the derivational networks, I counted two derivations that differ only in the aspect of the initial forms as one unit.

Dargwa has very few non-derived (simple) verbs (200–250 per dialect). Most verbs are derived from simple verbs by prefixation and/or composition. The prefixal verbs are taken into account in the derivational networks, with the exception of some verbs with highly idiomatic meaning.

45.2 Maximum derivational networks

With its rich inflection, productive patterns of class-to-class transitions, and common composition, Dargwa is not very rich in 'standard', 'European-type' derivation patterns. In most cases, it shows only 1st order derivations. Transcategorial affixes can be applied recursively, but in most cases their recursive use results in highly marginal forms (cf. above). That is why the derivational networks look very simple when compared with many Indo-European languages.

The calculations of the maximum derivational networks for all semantic categories are shown in Table 45.1.

Table 45.1: Maximum derivational networks per order of derivation for all three word-classes.

	1st order	2nd order	3rd order	4th order	5th order	Σ
Nouns	3	0	0	0	0	3
Verbs	5	14	0	0	0	5
Adjectives	4	0	0	0	0	4
TOTAL	12	14	0	0	0	12

45.3 Saturation values

Taking into account the small number of derivatives of the 2nd order and their total absence in the 3rd and further orders, we can state that the notion of saturation value is not as helpful for Dargwa as for Indo-European type languages (Tables 45.2–45.4).

Table 45.2: Saturation values per order of derivation, nouns.

Nouns		Saturation value (%)	1st order (%)	2nd order (%)	3rd order (%)	4th order (%)	5th order (%)
bone	lík:a	25	25	0	0	0	0
eye	ʕúʕli	50	50	0	0	0	0
tooth	cúla	50	50	0	0	0	0
day	béri	25	25	0	0	0	0
dog	x̣:₀eʕ	25	25	0	0	0	0
louse	nez	50	50	0	0	0	0
fire	c'a	0	0	0	0	0	0
stone	q:árq:a	25	25	0	0	0	0
water	šin	75	75	0	0	0	0
name	zu	25	25	0	0	0	0

Table 45.3: Saturation values per order of derivation, verbs.

Verbs		Saturation value (%)	1st order (%)	2nd order (%)	3rd order (%)	4th order (%)	5th order (%)
cut	b.alʙiž/b.ulʙiž	15.38	24	0	0	0	0
dig	b.urq:iž/uq:iž	38.46	40	35.71	0	0	0
pull	b.iʔiž/b.ilʔiž	12.82	20	0	0	0	0
throw	ix̣₀iž/irx̣₀iž	53.85	48	64.29	0	0	0
give	b.ič:iž/luč:iž	33.33	32	35.71	0	0	0
hold	b.uciž/b.urciž	79.49	68	100	0	0	0

Table 45.3 (continued)

Verbs		Saturation value (%)	1st order (%)	2nd order (%)	3rd order (%)	4th order (%)	5th order (%)
sew	b.arχiž/b.urχiž	46.15	48	42.86	0	0	0
burn	b.ič:iž/ič:iž	12.82	16	7.14	0	0	0
drink	d.erč:iž/ d.uč:iž	17.95	28	0	0	0	0
know	b.aχiž/b.alχiž	12.82	20	0	0	0	0

The verbs are cited in the infinitive; the two aspectual forms (perfective/imperfective) are given here.

Table 45.4: Saturation values per order of derivation, adjectives.

Adjectives		Saturation value (%)	1st order (%)	2nd order (%)	3rd order (%)	4th order (%)	5th order (%)
narrow	ʁ̥aˤrc'-	50	50	0	0	0	0
old	b.urq'-	100	100	0	0	0	0
straight	b.arx-	50	50	0	0	0	0
new	s:ák:a-	50	50	0	0	0	0
long	b.uqén-	75	75	0	0	0	0
warm	waná-	50	50	0	0	0	0
thick	b.abc-	75	75	0	0	0	0
bad	waˤ-	50	50	0	0	0	0
thin	b.uk'úl-	50	50	0	0	0	0
black	c'ut:aˤrá-	50	50	0	0	0	0

The average saturation values for each word-class are given in Table 45.5.

Table 45.5: Average saturation values per order of derivation for all three word-classes.

	1st order	2nd order	3rd order	4th order	5th order
Nouns	35.00	0	0	0	0
Verbs	34.40	32.31	28.57	0	0
Adjectives	60.00	0	0	0	0

45.4 Orders of derivation

With the exception of transcategorial suffixes and several verbal derivations, Dargwa confines itself to 1st order derivations. The maximum number of orders is two. In Table 45.6, we can see that the average number of orders of derivation for the nouns and adjectives is one or even less, while the average number for the verbs is 1.6.

Table 45.6: Maximum and average number of orders of derivation for all three word-classes.

	Maximum	Average
Nouns	1	0.9
Verbs	2	1.6
Adjectives	1	1

45.5 Derivational capacity

The maximum derivational capacity (the number of direct derivatives for each word) is 17. The average capacities are 2.4 for adjectives, 1.4 for nouns, and 8.6 for verbs (see Tables 45.7 and 45.8).

The adjectives and nouns do not show any derivations of the 2nd and further orders, while the verbs have no derivations of any order other than the 1st and the 2nd.

Table 45.7: Maximum and average derivational capacity for all three word-classes.

	Maximum	Average
Nouns	3	1.4
Verbs	17	8.6
Adjectives	4	2.4

Table 45.8: Average number of derivatives per order of derivation for all three word-classes.

	1st order	2nd order	3rd order	4th order	5th order
Nouns	1.4	0	0	0	0
Verbs	8.6	4.0	0	0	0
Adjectives	2.4	0	0	0	0

45.6 Correlation between semantic categories and orders of derivation

For the adjectives, the most characteristic derivations of the 1st order are nouns and adverbs denoting STATE and MANNER: they are derived from all 10 adjectives from the sample:

(9) s:ák:a(-se) 'new' > s:ák:a-dix 'novelty'
             > s:ák:a-le 'in a new way'

The most typical derivatives of the nouns are adjectives with the ORNATIVE (8 derivations) or AUGMENTATIVE meaning (derived from the plural form, 3 derivations):

(10) ʕúʕli 'eye' / ʕuʕl-be PL 'eyes' > ʕuʕl-b-ar 'having big eyes'
      zu 'name' / zu-me PL 'names' > zu-m-ar 'having many names'

Most verbs derive DIRECTIONAL forms marked with verbal prefixes (6 verbs in our sample), CAUSATIVE verbs with the suffix -aq (all 10 verbs in the sample), deverbal nouns with the suffix -ala denoting the AGENT, PATIENT or RESULT of an

ACTION (all 10 verbs in the sample) or deverbal nouns with the universal suffix -*dix:* denoting STATE (6 verbs).

The 2nd order is only attested in the verbal system: these are the CAUSATIVE verbs derived from simple verbs with prefixes, cf. example (11).

(11) *b.uciž* 'catch' (PF) > *gu-b.uciž* 'put someting under something (once)' > *gu-b.uc-aq-iž* 'make somebody put something under something (once)'

45.7 Semantic categories with blocking effects

The verbs allow only two prefixes: any second prefix blocks further prefixation irrespective of its meaning. For the nouns and adjectives, there are no principal blocks for the class-to-class transitions (cf. example (5)). But, as mentioned before, the resulting forms are usually marginal.

45.8 Typical combinations of semantic categories

The most typical combinations for the verbs are presented by the deverbal nouns expressing the meanings of AGENT-PATIENT (5 verbs) or PATIENT-RESULTATIVE (2 verbs):

(12) *ix(ₒ)-* PF (infinitive *išiž*) 'throw' > *ixₒ-ala* 'the one who has thrown' and 'something that has been thrown'
b.ik:(ₒ)- PF (infinitive *b-ič:iž*)   > *b.ikₒ-ala* 'something that has burnt' and 'burn (noun)'

45.9 Multiple occurrence of semantic categories

As mentioned in section 45.4, recursiveness is characteristic of nominal derivations to a certain degree. Most oblique case forms (genitive, comitative, locative cases) can be the base of productive attributive derivations with the suffix -*se*. The resulting forms can be used as both attributes and nouns. In the latter function, they can again attach all necessary case markers. The derived case forms may again be the base of the same productive derivation (cf. example (5) above).

45.10 Reversibility of semantic categories

In the data used for this study, there were no cases of semantic categories occurring in a reversed order.

45.11 Reasons for structurally poor derivational networks

The derivational possibilities in Dargwa seem poor from the point of view of the present research frame. However, this is not the case: derivation in Dargwa is just very different from the European-type patterns. The absence of such patterns is well compensated for in several domains of the grammar:
(1) Dargwa shows extremely rich inflection, which covers certain meanings that in European languages are covered by derivations: for example, any argument of a predicate can be encoded by a participle.
(2) Dargwa has productive derivation patterns, which can easily produce many occasional words with the necessary semantics, but are not counted in the derivational networks.
(3) Dargwa makes extensive use of word-formation devices other than affixation: first of all, composition, but to a certain degree also conversion.

45.12 Conclusions

As mentioned above, the morphological richness of Dargwa is not seen in the methodology of derivational networks. However, the verbs, which show the most complex and branched morphology, also show the richest derivational potential. Many of them have more than ten 1st order derivations and some derivations of the 2nd order. The adjectives and nouns – taking into account the terms and conditions of the suggested framework – do not show any non-direct derivations.

References

Abdullaev, Sajgid N. 1954. *Grammatika darginskogo jazyka (fonetika i morfologija)*. Maxačkala: Daggiz.

Musaev, Magomed-Said M. 1999. Darginskij jazyk. *Jazyki mira. Kavkazskie jazyki*, 357–369. Moskva: Academia.
Musaev, Magomed-Said M. 2002. *Darginskij jazyk*. Moskva: Academia.
Sumbatova, Nina. 2013. *Problema chastej rechi v darginskom jazyke* [The problem of parts of speech in Dargwa]. Moscow: Thesaurus.
Sumbatova, Nina. 2016. Dargwa. In Peter O. Müller, Ingeborg Ohnheiser, Susan Olsen & Franz Rainer (eds.), *Word-Formation. An International Handbook of the Languages of Europe, Vol. 5*, 3638–3658. Berlin & Boston: Mouton de Gruyter.
Sumbatova, Nina & Yuri Lander. 2014. *Darginskij govor selenija Tanti. Grammaticheskij ocherk. Voprosy sintaksisa*. Moscow: Jazyki russkoI kul'tury.
Van den Berg, Helma. 2001. *Dargi Folktales. Oral Stories from the Caucasus and an Introduction to Dargi Grammar*. Leiden: CNWS.
Xajdakov, Said M. 1985. *Darginskij i megebskij jazyki*. Moskva: Nauka.

Xabier Artiagoitia
46 Derivational networks in Basque

46.1 General notes

Compounding and derivation are the usual word-formation strategies in Basque, but the Basque lexicon has historically relied a great deal on borrowing (from neighbouring Romance languages, and directly from Latin in earlier times); as of today, neoclassical formations in Basque usually take the same form as in Spanish. Derivation in Basque is done mainly by suffixes (Artiagoitia, Hualde and Ortiz de Urbina 2016) and hardly ever by prefixes, which are just a few, either borrowed from Romance (e.g. *des-*; *eman* 'give' > *deseman* 'undo, cancel') or calqued from it (e.g. *ezagun*$_A$ 'known' > *ezezagun*$_A$ 'unknown'; *ez* 'not'); the prefix *ber-* (variant *bir-*) 're-' might be the only autochthonous one (de Rijk 2008: 891), e.g. *eman* 'give' > *berreman* 'give again'. It is also the case that all verb formation or derivation is done through conversion, a process that is highly productive for nouns, adjectives, and nouns bearing the allative adposition; cf. *ur*$_N$ 'water' > *urtu*$_V$ 'to melt', *mehe*$_A$ 'thin' > *mehetu*$_V$ 'to get thin/make something thin', *begietara*$_{PP}$ 'to the eyes' > *begietaratu*$_V$ 'to come/bring to the eyes'; *-tu* is the participial ending and also the citation form for verbs. Furthermore, conversion may affect comparative adjectives (i.e. it is possible after inflection) or quantifiers, e.g. from *mehe*$_A$ 'thin', *meheago*$_A$ 'thinner' > *meheagotu*$_V$ 'to become thinner/make something thinner'; from *gutxi*$_Q$ 'little' > *gutxitu*$_V$ 'to diminish'; or from the comparative *gutxiago*$_Q$ 'less' > *gutxiagotu*$_V$ 'to become less, lessen'.

Another factor that may be relevant for our research is the separation between compounding and derivation: in the Basque grammatical tradition, the usual decisive criterion for discriminating between a suffix and a word is whether the second member of a compound can stand independently as a word. This sweeps away some potential suffixes which are words in present Basque, even though their meaning as independent words has little to do with their use as bound morphemes, e.g. *muga*$_N$ 'border', *zain*$_{N/ADV}$ 'guard' and 'waiting', *mugazain*$_N$ 'border guard'; *zain* is hardly ever used to mean 'guard' in present Basque. Consequently, I have not considered suffixes second members of compounds that exist as independent words in the dictionary of the Basque Academy (Euskaltzaindia 2016), with the exception of *-tasun* '-ness' (e.g. *zuzen*$_A$ 'straight' > *zuzentasun*$_N$ 'straightness, justice'), a well-known suffix that was promoted as an independent word in the 20th century with the meaning 'feature', and *-tegi* (e.g. *su*$_N$ 'fire' > *sutegi*$_N$ 'forge, fireplace'), the meaning of which as a free word ('barn, storage room') is dialectally reduced. Conversely, suffixes that were independent words at some stage in the language but do not exist as such have been included, even though the Basque Academy still regards words containing them as compounds (Euskaltzaindia 1994); examples include -*dun* (e.g. *hezur*$_N$ 'bone' > *hezurdun*$_A$ 'vertebrate'), -*gin* (e.g. *harri*$_N$ 'stone' > *hargin*$_N$ 'stonemason'), or -*gile* (e.g. *su*$_N$ 'fire' > *sugile*$_N$ 'firemaker'). The result of these considerations is that, out of the 72 derivational suffixes listed by Villasante (1974: 160), 18 have been eliminated in this project; most of these are what de Rijk (2008) calls parasuffixes.

I have drawn the examples for this study from Sarasola's (2007) *Basque Dictionary*, which is itself the basis for the Basque Academy's dictionary (Euskaltzaindia 2016), and from Sarasola's ongoing dictionary, based on a 21st-century corpus (Contemporary Reference Prose). All examples are attested words, not possible words.[1]

46.2 Maximum derivational networks

Remarkably, Basque never gets beyond the 3rd order of derivation, or even the 2nd order in the case of verbs. Derivational networks only seem to be strong for the 1st order.

Table 46.1: Maximum derivational networks per order of derivation for all three word-classes.

	1st order	2nd order	3rd order	Σ
Nouns	36	18	2	56
Verbs	36	12	0	48
Adjectives	30	5	5	40
TOTAL	102	35	7	144

---

[1] I have avoided using the *Basque General Dictionary* (Mitxelena and Sarasola 1987–2011) because it provides the history of every single written Basque word, regardless of whether it has been used in the literature or whether it is the sole creation of a dictionary writer. Sarasola's (2007) dictionary, on the other hand, is based on words actually used by writers of all times and, thus, I find it a more reliable source.

Adjectives have the lowest number of derivatives, yet they are balanced between 2nd and 3rd order derivatives; however, all the 3rd order derivatives correspond to *berri* 'new'.

46.3 Saturation values

The mean saturation values for nouns range between 30% and 7%, as displayed in Table 46.2. The noun with the lowest saturation value is *zorri* 'louse', which also happens to be one of the three nouns with no 2nd order, together with *hezur* 'bone' and *txakur* 'dog'. The noun with the highest saturation value is *begi* 'eye'; this and *ur* 'water' (25%) are the only ones that get to the 3rd order.

Table 46.2: Saturation values per order of derivation, nouns.

Nouns		Saturation value (%)	1st order (%)	2nd order (%)	3rd order (%)
bone	hezur	17.86	27.78	0	0
eye	begi	30.36	27.78	33.33	50
tooth	hortz	21.43	22.22	22.22	0
day	egun	16.07	16.67	16.67	0
dog	txakur	16.07	25	0	0
louse	zorri	7.14	11.11	0	0
fire	su	17.86	22.22	11.11	0
stone	harri	28.57	33.33	22.22	0
water	ur	25	19.44	33.33	50
name	izen	17.86	13.89	27.78	0

With respect to verbs, no verb reaches the 3rd order of derivation, and three verbs fail to reach the 2nd order. The highest and lowest mean saturation values oscillate between 39% for *jakin* 'know' and 8% for *induskatu* 'dig'; the former has the highest values in the 1st and 2nd orders.

As regards the adjectives in Table 46.4, just four get to the 2nd order of derivation and only *berri* 'new' reaches the 3rd order; this is also the adjective with

Table 46.3: Saturation values per order of derivation, verbs.

Verbs		Saturation value (%)	1st order (%)	2nd order (%)
cut	ebaki	16.67	22.22	0
dig	induskatu	8.33	11.11	0
pull	erakarri	20.83	22.22	16.67
throw	bota	10.42	13.89	0
give	eman	22.92	27.78	8.33
hold	eutsi	20.83	22.22	16.67
sew	josi	16.67	13.89	25
burn	erre	20.83	22.22	16.67
drink	edan	35.42	33.33	41.67
know	jakin	39.58	36.11	50

Table 46.4: Saturation values per order of derivation, adjectives.

Adjectives		Saturation value (%)	1st order (%)	2nd order (%)	3rd order (%)
narrow	estu	15	20	0	0
old	zahar	27.5	36.67	0	0
straight	zuzen	22.5	26.67	20	0
new	berri	45	33.33	60	100
long	luze	32.5	36.67	40	0
warm	epel	12.5	13.33	20	0
thick	lodi	12.5	16.67	0	0
bad	txar	10	13.33	0	0
thin	mehe	12.5	16.67	0	0
black	beltz	17.5	23.33	0	0

the highest mean saturation value, viz. 45%; the lowest value of 10% is demonstrated by *txar* 'bad'.

Table 46.5 summarizes the average saturation values for the three categories. The average saturation values are very similar in the 1st order of derivation, and

Table 46.5: Average saturation values per order of derivation for all three word-classes.

	1st order	2nd order	3rd order
Nouns	21.94	16.66	10
Verbs	22.50	17.5	0
Adjectives	23.66	14	10

the same is true of the 2nd order. For the 3rd order, the average saturation values are identical for nouns and adjectives.

The conclusion that one draws upon looking into derivational networks in Basque is that derivational networks are not very strong cross-categorially in the language and, furthermore, that they behave in a balanced way in all three categories.

46.4 Orders of derivation

As for the average and maximum orders of derivation in the Basque data, the calculations are shown in Table 46.6. The results are in line with our comments on previous tables regarding the poverty of derivational networks in Basque.

Table 46.6: Maximum and average number of orders of derivation for all three word-classes.

	Maximum	Average
Nouns	3	1.9
Verbs	2	1.6
Adjectives	3	1.5

46.5 Derivational capacity

The maximum and average values for the three categories are relatively balanced, which reinforces the conclusion in section 46.3 regarding maximum derivational networks.

Table 46.7: Maximum and average derivational capacity for all three word-classes.

	Maximum	Average
Nouns	12	7.9
Verbs	13	8.1
Adjectives	11	7.1

As Table 46.8 shows, nouns have a higher level of derivatives compared to verbs and adjectives in the 2nd order, although the number is relatively low in any case. The categories seem to converge again for the 3rd order of derivation. The lower value of adjectival derivatives for the 2nd order might be due to the existence of alternative (and very productive) processes for adjective formation such as affective palatalization (e.g. zuzen$_A$ 'straight' > xuxen$_A$ 'rather straight') and reduplication (e.g. zuzen-zuzen$_A$ 'very straight').

Table 46.8: Average number of derivatives per order of derivation for all three word-classes.

	1st order	2nd order	3rd order
Nouns	7.9	3	0.2
Verbs	8.1	2.1	0
Adjectives	7.1	0.7	0.5

46.6 Correlation between semantic categories and orders of derivation

With respect to nouns, QUALITY (value 8) is the most characteristic semantic category in the 1st order, followed by COLLECTIVE and LOCATIVE (both value 6). In the 2nd order, AGENT (value 4) is most characteristic. In the case of QUALITY, the existence of two synonymous suffixes like -tsu and -dun is probably a helping factor, e.g. hezur$_N$ 'bone' > hezurdun$_A$ 'vertebrate', hezurtsu$_A$ 'bony'.

When it comes to verbs' derivational networks, AGENT (value 9) and ACTION (value 8) are the most salient semantic categories in the 1st order, followed by

ABILITY and RELATIONAL (value 6 for both categories) and RESULTATIVE (value 5). In the 2nd order, STATE (value 5) is by far the most characteristic semantic category. The fact that most verbs are action verbs and the existence of two synonymous suffixes (which usually alternate depending on the morphonemics of the verb) help explain the high value of AGENT, e.g. *edan*$_V$ 'drink' > *edale*$_{N/A}$ 'drinker', *erre*$_V$ 'burn, smoke' > *erretzaile*$_{N/A}$ 'smoker'. The category STATE has a value of 6 thanks to the suffix -*tasun*, which attaches to any (deverbal) adjective, e.g. *edan*$_V$ 'drink' > *edangarri*$_A$ 'drinkable' > *edangarritasun*$_N$ 'drinkability, state of being drinkable'.

Regarding adjectives, STATE (value 10) is the most characteristic semantic category in the 1st order, followed by DIMINUTIVE, MANNER and PEJORATIVE (all value 6). This has to do with the fact that the suffix -*tasun* 'ness' (e.g. *zahar*$_A$ 'old' > *zahartasun*$_N$ 'oldness') is again productive for virtually all adjectives; similar considerations apply to the suffixes -*txo* (*zahar*$_A$ 'old' > *zahartxo*$_A$ 'rather old'), -*ki* (*zuzen*$_A$ 'straight' *zuzenki*$_{ADV}$ 'straightly') and -*keria* (*zahar*$_A$ 'old' > *zaharkeria*$_N$ 'a despicable old thing'). No clear correlations can be established in the 2nd and 3rd orders.

46.7 Semantic categories with blocking effects

It is difficult to determine any blocking effect for specific semantic categories given that Basque derivational networks hardly ever reach the 3rd order. For adjectives, the categories AUGMENTATIVE, DIMINUTIVE, PEJORATIVE and STATE in the 1st order block further derivation. A similar claim can be made for the same categories with respect to nouns, with the addition of the category ACTION. In the case of verbs, the category ACTION also blocks further derivations, unlike most of the other semantic categories involved.

46.8 Typical combinations of semantic categories

Basque derivational networks are relatively short and, furthermore, one can hardly establish any typical combination of semantic categories; combinations never happen more than three times (e.g. CAUSATIVE + ABILITY/ACTION/AGENT, ABILITY + STATE, RELATIONAL + STATE, and MANNER + MANNER).

46.9 Multiple occurrence of semantic categories

There are three cases of MANNER occurring twice in a single derivational chain due to the possibility for the adverbial suffixes -*ki* and -*ro* to combine with one another, two of which are *epel*$_A$ 'warm' > *epelki*$_{ADV}$ 'warmly' > *epelkiro*$_{ADV}$ 'warmly' and *zuzen*$_A$ 'straight' > *zuzenki*$_{ADV}$ 'straightly' > *zuzenkiro*$_{ADV}$ 'straightly'. In the case of *berri*$_A$ 'new' > *berriro*$_{ADV}$ 'newly, again' > *berriroki*$_{ADV}$ 'newly, again', the order of the MANNER suffixes is reversed.

46.10 Reversibility of semantic categories

There are no instances of a reversed order of semantic categories, given that Basque networks only get to 3rd order derivations in a very limited number of cases.

46.11 Reasons for structurally poor derivational networks

As explained in the first section, the poverty of Basque derivational networks is partly accounted for by the high productivity of X > V conversion processes. The existence of alternative ways aside from derivational morphemes proper, such as affective palatalization, reduplication, or even compounding, to form nouns and adjectives may help explain the relative poorness of Basque derivational networks. Allowing conversion and affective palatalization into the calculation of derivational networks would have undoubtedly produced a higher number of 2nd and 3rd order derivatives, especially for nouns and adjectives.

46.12 Conclusions

Judging from the sample words used in this study, Basque appears to have a limited strength in producing derivational networks beyond the 2nd order (Table 46.1). This tendency is consistent for the three classes of words with respect to 1st order derivations (similar average saturation values and maximum and average derivational capacities, as shown in Table 46.7).

As can be seen in Table 46.1, nouns exhibit the highest derivational network (56), with the highest number in the 1st (tied with verbs) and 2nd orders, but they are outscored by adjectives in the 3rd order. The maximum derivational network for verbs is smaller (48) with no 3rd order derivatives, and adjectives come last (40 derivatives), yet they have the highest number of 3rd order derivatives. The overall saturation values (Table 46.5) for the three categories are in any case similar for the 1st and 2nd order of derivations; these range from 22% to 23% in the 1st order and from 14% to 16 in the 2nd order. My impression is that reduplication and affective palatalization is most productive with adjectives, which would compensate for their relatively low derivational capacity.

As a closing remark, Basque derivations cover 30 of the 49 semantic categories provided for this research. In principle, this fact suggests that Basque must resort to other means, whether phonological, morphological or syntactic, to convey the remaining semantic categories. The derivational capacity of the Basque language, however, appears to be quite robust and balanced in the three categories considered, given the number of categories represented in the sample, yet this robustness does not result in the formation of derivational networks beyond the 3rd order.

References

Artiagoitia, Xabier, José Ignacio Hualde & Jon Ortiz de Urbina. 2016. Basque. In Peter O. Müller, Ingeborg Ohnheiser, Susan Olsen & Franz Rainer (eds.), *Word-Formation. An International Handbook of the Languages of Europe*, Vol. 5, 3327–3348. Berlin: Mouton de Gruyter.
De Rijk, Rudolf P. G. 2008. *Standard Basque: A Progressive Grammar*. Boston: MIT Press.
Euskaltzaindia [Basque Academy]. 1994. Hitz elkarketa /4. *Hitz elkartuen osaera eta idazkera* [Compounding /4. The composition and writing of compound words]. Bilbao: Euskaltzaindia.
Euskaltzaindia [Basque Academy]. 2016. *Euskaltzaindiaren Hiztegia* [The Dictionary of the Basque Academy]. Bilbao: Euskaltzaindia.
Mitxelena, Luis & Ibon Sarasola. 1987–2011. *Diccionario General Vasco – Orotariko Euskal Hiztegia*, 2nd edn. Bilbao: Euskaltzaindia/Desclée de Brouwer.
Villasante, Luis. 1974. *Palabras vascas compuestas y derivadas*. Oñate: Editorial Franciscana de Aránzazu.

Sources

EH = Sarasola, Ibon. 2007. *Euskal Hiztegia* [Basque Dictionary]. San Sebastian: Elkar.
EEH = Sarasola, Ibon. 2018. *Egungo Euskararen Hiztegia* [The Dictionary of Contemporary Basque]. http://www.ehu.eus/eeh/.
EPG = Sarasola, Ibon, Pello Salaburu & Josu Landa. 2009. *Ereduzko Prosa Gaur* [Contemporary Reference Prose] https://www.ehu.eus/euskara-orria/euskara/ereduzkoa/.
Euskaltzaindia. 2016. *Euskaltzaindiaren Hiztegia* [The Dictionary of the Basque Academy]. http://www.euskaltzaindia.eus.

Manana Topadze Gäumann
47 Derivational networks in Georgian

47.1 General notes

Georgian belongs to the Kartvelian (South Caucasian) language family; it is an agglutinative language, and displays some inflectional features. Word-formation in Georgian is very productive. The most widespread devices of word-formation are affixation (prefixation, suffixation, circumfixation), composition and reduplication (Boeder 2005; Gogolashvili 2011; Harris 2002; Heinze 2008).

A wide range of derivational affixes are polysemous, i.e. different semantic categories can derive from one and the same affix: e.g. derivates with the suffix *-ian* can express the category of QUALITY or POSSESSION – *kud-i* 'hat' > *kud-ian-i* 'wearing a hat', *k'lde* 'rock' > *k'ld-ian-i* 'rocky'.

In reverse, different affixes can correspond to the same semantic category: e.g. words related to the semantic category of POSSESSION can derive from both the suffixes *-ian* and *-osan*: *c'ver-i* 'beard' > *c'ver-osan-i* / *c'ver-ian-i* 'bearded'.

Next to simple, monosyllabic prefixes and suffixes, there are a considerable number of compound affixes containing two or more fossilized morphemes, whose origin is not always transparent (Gogolashvili 2011: 214). For example, *-osan*, which has been grammaticalized as one suffix, consists of two formants: *-os* and *-an*. In the Georgian data set, compound affixes containing fossilized elements have been considered as simple ones.

In some circumstances, inflectional affixes may have derivational functions. This is the case with the genitive, instrumental and adverbial case markers *-is*, *-it* and *-ad*, which can be employed as derivational affixes (Gogolashvili 2011: 238), e.g. *uarq'opa* 'negation' > *uarq'op-it-i* 'negative', *aaleba* 'to inflame' > *aaleb-ad-i* 'inflammable'.

The suffixes *-it* and *-ad* in the cited examples clearly have a derivational value and can be regarded as polysemous morphemes. Therefore, instances of the above-mentioned type have been included in the present data set.

The data for the compiled derivational network have been extracted from the Georgian National Corpus (GNC, contains ca. 200 Mio tokens in Modern Georgian). Each item has been additionally verified in the *Explanatory Dictionary of the Georgian Language* (Arabuli 2008; Chikobava 1950–1964), which contains 129,755 entries.

Since Georgian lacks an infinitive, the imperfective forms of verbal nouns (masdars without a preverb) have been used instead. The only exception is the masdar *micema* 'to give', where the preverb *mi-* is lexicalized. Therefore, the whole word has been considered as one morpheme for the analysis.

Archaic and obsolete words attested uniquely in literary text or poetry as well as hapax legomena have been excluded from the sample.

47.2 Maximum derivational networks

The highest derivational productivity is displayed by verbs, which have the highest average in all orders of derivation followed by nouns and adjectives, as shown in Table 47.1. Nouns lack a 5th order of derivation.

Table 47.1: Maximum derivational networks per order of derivation for all three word-classes.

	1st order	2nd order	3rd order	4th order	5th order	Σ
Nouns	101	75	40	10	0	226
Verbs	108	342	280	62	12	804
Adjectives	79	104	87	24	4	298
TOTAL	288	521	407	96	16	1328

47.3 Saturation values

The highest saturation value encountered in nouns is for *tvali* 'eye' (64.29%), which is also the only noun with a 4th order derivation (100%). The lowest saturation value is shown by *kva* 'stone' (9.18%). Two nouns, *dzayli* 'dog' and *cecxli* 'fire', lack a 3rd order derivation (cf. Table 47.2).

As expected, the highest saturation value for the verbs is shown by *c'eva* 'to pull' (66.52%) and the lowest by *micema* 'to give' (4.91%), since *c'eva* can occur with all 15 preverbs (having a DIRECTIONAL, aspectual or attenuative function), whilst *micema* contains the lexicalized preverb *mi-* and cannot be combined with other preverbs (Table 47.3). One verb, *codna* 'to know', lacks a 3rd order derivation, while 4th order derivations are missing for *micema* 'give', *sma* 'drink' and *codna* 'know'. Only three verbs produce a 5th order derivation: *c'eva* 'pull' (16.67%), *c'va* 'burn' (83.33%) and *sma* 'drink' (100%).

Adjectives are less productive than nouns and verbs. The highest saturation is shown by *sc'ori* 'straight' (51.72%) and the lowest by *cudi* 'bad' (12.07%).

Table 47.2: Saturation values per order of derivation, nouns.

Nouns		Saturation value (%)	1st order (%)	2nd order (%)	3rd order (%)	4th order (%)	5th order (%)
bone	dzvali	15.31	39.29	9.09	3.7	0	0
eye	tvali	64.29	50	45.45	88.89	100	0
tooth	k'bili	15.31	28.57	15.15	7.41	0	0
day	dɣe	27.55	39.29	42.42	7.41	0	0
dog	dzaɣli	11.22	28.57	9.09	0	0	0
louse	t'ili	10.2	14.29	15.15	3.7	0	0
fire	cecxli	15.31	35.71	15.15	0	0	0
stone	kva	9.18	21.43	6.06	3.7	0	0
water	c'q'ali	30.61	53.57	30.3	18.52	0	0
name	saxeli	31.63	50	39.39	14.81	0	0

Table 47.3: Saturation values per order of derivation, verbs.

Verbs		Saturation value (%)	1st order (%)	2nd order (%)	3rd order (%)	4th order (%)	5th order (%)
cut	č'ra	58.93	48.28	63.04	68.92	39.13	0
dig	txra	50.89	44.83	51.09	62.16	34.78	0
pull	c'eva	66.52	44.83	72.83	77.03	47.83	16.67
throw	srola	42.86	37.93	34.78	62.16	30.43	0
give	micema	4.91	20.69	4.35	1.35	0	0
hold	č'era	27.23	27.59	33.7	21.62	26.09	0
sew	k'erva	45.09	41.38	44.57	51.35	43.48	0
burn	c'va	39.29	48.28	39.13	29.73	47.83	83.33
drink	sma	16.07	27.59	20.65	4.05	0	100
know	codna	7.14	31.03	7.61	0	0	0

Only four out of the 10 adjectives produce a 4th order derivation and only two a 5th order derivation (Table 47.4).

Table 47.4: Saturation values per order of derivation, adjectives.

Adjectives		Saturation value (%)	1st order (%)	2nd order (%)	3rd order (%)	4th order (%)	5th order (%)
narrow	vic'ro	20.69	26.92	42.42	7.89	0	0
old	dzveli	18.1	42.31	27.27	2.63	0	0
straight	sc'ori	51.72	30.77	45.45	63.16	62.5	100
new	axali	21.55	42.31	30.3	10.53	0	0
long	grdzeli	28.45	38.46	54.55	13.16	0	0
warm	tbili	41.38	34.62	45.45	47.37	37.5	0
thick	skeli	20.69	23.08	12.12	31.58	12.5	0
bad	cudi	12.07	23.08	21.21	2.63	0	0
thin	txeli	25.86	15.38	9.09	42.11	37.5	33.33
black	šavi	16.38	26.92	27.27	7.89	0	0

Table 47.5 gives an overview of the average saturation values per order of derivation for all three word-classes in Georgian. Verbs display the highest saturation for all five orders of derivation, followed by adjectives. Nouns lack a 5th order of derivation.

Table 47.5: Average saturation values per order of derivation for all three word-classes.

	1st order	2nd order	3rd order	4th order	5th order
Nouns	36.07	22.73	14.81	10	0
Verbs	37.24	37.18	37.84	26.96	20
Adjectives	30.39	31.51	22.9	15	13.33

47.4 Orders of derivation

Verbs and adjectives possess a maximum of five orders of derivation, whilst nouns possess only four.

47.5 Derivational capacity

The average derivational capacities do not vary strongly across the three word-classes. Typically, between 6.6 and 7.7 words derive from simple nouns, verbs and adjectives in the 1st order of derivation (cf. Tables 47.6 and 47.7).

Table 47.6: Maximum and average derivational capacity for all three word-classes.

	Maximum	Average
Nouns	15	6.66
Verbs	14	7.71
Adjectives	11	7.18

Table 47.7: Average number of derivatives per order of derivation for all three word-classes.

	1st order	2nd order	3rd order	4th order	5th order
Nouns	6.66	5	1.66	1	0
Verbs	7.71	5.10	4.91	5.64	2
Adjectives	7.18	5.78	3.63	2.4	1.33

As regards the average number of derivatives per order of derivation, we can see that in the 1st and 2nd orders, all three word-classes are almost equally productive. For the 3rd, 4th and 5th orders, verbs show the highest productivity, followed by adjectives.

47.6 Correlation between semantic categories and orders of derivation

47.6.1 Nouns

10 out of 10 nouns in the 1st order have derivatives within the semantic categories PRIVATIVE and SIMILATIVE, such as *dzvali*$_N$ > *udzvlo*$_A$ 'boneless' and *dzvlisebri*$_A$

'bonelike'. In the category SIMILATIVE, some nouns have 2 derivatives, since SIMILATIVE can be expressed by means of different suffixes, e.g. *-ebr, -vit,* or *-nair*. 8 of the 10 nouns produce derivatives in the categories of PURPOSE (e.g. *dzvali*$_N$ > *sadzvale*$_N$ 'ossuary'), QUALITY (e.g. *dzvali*$_N$ > *dzvliani*$_A$ 'bony') and ACTION (e.g. *dzvali*$_N$ > *gadzvaleba*$_V$ 'ossify').

The dominant category in the 2nd order is ABSTRACTION (with 8 derivates, e.g. *saxeli*$_N$ > *saxelovneba*$_N$ 'lustrousness') followed by QUALITY, produced by 7 out of the 10 nouns (e.g. *kva*$_N$ > *gakvavebuli*$_A$ 'petrified'). In the 3rd order, 4 out of the 10 nouns produce QUALITY derivatives and 3 produce PRIVATIVE ones.

Therefore, there are strong correlations between the 1st order of derivation and PRIVATIVE and SIMILATIVE, and between the 2nd order and ABSTRACTION.

47.6.2 Verbs

The dominant categories in the 1st order are PRIVATIVE (e.g. *c'va*$_V$ > *uc'vavi*$_A$ 'incombustible') and ACTION (*c'va*$_V$ > *šec'va*$_V$ 'to fry/to broil'), both with 8 derivates, followed by ENTITY and AGENT, produced by 7 out of the 10 verbs. Each of the 10 verbs (masdars) produces PRIVATIVE in the 2nd order of derivation, e.g. *c'va*$_V$ > *arac'vadi*$_A$ 'non-flammable'.

In the 2nd order of derivation, 9 out of the 10 verbs produce the categories of QUALITY, e.g. *sma*$_V$ > *šesasmeli*$_A$ 'to be drunk', AGENT, e.g. *sma*$_V$ > *šesma*$_V$ 'to drink a toast' > *šemsmeli*$_A$ 'who drinks a toast', and CAUSATIVE, e.g. *sma*$_V$ > *šesma*$_V$ 'to drink a toast' > *šesmevineba*$_V$ 'to let someone drink a toast'. The most characteristic category of the 3rd order is MANNER (8 derivates, e.g. *sma*$_V$ > *šesma*$_V$ 'to drink a toast' > *šeusmelad*$_{Adv}$ 'without drinking a toast') followed by QUALITY (7 derivates) and CAUSATIVE (7 derivates). In the 4th order of derivation, 6 out of the 10 masdars produce the category MANNER, e.g. *txra*$_V$ > *amoutxrelad*$_{Adv}$ 'without grubbing out'.

Thus, there are strong correlations between the 1st order of derivation and PRIVATIVE, ACTION, ENTITY and AGENT, and between the 2nd order and PRIVATIVE, QUALITY, AGENT and CAUSATIVE. The 3rd order correlates with MANNER, QUALITY and CAUSATIVE. The 4th order correlates with the semantic category of MANNER.

47.6.3 Adjectives

The most characteristic category in the 1st order of derivation is ACTION (10 derivates, e.g. *sc'ori*$_A$ > *gasc'oreba*$_V$ 'to make even') followed by MANNER (7 derivates, e.g. *sc'ori*$_A$ > *sc'orad*$_{Adv}$ 'evenly'), STATIVE (7 derivates, e.g. *dzveli*$_A$ > *sidzvele*$_N$

'oldness') and DIMINUTIVE (7 derivates, e.g. *tbili*₍ₐ₎ > *motbo*₍ₐ₎ 'tepid'). The dominant categories of the 2nd order are PRIVATIVE (8 derivates) and RESULTATIVE (8 derivates), followed by AGENT (6 derivates), ACTION (6 derivates) and PURPOSE (6 derivates). In the 3rd order, the most derived words are displayed in the categories of RESULTATIVE (7 derivates) and MANNER (6 derivates).

Consequently, there are strong correlations between the 1st order of derivation and ACTION, MANNER, STATIVE and DIMINUTIVE, and between the 2nd order and PRIVATIVE, RESULTATIVE, AGENT, ACTION and PURPOSE. The 3rd order correlates with RESULTATIVE, MANNER and PRIVATIVE. The 4th and 5th orders correlate with the semantic category of MANNER.

47.7 Semantic categories with blocking effects

As regards blocking effects, for nouns, the semantic categories of AGENT, DIMINUTIVE and SIMILATIVE block further derivations in the 1st order. LOCATION hinders further derivation in the 2nd order, and ABSTRACTION blocks further derivations in the 3rd order.

For verbs, the categories STATIVE, AUGMENTATIVE and LOCATION allow no further derivations in the 1st order. AGENT, PATIENT and LOCATION block further derivations in the 2nd order. In the 3rd order, RESULT, ENTITY and CAUSATIVE block further derivations. In the 4th order, MANNER hinders further derivation.

For adjectives, the semantic categories of STATE and DIMINUTIVE hinder further derivation. In the 2nd order, AGENT and ENTITY do not allow any further derivations. RESULT in the 3rd order and MANNER in the 4th block further derivations.

47.8 Typical combinations of semantic categories

Typical combinations of semantic categories for nouns are PRIVATIVE-MANNER (5 occurrences, e.g. *ucecxlo*₍ₐ₎ > *ucecxlod* ₍ₐdv₎ 'firelessly, in a fireless way'), QUALITY-ACTION (4 occurrences, e.g. *c'q'liani*₍ₐ₎ 'watery, aqueous' > *gac'q'lianeba*₍ᵥ₎ 'turning watery'), and ACTION-AGENT (4 occurrences, e.g. *dasaxeleba*₍ᵥ₎ 'to name' > *damsaxelebeli*₍N₎ 'someone who names').

Characteristic combinations for verbs seem to be ACTION-AGENT (8 occurrences, e.g. *asrola*₍ᵥ₎ 'throw up' > *amsroleli*₍N₎ 'who throws up'), PRIVATIVE-MANNER (8 occurrences, e.g. *unak'ero*₍ₐ₎ 'lacking seams, araphorostic' > *unak'erod*₍ₐdv₎ 'in an araphorostic way'), ACTION-CAUSATIVE (8 occurrences, e.g. *šek'erva*₍ᵥ₎ 'to sew' > *šek'erineba*₍ᵥ₎ 'to let someone sew'), ACTION-RESULT (7 occurrences, e.g. *dak'ereba*₍ᵥ₎ 'to darn' >

dak'erebuli₍ₐ₎ 'darned') and ENTITY-SIMILATIVE (5 occurrences, e.g. *namc'vi*₍ₙ₎ '(cigarette) stub' > *namc'visebri*₍ₐ₎ 'stub-like').

The typical combinations for adjectives are ACTION-RESULT (10 occurrences, e.g. *gatboba*₍ᵥ₎ 'to warm up' > *gamtbari*₍ₐ₎ 'warmed up'), ACTION-PRIVATIVE-MANNER (10 occurrences, e.g. *gagrdzeleba*₍ᵥ₎ 'to extend' > *gaugrdzelebeli*₍ₐ₎ 'non-extended' > *gaugrdzeleblad*₍ₐdᵥ₎ 'in a non-extended way/without extending') and ACTION-CAUSATIVE (6 occurrences, e.g. *gasc'oreba*₍ᵥ₎ 'to straighten' > *gasc'orebineba*₍ᵥ₎ 'to let someone straighten').

47.9 Multiple occurrence of semantic categories

Several cases of multiple occurrences of semantic categories can be observed in single derivational chains: ACTION-ACTION (e.g. *tvaliereba*₍ᵥ₎ 'to look at, examine' > *atvaliereba*₍ᵥ₎ 'to look up'), RESULT-RESULT (e.g. *gatvalisc'inebuli*₍ₐ₎ 'considered/taken into account' > *argatvalisc'inebuli*₍ₐ₎ 'not considered/not taken into account'), QUALITY-QUALITY (e.g. *moč'rili*₍ₐ₎ 'cut' > *amoč'rili*₍ₐ₎ 'cut out'), AGENT-AGENT (e.g. *msroleli*₍ₙ₎ 'thrower' > *amsroleli*₍ₙ₎ 'who throws up'), CAUSATIVE-CAUSATIVE (e.g. *srolineba*₍ᵥ₎ 'let someone throw' > *asrolineba*₍ᵥ₎ 'let someone throw up') and STATE-STATE (e.g. *tanasc'roba*₍ₙ₎ 'equality' > *utanasc'oroba*₍ₙ₎ 'inequality').

47.10 Reversibility of semantic categories

No semantic categories occurring in a reversed order were observed in the Georgian data set.

47.11 Conclusions

In the Georgian data set, the verbs show the highest number of derivational networks in all five orders (Table 47.1) as well as the overall highest saturation value: 37.24% in the 1st order (Table 47.5). Verbs and adjectives have five orders of derivation, whereas nouns only have four (Table 47.8). The average derivational capacity for all three word-classes varies between 6.66% (nouns) and 7.71% (verbs). 25 out of the 49 available semantic categories are covered by the Georgian data set. The missing categories are built by devices of word-formation other than derivation.

Table 47.8: Maximum and average number of orders of derivation for all three word-classes.

	Maximum	Average
Nouns	4	2.9
Verbs	5	3.8
Adjectives	5	3.6

References

Arabuli, Avtandil (ed.). 2008. ქართული ენის განმარტებითი ლექსიკონი [Explanatory Dictionary of the Georgian Language], vols. I and II. Tbilisi: Meridian Publishers. http://www.ena.ge/explanatory-online.

Boeder, Winfried. 2005. The South Caucasian Languages. *Lingua* 115 (1). 5–89.

Chikobava, Arnold (ed.). 1950–1964. ქართული ენის განმარტებითი ლექსიკონი [Explanatory Dictionary of the Georgian Language], vols. I–VIII. Tbilisi: Akademia. http://www.ena.ge/explanatory-online.

Georgian National Corpus. http://gnc.gov.ge.

Gogolashvili, Giorgi. (ed.). 2011. თანამედროვე ქართული ენის მორფოლოგია [Morphology of Present-Day Georgian Language]. Tbilisi: Arnold Chikobava Institute of Linguistics.

Harris, Alice C. 2002. The word in Georgian. In Robert M. W. Dixon and Alexandra Y. Aikhenvald (eds.), *Word: A Cross-linguistic Typology*, 227–242. Cambridge: Cambridge University Press.

Heinze, Sybilla. 2008. *Georgische Wortbildung: eine Betrachtung unter Berücksichtigung der Arbeit Friedrich Neissers.* Jena: VDM Verlag Müller.

Benjamin Saade
48 Derivational networks in Maltese

48.1 General notes

As the only Semitic language of the sample in this volume, Maltese certainly is an outlier in many respects regarding affixal derivation in general and the compilation of derivational networks in particular. The lexicon of Maltese is heavily mixed. A dictionary study (Brincat 2011: 407) puts the Semitic component at only 32.41%, with the Romance element (Italian, Sicilian) making up 52.46%. English, with 6.12%, and items with a local or unknown origin complete the lexicon. However, the influence of Italian/Sicilian does not extend to the core vocabulary to the same degree (Stolz 2003: 291).

The mixed lexicon is also mirrored in the morphology of Maltese, which shows an etymology-based compartmentalization: Semitic morphology applies to Semitic bases (and also Italian ones, mostly in verbal morphology), while Italian morphology applies almost exclusively to Italian bases. However, while most of the morphology in Maltese still follows a Semitic root-and-pattern schema, there are niches where Italian/Sicilian morphology (affixation) developed a certain amount of productivity, including with Semitic bases (Saade 2016, 2019). Conversely, there are areas where Semitic morphology is starting to lose ground (e.g. DIMINUTIVES).

Since the lexical items in the sample for this volume were chosen for their basicness, all except one of the translation equivalents for Maltese are of Semitic origin (29/30) with the item *dritt* 'straight' being the only item of Italian/Sicilian origin. This obscures the fact that, outside of the core vocabulary, the Italian lexicon and consequently Italian morphology plays a much more important role. An even more severe limitation lies in the fact that root-and-pattern morphology, which is used for the majority of formations in the compiled derivational networks, is not strictly affixal. Even if this major complication is accepted, the non-affixal nature of morphology makes the identification of the direction of derivation on a strictly formal basis extremely difficult, if not impossible, for many formations.

The procedure of creating the derivational networks was tripartite: firstly, all possible derivations for each item were extracted from the most comprehensive Maltese dictionary (Aquilina 1987, 1990). Secondly, each formation was checked in the 250-million-word MLRS corpus version 3.0 (Gatt and Čéplö 2013). Additional formations not found in the dictionary were also checked. As a last step, two native speakers of Maltese were asked to mark this maximum list of derivations for their existence or non-existence in Maltese. Only derivations that were either found in the corpus or marked as valid by one of the speakers were included in the networks. This decision was taken since the dictionary entries contain many archaic formations that are no longer in use in present-day Maltese, and even a 250-million-word corpus cannot completely replace the competence of a native speaker.

48.2 Maximum derivational networks

The total maximum derivational networks for nouns, verbs, and adjectives do not differ dramatically, with maximums of 13, 15 and 17 derivatives, respectively (Table 48.1). Verbs have the highest maximal number of derivatives in the 1st order, while adjectives exhibit the highest number in the 2nd, 3rd and 4th orders. Generally, the maximum derivational networks are quite small for all word-classes.

Table 48.1: Maximum derivational networks per order of derivation for all three word-classes.

	1st order	2nd order	3rd order	4th order	Σ
Nouns	8	4	1	0	13
Verbs	9	5	1	0	15
Adjectives	6	6	4	1	17
TOTAL	23	15	6	1	45

48.3 Saturation values

As can be seen from Table 48.2, saturation values for nouns in Maltese are low both on the individual level and on the general level. The very low average saturation in all orders can partly be explained by the three items *jum* 'day', *kelb* 'dog', *qamla* 'louse' having no valid derivations at all. However, even aside from these outliers, the lack of derivational depth for nouns in Maltese is quite striking, as only one of the sample words (*għajn*) exhibits a single derivation in the 3rd order.

The saturation values of individual Maltese verbs (Table 48.3) cluster more around the mean of the respective order, with the exception of *ġibed* 'pull' which has a high saturation, *xorob* 'drink' which has a low saturation, and *af* 'know' which has no valid derivatives at all. The verb *af* is a defective form that can be

Table 48.2: Saturation values per order of derivation, nouns.

Nouns		Saturation value (%)	1st order (%)	2nd order (%)	3rd order (%)
bone	għadam	30.77	37.5	25	0
eye	għajn	30.77	25	25	100
tooth	snien	15.38	12.5	25	0
day	jum	0	0	0	0
dog	kelb	0	0	0	0
louse	qamla	0	0	0	0
fire	nar	7.69	12.5	0	0
stone	ġebel	23.08	37.5	0	0
water	ilma	7.69	12.5	0	0
name	isem	38.46	25	75	0

Table 48.3: Saturation values per order of derivation, verbs.

Verbs		Saturation value (%)	1st order (%)	2nd order (%)	3rd order (%)
cut	qata'	40	44.44	20	100
dig	għażaq	40	44.44	40	0
pull	ġibed	60	55.56	80	0
throw	tefa'	33.33	33.33	40	0
give	ta	33.33	44.44	20	0
hold	żamm	33.33	44.44	20	0
sew	ħiet	46.67	55.56	40	0
burn	ħaraq	26.67	44.44	0	0
drink	xorob	13.33	22.22	0	0
know	af	0	0	0	0

related (at least diachronically) to the regular triliteral verb *għaraf* 'to recognize'. Since the focus of this study is synchronous, this relation was not included in the derivational network. However, verbs also have a very low derivational depth, with *qata'* 'cut' being the only verb with a derivative in the 3rd order.

Adjectives are the only word-class in Maltese that has derivatives in the 4th order (one instance, for *rqiq* 'thin'). Furthermore, all items at least have one derivative in the 1st order in contrast to nouns and verbs. Regarding saturation, adjectives possess the highest average across all orders for all word-classes (Table 48.4).

Table 48.4: Saturation values per order of derivation, adjectives.

Adjectives		Saturation value (%)	1st order (%)	2nd order (%)	3rd order (%)	4th order (%)
narrow	dejjaq	41.18	50	50	25	0
old	qadim	17.65	33.33	16.67	0	0
straight	dritt	5.88	16.67	0	0	0
new	ġdid	23.53	33.33	33.33	0	0
long	twil	41.18	33.33	33.33	75	0
warm	sħun	41.18	50	33.33	50	0
thick	oħxon	35.29	50	33.33	25	0
bad	ħażin	41.18	66.67	33.33	25	0
thin	rqiq	52.94	83.33	33.33	25	100
black	iswed	29.41	66.67	16.67	0	0

In summary, nouns in Maltese display the lowest saturation both by item and by order (Table 48.5). Saturation values for verbs and adjectives are almost three times higher than those of nouns. Adjectives display the highest average saturation in all orders including the 4th order, where it is the only word-class with any derivations.

Table 48.5: Average saturation values per order of derivation for all three word-classes.

	1st order	2nd order	3rd order	4th order
Nouns	16.25	15	10	0
Verbs	38.89	26	10	0
Adjectives	48.33	28.33	22.5	10

48.4 Orders of derivation

While the maximum number of orders is almost the same for all word-classes, the average number of orders differs dramatically from only 1.1 orders for nouns to 1.7 orders for verbs and 2.6 orders for adjectives (Table 48.6). The disparity between the maximum and average orders for nouns and verbs can partly be explained by the fact that only one sample word for each word-class displays a derivation in the 3rd order (*għajn* 'eye' and *qata'* 'cut').

Table 48.6: Maximum and average number of orders of derivation for all three word-classes.

	Maximum	Average
Nouns	3	1.1
Verbs	3	1.7
Adjectives	4	2.6

48.5 Derivational capacity

Once again, Maltese nouns display the lowest numbers for maximum and average derivational capacity across all orders (Table 48.7 and Table 48.8). Verbs have the highest average number of derivatives in the 1st order, while adjectives score highest in all following orders.

Table 48.7: Maximum and average derivational capacity for all three word-classes.

	Maximum	Average
Nouns	3	1.3
Verbs	5	3.5
Adjectives	5	2.9

Table 48.8: Average number of derivatives per order of derivation for all three word-classes.

	1st order	2nd order	3rd order	4th order
Nouns	1.3	0.6	0.1	0
Verbs	3.5	1.3	0.1	0
Adjectives	2.9	1.7	0.9	0.1

48.6 Correlation between semantic categories and orders of derivation

There are no characteristic semantic categories for any order of derivation for nouns (SINGULATIVE is applied in 3/10 cases for the 1st order). For verbs, ACTION (9/10) and ANTICAUSATIVE (8/10) are correlated with the 1st order. SINGULATIVE is weakly correlated (6/10) with the 2nd order. There are no correlations with individual semantic categories for verbs in the 3rd order. For adjectives, STATE and PROCESS (both 8/10) are correlated with the 1st order. CAUSATIVE and PROCESS (5/10) are weakly correlated with the 2nd order. There are no correlations with individual semantic categories for adjectives in the 3rd or 4th orders.

48.7 Semantic categories with blocking effects

For nouns, there is only the very weak blocking effect of QUALITY in the 1st order. For verbs, there is a strong blocking effect by ANTICAUSATIVE in the 1st order and SINGULATIVE in the 2nd order. For adjectives, there is a strong blocking effect by STATE and a weaker effect by DIMINUTIVE in the 1st order. PROCESS has a weak blocking effect in the 2nd order and PROCESS/QUALITY an equally weak effect in the 3rd order.

48.8 Typical combinations of semantic categories

For nouns, there are no characteristic combinations of semantic categories. For verbs, the combination ACTION-SINGULATIVE is systematic, while for adjectives it is the combination CAUSATIVE-ANTICAUSATIVE.

48.9 Multiple occurrence of semantic categories

Except for one instance of the multiple occurrence of PROCESS for adjectives, this phenomenon cannot be observed in the Maltese derivational networks.

48.10 Reversibility of semantic categories

There is only one instance of this phenomenon for the adjective *rqiq* 'thin'. Here, the derivational chain is *rqiq* 'thin' > *raqq* 'getting thin', PROCESS > *raqqaq* 'to make thin', CAUSATIVE > *traqqiq* 'the making thin, thinning', PROCESS. This phenomenon is not attested for nouns and verbs.

48.11 Reasons for structurally poor derivational networks

There are several reasons for the relative sparseness of the Maltese derivational networks. The first is due to the methodology employed in the compilation of the networks. As mentioned in section 48.1, items that were not found in a large corpus or confirmed by a native speaker were excluded, even if they were present in the dictionary. This concerns many formations that are not as productive as they used to be. For example, most DIMINUTIVE formations for the nouns in the sample were listed in the dictionary but were not verified by corpus examples or native speakers. In their overview of word-formation in Maltese, Brincat and Mifsud (2015: 3357) similarly state for nominal derivation that although Maltese possesses "[...] an impressive array of morphological tools [...] many of these tools became gradually less productive and their members were often reduced to closed lists without any clear connection between them in the mind of the speakers."

Furthermore, a part of the sparseness can be explained by the actual sample. Four individual items do not have any valid derivatives: one verb and three nouns. The verb *af* 'know' is extremely irregular and cannot be synchronically related to other derivatives, though this is possible diachronically. The nouns *jum* 'day', *kelb* 'dog' and *qamla* 'louse' also do not have valid derivatives, since some of the existing formally related derivations only have a distant or metaphorical semantic relationship to the base words. These sparse or even defective derivational paradigms are clearly an artefact of the choice of sample words.

Despite the sparsely populated derivational networks, Maltese is in no way deficient and just uses other strategies to express the same concepts. As an example, the concept 'daily', which is given as *jumieni* (derivative of *jum* 'day') in Aquilina's dictionary, is not verified by native speakers or corpus data. Instead, the construction *ta' kul.jum* (of every.day) is used to express the same concept in present-day Maltese, utilizing a combination of an analytical construction (prepositional phrase) and compounding. Another strategy employed by speakers of Maltese is the importation of either Italian or English lexical material for otherwise potentially derived concepts.

48.12 Conclusions

Overall, the derivational networks presented and analyzed here show that the productivity of Semitic root-and-pattern morphology is rather low in Maltese, resulting in relatively sparse networks, especially for the class of nouns, though less so for verbs and adjectives. Some of the sparseness can be explained by the choice of sample words, since four items do not have any valid derivatives at all. This is an artefact of the methodology and does not represent the derivational possibilities of Maltese to their full extent. A potential future replication of this study should include more lexical items pertaining to contemporary culture in order to give a more current picture of derivational morphology in Maltese. However, putting these reservations about representativeness aside, it still seems clear that derivational depth in Maltese (maximum and average number of derivational orders) in particular can be safely classified as very shallow. This lack of depth also explains the absence or at least rarity of many of the phenomena investigated in this chapter (typical combinations of semantic categories, multiple occurrences of semantic categories, and the reversibility of semantic categories). While morphological tools of derivation are available in Maltese derivation, they are no longer put to use as systematically as they used to be. It is important to state that the expressiveness of Maltese is in no way rendered deficient by the relative poverty of the derivational networks. Analytical constructions, lexical material borrowed from Italian and English and other strategies more than make up for the less productive derivational morphology. In conclusion, Maltese certainly represents an outlier regarding derivational capacity in the context of the languages of Europe, but its mixture of Arabic and Italian morphology plus different coping mechanisms to balance out the relative poverty of the derivational system make it a valuable point of reference in the sample of languages treated in this volume.

References

Aquilina, Joseph. 1987. *Maltese-English dictionary. Vol. I: A-L.* Sta Venera: Midsea Books.
Aquilina, Joseph. 1990. *Maltese-English dictionary. Vol. II: M-Z.* Sta Venera: Midsea Books.
Brincat, Joseph. 2011. *Maltese and other languages: A linguistic history of Malta.* Sta Venera: Midsea Books.
Brincat, Joseph & Manwel Mifsud. 2015. Maltese. In Peter O. Müller, Ingeborg Ohnheiser, Susan Olsen & Franz Rainer (eds.), *Word-formation. An international handbook of the languages of Europe, vol. 5,* 3349–3366. Berlin: De Gruyter Mouton.
Gatt, Albert & Slavomír Čéplö. 2013. Digital corpora and other electronic resources for Maltese. *Proceedings of Corpus Linguistics Conference 2013.* University of Lancaster.
Saade, Benjamin. 2016. Adverbial derivation in Maltese and Italian: A starting point for studies in cross-linguistic productivity. *STUF – Language Typology and Universals* 69 (4): 547–563.
Saade, Benjamin. 2019. Assessing productivity in contact: Italian derivation in Maltese. *Linguistics* 57 (1). https://doi.org/10.1515/ling-2018-0031.
Stolz, Thomas. 2003. Not quite the right mixture: Chamorro and Malti as candidates for the status of mixed language. In Yaron Matras & Peter Bakker (eds.), *The mixed language debate: theoretical and empirical advances (Trends in Linguistics 145),* 271–315. Berlin: Mouton de Gruyter.

Lívia Körtvélyessy, Alexandra Bagasheva, Pavol Štekauer,
Salvador Valera, Ján Genči

49 Derivational networks in European languages: A cross-linguistic perspective

The previous chapters described the specific features and richness of derivational networks in each of the 40 languages included in our research sample. In this final chapter, these preceding chapters and the 1,200 derivational networks on which they are based serve as an important and rich source of data and observations for drawing relevant cross-linguistic conclusions on the similarities and differences among the languages, as well as those language genera and/or languages that are sufficiently represented in our sample. In particular, we examine and compare the maximum derivational networks (section 49.1), saturation values (49.2), consistency of derivations at the language level (49.3) and at the genera level (49.4), correlations between saturation values and the paradigmatic capacity (49.5), maximum and average numbers of orders of derivation (49.6), numbers of derivatives (49.7), correlations between semantic categories and orders of derivation (49.8), semantic categories with blocking effects (49.9), combinations of semantic categories (49.10), multiple occurrences of semantic categories (49.11), reversibility of semantic categories (49.12) and the reasons for structurally poor derivational networks (49.13). The data are evaluated in terms of word-classes and orders of derivation, with a special focus on the role of genera and/or families, morphological types and the nature of the word-formation systems of individual languages. It is hypothesized that each of these five factors has an impact on (the possibility of) the generalization of our data.

49.1 Maximum derivational networks

The parameter of the maximum derivational network (MDN) serves to identify the maximum number of possible derivatives, i.e. the maximum potential number of words derivable from a basic simple word. Given our research sample, it is related to 10 basic underived words selected according to the criteria described in section 1.3.1. The MDN is calculated as a sum total of all the highest numbers of derivatives for a given semantic category from among all 10 sample words (in our case) of a given word-class (cf. Figure 1.4 and the related account of the calculation in section 1.2). This means that it shows the maximum number of derivatives that can theoretically be formed from each simple underived word, thus indicating the derivational potential of simple underived words belonging to the same word-class (with regard to the specific sample).

Analogically to the considerable differences between languages in terms of the number of affixation subtypes (Körtvélyessy et al. 2018) used for the formation of new complex words, substantial differences can be found in the MDNs. They are evident for the orders of both derivation and word-classes, and in what follows they are shown by word-class. Table 49.1 illustrates the situation in the word-class of nouns.

It is exclusively Slavic and Romance languages plus Basque that can be found among the top 10 languages for the 1st order derivation. The 2nd order situation is more varied: the top 10 languages include, in addition to these two main genera, the Uralic languages Hungarian and North Saami. In general, from the 2nd order onwards, the Uralic languages feature high values. Apart from Hungarian and North Saami, Finnish has a high MDN value, too. While the importance of Slavic and Romance languages gradually drops as the order of derivation grows, languages like Georgian and Turkish grow in importance.

The situation in the group of basic adjectives is similar. All top 10 positions in the 1st order of derivation are reserved for Slavic and Romance languages. Interestingly, the MDNs of the basic adjectives in Romance languages drop significantly from the 2nd order, from which point on none of them appear in the top 10. With the growing orders of derivation, the Uralic languages as well as Lithuanian, Georgian and Turkish grow in significance. In the latter two languages, this pattern is consistent with the one found in nouns, too.

The dominance of Slavic languages according to the parameter of MDNs among basic verbs is striking, which is primarily due to an extremely high number of prefixes expressing various shades of Aktionsart. In general, the MDNs of Germanic languages are low for all three word-classes. The differences between languages with the highest MDN values and the lowest ones are extremely large – much larger than in nouns and adjectives (Table 49.2).

In addition, Table 49.2 shows that the highest MDN value from among all word-classes and orders of derivation is found for Czech verbs in the 3rd order, where the MDN value is as high as 149. Slovak basic verbs produce 129 potential derivatives in their 2nd order, and the MDN of Serbian adjectives' 2nd order is 100. To remind the reader of the meaning of these values, they indicate the number of derivatives that can potentially be produced from each of the basic words of a particular word-class. The derivational potential in the languages with the highest MDN values is thus enormous.

Table 49.1: Languages with the highest and lowest MDN values, nouns.

1st order		2nd order		3rd order		4th order	
Language	No. of derivatives	Language	No. of derivatives	Language	No. of derivatives	Language	No. of derivatives
Italian	64	Croatian	76	Hungarian	40	Hungarian	15
Croatian	63	Italian	70	Czech	33	Georgian	10
Galician	54	Serbian	59	Croatian	29	Italian	9
Serbian	51	Czech	57	Georgian	27	North Saami	8
Danish	9	Icelandic	2	6 languages[a]	0	18 languages	0
Maltese	8	Danish	1				
Chechen	6	Chechen	0				
Dargwa	4	Dargwa	0				

[a]Chechen, Danish, Dargwa, English, Frisian, and Norwegian.

Table 49.2: Languages with the highest and lowest MDN values, verbs.

1st order		2nd order		3rd order		4th order	
Language	No. of derivatives	Language	No. of derivatives	Language	No. of derivatives	Language	No. of derivatives
Serbian	93	Slovak	129	Czech	149	Czech	64
Slovene	68	Serbian	124	Serbian	114	Serbian	55
Slovak	66	Georgian	122	Croatian	94	Slovene	39
Croatian	62	Czech	114	Georgian	74	Croatian	24
Danish	16	Norwegian	12				
Icelandic	15	Icelandic	8				
Norwegian	14	Maltese	5				
Maltese	9	Danish	1				

Table 49.3 provides a review of the average MDN values for all three word-classes by order of derivation. It is evident that the greatest potential for rich derivational networks is offered by basic verbs in each order of derivation. The average values significantly exceed those for nouns and adjectives. Adjectives seem to establish slightly better derivational conditions than nouns.

Table 49.3: Average MDNs for all three word-classes by orders of derivation.

Word-class	1st order	2nd order	3rd order	4th order	5th order
Nouns	28.45	25.89	11.03	2.76	0.53
Adjectives	27.47	26.45	15.03	4.55	0.66
Verbs	36.34	44.87	24.95	8.18	1.50

The distribution of the data can be advantageously represented by boxplots (see Diagrams 49.1–49.3 below). It is obvious that, with a rising order, the data are more scattered in each word-class, including the existence of outliers, i.e. the data which are at an abnormal distance from the median. Thus, the higher the order of derivation, the more scattered the MDN values. This is especially significant for the 3rd order of verbs. The boxplot for verbs also shows that four languages with MDN values above 100 cause a high average value of verbs in the 2nd order. With the exception of one language, these data are still on the whisker in comparison to the 3rd order, where languages with high MDN values are outliers. The number of outlier languages in the 3rd order of verbs is as many as five; in the case of adjectives, there are three outlier languages, and in the case of nouns, none of the languages display an outlier MDN value. This distribution confirms the data for the 3rd order in Table 49.3 – the high average value for verbs is caused by the languages with an extremely high MDN value in comparison to the median value. The boxplots also show that the number of languages with an MDN above 50 is generally much higher for verbs, especially in the 2nd order of derivation. This confirms our interpretation of the average values in Table 49.3 – the word-class of verbs has the highest potential for the derivation of new words.

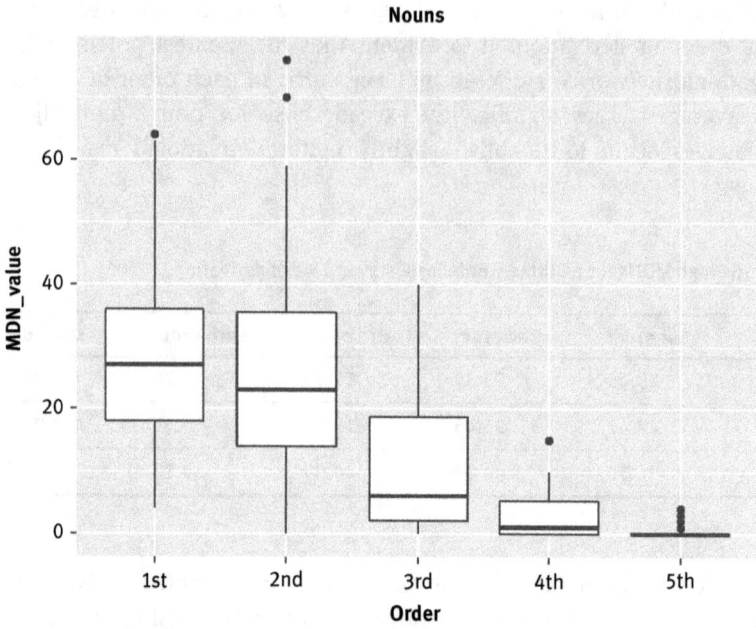

Diagram 49.1: Relation between MDNs and orders of derivation, nouns.

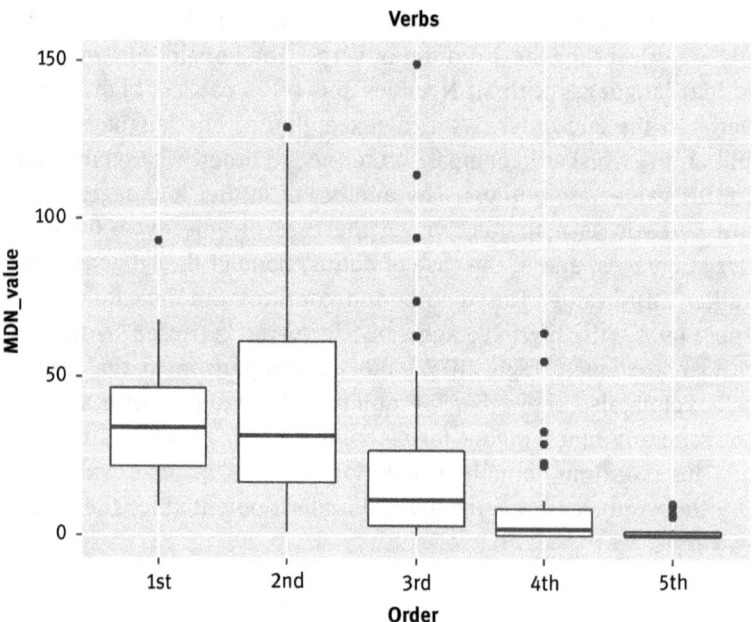

Diagram 49.2: Relation between MDNs and orders of derivation, verbs.

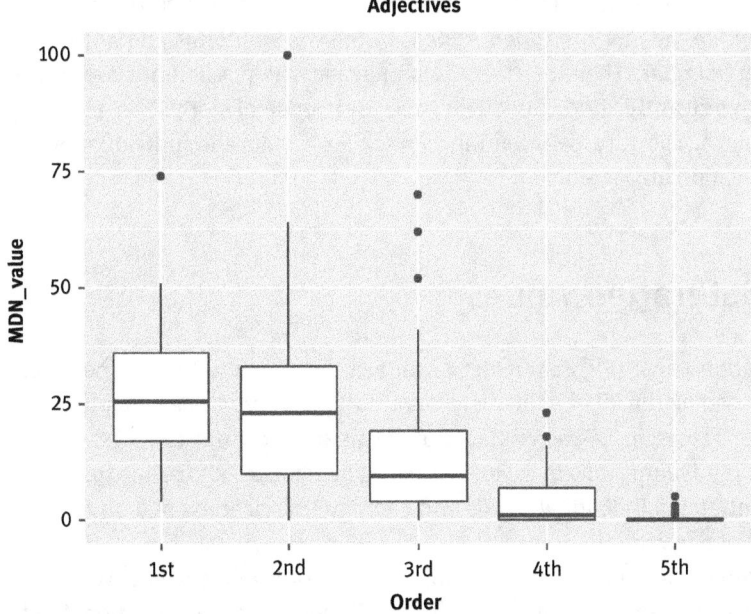

Diagram 49.3: Relation between MDNs and orders of derivation, adjectives.

Summary

(i) The highest potential for deriving rich derivational networks is clearly bound to simple underived *verbs*. They have the highest MDN value in every order of derivation, and these values are significantly higher than in the other two word-classes.//
(ii) The derivational potential of simple underived nouns and adjectives is *similar*, and in some orders almost identical.
(iii) The highest MDN values are featured mainly by *Slavic languages* and, in the higher orders of nominal derivation, also some other languages like Hungarian and Georgian.
(iv) *High MDN values* seem to be typical of *synthetic and agglutinating languages*. However, instances like Dargwa, which has a minimum MDN value, suggest that there is no systematic correlation between the morphological type of a language and the nature of its word-formation system, as also observed by Štekauer (2012). This important finding will be highlighted in several places in this chapter.

(v) If the orders of derivation are compared, the *highest derivational potential is bound to the first two orders* which, in the case of nouns and adjectives, are very similar. Then, as the orders increase, the possibilities for derivation significantly drop. For verbs, the 2nd order of derivation evidently dominates. The gaps between the average MDN values in individual orders of derivation are significant.

49.2 Saturation values

The saturation value (SV) parameter examines the degree to which the potential, expressed as the MDN value, is *actualized* by the individual sample words used in our research (cf. the explanation and examples in section 1.3.5). This parameter is advantageous in several respects, as it makes it possible to:
(i) concentrate on individual words and compare the richness of derivation by orders of derivation;
(ii) compare the saturation values of all sample words of a specific word-class and conclude on the degree of similarity/difference in the derivational richness of simple underived words of the same word-class that belong to the core vocabulary in all languages under research;
(iii) compare nouns, verbs and adjectives as a whole and find out which of these three word-classes establishes the best derivational opportunities; and
(iv) evaluate the data from the perspective of groups of languages (genera, families).

49.2.1 Cross-linguistic comparison of individual words by SV

For reasons of space, it is not possible to discuss all 30 words here. Therefore, we have picked out the noun *bone* (including its equivalents in the other sample languages) to illustrate
a) the range of findings offered by this method of analysis, and, by implication,
b) the possibilities of evaluating derivational networks inherent in the proposed approach.

The highest SV in the 1st order was identified for Dutch (81.82%). This means that *been*, the Dutch equivalent of *bone*, allows the actualization of over 80% of the derivational potential represented by the corresponding MDN for Dutch nouns. Dutch is followed by Greek (50%), German (42.86%), Lithuanian (41.38%)

and a group of 12 languages in the range of 30–40%, comprising five Slavic languages, one Germanic and two Romance languages, and Georgian (39.12%), Tatar (38.89%), Maltese (37.50%) and North Saami (34.78%). The language with the lowest SV in the 1st order is Icelandic (8.33%).

The 2nd order is dominated by Greek, which has an SV of as high as 69.57%, followed by French (66.67%), German (66.67%), Dutch (60%) and Slovak (48.89%).[1] The 2nd order for *bone* features much bigger differences in derivation among the sample languages in at least two respects:
(i) as per the preceding data, the highest SVs significantly exceed those of the 1st order; and
(ii) unlike the 1st order, there are languages without any derivatives: Icelandic, Tatar, Basque, Dargwa, and Chechen. Furthermore, there are languages with an SV of under 10%: Catalan, Spanish, Welsh, and Georgian.

The SVs for Galician were relatively low in the 1st and the 2nd orders (22.22% and 25.71%, respectively), but this increases substantially in the actualization of the 3rd order possibilities (66.67%). Greek also maintains a high SV level in the 3rd order (47.06%), and Slovak and North Saami are in a similar, but slightly lower range (40%). Apart from the five languages without derivations in the 2nd order, some other languages attest no derivations in the 3rd order, namely Italian, Portuguese, Spanish, Welsh, Latvian, Estonian and Maltese. The derivational capacity of the sample languages dramatically falls in the next orders of derivation.

Taking the total SV into consideration, Dutch is at the top with 65.22%, followed by Greek (56.45%), German (47.06%) and Slovak (41.60%). At the opposite end we find Icelandic, the only language with a total SV under 10%. All the data are summarized in Tables 49.4 and 49.5. The languages are listed by language genera/families.

Based on the total SVs for the word *bone*, languages can be divided into three groups. The SVs in the first group (high) are above 40%. In the second group (medium), they range from 40% to 20%. The last group (low) covers languages with saturation levels below 20%. This division is useful for further typological evaluations.

SVs can be projected onto a *saturation map*. In Map 49.1 below, the green colour indicates the highest total SVs for *bone* (Dutch, French, German, Slovak

---

[1] The topmost position is assumed by Danish with 100%. However, this value follows from the fact that Danish has only one derivative in the 2nd order. Therefore, it is not taken into consideration here.

Table 49.4: SVs of *bone* and its equivalents in the sample languages.

	Language	1st order	2nd order	3rd order	4th order	5th order	Total saturation value
kost	Bulgarian	36.67	26.09	26.67	0	0	28
kost	Croatian	22.22	23.68	6.9	0	0	19.54
kost	Czech	32.26	24.56	30.3	16.67	50	27.91
kość	Polish	33.33	35.71	12.5	0	0	30.3
кость	Russian	29.41	38.89	23.08	0	0	30.61
кост	Serbian	31.37	33.9	7.41	0	0	26.21
kosť	Slovak	36.17	48.89	40.74	40	0	41.6
kost	Slovene	22.5	24.32	23.53	100	0	25
кістка	Ukrainian	16	23.81	38.89	33.33	0	25.35
ben	Danish	33.33	100	0	0	0	36.36
been	Dutch	81.82	60	0	0	0	65.22
bone	English	30	45.45	0	0	0	35.48
bonke	Frisian	22.22	50	0	0	0	27.27
Knochen	German	45	55.56	33.33	0	0	45.45
bein	Icelandic	8.33	0	0	0	0	6.67
ben, bein	Norwegian	27.78	14.29	0	0	0	24
ben	Swedish	35.71	29.41	16.67	0	0	28.95
os	Catalan	26.83	8.11	25	0	0	18.18
os	French	38.1	66.67	100	0	0	60
óso	Galician	22.22	25.71	66.67	0	0	25
osso	Italian	25	20	0	0	0	18.07
osso	Portuguese	36.11	26.92	0	0	0	31.25
os	Romanian	34.15	32.61	23.81	0	0	30.09
hueso	Spanish	19.57	6.06	0	0	0	13.1
cnámh	Irish	17.65	26.32	33.33	0	0	21.43
asgwrn	Welsh	17.14	6.67	0	0	0	13.73

Table 49.4 (continued)

	Language	1st order	2nd order	3rd order	4th order	5th order	Total saturation value
kauls	Latvian	30.43	37.5	0	0	0	30.95
kaulas	Lithuanian	41.38	39.13	25	0	0	39.29
κόκκαλο	Greek	50	69.57	47.06	0	0	56.45
luu	Estonian	22.58	24	0	0	0	19.4
luu	Finnish	24.24	35.29	19.05	0	0	24.74
dákti	North Saami	34.78	23.68	40	25	0	29.9
csont	Hungarian	25.93	25.58	12.5	20	0	20.16
söyäk	Tatar	38.89	0	0	0	0	16.28
kemik	Turkish	25	20	12.5	0	0	16.44
hezur	Basque	27.78	0	0	0	0	17.86
ликка	Dargwa	25	0	0	0	0	25
da'ahk	Chechen	16.67	0	0	0	0	16.67
dzvali	Georgian	39.29	9.09	3.7	0	0	15.31
għadam	Maltese	37.5	25	0	0	0	30.77

Table 49.5: Languages according to the total SV of *bone* from highest to lowest SVs.

SV	Languages
HIGH	Dutch, French, Greek, German, Slovak
MEDIUM	Bulgarian, Czech, Danish, Dargwa, English, Finnish, Frisian, Galician, Hungarian, Irish, Latvian, Lithuanian, Maltese, North Saami, Norwegian, Polish, Portuguese, Romanian, Russian, Serbian, Slovene, Swedish, Ukrainian
LOW	Basque, Catalan, Chechen, Croatian, Estonian, Georgian, Icelandic, Italian, Spanish, Tatar, Turkish, Welsh

and Greek). The yellow areas are those with the lowest SVs (Croatian, Estonian, Catalan, Italian, Basque, Chechen, Turkish, Tatar, Georgian, Welsh, Spanish, and Icelandic). The areas in blue indicate languages with medium SVs.

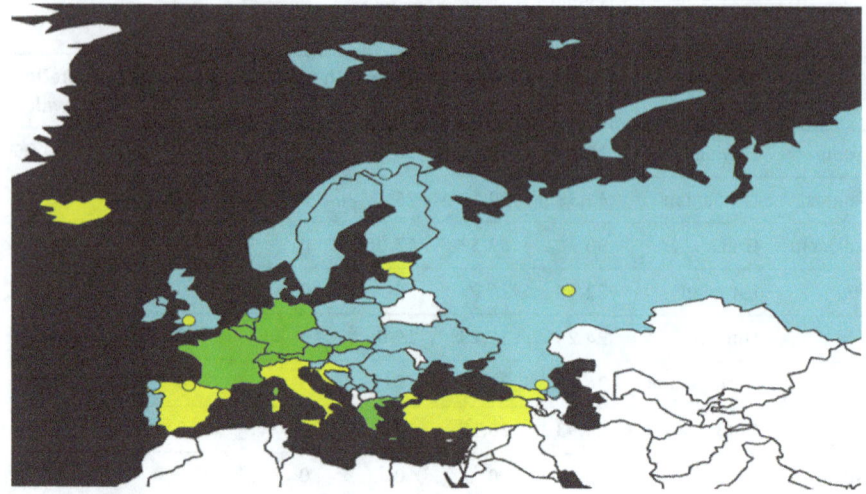

Map 49.1: Distribution of languages according to their SV (*bone*).

Map 49.1 indicates that the languages with the highest SV for *bone* constitute a *homogeneous strip* (with the exception of Greek), *stretching from the Atlantic coast to Central Europe*.

Another important parameter concerns the number of derivational orders employed in individual languages. In the case of *bone*, there is no language that derives words in all five orders. Five languages derive words in four orders, 18 languages in three orders, 12 languages in two orders and five languages only in one order. It follows from Table 49.6 that the highest number of derivational orders correlates with *Slavic and Uralic languages*, i.e. *synthetic languages*.

Table 49.6: Classification of languages according to the number of orders of derivation (*bone*).

Order of derivation	Languages
5 orders	–
4 orders	Hungarian, North Saami, Slovak, Slovene, Ukrainian (5 languages)
3 orders	Bulgarian, Catalan, Croatian, Czech, Finnish, French, Galician, Georgian, German, Greek, Irish, Lithuanian, Polish, Romanian, Russian, Serbian, Swedish, Turkish (18 languages)
2 orders	Danish, Dutch, English, Estonian, Frisian, Italian, Latvian, Maltese, Norwegian, Portuguese, Spanish, Welsh (12 languages)
1 order	Basque, Chechen, Dargwa, Icelandic, Tatar (5 languages)

The sample languages significantly differ in the *distribution* of the actualized derivational potential across individual orders of derivation. If we concentrate on the first three orders, Greek's SV is 50% and above in each order. Ukrainian manifests increasing SVs as the order increases (16%, 23.81%, 38.89%) and a high SV even in the 4th order (33.33%). The opposite can be observed in Lithuanian (41.38%, 39.13%, 25.00%). There are languages with a kind of falling-rising SV, such as Catalan (26.83%, 8.11%, 25.00%), languages with a rising-falling SV, for example, Finnish (24.24%, 35.29% 19.05%), and, importantly, languages that concentrate the derivation exclusively in the first two orders. Examples of this are numerous, including, for instance, Dutch, English, Italian, Spanish, and Estonian. In addition, there are languages that restrict their derivational activities to the 1st order (Icelandic and Tatar).

In the following analysis, the first three orders of derivation are taken into consideration. As a result, the sample of languages is reduced to 23 languages because 17 languages derive words from *bone* only in the first two orders (cf. Table 49.4).

The SVs of *bone* in these languages follow two basic tendencies: the SV either rises (the SV in the 2nd order is higher than the SV in the 1st order) or falls (the SV in the 2nd order is lower than the SV in the 1st order). Furthermore, for both of these basic cases, three patterns can be observed.

Rising (including rising-falling)

14 languages show this pattern (cf. Table 49.7). Half of them are Slavic languages. In the first pattern, the lowest SV is in the 1st order, and the highest in the 3rd order. The second and third patterns are rising-falling ones. In both of them, it is the 2nd order of derivation that features the highest SV. They differ in their position of the 3rd order relative to the 1st order.

Falling (including falling-rising)

In contrast to the former pattern, only two languages here are Slavic (Bulgarian and Czech). There are two Romance languages and two Uralic languages (Hungarian and North Saami). As in the previous case, three patterns can be identified: Pattern 1 shows gradually falling SVs, while Patterns 2 and 3 are falling-rising types (cf. Table 49.8). In all patterns, the SV in the 1st order of derivation is always higher than in the 2nd order. In Patterns 1 and 2, the SV in the 1st

Table 49.7: Patterns of rising SVs (bone).

	Description	Languages (Total 14)
Pattern 1	LOW-MEDIUM-HIGH	French, Galician, Irish, Turkish, Ukrainian (5 languages)
Pattern 2	MEDIUM-HIGH-LOW	Croatian, Finnish, German, Greek, Polish, Russian, Serbian (7 languages)
Pattern 3	LOW-HIGH-MEDIUM	Slovak, Slovene (2 languages)

Table 49.8: Patterns of falling SVs (bone).

	Description	Languages (Total 9)
Pattern 1	HIGH-MEDIUM-LOW	Georgian, Hungarian, Lithuanian, Romanian, Swedish (5 languages)
Pattern 2	HIGH-LOW-MEDIUM	Bulgarian, Catalan, Czech (3 languages)
Pattern 3	MEDIUM-LOW-HIGH	North Saami (1 language)

order is the highest and in the 2nd order it drops to either the lowest or the medium value. In the last pattern, the highest value is in the 3rd order.

This was an example of the possibilities for an analysis at the level of a single word. A more interesting and more telling analysis would be one that covered all ten words of each word-class.

49.2.2 Cross-linguistic comparison of word-classes by saturation value

Nouns

For each order of derivation, we classified languages into three groups according to their SV (Table 49.9). This perspective shows that the highest average SV in the 1st order for all ten nouns was found in Dutch (51.82%), followed by Greek (39.95%), German (39.05%), Georgian (36.07%), Dargwa (35.00%) and Swedish (34.29%). The SV for Maltese in the 1st order is as low as 16.25%. Dargwa is a special case in this series: it ranks highly in the 1st order, but this is the only order for the derivation of basic simple nouns in this language. German tops the 2nd order with 50.00%, as the SV of Dutch drops significantly to 28.00%. While the 3rd order is dominated by North Saami with 34.40%, German still maintains a high SV in this order (20.00%). Languages with only one order of derivation (Chechen and Dargwa) have high SVs in the 1st order (for obvious reasons). Dargwa belongs to the high SV group and Chechen to the medium group. With the exception of Danish, a similar situation can be observed for other languages with two orders (English, Frisian, and Norwegian).

Verbs

Table 49.10 classifies languages according to the SVs of verb-based derivations. Verb-based derivations are characterized by high SVs across all orders. Thus, Greek dominates the first two orders with values approaching 50% and German the 3rd order with an SV of 43.50%. Even the 4th order's top value is as high as 30%. In general, the SVs of verb-based derivational networks are fairly high. In the 1st order of derivation, there are as many as 20 languages that actualize their potential to more than 30%. In the 2nd order, there are 11 such languages. It is interesting that the top 10 values for the individual orders include genetically diverse languages, i.e. we do not witness the dominance of a specific genus.

Adjectives

The adjective-based derivations show very high top-level SVs (cf. Table 49.11). The highest SV in the 1st order reaches 60% (Dargwa), in the 2nd order it is 40.40% (Greek), in the 3rd order it is 48.89% (Greek) and in the 4th order it has the same

Table 49.9: Classification of languages according to SV by orders of derivation, nouns.

	High SV	Medium SV	Low SV	No derivatives
1st order	Czech, Dargwa, Dutch, Finnish, Georgian, German, Greek, North Saami, Romanian, Russian, Swedish (11 languages)	Basque, Bulgarian, Catalan, Chechen, Croatian, English, Estonian, Frisian, Galician, Hungarian, Irish, Italian, Latvian, Lithuanian, Norwegian, Polish, Portuguese, Serbian, Slovak, Slovene, Spanish, Tatar, Turkish, Ukrainian, Welsh (25 languages)	Danish, French, Icelandic, Maltese (4 languages)	
2nd order	Czech, Dutch, English, Estonian, Finnish, Frisian, German, Greek, Hungarian, Italian, North Saami, Slovak, Turkish (13 languages)	Bulgarian, Catalan, Croatian, Danish, Georgian, Latvian, Lithuanian, Norwegian, Romanian, Serbian, Swedish, Ukrainian (12 languages)	Basque, French, Galician, Icelandic, Irish, Maltese, Polish, Portuguese, Russian, Slovene, Spanish, Tatar, Welsh (13 languages)	Chechen, Dargwa (2 languages)
3rd order	Croatian, Czech, Finnish, German, Greek, Hungarian, Lithuanian, North Saami, Portuguese, Turkish (10 languages)	Bulgarian, Catalan, Estonian, Georgian, Irish, Italian, Latvian, Polish, Romanian, Russian, Serbian, Slovak, Slovene, Swedish, Ukrainian (15 languages)	Basque, Dutch, French, Galician, Icelandic, Maltese, Spanish, Tatar, Welsh (9 languages)	Chechen, Danish, Dargwa, English, Frisian, Norwegian (6 languages)

49 Derivational networks in European languages: A cross-linguistic perspective — 501

4th order	Croatian, German, North Saami (3 languages)	Bulgarian, Czech, Finnish, Hungarian, Italian, Romanian, Serbian, Slovak, Turkish, Ukrainian (10 languages)	Catalan, Estonian, Georgian, Polish, Russian, Slovene, Swedish (7 languages)	Basque, Chechen, Danish, Dargwa, Dutch, English, French, Frisian, Galician, Greek, Icelandic, Irish, Latvian, Lithuanian, Maltese, Norwegian, Portuguese, Spanish, Tatar, Welsh (20 languages)
5th order		Bulgarian, Croatian, Czech, Finnish, Hungarian, North Saami, Slovak, Turkish, Ukrainian (9 languages)		Basque, Catalan, Chechen, Danish, Dargwa, Dutch, English, Estonian, French, Frisian, Galician, Georgian, German, Greek, Icelandic, Irish, Italian, Latvian, Lithuanian, Maltese, Norwegian, Polish, Portuguese, Romanian, Russian, Serbian, Slovene, Spanish, Swedish, Tatar, Welsh (31 languages)

Legend:
1st order: HIGH = 30–52%; MEDIUM = 20–29%; LOW= <20%
2nd order: HIGH = 26–50%; MEDIUM = 20–25%; LOW= <20%
3rd order: HIGH = 20–34%; MEDIUM = 11–19%; LOW= <11%
4th order: HIGH = 20–27%; MEDIUM = 11–19%; LOW= <11%
5th order: ALL CATEGORIES = 10%

Table 49.10: Classification of languages according to SV by orders of derivation, verbs.

	High SV	Medium SV	Low SV	No derivatives
1st order	Czech, Dutch, French, Georgian, Greek, Maltese, North Saami, Turkish (8 languages)	Bulgarian, Catalan, Croatian, Dargwa, English, Estonian, Finnish, Frisian, Galician, German, Hungarian, Icelandic, Italian, Latvian, Lithuanian, Polish, Portuguese, Romanian, Slovak, Slovene, Spanish, Swedish, Tatar, Ukrainian (24 languages)	Basque, Chechen, Danish, Irish, Norwegian, Russian, Serbian, Welsh (8 languages)	
2nd order	Croatian, Dutch, Georgian, German, Greek, Hungarian, Latvian, Lithuanian, North Saami, Serbian, Turkish (11 languages)	Bulgarian, Catalan, Czech, Dargwa, English, Estonian, Finnish, Italian, Maltese, Polish, Portuguese, Romanian, Slovak, Slovene, Swedish, Tatar (16 languages)	Basque, Chechen, Danish, French, Frisian, Galician, Icelandic, Irish, Norwegian, Russian, Spanish, Ukrainian, Welsh (13 languages)	
3rd order	Croatian, Czech, Dutch, English, Georgian, German, Greek, Latvian, Lithuanian, North Saami, Serbian, Slovak, Slovene, Turkish (14 languages)	Bulgarian, Catalan, Estonian, Finnish, Galician, Hungarian, Irish, Italian, Polish, Romanian, Russian, Spanish, Swedish, Tatar, Welsh (15 languages)	Chechen, French, Frisian, Icelandic, Maltese, Norwegian, Portuguese (7 languages)	Basque, Danish, Dargwa, Ukrainian (4 languages)

	high	medium	low	zero
4th order	Croatian, Georgian, German, Latvian, Lithuanian, North Saami, Swedish (7 languages)	Czech, Estonian, Finnish, Hungarian, Italian, Polish, Russian, Serbian, Slovak, Slovene, Turkish, Welsh (12 languages)	Bulgarian, Dutch, Frisian, Norwegian, Romanian (5 languages)	Basque, Catalan, Chechen, Danish, Dargwa, English, French, Galician, Greek, Icelandic, Irish, Maltese, Portuguese, Spanish, Tatar, Ukrainian (16 languages)
5th order	—	Czech, Georgian, Slovak (3 languages)	Bulgarian, Croatian, Dutch, Estonian, Finnish, Hungarian, North Saami, Norwegian, Serbian, Slovene (10 languages)	Basque, Catalan, Chechen, Danish, Dargwa, English, French, Frisian, Galician, German, Greek, Icelandic, Irish, Italian, Latvian, Lithuanian, Maltese, Polish, Portuguese, Romanian, Russian, Spanish, Swedish, Tatar, Turkish, Ukrainian, Welsh (27 languages)

Legend:
1st order: HIGH = 35–50%; MEDIUM = 25–34%; LOW = <25%
2nd order: HIGH = 30–45%; MEDIUM = 20–29%; LOW = <20%
3rd order: HIGH = 20–44%; MEDIUM = 10–19%; LOW = <10%
4th order: HIGH = 20–30%; MEDIUM = 11–19%; LOW = <11%
5th order: HIGH = >10; LOW = <10

Table 49.11: Classification of languages according to SV by orders of derivation, adjectives.

	High SV	Medium SV	Low SV	No derivatives
1st order	Dargwa, Dutch, French, Lithuanian, Maltese (5 languages)	Basque, Bulgarian, Catalan, Croatian, Czech, English, Estonian, Finnish, Frisian, Galician, Georgian, German, Greek, Hungarian, Icelandic, Irish, Italian, Latvian, North Saami, Norwegian, Polish, Portuguese, Romanian, Russian, Serbian, Slovak, Slovene, Spanish, Swedish, Tatar, Turkish, Ukrainian, Welsh (33 languages)	Chechen, Danish (2 languages)	
2nd order	Estonian, French, Georgian, Greek, Hungarian, Lithuanian, North Saami, Turkish (8 languages)	Chechen, Croatian, Czech, Dutch, Finnish, Galician, German, Irish, Italian, Latvian, Maltese, Polish, Portuguese, Romanian, Serbian, Slovak, Slovene, Spanish, Swedish, Tatar, Ukrainian (21 languages)	Basque, Bulgarian, Catalan, Danish, English, Frisian, Icelandic, Norwegian, Russian, Welsh (10 languages)	Dargwa (1 language)
3rd order	Estonian, Finnish, Greek, Hungarian, Latvian, Lithuanian, North Saami, Turkish (8 languages)	Bulgarian, Croatian, Czech, Dutch, Georgian, German, Maltese, Tatar (8 languages)	Basque, Catalan, English, Frisian, Galician, Irish, Italian, Polish, Portuguese, Romanian, Russian, Serbian, Slovak, Slovene, Spanish, Swedish, Ukrainian, Welsh (18 languages)	Chechen, Danish, Dargwa, French, Icelandic, Norwegian (6 languages)

Order		
4th order	Greek, Latvian (2 languages)	Croatian, Estonian, Finnish, Lithuanian, Bulgarian, Catalan, Czech, Georgian, North Saami, Swedish, Turkish (7 languages)	German, Hungarian, Italian, Maltese, Polish, Romanian, Serbian, Slovak, Slovene, Tatar, Ukrainian, Welsh (16 languages)	Basque, Chechen, Danish, Dargwa, Dutch, English, French, Frisian, Galician, Icelandic, Irish, Norwegian, Portuguese, Russian, Spanish (15 languages)
5th order	Czech, Finnish (2 languages)	German, Georgian, Turkish (3 languages)	Bulgarian, Croatian, North Saami, Serbian, Slovene (5 languages)	Basque, Catalan, Chechen, Danish, Dargwa, Dutch, English, Estonian, French, Frisian, Galician, Greek, Hungarian, Icelandic, Irish, Italian, Latvian, Lithuanian, Maltese, Norwegian, Polish, Portuguese, Romanian, Russian, Slovak, Spanish, Swedish, Tatar, Ukrainian, Welsh (30 languages)

Legend:
1st order: HIGH = 40–60%; MEDIUM = 20–39%; LOW= <20%
2nd order: HIGH = 30–41%; MEDIUM = 20–29%; LOW= <20%
3rd order: HIGH = 30–50%; MEDIUM = 20–29%; LOW= <20%
4th order: HIGH = 30–40%; MEDIUM = 20–29%; LOW= <20%
5th order: HIGH = 20–25%; LOW= <20

value as in the 1st order – 60% (Dargwa). The highest SV in the 5th order is 25% (Finnish). These high SVs in all five orders also influence the division of languages into high, medium and low groups.

Family-wise, the top position in the 1st order is assumed by diverse languages. The most significant finding of this sort comes from the 3rd order, where half of the top languages are represented by Uralic languages.

Total word-class SV

A more generalized view is given by the *total word-class SV*, i.e. by the total SV per word-class in a given language. It is calculated as a proportion of all actualized derivatives and the maximum derivational network for a given word-class as a whole (10 basic words in our case).

Nouns

Table 49.12 below divides languages into three groups.

Table 49.12: Classification of languages according to total saturation value, nouns.

Total word-class SV	Languages
High (30–40%)	Dargwa, Dutch, German, Greek, North Saami
Medium (20–29.99%)	Bulgarian, Catalan, Chechen, Croatian, Czech, English, Estonian, Finnish, Frisian, Galician, Georgian, Hungarian, Irish, Italian, Latvian, Lithuanian, Norwegian, Portuguese, Romanian, Russian, Serbian, Slovak, Slovene, Spanish, Swedish, Turkish, Ukrainian
Low (< 20%)	Basque, Danish, French, Icelandic, Maltese, Polish, Tatar, Welsh

These results can be projected onto the following saturation map (Map 49.2).

It follows from Map 49.2 that there is no homogeneous territory of languages featuring the highest total word-class SV (dark green colour). This group of languages is heterogeneous in terms of their genetic origin: two Germanic languages, one North Caucasian language, one Uralic language, and Greek. The vast majority of languages (27 out of 40) belong to the medium group, suggesting that *the total word-class SV between 20 and 29.99% is characteristic for the word-class of nouns.* In other words, cross-linguistically, the

Map 49.2: Distribution of languages according to their total word-class SV, nouns.

word-class of nouns seems to actualize between 20% and 29.99% of its potential derivational capacity.

Verbs

Table 49.13, featuring the total word-class SVs for verbs, confirms the previous observation that the majority of languages feature medium SVs.

Table 49.13: Classification of languages according to total saturation value, verbs.

Total word-class SV	Languages
High (30–46%)	Dargwa, Dutch, Georgian, German, Greek, Lithuanian, Maltese, North Saami, Turkish
Medium (20–29.99%)	Basque, Bulgarian, Catalan, Croatian, Czech, English, Estonian, Finnish, French, Frisian, Galician, Hungarian, Icelandic, Italian, Latvian, Polish, Portuguese, Romanian, Serbian, Slovak, Slovene, Spanish, Swedish, Tatar, Ukrainian
Low (<20%)	Chechen, Danish, Irish, Norwegian, Russian, Welsh

The situation in the word-class of verbs is similar to that of nouns in concentrating the majority of languages in the range of 20–20.99% (25 out of 40 languages). This is again very telling of general patterns in the derivational networks of basic verbs. The topmost group includes the same languages as that of nouns, plus Turkish, Georgian, Maltese and Lithuanian. This means that it is also the case for verbs that the highest SV is characteristic of a heterogeneous group of languages, regardless of their genetic origin or geographical location. As shown in Map 49.3, these languages are scattered across Europe. In contrast, the light brown colour on the map indicates that languages with low SVs are mostly spoken in peripheral European areas and in Eastern Europe.

Map 49.3: Distribution of languages according to their total word-class SV, verbs.

Adjectives

Finally, Table 49.14 and Map 49.4 give the total SVs for adjectives. As with nouns and verbs, the majority of languages belong to the medium value (25 out of 40). With the exception of German, all the other topmost languages from the word-class of nouns feature high SVs in adjectives as well. In this word-class, however, the number of high-SV languages is higher than in nouns or verbs (12), thus leaving merely three languages in the lowest SV group. Nevertheless, they do not constitute a continuous territory. What is analogous with the previous word-classes is the geographically peripheral location (the eastern part of Europe) of the low-SV languages.

Table 49.14: Classification of languages according to total saturation value, adjectives.

Total word-class SV	Languages
High (30–60%)	Dargwa, Dutch, Estonian, French, Greek, Hungarian, Latvian, Lithuanian, Maltese, North Saami, Spanish, Turkish
Medium (20–29.99%)	Basque, Bulgarian, Catalan, Croatian, Czech, English, Finnish, Frisian, Galician, Georgian, German, Icelandic, Irish, Italian, Norwegian, Polish, Portuguese, Romanian, Serbian, Slovak, Slovene, Swedish, Tatar, Ukrainian, Welsh
Low (<20%)	Chechen, Danish, Russian

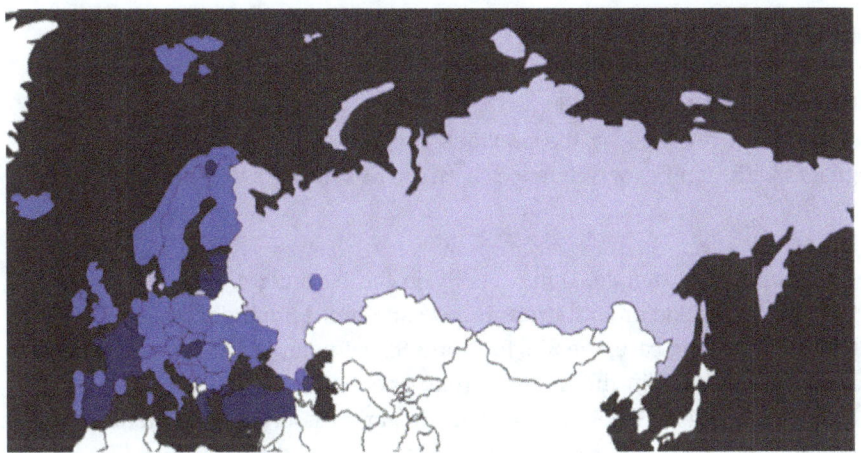

Map 49.4: Distribution of languages according to their total word-class SV, adjectives.

Word-class comparison

Tables 49.12–49.14 and Maps 49.2–49.4 enable us to draw some interesting conclusions about the tendencies of the actualization of derivational potential at the level of word-classes.

Summary

(i) Languages actualize 20–30% of the derivational potential of a word-class. This value indicates the degree of predictability of derivational networks.

This is almost identical for all three word-classes and is represented by 67.5% of languages for nouns and 62.5% of languages for both verbs and adjectives.

(ii) There is a core group of languages that keep high SVs across all three word-classes. They include Greek, Dutch, North Saami and Dargwa. This group might be completed by German, Turkish and Lithuanian, but these have high values in two word-classes and a medium SV in the third word-class.

(iii) There is no geographically homogeneous territory in which the languages of the topmost SVs are spoken. These languages are of various genetic origins and are scattered across Europe. In contrast, low-SV languages arrange themselves in geographically peripheral areas.

Distribution of SVs across orders of derivation

Patterns of SV distribution I

What is not revealed by the previous analysis is the fact that there are languages with significant differences between SVs in various orders of derivation.

Nouns

Let us take, for example, Dutch. Its SV in the 1st order of derivation is nearly 52%, but in the 2nd order it drops to 28% and in the 3rd order it is only 10%. To take a contrasting case, the SVs for North Saami noun-based derivatives always keep the language in the highest group and, at the same time, they are well balanced (33.04%, 30.79%, 34.40%). Hungarian is pretty consistent too: 12th position in the 1st order (29.26%), 13th position in the 2nd order (27.68) and 14th position in the 3rd order (23.50%). Czech ranks highly in the first two orders with 33.22% and 30.00%, respectively, then its SV drops to 24.24%. The same is basically true of Catalan, but with much lower SVs. Contrary to this, Georgian ranks 3rd in the 1st order with 36.07%, but 21st in the 2nd order (22.73%) and 24th in the 3rd order (14.81%). In general, however, it can be observed that the majority of languages maintain a specific level of SV throughout individual orders of derivation without substantial oscillations. This enables us to identify specific cases in terms of the richness of derivational networks at individual orders of derivation for a homogeneous group of words (simple underived nouns belonging to the core vocabulary, in our case).

As in the case of *bone*, languages can be classified in terms of falling and rising SVs (cf. Tables 49.15 and 49.16). In the word-class of nouns, the situation is surprisingly homogeneous. 34 languages derive new complex words in three orders of derivation. Out of these 34 languages, 26 follow the same pattern (a falling

Table 49.15: Patterns of rising saturation values, nouns.

	Description	Languages (Total 6)
Pattern 2		Estonian, Finnish, German, Latvian, Slovak (5 languages)
Pattern 3		Turkish (1 language)

Table 49.16: Patterns of falling saturation values, nouns.

	Description	Languages (Total 28)
Pattern 1		Basque, Bulgarian, Catalan, Croatian, Czech, Dutch, French, Galician, Georgian, Hungarian, Icelandic, Irish, Italian, Lithuanian, Maltese, Polish, Romanian, Russian, Serbian, Slovene, Spanish, Swedish, Tatar, Ukrainian, Welsh (25 languages)
Pattern 2		Portuguese (1 language)
Pattern 3		North Saami (1 language)

tendency, Pattern 1). Five languages represent the rising pattern (Pattern 2). Each of the three remaining languages belongs to a different type.

Verbs

As in the case of nouns, languages may also differ in the consistency of their SVs. Croatian, for example, keeps its SV above 30% (30.16%, 30.90%, 29.68%) in the first three orders of derivation. In contrast, German has a relatively low SV in the 1st order of derivation (29.71%), but in the 2nd and 3rd orders it rises above 40.00%. A significant drop can be observed in Spanish (30.91%, 17.93%, 14.00%). Welsh keeps its SVs between 20% and 10% in all three orders of derivation. 27 languages out of 36 follow the falling line, and 26 of them belong to the same pattern (Pattern 1) (cf. Tables 49.17 and 49.18). The second largest group consists of six languages and represents the rising pattern (Pattern 2) (cf. Table 49.17).

Table 49.17: Patterns of rising saturation values, verbs.

	Description	Languages (Total 9)
Pattern 2		Croatian, Hungarian, Italian, Latvian, Slovene, Turkish (6 languages)
Pattern 3		North Saami, Serbian (2 languages)
Pattern 4		German (1 language)

Table 49.18: Patterns of falling saturation values, verbs.

	Description	Languages (Total 27)
Pattern 1		Bulgarian, Catalan, Czech, Dutch, English, Estonian, Finnish, French, Frisian, Galician, Greek, Chechen, Icelandic, Irish, Lithuanian, Maltese, Norwegian, Polish, Portuguese, Romanian, Russian, Slovak, Spanish, Swedish, Tatar, Welsh (26 languages)
Pattern 3		Georgian (1 language)

Adjectives

Pattern 1 in the falling line is the most numerous group (22 languages) (cf. Table 49.20). Interestingly, a new pattern (Pattern 4) occurs in adjectives (cf. Table 49.19). The SV starts off low in the 1st order and gradually rises with the derivation order. This situation was found in the cases of Turkish and Greek.

Word-class comparison

The above shows that SVs fall gradually with rising orders of derivation for the vast majority of languages. This occurs in 28 languages for nouns, and in 27 languages for both verbs and adjectives. This suggests that the derivation of fewer words with an increasing order of derivation is independent of the word-class. Moreover, it is Pattern 1, i.e. the gradually falling SV with the increasing order, that evidently dominates: it is present in 26 languages in both nouns and verbs, and 22 languages in adjectives.

Table 49.19: Patterns of rising saturation values, adjectives.

	Description	Languages (Total 6)
Pattern 2		Estonian, Georgian, Slovene (3 languages)
Pattern 3		North Saami (1 language)
Pattern 4		Greek, Turkish (2 languages)

Table 49.20: Patterns of falling saturation values, adjectives.

	Description	Languages (26)
Pattern 1		Basque, Bulgarian, Catalan, Croatian, Czech, English, Frisian, Galician, Irish, Italian, Maltese, Polish, Portuguese, Romanian, Russian, Serbian, Slovak, Spanish, Swedish, Ukrainian, Welsh (21 languages)
Pattern 2		German, Hungarian, Latvian, Lithuanian (4 languages)
Pattern 3		Finnish, Tatar (2 languages)

Patterns of SV distribution II

If the focus is laid on the classification of languages according to Tables 49.12–49.14, i. e. into high, medium and low SV groups, and if we restrict our attention to the first three orders of derivation, we can observe the varying behaviours of languages.

Nouns

Some languages behave consistently across the orders of derivation. For example, Czech, Finnish, German, Greek and North Saami always have high SVs, while Bulgarian, Catalan, Latvian, Serbian and Ukrainian are always in the medium group. French, Icelandic and Maltese always feature low SVs. Eight languages never reach the group of high SVs: in the first three orders of derivation, they feature the patterns medium-low-low (Basque, Galician, Spanish, Tatar, Welsh) and medium-low-medium (Irish, Polish, Slovene). In contrast, 10 languages never drop to the low saturation group. They adhere to one of the following patterns: medium-high-medium (Italian, Estonian, Slovak), high-medium-medium (Swedish, Romanian, Georgian), medium-high-high (Turkish, Hungarian) or medium-medium-high (Croatian, Lithuanian). Table 49.21 gives an overview of all the patterns occurring in nouns.

Table 49.21: Classification of languages by saturation values in the first three orders of derivation, nouns.

Patterns for the first three orders	Languages
H-H-H	Czech, German, Greek, Finnish, North Saami
M-M-M	Bulgarian, Catalan, Latvian, Serbian, Ukrainian
L-L-L	French, Icelandic, Maltese
H-M-M	Georgian, Romanian, Swedish
M-M-L	Basque, Galician, Spanish, Tatar, Welsh
M-L-M	Irish, Polish, Slovene
M-H-M	Estonian, Italian, Slovak
M-H-H	Hungarian, Turkish
M-M-H	Croatian, Lithuanian
H-H-L	Dutch
H-L-M	Russian
M-L-H	Portuguese

Legend: H – high SV, M – medium SV, L – low SV.

Verbs

In this word-class, too, there are languages that maintain a high SV throughout the first three orders of derivation (Greek, Turkish, Georgian, Dutch and North Saami) (cf. Table 49.22). By contrast, French drops its SV in the 2nd order of derivation so dramatically that it has a low rank in the 2nd and 3rd orders (such that it has no derivatives in the 4th order). Czech oscillates between the high and medium groups (but with very small differences in SVs), while Maltese drops its SVs continuously: in the 1st order of derivation its SV is high, in the 2nd it is medium, and in the 3rd order it is low.

Table 49.22: Classification of languages by saturation values in the first three orders of derivation, verbs.

Patterns for the first three orders	Languages
H-H-H	Dutch, Georgian, Greek, North Saami, Turkish
M-M-M	Bulgarian, Catalan, Estonian, Finnish, Italian, Polish, Romanian, Swedish, Tatar
L-L-L	Chechen, Norwegian
H-M-H	Czech
M-M-L	Portuguese
M-L-M	Galician, Spanish
M-H-H	Croatian, Latvian, Lithuanian, German
M-M-H	English, Slovene, Slovak
M-H-M	Hungarian
H-L-L	French
M-L-L	Frisian, Icelandic
L-L-M	Irish, Russian, Welsh
L-H-H	Serbian
H-M-L	Maltese

Adjectives

Table 49.23 below illustrates that only one language (Lithuanian) has high SVs in all three orders of derivation. None of the languages feature low saturation in the first three orders. The largest number of languages (12) have medium SVs in the 1st and 2nd orders, dropping into the low group in the 3rd order. The table also shows that, while there are languages that are consistent in their SVs (Lithuanian, German, Croatian, Czech), there are also languages with considerable variations in their SVs.

Table 49.23: Classification of languages by saturation values in the first three orders of derivation, adjectives.

Patterns for the first three orders	Languages
H-H-H	Lithuanian
M-M-M	Croatian, Czech, German
M-M-L	Galician, Irish, Italian, Polish, Portuguese, Romanian, Serbian, Slovak, Slovene, Spanish, Swedish, Ukrainian
M-L-L	Basque, Catalan, English, Frisian, Russian, Welsh
H-M-M	Dutch, Maltese
M-L-M	Bulgarian,
M-H-H	Estonian, Greek, Hungarian, North Saami, Turkish
M-M-H	Finnish, Latvian, Tatar
M-H-M	Georgian

Comparison of word-classes

The data show that keeping a particular level of SV across the first three orders of derivation partly depends on the word-class and partly on the general derivational potential of individual languages. Two languages maintain the pattern H-H-H in nouns and verbs (Greek and North Saami) and two languages maintain the pattern M-M-M in nouns and verbs (Bulgarian and Catalan). There is no such correspondence between adjectives and the other two word-classes. In addition, there is no language that maintains the pattern L-L-L in at least two word-classes.

There are several prevailingly H languages. As mentioned above, they include Greek and North Saami as well as some other languages with predominantly high SVs across their orders of derivation in all three word-classes, which are Turkish, Czech, German, Hungarian and Lithuanian.

There are 10 prevailingly M languages: Bulgarian, Galician, Italian, Polish, Romanian, Slovak, Slovene, Spanish, Swedish and Tatar. Nine other languages with medium values in two word-classes can also be added to this group: Catalan, Croatian, Georgian, Latvian, Estonian, Finnish, Irish, Portuguese, and Serbian.

There is no prevailingly L language. Two languages have low SVs in two word-classes: low SVs occur in verb-based and adjective-based networks in Russian, and Welsh has medium SVs in nouns and low SVs in verbs and adjectives. The majority of low SVs can be found in languages with fewer than three orders of derivations in all or some word-classes, like Danish, Frisian, Icelandic,

English, Basque and Norwegian. An interesting case is that of French, which has fewer than three orders in adjectives; while it has low SVs in nouns, its verb-based network combines a high SV in the 1st order and low SVs in the 2nd and 3rd orders.

All this discussion can be represented by Diagrams 49.4–49.6, which illustrate the correlation between the number of orders and the total word-class SVs. Since the correlation coefficient for each word-class approaches 0 (nouns = − 0.01, verbs = 0.17, adjectives = − 0.22), there is no correlation between SVs and orders of derivation. The diagrams show that languages tend to have SVs between 20 and 30%.

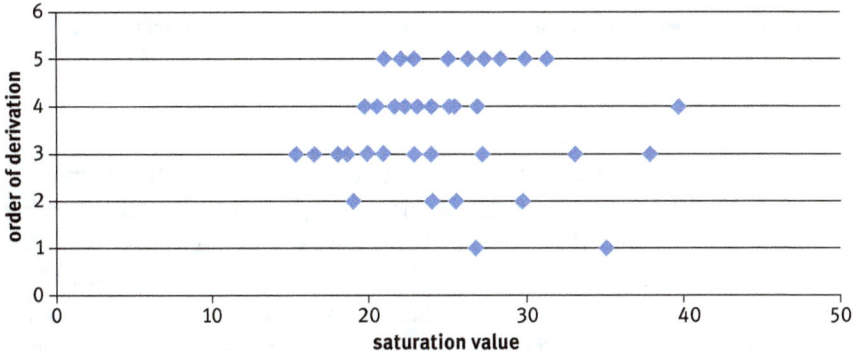

Diagram 49.4: Correlation of saturation values and orders of derivation, nouns.

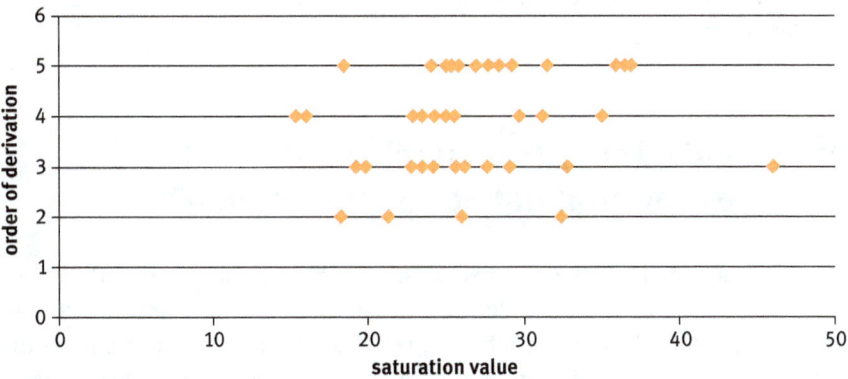

Diagram 49.5: Correlation of saturation values and orders of derivation, verbs.

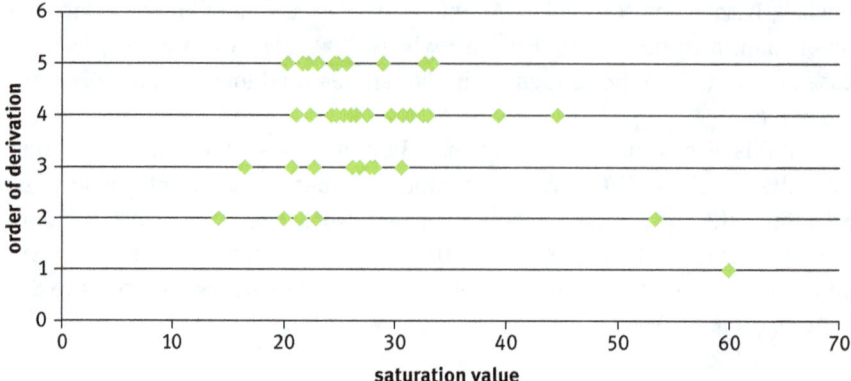

Diagram 49.6: Correlation of saturation values and orders of derivation, adjectives.

Summary

(i) The fundamental tendency for the majority of languages is the falling tendency, i.e. the saturation value is indirectly proportional to the growing order of derivation. This tendency is independent of the word-class of the basic word.
(ii) There are very few languages that maintain a consistent level in their saturation values across consecutive orders of derivation. The SV consistency of a particular language depends on the word-class of the basic word.
(iii) The SVs' consistency across orders of derivation is not affected by the genetic affiliation of a language.
(iv) In general, there is no correlation between saturation values and orders of derivation.

49.3 Consistency of derivation: Are the derivational networks predictable?

Any discussion of derivational networks should, by necessity, pursue the objective of answering one of the following central questions: are derivational networks predictable? If so, what is the degree of predictability? And what are the factors affecting the predictability of derivational networks? Therefore, further to the discussion in section 49.2, we aim to identify any patterns in saturation values for individual languages and individual orders of derivation in order to find out whether the saturation values for all 10 words of a given word-class are *consistent*. Consistency implies *predictability*. Certainly, this is not an either/or question. Instead, predictability is a cline, determined by the extent of deviations from the average saturation value. This can be evaluated by means of the parameter of *standard deviation* (SD). If the standard deviation is under 10%, we will consider the derivation within a particular word-class of a given language to be predictable in a given order of derivation. The data enable us to draw the following conclusions.

49.3.1 Nouns

In Table 49.24, languages are divided into three groups according to the SD. The table shows that 13 languages are ranked in the group with SD <10 in the 1st order of derivation. Two languages from this group (Bulgarian and Croatian) occur in the same SD group in the 2nd order as well, this time accompanied by Ukrainian. There is no language with SD <10 in the 3rd order of deviation. Furthermore, Bulgarian and Croatian behave differently in the 3rd order. While Bulgarian smoothly slips into the medium group, Croatian makes a jump into the group with the lowest consistency. The number gradually drops with the growing order.

The SD >20 group shows the opposite tendency. In the 1st order of derivation, there are only three languages with an SD of above 20, but in the 2nd order there are 12 languages, and in the 3rd the number of languages is 13. Dutch occurs repeatedly in this group in each order of derivation. So do Danish and Dargwa. However, Dargwa has only one order of derivation and Danish two.

The medium SD group (10–19.9) shows a dropping tendency too, but the numbers are more balanced (1st order: 24 languages; 2nd order: 20 languages; 3rd order: 15 languages). Seven languages (Czech, Polish, Russian, Serbian, Slovene, Catalan, and North Saami) belong to this group in each order of derivation.

Map 49.5 shows the consistency in the word-class of nouns in the 1st order of derivation. The darker the green colour, the more consistent the SVs in a given language. There is a stretch of areas in dark green running through Europe from north to south. This stretch divides Europe into western and eastern parts. The three light green locations are isolated territories of Danish, Dargwa and Dutch.

Nouns, 1st order

There are 13 languages with SDs under 10.00: Bulgarian, Croatian, Slovak, German, Icelandic, Norwegian, Italian, Welsh, Latvian, Finnish, Hungarian,

Table 49.24: Classification of languages by standard deviation per order of derivation, nouns.

Order SD	1st	2nd	3rd
0.1–9.9	Basque, Bulgarian, Croatian, Finnish, German, Hungarian, Icelandic, Italian, Latvian, Norwegian, Slovak, Turkish, Welsh	Bulgarian, Croatian, Ukrainian	
10–19.9	Catalan, Chechen, Czech, English, Estonian, French, Frisian, Galician, Georgian, Greek, Irish, Lithuanian, Maltese, North Saami, Polish, Portuguese, Romanian, Russian, Serbian, Slovene, Spanish, Swedish, Tatar, Ukrainian	Basque, Catalan, Czech, English, Frisian, Galician, German, Hungarian, Irish, Italian, Latvian, North Saami, Polish, Portuguese, Russian, Serbian, Slovak, Slovene, Spanish, Turkish	Bulgarian, Catalan, Czech, Finnish, Greek, Hungarian, Italian, North Saami, Polish, Russian, Serbian, Slovak, Slovene, Tatar, Ukrainian
>20	Danish, Dargwa, Dutch	Danish, Dutch, Estonian, Finnish, French, Greek, Icelandic, Lithuanian, Norwegian, Romanian, Tatar, Welsh	Basque, Croatian, Dutch, Estonian, French, Galician, German, Icelandic, Irish, Latvian, Lithuanian, Portuguese, Spanish, Swedish, Turkish, Welsh
No derivatives		Chechen, Dargwa, Georgian, Maltese, Swedish	Danish, Dargwa Chechen, English, Frisian, Georgian, Maltese, Norwegian, Romanian

Turkish and Basque. Their SDs range between 6 and 9.9, with Bulgarian featuring the most consistent SV across nouns (6.23). Importantly, no language exceeds an SD value of 20.

Nouns, 2nd order

Only three languages have an SD under 10.00: Bulgarian, Croatian and Ukrainian. Most of the other languages are within the range between 10.00 and 20.00. There are a few values above 20.

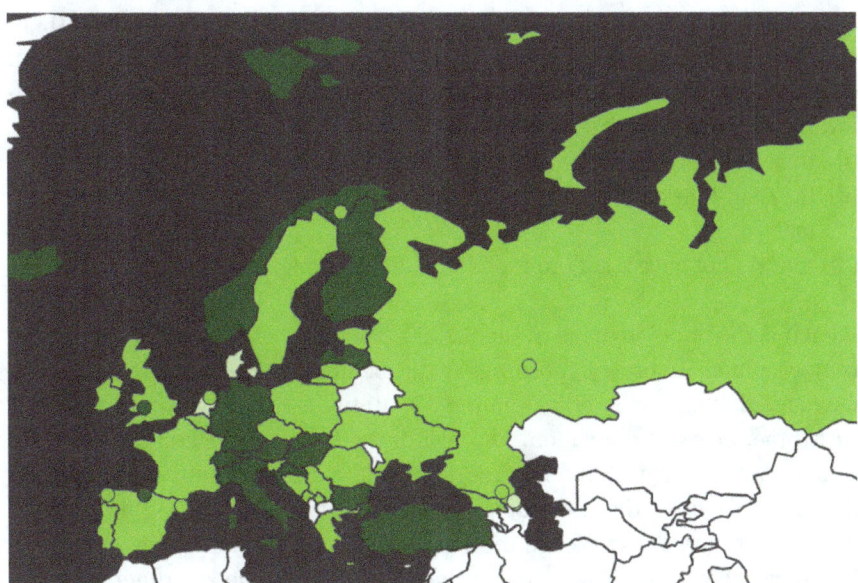

Map 49.5: Classification of languages by standard deviation in the 1st order, nouns.

Nouns, 3rd order

None of the languages with a standard deviation under 10 preserve their SV consistency in the 3rd order. The values for the individual nouns are apparently more scattered than in the 2nd order, and much more than in the 1st order.

49.3.2 Verbs

There are 11 languages in the SD <10 group in the 1st order of derivation (cf. Table 49.25). Only Serbian remains in the same group in the 2nd order, and there is no language in the 3rd order. As in the case of nouns, there is a falling tendency in terms of the number of languages.

In the least consistent group (SD >20), the 1st order is represented by one language (French), while the 2nd order counts seven languages and the 3rd order has 22 languages.

The highest number of languages occurs in the SD 10–19.9 group: 29 languages in the 1st order, 32 languages in the 2nd order and 15 languages in the 3rd order.

None of the languages, with the exception of Serbian, remain in the SD <10 group in the 2nd and 3rd orders of derivation. All languages (with the exception of Georgian) drop to the medium group. Afterwards, they follow one of the following options for the 3rd order:
(i) they stay in the medium group (Croatian, Estonian, Hungarian);
(ii) they fall into the SD >20 group (Latvian, North Saami, Turkish, Georgian); or
(iii) they do not have a 3rd order of derivation (Basque, Chechen).

French is the only language in the SD >20 group in the 1st order of derivation. In the 2nd and 3rd orders, it belongs to the medium group. Georgian is the only language that gradually falls from the SD <10 to the SD >20 group through the first three orders of derivation. The rest of the languages (Ukrainian, Danish, Dutch, Italian, Dragwa, and Maltese) start in the medium group and drop into the SD >20 group in the 2nd order. Afterwards, they either stay in this group or they do not have derivatives in the 3rd order. Languages in the medium group in the 1st order of derivation stay in the same group in the 2nd order. The prevailing number of Slavic languages, Tatar and Lithuanian also stay here in the 3rd order, while the majority of Germanic and Romance languages drop into the last deviation group, as do the Celtic languages and Greek.

Map 49.6 illustrates the consistency situation in the 1st order of derivation, where darker shades signal higher consistencies. Languages in dark brown are scattered throughout Europe. This is different from the situation with nouns. Nevertheless, the map confirms the observations that consistency in developing derivational networks is related to the genetic affiliation of a language.

Verbs, 1st order

In this case, 10 languages have an SD under 10.00: Serbian, Croatian, Estonian, Hungarian, Turkish, North Saami, Latvian, Basque, Georgian and Chechen. Serbian and Croatian have the lowest SDs (5.95 and 6.12, respectively). However, the SD of as many as 15 other languages falls within the range of 10.00 to 12.00. By implication, the predictability of derivation in this order of verbs appears to be very good, especially since there is only one language whose SD exceeds 20.00 (French: 21.00).

Table 49.25: Classification of languages by standard deviation per order of derivation, verbs.

Order SD	1st	2nd	3rd
0.1–9.9	Basque, Chechen, Croatian, Estonian, Georgian, Hungarian, Latvian, North Saami, Serbian, Turkish	Serbian	
10–19.9	Bulgarian, Catalan, Czech, Danish, Dargwa, Dutch, English, Finnish, Frisian, Galician, German, Greek, Icelandic, Irish, Italian, Lithuanian, Maltese, Norwegian, Polish, Portuguese, Romanian, Russian, Slovak, Slovene, Spanish, Swedish, Tatar, Ukrainian, Welsh	Basque, Bulgarian, Catalan, Chechen, Croatian, Czech, English, Estonian, Finnish, French, Frisian, Galician, German, Greek, Hungarian, Icelandic, Irish, Latvian, Lithuanian, North Saami, Norwegian, Polish, Portuguese, Romanian, Russian, Slovak, Slovene, Spanish, Swedish, Tatar, Turkish, Welsh	Bulgarian, Croatian, Czech, English, Estonian, Finnish, French, Hungarian, Lithuanian, Polish, Russian, Serbian, Slovene, Swedish, Tatar
>20	French	Danish, Dargwa, Dutch, Georgian, Italian, Maltese, Ukrainian	Catalan, Chechen, Dutch, Frisian, Galician, Georgian, German, Greek, Icelandic, Irish, Italian, Portuguese, Latvian, Maltese, North Saami, Norwegian, Romanian, Slovak, Spanish, Turkish, Welsh
No derivatives			Basque, Danish, Dargwa, Ukrainian

Verbs, 2nd order

No language is characterized by an SD below 10.00. The vast majority of them have a value between 10.00 and 20.00. High values of above 20.00 have been found for languages that do not have new derivatives in the 2nd order for several basic words (Danish, Ukrainian, Welsh, Dargwa and Maltese).

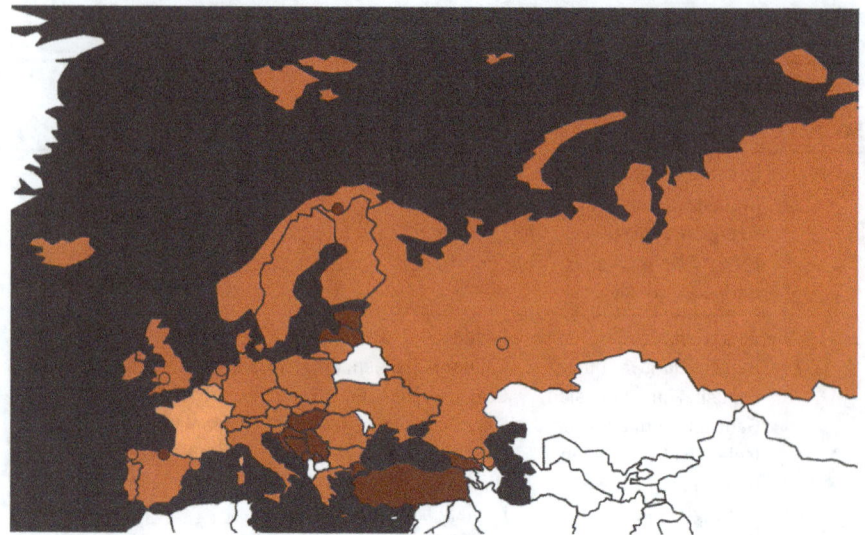

Map 49.6: Classification of languages by standard deviation in the 1st order, verbs.

Verbs, 3rd order

Like with nouns, none of the SD <10 languages preserve their SV consistency in the 3rd order. The most consistent languages in this order of derivation include Serbian (11.02), Swedish (12.75), Bulgarian (12.86), Slovene (13.01), French (15.27), four other Slavic languages (Czech, Russian, Croatian and Polish), three Uralic languages (Finnish, Estonian and Hungarian), English and Tatar, all of which have an SD value below 20.00.

49.3.3 Adjectives

In the word-class of adjectives, the group with SDs below 10 counts 12 languages in the 1st order of derivation, nine in the 2nd order and one in the 3rd order (cf. Table 49.26). This dropping tendency (higher order, fewer languages) is typical also of the medium group (20, 20 and 19 languages in the 1st, 2nd and 3rd orders, respectively). In the last group (above 20), the opposite tendency can be observed: there are two languages in the 1st order, 10 languages in the 2nd order and 20 languages in the 3rd order. Greek displays a very consistent behaviour throughout the orders of derivation and is always in the SD <10 group. At the other end of the scale is Dutch, which is always in the >20 group. The behaviour of Slavic languages in the SD <10 group in the 1st order of derivation is interesting. In the 2nd order, they either fall into the medium SD group (Bulgarian, Croatian, Polish, Slovene) or they stay in the SD <10 group. Consequently, they then continue in the medium SD group in the 3rd order. This behaviour is in contrast to non-Slavic languages in the SD <10 group. Greek has been already mentioned, and Catalan and Turkish pass into the medium group in the 2nd order and the SD >20 group in the 3rd order. Hungarian stays in the SD <10 group in the 2nd order and then jumps into the SD >20 group in the 3rd order. Basque descends from the SD <10 group in the 1st order to the SD >20 group in the 2nd and 3rd orders. To sum up, Slavic languages never go lower than the medium group for the 1st and 2nd orders of derivation. By contrast, no Germanic language is present in the SD <10 group.

Table 49.26: Classification of languages by standard deviation per order of derivation, adjectives.

Order SD	1st	2nd	3rd
0.1–9.9	Basque, Bulgarian, Catalan, Croatian, Greek, Hungarian, Polish, Russian, Slovene, Turkish, Ukrainian, Welsh	Estonian, Finnish, German, Greek, Hungarian, Lithuanian, North Saami, Russian, Ukrainian	Greek
10–19.9	Chechen, Czech, Danish, Dargwa, English, Estonian, Finnish, French, Frisian, Galician, German, Irish, Italian, Latvian, Lithuanian, Maltese, North Saami, Norwegian, Portuguese, Romanian, Serbian, Slovak, Spanish, Swedish, Tatar	Bulgarian, Catalan, Croatian, Czech, English, Frisian, Georgian, Irish, Italian, Latvian, Maltese, Norwegian, Polish, Romanian, Serbian, Slovak, Slovene, Swedish, Tatar, Turkish	Bulgarian, Croatian, Estonian, Finnish, German, Lithuanian, North Saami, Polish, Romanian, Russian, Slovene, Swedish, Tatar, Ukrainian
>20	Dutch, Icelandic	Basque, Chechen, Danish, Dutch, French, Galician, Icelandic, Portuguese, Spanish, Welsh	Basque, Catalan, Czech, Danish, Dutch, English, Frisian, Galician, Georgian, Hungarian, Irish, Italian, Latvian, Maltese, Portuguese, Serbian, Slovak, Spanish, Turkish, Welsh
No derivatives		Dargwa	Chechen, Dargwa, French, Icelandic, Norwegian

Map 49.7 below shows how Europe is divided in the 1st order of derivation if the consistency criterion is taken into consideration, where the darkest shade indicates the highest consistency. Western European areas mostly feature a medium level of consistency (SD between 10–19.9). Central Europe is a transition area, and eastern and southern European languages appear to be very consistent.

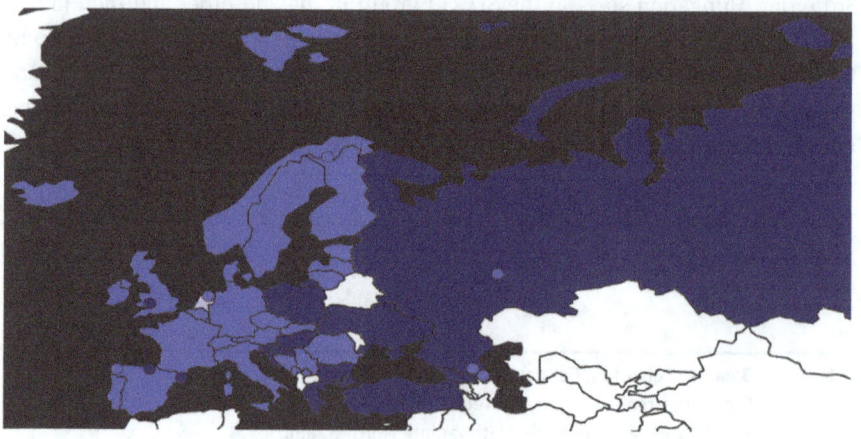

Map 49.7: Classification of languages by standard deviation in the 1st order, adjectives.

Adjectives, 1st order

Six out of the nine Slavic languages feature very high levels of consistency in deriving new words from basic adjectives. The SD of the remaining three is slightly above 10.00. From among the other languages, values under 10.00 have been found for Catalan, Welsh, Greek, Turkish, Basque and Georgian, i.e. 12 languages in total. The lowest values are for Russian (5.98), Turkish (6.14), Welsh (6.78) and Catalan (6.88). A fairly high level of consistency of derivation from basic adjectives in the 1st order is supported by there being no language with an SD above 20.00.

Adjectives, 2nd order

The standard deviation of five languages is below 10.00: Russian (6.46), Ukrainian (9.17), German (8.46), Lithuanian (9.82), and Greek (9.87). Note that all the other Slavic languages have standard deviation levels slightly above 10.00. As with nouns and verbs, high standard deviations (above 20.00) are mainly (but not exclusively – cf. Spanish and Portuguese, for example) due to the absence of derivatives within this order for several basic adjectives (e.g. in Danish, Dutch, Icelandic, French, Welsh, Basque, and Chechen).

Adjectives, 3rd order

Lithuanian is the only language with a high level of consistency in the 3rd order (6.68). While the standard deviation of German is also fairly low for this order of derivation (13.60), the derivation of most of Germanic languages is fairly unpredictable, which is especially due to the almost total absence of derivatives in this order. Relatively good values are characteristic of Uralic languages (Estonian, Finnish and North Saami), as well as Tatar, Greek and Romanian.

49.3.4 Comparison of word-classes

1st order
Croatian, Hungarian and Basque are in the most consistent group in the 1st order of derivation in each word-class. Czech, English, Frisian, Swedish, Galician, Portuguese, Spanish, Romanian, Irish, Lithuanian, and Maltese are always placed in the medium group. None of the languages occur repeatedly in the SD >20 group in the 1st order of derivation. The number of highly consistent languages (SD <10) per individual word-class is balanced (nouns – 13 languages; verbs – 10 languages; adjectives – 12 languages).

2nd order
None of the languages occur in the SD <10 group in each word-class. Ukrainian is the only language which can be found twice in this group (with nouns and adjectives). In comparison with the 1st order, the number of languages in the SD <10 group is relatively small: there are only three languages for nouns, one for verbs, and nine for adjectives. Czech, English, Frisian, Catalan, Irish, Latvian and Turkish are always in the medium group for each word-class, while Dutch and Danish are always in the SD >20 group in each word-class.

3rd order
Greek is the only language in the SD <10 group. Bulgarian, Czech, Polish, Russian, Slovene, Finnish and Tatar are always in the medium group. Dutch, Galician, Portuguese, Spanish, Irish, Latvian and Turkish are always in the SD >20 group.

Summary

(i) Derivational networks are most predictable in the 1st order. This is evidenced by a relatively high number of languages with SDs under 10.00 in all three word-classes (almost one third of all the sample languages), as well as by a relatively high level of consistency of this value in many other languages. This observation runs counter to previous views that suggested that derivational categories are "not part of any well-organized categorial system" (Plank 1994: 1672).

(ii) The consistency of the results falls as the order increases, which means that the derivational networks are much less predictable in higher orders of derivation.

(iii) The three languages (Croatian, Turkish and Basque) that are highly consistent in the 1st order of derivation across all three word-classes (SD < 10.00) belong to different language families and different morphological types. To this group of languages with consistent derivation, we may add languages with SDs that are below 10.00 in two word-classes and slightly higher in the third class, such as Bulgarian, Polish and Welsh.

(iv) A high level of consistency across all three orders in all three classes is rare, but it does occur in Bulgarian and Serbian (with the exception of the 3rd order of adjectives in the case of the latter).

(v) Regardless of the word-class, the most populous category is always the medium SV group in the 1st order of derivation, which counts 26 languages for nouns, 24 languages for verbs and 33 languages for adjectives. These three word-class-based groups overlap in 20 languages. Thus, 20 languages have medium SVs in each word-class in at least two orders of derivation. By implication, a medium SV (20–30%) can be considered the most common pattern.

49.4 The level of genera

49.4.1 Comparison of the genera

This section only includes those genera that are represented by a sufficient number of languages in our sample, i.e. only three Indo-European genera: the Slavic, Germanic and Romance languages. A comparison of average SVs by order of derivation and word-class is summarized in Table 49.27.

Table 49.27 shows a falling pattern in SVs as the order of derivation grows without exception, i.e. in all three word-classes for each genus.

Table 49.27: Comparison of selected genera by order of derivation and word-class.

	Genus	1st order (%)	2nd order (%)	3rd order (%)
Nouns	Germanic	29.94	27.86	17.08
	Romance	26.95	19.26	13.69
	Slavic	27.73	23.27	16.97
Adjectives	Germanic	28.62	22.45	19.40
	Romance	34.13	27.62	13.58
	Slavic	26.93	22.46	17.42
Verbs	Germanic	28.62	22.45	19.40
	Romance	30.72	22.01	13.52
	Slavic	28.73	25.00	20.70

Table 49.27 also shows that there are no striking differences in the average SVs in the 1st order with the exception of adjectives, where the average SV of Romance languages is higher by almost 6%. The SVs in the other cases are remarkably similar, ranging between 26.95% and 30.72, which indicates a general tendency to fill out derivational networks in the 1st order of the Slavic, Germanic and Romance genera. Similar conclusions apply to the 2nd order, where there is only one large difference in average SV, viz. between the Germanic and the Romance languages in noun-based derivations (27.86% vs. 19.26%). The average SV values in the 2nd order tend to be lower than in the 1st order by about 5%. In other words, the derivational richness of the 2nd order of derivation is on average lower than that of the 1st order by 5%. This drops in the 3rd order by an additional 7%.

It appears, then, that, like individual languages, the genera are sensitive to the word-class of basic words and the order of derivation. Thus, while for noun-based derivations the ranking of the language genera in all three examined orders is Germanic, Slavic, then Romance, the situation for adjective-based derivations changes by order of derivation: the Romance genus dominates in the 1st and the 2nd orders, but its average SV in the 3rd order is lowest of all. Similarly, for verb-based derivations, the Romance genus dominates in the 1st order, but has by far the lowest average SV in the 3rd order. The 2nd and 3rd orders are dominated by the Slavic genus.

49.4.2 Inside the genera

The analysis in section 49.4.1 shows a fairly high degree of consistency in the average saturation values of the three Indo-European genera as a whole. A look inside the individual genera, however, provides us with a less consistent picture. Taking the Slavic genus as an example, the difference between the highest SV (Czech: 33.22%) and the lowest SV (Slovene: 23.00%) in the 1st order of nouns is over 10%. The same is true of the 2nd order: Czech and Slovak (both 30%) exceed Polish by almost 15%. A similar difference between the highest SV (Czech) and the lowest SV (Russian) can also be found in the 3rd order. These findings raise the question of whether this level of variance is a general phenomenon across the three genera in question. The answer to this can be found in Table 49.28.

Table 49.28: Differences between the languages with the highest and lowest SVs.

	Genus	1st order (%)	2nd order (%)	3rd order (%)
Nouns	Germanic	32.93	28.89	20.00
	Romance	15.09	10.29	10.00
	Slavic	10.22	14.29	12.89
Adjectives	Germanic	25.00	14.62	20.00
	Romance	31.94	21.56	9.17
	Slavic	9.63	12.91	14.39
Verbs	Germanic	17.25	30.00	30.00
	Romance	5.08	11.91	7.75
	Slavic	22.63	16.15	14.49

Languages without a 3rd order of derivation are disregarded here.

Table 49.28 shows us that the SV differences between individual languages are considerable in all orders of derivation and in all three word-classes. This is not surprising if one realizes that the word-formation system of each language of a particular genus developed differently throughout its history, as evidenced by the degree of diversification[2] calculated, inter alia, for the three

---

[2] "This parameter indicates to what degree the WF systems of genetically related languages differ in their structural richness. By implication, it enables us to compare language genera/

above-discussed Indo-European genera in order to identify the degree of diversification of word-formation systems of languages belonging to the same genus (Körtvélyessy et al. 2018).

Summary

(i) There is an evident tendency for all language genera SVs: they fall in all three word-classes as the order of derivation grows without exception (for the examined genera).
(ii) The average SVs for the examined genera are remarkably similar and indicate that each of the genera actualizes about 25–30% of the potential in the 1st order, about 22% in the 2nd order, and about 13–18% in the 3rd order.
(iii) The genera tend to maintain very similar average SVs across the word-classes.
(iv) A different picture is obtained by comparing SVs for languages inside the genera: the differences are considerable in all three word-classes and all three orders of derivation.

49.5 Correlation between the saturation value and the paradigmatic capacity

An interesting piece of information about derivational networks from the cross-linguistic point of view is the (non-)existence of *correlation* between two variables: the *saturation value* and the *paradigmatic capacity*. Let us recall that the saturation value is calculated as the proportion between the number of actual derivatives and the maximum (i.e. potential) derivational network. The paradigmatic capacity is determined by the number of derivatives from the word-formation base in a particular order of derivation. The question is whether there is any relation between the number of words derivable from the basic simple word in the 1st order of derivation and the saturation value in the next orders. As is generally known, a correlation reflects the interdependence of two functions or data sets. A value of 1 therefore means that one data set copies the other one, suggesting a maximum correlation. Growing values in one set imply

---

families in terms of the degree of diversification of their WF systems from their protolanguage" (Körtvélyessy et al. 2018: 315).

proportionally growing values in the other. A value of –1 means indirect proportionality, and zero implies no interdependence.

The correlation value for the 1st order is necessarily 1, because we calculate the correlation of the 1st order saturation by means of the 1st order data. Since the SVs in the 2nd, 3rd, 4th and 5th orders are related to the 1st order data, the correlation values indicate a trend of the respective order's saturation relative to the 1st order data.

49.5.1 Nouns

Taking the whole sample of languages into consideration, one cannot observe any systematic correlation. Languages differ from one another significantly in this respect, ranging from 0.92 (Estonian) down to 0.07 (Basque) in the 2nd order, from 0.88 (Estonian) to 0.04 (Spanish, Polish) in the 3rd order, etc.

22 languages feature a correlation value above 0.5 in the 2nd order of derivation, compared to only five languages in the 3rd order, one language (Estonian) in the 4th order and no languages in the 5th order. In each order, the highest correlation value (0.92, 0.88, and 0.85, respectively) is found for Estonian. Georgian and Turkish are the only other languages in which the correlation exceeds the value of 0.5 in both the 2nd and the 3rd orders. Correlations can differ substantially for the same language in different orders of derivation. For illustration, while the correlation of French nouns in the 2nd order is 0.87, it is only 0.38 in the 3rd order.

Indirectly proportional correlation is rare. While there are several languages with minus values and their number increases with the order of derivation from the 2nd order to the 4th order, the only significant values are for Ukrainian (–0.66) in the 3rd order, Ukrainian (–0.57) and Slovak (–0.53) in the 4th order, and Slovak (–0.54) in the 5th order.

49.5.2 Verbs

Verbs are characterized by the highest number of languages with 2nd order correlation values above 0.5 (28 languages). Latvian, Lithuanian, Dargwa and Polish exceed the correlation value of 0.9. Nine languages exceed the correlation value of 0.5 in the 3rd order, with Lithuanian at the top. Welsh, Georgian and North Saami also feature high correlation values in each of these three orders of derivation. This contrasts to their values in the other two word-classes. The correlation of, for example, Welsh in the 2nd order of adjectives is as low as 0.24, and in the 3rd and the 4th orders it is –0.10.

49.5.3 Adjectives

While the observation of considerable differences among languages' correlation values in each order of derivation has been confirmed for adjectives as well, what strikes one at first sight is that the correlations may differ significantly for different word-classes within the same language. While Estonian clearly dominates this parameter for nouns, its correlation values for adjectives are much lower for individual orders (0.55, −0.35, −0.12). The same is true of, for example, Serbian: its values for nouns in the first two orders (0.87, 0.53) are much higher than those for adjectives (0.58, 0.23).

The highest number of languages with a correlation above 0.5 can be found in the 2nd order of adjectives (22 languages). In this case, Slovak manifests the strongest correlation (0.87), followed by Croatian (0.83) and Czech (0.81). In the 3rd order, there are only three languages above 0.5 (Croatian 0.64, North Saami 0.56, Galician 0.53). In the 4th order, there are also three languages above 0.5 (Ukrainian 0.69, North Saami 0.63, Maltese 0.62).

49.5.4 Word-class comparison

Taking all three word-classes into consideration, only one language exceeds the correlation value of 0.50 in the 5th order of derivation: North Saami, with 0.68 for adjectives. North Saami is also an example of a language with high correlation values that are almost constantly above 0.50, with the exception of the 3rd and 4th orders of nouns.

Summary

(i) No significant correlation seems to exist between saturation value and paradigmatic capacity for our sample of languages as a whole.
(ii) The correlation depends on the interplay of three factors:
   – the specific language
   – the word-class of the basic word
   – the order of derivation

Generalizations are therefore difficult to make, and no clear tendencies emerge from the data in relation to a possible correlation between saturation value and paradigmatic capacity.

49.6 Maximum and average number of orders of derivation

Languages differ in the number of possible affixes attached to the basic word. This section examines the possibility of generalizing the number of orders of derivation with regard to the specific word-class of basic words, the morphological type of a specific language, the nature of its word-formation system, as well as its genetic affiliation.

49.6.1 Nouns

As it follows from Table 49.29, only nine languages derive nouns in five orders, including five Slavic, two Uralic, and Turkish. All these languages are usually described as synthetic languages, and three of them are agglutinating (Finnish, Hungarian, Turkish).

Table 49.29: Classification of languages according to the maximum number of orders of derivation, nouns.

No. of orders	Languages
5 orders	Bulgarian, Croatian, Czech, Finnish, Hungarian, Slovak, Turkish, Ukrainian (8 languages)
4 orders	Catalan, Estonian, Georgian, German, Italian, North Saami, Polish, Romanian, Russian, Serbian, Slovene, Swedish, Tatar (13 languages)
3 orders	Basque, Dutch, French, Galician, Greek, Icelandic, Irish, Latvian, Lithuanian, Maltese, Portuguese, Spanish, Welsh (13 languages)
2 orders	Danish, English, Frisian, Norwegian (4 languages)
1 order	Chechen, Dargwa (2 languages)

At the other end of the scale are two Nakh-Daghestanian languages (Chechen, Dargwa) with only one order of derivation. Two orders of derivation are available in Danish, English, Frisian and Norwegian. All of them are Germanic languages with isolating morphology.

49.6.2 Verbs

Each language has at least two orders of derivation. Basque, Danish, Dargwa and Ukrainian do not make use of more than two orders. The languages are genetically and geographically distant, and they also differ morphologically. Thus, no association between the number of orders of derivation and their classification can be observed. On the other hand, all the other Slavic languages in our sample make use of more than three orders of derivation. One of them has six orders of derivation, while five of them have five orders of derivation. All agglutinating languages in our sample have five derivational orders.

Table 49.30: Classification of languages according to the maximum number of orders of derivation, verbs.

No. of orders	Languages
6 orders	Slovak (1 language)
5 orders	Bulgarian, Croatian, Czech, Dutch, Estonian, Finnish, Georgian, Hungarian, Norwegian, Serbian, Slovene, Turkish (12 languages)
4 orders	Frisian, German, Italian, Latvian, Lithuanian, North Saami, Polish, Romanian, Russian, Swedish, Welsh (11 languages)
3 orders	Catalan, Chechen, English, French, Galician, Greek, Icelandic, Irish, Maltese, Portuguese, Spanish, Tatar (12 languages)
2 orders	Basque, Danish, Dargwa, Ukrainian (4 languages)
1 order	No languages

49.6.3 Adjectives

There is one language with only one order of derivation (Dargwa). Five languages have two orders of derivation, and nine languages have three orders. The biggest group is represented by languages with four orders of derivation. Five orders of derivation were identified in ten languages (cf. Table 49.31).

The low number of orders of derivation in Dargwa is balanced out by a high SV in the 1st order. It is the highest SV in this word-class (60%). A low number of orders compensated with a high SV in the 1st order can also be observed in French. French has only two orders of adjective-based derivations. The SV in the 1st order is the second highest (57.14). On the other hand, three other languages with a low number of orders of derivation have low SVs in both orders of saturation, e.g. for Danish it is 15% in the 1st order and 10% in the 2nd. This means that it is not possible to speak about a general tendency to compensate for a low number of orders of derivation with a high SV in these orders. Analogically, there is no strict correlation between a high number of orders of derivation and high SVs. While, for example, Turkish, Czech and North Saami, with five orders of derivation in each word-class, are characterized by high SVs in the first three orders in all three word-classes, Greek, with high SVs across word-classes and orders of derivation, has only three orders for nouns and verbs and four for adjectives. From this, it follows that SVs do not necessarily correlate with the number of derivational orders.

Table 49.31: Classification of languages according to the maximum number of orders of derivation, adjectives.

No. of orders	Languages
5 orders	Bulgarian, Croatian, Czech, Finnish, German, Georgian, North Saami, Serbian, Slovene, Turkish (10 languages)
4 orders	Catalan, Estonian, Greek, Hungarian, Italian, Latvian, Lithuanian, Maltese, Polish, Romanian, Slovak, Swedish, Tatar, Ukrainian, Welsh (15 languages)
3 orders	Basque, Dutch, English, Frisian, Galician, Irish, Portuguese, Russian, Spanish (9 languages)
2 orders	Chechen, Danish, French, Icelandic, Norwegian (5 languages)
1 order	Dargwa (1 language)

Examples of words with six and five orders of derivation, ranging over all three word-classes, are given in examples (1) and (2), respectively.

(1) *6 orders*
Slovak: *pri-s-ťah-ov-alec-k-y*
DIR-REMOVE-pull-DURATIVE-AGENT-?-MANNER
'immigration.ADV'

(2) *5 orders*
Noun-based
Ukrainian

на-йм-ен-ува-нн-ячк-о
RESULTATIVE-name-CAUS-CAUS-CAUS-DIM-INFLECTION
'nice, short name'

Hungarian
meg-szem-ély-es-ít-és
RESULTATIVE-eye-NOMINALIZER-ATTRIBUTIVE-CAUSATIVE-NOMINALIZER
'personalization'

Finnish
päiv-it-t-y-mättö-myys
day-CAUS-CAUS-ANTICAUS-PRIVATIVE-STATE
'being impossible to be updated by itself'

Verb-based
Dutch
on-weet-en-schap-elijk-heid
NEG-know-INFINITIVE-NOM-ADJ-NOM
'unscientificness'

Estonian
tead-v-us-ta-matu-s
know-ABILITY.ADJ-ABILITY.NOUN-CAUSATIVE-PRIVATIVE-STATIVE
'unconsciousness, subliminality'

Hungarian
meg-ad-ó-z-tat-ás
RESULTATIVE-give-NOMINALIZER-DURATIVE-CAUSATIVE-NOMINALIZER
'taxing.N'

Adjective-based
Czech
nej-úzk-ost-n-ě-ji
AUGMENTATIVE-narrow-ABSTRACTION-RELATIONAL-MANNER-AUGMENTATIVE
'most anxiously'

Georgian
ga-mo-u-sc'or-eb-l-oba
ACTION-ACTION-PRIVATIVE-straight-RESULT-ABSTRACTION
'irreparability'

North Saami
njulg-e-st-adda-goahti-n
right/straight-CAUSATIVE-SUBITIVE-ITERATIVE-INCHOATIVE-ACTION
'straightening (out) quickly several times'

49.6.4 Comparison of word-classes

Our data show that the maximum number of orders of derivation, i.e. the maximum number of affixes attached to a simple underived base, is six. Five orders occur with all three word-classes, including eight languages for noun-based affixation, 10 languages for adjective-based affixation, and 12 languages for verb-based affixation. By implication, the verbal base appears to be the most productive source of affixation.

Five orders of derivation have been identified in all three word-classes for Bulgarian, Croatian, Czech, Turkish and Finnish, i.e. none of the Germanic or Romance languages in the sample produce affixation chains of a maximum length in all three word-classes. German and Danish can produce five-affix words from adjectives, and Norwegian also can from verbs. No Romance language can derive words with five affixes. On the other hand, Romance languages are very consistent in the number of orders of derivation: in all three word-classes, they have either three or four orders of derivation. The only exception is French with two orders in the case of adjectives. This word-formation feature is dominated by Slavic and Uralic languages. At the opposite end of the scale, there are two languages that can attach only one affix to the basic noun (Chechen, Dargwa), while English, Frisian and Norwegian can attach two affixes. With adjectives, Dargwa is a single-affixation language; Chechen, French, Icelandic and Norwegian cannot attach more than two affixes. With verbs, only two affixation steps are possible in Dargwa, Basque and Ukrainian.

These results are confirmed by the average numbers of affixation steps. Out of 11 languages with an average value of three or more, seven are Slavic, three are Uralic, and then there is also Turkish. A similar dominance has also been found for adjectives and verbs.

Verbs and adjectives serve as the most prolific starting point for affixation processes, having on average 2.78 and 2.76 affixation steps, respectively, for the whole language sample. These values are higher than the average of 2.46 affixation steps for nouns.

Obviously, the highest number of languages can be found in the 1st order of derivation, and the lowest number in the 5th order (cf. Table 49.32). The number of languages that can derive new words in individual orders of

Table 49.32: Number of languages per order of derivation.

Order of derivation	1st	2nd	3rd	4th	5th
Nouns	40	38	34	20	8
Verbs	40	40	36	24	12
Adjectives	40	31	34	25	10

derivation are more or less equally distributed in terms of word-classes. For example, in the 1st order, each of the 40 sample languages derives new words; in the 3rd order, the difference is merely two languages; and in the 4th and 5th orders, it is four languages. This balanced representation of languages for each order of derivation in each word-class is violated by adjectives in the 2nd order.

The sample languages were divided into morphological types. According to Sapir (1921), two criteria can be applied: the index of synthesis and the index of fusion. While the index of synthesis considers how many morphemes a word is built from, the index of fusion focuses on the technique or the process of building words. In our case, the number of derivational orders expresses the number of attached affixes. Consequently, we can discuss the index of synthesis and its relation to the number of derivational orders. The morphological types of individual languages were identified on the basis of various sources (Müller et al. 2015–2016; Štekauer et al. 2012; *Ethnologue*). We are aware that this kind of classification cannot be precise, because it is not possible to match one language as a whole with one type. In our approach, we take the type of prevailing feature as a determinant of the morphological language type.

Given these methodological restrictions, three morphological types were identified in our sample: 25 inflectional languages (Bulgarian, Catalan, Croatian, Czech, Dutch, French, Galician, German, Greek, Icelandic, Irish, Italian, Latvian, Lithuanian, Maltese, Polish, Portuguese, Romanian, Russian, Serbian, Slovak, Slovene, Spanish, Ukrainian, Welsh); 10 agglutinating languages (Basque, Dargwa, Estonian, Finnish, Georgian, Hungarian, Chechen, North Saami, Tatar, Turkish); and five analytical languages (Danish, English, Frisian, Norwegian, Swedish). Based on the maximum number of orders of derivation, the sample languages were divided again into three further groups (cf. Table 49.33):
(i) languages with a high number of orders (4–5);
(ii) languages with a medium number of orders (3); and
(iii) languages with a low number of orders (1–2).

Table 49.33: Classification of languages by the number of orders of derivation and word-classes.

	Nouns	Verbs	Adjectives
HIGH	Bulgarian, Catalan, Croatian, Czech, Estonian, Finnish, Georgian, German, Hungarian, Italian, North Saami, Polish, Romanian, Russian, Serbian, Slovak, Slovene, Swedish, Tatar, Turkish, Ukrainian (21 languages)	Bulgarian, Croatian, Czech, Dutch, Estonian, Finnish, Frisian, Georgian, German, Hungarian, Italian, Latvian, Lithuanian, North Saami, Polish, Romanian, Russian, Serbian, Slovak, Slovene, Swedish, Turkish, Welsh (23 languages)	Bulgarian, Catalan, Croatian, Czech, Estonian, Finnish, Georgian, German, Greek, Hungarian, Italian, Latvian, Lithuanian, Maltese, North Saami, Polish, Romanian, Russian, Serbian, Slovak, Slovene, Swedish, Tatar, Turkish, Ukrainian, Welsh (26 languages)
MEDIUM	Dutch, French, Galician, Greek, Icelandic, Irish, Latvian, Lithuanian, Maltese, Portuguese, Spanish, Welsh (12 languages)	Basque, Catalan, English, French, Galician, Greek, Icelandic, Irish, Maltese, Portuguese, Spanish, Tatar (12 languages)	Basque, Dutch, English, Frisian, Galician, Irish, Portuguese, Spanish (8 languages)
LOW	Basque, Chechen, Danish, Dargwa, English, Frisian, Norwegian (7 languages)	Danish, Dargwa, Chechen, Norwegian, Ukrainian (5 languages)	Chechen, Danish, Dargwa, French, Icelandic, Norwegian (6 languages)

The following languages are always in the HIGH group:
(i) Inflectional: Bulgarian, Croatian, Czech, German, Italian, Polish, Romanian, Serbian, Slovak, Slovene;
(ii) Agglutinating: Estonian, Finnish, Georgian, Hungarian, North Saami, Turkish; and
(iii) Analytic: Swedish.

These languages can be completed with those which occur in the MEDIUM group only once, e.g. Catalan features a high number of derivational orders for nouns and adjectives, and a medium number for verbs. All these languages are either inflectional (Catalan, Latvian, Lithuanian, Russian, Welsh) or agglutinating (Tatar).

Based on this summary, it can be concluded that a high number of derivational orders is associated with inflectional and agglutinating types of languages. There are four groups of exceptions to this:

(i) There are four inflectional languages (Galician, Irish, Portuguese, Spanish) which are MEDIUM in each word-class. Interestingly, three of them are Romance languages. Altogether, there are six Romance languages in our sample. While two of them follow the above-mentioned tendency specified for the relation between inflectional languages and the number of derivation orders, four do not. Obviously, Romance inflectional languages behave differently from Slavic inflectional languages. By implication, it is not only the morphological type of a language but also its genetic affiliation that influences its derivational nature.
(ii) There are four other inflectional languages that do not have a high number of derivational orders: Icelandic, Dutch, Ukrainian and Greek. Dutch and Greek occur in the MEDIUM group twice and once in the HIGH group, so they are still very close to meeting the criteria for the above-mentioned tendency. The same is true of Ukrainian, which occurs twice in the HIGH group and once (verbs) in the LOW group. Icelandic is in the MEDIUM group twice and once in the LOW group.
(iii) There are three agglutinating languages (Basque, Dargwa and Chechen) that feature very low numbers of derivational orders (Dargwa is always in the LOW group; Basque and Chechen are in the LOW group twice and once in the MEDIUM group).
(iv) Swedish is usually described as an analytical language. In our sample, it is the only analytical language that features a high number of derivational orders. The remaining four analytical languages are not consistent in their behaviour: Norwegian has a LOW number of derivational orders for nouns and adjectives but a HIGH number for verbs; English occurs twice in the MEDIUM group (verbs, adjectives) and once in the LOW group; Frisian is HIGH for verbs, MEDIUM for adjectives and LOW for nouns; and finally, Danish is always LOW. Interestingly, all analytical languages are in the LOW group for nouns. If they are ever in a HIGH group (Frisian and Norwegian), it is for verbs.

Summary

(i) The maximum number of orders of derivation in our sample of languages is six.
(ii) In most languages with five orders of derivation, the 5th order is saturated in the word-class of verbs. In general, the verbal base correlates with a high number of orders of derivation.

(iii) If the average values of derivational orders across all three word-classes are taken into consideration, the verb-based and adjective-based networks are significantly richer than the noun-based networks.
(iv) Inflectional and agglutinating languages tend to have a high number of derivational orders, which naturally follows from the 'synthetic' nature of their morphological systems.
(v) Genetically, this corresponds to Slavic and Uralic languages. None of the Germanic or Romance languages reach the level of five orders of derivation.
(vi) While some languages compensate for their low number of orders of derivation with a high SV in the 1st order, this is not a hard and fast rule.
(vii) Conversely, high SVs are also present in languages with a high number of orders of derivation.
(viii) The lack of absolute homogeneity of languages belonging to the same morphological type can also be accounted for by: (a) the unequal development of the word-formation systems of languages belonging to the same language genus (see above, section 49.4.2); and (b), as demonstrated by Štekauer (2012), the typology of word-formation systems does not correspond with the morphological typology. In other words, "there does not seem to be any strong and systematic correlation between the traditional morphological classification and the use of word-formation rules in these languages" (Štekauer 2012: 725).

49.7 Number of derivatives

The number of derivatives shows the extent of the actually realized potential of derivational networks. As such, it is an important indicator of their richness.

49.7.1 Average number of derivatives

Table 49.34 shows that the most prolific base for the derivation of complex words is the verb. The average of verb-based derivatives clearly outnumbers the figures for adjectives and nouns. Furthermore, the 2nd order of verb-based derivations features the highest average number of derivatives in general. The values for adjective-based derivations are slightly higher than those for noun-based derivations. This result tallies with the data on the maximum derivational networks for individual word-classes, the data on the average number of orders of derivation, as well as the data on the correlation between

Table 49.34: Average number of derivatives by order of derivation for all languages.

	1st order	2nd order	3rd order	4th order	5th order
Nouns	7.71	6.26	2.21	0.43	0.06
Verbs	10.82	12.84	6.13	1.46	0.18
Adjectives	8.17	6.86	3.56	0.86	0.09

SVs and paradigmatic capacity in terms of the number of languages with a correlation above 0.5.

Language-wise, the highest average number of derivatives occurs in the 2nd order of Serbian verbs (39.10), followed by Croatian, Slovak, Georgian, Czech and Lithuanian, all of which exceed 30 derivatives. Interestingly, the average value for verbs is higher in the 2nd order than in the 1st order. Verb-based derivations are dominated by Slavic languages (Serbian, Croatian, Czech and Slovak). The maximum average values per language in adjective-based derivations are much lower than those in verbs and do not exceed 20 words, with the sole exception of the Serbian 2nd order (20.10). While the first three orders are clearly dominated by Slavic languages, Finnish gradually gains in importance as the order of derivation grows.

While the previously mentioned Slavic languages maintain high positions in noun-based derivations throughout all five orders, the roles of Italian in the first two orders and of Hungarian in the 3rd and the 4th orders are strikingly significant.

49.7.2 Sensitivity to absence of a word-formation process

Körtvélyessy et al. (2018) evaluated a sample of European languages by way of, inter alia, the calculation of the SV of individual word-formation processes.[3] This enables us to test the interrelation between the absence of a given word-formation process or its low SV in word-formation and the number of derivatives. The question, therefore, is whether such an absence has an impact on the richness of a derivational network. For this purpose, we chose to analyze the

---

[3] The saturation value in word-formation reflects the structural richness of a word-formation process. It is calculated as the proportion between the number of word-formation types actually employed for the formation of new complex words and the number of possible word-formation types within a given word-formation process.

class of verbs, owing to the phenomenon of Aktionsart that is reflected in a large number of derivatives coined by prefixes.

In the following analysis, the SVs of prefixation identified by Körtvélyessy et al. (2018) are compared with the number of derivatives in the word-class of verbs. Two groups of languages are contrasted: languages with a high prefixation SV (high PrefSV), namely Romanian, Catalan, Dutch, German and Maltese, and languages with a low or zero prefixation SV (low PrefSV), including Estonian, Hungarian, Tatar and Finnish. Languages with a high PrefSV are, with the exception of Maltese, Indo-European languages from two language genera (Romance and German). Languages with a low PrefSV are Uralic and Altaic. Both Tatar and Turkish are members of the Turkic genus. Hungarian is an Ugric language; Estonian and Finnish belong to the Finnic genus. Thus, if Maltese is excluded, the Romance and Germanic languages are at one end of the scale (high PrefSV), and Turkic, Ugric and Finnic at the other (low PrefSV). Interestingly, languages of both groups are homogeneous also from the perspective of the morphological classification of languages. Romanian, Catalan, Dutch and German from the high PrefSV group are synthetic, while all languages from the low PrefSV are agglutinating languages.

Table 49.35 below orders languages according to their prefixation SVs. The number of derivatives is given as an average value.

Table 49.35: Languages by SV and number of derivatives.

Prefixation SV	Language	Number of derivatives				
		1st order	2nd order	3rd order	4th order	5th order
47.06	Romanian	12.3	11.2	2.9	0.2	0
41.18	Catalan	11.5	8.6	0.5	0	0
41.18	Dutch	5.4	4.8	0.8	0.2	0.1
41.18	German	10.4	12.4	6.4	1.2	0
41.18	Maltese	3.5	1.3	0.1	0	0
11.76	Estonian	11.6	11.9	4.7	1.2	0.2
11.76	Finnish	11.3	10.5	3.7	1.2	0.1
0	Hungarian	11.9	16.1	5.8	1.1	0.2
0	Tatar	8.9	6.7	1.5	0	0
0	Turkish	9.9	14.5	7.7	1.6	0.2

Vertical evaluation

In the 1st order of derivation, the number of derivatives is not proportional to the corresponding prefixation SV. While Romanian and Catalan are from the high PrefSV group and Estonian, Finnish and Hungarian belong to the low PrefSV group, their average numbers of derivatives are roughly identical.

The same observation applies to the 2nd order of derivation: all Uralic languages have a high number of derivatives and so do Romanian and Catalan. Besides genetic classification, the morphological type of a language plays an important role. Finnish, Hungarian and Estonian are agglutinating languages, while Romanian and Catalan are synthetic. From the 3rd order of derivation downwards, all languages with a high PrefSV show a decline and the number of derivatives is very low: in the 5th order there is only one derivative in Dutch, and there are no derivatives in Romanian, Catalan or German. In the low PrefSV languages, a different pattern of behaviour (with the exception of Tatar) can be observed: the number of derivatives drops with the higher degree of derivation in these languages as well but, if the position of a language (from the perspective of the number of derivatives) is taken into consideration, Turkish and the Uralic languages occupy the top positions in both the 4th and 5th orders.

What factors, then, affect the number of derivatives in individual languages? No doubt, there is not just a single reason. Instead, a combination of factors appears to be at play.

It is primarily, but not exclusively, a language's genetic membership that influences the number of derivatives rather than the absence or presence of prefixation in its word-formation system. As is evident from Table 49.35, German and Dutch have identical prefixation SVs, but significantly differ in their average number of derivatives in the 1st order. Similar cases abound. The *morphological type of a language* is also influential, but we must take into account that there is no systematic relation between the morphological type of a language and the nature of its word-formation system (Štekauer 2012). It is also necessary to reiterate the fact that the *word-formation systems of individual languages of the same genus diversified in the course of their development from their protolanguage*. Last but not least, we must mention the *compensation strategies* discussed in detail in individual language-specific chapters: each language finds its own word-formation strategy to compensate for its low/limited affixation capacity.

Horizontal evaluation

Generally, the number of derivatives drops as the degree of derivation increases. There are exceptions to this rule, however: German (high PrefSV) has a higher number of derivatives in the 2nd order, and so do Estonian, Hungarian and Turkish (low PrefSV). Thus, it can be concluded that this dropping line is not typical of languages with low prefixation SVs. With the exception of Tatar, languages with a low PrefSV have derivatives in each order of derivation. It is not so in the case of languages in the high PrefSV group: Catalan and Maltese do not derive new words in the 4th order, and in the 5th order, only one language from this group derives new words: Dutch (in fact, there is only one derivative for the verb *weten* 'to know').

The highest number of derivatives has been found for Hungarian in the 2nd order of derivation. In the 1st order it is Romanian (12.3), closely followed by Hungarian, Estonian and Finnish. From the 3rd order of derivation it is always a language from the low PrefSV group that assumes the top position. Thus, languages with low or no prefixation derive more verbs in individual orders of derivation.

Discussion

Disregarding Tatar, it can be concluded that languages that lack prefixation (or wherein the saturation value of prefixation is very low) derive new words in all orders of derivation. Languages with high prefixation SVs are typical of balanced numbers of derivatives in the 1st and 2nd orders, and the number of their derivatives dramatically drops from the 3rd order. A higher number of derived words in individual orders of derivation is typical of languages that lack prefixation or have low prefixation SVs. These observations can also be associated with the morphological type of languages and their genetic affiliation. All five languages with no prefixation (or with very low prefixation SVs) are agglutinating and fall into two language families. With the exception of Maltese, all languages from the high PrefSV group belong to the Indo-European language family representing two genera (Romance and Germanic), and they are synthetic languages.

Summary

(i) Verb-based derivational networks feature the highest number of derivatives.
(ii) The highest numbers of derivatives are produced by Slavic languages.

(iii) The absence of a particular derivational process does not seem to affect the number of derivatives because it is usually compensated for by other word-formation processes.
(iv) The number of derivatives appears to be the result of the interplay of several factors: the genetic affiliation of the language, which is reflected in its morphological type (synthetic type), which is itself reflected in high MDN values and high orders of derivation.

49.8 Correlations between semantic categories and orders of derivation

Even though they are not as rigorous and straightforward as form-based conclusions, some observations are worth mentioning that relate to emergent patterns based on the comparative semantic categories employed for describing the networks in the sample of 40 European languages (cf. Bagasheva 2017).

Two methodological clarifications are in order here. A correlation between an order of derivation and semantic categories here means a consistent representation of a specific semantic category by derivations from the majority of base words within a word-class group. Second, a majority here means an incidence between 10 (all base words) and 7 or 6 base words.

DIMINUTIVE, QUALITY, PRIVATIVE, RELATIONAL and ACTION are the semantic categories that are most clearly correlated with the 1st order of derivation from nominal bases across the language sample. Thus, for example, DIMINUTIVE correlates with the 1st order of derivation of Spanish nouns (e.g. *hueso* 'bone' vs. *huesito* 'small bone') and adjectives (e.g. *delgado* 'thin' vs. *delgadito* 'slightly thin'). DIMINUTIVE is actually the semantic category in which most correlations can be found in the sample: DIMINUTIVE is correlated with the 1st order of derivation in nine Slavic languages, six Romance languages, three Germanic languages, two Baltic languages, two Uralic languages and in Greek, Tatar and North Saami, i.e. in 25 languages from the sample altogether.

Even though a clear correlation for DIMINUTIVE can be identified in the majority of languages, AUGMENTATIVE is neither so copiously represented, nor so clearly correlated with the 1st order. Even though the two semantic categories are supposedly members of a common supercategory – EVALUATIVE – and denote opposite markedness or direction from a perceived standard, only DIMINUTIVE can be said to be strongly represented across language types, families, genera, and areal distribution. This is understandable, as witnessed by the findings presented by Körtvélyessy (2015: 119): out of the 71 European languages in her sample, 60 have evaluative morphology; 39 of these languages have both DIMINUTIVES and AUGMENTATIVES, while 21 languages only have DIMINUTIVES. No language has AUGMENTATIVES without also having DIMINUTIVES. Her results thus give additional support to the statement by Bakema and Geeraerts (2000: 106), who maintain that "[A]UGMENTATIVES are less widespread than DIMINUTIVES. The two categories are related by an implicational universal: the existence of AUGMENTATIVES in a language implies the presence of DIMINUTIVES, but the reverse does not hold."

The semantic categories that are better represented in 1st order derivations from nominal bases in the sample are QUALITY, PRIVATIVE and RELATIONAL (cf. Table 49.36). QUALITY is correlated with 1st order derivatives from nominal bases in 21 languages, while PRIVATIVE is in 14 and RELATIONAL in 11, as in the following examples:

(3) QUALITY
English: *fire fiery*
PRIVATIVE
Slovak: *bezmenný   bezzubý*
          'nameless' 'toothless'
RELATIONAL
Bulgarian: *kuče   kučeški*
            'dog' 'related to a dog/of a dog'

Besides these clear associations, no further discernible patterns can be established.

Table 49.36: Correlation between the 1st order of derivation and semantic categories.

DIMINUTIVE	QUALITY	PRIVATIVE	RELATIONAL
	Basque		
Bulgarian	Bulgarian		Bulgarian
Catalan	Catalan		Catalan
Croatian			Croatian
Czech			Czech
	Chechen		
Dutch			
	English	English	

Table 49.36: (continued)

Diminutive	Quality	Privative	Relational
Estonian		Estonian	
	Finnish	Finnish	
Frisian			
Galician		Galician	
German	German	German	
	Georgian	Georgian	
Greek			
Hungarian	Hungarian	Hungarian	
	Icelandic		
	Irish		
Italian	Italian	Italian	Italian
Latvian		Latvian	
Lithuanian		Lithuanian	Lithuanian
North Saami	North Saami	North Saami	
	Norwegian		
Polish	Polish		
Portuguese			
Romanian			Romanian
Russian	Russian		
Serbian	Serbian		
	Swedish		
Slovak		Slovak	Slovak
Slovene			Slovene
Spanish			
Tatar		Tatar	
	Turkish	Turkish	
Ukrainian	Ukrainian		
	Welsh		Welsh

Examples of complex words derived from a nominal base which include these semantic categories in the 1st order are given in (4):

(4) DIMINUTIVE
Polish: *pies-ek*
dog-DIM
'doggy'
ACTION
Spanish: *oj-ear*
eye-ACTION
'to eye'
QUALITY
Icelandic: *nafn-laus*
name-QUALITY
'nameless'
PRIVATIVE
Turkish: *kemik-siz*
bone-PRIVATIVE
'boneless'

As the order of derivation increases, the number of semantic categories for which a bias to correlation can be detected decreases. Only two semantic categories can be said to show a bias to correlation with the 2nd order of derivation from noun bases: ACTION and STATIVE. The incidence of these correlations was established in 15 languages for the former category and in nine for the latter. Table 49.37 represents the incidence of the most frequent semantic categories that correlate with the 2nd order of derivation from nominal bases.

Examples of complex words derived from a nominal base which include these semantic categories in the 2nd order are given in (5):

(5) ACTION
Croatian: *zub-ar-iti*
tooth-AGENT-ACTION
'to perform a dentist's work'
STATIVE
English: i) *tooth-less-ness*
ii) *tooth-i-ness*

Table 49.37: Correlation between the 2nd order of derivation and semantic categories in noun-based derivational networks.

ACTION	STATIVE
Catalan	
	English
Finnish	Finnish
Galician	
German	German
Greek	
Hungarian	Hungarian
	Icelandic
Irish	
Italian	
Lithuanian	
North Saami	
Norwegian	Norwegian
Portuguese	
	Russian
Swedish	Swedish
Turkish	Turkish
Ukrainian	

While Slavic languages stand out disproportionately in the sample in relation to the saturation of DIMINUTIVE in the 1st order of noun-based derivations, Germanic languages seem to be the ones wherein the majority of STATIVE derivations are consistently saturated in the 2nd order, while ACTION is saturated in the 2nd order in the greatest number of Romance languages.

As far as derivations from verb bases are concerned, the following tendencies are noticeable: there is a correlation between the 1st order of derivation and the semantic categories ACTION and AGENT (in 24 and in 21 languages, respectively). The remaining two semantic categories that are systematically saturated in the

1st order of derivation from verb bases, RESULTATIVE and ABILITY, are represented in 15 and 11 languages, respectively. Unlike in noun-based derivatives, DIMINUTIVE is correlated with the 1st order of derivation from verb bases in only seven languages, four of which are Slavic languages (Bulgarian, Russian, Slovak and Slovene), with the remainder being two Romance languages (Galician and Italian) and Greek. As with derivations from nominal bases, the pattern of an increase in the order of derivation being associated with a decrease in the number of semantic categories for which a bias to correlation can be detected is still present. Only two semantic categories can be said to show a tendency to correlate with the 2nd order of derivation from verb bases: ACTION and AGENT. ACTION seems to be frequently realized by 2nd order verb-based derivatives, being so in 14 languages; AGENT is realized in 10 languages. In the 2nd order, the tendencies are not as strong or clear as in the 1st order. No clear and consistent patterns can be found for the 3rd order of derivation in the set of derivational networks from verb bases. Table 49.38 summarizes the established patterns in the saturation of semantic categories per order of derivation in verb-based derivational networks.

The distribution of the first two categories in the 1st order of derivation is as follows: ACTION in 15 Indo-European languages (six Germanic, five Romance, two Baltic, one Celtic, and one Slavic), three Uralic languages, two Nakh-Daghestanian languages, one Altaic language, Basque, and one Afro-Asiatic language. For AGENT, the distribution is as follows: 15 Indo-European languages (six Romance, five Germanic, two Baltic, one Slavic, and one Celtic), two Nakh-Daghestanian languages, Basque, one Uralic language, and one Altaic language. It appears that Germanic languages tend towards ACTION, while Slavic languages seem to be significantly underrepresented. This can be accounted for by a methodological decision (cf. Chapter 2) that affected the data gathering stage, namely, to consider the derivation of ACTION (*nomina actionis*) so regular and predictable in Slavic languages that it was to be treated as falling under the scope of inflection. The absolute absence of any Slavic languages among the languages in which verb-based derivatives systematically saturate the semantic category ABILITY cannot be explained away by a methodological decision, however. This conspicuous absence is definitely associated with the features of this group of languages.

It is also worth noting that ACTION appears in both the 1st and 2nd order of derivation from verbal bases in the following languages: Latvian, Lithuanian, Estonian, Finnish, Hungarian, German, Icelandic, Norwegian, Catalan, Russian, and Turkish. This presupposes the occurrence of this semantic category in subsequent orders of derivation (see section 49.9). As for the semantic category AGENT, it appears repeatedly in subsequent orders of derivation from verb bases in the following languages: Latvian, Lithuanian, Georgian, Finnish, Swedish, Italian, and Romanian.

Table 49.38: Semantic categories per order of derivation in verb-based derivational networks.

Language	1st order of derivation	2nd order of derivation
Basque	ABILITY ACTION AGENT	
Bulgarian	DIMINUTIVE	
Catalan	ACTION AGENT RESULTATIVE	ACTION
Chechen	ACTION	
Croatian		TERMINATIVE ABSTRACTION REFLEXIVE RELATIONAL
Czech	DIRECTIONAL FINITIVE ITERATIVE	ABILITY Relational
Dargwa	AGENT RESULTATIVE	
Dutch	AGENT	
English	ABILITY ACTION AGENT	
Estonian	ABILITY ACTION RESULTATIVE	ACTION Agent
Finnish	ACTION AGENT	ACTION Agent
French	ABILITY AGENT	
Frisian	ACTION AGENT RESULTATIVE	
Galician	ABILITY ACTION AGENT DIMINUTIVE RESULTATIVE	
Georgian	ACTION AGENT	AGENT
German	ABILITY ACTION AGENT	ACTION

(continued)

Table 49.38 (continued)

Language	1st order of derivation				2nd order of derivation	
Greek				DIMINUTIVE		
Hungarian	ACTION				RESULTATIVE	
Icelandic	ACTION				ACTION	AGENT
Irish	ACTION	AGENT				
Italian	ABILITY	ACTION	AGENT	DIMINUTIVE	RESULTATIVE	
Latvian	ACTION	AGENT			ACTION	AGENT
Lithuanian	ACTION	AGENT			ACTION	AGENT
Maltese	ACTION					
North Saami	ACTION	AGENT			RESULTATIVE	
Norwegian	ACTION				ACTION	
Polish				DIMINUTIVE	RESULTATIVE	
Portuguese	ACTION	AGENT				
Romanian	ABILITY		AGENT			AGENT
Russian	ACTION				ACTION	
Serbian				DIMINUTIVE	RESULTATIVE	
Slovak					RESULTATIVE	

Language	ABILITY	ACTION	AGENT	DIMINUTIVE	RESULTATIVE	AGENT	ACTION
Slovene			AGENT		RESULTATIVE		
Spanish	ABILITY	ACTION			RESULTATIVE		
Swedish	ABILITY	ACTION	AGENT			AGENT	
Ukrainian				DIMINUTIVE	RESULTATIVE		
Tatar			AGENT				
Turkish		ACTION			RESULTATIVE		ACTION
Welsh	ABILITY						

In adjective-based derivations, the most conspicuous tendency of correlation in the 1st order is detected for the categories STATIVE, MANNER, DIMINUTIVE and AUGMENTATIVE, which are represented in 23, 21, 17 and 15 languages, respectively. Table 49.39 lists the languages in which the correlation has been established.

Table 49.39: Correlation between semantic categories and the 1st order of derivation from adjective bases.

MANNER	STATIVE	DIMINUTIVE	AUGMENTATIVE
Basque	Basque	Basque	
Bulgarian	Bulgarian	Bulgarian	
		Catalan	Catalan
Czech			
	Chechen		
Dargwa	Dargwa		
	Dutch		
English	English		
Estonian			
Finnish	Finnish	Finnish	
French			French
Galician	Galician	Galician	Galician
Georgian	Georgian	Georgian	
	German		German
Greek		Greek	Greek
Hungarian			
Icelandic		Icelandic	
			Irish
Italian		Italian	Italian
Latvian			
Lithuanian			Lithuanian
	Maltese		

Table 49.39 (continued)

MANNER	STATIVE	DIMINUTIVE	AUGMENTATIVE
	North Saami		
	Norwegian		
Polish		Polish	
	Portuguese	Portuguese	Portuguese
	Romanian	Romanian	Romanian
		Russian	
Slovak	Slovak	Slovak	
Slovene			Slovene
Spanish	Spanish	Spanish	Spanish
	Tatar		
	Turkish	Turkish	Turkish
	Swedish		Swedish
Ukrainian	Ukrainian	Ukrainian	Ukrainian
	Welsh		

The distribution is as follows: STATIVE in 14 Indo-European languages (six Germanic, four Romance, three Slavic, and one Celtic), two Nakh-Daghestanian languages, one Kartvelian language, Basque, and three Uralic languages. MANNER appears in 18 Indo-European languages (six Slavic, four Romance, three Uralic, two Baltic, two Germanic, and Greek), two Nakh-Daghestanian languages, and Basque. Unlike in noun-based derivatives, in adjective-based ones, the occurrence of both AUGMENTATIVE and DIMINUTIVE is almost balanced across languages – AUGMENTATIVE systematically appears in 1st order derivatives from adjective bases in 15 languages and DIMINUTIVE in 16. Worth mentioning is also the fact that the semantic category ACTION makes consistent appearances in both the 2nd and 3rd order of derivation, in 17 and 12 languages respectively. No other remarkable patterns can be isolated for the 2nd and 3rd orders.

Summary

(i) In general, correlations appear to depend on the base.
(ii) Correlations between semantic categories and orders of derivation occur mainly in the first two orders of derivation: they occur steadily in virtually all languages in the 1st order, and in most languages in the 2nd order.
(iii) By contrast, beyond the 2nd order of derivation, correlations become obscure: in several languages a correlation between the 3rd order and specific semantic categories has been established, but the semantic categories are diverse and only six languages coincide here as regards which semantic categories correlate. From that order onwards, no clear correlations were observed.
(iv) Regarding semantic categories, DIMINUTIVE appears to be correlated with the 1st order of derivation from all three types of base.

49.9 Semantic categories with blocking effects

There has been some fairly extensive research into the combinability of affixes and the blocking effects of affixes (so-called terminal affixes). The underlying idea of this direction of investigation concerns the fact that affixes cannot be combined arbitrarily. Instead, there are strict rules in each language that govern the possibility of the attachment of various affixes to the base (such as various base-driven and affix-driven approaches; cf. Fabb 1988; Plag 1996; Giegerich 1999; Gaeta 2005, among others) as well as the ordering and combinations of affixes (cf., for example, Aronoff and Fuhrhop 2002; Hay and Plag 2004; Manova and Aronoff 2010; Saarinen and Hay 2014; Manova 2015). While the approaches to affix ordering vary (Manova and Aronoff (2010) identify eight approaches: phonological, morphological, syntactic, semantic, statistical, psycholinguistic, cognitive and templative), the point of departure in each of them is an affix. Our approach is different and, in a way, complementary. We take a semantic category (which, usually, can be represented by more than one synonymous affix) as the starting point and examine their combinability as well as their capacity to block any subsequent derivation. Certainly, in a form of typological research, we necessarily have to try to identify any regularities and tendencies across languages. Our findings are presented in sections 49.9 and 49.10.

Blocking is reported to be conditioned by specific suffixes and also by specific semantic categories. The former is reported for languages like Estonian and Norwegian in the language sample, but the focus of this section is on the latter, i.e. blocking by semantic categories, such as blocking by the semantic category MANNER in Portuguese (e.g. *novamente* 'newly') or by the semantic category STATIVE in German (e.g. *Schneidbarkeit* 'cuttability').

Semantic categories with blocking effects are reported in all the languages of the sample except Welsh. A bias towards specific blocking categories can also be identified, such that the same semantic category has a blocking effect through all the word-classes, regardless of the order of derivation. Thus, for example, in North Saami the category ACTION blocks further derivation in verbs from the 1st order onwards, and in nouns and adjectives from the 2nd order onwards. This can be attested for specific semantic categories across languages as follows:

(i)	Finnish:	STATIVE	
(ii)	Georgian:	AGENT	
(iii)	Hungarian:	MANNER	PROCESS
(iv)	Icelandic:	ACTION	PROCESS
		AGENT	QUALITY
		MANNER	STATIVE
(v)	Lithuanian:	ACTION	
(vi)	North Saami:	ACTION	PROCESS
		AGENT	
(vii)	Slovene:	DIMINUTIVE	FEMALE
(viii)	Spanish:	MANNER	
(ix)	Swedish:	AGENT	INSTRUMENT
		AUGMENTATIVE	MANNER
		ENTITY	PATIENT
(x)	Ukrainian:	AGENT	

Again, considerable variation can be identified here, ranging from languages where blocking is reported for only one category (Finnish, Georgian, Lithuanian, Spanish, Ukrainian) to languages where up to six categories have a blocking effect (Icelandic, Swedish). Remarkably, the number of semantic categories with blocking effects through all word-classes is comparatively low: 12 categories out of a possible 41. It is also remarkable how, of these blocking categories, the category AGENT occurs in half of the languages reported above.

By word-class, in adjective-based derivations, the most conspicuous associations in the 1st order are detected for STATE and DIMINUTIVE, as follows:

(i)	DIMINUTIVE:	Czech	Greek	Slovene
		Georgian	Maltese	Turkish

(ii) STATE: Bulgarian   Georgian   Maltese
              Chechen   Hungarian Tatar
              Finnish   Icelandic Ukrainian

In the 2nd order of derivation, they are for AGENT, MANNER and PROCESS, as follows:

(i)   AGENT: Georgian   Lithuanian   Swedish
                Icelandic   North Saami   Ukrainian

(ii) MANNER: Finnish   Lithuanian   Spanish
                Hungarian   Polish

(iii) PROCESS: Hungarian   Maltese
                Icelandic   North Saami

In the 3rd order of derivation, they are for ACTION and MANNER, as follows:

(i)   ACTION: Hungarian   Lithuanian   Turkish
                Icelandic   North Saami   Ukrainian

(ii) MANNER: Czech   Greek   Spanish
                Finnish   Hungarian

In the 4th order of derivation, it is for ACTION, as follows:

(i)   ACTION: Lithuanian   North Saami

These data are summarized in Table 49.40.

According to this, Hungarian, Icelandic, Lithuanian and North Saami record consistent blocking by semantic categories across orders of derivation within the adjective word-class.

In the orders of derivation where several semantic categories are reported to have a blocking effect, the tendency is for each language to have only one semantic category with a blocking effect, e.g. Bulgarian with respect to STATE in the 1st order. However, some languages report several, e.g. Georgian reports three (DIMINUTIVE, STATE, AGENT) and Maltese reports two (DIMINUTIVE, STATE), both in the 1st order. Similarly, Hungarian, Lithuanian and North Saami report two categories each in the 2nd order, and Hungarian does so again in the 3rd order. Few languages report blocking in the 4th order of derivation. Otherwise,

Table 49.40: Semantic categories with blocking effects in adjectives.

Language	1st order	2nd order	3rd order	4th order
Bulgarian	STATE			
Chechen	STATE			
Czech	DIMINUTIVE		MANNER	
Finnish	STATE	MANNER	MANNER	
Georgian	DIMINUTIVE STATE AGENT			
Greek	DIMINUTIVE		MANNER	
Hungarian	STATE	MANNER PROCESS	ACTION MANNER	
Icelandic	STATE AGENT	PROCESS	ACTION	
Lithuanian	AGENT MANNER		ACTION	ACTION
Maltese	DIMINUTIVE STATE	PROCESS		
North Saami	AGENT	PROCESS	ACTION	ACTION
Polish		MANNER		
Slovene	DIMINUTIVE			
Spanish		MANNER	MANNER	
Swedish		AGENT		
Tatar	STATE			
Turkish	DIMINUTIVE		ACTION	
Ukrainian	STATE AGENT		ACTION	

no pattern of distribution can be identified here in relation to language type, language family, or genus or areal specification.

In noun-based derivations, the most conspicuous associations in the 1st order are detected for DIMINUTIVE, MANNER and SIMILATIVE, as follows:

(i) DIMINUTIVE: Georgian Polish Turkish
Hungarian North Saami Ukrainian
Latvian Slovene
Lithuanian Tatar

(ii) MANNER: Chechen North Saami
Icelandic Swedish

(iii) SIMILATIVE: Georgian Tatar
Slovene Turkish

In the 2nd order of derivation, they are for ACTION and MANNER, as follows:

(i) ACTION: Hungarian North Saami
Latvian Turkish

(ii) MANNER: Czech Hungarian Spanish
Finnish Latvian Swedish

In the 3rd order of derivation, it is for ACTION, as follows:

(i) ACTION: Hungarian North Saami
Lithuanian Turkish

In the 4th order of derivation, it is again for ACTION, as follows:

(i) ACTION: Hungarian Turkish
North Saami

These data are summarized in Table 49.41.

According to this, Hungarian, North Saami and Turkish record consistent blocking by semantic categories across orders of derivation within the noun word-class.

As with adjectives, in the orders of derivation where several semantic categories have a blocking effect, many languages report only having one semantic category with a blocking effect, e.g. Chechen with respect to MANNER in the 1st order. However, some languages report several, e.g. Georgian, Slovene, Tatar and Turkish report two blocking categories in the 1st order, and Hungarian and Latvian also report two blocking categories in the 2nd order. Few languages report blocking in the 3rd or 4th order of derivation. Otherwise, no pattern of distribution can be identified here in relation to language type, language family, or genus or areal specification.

In verb-based derivations, the most conspicuous associations in the 1st order are detected for ACTION, AGENT, ENTITY and LOCATION, as follows:

Table 49.41: Semantic categories with blocking effects in nouns.

Language	Order of derivation			
	1st order	2nd order	3rd order	4th order
Chechen	MANNER			
Czech		MANNER		
Finnish		MANNER		
Georgian	DIMINUTIVE	SIMILATIVE		
Greek				
Hungarian	DIMINUTIVE	ACTION MANNER	ACTION	ACTION
Icelandic	MANNER			
Latvian	DIMINUTIVE	ACTION MANNER		
Lithuanian	DIMINUTIVE		ACTION	
North Saami	DIMINUTIVE MANNER	ACTION	ACTION	ACTION
Polish	DIMINUTIVE			
Slovene	DIMINUTIVE	SIMILATIVE		
Spanish		MANNER		
Swedish	MANNER	MANNER		
Tatar	DIMINUTIVE	SIMILATIVE		
Turkish	DIMINUTIVE	SIMILATIVE ACTION	ACTION	ACTION
Ukrainian	DIMINUTIVE			

(i) ACTION: Basque, Lithuanian, Slovene, Latvian, North Saami, Tatar

(ii) AGENT: Greek, Icelandic, Swedish, Hungarian, North Saami, Tatar

(iii) ENTITY: Greek, Swedish, North Saami, Ukrainian

(iv) LOCATION: Bulgarian, Greek, Ukrainian, Georgian, Swedish

In the 2nd order of derivation, they are for ACTION and DIMINUTIVE, as follows:

(i) ACTION: Hungarian   North Saami
                 Icelandic   Tatar

(ii) DIMINUTIVE: Czech   Slovene
                 Greek   Tatar

In the 3rd order of derivation, they are for ACTION and MANNER, as follows:

(i) ACTION: Hungarian   North Saami
              Latvian   Turkish

(ii) MANNER: Czech   Hungarian   Spanish
              Finnish   Latvian   Swedish

In the 4th order of derivation, it is for ACTION, as follows:

(i) ACTION: Hungarian North Saami

These data are summarized in Table 49.42.

Table 49.42: Semantic categories with blocking effects in verbs.

Language	Order of derivation			
	1st order	2nd order	3rd order	4th order
Basque	ACTION			
Bulgarian		LOCATION		
Czech		DIMINUTIVE	MANNER	
Finnish				
Georgian		LOCATION		
Greek	AGENT ENTITY LOCATION	DIMINUTIVE		
Hungarian	AGENT	ACTION	ACTION MANNER	ACTION
Icelandic	AGENT	ACTION		
Latvian	ACTION		ACTION	

Table 49.42 (continued)

Language	Order of derivation			
	1st order	2nd order	3rd order	4th order
Lithuanian	ACTION			
North Saami	ACTION AGENT ENTITY	ACTION	ACTION	ACTION
Slovene	ACTION	DIMINUTIVE		
Spanish			MANNER	
Swedish	AGENT ENTITY LOCATION			
Tatar	ACTION AGENT	ACTION DIMINUTIVE		
Turkish			ACTION	
Ukrainian	ENTITY LOCATION			

According to Table 49.42, Greek, Hungarian, North Saami, Swedish and Tatar record consistent blocking by semantic categories across orders of derivation within the verb word-class.

As for adjectives and nouns, in the orders of derivation where several semantic categories have a blocking effect, the tendency is for languages to have only one semantic category with a blocking effect, even if some languages report several, e.g. Greek, North Saami, Swedish, Tatar and Ukrainian in the 1st order, Tatar in the 2nd order, and Hungarian in the 3rd order. Few languages report blocking in the 4th order of derivation. Otherwise, no pattern of distribution can be identified here in relation to language type, language family, or genus or areal specification.

The opposite scenario, i.e. the identification of semantic categories that do not occur at all in specific languages, is also possible, but the combinations are too many to list here. A set of semantic categories that rarely have a blocking effect in the sample can, however, be listed here. The following selections are reported only in one case, regardless of the word-class or the order of derivation:
(i) ATTENUATIVE, in the 2nd order of Greek nouns
(ii) ANTICAUSATIVE, in the 1st order of Maltese verbs
(iii) CONCOMITANT, in the 1st order of Greek verbs
(iv) CUMULATIVE, in the 2nd order of Ukrainian verbs
(v) DISTRIBUTIVE, in the 3rd order of Polish verbs
(vi) INCEPTIVE, in the 1st order of Ukrainian verbs
(vii) POSSESSIVE, in the 1st order of Hungarian nouns

Summary

(i) All languages in the sample, irrespective of genus or family, report semantic categories with blocking effects. The only exception is Welsh.
(ii) Semantic categories do not report blocking effects through all the word-classes in the same order of derivation. DIMINUTIVE, MANNER and ACTION cut across word-classes, albeit in different orders of derivation for the three word-classes.
(iii) Blocking in the 4th order of derivation is reported to be base-insensitive and is limited to both one semantic category (ACTION) and few languages (Hungarian and North Saami for all three word-classes, and Lithuanian and Turkish for nouns).
(iv) Several languages record consistent blocking by semantic categories across orders of derivation, e.g. Hungarian and North Saami.
(v) In the orders of derivation where several semantic categories have a blocking effect, the tendency is for languages to have only one semantic category with a blocking effect, except for some languages which consistently report several, regardless of the word-class or order of derivation, e.g. Hungarian and Tatar.

49.10 Combinations of semantic categories

By 'combinations of semantic categories', we mean the occurrence of semantic categories in successive orders of derivation in the networks of five or more of the base words in a particular word-class, e.g. in Catalan (nouns as base): LOCATION-base > ACTION > RESULTATIVE (e.g. *magatzem* 'warehouse' > *emmagatzemar* > *desemmagatzemar*); in Croatian (nouns as base): AGENT (or EXPERIENCER, PATIENT) – POSSESSIVE (e.g. *pas* 'dog' > *pset-ar* 'dog holder' – *pset-ar-ev* 'dog holder's'), AGENT – FEMININE – POSSESSIVE (*zub* > *zub-ar* – *zub-ar-ica* – *zub-ar-ič-in* 'female dentist's'); and in English (verbs as base): combinations of ABILITY in the 1st order with ABILITY and PRIVATIVE in the 2nd order (*cuttable* > *cuttability*, *cuttable* > *uncuttable*). Combinations of semantic categories are reported for all the languages in the sample except Welsh. A number of languages also do not attest frequent combinations for specific word-classes, e.g. there are no frequent combinations for adjectives in Dargwa, for nouns in Chechen, Dargwa, Maltese and Polish, or for verbs in Irish.

The combinability of semantic categories (which, for methodological reasons, can only be traced in combinations between 1st and 2nd order derivatives onwards) is astoundingly varied, and no recurrent patterns could be established across the language sample for frequent combinations across the board. Still, some cases can be highlighted.

(i) Each word-class starts out with specific combinations, such that the same sequence is often not found across the three word-classes in the sample, except in certain languages, as in example (5) and as summarized in Table 49.43.

Table 49.43: Languages in which frequent combinations occur regardless of word-class.

Language	Combination		
	Adjectives	Nouns	Verbs
Czech	QUALITY + ABSTRACTION	QUALITY + ABSTRACTION	QUALITY + ABSTRACTION
	QUALITY + PATIENT	QUALITY + PATIENT	QUALITY + PATIENT
	RELATIONAL + MANNER	RELATIONAL + MANNER	RELATIONAL + MANNER
Georgian		ACTION + AGENT	ACTION + AGENT
	ACTION + CAUSATIVE	ACTION + CAUSATIVE	ACTION + CAUSATIVE
	ACTION + RESULT		ACTION + RESULT
Greek	ACTION + SATURATIVE + PATIENT	ACTION + SATURATIVE + PATIENT	
	ACTION + ITERATIVE + PATIENT	ACTION + ITERATIVE + PATIENT	
	ACTION + ATTENUATIVE + PATIENT	ACTION + ATTENUATIVE + PATIENT	
Icelandic	QUALITY + QUALITY	QUALITY + QUALITY	QUALITY + QUALITY
Irish	CAUSATIVE + ACTION	CAUSATIVE + ACTION	
Latvian		CAUSATIVE + FINITIVE + ACTION	CAUSATIVE + FINITIVE ACTION
North Saami	RESULTATIVE + PROCESS	RESULTATIVE + PROCESS	
	RESULTATIVE + INCHOATIVE + PROCESS	RESULTATIVE + INCHOATIVE + PROCESS	

(5) Icelandic
 Noun: *nafnlaus* > *nafnleysi*
 'nameless' 'anonymity'
 Verb: *brennanlegur* > *torbrennanlegur*
 'burnable' 'difficult to burn'
 Adjective: *langsamur* > *langsamlega*
 'prolonged' 'by far'

No associations can be identified here with regard to language type, language family, or genus or areal distribution.

(ii) The opposite scenario, i.e. frequent combinations which are specific to word-classes, can also be found in several languages, but with considerably more restrictions, as in example (6) and as summarized in Table 49.44.

Table 49.44: Word-class-specific frequent combinations across languages.

Language	Combination		
	Adjectives	Nouns	Verbs
Chechen	QUALITY + STATE		
English	QUALITY + STATE		
Ukrainian	QUALITY + STATE		

(6) Chechen:
 Adjective *vokkha* > *vokkhalla*
 'old, senior, elder' 'an old age, seniority, eldership'

It follows from Table 49.44 that it is only the class of adjectives that manifests frequent combinations of semantic categories across languages. No associations can be identified here with regard to language type, language family, or genus or areal distribution.

(iii) The various possible arrangements and the size of the sample do not allow us even to hint at combinations that otherwise typically occur. It is, however, possible to identify typical starting categories that are particularly frequent in each word-class (Table 49.45) and typical starting categories that occur in each word-class even if they are not particularly frequent in a language (Table 49.46).

Table 49.45 above shows specific biases of certain languages towards specific categories in specific word-classes, e.g. Bulgarian adjectives towards PATIENT, in contrast to North Saami adjectives towards RESULTATIVE or Tatar adjectives towards UNDERGOER, to name just one of the possible contrasts that can be found. More relevantly, it also shows, as also confirmed in Table 49.46, that certain categories stand out for their frequency regardless of their word-class or language, such as:

a. ABILITY, AGENT, ACTION, CAUSATIVE, QUALITY or SIMILATIVE in the adjective word-class. Examples of combinations that occur in several languages are:
QUALITY + AUGMENTATIVE in German, Swedish and Ukrainian
PRIVATIVE + MANNER in Italian, Polish and Russian
SIMILATIVE + MANNER in Czech, Latvian, Lithuanian and Polish

b. AGENT, QUALITY, PRIVATIVE and SIMILATIVE in the noun word-class. Examples of combinations that occur in several languages are:
QUALITY + STATIVE in Bulgarian, English, Norwegian and Serbian
CAUSATIVE + ACTION in Basque, Irish, Norwegian and Spanish

c. AGENT, CAUSATIVE, DIRECTIONAL, FINITIVE, PROCESS and QUALITY in the verb word-class. Examples of combinations that occur in several languages are:
AGENT + FEMALE in Bulgarian, Dutch, German, Serbian and Slovene
CAUSATIVE + ACTION in Finnish and Swedish
CAUSATIVE + AGENT in Finnish and Swedish

No pattern can be identified by language type, language family, or genus or areal distribution for these combinations.

(iv) Despite the apparent bias towards a set of starting categories, the possible observations of combinations are thus very limited:
  a. Certain combinations with a range of subsequent categories can be attested at least four times across languages in the language sample for a specific word-class:
    i. In the adjective word-class:
       QUALITY + STATE (+) in Chechen, English, German and Ukrainian
    ii. In the verb word-class:
       AGENT + FEMALE (+) in Bulgarian, Croatian, German, Serbian and Slovak

Table 49.45: Initial categories in frequent combinations across languages.

Language	Combination	
	Adjectives	Nouns
Bulgarian		PATIENT
Catalan	QUALITY	
Croatian	AGENT	AGENT
Czech		
Finnish		
Galician		
Georgian	ACTION	ACTION
German	ABILITY / QUALITY	ABILITY
Greek	ACTION	ACTION
Hungarian	QUALITY	
Icelandic	QUALITY	
Lithuanian	CAUSATIVE PROCESS	
North Saami	RESULTATIVE	
Portuguese		
Romanian	CAUSATIVE	CAUSATIVE
Russian		
Tatar		UNDERGOER
Ukrainian	QUALITY	

The presented semantic categories in Table 49.45 are characterized by a frequency above three attested combinations per language, regardless of word-class.

				Combination			
				Verbs			
ENTITY				ACTION			
				AGENT			
						DURATIVE	
					CAUSATIVE		PROCESS
				AGENT			
				ACTION			
	QUALITY		ABILITY	AGENT			QUALITY
	QUALITY						QUALITY
	QUALITY						QUALITY
	PROCESS				DIRECTIONAL		
		RESULTATIVE		CAUSATIVE			
DIMINUTIVE							
				CAUSATIVE			
				ACTION			
				AGENT			UNDERGOER
				ACTION			

Table 49.46: Initial categories in typical combinations across languages.

Language	Semantic categories that	
	Adjectives	Nouns
Bulgarian		
Catalan	QUALITY	
Chechen	QUALITY	
Croatian	AGENT	AGENT CAUSATIVE
Czech		AGENT
Dargwa		
English	ABILITY QUALITY	PRIVATIVE
Finnish		
Galician		
Georgian	ACTION	ACTION PRIVATIVE
German	ABILITY AGENT	QUALITY ABILITY AGENT
Greek	ACTION	ACTION
Hungarian	QUALITY	
Icelandic	QUALITY	
Irish	CAUSATIVE QUALITY	CAUSATIVE
Latvian	CAUSATIVE SIMILATIVE	
Lithuanian	CAUSATIVE PROCESS SIMILATIVE	
Maltese	CAUSATIVE	
North Saami		PRIVATIVE
Polish	PRIVATIVE SIMILATIVE	
Portuguese		
Romanian		
Russian		
Slovene	CAUSATIVE	
Swedish		
Tatar		
Ukrainian	QUALITY	

The presented initial semantic categories are with a frequency above four attested combinations, regardless of language.

start combinations

		Verbs			
QUALITY	AGENT	DIRECTIONAL			
	ACTION				
	ACTION				
	AGENT				
QUALITY SIMILATIVE		DIRECTIONAL FINITIVE			SIMILATIVE
	AGENT				
			PRIVATIVE		
	CAUSATIVE		PROCESS		
QUALITY			PRIVATIVE		
QUALITY SIMILATIVE ABILITY	AGENT			QUALITY	
QUALITY				QUALITY	
QUALITY				PROCESS	
QUALITY	CAUSATIVE	DIRECTIONAL FINITIVE			
PROCESS		DIRECTIONAL FINITIVE			
	CAUSATIVE				
			PROCESS		
	CAUSATIVE				
				QUALITY	
	AGENT	DIRECTIONAL FINITIVE			
	CAUSATIVE				
	AGENT CAUSATIVE				

b. Certain combinations are attested only once in the language sample, even regardless of the word-class, which is sometimes because their starting category occurs only once, even in the same language:
   i. In the noun word-class:
      TEMPORAL + QUANTITY (+) in Catalan
   ii. In the verb word-class:
      ANTICAUSATIVE + ENTITY in Icelandic
      CONCOMITANT + PATIENT in Greek
      DISTRIBUTIVE + DURATIVE (+) in Czech

Summary

(i) Frequent combinations of semantic categories are reported for most of the languages in the sample, and also regularly for each word-class. However, each word-class starts out with its own specific combinations, such that the same sequence is typically not found across the three word-classes in the sample.

(ii) Few frequent combinations specific to word-classes can be found across languages, e.g. QUALITY + STATE in adjectives in Chechen, English and Ukrainian, so few biases of certain languages towards combinations of specific categories in specific word-classes can be detected.

(iii) Some starting categories that occur in each word-class can be identified as showing categories that stand out for their frequency regardless of word-class and language, e.g. QUALITY.

(iv) Unique combinations can be attested in the sample too, e.g. ANTICAUSATIVE + ENTITY occurs only once in the sample (Icelandic).

(v) No pattern can be identified by language type, language genus, or family or areal distribution, but certain combinations with a range of subsequent categories can be attested across languages.

49.11 Multiple occurrence of semantic categories

The multiple occurrence of semantic categories in subsequent orders of derivation is a relatively frequent phenomenon in the 40 European languages under study. This phenomenon is manifested in the recurrence of the same semantic category in successive orders of derivation, as in the examples below:

- Basque: e.g. QUALITY – QUALITY: *epel*$_A$ 'warm' > *epelki*$_{ADV}$ 'warmly' > *epelkiro*$_{ADV}$ 'warmly'; *zuzen*$_A$ 'straight' > *zuzenki*$_{ADV}$ 'straightly' > *zuzenkiro*$_{ADV}$ 'straightly'; *berri*$_A$ 'new' > *berriro*$_{ADV}$ 'newly, again' > *berriroki*$_{ADV}$ 'newly, again'.
- Croatian: e.g. QUALITY – QUALITY: *zl-o-ba-n* 'malicious' – *na-zl-o-ba-n* 'malicious'.
- Frisian: e.g. *witt* 'know' > ABSTRACTION in 1st order verb: *witten* > ABSTRACTION *wittenskip* 'science' > ABSTRACTION in 4th order: *wittenskiplikens* 'scientific character'.
- Georgian: e.g. ACTION – ACTION: *tvaliereba*$_V$ 'to look at, examine' > *atvaliereba*$_V$ 'to look up'; QUALITY – QUALITY: *moč'rili*$_A$ 'cut' > *amoč'rili*$_A$ 'cut out'; AGENT – AGENT: *msroleli*$_N$ 'thrower' > *amsroleli*$_N$ 'who throws up'; CAUSATIVE – CAUSATIVE: *srolineba*$_V$ 'let someone throw' > *asrolineba*$_V$ 'let someone throw up'.

Multiple occurrence has been identified in 26 out of the 40 languages: Basque, Bulgarian, Catalan, Chechen, Dargwa, Finnish, Frisian, Georgian, German, Greek, Hungarian, Icelandic, Latvian, North Saami, Polish, Portuguese, Romanian, Russian, Serbian, Slovak, Slovene, Spanish, Swedish, Tatar, Turkish and Ukrainian.

These languages cover all language types and all language families, with the exception of the Afro-Asiatic family (Maltese), represented in the sample, as shown in Tables 49.47 and 49.48.

Table 49.47: Languages where the multiple occurrence of semantic categories is attested by language type.

Language type	Languages
Inflectional	Bulgarian, Catalan, German, Greek, Icelandic, Latvian, Polish, Portuguese, Romanian, Russian, Serbian, Slovak, Slovene, Spanish, Ukrainian
Agglutinating	Basque, Chechen, Dargwa, Finnish, Georgian, Hungarian, North Saami, Tatar, Turkish
Analytical	Frisian, Swedish

Of these, Table 49.47 maintains in the main the proportions of the language types represented in the sample, whereas Table 49.48 lends itself to further comment in that the proportions of the language sample are not replicated to the extent that Slavic languages, compared with other language genera of the Indo-

Table 49.48: Languages where the multiple occurrence of semantic categories is attested by language family.

Afro-Asiatic	Altaic	Basque	Language family/genus							Kartvelian	Nakh-Daghestanian	Uralic
			Indo-European									
			Baltic	Celtic	Germanic	Greek	Romance		Slavic			
	Tatar	Basque	Latvian		Frisian	Greek	Catalan		Bulgarian	Georgian	Chechen	Finnish
	Turkish				German		Portuguese		Polish		Dargwa	Hungarian
					Icelandic		Romanian		Russian			North Saami
					Swedish		Spanish		Serbian			
									Slovak			
									Slovene			
									Ukrainian			

49 Derivational networks in European languages: A cross-linguistic perspective — 577

European family, display multiple occurrence in seven out of nine languages in this genus, in contrast to four out of eight Germanic languages or three out of seven Romance languages.

With regard to the opposite case, i.e. the languages wherein multiple occurrence is not recorded, Tables 49.49 and 49.50 show that no relevant pattern can be identified, as the languages arrange themselves across language types and language families or genera in an approximate proportion to the number of languages of each case represented in the sample.

Table 49.49: Languages where the multiple occurrence of semantic categories is not attested by language type.

Language type	Languages
Inflectional	Dutch, French, Galician, Italian[a]
Agglutinating	Estonian
Analytical	Danish, English

[a]Here recorded as negligible.

Table 49.50 is congruent with Table 49.46 in that it contains a fair number of the most represented language genera, i.e. Germanic and Romance, and in that it shows the opposite results to Table 49.46, i.e. a disproportional underrepresentation of Slavic languages.

The above does not take into consideration 10 languages, not listed above, for which occasional, rare or sporadic occurrences of semantic categories are reported. These languages are Croatian, Czech, Estonian, Irish, Lithuanian, Maltese, Norwegian, Romanian, Tatar and Welsh.

There is considerable variation as to which categories occur multiple times, in which orders of derivation they occur, and for which word-classes. Languages thus display arrangements that may differ considerably in several ways:

(i) There may be considerable variation within languages with regard to semantic categories and how they occur multiple times with respect to word-classes, e.g.:
    a. Greek records multiple occurrences of the category DIMINUTIVE in all three word-classes, whereas German displays multiple occurrences of AUGMENTATIVE in adjectives and verbs, but not in nouns. The latter, a rather specific pattern, may find similar arrangements in other languages, e.g. in Tatar, where the multiple occurrence of the semantic

Table 49.50: Languages where the multiple occurrence of semantic categories is not attested by language family.

| Afro-Asiatic | Altaic | Basque | Language family/genus ||||||| Kartvelian | Nakh-Daghestanian | Uralic |
| | | | Indo-European |||||| | | |
			Baltic	Celtic	Germanic	Greek	Romance	Slavic			
					Danish		French				Estonian
					Dutch		Galician				
					English		Italian				

category CAUSATIVE is recorded in adjectives and verbs but, like German for AUGMENTATIVE, not in nouns.
   b. Bulgarian records multiple occurrences of the categories QUALITY in nouns and PLURIACTIONALITY in verbs, but none in adjectives, whereas Latvian, for example, records multiple occurrences of SIMILATIVE precisely in adjectives.
(ii) There may be considerable variation between languages with regard to semantic categories and how they occur multiple times with respect to word-classes, e.g.:
   a. Frisian reports multiple occurrences of a limited set of semantic categories per word-class:
      i. Adjectives: ACTION
      ii. Nouns: QUALITY
      iii. Verbs: ABSTRACTION
   b. This contrasts sharply with the set of semantic categories recorded for Polish or for Slovene, of which, for brevity, only the former is shown for illustration:
      i. Adjectives: DIMINUTIVE, LOCATION, MANNER, QUALITY, REFLEXIVE and RESULTATIVE
      ii. Nouns: COLLECTIVE, DIMINUTIVE, LOCATION, QUALITY, RELATIONAL and RESULTATIVE
      iii. Verbs: ACTION, AGENT, AUGMENTATIVE, DIMINUTIVE, DISTRIBUTIVE, FEMALE, ITERATIVE, LOCATION, REFLEXIVE, RELATIONAL, and RESULTATIVE

The possibility of the multiple occurrence of a semantic category in successive orders of derivation can be explored in several senses. The first is whether the categories reoccur successively with or without a different intermediate semantic category. The two cases are recorded in the sample.
(i) Multiple occurrence of a semantic category without a different intermediate category, e.g.:
   a. Frisian:
      i. Adjectives: ACTION + ACTION
      ii. Nouns: QUALITY + QUALITY
      iii. Verbs: ABSTRACTION + ABSTRACTION + ABSTRACTION

(ii) Multiple occurrence of a semantic category with a different intermediate category, e.g.:

a. Slovene:
   i. Adjectives: PROCESS + PROCESS
   MANNER + MANNER
   ii. Nouns: ACTION + ACTION
   DIMINUTIVE + DIMINUTIVE
   PROCESS + FINITIVE + PROCESS
   RELATIONAL + ENTITY + RELATIONAL
   iii. Verbs: QUALITY + QUALITY
   FINITIVE + QUALITY + PRIVATIVE + QUALITY

Concerning which semantic categories occur on multiple occasions, certain ones stand out in this respect because they appear consistently, as shown in Table 49.51.

Table 49.51: Most frequently recorded semantic categories with multiple occurrences.

Semantic category	Languages
QUALITY (10 languages)	Bulgarian, Catalan, Chechen, Frisian, Georgian, Icelandic, Polish, Serbian, Slovene, Ukrainian
ACTION (11 languages)	Catalan, Chechen, Frisian, Georgian, Icelandic, North Saami, Polish, Slovene, Spanish, Swedish, Ukrainian
DIMINUTIVE (6 languages)	Bulgarian, Greek, Polish, Portuguese, Romanian, Slovene
CAUSATIVE (9 languages)	Chechen, Finnish, Georgian, North Saami, Romanian, Swedish, Tatar, Turkish, Ukrainian

These categories occur multiply in both language types and language families and genera, as shown in the following table.

The data are not sufficient to make any typological conclusions or generalizations. Table 49.51 above maintains in the main the proportions of the language types represented in the sample, except that it lends itself to further comment in that the proportions of the language sample are not replicated by:
(i) DIMINUTIVE, in that its multiple occurrence is not recorded in any agglutinating or analytical language; and
(ii) CAUSATIVE, in that it is recorded in more agglutinating than inflectional languages, despite their different proportions in the language sample.

Tables 49.51 and 49.52 hint at different behaviours for each of the main language genera:

49 Derivational networks in European languages: A cross-linguistic perspective — 581

Table 49.52: Semantic categories for which multiple occurrence is attested by language type.

Language type	Semantic categories			
	QUALITY	ACTION	DIMINUTIVE	CAUSATIVE
Inflectional	Bulgarian, Catalan, Icelandic, Polish, Serbian, Slovene, Ukrainian	Catalan, Icelandic, Polish, Slovene, Spanish, Ukrainian	Bulgarian, Greek, Polish, Portuguese, Romanian, Slovene	Romanian, Ukrainian
Agglutinating	Chechen, Georgian	Chechen, Georgian		Chechen, Finnish, Georgian, North Saami, Tatar, Turkish
Analytical	Frisian	Frisian, Swedish		Swedish

(i) Germanic languages do not maintain their proportion with respect to other language genera in this regard, except for the category ACTION and, to a much lesser degree, QUALITY.
(ii) Romance languages do not maintain their proportion with respect to other language genera, except for the categories ACTION and DIMINUTIVE, both to a low degree.
(iii) Slavic languages maintain their proportion with respect to other language genera for the semantic categories QUALITY, ACTION and DIMINUTIVE, but not for CAUSATIVE.

This confirms what Table 49.51 suggests concerning the multiple occurrence of semantic categories in Slavic languages in general, in this case also with regard to certain individual semantic categories (QUALITY, ACTION and, less markedly, DIMINUTIVE), but not with respect to others (CAUSATIVE). The limited data do not allow similar specific claims to be made with regard to individual semantic categories in Altaic, Nakh-Daghestanian or Uralic languages, which are also suggested as being language families in which the phenomenon of multiple occurrence is identified (Table 49.48).

Various other patterns are hinted at by the data (cf. Tables 49.53 to 49.56), but again these are of a tentative kind, in the absence of a bigger data set, e.g.:
(i) Multiple occurrences of the semantic category PROCESS are only recorded in inflectional languages (Catalan, Polish, Russian and Slovene), but not in all the inflectional languages wherein multiple occurrence is recorded (not in Bulgarian, German, Greek, Icelandic, Latvian, Portuguese, Romanian, Serbian, Slovak, Spanish or Ukrainian).

Table 49.53: Multiple occurrences of the semantic category QUALITY by language family.

Afro-Asiatic	Altaic	Basque	Language family/genus						Kartvelian	Nakh-Daghestanian	Uralic
			Indo-European								
			Baltic	Celtic	Germanic	Greek	Romance	Slavic			
					Frisian Icelandic		Catalan	Bulgarian Polish Serbian Slovene Ukrainian	Georgian	Chechen	

Table 49.54: Multiple occurrences of the semantic category ACTION by language family.

Afro-Asiatic	Altaic	Basque	Language family/genus						Kartvelian	Nakh-Daghestanian	Uralic
			Indo-European								
			Baltic	Celtic	Germanic	Greek	Romance	Slavic			
					Frisian Icelandic Swedish		Catalan Spanish	Polish Slovene Ukrainian	Georgian	Chechen	

Table 49.55: Multiple occurrences of the semantic category DIMINUTIVE by language family.

			Language family/genus							
Afro-Asiatic	Altaic	Basque	Indo-European					Kartvelian	Nakh-Daghestanian	Uralic
			Baltic	Celtic	Germanic	Greek	Romance	Slavic			
						Greek	Portuguese	Bulgarian			
							Romanian	Polish			
								Slovene			

Table 49.56: Multiple occurrences of the semantic category CAUSATIVE by language family.

			Language family/genus							
Afro-Asiatic	Altaic	Basque	Indo-European					Kartvelian	Nakh-Daghestanian	Uralic
			Baltic	Celtic	Germanic	Greek	Romance	Slavic			
	Tatar				Swedish			Ukrainian	Georgian	Chechen	Finnish
	Turkish										North Saami

(ii) Multiple occurrence of the semantic category ENTITY are only recorded in Slavic languages (Russian, Serbian, Slovak, and Slovene), but not in all the Slavic languages wherein multiple occurrence is recorded (not in Bulgarian, Polish or Ukrainian).

Specific specialized combinations of languages and semantic categories can also be identified in one of two ways:
(i) With regard to the specialization of languages, in that several languages record multiple occurrences of very few semantic categories, e.g.:
    a. Basque: MANNER and STATE
    b. Finnish: CAUSATIVE
    c. German: AUGMENTATIVE
    d. Greek: DIMINUTIVE
    e. Latvian: SIMILATIVE
    f. Portuguese: DIMINUTIVE
    g. Romanian: CAUSATIVE and DIMINUTIVE
    h. Serbian: ENTITY and QUALITY
    i. Spanish: ACTION
    j. Turkish: CAUSATIVE

(ii) With regard to the specialization of semantic categories, in that certain semantic categories occur repeatedly in very few or in just one language, e.g.:
    a. AUGMENTATIVE: German and Polish
    b. DISTRIBUTIVE: Polish
    c. FEMALE: Polish
    d. FINITIVE: Slovene
    e. INSTRUMENT: Polish and Russian
    f. ITERATIVE: Polish and Tatar
    g. LOCATION: Polish
    h. PERCEPTIVE: Tatar
    i. PLURIACTIONAL: Bulgarian
    j. REFLEXIVE: Polish and Russian
    k. SIMILATIVE: Latvian
    l. UNDERGOER: Tatar

The multiple occurrence of semantic categories thus gives rise to a number of combinations between languages/language families and categories. Of these, the clearest association is between Slavic languages and the repetitive occurrence of semantic categories in subsequent orders of derivation.

Summary

(i) Semantic categories occur on multiple occasions in successive orders of derivation, especially in Slavic languages, but which categories do so and how they arrange themselves within languages may vary considerably. This holds both across word-classes and within word-classes.
(ii) This multiple occurrence may be mediated by an intervening category, or not. Semantic categories may reoccur successively with or without a different intermediate semantic category, as in the sequences ACTION + ACTION vs. PROCESS + FINITIVE + PROCESS, both found in Slovene nouns.
(iii) Differences can be found between language genera as regards the multiple occurrence of semantic categories, e.g. Germanic and Romance languages do not maintain their proportions compared with other languages, except for the semantic categories ACTION and QUALITY in the former case, and ACTION and DIMINUTIVE in the latter case. The opposite is found for Slavic languages: they maintain their proportion compared with other genera for the semantic categories QUALITY, ACTION and DIMINUTIVE, but not for CAUSATIVE.
(iv) The data are not sufficient to make any typological conclusions or generalizations, except in specific cases, e.g. multiple occurrences of DIMINUTIVE are not recorded in any agglutinating or analytical language, while those of CAUSATIVE are recorded in more agglutinating than inflectional languages, despite their different proportions in the language sample.
(v) Very specific combinations of languages and semantic categories can be identified, such that several languages record multiple occurrences of very few semantic categories, and certain semantic categories occur in very few or in just one language.
(vi) There is no correlation between the number of orders of derivation and the multiple occurrences of semantic categories. This applies to all word-classes. It is best represented in languages with four and five orders of derivation, though it has also been registered in languages with only two orders of derivation, e.g. adjectives in Chechen or nouns in Frisian.

49.12 Reversibility of semantic categories

The reversibility of semantic categories in subsequent orders of derivation, i.e. the occurrence of derivatives of both AB and BA orders of two semantic categories in a language, is not a frequent or well-represented phenomenon in the 40 European languages under study. Reversibility has been identified in 14 out of the 40 languages: in their derivational networks, Croatian, English, Estonian, Finnish, German, Greek, Hungarian, Maltese, Romanian, Slovene, Spanish, Tatar, Turkish and Welsh display a reversed ordering of semantic categories in subsequent orders of derivation.

These languages cover all languages types and five out of the seven language families represented in the sample, as shown in Tables 49.57 and 49.58.

Table 49.57: Languages where the reversibility of semantic categories can be attested by language type.

Language type	Languages
Inflectional	Croatian, German, Greek, Maltese,[a] Romanian, Slovene, Spanish, Welsh
Agglutinating	Estonian, Finnish, Hungarian, Tatar, Turkish
Analytical	English

[a]Maltese is generally not recognized as an inflectional language. At best, it could be described as a hybrid language combining introflection (root-and-vowel pattern) and affixation. Adhering to Sapir's typological classes, we consider it best, with the qualifications made here, to include Maltese in the group of languages with inflectional typological characteristics.

Of these, Table 49.57 maintains in the main the proportions of the language types represented in the sample, whereas Table 49.58 lends itself to further comment in that the proportions of the language sample are not replicated by:

(i) Germanic, Romance or Slavic languages with respect to less represented language genera or families in the total language sample, but which attest the same number of languages in this regard, e.g. Turkish from the Altaic family and Uralic.
(ii) Altaic languages, insofar as the two languages of the group included in the sample are represented here.
(iii) Latvian and Lithuanian, which are not reported here for the reason that, in Baltic languages, instances of reversibility are perceived as and reported in terms of alternative derivational interpretations – e.g. Lithuanian *deg-ti* 'burn (intr.)' > suffixal CAUSATIVE, *deg-in-ti* 'burn (tr.)' > prefixal FINITIVE **su**-*deg-in-ti* 'burn down (tr.)'.

Other languages not listed above report occasional or exceptional reversibility (Czech) or, in the case of the Baltic genus, the phenomenon is reinterpreted in different terms.

Table 49.58: Languages where the reversibility of semantic categories can be attested by language family.

			Language family/genus							
Afro-Asiatic	Altaic	Basque	Indo-European					Kartvelian	Nakh-Daghestanian	Uralic
			Baltic	Celtic	Germanic	Greek	Romance	Slavic			
Maltese	Tatar		Estonian	Welsh	English	Greek	Romanian	Croatian			Finnish
	Turkish				German		Spanish	Slovene			Hungarian

Among these, the possibilities are rather limited in number and refer to one or two combinations of reversible semantic categories. Only in three languages (Romanian, Tatar, Welsh) are the categories not limited to one or two pairs of semantic categories that permit a sequential exchange, as summarized in Table 49.59.

Table 49.59 shows that the languages wherein most reversible combinations of semantic categories occur are as follows:

(i) Romanian:
   a. ABILITY + ITERATIVE
   b. CAUSATIVE + ENTITY
   c. PRIVATIVE + STATIVE
   d. QUALITY + STATIVE

(ii) Tatar:
   a. ABSTRACTION + QUALITY CAUSATIVE + PLURIACTIONALITY/RECIPROCAL/UNDERGOER/REFLEXIVE/PROCESS
   b. ITERATIVE + RECIPROCAL
   c. QUALITY + STATIVE
   d. AGENT + STATIVE
   e. ABSTRACTION + QUALITY
   f. QUALITY + UNDERGOER

(iii) Welsh:
   a. ABSTRACTION + PRIVATIVE
   b. ABSTRACTION + QUALITY
   c. ABSTRACTION + REFLEXIVE
   d. CAUSATIVE + QUALITY
   e. PRIVATIVE + QUALITY

The limited amount of data does not allow the identification of patterns in the distribution of these reversible combinations by language type, by language genus or family, or by areal distribution. Similarly, there is no pair of semantic categories that are clearly the most frequent pair across the board. The most frequent reversible categories are:

(i) CAUSATIVE (in three combinations and in five languages)
(ii) PRIVATIVE (in five combinations and in five languages)
(iii) QUALITY (in five combinations and in five languages)

The most frequent combinations of reversible categories are as follows, but again no pattern can be identified in their distribution due to the limited amount of data:

(i) CAUSATIVE + PROCESS
(ii) QUALITY + STATIVE

Table 49.59: Languages where the reversibility of semantic categories can be attested.

Language	Semantic categories (in one of the possible orders)
Croatian	ATTENUATIVE RELATIVE
English	ABILITY PRIVATIVE
Estonian	CAUSATIVE PROCESS
Finnish	QUALITY MANNER
German	ABILITY PRIVATIVE
Greek	PATIENT SATURATIVE
Hungarian	QUALITY STATIVE[a]
Maltese	CAUSATIVE PROCESS
Romanian	ABILITY ITERATIVE; CAUSATIVE ENTITY; QUALITY STATIVE; STATE PRIVATIVE
Slovene	PRIVATIVE MANNER
Spanish	QUALITY STATIVE
Tatar	CAUSATIVE + various types e.g. REFLEXIVE, UNDERGOER; QUALITY STATIVE
Turkish	AGENT STATE; CAUSATIVE PROCESS
Welsh	ABSTR. PRIVATIVE; ABSTR. QUALITY; ABSTR. REFLEXIVE; CAUSATIVE QUALITY; PRIVATIVE QUALITY

[a] In this case, STATIVE/ABSTRACTION.

Summary

(i) The systematic reversibility of semantic categories is represented in five out of the seven language families of the sample.
(ii) No patterns can be identified as regards language type, language genus or family, or areal distribution, due to the limited amount of data.

49.13 Reasons for structurally poor derivational networks

The size and diversity of the data sample used here also have an effect on the overall picture as regards, firstly, whether the derivational networks can be considered comparatively rich or poor and, secondly, the reasons for comparatively poorer networks.

Restrictions for richer derivational networks have been identified in 16 out of the 40 languages: Basque, Chechen, Danish, Dargwa, Dutch, English, French, Frisian, Icelandic, Irish, Latvian, Maltese, Norwegian, Portuguese, Tatar and Welsh.

These languages cover all languages types and five out of the seven language families represented in the sample, as shown in Table 49.60.

Table 49.60: Languages for which restrictions on derivational networks have been identified by language type.

Language type	Languages
Inflectional	Dutch, French, Icelandic, Irish, Latvian, Maltese, Portuguese, Welsh
Agglutinating	Basque, Chechen, Dargwa, Tatar
Analytical	Danish, English, Frisian, Norwegian

Notably, the proportion of language types is not maintained here, and analytical languages stand out as not producing rich derivational networks (4 out of 5), compared to agglutinating languages (4 out of 10) and inflectional languages (8 out of 25). Although these percentages do not lend themselves to strong statements, they contrast sharply with what appears to be a rather even distribution as regards language genus or family, as shown in Table 49.61.

Table 49.61: Languages for which restrictions on derivational networks have been identified by language family.

			Language family/genus							
			Indo-European							
Afro-Asiatic	Altaic	Basque	Baltic	Celtic	Germanic	Greek	Romance	Slavic	Kartvelian	Nakh-Daghestanian	Uralic
Maltese	Tatar	Basque	Latvian	Irish	Danish Dutch English		French			Chechen	
				Welsh	Icelandic Frisian Norwegian		Portuguese			Dargwa	

It is worth noting, however, that no Slavic language reports poor derivational networks, especially when compared with the other two language genera that are the same approximate size and report limited derivational networks (Germanic and Romance).

Several languages make less use of the derivation resources studied here only by comparison with other languages, e.g. Dargwa, which is reported to produce apparently poor derivational networks, but only when compared with the networks of other languages. This is not relevant in this section, however.

In the languages where poor derivational networks are reported, two major arguments are cited:

(i) Limitations as a result of methodological decisions. These are as a consequence of three decisions:
   a. The sample under study, as the lexical entries that make up the sample for the production of derivational networks may not lend themselves to derivation, especially in:
      i. Dutch
      ii. Finnish, as the entries of the sample do not cover all possible morphological and semantic types
      iii. German, due to the representation of certain semantic categories in verbs (even if some of these have been interpreted not only as derivation but also as compounding)
      iv. Maltese
      v. Tatar, although in this case, specific entries are referred to rather than the sample in general
   b. The processes excluded from the concept of the 'derivational paradigm', that is, processes that play a major role in the formation of new words in a given language but which are not covered by this piece of research. The processes cited in this respect are relatively few, and refer systematically to the following:
      i. Suppletion or morphologically simple forms[4]:
         1. French
      ii. Conversion, which is reported to be responsible for a large amount of word-formation in the following languages[5]:
         1. Basque, specifically with regard to conversion to verbs
         2. Dargwa
         3. English

---

4 This is also cited as a constraint on richer derivational paradigms in Romanian.
5 This is also cited as a constraint on richer derivational paradigms in Dutch and Romanian.

4. French, especially for derivation of nouns from adjectives and verbs
        5. Icelandic
        6. Portuguese
    iii. Compounding, which is reported to be responsible for a large amount of word-formation in the following languages:
        1. English
        2. French
        3. Icelandic
        4. Irish
        5. Latvian, specifically for nouns
        6. Norwegian
        7. Portuguese
        8. Tatar
        9. Welsh
    iv. Reduplication, especially for the expression of evaluative meaning:
        1. French
    v. Participial forms, which occur in:
        1. Finnish
        2. Portuguese
    vi. Bound forms or affixoids, which occur in:
        1. Icelandic
        2. Welsh
    vii. Particle verbs, which are cited as being frequent only for Dutch.
  c. The attestation method, which may in some languages create difficulties due to limited resource availability:
    i. Underdeveloped lexicographical resources:
        1. Chechen
    ii. Irregular attestation, such that entries that are not attested in corpora could have been attested in dictionaries or by native speakers:
        1. Maltese
(ii) Limitations inherent to each language. These are language-specific conditions, and cover the following:
  a. Constraints in the formation of neologisms:
    i. Chechen
  b. Constraints in the use of derivation for word-formation:
    i. Danish

ii. Frisian, in this case also with a rapidly decreasing number of derivatives from one order of derivation to the next
iii. Slovak, as nouns are reported to function as motivated units instead of as motivating units
c. The influence of bilingualism, specifically where a contact language supplies word-formation resources that partly replace the word-formation resources of the language under study:
   i. Chechen
d. The influence of native and borrowed morphology:
   i. English
   ii. Irish
   iii. Portuguese, in this case relating to the borrowing of morphemes, not whole words
e. The use of compensating naming strategies, specifically:
   i. Morphological resources:
      1. Icelandic, especially with regard to a rich use of inflection for the representation of some of the semantic categories under study
      2. Swedish, for the semantic categories not represented, even if, in general, the derivational networks of Swedish are not comparatively poor
      3. Ukrainian, even if the derivational capacity of the semantic categories recorded is quite rich
      4. Basque, especially with regard to affective palatalization and reduplication
   ii. Syntactic resources, like phrases:
      1. French, e.g. with constructions involving several word-classes
      2. Frisian, e.g. with prepositional phrases where the derivational meaning is represented lexically
      3. Icelandic
      4. Irish
      5. Norwegian
      6. Swedish, again for the semantic categories not represented, even if, in general, the derivational networks of Swedish are not comparatively poor
      7. Ukrainian, even if the derivational capacity of the semantic categories recorded is quite rich
      8. Welsh

iii. Semantic resources, like semantic extension/narrowing, borrowing, or the reuse of old vocabulary[6]:
    1. Irish

Both of these types of limitations lend themselves to further analysis. Some limitations, specifically the role of alternative resources for the expression of certain semantic categories, are both methodological and language-specific, and could have been listed as either. The focus is, thus, on point b) of the methodological limitations and point e) of the language-specific limitations, in that they hint at the strategies employed as compensating mechanisms, or, more precisely, as alternative naming procedures to derivation.

Three cases stand out here. The first is compounding, which is reported in nine languages, but no relevant pattern can be found therein because the languages in question replicate, in the main, a cross-section of the entire language sample:
(i) as regards language type, of these nine languages, six are inflectional, two are analytical, and one is agglutinating.
(ii) as regards the language genus or family, of these nine languages, three are Germanic, two are Celtic, two are Romance, one is Baltic and one belongs to the Altaic family.

These data are shown in Tables 49.62 and 49.63.

Table 49.62: Languages where compounding is reported as an alternative process for derivation and is partly responsible for comparatively poor derivational networks by language type.

Language type	Languages
Inflectional	French, Icelandic, Irish, Latvian, Portuguese, Welsh
Agglutinating	Tatar
Analytical	English, Norwegian

Table 49.63 lends itself to further comment in that the proportions of the language sample are not replicated by:

---

[6] This is also cited as a constraint on richer derivational paradigms in Latvian, Romanian and Ukrainian.

Table 49.63: Languages where compounding is reported as an alternative process for derivation and is partly responsible for comparatively poor derivational networks by language family.

Afro-Asiatic	Altaic	Basque	Language family/genus					Kartvelian	Nakh-Daghestanian	Uralic
			Indo-European							
			Baltic	Celtic	Germanic	Greek	Romance	Slavic		
	Tatar		Latvian	Irish Welsh	English Icelandic Norwegian		French Portuguese			

(i) Celtic languages, insofar as the two languages of the sample are cited here.
(ii) Slavic languages, insofar as none of the nine languages of the sample are cited here.

The second case that stands out here is conversion, but to a lesser degree: it is reported in six languages where no relevant pattern can be found, because the languages in question replicate, in the main, a cross-section of the entire language sample:
(i) as regards language type, of these six languages, four are inflectional, one is analytical, and one is agglutinating.
(ii) as regards the language genus or family, of these six languages, three are Germanic, two are Romance, and the last one is Basque.

These data are shown in Tables 49.64 and 49.65.

Table 49.64: Languages where conversion is reported as an alternative process for derivation and is partly responsible for comparatively poor derivational networks by language type.

Language type	Languages
Inflectional	Dutch, French, Icelandic, Portuguese
Agglutinating	Basque
Analytical	English

Just as for compounding, the latter table (Table 49.67) lends itself to further comment in that the proportions of the language sample are not replicated by Slavic languages, insofar as none of the nine languages of the sample are cited here.

The third case is the use of syntactic structures for the expression of semantic categories, often in the form of phrases involving lexical bases that instead use derivation in other languages of the sample.[7] These cases are shown in Tables 49.66 and 49.67.

Table 49.66 hints that the language sample is not fully represented in this respect, in that agglutinating languages are not reported as using this resource.

Table 49.67 lends itself to further comment in that the proportions of the language sample are not replicated by:

---

[7] This is also cited as a constraint on richer derivational paradigms in Swedish and Ukrainian.

Table 49.65: Languages where conversion is reported as an alternative process for derivation and is partly responsible for comparatively poor derivational networks by language family.

Afro-Asiatic	Altaic	Basque	Language family/genus						Kartvelian	Nakh-Daghestanian	Uralic
			Indo-European								
			Baltic	Celtic	Germanic	Greek	Romance	Slavic			
		Basque			Dutch		French				
					English		Portuguese				
					Icelandic						

Table 49.66: Languages where syntactic resources are reported as an alternative process for derivation and are partly responsible for comparatively poor derivational networks by language type.

Language type	Languages
Inflectional	French, Icelandic, Irish, Welsh
Agglutinating	
Analytical	Frisian, Norwegian

(i) Multiple language families, insofar as only genera from the Indo-European family are cited here.
(ii) Celtic languages, insofar as the two languages of the sample are cited here.
(iii) Romance and Slavic languages, insofar as only one of their seven and nine languages are cited here.

The sample also reveals constraints in the representation of certain semantic categories, which results in poorer derivational networks. These constraints refer to the rare use of the categories represented in the languages listed in Table 49.68.

Finnish is used as an exemplar here to showcase lack of or rare occurrence of specific semantic categories in languages. There is great variability in terms of the specific semantic categories reported by different languages.

Without making a mountain out of a molehill, it can safely be suggested that comparative semantic categories are very useful as a means to an end, i.e. they are indispensable for generating derivational networks and establishing correlations between orders of derivation and preferences for their expression in respective orders per language and per group. Despite the enormous diversity in their combinability, such comparative concepts can be used as a criterion for descriptive generalizations for particular groups.

Summary

(i) Constraints on derivational networks are relatively rare compared with derivational networks, where no major restrictions apply.
(ii) Slavic languages stand out by not reporting poor derivational networks in any case.
(iii) Alternatives to derivation refer mainly to compounding, conversion, and syntactic structures.

Table 49.67: Languages where syntactic resources are reported as an alternative process for derivation and are partly responsible for comparatively poor derivational networks by language family.

Afro-Asiatic	Altaic	Basque	Language family/genus						Kartvelian	Nakh-Daghestanian	Uralic
				Indo-European							
			Baltic	Celtic	Germanic	Greek	Romance	Slavic			
				Irish Welsh	Frisian Icelandic Norwegian		French				

Table 49.68: An illustration of semantic categories not attested or reported to be rare in languages.

	Languages						
Finnish	Frisian	Georgian	German	Norwegian	Ukrainian	Welsh
ANTICAUSATIVE							
AUGMENTATIVE							
COLLECTIVE							
DIMINUTIVE							
ENTITY							
EXPERIENCER							
INSTRUMENTATIVE							
LOCATION							
REFLEXIVE							
RESULTATIVE							
SUBITIVE							

49.14 Conclusions

The typological research presented in this chapter is based on all the language-specific descriptions in the preceding chapters. Our observations can be summarized as follows:

(i) There are considerable *differences among languages in their derivational capacity*, which is reflected in the number of derivatives in derivational networks. It suffices to compare any derivational network of, for example, Croatian to a derivational network of, for example, English. This difference usually amounts to several dozen derivatives.

(ii) If we compare the average maximum derivational network (MDN) values by word-class and by order of derivation, it is obvious that the derivational potential of simple underived nouns and adjectives is very similar, and in some orders almost identical. *Verbs clearly have the highest MDN values* in every order of derivation, and they are significantly higher than those of the other two word-classes. This is especially due to the extreme derivational potential of those languages that employ prefixes for the expression of the category of Aktionsart. One possible explanation for this supremacy of verbs can be sought in the *derivational construal* (Croft 2012: 17) potential of verbs in view of the fact that, onomasiologically speaking, they are the locus of the lexical semantic encoding of event structure (i.e. they can function as lexicalized construal carriers of both aspectual and causal structure[8]).

(iii) The richness of derivational networks is *sensitive to the word-class* of the basic word. This means that, for the majority of languages, the richness of derivational networks varies depending on the word-class of the basic words. High consistency across all three orders in all three classes is rare, but it does occur in Bulgarian and Serbian. When restricted to the 1st order, highly consistent networks in all three word-classes have been identified for Croatian, Turkish and Basque and, to an extent, Bulgarian, Polish and Welsh.

(iv) The richness of derivational networks is *sensitive to the order of derivation*.

(v) The richness of derivational networks is probably also sensitive to the semantics of base words, but this hypothesis is in need of further empirical corroboration.

(vi) There is a tendency for languages to actualize 20%–29.99% of the derivational potential of a word-class. This tendency is almost identical for all three word-classes and is represented by 67.5% of languages for nouns and 62.5% of languages for both verbs and adjectives.

(vii) There is a *core group* of languages that keep *high saturation values (SVs) across all three word-classes*. This comprises Greek, Dutch, Dargwa and North Saami. These might be joined by German, Turkish and Lithuanian, which have high values in two word-classes and a medium SV in the third word-class.

(viii) There is an unambiguous tendency for SVs to fall gradually as the order of derivation rises *in all three word-classes*. It occurs in 28 languages for nouns, and 27 languages for both verbs and adjectives. This suggests that the tendency to derive fewer words as the order of derivation increases is independent of the word-class.

(ix) The SVs do not vary for the examined genera in a significant way in any of the word-classes, which indicates that *it is possible to predict the level of richness of derivational networks for language genera*.

---

8 See Croft (2012) for an elaborate account of the way in which verbs can, in terms of construction grammar and cognitive linguistics, lexically map various profiles of a concept via derivational construal.

(x) A *medium SV* (20%–30%) can be considered the most typical SV for all word-classes and for the first three orders of derivation.

(xi) There is no geographically homogeneous territory in which the languages of the topmost SVs are spoken. These languages are of various genetic origins and are scattered across Europe. What can be considered as a general tendency, however, is *the use of low-SV languages in geographically peripheral areas* of Europe.

(xii) The data suggest that derivational networks are *most predictable in the 1st order*. This is manifested by a high number of languages with a level of standard deviation (SD) below 10.00 as well as by the generally relatively high consistency of this value in the other languages. The consistency of results falls as the order grows, which means that derivational networks are much less predictable in the higher orders of derivation.

(xiii) The correlation between SV and paradigmatic capacity may differ significantly in the same language in different word-classes and different orders of derivation.

(xiv) The maximum number of orders of derivation, i.e. the maximum number of affixes attached to a simple underived word, is five for all three word-classes. There are six languages that reach five orders of derivation in all three word-classes, none of which belong to the Romance or Germanic genera. The average number of affixation steps is very similar for verb-based and adjective-based derivations (2.78 and 2.76, respectively). This figure is lower for nouns (2.46).

(xv) In terms of the total number of derivatives, verbs have the most prolific base. The average number of verb-based derivatives is clearly greater than the figures for adjectives and nouns. This word-formation feature is dominated by Slavic and Uralic languages. The values for adjective-based derivations are slightly higher than those for noun-based derivations. This result tallies with the data on the maximum derivational networks for individual word-classes, the data on the average number of orders of derivation, as well as the data on the correlation between the SV and the paradigmatic capacity.

(xvi) The non-existence of a particular word-formation process or a minimum number of word-formation types of a particular word-formation process does not correlate with the richness of a derivational network.

(xvii) Inflectional and agglutinating languages tend to have a high number of derivational orders. However, the genetic factor might be influential, too. Romance inflectional languages have a smaller number of derivational orders than Slavic languages. While Nakh-Daghestanian languages, classified as agglutinating, tend to have a very low number of derivational orders, Uralic languages, which are also agglutinating, feature high numbers of orders of derivation. Analytical languages are not consistent in their behaviour. Generally, however, they have a lower number of derivational orders, especially in the case of nouns.

(xviii) Correlations between semantic categories and orders of derivation are reported in almost all languages as systematic occurrences in the 1st order of derivation and by the majority in the 2nd order of derivation, although only those semantic categories with a notable occurrence (i.e. those that were present in a significant number of the languages in the sample) were discussed above.

(xix) Regarding correlations, DIMINUTIVE appears to be correlated with the 1st order of derivation from all three types of bases. Otherwise, it appears that the correlations are base-sensitive. In several languages, a correlation between the 3rd order of derivation and specific semantic categories has been established, but the semantic categories are so diverse that there are no more than six languages in which the same category correlates with this order of derivation. No clear correlations for the 4th and 5th orders of derivation were observed. Only one language (Norwegian) reports a correlation between the 5th order of derivation from all three bases (i.e. nominal, verbal and adjectival) and the semantic category STATIVE.

(xx) Semantic categories with blocking effects are reported in all the languages of the sample except Welsh. However, few semantic categories report blocking effects through all the word-classes. Similarly, few languages report blocking in the 4th order of derivation. Several languages record consistent blocking by semantic categories across orders of derivation, e.g. Hungarian and North Saami. In the orders of derivation where several semantic categories have a blocking effect, the tendency is for languages to have only one semantic category with a blocking effect; however, there are some languages that consistently report several blocking effects, regardless of the word-class or order of derivation, e.g. Hungarian and Tatar.

(xxi) No language type, language genus, or family or areal distribution pattern can be identified as regards the distribution of semantic categories with a blocking effect, but a set of semantic categories that rarely have a blocking effect in the sample can be listed:
   a. ATTENUATIVE, in the 2nd order of Greek nouns
   b. ANTICAUSATIVE, in the 1st order of Maltese verbs
   c. CONCOMITANT, in the 1st order of Greek verbs
   d. CUMULATIVE, in the 2nd order of Ukrainian verbs
   e. DISTRIBUTIVE, in the 3rd order of Polish verbs

f. INCEPTIVE, in the 1st order of Ukrainian verbs
g. POSSESSIVE, in the 1st order of Hungarian nouns

(xxii) Frequent combinations of semantic categories are reported for most of the languages in the sample (though not for Welsh) and regularly for each word-class (though not, for example, for adjectives in Dargwa, nouns in Chechen, Dargwa, Maltese and Polish, or verbs in Irish). Each word-class starts out with specific combinations, such that the same sequence is not found across the three word-classes in the sample, except in certain languages, e.g. QUALITY + ABSTRACTION in Czech adjectives, nouns and verbs, or ACTION + AGENT in Georgian nouns and verbs. No associations can be identified here with regard to language type, language genus, or family or areal distribution. Few frequent combinations that are specific to word-classes can be found across languages: an exception is QUALITY + STATE in Chechen, English, German and Ukrainian adjectives. Again, no associations can be identified here with regard to language type, language genus, or family or areal distribution.

(xxiii) Starting categories that are frequent in each word-class can be identified to show biases of certain languages towards specific categories in specific word-classes, e.g. Bulgarian adjectives towards PATIENT. Starting categories that occur in each word-class can be identified to show categories that stand out due to their frequency, regardless of word-class and language, e.g.:
a. In adjectives, ABILITY, ACTION, AGENT, CAUSATIVE, QUALITY and SIMILATIVE
b. In nouns, AGENT, QUALITY, PRIVATIVE and SIMILATIVE
c. In verbs, AGENT, CAUSATIVE, DIRECTIONAL, FINITIVE, PROCESS and QUALITY
No pattern can be identified by language type, language genus, or family or areal distribution for these combinations, but certain combinations that have a range of subsequent categories can be attested at least four times across languages:
d. In adjectives, QUALITY + STATE (+) in Chechen, German, English and Ukrainian
e. In verbs, AGENT + FEMALE (+) in Bulgarian, Croatian, German, Serbian and Slovak
Certain combinations are attested only once, even regardless of the word-class, e.g. TEMPORAL + QUANTITY (+) in Catalan nouns or ANTICAUSATIVE + ENTITY in Icelandic verbs, to name only two examples.

(xxiv) The multiple occurrence of a semantic category (i.e. its recurrence in successive orders of derivation) is a relatively frequent phenomenon in the 40 European languages under study. It is comparatively higher in Slavic languages than in other language genera or families in the sample.

(xxv) There is considerable variation in the multiple occurrences of semantic categories, ranging from languages where only one category reoccurs to languages where over ten categories may reoccur for one word-class. Semantic categories may reoccur successively with or without a different intermediate semantic category. Differences can be found between language types as regards the multiple occurrence of semantic categories:
   a. DIMINUTIVE is not recorded in any agglutinating or analytical language.
   b. CAUSATIVE is recorded in more agglutinating than inflectional languages, despite their different proportions in the language sample.
(xxvi) Differences can be found between language genera as regards the multiple occurrence of semantic categories, which hint that:
   a. Germanic languages are biased towards the category ACTION and, to a much lesser degree, QUALITY.
   b. Romance languages are biased towards the categories ACTION and DIMINUTIVE, both to a low degree.
   c. Slavic languages are biased towards the categories QUALITY, ACTION and DIMINUTIVE, but not for CAUSATIVE.

   Very specific combinations can be identified, such that several languages record multiple occurrences of very few semantic categories, and certain semantic categories occur in very few or in just one language.
(xxvii) The systematic reversibility of semantic categories is not a characteristic property of European languages. The languages that display semantic reversibility do this only with regard to one or two categories, so only exceptionally do a higher number of categories or combinations allow reversibility. No patterns can be identified as regards language type, language genus, or family or areal distribution, due to the limited amount of data.
(xxviii) Constraints on derivational networks are relatively infrequent compared with derivational networks where no major restrictions apply. Slavic languages stand out due to not reporting any cases of poor derivational networks, especially compared with the other two language genera that are their same approximate size and report limited derivational networks (Germanic and Romance). Poor derivational networks may be due to methodological decisions or language-inherent issues. The method used constrained the derivational networks due to the lexical sample used, due to what was considered to fall within the scope of derivation, and due to limitations in the attestation method used. Alternatives to derivation refer mainly to compounding, conversion and syntactic structures, but apparently comparatively less frequently in agglutinating languages and, as mentioned above, in Slavic languages.

References

Aronoff M. & N. Fuhrhop. 2002. Restricting suffix combinations in German and English: Closing suffixes and the monosuffix constraint. *Natural Language and Linguistic Theory* 20. 451–490.
Bagasheva, Alexandra. 2017. Comparative semantic concepts in affixation. In J. Santana-Lario and S. Valera (eds.), *Competing patterns in English affixation*, 33–65. Bern: Peter Lang.
Bakema, P. & D. Geeraerts. 2000. Diminution and augmentation. In G. E. Booij, Ch. Lehmann & J. Mugdan (eds.), *Morphologie/Morphology. Ein internationales Handbuch zur Flexion und Wortbildung / An International Handbook on Inflection and Word Formation, Vol. 1*, 1045–1052. Berlin: de Gruyter.
Croft, W. 2012. *Verbs. Aspect and causal structure*. Oxford: Oxford University Press.
Fabb, N. 1988. English suffixation is constrained only by selectional restrictions. *Natural Language and Linguistic Theory* 6. 527–539.
Gaeta, L. (2005). Combinazioni di suffissi in Italiano. In M. Grossmann & A. Thornton (eds.), *La Formazione delle Parole. Atti del XXXVII Congresso Internazionale di Studi della Societa di Linguistica Italiana (SLI)*, 229–247. Roma: Bulzoni.
Giegerich, H. J. 1999. *Lexical strata in English. Morphological causes, phonological effects*. Cambridge: Cambridge University Press.
Hay J. & I. Plag. 2004. What constrains possible suffix combinations? On the interaction of grammatical and processing restrictions in derivational morphology. *Natural Language and Linguistic Theory* 22. 565–596.
Körtvélyessy, Lívia. 2015. *Evaluative morphology from a cross linguistic perspective*. Newcastle: Cambridge Scholars Publishing.
Körtvélyessy, L., P. Štekauer, J. Genči & J. Zimmermann. 2018. Word-Formation in European languages. *Word Structure* 11 (3). 313–358.
Manova, S. (ed.). 2015. *Affix ordering across languages and frameworks*. Oxford: Oxford University Press.
Manova, S. & Aronoff, M. 2010. Modelling affix order. *Morphology* 20 (1). 109–131.
Müller, P.O., Ohnheiser, I., Olsen, S. & Rainer, F. (eds.). 2015–2016. *Word-Formation. An international handbook of the languages of Europe*. Berlin: Mouton de Gruyter.
Plag, I. 1996. Selectional restrictions in English suffixation revisited. A reply to Fabb (1988). *Linguistics* 34. 769–798.
Plank, F. 1994. Inflection and derivation. In R. E. Asher (ed.), *The encyclopedia of language and linguistics, vol. 3*, 1671–1678. Oxford: Pergamon Press.
Saarinen, P. & J. Hay. 2014. Affix ordering in derivation. In R. Lieber & P. Štekauer (eds.), *The Oxford handbook of derivational morphology*, 370–383. Oxford: Oxford University Press.
Sapir, Edward. 1921. *Language: An introduction to the study of speech*. New York: Harcourt, Brace and Company.
Štekauer, P. 2012. Morphological types vs. word-formation: Any correlation? In E. Cyran, H. Kardela & B. Szymanek (eds.), *Sound structure and sense. Studies in memory of Edmund Gussmann*, 711–728. Lublin: KUL.
Štekauer, P., S. Valera & L. Körtvélyessy. 2012. *Word-formation in the world's languages. A typological survey*. Cambridge: Cambridge University Press.

Index

Actualization 23, 259, 492, 493, 509
Adposition 157, 455
Affixoid 21, 33, 43, 127, 137, 147, 180, 187, 203, 310, 317, 347, 386, 409, 427, 431, 593
Affix stacking 65, 69
Aktionsart 63, 386, 392, 395, 486, 544, 602
Allomorphy 215, 240, 279, 282
Aspect V, 27, 28, 53, 66, 93, 115, 116, 297, 310, 320, 386, 446

Bilingualism 157, 441, 594

Circumfixation 93, 323, 465
Class-changing 7
Class-maintaining 285
Combining form 21, 33, 127, 147, 203, 215, 252, 273
Comparative concept 2, 18, 19, 599
Compounding 33, 43, 85, 105, 115, 120, 127–130, 154, 155, 157, 167–169, 179, 188, 190, 196, 200, 203, 208, 215, 217, 237, 239, 252, 273, 299, 306, 309, 318, 347, 372, 373, 399, 409, 421, 423, 431, 455, 462, 482, 592, 593, 595, 597, 599, 606
Confix 190
Conversion 21, 27–30, 36, 53–55, 85, 105, 120, 127, 128, 144, 151, 154, 155, 157, 167, 168, 179, 187, 191, 213, 214, 237, 242, 251, 270, 271, 273, 277, 283, 285, 295–297, 310, 362, 363, 385, 386, 409, 423, 427, 431, 435, 452, 455, 462, 592, 597, 599, 606
Core vocabulary 12, 293, 386, 475, 492, 510
Cross-paradigm 6

Derivation
– heterogeneous 239, 248
– prefixal-suffixal 65, 92, 239, 246–248, 261, 285
Derivational nest V, 3, 4
Derivational series 3, 4, 373
Direct derivative V, 10, 11, 221, 278, 283, 314

Elative 215, 257, 258
Ethnologue 16, 17, 539
Evaluative 103, 116, 217, 218, 229, 237, 239, 245–247, 252, 257–259, 261, 262, 266, 269, 270, 281, 285, 290, 293, 352, 548, 593

Family V, 22, 33, 229, 347, 361, 409, 443, 465, 506, 546, 561, 562, 565, 566, 568, 569, 574–578, 582, 583, 586–588, 590, 591, 595–597, 599, 600, 604–606
– derivational V, 4, 5, 36
– morphological 6

Genus V, 22, 499, 528–531, 542, 544, 545, 561, 562, 565, 566, 568, 574, 576–578, 582, 583, 586–588, 590, 595, 597, 604–606
Gradation 21, 105, 121
Grammaticalization 179, 213

Homonymy 53, 295

Imperfectivization 27, 105
Inflection
– inherent 28
– non-prototypical 27

Language
– agglutinating 33, 365, 385, 491, 534, 539–542, 544–546, 575, 577, 580, 581, 585, 586, 590, 595, 597, 599, 603, 604, 606
– analytical 196, 539–541, 575, 577, 580, 581, 585, 586, 590, 595, 597, 599, 604, 606
– inflectional 33, 43, 53, 539–542, 575, 577, 580, 581, 585, 586, 590, 595, 597, 599, 603, 606
– synthetic 43, 200, 347, 411, 491, 496, 534, 542, 544–547

Morphological subtraction 239
Motivation 3, 65, 251

https://doi.org/10.1515/9783110686630-050

Nominalization 90, 273, 283, 295

Ontological type 19

Paradigm
– derivational V, 1, 3–10, 270, 395, 431, 481, 592, 595, 597
– inflectional V, 6–10, 27, 28, 53, 150, 336
Paradigmatic capacity 1, 10–12, 23, 231, 421, 485, 531, 533, 543, 603
Paradigm-based model 4, 5
Particle verb 127, 137, 144, 157, 168, 203, 593
Past participle 20, 21, 127, 203, 214, 240, 251, 271, 273, 297, 310, 358, 386
Perfectivization 27, 28
Polysemy 20, 21, 53, 65, 295, 296
Postfixation 37, 44, 65, 93
Prefixation 28, 43, 53–55, 59, 65, 68, 69, 85, 92, 93, 99, 102, 105, 115, 147, 150, 161, 162, 179, 187, 203, 211, 217, 234, 235, 247, 251, 261, 273, 285, 319, 323, 333, 347, 361, 373, 446, 449, 451, 465, 544, 545
Prefixoid 180, 365

Reduplication 460, 462, 463, 465, 593, 594
Reflexivization 28, 36, 93

Semantic shift 21
Structural richness 1, 12, 40, 62, 112, 230, 274, 530, 543
Suffixation 28, 43, 53–55, 65, 85, 92, 93, 102, 105, 115, 145, 147, 153, 174, 179, 187, 203, 211, 214, 217, 225, 239, 246–248, 251, 257, 261, 265, 266, 271, 273, 285, 319, 323, 333, 347, 373, 423, 435, 465
Superlative 115, 127, 157, 167, 168, 214, 223, 251, 252, 261, 265
Suppletion 230, 233, 237, 240, 241, 275, 283, 286, 592

Transflexion/transflection 21, 93, 98, 213, 251
Transgressive 30, 54
Transposition 21, 115, 191

Word
– actual 10, 13, 20, 33, 348, 531
– possible 20, 147, 150, 270, 347, 348, 456
– potential 33, 41, 169

www.ingramcontent.com/pod-product-compliance
Lightning Source LLC
Chambersburg PA
CBHW050522300426
44113CB00012B/1927